Publications of the
Carnegie Endowment for International Peace
Division of International Law
Washington

THE UNITED STATES OF AMERICA:
A STUDY IN INTERNATIONAL
ORGANIZATION

By the Author of and Uniform with This
Study in International Organization:

Judicial Settlement of Controversies Between States of the American Union

Cases decided in the Supreme Court of the United States
(2 vols., 4to)

An Analysis of Cases decided in the Supreme Court of the United States
(1 vol., 4to)

I can not refrain from asking your Lordships to consider how the subject has been viewed by our brethren in the United States of America. They carried the common law of England along with them, and jurisprudence is the department of human knowledge to which, as pointed out by Burke, they have chiefly devoted themselves, and in which they have chiefly excelled. (*Lord Campbell in Regina v. Millis, 10 Clark & Finnelly, 777, decided in 1844.*)

Sitting, as it were, as an international, as well as a domestic tribunal, we apply Federal law, state law, and international law, as the exigencies of the particular case may demand. (*Chief Justice Fuller in Kansas v. Colorado, 185 United States, 125, 146–147, decided in 1902.*)

Confederations have existed in other countries than America; republics have been seen elsewhere than upon the shores of the New World; the representative system of government has been adopted in several states of Europe; but I am not aware that any nation of the globe has hitherto constituted a judicial power in the same manner as the Americans. (*Alexis de Tocqueville, De la Démocratie en Amérique, 2 Vols., 1835, Vol. I, p. 158.*)

The Supreme Court of the United States, which is the American Federal institution next claiming our attention, is not only a most interesting but a virtually unique creation of the founders of the Constitution. . . . The success of this experiment has blinded men to its novelty. There is no exact precedent for it, either in the ancient or in the modern world. (*Sir Henry Sumner Maine, Popular Government, 1886, pp. 217–218.*)

American experience has made it an axiom in political science that no written constitution of government can hope to stand without a paramount and independent tribunal to determine its construction and to enforce its precepts in the last resort. This is the great and foremost duty cast by the Constitution, for the sake of the Constitution, upon the Supreme Court of the United States. (*Edward John Phelps, The United States Supreme Court and the Sovereignty of the People, 1890, Orations and Essays, 1901, pp. 58–59.*)

The extraordinary scope of judicial power in this country has accustomed us to see the operations of government and questions arising between sovereign states submitted to judges who apply the test of conformity to established principles and rules of conduct embodied in our constitutions.

It seems natural and proper to us that the conduct of government affecting substantial rights, and not depending upon questions of policy, should be passed upon by the courts when occasion arises. It is easy, therefore, for Americans to grasp the idea that the same method of settlement should be applied to questions growing out of the conduct of nations and not involving questions of policy. (*Elihu Root, Judicial Settlement of International Disputes, 1908, Addresses on International Subjects, 1916, pp. 151–2.*)

THE UNITED STATES OF AMERICA:
A STUDY IN INTERNATIONAL
ORGANIZATION

BY

JAMES BROWN SCOTT, A.M., J.U.D., LL.D.

Technical Delegate of the United States to the Second Hague Peace
Conference, 1907; Technical Delegate of the United States
to the Peace Conference at Paris, 1919.

"I send you enclos'd the propos'd new Federal Constitution for these States. I was engag'd 4 Months of the last Summer in the Convention that form'd it. It is now sent by Congress to the several States for their Confirmation. If it succeeds, I do not see why you might not in Europe carry the Project of good Henry the 4th into Execution, by forming a Federal Union and One Grand Republick of all its different States & Kingdoms; by means of a like Convention; for we had many Interests to reconcile." Benjamin Franklin to Mr. Grand, October 22, 1787.—*Documentary History of the Constitution of the United States of America, Vol. IV, 1905, pp. 341-2.*

NEW YORK
OXFORD UNIVERSITY PRESS
AMERICAN BRANCH: 35 WEST 32ND STREET
London, Toronto, Melbourne and Bombay
1920

TO
ROBERT BACON
IN AFFECTIONATE ADMIRATION

PREFACE

The United States of America constitute a union of States, "a more perfect Union," to use the language of the preamble to the Constitution, than that under the Articles of Confederation which the Constitution was devised to supplant. On July 4, 1776, the thirteen British colonies lying between the Gulf of Mexico and Canada, to the east of the Mississippi, abjured allegiance to the British Crown and solemnly published and declared themselves to be " Free and Independent States " possessing, as the Declaration of Independence stated, " full power to levy War, conclude Peace, contract Alliances, establish Commerce, and to do all other Acts and Things which Independent States may of right do." Availing themselves of their right to contract alliances, they entered into " a firm league of friendship with each other, for their common defence, the security of their liberties, and their mutual and general welfare, binding themselves to assist each other, against all force offered to, or attacks made upon them, or any of them, on account of religion, sovereignty, trade, or any other pretence whatever." " Stiling " this confederation " The United States of America," and declaring in explicit terms that " each State retains its sovereignty, freedom and independence, and every power, jurisdiction and right, which is not by this confederation expressly delegated to the United States, in Congress assembled," the Articles of Confederation creating this union of the States were approved by their delegates in Congress November 15, 1777, and ratified by the last of the thirteen States on March 1, 1781.

The firm league of friendship failing of the purposes for which it was created by the delegates of the States in Congress assembled and ratified by the States themselves, the Congress on February 21, 1787, resolved it to be expedient that " on the second Monday in May next, a Convention of Delegates, who shall have been appointed by the several States, be held at Philadelphia, for the sole and express purpose of revising the Articles of Confederation, and reporting to Congress and the several Legislatures, such alterations and provisions therein, as shall, when agreed to in Congress, and confirmed by the States, render the federal Constitution adequate to the exigencies of Government, and the preservation of the Union." In pursuance of this resolution the delegates of twelve of the States met in convention in the month of May and adjourned on September 17, 1787, having drafted a constitution for a more perfect Union of the United States which, ratified by the thirteen original States in the course of the ensuing three years, today controls the conduct of forty-eight States and which in practice as well as in theory has proved adequate to the " exigencies of government and the preservation of the Union."

In the belief that the experience of the American States proclaimed to be free and independent in their Declaration of Independence, each retaining " its sovereignty, freedom and independence " under the Articles of Confederation, would be of value in any attempt to strengthen that larger union of States which we call the Society of Nations, the undersigned has ventured to treat within the compass of a volume some of the international problems met and solved by the framers of a more perfect Union under the caption of " The United States of America: A Study in International Organization."

JAMES BROWN SCOTT.

WASHINGTON, D. C.,
November 11, 1918.

POSTSCRIPTUM, *May 11, 1920.* — Absence from the country and difficulties in printing have delayed the appearance of the present volume. The text, however, speaks from Armistice Day, 1918.

Two additions of a later date have been made in the extracts prefixed to chapters: the first is the text of the settlement of the controversy between Virginia and West Virginia (Chapter XIII); the second is Mr. Root's definition of a justiciable question (Chapter XX). The text of the Eighteenth Amendment to the Constitution of the United States as printed in the Appendix has also been added.

I have left untouched the dedication to my beloved friend, Robert Bacon, whose noble life ended on May 29, 1919. — J. B. S.

TABLE OF CONTENTS

CHAPTER I

Rise of the Idea of Union

CHAPTER II

Independence Declared

CHAPTER III

A Confederation of Sovereign States

CHAPTER IV

EARLY BACKGROUNDS OF THE AMERICAN CONSTITUTION: THE TRADING COMPANIES

CHAPTER V

FURTHER COLONIAL PRECEDENTS

CHAPTER VI

ESTABLISHMENT OF STATE CONSTITUTIONS

CHAPTER VII

THE FEDERAL CONVENTION: AN INTERNATIONAL CONFERENCE

CHAPTER VIII

CREATION OF THE FEDERAL LEGISLATURE

CHAPTER IX

CREATION OF THE EXECUTIVE

CHAPTER X

THE FIRST PERMANENT TRIBUNAL OF THE STATES

CHAPTER XI

TEMPORARY JUDICIAL COMMISSIONS

CHAPTER XII

CREATION OF THE SUPREME COURT

CHAPTER XIII

PROTOTYPE OF A COURT OF INTERNATIONAL JUSTICE

CHAPTER XIV

THE ADMISSION OF NEW STATES

CHAPTER XVIII

POWERS OF THE SUPREME COURT

CHAPTER XIX

EXTENT AND EXERCISE OF JUDICIAL POWER

CHAPTER XX

CASE — CONTROVERSY — SUIT

CHAPTER XXI

JUDICIAL POWERS AND THEIR RELATION TO LAW AND EQUITY, TO ADMIRALTY, MARITIME AND INTERNATIONAL LAW

CHAPTER XXII

IMMUNITY OF STATES AND NATIONS FROM SUIT

CHAPTER XXIII

A MORE PERFECT SOCIETY OF NATIONS

APPENDIX

A. PLANS OF UNION FOR THE COLONIES AND THE STATES OF NORTH AMERICA

THE UNITED STATES OF AMERICA: A STUDY IN INTERNATIONAL ORGANIZATION

I. RISE OF THE IDEA OF UNION

A prima descendit origine mundi
Causarum series. (*Lucan, Pharsalia, Book VI.*)

The appreciation of a great and vital want will account for the origin of the idea of a common union. A study of its embodiment reveals the feature of growth. It is so original and peculiar, that it may be termed American. (*Richard Frothingham, The Rise of The Republic of the United States, 1872, p. 28.*)

Often, too, an institution may appear to be the result of direct imitation, when in fact it may be the product of a common race instinct, as in the case of the representative system reproducing itself in all the branches of the Teutonic race. . . . The law of historical continuity, or political inheritance, is not inconsistent with the law of historical variation, or political originality. In fact, the greater the accumulations of past experiences, the greater will be the capacity to solve by original methods the problems presented by new experiences. (*William C. Morey, The First State Constitutions, 1893, Annals of the American Academy of Political and Social Science, Vol. IV, part I, p. 203.*)

Mr. Gladstone recently pronounced it the most wonderful work ever struck off at a given time by the brain and purpose of man.

John Stuart Mill said, in his essay on De Tocqueville's "Democracy in America," that "the whole edifice was constructed, within the memory of man, upon abstract principles."

If we are to understand these expressions as meaning that the Constitution sprang into being, like Athené from the brain of Zeus, or that it was the work of doctrinaires endeavoring to found an ideal republic, it would be easy to show their falsity. The Constitution "has its roots deep in the soil of the past." No one generation, whatever its experience, could have invented such a system. It is a development, under a new environment, of old forms of government. Everything in it that was new was a "conservative innovation." (*W. T. Brantly, Of the Influence of European Speculation in the Formation of the Federal Constitution, 1880, in Southern Law Review, New Series, Vol. VI, p. 351.*)

Yet it is a characteristic of the race both in England and America that it has never really broken with the past. Whatever of novelty may appear from time to time, there is ever under all the great and steady force of historic continuity. (*C. Ellis Stevens, Sources of the Constitution of the United States, 1894, 2nd edition, p. xvii.*)

In fact, the distribution of political powers between co-ordinate governments — a system which sprang up in Plymouth, Massachusetts Bay, Connecticut and Rhode Island — had no existing counterpart in the countries of the civilized world. It can be historically explained only as the instinctive reproduction of primitive institutions under the influence of a primitive environment. (*William C. Morey, The Sources of American Federalism, 1895, The American Academy of Political and Social Science, Vol. VI, p. 211.*)

The new political system was a modification neither of the Confederation of 1781, nor of the Albany Union of 1754, nor of the New England Confederacy of 1643. These superficial alliances served, it is true, to bring the colonies and States into more amicable relations, by which they could aid each other against their common foes. But none of them contained the essential and distinctive features of that composite state-system which was established by the Constitution of 1787. We must search deeper into American political life, and perhaps into the common political life of our Teutonic, and even our Aryan ancestors to find the true historical sources of American federalism. (*William C. Morey, The Sources of American Federalism, 1895, The American Academy of Political and Social Science, Vol, VI, p. 204.*)

In the old system assemblies were not formally instituted, but grew up of themselves because it was the nature of Englishmen to assemble. (*Sir John Robert Seeley, The Expansion of England, 1883, American edition, p. 67.*)

A proposition for a Union was suggested at a meeting of Connecticut magistrates and ministers in Boston, in 1637. (*Richard Frothingham, The Rise of The Republic of the United States, 1872, p. 39.*)

The New-England Confederacy recognized the equality of the colonies that were parties to it, and the inviolability of their local governments; but the provisions designed to promote the common welfare were a crude embodiment of the union element. (*Richard Frothingham, The Rise of The Republic of the United States, 1872, p. 72.*)

But it is beginning to be realized that the Constitution of the United States, though possessing elements of novelty, is not, after all, the new creation that this idea would imply. It is not, properly speaking, the original composition of one body of men, nor the outcome of one definite epoch,— it is more and better than that. It does not stand in historical isolation, free of antecedents. It rests upon very old principles,— principles laboriously worked out by long ages of constitutional struggle. It looks back to the annals of the colonies and of the mother-land for its sources and its explanation. And it was rendered possible, and made what it is, by the political development of many generations of men. (*C. Ellis Stevens, Sources of the Constitution of the United States, 1894, 2nd edition, pp. viii-ix.*)

The best reason for American pride in the Constitution lies, not in the creative genius of its framers, nor in the beauty and symmetry of their work, but in the fact that it was and is a perfect expression of the institutional methods of its people. It is for that reason that it meets their needs as well to-day as in 1787–89. So long as they shall continue in the ways of their fathers; so long as they shall regard with pronounced disfavor the political quacks who constantly beg them to hazard a trial of never-tested remedies; so long may they continue to take a just pride in their Constitution, under all its possible coming changes, as one which has been "adequately discussed," and the results of the discussion of which have been fully "tested by experiment." (*Alexander Johnston, The First Century of the Constitution, The New Princeton Review, Vol. IV, No. 2, 1887, p. 190.*)

CHAPTER I

RISE OF THE IDEA OF UNION

On the 11th day of November, according to the old, but on the 21st day of November, 1620, according to the new order of things, some forty-one passengers of the *Mayflower,* whom a grateful posterity calls the Pilgrims, bringing to the New World a new type of men and a new spirit which we may with just pride call the American spirit, entered into a compact for their government when they should leave the little vessel which had carried them across a stormy ocean out of their course to the Hudson, for which region they had a patent, to the inhospitable shores of New England, for which they had no patent. The passage across the Atlantic had been stormy in more ways than one, for, in the absence of a patent from the New England Company, the Pilgrims were without title to the soil upon which they were soon to set foot. In the absence of a charter from the Crown, they were without authority to govern themselves as a body politic. Because of these things and also because of the frailties to which even some of their number were subject, the better part of them, believing that government as instituted among men derives its just powers from the consent of the governed and that this consent was in itself a compact on their part, entered into that agreement which we today call the Mayflower Compact, which they thus happily expressed:

> In ye name of God, Amen. We whose names are underwriten, the loyall The Mayflower Compact subjects of our dread soveraigne Lord, King James, by ye grace of God, of Great Britaine, Franc, & Ireland king, defender of ye faith, &c., haveing undertaken, for ye glorie of God, and advancemente of ye Christian faith, and honour of our king & countrie, a voyage to plant ye first colonie in ye Northerne parts of Virginia, doe by these presents solemnly & mutualy in ye presence of God, and one of another, covenant & combine our selves togeather into a civill body politick, for our better ordering & preservation & furtherance of ye ends aforesaid; and by vertue hearof to enacte, constitute, and frame such just & equall lawes, ordinances, acts, constitutions, & offices, from time to time, as shall be thought most meete & convenient for ye generall good of ye Colonie, unto which we promise all due submission and obedience.[1]

Just as the separatists, whom we call the Pilgrim fathers, traversed a waste of waters from the Old World to the New, so separatists in the political sense

---

[1] William Bradford, History of Plymouth Plantation, *Collections of the Massachusetts Historical Society, 1856, 4th Series,* Vol. iii, pp. 89–90.

of the word traversed a waste of wilderness and left three of the then eight towns of Massachusetts Bay in 1635, pushing to the west — with the permission, be it said, of that commonwealth, or rather, acting under a commission of its General Court for a twelvemonth. Establishing three towns on the western bank of the Connecticut River, they laid the foundation of the State of that name; furnishing in its constitution of 1639, known as the Fundamental Orders of Connecticut, what has been called the first written constitution in the modern sense of the term as a permanent limitation on governmental powers known in history, and suggesting, it has been claimed, by the confederation of its towns, which, however, retained the power not delegated to the State, the idea of that more perfect Union composed of the American States.

The spirit which pervaded these newer Pilgrims, and which today pervades the western world, was stated by Thomas Hooker, one of the chief settlers, from his pulpit in Hartford some seven months before the Fundamental Orders were drafted and went into effect. He chose for his text the 13th verse of the first chapter of Deuteronomy: "'Take you wise men, and understanding, and known among your tribes, and I will make them rulers over you.' Captains over thousands, and captains over hundreds — over fifties — over tens, &c." In the course of his sermon he is reported to have said, under the caption of *Doctrine,* in the brief extract of it made by one of the congregation:

I. That the choice of public magistrates belongs unto the people, by God's own allowance.

II. The privilege of election, which belongs to the people, therefore, must not be exercised according to their humours, but according to the blessed will and law of God.

III. They who have power to appoint officers and magistrates, it is in their power, also, to set the bounds and limitations of the power and place unto which they call them.

And the American Hooker is reported as giving for his American polity the following *Reasons:*

1. Because the foundation of authority is laid, firstly, in the free consent of the people.

2. Because, by a free choice, the hearts of the people will be more inclined to the love of the persons [chosen] and more ready to yield [obedience].

3. Because, of that duty and engagement of the people.[1]

In the preamble to the Fundamental Orders, the American theory of government is thus stated, omitting provisions concerning churches, in which membership, however, was not essential to the exercise of civil rights:

[1] Abstracts of Two Sermons by Rev. Thomas Hooker, from the short-hand notes of Mr. Henry Wolcott, *Collections of the Connecticut Historical Society,* 1860, Vol. i, p. 20.

Forasmuch as it hath pleased the Allmighty God by the wise disposition of his diuyne p^{r}uidence so to Order and dispose of things that we the Inhabitants and Residents of Windsor, Harteford and Wethersfield are now cohabiting and dwelling in and vppon the River of Conectecotte and the Lands thereunto adioyneing; And well knowing where a people are gathered togather the word of God requires that to mayntayne the peace and vnion of such a people there should be an orderly and decent Gouernment established according to God, to order and dispose of the affayres of the people at all seasons as occation shall require; doe therefore assotiate and conioyne our selues to be as one Publike State or Comonwelth; and doe, for our selues and our Successors and such as shall be adioyned to vs att any tyme hereafter, enter into Combination and Confederation togather, to mayntayne and p^{r}searue the liberty and purity of the gospell of our Lord Jesus wch we now p^{r}fesse . . . ; As also in o^r Ciuell Affaires to be guided and gouerned according to such Lawes, Rules, Orders and decrees as shall be made, ordered & decreed . . .[1]

As in the case of Plymouth, so in the settlements in the Connecticut valley, there was apparently no grant of title to land and there was no charter from the Crown. In the Mayflower Compact, the signers profess loyalty and obedience to their " dread soveraigne Lord," but find in themselves authority " to enacte, constitute, and frame such just & equall laws, ordinances, acts, constitutions, & offices, from time to time," which they themselves shall consider to be in the general interest and good of the colony. In the Fundamental Orders there is no reference to their " dread soveraigne Lord," and the confederating towns, recognizing that in their case government derives its just consent from their inhabitants and residents, proceed without further ado to provide for the election of a governor, magistrates and deputies to the general assemblies or courts " for makeing of lawes, and any other publike occation, wch conserns the good of the Comonwelth." [2]

The views of the Pilgrim fathers and of the Connecticut settlers in the matter of compact and the action of the Connecticut settlers in framing a system of government for their self-created body politic have been selected, not for the purpose of establishing priority in behalf of one or the other but as showing how, freed from the environment of the Old, the settlers of the New World stated and put into practice the doctrines held by them as individuals when unrestrained by the provisions of a charter or instructions from the Crown, and as indicating the conceptions of government likely to take visible form and effect in this western world when the inhabitants of the colonies were free to devise constitutions for their States and a union of those States.

[1] F. N. Thorpe, *The Federal and State Constitutions, Colonial Charters, and Other Organic Laws of the United States of America,* 1909, Vol. I, p. 519; B. P. Poore, *The Federal and State Constitutions, Colonial Charters, and Other Organic Laws of the United States,* 1877, p. 249.

[2] Thorpe, *ibid.,* p. 520; Poore, *ibid.,* p. 250.

Early Plans
of Union

The possibility of union was present to the minds of the American colonists even in the 17th century, shown by the New England Confederation, organized in 1643 and surviving the restoration of the Stuarts in 1660. William Penn, a great and a good man, held in grateful remembrance not only by the Commonwealth which bears his name but by the American people, and indeed the world at large, proposed a union of the colonists as far back as 1697. A plan proposed by Dr. Franklin in 1754 was, as its author aptly said, rejected in America because it had too much of the prerogative, and in England because it was too democratic, and was therefore not in accord with the plans of the home government.

These plans are of interest as showing how propinquity leads to union, and in our case to a union recognizing the greater interest of the whole without degrading the colonies or the states into provinces.

New England
Confederation

The aim or purpose of the New England Confederation, as it is generally called, is admirably and quaintly set forth in what may be called the preamble, or inducement to it, and the first article runs as follows:

> Whereas we all came into these parts of *America* with one and the same end and ayme, namely, to advance the Kingdome of our Lord Jesus Christ, and to enjoy the liberties of the Gospel, in purity with peace; and whereas in our settling (by a wise providence of God) we are further dispersed upon the Sea-Coasts and Rivers, then was at first intended, so that we cannot (according to our desire) with convenience communicate in one Government and Jurisdiction; and whereas we live encompassed with people of severall Nations, and strange languages which hereafter may prove injurious to us and our posterity: And forasmuch as the Natives have formerly committed sundry insolencies and outrages upon severall Plantations of the English, and have of late combined themselves against us. And seeing by reason of the sad Distractions in *England,* which they have heard of, and by which they know we are hindered both from that humble way of seeking advice or reaping those comfortable fruits of protection which, at other times, we might well expect; we therefore doe conceive it our bounden duty, without delay, to enter into a present Consotiation amongst our selves, for mutuall help and strength in all our future concernments, that, as in Nation, and Religion, so, in other respects, we be, and continue, One, according to the tenour and true meaning of the ensuing Articles.
>
> I. Wherefore it is fully Agreed and Concluded by and between the parties, or Jurisdictions above named, and they doe joyntly and severally by these presents agree and conclude, That they all be, and henceforth be called by the name of *The United Colonies of New-England.*[1]

The second article states that the United Colonies entered into this " firm and perpetuall league of friendship and amity, for offence and defence, mutuall advice and succour . . . and for their own mutuall safety, and wellfare."

The third article limits the Union to the colonies of Massachusetts, Ply-

---

[1] *Records of the Colony or Jurisdiction of New Haven from May, 1653, to the Union,* Charles J. Hoadly, ed., 1858, p. 562.

mouth, Connecticut and New Haven, leaving out Rhode Island unless it would acknowledge the jurisdiction either of Massachusetts or of Plymouth. This the Rhode Island settlement refused to do and its application for admission was rejected. This little community has had a mind of its own. It was not a member of the first Union; it failed to send delegates to the Constitutional Convention of 1787, and it left itself out of that greater Union which we call the United States until it, the smallest, decided to throw in its lot with the other and larger States.

The fourth article provided that the expenses of warfare,— wars were to be just,— offensive or defensive, "both in men, provisions, and all other disbursements," should be borne according to the males within each of the colonies "from sixteen yeares old, to threescore, being inhabitants there," and the spoils of war, if any there should be, were to be "proportionably divided among the said Confederates."

The fifth article declared that Massachusetts, as the larger colony, should furnish against the enemy one hundred armed men, and that each of the others should furnish forty-five, and in this proportion if more or less were needed. This was, however, only to apply to just wars. A method was needed and provided for determining whether the wars were just, for if they were not the "Confederates" were not to be saddled with the expense of the member causing an unjust war. The commissioners of the Confederation were to determine this, "and if it appear, that the fault lay in the party so invaded, that then, that Jurisdiction, or Plantation, make just satisfaction, both to the invaders, whom they have injuried, and bear all the charges of the war themselves, without requiring any allowance from the rest of the Confederates toward the same." [1]

After having stated the general aims and purposes of the Confederation to be for mutual protection, and the part which each should play in case of war, which the Union evidently contemplated as a defensive measure, the articles pass to a question no less important and more germane to the present purpose. In the sixth article the Confederation is looked upon as having interests of its own, superior to and different from the interests of the contracting parties, and a careful line of demarcation is drawn between the league on the one hand and the members thereof on the other. Equality, however, was the life and breath of the agreement. Each of the four jurisdictions was to appoint two commissioners, fully empowered by each of the colonies "to hear, examine, weigh, and determine all affaires of war, or peace, leagues, ayds, charges, and numbers of men for war, division of spoyles, or whatsoever is gotten by conquest, receiveing of more Confederates, or Plantations into Combination with any of these Confederates," but "not intermedling with the Government of

[1] *Ibid.*, p. 564.

any of the Jurisdictions which by the third Article is to be " preserued intirely to themselves." Six of the eight commissioners were empowered " to settle, and determine the businesse in question," but if this number should fail to agree then the matter was to be referred to the colonies, and if " the businesse so referred, be concluded, then to be prosecuted by the Confederates, and all their Members." A meeting was to be held the first Thursday in each September of the year and in regular rotation at each capital of the contracting colonies.

By the seventh article, a president of the commissioners was to be elected by them, or any six of them, but he was to be a presiding officer, not an executive.

The eighth article has some prophetic provisions. Thus, the commissioners were to " endeavoure to frame and establish Agreements and Orders in generall cases of a civil nature, wherein all the Plantations are interested, for preserving peace amongst themselves, and preventing (as much as may be) all occasions of war, or differences with others, as about the free and speedy passage of Justice in each Jurisdiction, to all the Confederates equally, as to their own, receiving those that remove from one Plantation to another, without due Certificates." And in the last of these prophetic provisions are the surrender upon request of " any Servant run away from his Master, into any other of these Confederated Jurisdictions," and the surrender of escaped prisoners or fugitives from justice upon request of the magistrates of the colony from which the escape was made.

The ninth article is also reminiscent, as it were, of the future, stipulating that, as " the justest Wars may be of dangerous consequence, especially to the smaller Plantations in these *United Colonies,*" it was agreed that none of them should " at any time hereafter begin, undertake or engage themselves, or this Confederation, or any part thereof in any War whatsoever (sudden exigents with the necessary consequences thereof excepted . . .) without the consent and agreement of the forenamed eight Commissioners, or at least six of them, as in the sixt Article is provided."

The tenth article permitted, in default of the attendance of all the commissioners duly notified to attend, four to act, but six were nevertheless required to determine the justice of the war, and in the eleventh article it was agreed:

> That if any of the Confederates shall hereafter break any of these present Articles, or be any other way injurious to any one of the other Jurisdictions such breach of Agreement, or injury shalbe duly considered, and ordered by the Commissioners for the other Jurisdictions, that both peace, and this present Confederation, may be intirely preserved without violation.[1]

The commissioners of the contracting parties, other than Plymouth, were

[1] *Records of the Colony of New Haven,* p. 566.

duly authorized to sign the agreement, which they did on May 19 / 29, 1643. It was therefore allowed that the articles and agreements of " this perpetuall Confederation " should be submitted to the good people of Plymouth, and

> That, if Plimoth consente, then the whole treaty as it stands in these present articls is, and shall continue, firme & stable without alteration. But if Plimoth come not in, yet yᵉ other three confederats doe by these presents confeirme yᵉ whole confederation, and yᵉ articles therof.[1]

The General Court of Plymouth authorized its commissioners to ratify and confirm the articles August 29/September 7, 1643, which they did at Boston, at which time and place the other commissioners subscribed the Articles of Union on behalf of their respective colonies.

The Mayflower Compact of November 11 / 21, 1620, had set forth the American conception of the State as the agent of the people creating it, and here in this little confederation of four straggling colonies, there lies hidden the germ of a greater Union, in which the members should be States, not provinces, determining their internal affairs, and be represented by two commissioners, chosen by each of them upon a footing of equality in a larger council. It is not meant, of course, that this larger union was the outgrowth of the smaller, but merely that the spirit which produced this greater union was already in evidence in the New World.[2]

The idea of union dwelt in the mind of William Penn. Peace with Penn was a passion. In 1693 he published his well known essay *Toward the Present and Future Peace of Europe,* proposing the establishment of an European diet, parliament or estates, moved thereto, as he says, by the project of Henry IV; and it is interesting to note, in passing, that Penn's larger project is still before the world, for it is today the basis of projects of leaders of thought on both sides of the Atlantic. It can well be imagined, therefore, that, as the proprietor and founder of the Commonwealth which bears his name, he had a special interest that it should dwell in peace, as well as a general desire that the plantations, which already had within them the possibilities of statehood, should dwell in peace and harmony. Therefore, four years after

William Penn's " Scheam "

[1] William Bradford, History of Plymouth Plantation, *Collections of the Massachusetts Historical Society,* 1856, 4th Series, Vol. III, p. 422.

[2] Of the Confederation, embracing four colonies, thirty-nine towns with a population of 24,000 souls, a well informed and just historian has said: "A great principle was at the bottom of the confederation; but, noble as were the aims of those who handled it, they had not yet attained to sufficient breadth of view to apply it even to the whole of New England." Richard Frothingham, *The Rise of the Republic of the United States,* 1872, p. 43.

The importance of the Union of the struggling colonies as a precedent was however not lost on the British chronicler, Chalmers, who said, properly enough, that it "offers the first example of collition in colonial story and showed to party leaders in after times the advantages of concert." George Chalmers, *Political Annals of the Present United Colonies from their Settlement to the Peace of 1763* (1780), p. 177.

his international proposal, he suggested a colonial plan of union, entitling his plan:

A Briefe and Plaine Scheam how the English Colonies in the North parts of America Viz: Boston Connecticut Road Island New York New Jersey, Pensilvania, Maryland, Virginia and Carolina may be made more usefull to the Crowne, and one anothers peace and safty with an universall concurrance.

The colonies were to meet by their stated and appointed deputies once a year, and oftener if need be, during the war which then raged in Europe and involved the American colonies as at this writing it does the American States, and in times of peace at least once in two years, " to debate and resolve of such measures as are most adviseable for their better understanding, and the publick tranquility and safety; " that each colony was to be represented by two persons, as Penn was careful to point out, " well qualified for sence sobriety and substance." These were to compose the Congress, as the assembly was to be called, of twenty persons, to be under the presidency of the King's Commissioner — who was to be in this case the Governor of the colony of New York, as, according to the plan, the Congress was to meet " near the Center of the Colonies; " and in time of war the King's Commissioner was to be commander of the colonial quotas. In the sixth article the gist of the plan is given, and of the activities of the deputies it is said:

That their business shall be to hear and adjust all matters of Complaint or differences between Province and Province, As 1st where persons quit their own Province and goe to another, that they may avoid their just debts tho they be able to pay them, 2d where offenders fly Justice, or Justice cannot well be had upon such offenders in the Provinces that entertaine them, 3dly to prevent or cure injuries in point of commerce, 4th, to consider of ways and means to support the union and safety of these Provinces against the publick enemies. In which Congresse the Quotas of men and charges will be much Easier, and more equally sett, then it is possible for any establishment made here [in England] to do; for the Provinces, knowing their own condition and one anothers, can debate that matter with more freedome and satisfaction and better adjust and ballance their affairs in all respects for their common safty.[1]

In this plan we have a forerunner of the Continental Congress, for it is to embrace all English colonies in the " North parts of America." Congress it is called, and it is provided with a presiding officer.

With unerring instinct Penn laid his finger, in this first of federal projects for the English-speaking colonies of the continent, on what was in fact the object of the American.revolution, the better government of themselves and the safeguarding of their interests by the colonials in America, rather than by

[1] William Penn's Plans for a Union of the Colonies, 8th February, 1696–97, *The Pennsylvania Magazine of History and Biography,* Vol. xi, 1887, p. 496.

the English in England. Here again it will be observed that each colony, irrespective of size or population, has an equal voice and an equal number of representatives, and here again the number is, as in the New England Confederation and in the Constitution of the United States, two for each Colony or State. As in the case of the Confederation, it is not meant to suggest that Penn's plan gave birth to our instrument of government, but as the articles of the New England Confederation show the advantages of union for their general welfare, so this plan shows, on the part of an enlightened Englishman, the method which, put into practice, might have made of the colonies great, self-governing dominions, as is Canada today to the north of the great Republic.

The next proposal which can be said to have had an important influence upon the destinies of the colonies was made in 1753 by Great Britain, which viewed with alarm and apprehension the encroachments of France in America, and which therefore directed the Governors of the American colonies to appoint delegates to a Congress which was to meet at a time and a place to be fixed by the Governor of New York, in order to treat with the Six Nations of Indians of that colony, to secure their alliance in case of war with France and to concert measures against that power. This body, called the Albany Congress from the name of the place in which it assembled, was composed of delegates from seven colonies and met on June 19, 1754. There were present four delegates from New Hampshire, five from Massachusetts, two from Rhode Island, three from Connecticut, five from New York, four from Pennsylvania, and two from Maryland.

There was, from the opening of the Congress, a strong sentiment in favor of a union of the Colonies, which on the 24th was unanimously declared " at present absolutely necessary for their security and defence."[1] A committee of one from each of the seven colonies present was appointed to prepare a plan of union. On July 9th, Dr. Franklin, who represented Pennsylvania, was **Benjamin Franklin's Plan** " desired to make a draught of it." [2] On the following day a draft of Union, largely drawn by him, was presented and adopted, and on July 11, 1754, the Congress adjourned.

By the " Albany " or " Dr. Franklin's " plan of union (it is known by either name), the Union was to consist of all the British colonies in North America, with the exception of Georgia, which had been but recently founded, of Delaware, which was not yet independent of Pennsylvania, and of Vermont, which was not yet a distinct colony. The purpose of the Union was stated to be " for their mutual Defence and Security, and for extending the British Settlements in North America." The method by which the union was to be effected is thus set forth:

[1] *Documents Relative to the Colonial History of the State of New York,* J. R. Brodhead ed., 1855, Vol. vi, p. 859.
[2] *Ibid.,* p. 885.

That humble application be made for an Act of the Parliament of Great Brittain, by virtue of which, one General Govern[t] may be formed in America, including all the said Colonies, within, and under which Govern[t] each Colony may retain each present constitution, except in the particulars wherein a change may be directed by the said Act, as hereafter follows.[1]

The government of the union was to consist of a President-General, appointed by the Crown, and a Grand Council, chosen by the representatives of the people of the several colonies. The members of the Grand Council were to be appointed by the House of Representatives of each of the colonies, but not upon a footing of equality, the larger colonies having a larger representation, as Franklin says in his interesting commentary, "in some degree according to the proportion it contributed to the general treasury." [2]   Forty-eight in all were to be chosen, of which the then largest colonies, Massachusetts Bay and Virginia, were to have seven, and the smallest, New Hampshire and Rhode Island, two each, the members of the council meeting for the first time in the city of Philadelphia upon the call of the President-General.

The members thus selected were to sit for a period of three years, the number of delegates allowed each colony was to be revised after the first three years of the union, and " from time to time, in all ensuing elections," to be based upon " the proportion of money arising out of each colony to the general treasury." The council thus composed was to meet yearly, and oftener if required, at such time and at such place as agreed to before adjournment, or in case of emergency, as was to be determined by the President-General upon the written consent of seven members of the council " with due and timely notice to the whole." The council itself was to choose its speaker, and it was neither to be dissolved nor prorogued, nor to sit longer than six weeks at any one time, without their own consent " or the special command of the crown." The members were to be allowed ten shillings per diem during their session and journey to and from the place of meeting, and twenty miles were to be reckoned a day's journey.

The assent of the President-General was necessary to all acts of the Council which he should execute and he was authorized, in words which suggest the language of that greater instrument in whose framing the author of the Albany plan subsequently took part, " with the advice of the Grand Council " to make treaties with the Indians and also to declare peace or war with Indian nations. The President and Council were to regulate trade with the Indians, to act for the Crown, which henceforth was to be the sole purchaser of lands from the Indians, to grant settlements " till the crown shall think fit to form them into particular governments." The President and Council were likewise to raise

---

[1] *Documents Relative to the Colonial History of New York*, Vol. vi, p. 889.
[2] A. H. Smyth, *The Writings of Benjamin Franklin* (New York, the Macmillan Company, 1907), Vol. iii, p. 212. See also Jared Sparks, *The Works of Benjamin Franklin*, Vol. iii, p. 41.

soldiers and build forts, to equip vessels for their defense and the protection of their trade, but not to " impress men in any colony, without the consent of the legislature." For these purposes the President-General and the Council were empowered " to make laws, and lay and levy such general duties, imposts, or taxes, as to them shall appear most equal and just (considering the ability and other circumstances of the inhabitants in the several colonies), and such as may be collected with the least inconvenience to the people; rather discouraging luxury, than loading industry with unnecessary burthens."

Provision was made for the appointment of a general and a particular treasurer when necessary, with the proviso that no money was to be paid out except " by joint orders of the President-General and Grand Council " and in pursuance of law, and that accounts were to be yearly settled and reported to the assemblies of the different colonies.

The quorum for the Grand Council was fixed at twenty-five members, provided there be a representative from the majority of the colonies. The President-General and the Grand Council were a law-making body, and the article on this important head reads:

> That the laws made by them for the purposes aforesaid shall not be repugnant, but, as near as may be, agreeable to the laws of England, and shall be transmitted to the King in Council for approbation, as soon as may be after their passing; and if not disapproved within three years after presentation, to remain in force.[1]

In case of the death of the President-General the speaker of the Grand Council was to act " till the King's pleasure be known."

The provision concerning the officers is interesting, as this in one respect suggests the device of a later plan of union, in that all military and naval officers " to act under this general constitution " were to be nominated by the President-General with the approval of the Grand Council. But civilian officers were themselves to be nominated by the Council and to receive the President-General's approbation before entering upon the performance of their duties. It was foreseen that vacancies would occur either by death or removal of the military and civil officers appointed under this Constitution, and it was therefore provided that the Governor of the province should appoint others in their place " until the pleasure of the President-General and Grand Council can be known." Here again there is a suggestion of appointments to be made subject to the confirmation of the grand council known as the Senate of the United States.

The plan ended with a very important provision, safeguarding the colonies against usurpation on the part of the proposed government, for the military and civil establishments in each colony were to remain " in their present state, the general constitution notwithstanding," and a right was expressly granted to

[1] Smyth, *ibid.,* p. 223; Sparks, Vol. iii, p. 52.

each colony, contrary to the provisions of the constitution, to defend itself on a sudden emergency at the expense of the union.

Dr. Franklin's plan was premature. The colonies did not as yet feel the necessity of union in order to protect themselves against what they regarded as unjustifiable oppression on the part of the mother country, and they were therefore unwilling to make what they were pleased to call the concessions contained in the Albany plan. The home authorities, on the other hand, were apparently not ready to consolidate their colonial empire in America, and in any event they were likewise unwilling to make the concessions to self-government recommended in the Albany plan. As Dr. Franklin himself said, " the Crown disapproved it, as having too much Weight in the Democratic Part of the Constitution; and every Assembly as having allowed too much to Prerogative. So it was totally rejected." Many years after the Albany Convention, and two years after the adoption of the Constitution of the more perfect Union, the venerable Dr. Franklin recurred to the Albany plan and thus expressed himself concerning the results which in his opinion would have followed, had his plan of Union been adopted:

> On Reflection it now seems probable, that if the foregoing Plan or some thing like it had been adopted and carried into Execution, the subsequent Separation of the Colonies from the Mother Country might not so soon have happened, nor the Mischiefs suffered on both sides have occurred perhaps during another Century. For the Colonies, if so united, would have really been, as they then thought themselves, sufficient to their own Defence, and being trusted with it, as by the Plan, an Army from Britain, for that purpose would have been unnecessary; The Pretences for framing the Stamp Act would then not have existed, nor the other projects for drawing a Revenue from America to Britain by Act of Parliament, which were the Causes of the Breach & attended with such terrible Expense of Blood and Treasure; so that the different Parts of the Empire might still have remained in Peace and Union.[1]

By 1754 events were moving rapidly. The man who was destined to lead the Revolutionary armies was already in the field as a subaltern in the French and Indian War, which is the name by which the Seven Years' War of Europe is known in America. Franklin, who was to render hardly less distinguished service to his age, typified American thinking at its best. The conquest of Canada had given Great Britain an unbroken domain from the Gulf of Mexico northward. The Treaty of Peace had left a clear title to the territory from the Atlantic Ocean to the Mississippi River, with only Spain to the west of that water. The times seemed ripening for a uniform system of government. There was no longer a formidable enemy threatening the existence of the colonies from without; the home authorities felt that henceforth

---

[1] A. H. Smyth, *The Writings of Benjamin Franklin,* Vol. iii, p. 226 note.

they were to have a free hand in moulding the colonies to their will, and the servants of the Crown had begun to put the imperial house in order.

Without indulging in criticism of the Crown and its advisors, and without commendation of the colony and its advocates, it was not unreasonable, from the standpoint of the mother country, that the colonies should be subjected to a centralized control, that they should contribute to their own support, that they should be made to feel that they were an integral portion of the empire, and that therefore they should assume their share of the imperial burden, to be determined by the imperial, not by the colonial, authorities. Nor were the views of the colonists unreasonable from their own point of view, in that they had opened up and settled the New World, that they had brought with them the common law and the rights of Englishmen, that they were not only inherently entitled to the blessings of local government, but that they deserved such government by the services they had rendered, and that, while far from unwilling to perform their full duty to the empire, they nevertheless believed that the money raised by taxing them should be spent in America in accordance with their judgment and that they themselves should determine what their contributions should be, instead of having them determined by authorities across the seas, before whom they were not represented, and whose action they could neither influence nor control. The home government looked at the colonies from the standpoint of the past, as though they existed for the benefit of the home country and that the home authorities were naturally superior to them. The colonies, on the other hand, looked at their relations with the mother country from the standpoint of the future, in which they were to be integral parts of a great empire and in the economy of which they were to be practically self-governing dominions, united by language, tradition, and enlightened interest, but in which there was to be no mark or suggestion of inferiority. The new wine broke the old bottles.

It was foreseen that the adoption of a Declaration of Independence would necessitate some form of general government, because, in the opinion of the colonists, such a Declaration would break the bonds of allegiance to England, create of the erstwhile colonies free and independent States, and in the absence of a superior they would be obliged to devise some form of agreement and cooperation; otherwise their efforts would be unavailing. It was further foreseen by some in the Congress that the resort to arms would lead inevitably to independence, and that some agreement upon a union and a method of government should precede any declaration as it would inevitably have to follow it. The shrewdest mind in the country, and therefore in the Congress, was, it need hardly be said, Benjamin Franklin, and he was ready with a " plan " in 1775 as he had been ready with a plan of union twenty-one years earlier at the first Congress of the colonies at Albany. Therefore, on July 21, 1775, he laid his second plan before Congress, providing for a union of the colonies, soon to be independent States.[1] But the Congress, apparently, did not then measure aright the consequences of standing by Massachusetts in its armed resistance.

Dr. Franklin's plan provided for the union of the colonies for purposes of resistance against Great Britain, but apparently contemplated the possibility of a redress of grievances and a reconciliation with the mother country, whereupon the colonies were to " return to their former connexion and friendship with Britain." It was, however, foreseen by the venerable statesman, because of his intercourse with British men of affairs and his knowledge of the British people, that the reconciliation might not take place, and the last clause of his plan therefore runs: " But on Failure thereof this Confederation is to be perpetual." [2]

Notwithstanding the fact that his project was one primarily for colonies, not for States, the union which he proposed was of a very close nature, and would have rested upon the people rather than upon the colonies, although the rights of the colonies as such, or rather of the people within the colonies, were safeguarded. For example, there was to be a general congress, composed of delegates selected by each colony, but the number thereof for each was to depend upon the population of the colony, and a delegate was to be allowed for every five thousand male inhabitants, or, as the good Doctor put it, " male polls between sixteen and sixty years of age." The congress composed in this way would not represent solely the colonies but the people who happened to reside within their territorial limits, and as the Congress was therefore the representative of the people it was natural that the Congress should be empowered to provide for the general welfare and to enact laws for this purpose. It was to be the power and the duty of Congress, by Article V, to pass upon questions of war and peace, to send and to receive ambassadors and to contract alliances, to settle all disputes and differences between the colonies, and, apparently, as an afterthought, for it is in brackets, to bring about " (the reconciliation with Great Britain)." The Congress also was, in Dr. Franklin's language, to plant new colonies when proper. It was also to make " such general ordinances as, though necessary to the general welfare, particular Assemblies cannot be competent to," and among these he specified " those that may relate to our general commerce, or general currency; the establishment of posts; and the regulation of our common forces." The Congress also was to appoint " all general officers civil and military, appertaining to the general confederacy, such as general treasurer, secretary, &c." As representation in the Congress was to be based upon population, not upon the colonies as such, it was natural

[1] Smyth, *Writings of Benjamin Franklin,* Vol. vi, p. 420; Sparks, Vol. v, p. 91.
[2] Smyth, p. 425; Sparks, p. 96.

that the inhabitants having the largest representation should also bear a larger proportion of the burdens of government. Therefore, charges of war, " and all other general expenses to be incurred for the common welfare " were to be " defrayed out of a common treasury . . . to be supplied by each colony in proportion to its number of male polls between sixteen and sixty years of age," and the proportion of each colony was " to be laid and levied by the laws of each colony."

As still further showing the continental as distinct from the colonial idea, the quorum of the Congress was to consist of " one half of the members," and in the Congress itself and in the transaction of business each delegate was to " have a vote in all cases." The delegates to the Congress were to be elected annually and to meet at such time and place as should be agreed to in the next preceding Congress by rotation in the different colonies. In addition there was to be an executive council, appointed by the Congress out of its own body, to consist of twelve persons, and which was apparently to represent the Congress during its recess, " to execute what shall have been enjoined thereby; to manage the general Continental business and interests; to receive applications from foreign countries; to prepare matters for the consideration of the Congress; to fill up, *pro tempore,* continental offices that fall vacant; and to draw on the general treasurer for such moneys as may be necessary for general services, appropriated by the Congress to such services."

It has been stated that the existence of the colonies was recognized, although they were not made the basis of representation and they were apparently to be denied an equal share in providing for the general welfare, for which purpose the plan of government was proposed. Dr. Franklin's further views are set forth in the third Article, which reads:

> That each Colony shall enjoy and retain as much as it may think fit of its own present Laws, Customs, Rights, Privileges, and peculiar jurisdictions within its own Limits; and may amend its own Constitution as shall seem best to its own Assembly or Convention.[1]

The plan in all its parts displays not merely a keen and penetrating mind but shows its author to be a resident of a large and populous State, which could safely entrust its interest to a general assembly in the full knowledge that its greatness, its extent and its power would secure it an ample return for the concessions, always more specious than real, of great bodies and of great persons. The little States apparently did not take kindly to the plan of the great Doctor; for although read by its author to the Congress on July 21, 1775, it was neither adopted nor considered. There is no record in the Journal of the Congress of its having been read, and indeed the only testimony we have to that effect is the endorsement in Dr. Franklin's hand that it was read

[1] Smyth, *ibid.,* p. 421; Sparks, Vol. v, p. 92.

before Congress on the stated date.   It is mentioned, however, in this connection, for a twofold reason: to show that in July, 1775, a shrewd man of the world, who had suffered indignities at the hands of the British Government, was contented with a temporary union of the colonies, in the hope of a reconciliation with the mother country instead of advocating separation from Great Britain, and because Dr. Franklin's text seems to have been known to his friend and colleague John Dickinson, who a year later, as chairman of the committee formed for that purpose, prepared and presented a draft of the Articles of Confederation, after the independence of the colonies had been proclaimed.

II

INDEPENDENCE DECLARED

The archbishop of Canterbury (Laud) kept a jealous eye over New-England. One Burdett of Piscataqua was his correspondent. A copy of a letter to the archbishop wrote by Burdett was found in his study and to this effect, viz. "That he delayed going to England that he might fully inform himself of the state of the place as to allegiance, for it was not new discipline which was aimed at but sovereignty, and that it was accounted perjury and treason in their general court to speak of appeals to the King." (*Thomas Hutchinson, The History of the Colony of Massachusets-Bay, Vol. I, 1764, p. 86.*)

There were no reason that one man should take upon him to be lord or judge over another; because, although there be according to the opinion of some very great and judicious men a kind of natural right in the noble, wise, and virtuous, to govern them which are of servile disposition; nevertheless for manifestation of this their right, and men's more peaceable contentment on both sides, the assent of them who are to be governed seemeth necessary. (*Richard Hooker, Of the Laws of Ecclesiastical Polity, 1594, Church edition, 1868, Book I, Section 10, p. 54.*)

For there are no Examples so frequent in History, both sacred and prophane, as those of Men withdrawing themselves, and their Obedience, from the Jurisdiction they were born under, and the Family or Community they were bred up in, and *setting up new Governments* in other Places; from whence sprang all that number of petty Commonwealths in the Beginning of Ages, and which always multiplied, as long as there was room enough, till the stronger, or more fortunate, swallowed the weaker; and those great ones again breaking to Pieces, dissolved into lesser Dominions. (*John Locke, Two Treatises of Government, 1690, Book II, Ch. VIII, section 115, Works, Edition of 1714, Vol. II.*)

Thus, though looking back as far as Records give us any account of peopling the World, and the History of Nations, we commonly find the *Government* to be in one Hand; yet it destroys not that which I affirm, viz. That the *Beginning of politick Society* depends upon the Consent of the Individuals, to joyn into, and make one Society; who, when they are thus incorporated, might set up what Form of Government they thought fit. (*John Locke, Two Treatises of Government, 1690, Book II, Ch. VIII, section 106, Works, Edition of 1714, Vol. II.*)

Men being, as has been said, by Nature, all free, equal, and independent, no one can be put out of this Estate, and subjected to the political Power of another, without his own Consent. The only Way whereby any one devests himself of his natural Liberty, and puts on the *Bonds of civil Society* is by agreeing with other Men to joyn and unite into a Community, for their comfortable, safe, and peaceable Living one amongst another, in a secure Enjoyment of their Properties, and a greater Security against any, that are not of it. (*John Locke, Two Treatises of Government, 1690, Book II, Ch. VIII, section 95, Works, Edition of 1714, Vol. II.*)

Section 1. That all men are by nature equally free and independent, and have certain inherent rights, of which, when they enter into a state of society, they cannot, by any compact, deprive or divest their posterity; namely, the enjoyment of life and liberty, with the means of acquiring and possessing property, and pursuing and obtaining happiness and safety.

Sec 2. That all power is vested in, and consequently derived from, the people; that magistrates are their trustees and servants, and at all times amenable to them.

Sec. 3. That government is, or ought to be, instituted for the common benefit, protection, and security of the people, nation, or community; of all the various modes and forms of government, that is best which is capable of producing the greatest degree of happiness and safety, and is most effectually secured against the danger of maladministration; and that, when any government shall be found inadequate or contrary to these purposes, a majority of the community hath an indubitable, inalienable, and indefeasible right to reform, alter, or abolish it, in such manner as shall be judged most conducive to the public weal. (*Virginia Bill of Rights adopted June 12, 1776. Ben: Perley Poore, The Federal and State Constitu-*

tions, Colonial Charters, and other Organic Laws of the United States, Part II, 1877, pp. 1908–1909.)

We, therefore, the Representatives of the united States of America, in General Congress, Assembled, appealing to the Supreme Judge of the world for the rectitude of our intentions, do, in the Name, and by Authority of the good People of these Colonies, solemnly publish and declare, That these United Colonies are, and of Right ought to be Free and Independent States; that they are Absolved from all Allegiance to the British Crown, and that all political connection between them and the State of Great Britain, is and ought to be totally dissolved; and that as Free and Independent States, they have full power to levy War, conclude Peace, contract Alliances, establish Commerce, and to do all other Acts and Things which Independent States may of right do. And for the support of this Declaration, with a firm reliance on the Protection of Divine Providence, we mutually pledge to each other our Lives, our Fortunes and our sacred Honor. (*The unanimous Declaration of Independence of the thirteen united States of America, in Congress, July 4, 1776, Revised Statutes of the United States, 1878, p. 5.*)

The writer whose ideas and phrases are most deeply impressed upon American political history is, beyond all doubt, John Locke. It is not difficult to explain the cause of his great influence. His "Treatise on Government," published in 1690, was a justification of the Revolution of 1688. The principles of that Revolution, as expounded by him, became the orthodox Whig doctrine. "His treatise," says Mr. Leslie Stephen, in his able "History of English Thought in the Eighteenth Century," "became the political bible of the following century." Hallam says that it opened a new era of political opinion in Europe, and that the theory there propounded has been fertile of great revolutions and perhaps pregnant with more.

From the beginning of their dispute with England, the colonists found themselves fully sustained by the great Whig philosopher. What could be more acceptable than the doctrine that a people are absolved from obedience when illegal attempts are made upon their liberties, and that it is then their duty to make an appeal to heaven? When the colonies in 1776 formed their Bills of Rights, the great authority as to those rights was Locke. The Bills of Rights of Massachusetts, Pennsylvania, Maryland, and other States set forth, almost in the exact language of Locke, that "all government of right originates from the people, is founded in compact only, and instituted solely for the good of the whole."

The Declaration of Independence, which has long ago been apotheosized, did not escape contemporary criticism. Adams said that it was a commonplace compilation. Richard Henry Lee charged that it was copied from Locke's treatise on Government. To this charge it is certainly open. All those truths which the Declaration holds to be self-evident are set forth with just as much clearness and force in Locke's treatise. (*W. T. Brantly, Of the Influence of European Speculation in the Formation of the Federal Constitution, 1880, in Southern Law Review, New Series, Vol. VI, pp. 352–353.*)

The doctrine of the equality of all men, which is so striking in the Declaration, was accepted without controversy. This acquiescence was partly due to the condition of the country as a settlement in a wilderness. Before the Revolution, a common characteristic of all the colonies was the essential equality of the people. It is sometimes said, however, that we derived the doctrine of the equality of mankind from a French source. Sir Henry Maine observes, in his "Ancient Law," that the opinions then fashionable in France led Jefferson to join what he denominates the specially French assumption, that all men are born equal, with the assumption, more familiar to Englishmen, that all men are born free. Mr. Morley, in the *Fortnightly Review* for October, 1879, declares that "nobody who has examined so much as the surface of the question would dream of denying that the French theories of society played an important part in the preparation of American independence." (*W. T. Brantly, Of the Influence of European Speculation in the Formation of the Federal Constitution, 1880, in Southern Law Review, New Series, Vol. VI. pp. 353–354.*)

It is true that Jefferson afterwards "drank a deep draught from the intoxicating cup of the French Revolution," but we do not think that in 1776 he had felt the French political influence. He was, we know, a student of Locke, and Locke asserted the natural equality of man as strongly as his natural liberty. In Jefferson's original draft of the Declaration, now in the State Department, we see that he first wrote "all men are created equal and independent," and afterwards erased the words "and independent." In the second chapter of the "Treatise on Government," Locke says: "To understand political power aright, we must understand what state men are naturally in, and that is a state of perfect freedom. . . . A state also of equality. . . . In the state of nature, men are all *equal and independent*,"—the very phrase first employed by Jefferson. (*W. T. Brantly,*

Of the Influence of European Speculation in the Formation of the Federal Constitution, 1880, in Southern Law Review, New Series, Vol. VI. p. 354.)

The Declaration of Independence is singularly suggestive of the Virginia Bill of Rights which was adopted on June 12, 1776. They are both streams from the same prolific fountain. The first article of the Virginia Bill declares, "that all men are by nature equally free and independent, and have certain inherent rights the which, when they enter into a state of society, they cannot, by any compact, deprive or divest their posterity,— namely, the enjoyment of life and liberty with the means of acquiring and possessing property and pursuing and obtaining happiness and safety." The Virginia Bill was the work of George Mason, a man deeply versed in English parliamentary history, but who was not indebted for any of his opinions to French literary men. (*W. T. Brantly, Of the Influence of European Speculation in the Formation of the Federal Constitution, 1880, in Southern Law Review, New Series, Vol. VI. p. 354.*)

The origin of the idea of a state of nature wherein all men are equal has been traced to the Roman lawyers. Locke received it from Hobbes and Grotius. But it was so stamped with the authority of the Whig philosopher that it colored all the political thinking of the last century in America. The conception of man as the signatary of a social compact is an absurd one, and has long since fallen into disrepute with the best thinkers. Hume's refutation of the theory is complete, but it is not without advocates at the present day. Sir Henry Maine is astonished at the extraordinary vitality of this speculative error. The circumstance that the Bills of Rights of so many of these States continue to assert in terms that all government is founded in compact, may serve to show us that the value of a sonorous maxim in politics is not proportioned to its credit with philosophers. (*W. T. Brantly, Of the Influence of European Speculation in the Formation of the Federal Constitution, 1880, in Southern Law Review, New Series, Vol. VI. pp. 357–358.*)

That there were thirteen colonies, with separate governments in each, without any control by one over another, is admitted; that they assembled by different representations; that they voted, acted, and signed the declaration by their separate delegates, is apparent on the journals of congress, and the face of the paper. The members who assembled as the delegates of colonies, were the same, who, as the representatives of the states, made the declaration in the name, and by the authority of the good people of these colonies; which was :—" That these united colonies are, and of right ought to be, free and independent states." (*Mr. Justice Baldwin, A General View of the Origin and Nature of the Constitution and Government of the United States, 1837, p. 78.*)

CHAPTER II

INDEPENDENCE DECLARED

O<small>N</small> July 4, 1776, the representatives of the United States of America in Congress assembled proclaimed their independence in a declaration setting forth the right and the duty of all peoples to organize themselves into nations, with governments of their own choice, to change those forms of government when they have not subserved the purpose for which they were created by the peoples, and submitted facts to a candid world justifying the Declaration of Independence in their particular case. With the facts submitted by the Congress to a candid world we are not here concerned. We are, however, concerned with the right to set up a government for themselves, which the signers of the Declaration asserted, claimed and exercised. For, if the right exist, its exercise becomes a matter of expediency, and the facts merely the cause or pretext of its exercise by peoples bent on exercising the right.

The Funda-
mental Right

Before dealing with this matter, it is advisable to advert to the state of things which produced the Declaration and called into being the United States of America. The thirteen American colonies forming the original thirteen United States and extending from Florida, on the south, to Canada, on the north, were either settled originally by British subjects or had passed into the possession of Great Britain. These colonies, whether under a charter such as Connecticut; under a charter to a proprietor as in the case of Maryland; or governed directly as a province by the crown as Virginia, claimed the right of local self-government by means of assemblies of their own choice; for, to quote Sir John Seeley, "assemblies were not formally instituted, but grew up of themselves, because it was the nature of Englishmen to assemble." [1] Recognizing themselves as subjects of the mother country, provided such regulation was external and they were left to settle their internal affairs as seemed to them to be just in view of local conditions, with which they were familiar and of which they felt that the mother country was not cognizant, naturally, the colonists looked at their relations with the mother country from the colonial point of view. The recognition that there was a mother country implied another point of view, which did in fact exist.

Colonial
View

Great Britain held that the colonists were British subjects and possessed of the rights and liberties of such; that the colonists could have no greater rights than British subjects, and that, as such, they were subject to the Crown, the Parliament, or both, as were their fellow-countrymen of Great Britain; that the colonies were, as trading companies and bodies politic, entitled to

Imperial
View

[1] Sir John Robert Seeley, *The Expansion of England,* 1883, p. 67.

make laws within the charter but not *ultra vires,* and therefore subordinated to the law and the control of their creator; that, as colonists, they were subject to the burdens of the empire, as were their fellow-countrymen at home, and as colonies they were subject to regulation and control, internal as well as external; that the nature and extent of the duties to be imposed upon the colonists and the supervision and control of the colonies were matters of expediency, to be determined by the King, Lords and Commons of Great Britain, the supreme authority in all matters domestic, colonial, foreign. As was natural, the mother country looked upon its relations with the colonies from the standpoint of the empire.

The colonists, if admitting these rights in point of law, were unwilling to allow the mother country to exercise them in fact or to determine the matter of expediency. The mother country, possessing the rights, was unwilling to allow the colonists to determine the expediency of their exercise. There was no indifferent party to which the colonists could, or to which the mother country would, submit their differences. Each, therefore, appealed eventually to the arbitrament of the sword.

To obviate the resort to force which lurked in the background, the colonists petitioned the Crown, the Parliament and the people of Great Britain for a redress of grievances, and, conscious that the cause of each was the cause of every colony, a congress of their delegates assembled in 1774, in Philadelphia, just as Hutchinson happily said that, in 1619, "a house of burgesses broke out in Virginia." This assembly, extending beyond the confines of a colony and affecting the destinies of a continent, they aptly called a Continental Congress, and the first of these bodies, composed of representatives of all the colonies, with the exception of Georgia, met, in 1774, in the city of Philadelphia in the month of September.

A Continental Congress

As the blow which threatened all the colonies had first fallen in Massachusetts, it was natural that that province should have taken the initiative. Therefore, on June 17, 1774, one year to a day before the battle of Bunker Hill, the Massachusetts House of Representatives, under the leadership of Samuel Adams, resolved:

> That a meeting of Committees from the several Colonies on this Continent is highly expedient and necessary, to consult upon the present state of the Colonies, and the miseries to which they are and must be reduced by the operation of certain acts of Parliament respecting America, and to deliberate and determine upon wise and proper measures, to be by them recommended to all the Colonies, for the recovery and establishment of their just rights & liberties, civil & religious, and the restoration of union & harmony between Great Britain and the Colonies, most ardently desired by all good men. Therefore, Resolved, that the Honble. James Bowdoin, esq^r., the Honble. Thomas Cushing, esq^r., Mr. Samuel Adams, John Adams, & Robert Treat Paine, esq^rs., be, and they are hereby appointed a Committee on the part of this province, for the purposes aforesaid, any three of whom to be a quorum, to meet such committees or delegates from the other Colonies as have been or

may be appointed, either by their respective houses of Burgesses, or representatives, or by convention, or by the committees of correspondence appointed by the respective houses of Assembly, in the city of Philadelphia, or any other place that shall be judged most suitable by the Committee, on the first day of September next; & that the Speaker of the House be directed, in a letter to the speakers of the houses of Burgesses or representatives in the several Colonies, to inform them of the substance of these Resolves.[1]

On September 5th the delegates of all but three colonies met. On the 14th those of North Carolina appeared. The Congress organized with Peyton Randolph, of Virginia, as President. On September 7th a committee, consisting of two members from each colony, was appointed " to State the rights of the Colonies in general, the several instances in which those rights are violated or infringed, and the means most proper to be pursued for obtaining a restoration of them." And it was decided " that the Congress do confine themselves, at present, to the consideration of such rights only as have been infringed by acts of the British parliament since the year 1763." [2]

In this the colonists were well advised, for 1763 marked an epoch in the relations between America and Great Britain. Before that date the colonies had been looked upon as separate and distinct plantations, to be protected, if need be, against the aggression of France from the north in Canada and the west in Louisiana. The conquest of Canada, in which the colonies participated, and its cession by the treaty of 1763 to Great Britain, the cession of Louisiana to Spain and the recognition of the Mississippi as the boundary, caused the Crown and its advisers, apparently for the first time, to consider the colonies as a unit and to govern them as such, and, in pursuance of this policy, to pass the various statutes whereof the colonists complained.

Declaration and Resolves

They therefore adopted a declaration. On October 14th a report on the rights and grievances of the colonies was adopted, known as the Declaration and Resolves of the First Continental Congress.[3]

The declaration consists of eleven resolutions framed by representatives of " the good people of the several Colonies" with the exception of Georgia which, however, was later to be represented in the Congress. The first ten of the resolutions state the rights of the colonies as their respective representatives believed them to be on the eve of the Revolution, and the eleventh is an enumeration of the acts of parliament which they considered to be inconsistent with the declaration of rights and which therefore should be repealed " in order to restore harmony between Great Britain and the American colonies." The preamble asserts that Parliament has claimed " a power of right to bind the people of America, by statute in all cases whatsoever," that Parliament

[1] *Journals of the Continental Congress* (1904—), Vol. i, pp. 15–16. For documents and correspondence relating to proceedings of the Continental Congress and the Colonial Congresses, see also Force's *American Archives, Fourth Series,* 1837.

[2] *Ibid.,* p. 42.

[3] *Ibid.,* pp. 63-73.

had " in some acts expressly imposed taxes on them," and that Parliament " under various pretences, but in fact for the purpose of raising a revenue," had " imposed rates and duties payable in these colonies." Because of this action on the part of Great Britain, the colonies deemed it essential to set forth their rights in the premises. Therefore they declared:

That they were " entitled to life, liberty, & property," and that they had never renounced the right to dispose thereof to any foreign power without their consent;

That their ancestors were, at the time of their emigration, " entitled to all the rights, liberties, and immunities of free and natural-born subjects, within the realm of England; "

That these rights were not lost by emigration and that their descendants were therefore " entitled to the exercise and enjoyment of all such of them, as their local and other circumstances enable them to exercise and enjoy; "

That the inhabitants of the colonies could not, because of local conditions, be properly represented in Parliament, but only in their local legislatures, where by their representatives, they consented to taxation; recognizing, however, the right of the British Parliament to regulate their " external commerce, for the purpose of securing the commercial advantages of the whole empire to the mother country, and the commercial benefits of its respective members; excluding every idea of taxation, internal or external, for raising a revenue on the subjects, in America, without their consent; "

That the colonies were entitled " to the common law of England," and more especially to the " inestimable privilege " of trial by jury;

That they were " entitled to the benefits of such of the English statutes as existed at the time of their colonization," and which had been found applicable to local conditions;

That they were entitled to " all the immunities and privileges granted & confirmed to them by royal charters, or secured by their several codes of provincial laws; "

That they possessed the right, and without restraint, peaceably to assemble, to consider their grievances, and to petition the king for a redress thereof;

That the maintenance of a standing army in the colonies in times of peace without the consent of the colonial legislatures was against law;

That the branches of the legislature should be independent of each other; and therefore that the exercise of legislative power by a council appointed by the Crown and serving during its pleasure, " is unconstitutional, dangerous, and destructive to the freedom of American legislation; "

And finally, that these " their indubitable rights and liberties " could not be " legally taken from them, altered or abridged by any power whatever, without their own consent, by their representatives in their several provincial legislatures."

This document, which would have justified in itself the call and the meeting of the Congress, does not, however, stand alone; for the representatives of the colonies did not content themselves with a statement of grievances but considered " the means most proper to be used for the restoration " of colonial rights.

An Asso-ciation

Sharing, no doubt, the view of John Adams that the various Navigation Acts and Acts of Trade were the cause of strained relations leading in the end to revolution, the members of Congress were of the opinion that " a Non-Importation, Non-Consumption, and Non-Exportation Agreement, faithfully adhered to," would prove " the most speedy, effectual, and peaceable measure." Therefore a report, advocating an association to cut off all trade between the colonies, Great Britain and its other possessions, was reported on the 12th, agreed to on the 18th and signed on October 20, 1774, by fifty-three members of the Congress, by which they solemnly bound themselves and their constituents to adhere to the Association until the grievances whereof they complained were redressed; and they recommended it " to the provincial conventions, and to the committees in the respective colonies, to establish such farther regulations as they may think proper, for carrying into execution this association." [1]   Whereupon, the Congress adjourned on October 26th, having invited all the colonies to send delegates to another Congress, to meet on the 10th day of May, 1775, unless their grievances had been redressed in the meantime.

It is to be observed that, although no union, an association of the colonies was formed which was rapidly to develop into a union in law as well as in fact.   On April 19, 1775, the British forces in Boston deemed it advisable to seize and destroy some powder magazines at Concord in the province of Massachusetts.   The intention of the British commander became known and, when his troops entered the little town of Lexington at day-break, on the way to Concord, they found drawn up a small body of provincials, which they quickly dispersed and continued their march to Concord, where they indeed effected their purpose, but found larger bodies of provincials drawn up to resist them. Blood had been drawn at Lexington; it was freely shed at Concord, and before " the embattled farmers " the British troops hurriedly fell back to avoid the capture which threatened them.

When, therefore, the second Continental Congress met in Philadelphia on May 10, 1775, it was composed of representatives of all the thirteen colonies including those of Georgia, which by this time had made up its mind to cast its lot with the other colonies.   Peyton Randolph was again elected President, but, absenting himself in Virginia to attend to matters of the province, he was, on May 24, 1775, succeeded by John Hancock of Massachusetts.

Finding themselves in the midst of war, the colonies in Congress accepted

[1] *Journals of the Continental Congress,* Vol. i, p. 80.

the gauge of battle by electing on June 15th, by unanimous ballot, one of their members, George Washington, to be commander-in-chief of the armies raised and to be raised in order that " the liberties of the country receive no detriment." [1]

The Congress, recognizing the importance of this action, adopted on July 6, 1775, a carefully prepared and moderate " Declaration of the Causes and Necessity of Taking up Arms," which was " to be published by General Washington upon his arrival at the camp before Boston," in which city the British army was then besieged by the provincial troops and volunteers already pouring in from the adjoining colonies.   At the same time, every effort was made by the Congress to effect a reconciliation with the mother country, and the declaration of the 6th was accompanied on the 8th by a petition to the King, each drafted by the patriotic yet cautious and conciliatory Dickinson.

Another Declaration and a Petition

In the interval between the first and second Congress, Lord North, then Prime Minister of Great Britain, held out the olive branch in the form of a Conciliatory Resolution of February 27, 1775, by the terms of which the Imperial Parliament declared its intention to abstain from internal taxation, and only to regulate commerce, provided each colony or province should contribute its portion " to the common defence," and " engage to make provision also for the support of the Civil Government, and the Administration of Justice, in such Province or Colony." [2]   The conciliatory act was meant to be a concession, not a surrender, and it was shortly followed by the New England Restraining Act of March 30, 1775, cutting off all trade between the

[1] On June 16, 1775

The president from the chair informed Geo: Washington esq[r]. that he had the order of the Congress to acq[ain]t him, that the Congress had by a unanimous vote made choice of him to be general and commander in chief to take the supreme command of the forces raised and to be raised, in defence of American Liberty, and desired his acceptance of it.   Whereupon Colonel Washington, standing in his place, spoke as follows:

" Mr. President,

" Tho' I am truly sensible of the high Honour done me, in this Appointment, yet I feel great distress, from a consciousness that my abilities and military experience may not be equal to the extensive and important Trust: However, as the Congress desire it, I will enter upon the momentous duty, and exert every power I possess in their service, and for support of the glorious cause.   I beg they will accept my most cordial thanks for this distinguished testimony of their approbation.

" But, lest some unlucky event should happen, unfavourable to my reputation, I beg it may be remembered, by every gentleman in the room, that I, this day, declare, with the utmost sincerity, I do not think myself equal to the Command I am honored with. . . ." *Journals,* Vol. ii, pp. 91–2.

On June 26th the New York Provincial Congress submitted an address to General Washington expressing satisfaction at his appointment.   In the course of his reply he said:

" May your warmest wishes be realized in the success of *America* at this important and interesting period; and be assured that every exertion of my worthy colleagues and myself will be equally extended to the reestablishment of peace and harmony between the Mother Country and these Colonies, as to the fatal but necessary operations of war.   When we assumed the soldier we did not lay aside the citizen; and we shall most sincerely rejoice with you in that happy hour when the establishment of *American* liberty, on the most firm and solid foundations, shall enable us to return to our private stations in the bosom of a free, peaceful, and happy Country."   See *Journal of New York Provincial Congress* for June 26, 1775.   Here reprinted from *American Archives, Fourth Series,* 1839, Vol. 2, p. 1322.

[2] *Archives, Fourth Series,* 1837, Vol. 1, p. 1611.

colonies and foreign countries and restraining their trade to Great Britain. In April the southern colonies were likewise restrained, and these various measures were later superseded by the general act of December 22, 1775, prohibiting trade and intercourse with America.

On July 31, 1775, the Congress, in a report written by Thomas Jefferson, rejected Lord North's conciliatory resolution, which had been laid before that body in the month of May, 1775. On its part, Great Britain was not slow to take action. The battles of Lexington and Concord on April 19th and of Bunker Hill on June 17th, between British troops and the colonists, and the appointment of Washington as commander-in-chief, likewise convinced the British Government that war was on, and on August 23, 1775, it issued a proclamation of rebellion appropriately ending with "God Save the King." The resort was indeed made to conciliation, but the appeal had already been made to the sword. Too late for the American colonies on the Continent, it was not too late to save the other colonies which Great Britain then had or has since acquired, and which are now self-supporting dominions proud of their connection with the mother country. This was the famous Taxation of Colonies Act (18 Geo. III, c. 12) providing that Parliament " will not impose any duty, tax, or assessment whatever, payable in any of his Majesty's colonies, provinces, and plantations in North America or the West Indies; except only such duties as it may be expedient to impose for the regulation of commerce; the net produce of such duties to be always paid and applied to and for the use of the colony, province, or plantation, in which the same shall be respectively levied, in such manner as other duties collected by the authority of the respective general courts, or general assemblies, of such colonies, provinces, or plantations, are ordinarily paid and applied." Upon this act, caused by the revolt of the American colonies and the attitude of Great Britain toward its colonies of today, a competent British authority says: " This renunciation by the Imperial Parliament of the right to impose taxes upon a colony, whether a self-governing colony or not, has passed through two stages. Since 1783 taxation imposed by an Imperial Act has always been, even in the case of a Crown colony, imposed for the benefit of the colony, and the proceeds thereof have been paid to the colony. But until the repeal of the Navigation Laws in 1849 Parliament, in support of our whole navigation system, retained the practice of imposing duties on goods imported into the colonies, though the proceeds thereof were paid to the colonies so taxed. Since 1849 no Imperial Act has been passed for the taxation of any colony, and no colony is compelled by the Imperial Parliament to contribute anything in the way of taxation towards the cost of the government of the United Kingdom or towards the defence of the British Empire." [1]

No answer other than this proclamation and the prohibition of trade and

[1] Albert Venn Dicey, *Law of the Constitution,* 1915 ed., p. xxvi, Note 2.

intercourse with America was made to the petition of Congress of July 8, 1775 — consequently, the last offer of reconciliation made by Congress. The members of that famous body were confronted with prudent submission or armed resistance. The question of independence forced itself upon them and the succeeding months were devoted to its consideration, and certain steps taken before its declaration, which presupposed its adoption. Thus, on November 3, 1775, within four days of the news of the rejection of the petition to the King, the Congress recommended the Provincial Convention of New Hampshire " to call a full and free representation of the people, and that the representatives, if they think it necessary, establish such a form of government as, in their judgment, will best produce the happiness of the people, and most effectually secure peace and good order in the province, during the continuance of the present dispute between G[reat] Britain and the colonies." [1] And on May 15, 1776, the Congress, taking general action, resolved " That it be recommended to the respective assemblies and conventions of the United Colonies, where no government sufficient to the exigencies of their affairs have been hitherto established, to adopt such government as shall, in the opinion of the representatives of the people, best conduce to the happiness and safety of their constituents in particular, and America in general." [2]

The Notion of Independence

There was but one further step to take, as the Congress then thought and as we today see, and that step was finally taken on July 4, 1776. Therefore, by way of preparation, Richard Henry Lee, on behalf of the delegates from Virginia, made the following motion on June 7th:

The Final Step

> That these United Colonies are, and of right ought to be, free and independent States, that they are absolved from all allegiance to the British Crown, and that all political connection between them and the State of Great Britain is, and ought to be, totally dissolved.
> That it is expedient forthwith to take the most effectual measures for forming foreign Alliances.
> That a plan of confederation be prepared and transmitted to the respective Colonies for their consideration and approbation. [3]

This motion, appropriately made by Mr. Lee on behalf of the leading southern colony, was appropriately seconded by John Adams of the northern colony of Massachusetts. George Washington, of Virginia, had been appointed commander-in-chief upon motion of Maryland, seconded by John Adams of Massachusetts. The committee to draft the Declaration of Independence had as its chairman Thomas Jefferson of the colony, by virtue of that Declaration to be the State, of Virginia, in lieu of Richard Henry Lee, absent on account of illness in his family, who might otherwise have presided over the committee and drafted its report.

The committee, consisting of Thomas Jefferson of Virginia, John Adams

[1] *Journals of the Continental Congress,* Vol. iii, p. 319.
[2] *Ibid.,* Vol. iv, p. 342.
[3] *Ibid.,* Vol. v, p. 425.

of Massachusetts, Benjamin Franklin of Pennsylvania, Roger Sherman of
Connecticut, and Robert R. Livingston of New York, was elected by ballot
" to prepare a declaration to the effect of the said first resolution."   On the
28th of June the committee brought in a draft of a Declaration of Independence, written by Thomas Jefferson with slight emendations on the part of Dr.
Franklin and John Adams, still to be seen in their handwriting on Mr. Jefferson's manuscript.   On July 2nd, Richard Henry Lee's resolution was adopted.
On the 4th day of July the Declaration of Independence, as reported by the
committee, was agreed to with sundry amendments [1] both of form and substance, and signed by John Hancock as President of the Congress, by Charles
Thompson as Secretary, and by its members on August 2nd.   The Declaration was published immediately, and in fact as well as in law the independence
of the United States dates from the 4th day of July, 1776.   On this same
eventful day the Congress directed that copies be sent " to the several assemblies, conventions, and committees, or councils of safety, and to the several
commanding officers of the continental troops; that it be proclaimed in each
of the United States, and at the head of the army." [2]

The Declaration Signed and Pro-claimed

The document consists of what may be called a preamble, stating the right
of peoples to set up for themselves and to change their forms of government
at their sovereign pleasure; of an imposing list of grievances suffered at the
hands of George III, then King of Great Britain; and of a Declaration of
Independence, based upon the right in behalf of the colonies asserted in the
preamble and justified by the enumeration of grievances set forth in the body
of the instrument, " to assume, among the Powers of the earth, the separate
and equal station to which the Laws of Nature and of Nature's God entitle
them; " and " for the support of this Declaration, with a firm reliance upon the
protection of divine Providence," the delegates of the erstwhile colonies, speak-

---

[1] For an account of the drafting of the Declaration and the amendments suggested by
John Adams and Benjamin Franklin, see John H. Hazelton, *The Declaration of Independence — Its History*, 1906, Chapter VI.

In a letter to Mr. Madison, dated August 30, 1823, forty-seven years after " the transactions of Independence," Mr. Jefferson made the following statement:

the committee of 5. met, no such thing as a subcommittee was proposed, but they unanimously pressed on myself alone to undertake the draught. I consented; I drew it; but before I reported it to the committee, I communicated it *separately* to Dᴿ. Franklin and m̃r.
Adams requesting their corrections; because they were the two members of whose judgments and amendments I wished most to have the benefit before presenting it to the Committee; . . . their alterations were two or three only, and merely verbal. . . . Pickering's
observations, and m̃r. Adams's in addition, ' that it contained no new ideas, that it is a common place compilation, it's sentiments hacknied in Congress for two years before, and it's
essence contained in Otis's pamphlet,' may all be true. of that I am not to be the judge.
Richᵈ. H. Lee charged it as copied from Locke's treatise on government. Otis's pamphlet
I never saw, & whether I had gathered my ideas from reading or reflection I do not know.
I know only that I turned to neither book or pamphlet while writing it. I did not consider
it as any part of my charge to invent new ideas altogether & to offer no sentiment which
had ever been expressed before. Hazelton, pp. 144–145. See also Ford, *The Writings of
Thomas Jefferson*, Vol. x, pp. 267–8.

[2] *Journals of the Continental Congress*, Vol. v, p. 516.

ing now and the first time for the States, mutually pledged their lives, their fortunes, and their sacred honor.

For present purposes it is only necessary to state and to analyze the political philosophy contained in the preamble and the conclusion of this remarkable document, which, as the historian Buckle has, as we believe, aptly said, of the Declaration as a whole, " ought to be hung up in the nursery of every king, and blazoned on the porch of every royal palace." [1]

Its Political Philosophy

In the preamble to this most famous of American state papers, the members of the Second Continental Congress set forth not only the reasons which impelled them to separate but the rights which they believed to be inherent and the principles which should lie at the basis of every form of government, expressed in language as classic as the thought was impressive:

> When, in the Course of human events, it becomes necessary for one people to dissolve the political bands which have connected them with another, and to assume, among the Powers of the earth, the separate and equal station to which the Laws of Nature and of Nature's God entitle them, a decent respect to the opinions of mankind requires that they should declare the causes which impel them to the separation.[2]

Fortunately, this language is so clear and so broad that it is understood today as it was then, and its application to all states and conditions of men is seen by us of the present day, quite as it was felt by them to be applicable to the thirteen United Colonies. Certain observations of a very general nature may, however, be apposite.

The dissolution of the political bands connecting a people with another is looked upon as necessary in the course of human as distinct from divine events. The consequence of this dissolution is not the gathering of that people into a province or subordinate political community, but the creation of a power, separate and distinct from all other powers and possessed of an equal rank and station to which, according to the statesmen of that day, " the laws of Nature and of Nature's God entitle them." The matter is not labored or argued, it is merely stated, with its consequences. It was apparently felt that, although such action was in conformity with the laws of Nature and of Nature's God, it might not appear to be such to the princes and peoples of the old world. Therefore, " a decent respect to the opinions of mankind " suggested and required that they should declare the causes which impelled them to separate. Accordingly, fitting practice to precept, they thereupon stated the causes, basing them in the first instance upon certain principles, which they thus enumerated:

> We hold these truths to be self-evident, that all men are created equal, that they are endowed by their Creator with certain unalienable Rights, that among these, are Life, Liberty, and the pursuit of Happiness. That, to se-

[1] H. T. Buckle, *History of Civilization in England,* Am. ed., 1857, Vol. i, p. 846.
[2] *Journals,* Vol. v, p. 510.

cure these rights, Governments are instituted among Men, deriving their just Powers from the consent of the governed. That, whenever any form of Government becomes destructive to these ends, it is the Right of the People to alter or to abolish it, and to institute new Government, laying its foundation on such Principles, and organizing its Powers in such form, as to them shall seem most likely to effect their Safety and Happiness.[1]

By way of comment, it may be premised that the members of the Congress abstained from argument in laying down these truths, which, when stated, they proceed to apply in the form of conclusions rather than as premises to be proved. It is to be observed that, although convinced in their own minds, they are not dogmatic, inasmuch as they do not say, except by way of implication, that the truths they lay down are self-evident, but that they themselves hold them to be self-evident. In any event, they were to be self-evident in the New World, and the States of the New World, to be combined later into a more perfect Union, were to be based upon these truths.

It is further to be observed that these rights with which men are endowed by their Creator were, in their conception, inalienable, and that life, liberty and the pursuit of happiness were so important as to be singled out as among these, not that life, liberty, and the pursuit of happiness were the only inalienable rights with which men were endowed by their Creator. They were, however, the fundamental as well as inalienable rights, because to secure them governments were instituted among and by men which thus received whatever powers they were to exercise from the consent of the governed; the meaning of which seems to be as plain as words can make it, that States or nations do not confer powers upon the governed, but that the people composing the State or nation confer upon the Government of that State or nation all the powers which it possesses, and therefore may lawfully exercise.

In the next clause, taking note of history, it is declared that if, instead of securing to men the inalienable rights to life, liberty, and the pursuit of happiness for which governments are instituted, they have proved to be " destructive of these ends," the people have the right to alter or to abolish them, and by implication a duty is raised to institute a new government which shall be based upon such principles, and its powers organized in such form as shall seem to the people composing the State or nation most likely " to effect their Safety and Happiness."

There is assuredly here no divine right to govern wrong. The State is composed of men and women grouped together and it only exists for the convenience and security of the people residing within the boundaries thereof. The Government of the State is for the benefit of the people, not the people for the benefit of the governors; and the form of government failing to effect the purpose for which the State exists, and for which the form of government

[1] *Journals of the Continental Congress,* Vol. v, p. 510.

has been framed is to be brushed ruthlessly aside if it fail, and to be supplanted by one having a better chance of pleasing the individuals taken together, in whom the sovereignty, elsewhere attributed to the State or nation, resides.

Such was the American conception then, such is the American conception today, of the origin of their government and the purpose of government in general. Because of the principles laid down in the preamble, and the grievances specifically stated in the document, the Declaration thus draws in measured and unanswerable terms the consequences of one and the other:

> We, therefore, the Representatives of the United States of America, in General Congress assembled, appealing to the Supreme Judge of the World for the rectitude of our intentions, do, in the Name, and by Authority of the good People of these Colonies, solemnly publish and declare, That these United Colonies are, and of Right, ought to be Free and Independent States; that they are Absolved from all Allegiance to the British Crown, and that all political connetion between them and the State of Great Britain, is and ought to be totally dissolved; and that, as Free and Independent States, they have full Power to levy War, conclude Peace, contract Alliances, establish Commerce, and to do all other Acts and Things which Independent States may of right do. And for the support of this Declaration, with a firm reliance on the Protection of Divine Providence, we mutually pledge to each other our Lives, our Fortunes and our sacred honour.[1]

Because of these premises and conclusions, the people of the Colonies, by their representatives in Congress assembled, declared the Colonies to be free and independent States, absolving them from allegiance to the British Crown and dissolving the political connection between them and the State of Great Britain, apparently applying the word "State" to Great Britain and erstwhile colony with a like significance. And the free and independent States, no longer spoken of as united or in union, are declared to have "full power to levy War, conclude Peace, contract Alliances, establish Commerce, and to do all other Acts and Things which Independent States may of right do."

The immediate and the proximate results of this Declaration on the part of the Congress, drafted in faultless language by Jefferson, are thus stated by James Monroe, a younger contemporary, destined to be an illustrious successor of Jefferson in the Presidency: *Monroe's Conception of the Results*

> The first is that in wresting the power, or what is called the sovereignty, from the Crown it passed directly to the people. The second, that it passed directly to the people of each Colony and not to the people of all the Colonies in the aggregate; to thirteen distinct communities and not to one. To these two facts, each contributing its equal proportion, I am inclined to think that we are in an eminent degree indebted for the success of our Revolution.[2]

[1] *Journals*, Vol. v, p. 514.
[2] Views of the Presidents of the United States on the Subject of Internal Improvements — Stanislaus Murray Hamilton, *The Writings of James Monroe*, 1902, Vol. 6, p. 224. See also James D. Richardson, *Compilation of the Messages and Papers of the Presidents, 1789-1897* (1896), Vol. 2, p. 149.

And yet, although the colonies were declared by this instrument to be free and independent States, or thirteen distinct communities, in Monroe's gloss, they nevertheless may be considered by the agreement of association or by the Declaration of Independence, or by their mere association, without the agreement of 1774 or the Declaration of 1776, to form a body politic, as they were expressly held to be by a signer of the Declaration of Independence, in the case of *Respublica* v. *Sweers* (1 Dallas, 41), decided in the Supreme Court of Pennsylvania in 1779, approximately two years before the Articles of Confederation, making of them a perpetual Union, had gone into effect.

A New
Body
Politic

The facts of this case are very interesting, in that one Cornelius Sweers, a deputy Commissary-General of Military Stores in the armies of the United States of America, was indicted in a Pennsylvania court held in Philadelphia, — because the United States did not then possess courts of their own,— in November, 1778, for forgery upon two bills with intent to defraud the United States.   On the 14th of April, 1779, he was convicted upon both indictments, and five days later the exceptions taken by his counsel were overruled and sentence pronounced by the court.   Mr. Chief Justice McKean said, in over-ruling the exceptions to the form and substance of these indictments, and in sentencing the defendant, convicted upon both of them:

> The *first* exception was, "that, at the time of the offence charged, the *United States* were not a body corporate known in law."   But the Court are of a different opinion.   From the moment of their association, the *United States* necessarily became a body corporate; for, there was no superior from whom that character could otherwise be derived.   In *England,* the king, lords, and commons, are certainly a body corporate; and yet there never was any charter or statute, by which they were expressly so created.

After examining certain technicalities of pleading, immaterial to the matter in hand, the Chief Justice thus continued:

> Upon the whole, we are of opinion, that your conviction has been legal, as well as just; and, therefore, it only remains to pronounce the sentence of the court.

The sentence, alike important and interesting both to the defendant and to the reader, is happily expressed in terms of the independence of the United States:

> Sentence, on the first indictment:— A fine of £70 and imprisonment un-til the 4th of July, the anniversary of *American* Independence.
> Sentence, on the second indictment:— A fine of £1020 and imprisonment until the next annual election for *Pennsylvania,* and standing in the pillory for one hour.

Our First and
Only Ally

Reverting to the second of the three resolutions introduced by Richard Henry Lee on June 7, 1776, "that it is expedient forthwith to take the most effectual measures for forming foreign Alliances," it is sufficient to say, in this connection, that a committee of five was chosen on the 12th in order to prepare a plan of treaties to be proposed to foreign powers, and that Benjamin Franklin, a member of the committee on the Declaration of Independence, was, by the Congress, sent as our first minister to France, with which country he negotiated, on February 6, 1778, in conjunction with Silas Dean and Arthur Lee, an offensive and defensive treaty of alliance, by virtue of which France came to the aid of the United States, resulting in the acquisition of independence of the Colonies then, and today in the cooperation of the armies of these United States upon French soil to preserve inviolate the independence of our first and our only ally.

It could be shown, if time and space permitted, that the ideas and the language of the Declaration of Independence came from English philosophers, from Hooker to Locke; that every important phase of the preamble is to be found in one form or another in Locke's two discourses on Civil Government; and that, indeed, the important phrases of the preamble can be found in Locke's exact language.

But admitting that to be so, it does not detract from the importance of the document, because Locke spoke as an individual, justifying the Revolution of 1688, whereas the Congress spoke as a political body making the Revolution of 1776.   And it is believed that the Second Continental Congress is the first parliament, legislature, or congress that ever adopted and proclaimed these doctrines, and that the United States is the first country which ever put them into effect in the form in which they were stated.

The doctrines are in truth the doctrines of English liberty.   They are not, *Origin of the Doctrines* as has been so often asserted, the doctrines of Rousseau.   At least, they were not borrowed from him, and if they are to be found in Rousseau's *Social Contract,* they were taken from Locke, as Rousseau is known to have drawn heavily upon Locke for this little work.

The supposed influence of Rousseau is perhaps best stated by two careful and thoughtful investigators and writers.   Thus, Sir Henry Sumner Maine says in his *Ancient Law:*

> The American lawyers of the time, and particularly those of Virginia, appear to have possessed a stock of knowledge which differed chiefly from that of their English contemporaries in including much which could only have been derived from the legal literature of continental Europe.   A very few glances at the writings of Jefferson will show how strongly his mind was affected by the semi-juridical, semi-popular opinions which were fashionable in France, and we cannot doubt that it was sympathy with the peculiar ideas of the French jurists which led him and the other colonial lawyers who guided the course of events in America to join the specially French assumption that " all men are born equal " with the assumption, more familiar to Englishmen, that all men are born free, in the very first lines of their Declaration of Independence.   The passage was one of great importance to the history of the doctrine before us.   The American lawyers, in thus prominently and emphatically affirming the fundamental equality of human beings, gave an impulse to political movements in their own country, and in a less degree in

Great Britain, which is far from having yet spent itself; but beside this they returned the dogma they had adopted to its home in France, endowed with vastly greater energy and enjoying much greater claims on general reception and respect.[1]

In speaking of the influence of Rousseau and his followers, John Morley said, in his life of Rousseau, first published in 1873, that:

It was that influence which, though it certainly did not produce, yet did as certainly give a deep and remarkable bias, first to the American Revolution, and a dozen years afterwards to the French Revolution.[2]

In The *Fortnightly Review* for 1879, Mr. Morley, returning to the subject, declared that:

Nobody, however, who has examined so much as the mere surface of the question, would now dream of denying that the French theories of society played an important part in the preparation of American independence.[3]

As a colonist, Jefferson was, in his earlier days, influenced by English liberal writers, for the purpose of the colonists was to show that as Englishmen they were entitled to English liberty as laid down in English writers of repute. The Declaration of Independence naturally and necessarily embodied the views and the conception of government upon which the colonists had made their stand.

As a statesman, and especially after his return from France, where he succeeded Franklin as American Minister, Jefferson may, indeed, have been influenced by French ideas and conceptions.[4]

For the body of his countrymen who had not visited, much less resided in France, the French philosophers came with the French troops to America, and remained after the French Army departed, having accomplished its purpose at Yorktown. It is believed that in the matter of philosophy and democratic doctrine, they returned with more than they brought.

[1] Sir Henry Sumner Maine, *Ancient Law,* 10th Edition, 1884, pp. 91–92. In a note to this passage, published in his edition of *Ancient Law,* p. 409, Sir Frederick Pollock thus states what is believed to be the correct and the prevailing views on this subject:
" This is not the place to speak at large of Rousseau's influence on the founders of American independence and the leaders of the French Revolution; but the careful research of American scholars has lately shown that the Principles of 1789 owed more to the American Declaration of Independence and the earlier Bills of Rights of several States than we used to suppose, and less to Rousseau, and that the language of the American constitutional instruments proceeded from the school not of Rousseau but of Locke." (Scherger, *The Evolution of Modern Liberty,* New York, 1904).
[2] John Morley, *Rousseau,* 1873, Vol. 1, p. 188.
[3] John Morley, *A Word with Some Critics, The Fortnightly Review,* October, 1879, p. 584.
[4] It is true that Jefferson afterwards " drank a deep draught from the intoxicating cup of the French Revolution," but we do not think that in 1776 he had felt the French political influence. He was, we know, a student of Locke, and Locke asserted the natural equality of man as strongly as his natural liberty. (W. T. Brantly, *Of the Influence of European Speculation in the Formation of the Federal Constitution, 1880, Southern Law Review, New Series, Vol. VI, p. 354.*)

III

A CONFEDERATION OF SOVEREIGN STATES

As preliminary to the very able discussions of the constitution, which we have heard from the bar, and as having some influence on its construction, reference has been made to the political situation of these states, anterior to its formation. It has been said, that they were sovereign, were completely independent, and were connected with each other only by a league. This is true. (*Chief Justice Marshall in Gibbons* v. *Ogden, 9 Wheaton, I, 187, decided in 1824.*)

In *June* 1776, the Convention of *Virginia formally* declared, that *Virginia* was a free, sovereign, and independent state; and on the 4th of *July,* 1776, following, the *United States,* in Congress assembled, declared the *Thirteen United Colonies* free and independent states; and that as *such,* they had full power to levy war, conclude peace, &c. I consider this as a declaration, not that the United Colonies *jointly,* in a *collective* capacity, were independent states, &c. but that *each* of them was a sovereign and independent state, that is, that *each* of them had a right to govern itself by its own authority, and its own laws, without any controul from any other power upon earth.

Before these solemn acts of separation from the Crown of *Great Britain,* the war between *Great Britain* and the United Colonies, *jointly,* and *separately,* was *a civil* war; but *instantly,* on that great and ever memorable event, the war changed its *nature,* and became a PUBLIC war between *independent governments;* and immediately thereupon ALL the *rights* of *public* war (and all the other rights of an independent nation) attached to the government of *Virginia;* and all the *former political* connexion between *Great Britain* and *Virginia,* and also between their respective subjects, were totally dissolved; and not only the *two nations,* but all the subjects of each, were in a state of war; precisely as in the present war between *Great Britain* and *France. Vatt. lib. 3. c. 18. s. 292, 295. lib. 3. c. 5, s. 70, 72, and 73.*

From the 4th of *July,* 1776, the *American* States were *de facto,* as well as *de jure,* in the possession and actual exercise of *all* the *rights* of independent governments. On the 6th of *February,* 1778, the King of France entered into a treaty of *alliance* with the *United States;* and on the 8th of *Oct.* 1782, a treaty of Amity and Commerce was concluded between the *United States* and the States General of the *United Provinces.* I have ever considered it as the established doctrine of the *United States,* that their independence originated from, and commenced with, the declaration of Congress, on the 4th of *July,* 1776; and that *no other period* can be fixed on for its commencement; and that all laws made by the legislatures of the several states, *after* the declaration of independence, were the laws of sovereign and independent governments. (*Mr. Justice Chase in Ware* v. *Hylton, 3 Dallas 199, pp. 224–225, decided in 1796.*)

The court entertains no doubt that after the 4th of October 1776, he became a member of the new society, entitled to the protection of its government, and bound to that government by the ties of allegiance.

This opinion is predicated upon a principle which is believed to be undeniable, that the several states which composed this Union, so far at least as regarded their municipal regulations, became entitled, from the time when they declared themselves independent, to all the rights and powers of sovereign states, and that they did not derive them from concessions made by the British king. The treaty of peace contains a recognition of their independence, not a grant of it. From hence, it results, that the laws of the several state governments were the laws of sovereign states, and as such were obligatory upon the people of such state, from the time they were enacted. (*Mr. Justice Cushing in McIlvaine* v.*Coxe, 4 Cranch, 209, 212, decided in 1808.*)

This Court has decided, "That there was no territory within the United States, that was claimed in any other right than that of some one of the confederated states; therefore, there could be no acquisition of territory made by the United States, distinct from, or independent of, some one of the states; the soil and sovereignty were as much theirs at the declaration of independence, as at this hour." (1827.) "Thus stood the rights of the parties at the commencement of the revolution; . . ." (*Mr. Justice Baldwin, A General View of the Origin and Nature of the Constitution and Government of the United States, 1837, p. 86.*)

The People of this State, being by the Providence of God, free and independent, have the sole and exclusive Right of governing themselves as a free, sovereign, and independent State; and having from their Ancestors derived a free and excellent Constitution of Government whereby the Legislature depends on the free and annual Election of the People, they have the best Security for the Preservation of their civil and religious Rights and Liberties. And forasmuch as the free Fruition of such Liberties and Privileges as Humanity, Civility and Christianity call for, as is due to every Man in his Place and Proportion, without Impeachment and Infringement, hath ever been, and will be the Tranquility and Stability of Churches and Commonwealths; and the Denial thereof, the Disturbance, if not the Ruin of both.

Paragraph 1. *Be it enacted and declared by the Governor, and Council, and House of Representatives, in General Court assembled,* That the ancient Form of Civil Government, contained in the Charter from *Charles* the Second, King of *England,* and adopted by the People of this State, shall be and remain the Civil Constitution of this State, under the sole authority of the People thereof, independent of any King or Prince whatever. And that this Republic is, and shall forever be and remain, a free, sovereign and independent State, by the Name of the STATE OF CONNECTICUT. (*Constitution of Connecticut, 1776, Ben: Perley Poore, The Federal and State Constitutions, Colonial Charters, and other Organic Laws of the United States, 1877, Part I, pp. 257–258.*)

The people inhabiting the territory formerly called the province of Massachusetts Bay do hereby solemnly and mutually agree with each other to form themselves into a free, sovereign and independent body-politic or State, by the name of the commonwealth of Massachusetts. (*Constitution of Massachusetts, 1780, Part The Second, The Frame of Government, Ben: Perley Poore, The Federal and State Constitutions, Colonial Charters, and other Organic Laws of the United States, 1877, Part I, p. 960.*)

This alliance, league, or confederacy of the states with each other, can leave no doubt, that up to the time of the final ratification in March, 1781, each state was separately sovereign in its own inherent right; and so remained as to all power not expressly delegated, as was declared in the second article [of Confederation]. The third article is also conclusive, that the object of the alliance was to maintain and perpetuate their separate sovereignty. This is the more manifest, when these articles are taken in connection with the alliance of the states with France. . . .

"The essential and direct end of the present defensive alliance, is to maintain effectually, the liberty, sovereignty, and independence, *absolute* and *unlimited,* of the said United States, as well *in matters of government,* as *of commerce."* In the 11th article, the parties make a mutual guaranty; in that of France, "His most Christian majesty guaranties, on his part, to the United States, their liberty, sovereignty, and independence, *absolute* and *unlimited,* as well *in matters of government as commerce;* also *their posseesions,* and the additions or conquests that *their confederation* may make during the war," &c. 1 Laws, 95, 98.

This guaranty was fulfilled by the treaty of peace, in which "His Britannic majesty acknowledges the said United States, to wit: New Hampshire, &c., to be free, sovereign and independent states." I Laws, 196. This recognition, relating back to the separate or unanimous declarations by the states, as this Court have held it; has the same effect, as if the states had then assumed the same position, by the previous authority of the king; the treaty not being a grant, but a recognition, and subsequent ratification of their pre-existing condition; and all acts which had declared and defined it previous to the treaty, related back to 1776.

Such being the relations of the several states, in their federal and foreign concerns, it follows, that as to their internal concerns, they were in the same attitude of absolute and unlimited sovereignty, before the articles of confederation, as they were afterwards, except so far as they abridged it. Each was a party to the treaty of alliance and peace, and each was bound by the guarantee to France, after the confederation was abolished, and the constitution was established, as firmly as before: the states who delayed their ratification remained so bound, for they could by no act of their own, impair the rights of France: and they were equally entitled to the effects of the treaty of peace, whether they became constituent parts of the Union, by ratifying the constitution, or remained foreign states, by not adopting it. Their state constitutions and governments, remained unimpaired by any surrender of their rights; so that of consequence, their sovereignty was perfect, so long as they continued free from any federal shackles; so the states acted, and so the people of each declared, in all their conventions, from 1776 to 1780. (*Mr. Justice Baldwin, A General View of the Origin and Nature of the Constitution and Government of the United States, 1837, pp. 79–81.*)

The problem before the Convention was to form a confederation of States which should possess the requisite vigor without being a consolidation of the States. They knew that the latter plan would be rejected by their constituents, although Alexander Hamilton and others thought that there could be no other permanent solution of the problem. The Convention sought for light and guidance in the example of other confederated governments. They looked abroad to see how other countries had extricated themselves from similar difficulties. They examined the history of all federations. Americans at that time had no need to refer to any experience but their own, if they would learn the peculiar danger of a confederation. They had too often seen the Continental Congress in the attitude of a helpless suppliant before States that made a jest of its requisitions, to suppose that any national government which could not raise a revenue of its own would be adequate to the exigencies of the Union. We are therefore principally indebted to the distresses of the Confederation for the greatest political invention of the Constitution. All previous confederacies of which history contains any record had acted on the component States, and not on individuals. The Constitution, by its provision for operating upon the individual citizen, affords a far better guarantee of permanence than the hegemony of any powerful member of the Confederation could do. The Constitution thus gave a new maxim of unquestionable value to the science of politics. The Swiss Union of 1848 imitated it in this regard, and thus finally healed the dissensions between the cantons. (*W. T. Brantly, Of the Influence of European Speculation in the Formation of the Federal Constitution, 1880, in Southern Law Review, New Series, Vol. VI. pp. 361–362.*)

CHAPTER III

A CONFEDERATION OF SOVEREIGN STATES

UNDER the third resolution proposed by Richard Henry Lee on June 7, 1776, that "a plan of confederation be prepared and transmitted to the respective Colonies for their consideration and approbation," a committee of one from each colony was chosen on the 12th to report a form of confederation. This committee consisted of "a member from each colony" with

Mr. Dickinson's Plan

John Dickinson of Delaware as chairman. A plan drafted by Mr. Dickinson was reported on July 12th [1] and was considered twelve days later in the committee of the whole house and was the subject of debate from time to time until November 15, 1777, when it was adopted by the Congress with some important amendments.[2] The Congress directed that "these articles shall be proposed to the legislatures of all the United States, to be considered, and if approved of by them, they are advised to authorize their delegates to ratify the same in the Congress of the United States; which being done, the same shall become conclusive."[3] A circular letter to accompany the articles, in accordance with this resolution, was adopted on November 17, 1777. A form of ratification was adopted June 26, 1778. At various dates the States approved the Articles in the manner recommended by the Congress, the last State being Maryland, whose delegates signed on behalf of that State, March 1, 1781. Thereupon the United States had, for the first time, a form of government in law as well as in fact and on the succeeding day the Congress met for the first time under this form of government.

It may be observed in this connection, before proceeding to an examination of the successive steps by which the Articles of Confederation assumed

A United States Congress

form and shape, that the Congress, during this period, was intent upon winning the independence which the Articles were to regulate, and they were therefore of secondary importance; that, for one reason or another, the membership of the committee changed so that, at the date of their adoption by Congress, only one of the original members of the committee was still a member thereof and that even he was absent on that occasion. Changing membership, changing conditions, the differences between the States and the difficulty of reconciling them consumed time and patience, with the inevitable result that

---

[1] *Journals of the Continental Congress,* Vol. v, pp. 546–554.
[2] *Ibid.,* Vol. ix, pp. 907–928.
[3] *Ibid.,* p. 925.

the Articles of Confederation were a compromise, just as the Constitution of 1787 creating the more perfect Union of the States was a compromise. In the Congress as in the Convention, the large States wanted a larger influence than the smaller, to which the reply was then, as now in the society of nations: a little colony has its all at stake as well as a great one; our identity is a precious thing; we do not propose to be swallowed up. Large and Small States

In addition to this difference of view as to the rights of the States, large and small, the motives of the sections were questioned and a lack of confidence expressed, impossible to overcome on the moment, and indeed overcome in the Constitutional Convention only after years of suffering in a common cause when the statesmen of all the sections had learned to know, and therefore rightly to appreciate one another. New England, which may be said to have brought about the Revolution, was not popular and was viewed with suspicion and jealousy, Benjamin Harrison of Virginia saying that " the Yankees " ruled as absolutely in Congress " as the Grand Turk in his dominions." [1] This idea did not stop with Virginia, but pervaded the south, for Edward Rutledge of South Carolina, wrote:

> The Force of their Arms I hold exceeding Cheap, but I confess I dread their over-ruling Influence in Council. I dread their low Cunning and those . . . Principles which Men without Character and without Fortune in general possess, which are so captivating to the lower class of Mankind.[2]

New England, on its part, viewed its neighbors to the south with equal suspicion and distrust, not unmixed with contempt, if John Adams is to be credited, who says of them:

> The dons, the bashaws, the grandees, the patricians, the sachems, the nabobs, call them by what name you please, sigh, and groan, and fret, and sometimes stamp, and foam, and curse, but all in vain.[3]

In view of such circumstances the wonder is that the confederation took place, not that the instrument of confederation was faulty.

The Articles exist in two forms, in the draft in Dickinson's handwriting, laid before the Congress on July 12, 1776, and in the amended form in which Dickinson's draft was approved by the Congress on November 15, 1777, recommended to the States for their ratification and ultimately ratified by them.[4] The essentials of the completed instrument are contained in Dickinson's draft, which suggests a familiarity with Franklin's project, notably The Two Forms of the Articles

---

[1] E. P. Oberholtzer, *Robert Morris*, 1903, p. 37.

[2] To John Jay, June 29, 1776. *The Correspondence and Public Papers of John Jay*, H. P. Johnston ed., Vol. i, p. 67.

[3] To Patrick Henry, June 3, 1776. *The Works of John Adams*, C. F. Adams ed., Vol. ix, p. 387.

[4] The dates of ratification were: Massachusetts, Rhode Island, Connecticut, New York, Pennsylvania, Virginia, South Carolina, July 9, 1778 — North Carolina, July 21, 1778 — Georgia, July 24, 1778 — New Jersey, November 26, 1778 — Delaware, February 22, 1779 — Maryland, March 1, 1781.

in the fact that the States, although independent, are spoken of as colonies. Some of the amendments are far from happy, especially those indicating the amounts of revenue which each colony is to raise and to contribute to the general government. In the eleventh article of Dickinson's draft it is provided that " All Charges of Wars and all other Expences that shall be incurred for the common Defence, or general Welfare, and allowed by the United States assembled, shall be defrayed out of a common Treasury, which shall be supplied by the several Colonies in Proportion to the Number of Inhabitants of every Age, Sex and Quality, except Indians not paying Taxes, in each Colony . . ." [1] In the amended text the contributions of the States are to be " in proportion to the value of all land within each State,"— an amendment, it may be said in passing, which appears to have made the Articles unworkable in practice, however acceptable it may have been in theory.

It is not meant, in this connection, to express a preference for a poll as distinguished from a land tax, but the shifts to which the Congress was put to increase the value of land, and thus increase the State quotas, exposed that body to ridicule and brought the government into contempt in a way which would not have been possible if the text of the original draft had been adopted.

Nature of the Union

The government of the Confederacy was to be styled the United States of America, in which each State retained " its sovereignty, freedom and independence, and every power, jurisdiction and right," not " expressly delegated to the United States, in Congress assembled." The framers of this instrument were well informed as to the nature of the government which they were establishing. It was to be a Union of States, not a single State. It was to be a perpetual " league of friendship," " for their common defence, the security of their liberties and their mutual and general welfare," in which the States pledged themselves to protect one another against attack of any kind and from any quarter.

For the management of the general interests of the United States there was to be a Congress, which should meet once a year and exercise the powers with which the Confederation was vested. Each of the States was to be represented by not less than two nor more than seven delegates, appointed and paid by them, who might not serve as delegates more than three years out of any six. The States had an equal voice, each retaining and casting a single vote, notwithstanding the greater or less number of deputies which they might choose to send to Congress.

Powers Renounced

It was recognized that the purpose for which the Union was formed could not be effected if the States did not, in addition to the powers conferred upon the Congress, renounce the exercise of some of the powers inherent in sovereignty, freedom and independence. They therefore expressly renounced

[1] *Journals of the Continental Congress,* Vol. v, p. 548.

the right of making treaties with foreign countries or of entering into treaties or alliances between themselves without the consent of the Congress, and they pledged themselves not to lay any imposts or duties which might interfere with the treaties which the Confederation might make with foreign countries. While maintaining the right to keep up a militia, they renounced the right to create and maintain an army or navy without the consent of Congress, and they likewise renounced the right to engage in war, without the consent of Congress, except when actually attacked. They reserved to themselves the right to appoint regimental officers of the regiments raised for continental service, but vested the appointment of the general officers in Congress.

They endowed the general Congress with broad powers, suggesting but not actually making of the States a nation — powers with which the Congress under the Constitution has been invested and which with sundry additions have been deemed adequate, doubtless due to the fact that the government under the latter instrument acts directly upon the people of the States, thus executing the powers with which it is invested instead of relying upon the States as its agents. Among these powers were the sole right of declaring war and concluding peace, of sending and receiving embassies, of entering into treaties and alliances, of issuing currency, of fixing a standard of weights and measures, of establishing and regulating post offices throughout the United States, of appointing all officers of the army with the exception of regimental officers of contingents raised by the States, and all naval officers, and of making rules for the government of the land and naval forces and directing their operations. The Congress was also empowered to ascertain the sums of money necessary for the service of the United States and to apply it to the public service, to borrow money or emit bills of credit, to build and equip a navy, to agree upon the number of land forces and to make requisitions, binding each State to furnish its quota " in proportion to the number of white inhabitants in each State." In addition, the Congress was specifically authorized to appoint a committee of States, consisting of a delegate from each State, to sit during the recess of the Congress and to carry on the government during such recess, to appoint other committees and civil officers necessary for the management of the general forces of the United States under their direction, and to appoint from the members of Congress a president, who should not preside for more than one in any term of three years.

These powers were granted because they were felt to be necessary to secure the independence of the United States and to maintain peace and harmony among the States themselves, but in granting them the States placed what they conceived to be a salutary check upon their exercise, providing that the more important of them, which they specified, should be exercised only with the consent of nine States, and in the tenth of the Articles they

Powers of Congress

Peace and War

vested the committee of the States, or any nine of them, with power to execute during the recesses of Congress such powers as the Congress might delegate to the committee, or any nine of them, but withheld from them any power which the Congress itself could exercise only with the consent of nine States, all of which were specified and enumerated in the following paragraph of the ninth article, which also stated specifically the requirement of a majority in all other matters:

> The United States, in Congress assembled, shall never engage in a war, nor grant letters of marque and reprisal in time of peace, nor enter into any treaties or alliances, nor coin money, nor regulate the value thereof, nor ascertain the sums and expenses necessary for the defence and welfare of the United States, or any of them: nor emit bills, nor borrow money on the credit of the United States, nor appropriate money, nor agree upon the number of vessels of war to be built or purchased, or the number of land or sea forces to be raised, nor appoint a commander in chief of the army or navy, unless nine states assent to the same; nor shall a question on any other point, except for adjourning from day to day, be determined, unless by the votes of a majority of the United States, in Congress assembled.

The renunciation of the right which sovereign States possess, and unfortunately exercise, of engaging in war among themselves, and also the renunciation of the right to enter into treaties and agreements with themselves without the consent of the Congress, made it necessary to provide some method of settling disputes which might arise between the States, and which otherwise would remain unsettled because of the renunciation of war and of diplomatic negotiation. In certain cases of an international character, which might, in addition, give rise to disputes among the States, the Congress was authorized to establish " rules for deciding, in all cases, what captures on land or water shall be legal, and in what manner prizes, taken by land or naval forces in the service of the United States, shall be divided or appropriated;" to appoint " courts for the trial of piracies and felonies committed on the high seas;" and to establish " courts for receiving and determining, finally, appeals in all cases of captures; provided, that no member of Congress shall be appointed a judge of any of the said courts."

Congress
with
Appellate
Jurisdiction

For disputes that might arise between themselves, for which no tribunal existed, it was provided in the ninth article " that the United States, in Congress assembled, shall also be the last resort on appeal in all disputes and differences now subsisting, or that hereafter may arise between two or more states concerning boundary, jurisdiction or any other cause whatever," and specifically mentioning " all controversies concerning private right of soil, claimed under different grants of two or more states." The article likewise provided the method of settlement, which was, briefly:

The agents of the States in controversy appeared before the Congress, stating their controversy and asking for the appointment of commissioners to form a temporary court or tribunal. If the agents agreed upon the members of the court it was organized and the case referred to it. If, however, the agents did not agree upon the members of the court, the Congress selected three persons from each of the thirteen States, and from the thirty-nine thus chosen the names were to be struck, beginning with the defendant, until thirteen names were left. From this list of thirteen not less than seven nor more than nine were to be drawn by lot, and of this number any five could form the court. In the absence of the agent of any one of the litigating States, or upon his refusal to strike as provided by the article, the Secretary of the Congress was to act in his stead.

It was foreseen that changes in the Articles of Confederation might be necessary, but as the instrument was a diplomatic agreement no alteration was to be made unless agreed to in the Congress and "afterwards confirmed by the legislatures of every State."

From this brief summary it will be observed that the Articles of Confederation provide a government, with limited and specifically enumerated powers, which were only to be exercised with the consent of nine or of a majority of the sovereign, free and independent States of which the Confederation was composed. It will be further observed that the legislative was likewise the executive branch of the government, in so far as either existed, because the President of the Congress was the presiding officer but possessed of no independent powers, and the committee of the States was appointed by the Congress for the exercise of certain, but not all, of the powers of the Congress during its recess. There is no doubt a suggestion of a judiciary, but the judiciary, such as it was, was only constituted in the case of the court of appeals for prize cases, and from time to time temporary tribunals were to be chosen by the Congress for the trial of controversies between the States; cases involving piracies and felonies were to be tried by the private courts of the States.

There is here no clear and conscious recognition of the threefold division of government so conspicuous in the Constitutions of each of the thirteen States composing the Confederation and a fundamental though unexpressed principle of the Constitution which succeeded the Articles of Confederation, a conception which was reenforced from French sources, due to the alliance of France which so powerfully contributed to making the Declaration of Independence a reality.

The defects of the Articles of Confederation have been pointed out by every historian of the United States who has had occasion to deal with this period of our history. The Articles were indeed defective. They were not however so defective as the critics would have us believe, and even if they were it would seem to be wiser to consider the difficulties of the situation and to

Suggestion of a Judiciary

Defects

regard the Articles of Confederation as a step to a more perfect Union, and a very important one, than to deny them any claim upon our consideration. The Articles were not to blame if faulty; it was the defective vision of the statesmen who drafted them and of the States which were unwilling to grant a general government more extensive powers. It is easy for us to see the advantages of a closer union, because we have benefited by its blessings, but a union of the kind of the Constitution was hitherto unknown in the history of nations, and the necessity of a broader and more powerful general government, acting directly upon the States and not through the States, was not likely to be granted by colonies which had revolted because of the attempt of the mother country to impose its authority from above, and to impose the acts of a supreme legislature upon the colonies, overriding the local legislatures, in order to make the acts of Parliament apply to the individual without consideration of the colonies as such.

The purpose of the Revolutionary statesmen was to overthrow what they considered the tyranny of the mother country, claiming supremacy in all matters; it was not to create a domestic tyrant in the place of the imperial Parliament. Without compromise and concession and the safeguarding of the States and their peoples against the aggression of the general government, American statesmen would not have agreed to the provisions of the Constitution of the United States; and the different States, in agreeing to it, insisted upon certain amendments, which were proposed by the first Congress under the Constitution in 1789 and added to that instrument two years later. And even then two States, North Carolina and Rhode Island, refused to ratify the Constitution and did so only after it had gone into effect and the ten amendments to it had been proposed and, in the case of Rhode Island, ratified.

Excellences

While recognizing the defects of the Confederation, which were indeed obvious to those who wished union under a constitution rather than a diplomatic union, competent judges nevertheless recognized its excellences. It is noteworthy that George Washington, who had suffered from the defects of the Confederation more than any man living, nevertheless had a good word to say for the union.[1] John Jay was also qualified to speak, as he had been President of the Congress and as Secretary of Foreign Affairs he felt the imperfections of the system, especially in so far as foreign relations were concerned. Yet he was not pessimistic, saying of it: "Our federal govern-

---

[1] In a letter to Benjamin Harrison dated January 18, 1784, General Washington said:
"That the prospect before us is fair . . . none can deny; . . . I believe all things will come right at last, . . . The disinclination of the individual States to yield competent powers to Congress for the federal government, . . . will, if there is not a change in the system, be our downfall as a nation." An extension of federal powers, he believed, would "make us one of the most wealthy, happy, respectable and powerful nations that ever inhabited the terrestrial globe." W. C. Ford, *The Writings of George Washington*, Vol. x, pp. 344-6. See also Sparks, *Writings of George Washington*, Vol. ix, p. 11.

ment has imperfections, which time and more experience will, I hope, effectually remedy." [1]   Thomas Jefferson, it will be admitted, was also qualified to speak, and he probably expressed the view of most men of his day when he said that " with all the imperfections of our present government it is without comparison the best existing, or that ever did exist." [2]   John Marshall, whom many regard as the creator of our union through his opinions as Chief Justice of the Supreme Court, felt that if the Articles of Confederation preserved the idea of union until a more efficient system was adopted, which they certainly did and more, that then " this alone is certainly sufficient to entitle that instrument to the respectful recollection of the American people and its framers to their gratitude." [3]

From a national point of view the Articles were defective; from an international point of view they offered an example of a union of sovereign, free and independent States much closer than that of the society of nations, and, in spite of their imperfections, indeed because of their imperfections, they show, it is believed, how the society of nations can be organized as a Confederation without involving the sacrifice of sovereignty, should the members of that society be inclined to consider a conscious and closer union than exists today.

International Significance

While the defects of the Confederation were the subject of debate in the Congress, of discussion in the press, the talk alike of men of affairs and of private citizens, and the topic of correspondence if not its cause, among leaders of thought of the period, James Madison, to whose untiring efforts the world is principally indebted for the American Constitution, has, as was to be expected, stated more elaborately than any one of his contemporaries the weakness and the inadequacy of the Articles of Confederation in a memorandum prepared on the eve of the Convention, called for the sole and express purpose of recommending " a Federal constitution adequate to the exigencies of government and the preservation of the Union."

James Madison's Summary of the Weakness

In a paper written well nigh fifty years after the event, intended, apparently, as a preface to the Debates of the Convention, which he himself attended and reported with his own hand, he gives in the following passage the reasons why his testimony on this point should be accepted.

Having served as a member of Cong[s]. through the period between Mar. 1780 & the arrival of peace in 1783, I had become intimately acquainted with the public distresses and the causes of them.   I had observed the successful opposition to every attempt to procure a remedy by new grants of power to

[1] Letter to Lord Lansdown, April 16, 1786. William Jay, *The Life of John Jay,* 1833, Vol. ii, p. 183.

[2] Letter to E. Carrington, Paris, August 4, 1787. *Writings of Thomas Jefferson,* Ford ed., Vol. iv, p. 424.

In a letter to M. de Meusnier, Jan. 24, 1786, Mr. Jefferson said:

" The Confederation is a wonderfully perfect instrument considering the circumstances under which it was formed." (Ford ed., iv, 141.)

[3] *The Life of George Washington,* by John Marshall, Philadelphia, 1805, v. 4, p. 416.

Cong⁸. I had found moreover that despair of success hung over the compromising provision of April 1783, for the Public necessities, which had been so elaborately planned and so impressively recommended to the States. Sympathizing, under this aspect of affairs, in the alarm of the friends of free Govᵗ. at the threatened danger of an abortive result to the great & perhaps last experiment in its favour, I could not be insensible to the obligation to co-operate as far as I could in averting the calamity. With this view I acceded to the desire of my fellow Citizens of the County that I should be one of its representatives in the Legislature, hoping that I might there best contribute to inculcate the critical posture to which the Revolutionary cause was reduced, and the merit of a leading agency of the State in bringing about a rescue of the Union, and the blessings of liberty staked on it, from an impending catastrophe.

It required but little time after taking my seat in the House of Delegates in May 1784, to discover that however favorable the general disposition of the State might be towards the Confederacy the Legislature retained the aversion of its predecessors to transfers of power from the State to the Govᵗ. of the Union; notwithstanding the urgent demands of the Federal Treasury; the glaring inadequacy of the authorized mode of supplying it, the rapid growth of anarchy in the Fedˡ. System, and the animosity kindled among the States by their conflicting regulations.[1]

It is evident to us of the present day, from an inspection of his writings and from his leadership in the Constitutional Convention, that James Madison was the fittest by study and experience to propose the basis of a Constitution for the more perfect union, and his contemporaries, without the means of knowledge at our disposal, so considered him. One of his colleagues in the Federal Convention, writing of him, says:

Mʳ. Maddison is a character who has long been in public life; and what is very remarkable every Person seems to acknowledge his greatness. He blends together the profound politician, with the Scholar. In the management of every great question he evidently took the lead in the Convention, and tho' he cannot be called an Orator, he is a most agreeable, eloquent, and convincing Speaker. From a spirit of industry and application which he possesses in a most eminent degree, he always comes forward the best informed Man of any point in debate. The affairs of the United States, he perhaps, has the most correct knowledge of, of any Man in the Union. He has been twice a Member of Congress, and was always thought one of the ablest Members that ever sat in that Council.[2]

It was not by chance that Mr. Madison made this impression upon his fellow delegate, who in this matter spoke for his contemporaries. He had represented his State in the Continental Congress and was aware of the defects of the Confederation from actual experience in that body. He was familiar with every detail of the Articles of Confederation, and as a preparation for his work in the Convention he had set forth in connected form the defects of the Confederation in a memorandum, and he had likewise

---

[1] *The Writings of James Madison*, Gaillard Hunt ed., Vol. ii, pp. 396–7.
[2] Notes of Major William Pierce on the Federal Convention of 1787, *American Historical Review*, Vol. iii, p. 331.

embodied in another memorandum the defects of the known instances of confederations, in so far as they could be gathered from historical records then at his disposal.[1] He arranged the defects of the Confederation under eleven headings and accompanied each with apt illustrations.[2] Of this important document, which is unfortunately too long to be quoted in its entirety, as it deserves to be, the following is a brief analysis:

1. Failure of the States to comply with the Constitutional requisitions.

This defect Mr. Madison considered to be so obvious as to require neither illustration nor argument. It resulted, he said, " so naturally from the number and independent authority of the States, and has been so uniformly exemplified in every similar Confederacy, that it may be considered as not less radically and permanently inherent in, than it is fatal to the object of, the present system."

2. Encroachments by the States on the federal authority.

As examples of this defect he cites the wars and treaties of Georgia with the Indians, the compacts between Virginia and Maryland and between Pennsylvania and New Jersey, the troops raised and kept up by Massachusetts without the consent of the Confederation, as required by the sixth of the articles.

3. Violations of the law of nations and of treaties.

Under this heading he said that " not a year has passed without instances of them in some one or other of the States," and as examples he cites the Treaty of Peace with Great Britain, the treaty with France, the treaty with Holland, each one of which had been violated, and although these nations had been forebearing, or, as Madison said, " have not been rigorous in animadverting on us," indulgence was not always to be expected in the future.

4. Trespasses of the States on the rights of each other.

Under this caption Mr. Madison has a somewhat imposing and alarming list, citing specifically the law of his own State restricting foreign vessels to certain ports, and the laws of Maryland and New York in favor of vessels of their own citizens. Among the additional examples he mentions are the issue of paper money, making property a legal tender, acts of the debtor State in favor of debtors, affecting not only citizens of the other States but citizens or subjects of foreign nations, and finally the practice of many States in violating the spirit of the Articles of Confederation by putting the goods and products of the members of the Union upon the same footing with those of foreign countries.

5. Want of concert in matters where common interest requires it.

[1] *Writings of Madison,* Hunt ed., Vol. ii, pp. 369–390. See also memorandum contained in *Letters and Other Writings of James Madison,* pub. by order of Congress, 1865, Vol. i, pp. 389–398.
[2] *Ibid.,* pp. 361–369. Also see pp. 391–412 for sketch on the origin of the Constitutional Convention.

To this defect Mr. Madison attributes the deplorable state of commerce throughout the States, a weakness also affecting the national dignity, interest and revenue. To this clause he also traces inferior but still important defects, such as the want of uniformity in laws concerning naturalization and literary property, the lack of provision for national seminaries, for grants of incorporation for national purposes, for canals and other works of general utility.

6. Want of guaranty to the States of their Constitutions and laws against internal violence.

The hands of the Confederation were, he says, tied in this matter, because the Articles are silent as to it, and a very distressing example of this is mentioned in his correspondence, that of Shays' rebellion in Massachusetts in 1787, which also produced a profound impression upon contemporary opinion.

7. Want of sanction to the laws, and of coercion in the Government of the Confederacy.

Mr. Madison considered a sanction as essential to the idea of law as coercion is to that of government. This defect of the Confederation was due to the fact that the Articles did not form a " Political Constitution," but were, as he says, " nothing more than a treaty of amity, of commerce, and of alliance between independent and Sovereign States." Therefore, there was no central government and there was a lack of power in the Congress to compel obedience to law; and in Madison's opinion coercion in government was as essential as the sanction of law. The experience of the Congress had, he said, demonstrated " that a unanimous and punctual obedience of 13 independent bodies to the acts of the federal Government ought not to be calculated on," and without the supremacy of the acts of the Union, interpreted and applied in the sense in which they were meant by the Congress, it was impossible to better conditions or indeed to preserve the Union.

8. Want of ratification by the people of the Articles of Confederation.

Mr. Madison attached very great importance to this defect, as appears from his correspondence and also from his attitude in the Convention, recognizing clearly that a ratification by the people within a State would make it the law of the people, as well as of the State, and that an act or law ratified by the people would give the government a right to proceed directly against the person violating the act or law, instead of appealing to the State to correct the violation.

These consequences he considered as characteristic of what he called a political constitution, whereas in the Confederation, which he properly regarded as a league of sovereign powers and not as a political constitution, the Union could only act upon the State and through the State upon its citizens. In this connection, he also pointed out the danger to the Union of the violation of the compact by a State, which would give to the other members of the diplomatic union the right to withdraw and thus to destroy the Confederation.

9. Multiplicity of laws in the several States.

This is a defect in a nation or in a State, which apparently can not be corrected without a change of mind, heart and conduct on the part of members of legislatures. If Mr. Madison expected far less under a " Political Constitution " his reputation as a prophet would be shattered, for the laws of the Congress under the Constitution and of the different States since the date of its adoption are so constantly amended that we do not know whether our knowledge, so painfully acquired during a recess of these lawmaking bodies, has been repealed overnight by their action when in session. His comments on this point are, however, so interesting that they are quoted rather than paraphrased. Thus he says:

> Among the evils then of our situation, may well be ranked the multiplicity of laws from which no State is exempt. As far as laws are necessary to mark with precision the duties of those who are to obey them, and to take from those who are to administer them a discretion which might be abused, their number is the price of liberty. As far as laws exceed this limit they are a nuisance; a nuisance of the most pestilent kind. Try the Codes of the several States by this test, and what a luxuriancy of legislation do they present. The short period of independency has filled as many pages as the century which preceded it. Every year, almost every session, adds a new volume. This may be the effect in part, but it can only be in part, of the situation in which the revolution has placed us. A review of the several Codes will shew that every necessary and useful part of the least voluminous of them might be compressed into one-tenth of the cor...pass, and at the same time be rendered ten-fold as perspicuous.

10. Mutability of the laws of the States.

Mr. Madison was aware that his previous heading practically included this one. Nevertheless he stated it for the sake of completeness and as his observations upon it have not lost their point they are quoted to give full effect to the previous objections. Thus he says:

> This evil is intimately connected with the former, yet deserves a distinct notice, as it emphatically denotes a vicious legislation. We daily see laws repealed or superseded before any trial can have been made of their merits, and even before a knowledge of them can have reached the remoter districts within which they were to operate. In the regulations of trade, this instability becomes a snare not only to our citizens, but to foreigners also.

11. Injustice of the laws of the States.

This subject is likewise connected with the previous ones, because it is not merely the multiplicity of the laws and the numerous changes involved to which he objects. They were even at times unjust, in addition to other vices, and he was especially anxious to find the reasons for the injustice of the laws of the different States, in the belief that when the reasons had been disclosed the remedy would follow close upon their footsteps.   The causes of the evils he held to be, first, in the representative bodies, and second, in the people themselves; in the representative bodies because representative appointments are, he says, sought from three motives: "1. Ambition.   2. Personal interest.   3. Public good."   And he felt obliged to state that "Unhappily, the two first are proved by experience to be most prevalent."

But he regarded, and properly, the people to be more at fault, because if they wanted different representatives they could have them, and if they insisted upon just laws their representatives would frame them.   He finds the chief fault to be in the fact that civilized societies are divided into different interests and factions, "creditors or debtors, rich or poor, husbandmen, merchants, or manufacturers, members of different religious sects, followers of different political leaders, inhabitants of different districts, owners of different kinds of property, &c., &c."   He mentions three correctives, but finds them to be wanting whenever the interest of the individual seems to suggest their viola-

Personal
Interests

tion.   They are: "1. A prudent regard to their own good, as involved in the general and permanent good of the community."   As a result of experience Mr. Madison holds that this consideration lacks decisive weight, and he includes nations as well as individuals, saying, "It is too often forgotten, by nations as well as by individuals, that honesty is the best policy."   The second is a respect for character, and here again he finds that this corrective does not prevent injustice, because, as he says, "In a multitude its efficacy is diminished in proportion to the number which is to share the praise or the blame," and even if it prevails within a society it is doubtful if it crosses the frontier and extends into adjoining provinces or States, inasmuch as actions are constantly committed within one State affecting strangers beyond its confines.   The third is religion, which he mentions only to reject, saying, "The conduct of every popular assembly acting on oath, the strongest of religious ties, proves that individuals join without remorse in acts, against which their consciences would revolt if proposed to them under the like sanction, separately in their closets."

Sovereignty

As the result of his careful and prolonged study of this subject, he finds that "The great desideratum in Government is such a modification of the sovereignty as will render it sufficiently neutral between the different interests and factions to controul one part of the society from invading the rights of another, and, at the same time, sufficiently controuled itself from setting up an interest adverse to that of the whole society," and he concludes by considering the different forms of government and the extent to which they may be counted upon to meet his requirements.   Thus he says:

> In absolute Monarchies the prince is sufficiently neutral towards his subjects, but frequently sacrifices their happiness to his ambition or his avarice.

In small Republics, the sovereign will is sufficiently controuled from such a sacrifice of the entire Society, but is not sufficiently neutral towards the parts composing it. As a limited monarchy tempers the evils of an absolute one; so an extensive Republic meliorates the administration of a small Republic.

The form of government which he himself felt necessary was later laid before the Federal Convention by Mr. Randolph in what has been called the Virginia plan, which not only bears the impress of his experienced and scholarly mind but is in his own handwriting as well. He was not, however, unconscious of the fact that something was needed above and beyond the form of government, and it is the conscious expression of this fact that gives point and value to his observations. Governors of the States must be worthy of the trust, and with this he aptly closes his observations: *Mr. Madison's View of Public Officers*

> An auxiliary desideratum for the melioration of the Republican form is such a process of elections as will most certainly extract from the mass of the society the purest and noblest characters which it contains; such as will at once feel most strongly the proper motives to pursue the end of their appointment, and be most capable to devise the proper means of attaining it.

Before the ratification of the Articles of Confederation by the last of the thirteen States on March 1, 1781, a movement had begun to amend the Articles in order to make them more adequate for governmental purposes, which, prolonged through a series of years, led to the call of the Constitutional Convention which met in Philadelphia in the summer of 1787, an assembly which replaced the Articles by a newer and more perfect instrument of government called the Constitution, under which the United States on the one hand and the States on the other have waxed great and have prospered. The Congress recognized that the work of its hands was imperfect, but its members felt that the Articles of Confederation embodied all of the concessions from the States which they could obtain at that time, and they did not recognize, perhaps, before experiencing them, the defects of that instrument of government which is known as the Articles of Confederation. *Dissatisfaction*

Jonathan Elliot, to whom we are under the deepest obligation for his Debates in the State Conventions on the adoption of the Federal Constitution, and the debates in the Convention itself, entitled the section devoted to the period between the ratification of the Articles and the call of the Convention, " Proceedings which led to the Adoption of the Constitution of the United States." [1] And in this section he enumerates four proposals, which failed — but they may be termed happy failures, for it is because of them that the call went out for a convention which framed the more perfect Union. These four are: *Four Proposals that Failed*

First, the proposal to amend the eighth of the Articles of Confederation, in

[1] Jonathan Elliot, *The Debates in the Several State Conventions on the Adoption of the Federal Constitution,* 1836, Vol. i, pp. 92–120.

order to base the quotas upon population which the States should contribute to the government rather than upon the value of the realty in each of the States;

Second, a proposal to authorize the Congress to levy a duty of five per cent. *ad valorem* upon all goods, wares, and merchandise of foreign growth and manufacture imported into the United States after the 1st day of May, 1781, and to authorize the United States to levy a like duty of five per cent. on all prizes and prize goods condemned in the court of admiralty of any of the States, in order that the revenues arising therefrom should be used to discharge the principal and interest of the debts contracted or which should be contracted on the faith of the United States during the " present war ";

Third, a proposal to invest the United States with the power to levy duties upon certain specified goods imported into the United States from any foreign port, island or plantation during a period of twenty-five years, to raise from the States for a period of twenty-five years a revenue of $1,500,000 annually to extinguish the debt contracted on the faith of the United States according to quotas specified in the resolution;

Fourth, to amend the Articles of Confederation by investing the United States in Congress assembled, for a period of fifteen years, with the power to forbid the States to import or to export goods in vessels belonging to nations with which the United States did not have treaties of commerce, and to empower Congress, for a like period of fifteen years, to forbid the subjects of foreign States residing within the United States to export goods, wares or merchandise unless authorized so to do by treaty.

Economic
Troubles

Finance and commerce were the rocks upon which the little ship of state well nigh foundered, but the failure of the States to respond to the recommendations, indeed we might almost say the prayers, of the Congress led to private initiative, in the hope that it might succeed where public initiative had failed. The trouble, as we see today, was one that might be remedied without affecting the rights of the States, by investing the Congress, through its own agents, with the power of collecting revenue at the source, in accordance with the consent and the authorization of the States. In this way the general government would have been able to sue and to collect the revenue from the individual, whereas the government could not, under the law of nations, sue a sovereign, free and independent State to collect the quotas fixed by the Congress for the States in accordance with the Articles of Confederation; and the States were unwilling to invest the United States in Congress assembled with the right to sue the State, and to compel by force, if necessary, compliance with its obligations. The framers of the Confederation did not see, because they lacked experience, that a provision of this kind would not only provide the revenue needed by the general government, but would obviate quarrels and ill feeling between the States and their citizens, as the State would not need, for the purpose of the Union, to thrust its hand into the pockets of its citizens.

This matter has never been put more clearly than by Alexander Hamilton in his speech in the New York Convention advocating the ratification of the Constitution. "It has been observed," he said, that "to coerce the states is one of the maddest projects that was ever devised." And he asked, "can we believe that one state will ever suffer itself to be used as an instrument of coercion?" In his opinion, and Hamilton was no advocate of state rights, it could not be done, and it should not be tried. "The thing is a dream," he said, "it is impossible." On the theory of government which had been tried and found wanting, he added, "Then we are brought to this dilemma — either a federal standing army is to enforce the requisitions or the federal treasury is left without supplies, and the government without support." What was to be done, or as he expressed it in the language of debate: "What, sir, is the cure for this great evil?" This question he answered, in such a way as to show not merely the nature of the solution but the solution itself: "Nothing, but to enable the national laws to operate on individuals, in the same manner as those of the states do. This is the true reasoning upon the subject, sir." [1]

Coercion of States

But to return to the rôle of private initiative in the creation of the more perfect Union. The situation of the States in matters of commerce was that which would arise between sovereign, free and independent States in which there was not a customs union, such as the German States were wise enough to conclude in the middle of the 19th Century. As stated by a keen-eyed observer of the period: "The states," Mr. Madison said, "having no convenient ports for foreign commerce, were subject to be taxed by their neighbors, thro' whose ports, their commerce was carried on. New Jersey, placed between Phil^a & N. York, was likened to a cask tapped at both ends; and N. Carolina, between Virg^a & S. Carolina to a patient bleeding at both Arms." [2] The Congress foresaw the consequences of such a condition, and had already laid it before the States, but without avail, in the following impressive language:

> The situation of commerce at this time claims the attention of the several states, and few objects of greater importance can present themselves to their notice. The fortune of every citizen is interested in the success thereof; for it is the constant source of wealth and incentive to industry; and the value of our produce and our land must ever rise or fall in proportion to the prosperous or adverse state of trade. [3]

Private initiative supplied the remedy. Maryland and Virginia were interested in the navigation of Chesapeake Bay and its tributaries and they had come to a satisfactory working agreement in the matter. But Pennsylvania

Private Initiative

[1] Elliot, *Debates*, Vol. ii, pp. 232, 233.
[2] *Writings of Madison*, Hunt ed., Vol. ii, p. 395.
[3] Elliot, *Debates*, Vol. i, p. 107.

and Delaware were likewise interested parties, either as bordering on the Bay and its tributaries or as affected by their regulation. In a less degree all the States were interested in as far as they were affected, whereas the adjoining States were primarily concerned. Hence, it occurred to Mr. Madison to have Virginia propose a meeting of delegates of the States, in order to see what could be done or what could be proposed to better conditions in that matter of trade and commerce. Therefore, on January 21, 1786, the Virginia legislature appointed certain persons, among whom may be mentioned Edmund Randolph, James Madison and George Mason, as commissioners to " meet such commissioners as may be appointed by the other states in the Union, at a time and place to be agreed on, to take into consideration the trade of the United States; to examine the relative situation and trade of the said States; to consider how far a uniform system in their commercial regulations may be necessary to their common interest and their permanent harmony; and to report to the several states such an act relative to this great object as, when unanimously ratified by them, will enable the United States in Congress assembled effectually to provide for the same; that the said commissioners shall immediately transmit to the several states copies of the preceding resolution, with a circular letter requesting their concurrence therein, and proposing a time and place for the meeting aforesaid." [1]

Convention at Annapolis

In response to this invitation — for which there was no authority in the Articles of Confederation, and indeed there had been no authorization for the action of Maryland and Virginia in regulating their interests in the Chesapeake and its tributaries — issued by the State of Virginia, nine States appointed delegates to meet at Annapolis on the first Monday in September, 1786. When the day came delegates had arrived only from the five States of New York, New Jersey, Pennsylvania, Delaware and Virginia; but among these delegates were well known names — Alexander Hamilton and Egbert Benson of New York, William Patterson of New Jersey, John Dickinson of Delaware, Edmund Randolph and James Madison of Virginia. The distinguished veteran and colonial statesman, John Dickinson, was elected chairman of the Convention, which met on September 11, 1786, but in the absence of the other States the members present wisely limited themselves to a recommendation drafted by Hamilton, stating it to be " their unanimous conviction, that it may essentially tend to advance the interests of the Union, if the states, by whom they have been respectively delegated, would themselves concur, and use their endeavors to procure the concurrence of the other states, in the appointment of commissioners, to meet at Philadelphia on the second Monday in May next [1787], to take into consideration the situation of the United States, to devise such further provisions as shall appear to them necessary to render

Another Convention Proposed

[1] Elliot, *Debates,* Vol. i, pp. 115–6.

the Constitution of the Federal government adequate to the exigencies of the Union, and to report such an act for that purpose to the United States in Congress assembled, as, when agreed to by them, and afterwards confirmed by the legislatures of every State, will effectually provide for the same." [1]

The Convention was somewhat embarrassed in the matter of Congress, as the meeting at Annapolis was without its consent and therefore unconstitutional. As, however, Congress would have to act if the Articles of Confederation were to be amended " in order to render the Constitution of the Federal government adequate to the exigencies of the Union," it would be necessary not only to inform the Congress but to have it take appropriate action, in accordance with the thirteenth of the Articles of Confederation which provided that no " alteration at any time hereafter be made in any of them; unless such alteration be agreed to in the Congress of the United States and be afterward confirmed by the legislatures of every state." The commissioners prepared a report to their respective governments, and dealt with the delicate congressional situation in the following concluding paragraph:

> Though your commissioners could not with propriety address these observations and sentiments to any but the states they have the honor to represent, they have nevertheless concluded, from motives of respect, to transmit copies of this report to the United States in Congress assembled, and to the executive of the other states.[2]

Virginia at once took action, agreeing to the convention to be held at Philadelphia for the purposes specified in the report, and appointed commissioners or delegates to meet with the delegates of the other States to consider the revision of the Articles of Confederation. New Jersey, Pennsylvania, North Carolina, Delaware, and Georgia did likewise; whereupon the Congress, seeing that the Convention was to take place, and not unwilling to make a recommendation which was likely to be followed, as well as to aid in securing for the general government powers which it had repeatedly but vainly urged, gave its approval for the call of the convention in the following resolution, adopted February 21, 1787:

Congressional Approval

> Whereas there is provision, in the Articles of Confederation and Perpetual Union, for making alterations therein, by the assent of a Congress of the United States, and of the legislatures of the several states; and whereas experience hath evinced that there are defects in the present Confederation; as a mean to remedy which, several of the states, and particularly the state of New York, by express instructions to their delegates in Congress, have suggested a convention for the purposes expressed in the following resolution; and such convention appearing to be the most probable mean of establishing in these states a firm national government,—
>
> *Resolved,* That, in the opinion of Congress, it is expedient that, on the second Monday in May next, a convention of delegates, who shall have been ap-

---

[1] *Ibid.,* p. 118.
[2] *Ibid.*

pointed by the several states, be held at Philadelphia, for the sole and express purpose of revising the Articles of Confederation, and reporting to Congress and the several legislatures such alterations and provisions therein as shall, when agreed to in Congress, and confirmed by the states, render the federal Constitution adequate to the exigencies of government and the preservation of the Union." [1]

Authorized by the Congress, there was no reason why the States should hesitate, and with the exception of Rhode Island all of the thirteen States then composing the Union appointed delegates. They did not reach Philadelphia on " the second Monday in May next." It was not until the 25th that the delegates of seven States arrived. New Hampshire did not appoint its delegates until the 27th of June because of a lack of funds necessary to their maintenance, and the delegates appointed and accepting the appointment made their appearance only late in July, when the work of the Convention was well along, but fortunately in time to share in some of its most important proceedings.

Union of Sovereign States

It may be disputed whether a union of the States existed in law, although it may have existed in fact, before the 1st day of March, 1781, when the Articles of Confederation creating a perpetual Union were ratified by the last of the thirteen States upon the signature of the Articles by the delegates of Maryland, authorized and directed so to do by that State. There can be no doubt, however, that, after that date the thirteen American States formed a Confederation and remained confederated until the dissolution of the Confederation by the adoption of the Constitution and the organization of the government of the more perfect Union thereunder in 1789.

The question of the relation of the States to one another and to the Confederation established by the Articles has been the subject of no little debate. Yet there seems to be no reasonable doubt on this head, if the language of the Articles means what it says and if the decisions of the Supreme Court of the United States are entitled to respect. No doubt the States could have merged their personality in the Union of their creation, but there is no doubt that they did not do so; for, after stating in the first article that " the stile of this Confederacy shall be ' the United States of America,' " the very next article, and the first in which the relation of the States is considered, provides that " each State retains its sovereignty, freedom, and independence, and every power, jurisdiction and right which is not by this Confederation expressly delegated to the United States in Congress assembled."

As in the case of *Respublica* v. *Sweers* (1 Dallas, 41), decided in 1779, the Supreme Court of Pennsylvania considered the States to form a body corporate from the moment of their association, so in *Nathan* v. *Commonwealth of Virginia* (1 Dallas, 77, *note*), decided in the September term of 1781,

[1] Elliot, *Debates,* Vol. i, p. 120.

within a few months of the final ratification of the Articles of Confederation on March 1, 1781, the Supreme Court of Pennsylvania determined that the States under the Articles of Confederation were sovereign, free and independent States in the sense of international law. In the official report of this case it is stated that

> A foreign attachment was issued against the Commonwealth of Virginia, at the suit of Simon Nathan; and a quantity of cloathing, imported from France, belonging to that state, was attached in Philadelphia. The delegates in Congress from Virginia, conceiving this a violation of the laws of nations, applied to the supreme executive council of Pennsylvania, by whom the sheriff was ordered to give up the goods. The counsel for the plaintiff, finding that the sheriff suppressed the writ, and made no return of his proceedings, obtained, September 20, 1781, a rule that the sheriff should return the writ, unless cause was shewn.
>
> They contended, that the sheriff was a ministerial officer; that he could not dispute the authority of the court out of which the writ issues, but was bound to execute and return it at his own peril. 6 Co. 54. That those cases in England, where the sheriff was not compelled to return writs issued against ambassadors or their retinue, depended upon the stat. 7 Ann., c. 12, which did not extend to this state.
>
> The *Attorney-General*, on the part of the sheriff, and by direction of the supreme executive council, shewed cause, and prayed that the rule might be discharged. He premised, that though the several states which form our federal republic, had, by the confederation, ceded many of the prerogatives of sovereignty to the United States, yet these voluntary engagements did not injure their independence on each other; but that each was a sovereign, "with every power, jurisdiction, and right, not expressly given up." He then laid down two positions. First: that every kind of process, issued against a sovereign, is a violation of the laws of nations; and is in itself null and void. Second: that a sheriff can not be compelled to serve or return a void writ.

After elaborate argument by the Attorney General and counsel for plaintiff in support of their respective contentions, "the Court," to quote the official report, "held the matter some days under advisement — and at their next meeting the President delivered it as the judgment of the court.

" ' That the rule made upon the sheriff, to return the writ issued against the commonwealth of Virginia, at the suit of Simon Nathan, should be discharged.' "

To the same effect are the opinions of Chief Justice Marshall in the leading case of *Sturges* v. *Crowninshield* (4 Wheaton, 192), decided in 1819, in which that eminent jurist said:

> It must be recollected, that previous to the formation of the new constitution, we were divided into independent states, united for some purposes, but in most respects, sovereign.

And in the leading case of *Gibbons* v. *Ogden* (9 Wheaton, 1, 187), decided in 1824, Chief Justice Marshall again said:

As preliminary to the very able discussions of the constitution, which we have heard from the bar, and as having some influence on its construction, reference has been made to the political situation of these states anterior to its formation. It has been said, that they were sovereign, were completely independent, and were connected with each other only by a league. This is true.

As far, therefore, as the United States were concerned, they were independent from July 4, 1776; and from March 1, 1781, they formed a Confederation under the Articles of Confederation and Perpetual Union. As far as the outer world was concerned, their independence of Great Britain and membership in the society of nations was recognized by treaties with France of February 6, 1778, with the Netherlands of October 8, 1782, with Sweden of April 3, 1783, and with Great Britain itself of September 3, 1783. The Declaration of Independence had ceased to be a hope or a promise; it had become a fact, and it was alike the task and the test of the Statesmen of the day to secure that form of government which to them and their successors should seem most likely to effect their safety and happiness.

IV

EARLY BACKGROUNDS OF THE AMERICAN CONSTITUTION — TRADING COMPANIES

I do confess I did ever think that trading in companies is most agreeable to the English nature, which wanteth that same general vein of a republic which runneth in the Dutch and serveth to them instead of a company. (*Sir Francis Bacon, 1616, Letters and Life of Francis Bacon, James Spedding, Editor, Vol. v, 1869, p. 259.*)

Their story [The Merchants of the Staple] is the story of the beginning of English exports on any considerable scale, and of a system which was devised for the purpose. The main interest of the system lies in the fact that the Government worked through private merchants, and used them as machinery for State purposes. (*Sir C. P. Lucas, The Beginnings of English Overseas Enterprise, 1917, p. 55.*)

Henry by the grace of God King of England and France and Lord of Ireland, to all to whom these present letters shall come, greeting.
Know ye that, . . .
We, . . .
Do will and grant, by the tenor of these presents, to the said merchants, that they may freely and lawfully assemble and meet together as often and whensoever they please, in some convenient and fitting place, where they shall think good, and that they may choose and elect among themselves certain sufficient and fit persons for their governors in those parts at their good liking;
And furthermore we give and grant to the said Governors which are in such sort to be chosen by the aforesaid merchants, as much as in us lieth, special power and authority to rule and govern all and singular the merchants our subjects remaining in those parts and which hereafter shall come and repair to those parts, either by themselves or by their sufficient deputies, and to do unto them and every one of them in their causes and quarrels whatsoever, which are sprung up or shall hereafter spring up among them in the parts aforesaid, full and speedy justice, . . .
And, by the common consent of the aforesaid merchants our subjects, to make and establish statutes, ordinances and customs as shall seem expedient in that behalf for the better government of the state of the said merchants our subjects,
And to punish reasonably according to the quantity of their offence in that behalf all and singular the merchants our subjects which shall withstand, resist or disobey the aforesaid governors so to be chosen, or their deputies, or any of them, or any of the aforesaid statutes, ordinances and customs,
Moreover we do ratify, confirm and approve, and as ratified, confirmed and approved we command firmly and inviolably then to be observed all just and reasonable statutes, ordinances and customs which shall be made and established by the said governors, so to be chosen in the form aforesaid, . . . (*Charter Granted by Henry IV to the English Merchants in Holland, Zeeland, Brabant, and Flanders, February 5th, 1406/7, Sir C. P. Lucas, The Beginnings of English Overseas Enterprise, 1917, pp. 184–186.*)

The Adventurers were given authority to meet at Calais and elect a governor, and " four and twenty of the most sad discreet and honest persons of divers fellowships of the said Merchants Adventurers " to be his assistants, thirteen to form a quorum. To the governor and his deputies, with the twenty-four assistants, was entrusted the power of making laws for the fellowship. (*Charter of 1505, Sir C. P. Lucas, The Beginnings of English Overseas Enterprise, 1917, p. 71.*)

The first embryo of the chartered company is no less important and no less interesting, in its bearing upon the Empire that was to be, than the growth and evolution of the system. We have seen of what sort was the earliest charter to the Merchant Adventurers. It was not a charter to give a trade monopoly, it was a charter to grant a constitution, a charter to enable Englishmen sojourning in foreign parts to govern themselves. The preamble sets forth the mischief that has occurred and is likely to grow, " through want of good and discreet rule and government," unless the king intervenes " for the procuring of better government." With this end in view, the charter prescribes that the merchants "may freely and lawfully assemble and meet together," when and where they please, to elect governors "in those parts at their good liking." The governors are empowered to rule and administer justice to all English merchants resorting to those parts, to adjust disputes among the English merchants themselves, and disputes between English merchants and the merchants of the soil, to punish, to enforce, "and by the common consent of the aforesaid merchants our subjects, to make and establish statutes, ordinances and customs as shall seem expedient in that behalf for the better government of the state of the said merchants our subjects." . . . The one and only object of the charter is better government, and the way in which better government is to be attained is by granting self-government. The king knew well, and the merchants knew well, that, given law and order, English trade would prosper without government assistance; regulated companies were the early companies, regulated trade is what they stood for, as opposed to promiscuous and disorderly traffic. The king knew well, and the merchants knew well, that among Englishmen the golden road to law and order is to give them definite authority to govern themselves, to choose their own rulers and make their own laws. Exactly two hundred years later, in 1606, the continuous history of the British Empire beyond the seas began with the grant of a royal charter to the Virginia Company; the charter which was given to the English merchants in the Low Countries for their better government in 1407 might almost have been a model for the founding of English colonies in America. (*Sir C. P. Lucas, The Beginnings of English Overseas Enterprise, 1917, pp. 149–151.*)

In good truth his company was a plentiful nursery, for the forerunner and ancestor of all the chartered companies was the fellowship of the Merchant Adventurers: they made the first experiments and took the first risks: "one day still being a schoolmaster unto the other," they gradually evolved the machine which built up the British Empire. (*Sir C. P. Lucas, The Beginnings of English Overseas Enterprise, 1917, p. 149.*)

The Merchant Adventurers had a definite, continuous, working life, in one phase or another, from the central years of the Middle Ages till the beginning of the nineteenth century. . . . They embodied, to quote Carlyle's words, the English instinct "to expand, if it be possible, some old habit or method, already found fruitful, into new growth for the new need." Born of a guild, they became, as a regulated company, a guild enlarged and expanded to meet wider calls than those of a particular trade in an English city: they embodied "the development of national commerce along lines which were familiar in municipal life." That continuity, which has been an outstanding feature of English character and English history, was at once illustrated and up held by the Merchant Adventurers. . . .

The actual beginnings of the Overseas Empire of Great Britain coincided roughly with the beginnings of joint-stock companies, and in the construction of the Empire joint stock played a part which can hardly be over-estimated. (*Sir C. P. Lucas, The Beginnings of English Overseas Enterprise, 1917, pp. 141–143.*)

This third charter of Virginia thus erected the London Trading Company into a body-politic, democratic in its organization, with powers vested in a chief executive, a council, and an assembly, having full authority to legislate and to establish a form of government for the colony confided to its care.

The charter just described possessed all the essential elements of a written constitution. It established a frame of government and distributed executive, judicial, and legislative functions. It was, however, merely the constitution of an English trading company. (*William C. Morey, The Genesis of a Written Constitution, Annals of the American Academy of Political and Social Science, 1890–91, Vol. I, p. 541.*)

As we trace the various political institutions of the American colonies back to a common source we find that they were in the first instance derived from certain powers delegated by the English crown and embodied in charters granted to trading companies or proprietors. The first colonies, whether they were established by the authority of their superiors, or whether they were organized by their own independent efforts, acquired a form similar to that of the trading company. In its most primitive and typical form the colonial government, like that of the company, consisted of a governor, a deputy-governor, a council of assistants, and a general assembly. In this simple political body there was at first little differentiation of functions. The most important business, whether legislative, judicial or administrative, was performed by the whole corporate body, assembled in a "General Court." Matters of minor importance gradually came to be left to the official part of the body, that is, the governor, the deputy-governor, and the assistants, sitting together under the name of a "Court of Assistants," or "Council." Taking this simple and almost homogeneous political organism as a starting point, it will not be difficult for us to trace the growth of those more complex institutions which characterized the later colonies, and which became embodied in the first State constitutions. (*William C. Morey, The First State Constitutions, Annals of the American Academy of Political and Social Science, 1893, Vol. 4, pt. 1, p. 204.*)

These illustrations are, doubtless, sufficient to show that the form of government which prevailed in the southern colonies was modelled after that of the parent colony of Virginia, which, in turn, was derived from the form of government established by royal charter for the London Trading Company; and also that the constitutions of the southern colonies came into being, not as the result of mere custom, but as the product of statutory legislation.

As we turn to New England we shall see that the typical government of the Northern colonies was not patterned after that of a trading company. It was itself the government of a trading company. In the case of Virginia, the company sent out the colony and established a government over it. In the case of Massachusetts, the company became the colony, and brought its government with it. (*William C. Morey, The Genesis of a Written Constitution, Annals of the American Academy of Political and Social Science, 1890–91, Vol. I, p. 548.*)

CHAPTER IV

EARLY BACKGROUNDS OF THE AMERICAN CONSTITUTION — THE TRADING COMPANIES

A DISTINGUISHED statesman has observed that "as the British Constitution is the most subtile organism which has proceeded from . . . progressive history, so the American Constitution is . . . the most wonderful work ever struck off at a given time by the brain and purpose of man." [1] With this commendation of the Constitution the layman is likely to agree, but the historian would dissent, unless Mr. Gladstone's statement, for it was he who made the remark, is to be construed in such a way that the American like the British constitution be looked upon as the most subtile organism which has proceeded from progressive history. For the fact is that, with the Saxon conquest of England, progressive history began in England, and with the advent of the first English settler to America, progressive history began in America, and the culminations were the unwritten constitution of Great Britain on the one hand and the written Constitution of the United States on the other. If, however, the constitution of Great Britain were that of America, it would not have required the calling of a convention to reduce it to writing, and although it was undoubtedly in the minds of those who framed the American instrument of government, it was not the British constitution of 1787 but the British constitution as expressed in colonial charters adjusted to the conditions and circumstances of the new environment and incorporated in the Constitutions of the several independent states of America (to quote the title of a Congressional publication of 1781 [2]), which formed the firm and sure foundation upon which the new structure was reared.

Colonial
Charters

It is common knowledge that the territories which formed the thirteen British colonies, and ultimately the thirteen original States, were settled under charters granted by the Crown; that the earliest of these charters, to the London and New England Companies, were in form and content similar to, if not identical with the charters granted to the Trading Companies of England, of which the East India Company is the most famous and typical example;

---

[1] William E. Gladstone, *Gleanings of Past Years*, 1843–78, Vol. i, p. 212.
[2] *The Constitutions of the several independent states of America; the Declaration of independence; the Articles of confederation between the said states; the treaties between His Most Christian Majesty and the United States of America.* Published by order of Congress, Philadelphia, 1781.

that the form of government developed in Virginia under its charter was followed by the colonies south of Mason and Dixon's line; and that the form of government developed in Massachusetts under its charter, was followed by the colonies to the north of that line. It is important to dwell upon these facts, because they show how naturally the framers of the American Constitution were consciously or unconsciously influenced by generations of colonial experience and practice to authorize the judicial power of the United States to declare unconstitutional those acts of Congress and of the States forming the American union inconsistent with that charter which we call the Constitution, just as the courts of the mother-country had from time to time declared null and void legislation on the part of the colonies in excess of the grants contained in the charters creating these bodies politic.

Genesis of Authority of Supreme Court in Questions of Constitutionality

In the first volume of his history of Massachusetts, published in 1764, Thomas Hutchinson, then Chief Justice and Lieutenant Governor, and soon to become the last Royal Governor of that Commonwealth, said, in speaking of the original charter of the colony granted on March 4, 1628:

> It is evident from the charter that the original design of it was to constitute a corporation in England, like to that of the East-India and other great companies, with powers to settle plantations within the limits of the territory, under such forms of government and magistracy as should be fit and necessary.[1]

More recently Mr. George Cawston, a specialist in such matters and an incorporator of the British South African Company, has said:

> Most of the colonial possessions of this Empire were in the first place settled through the agency of Chartered Companies, and that our foreign trade and commerce principally originated in the same manner.

In his interesting and instructive volume entitled *The Early Chartered Companies,* Mr. Cawston quotes with approval in the preface that " individuals cannot extend society to distant places without forming a compact amongst themselves, and obtaining some guarantee for its being observed," to which he adds upon his own authority:

> All the old and most successful British colonies in America, Virginia, Massachusetts, Connecticut, Rhode Island, Pennsylvania, Maryland, and Georgia, which formed the basis of that most wonderful country, the United States of America, were founded by individuals whose public spirit, prudence, and resolution were not otherwise assisted by the Government of their country. The charter from the Crown simply erected each of those bodies of individuals into a corporation, with authority required for accomplishing, to use the words of several of these charters, " their generous and noble purpose." [2]

[1] Thomas Hutchinson, *The History of the Colony of Massachusets-Bay,* 1764, p. 13.
[2] George Cawston and A. H. Keane, *The Early Chartered Companies,* 1896, Preface, pp. vii–viii.

In Chapter X of the volume to which reference has been made, a careful and readable account is given of " The Virginia and New England Companies and Provincial Charters," in the course of which attention is directed to a distinction which should have been made by the Crown on its own motion, but which was ultimately wrung from the mother country as the result of a bitter experience:

Two
Kinds of
Charters

> And here a distinction should be drawn between charters granted to English trading companies, which on the whole were injurious, and charters granted to the settlers themselves, which were often beneficial and highly prized as legal instruments affording protection against the oppressive or unconstitutional measures of the Crown and the provincial Governors.   In general it may be said that charters of this second category should alone have been granted, or at least the others should have been withdrawn as soon as the colonists felt themselves strong enough for self-government.   Indeed, there was a natural tendency in this direction, and the control of the trading associations was ultimately everywhere replaced by representative assemblies.
>
> But the change was not always effected without considerable friction, which was due to the fact that the Home Government was slow to recognize the true relations that ought to have prevailed from the first between the colonies and the mother country.   Those colonies were, and should have been regarded as, mere extensions of England beyond the seas, as Professor Seeley has clearly shown in his ' Expansion of England,' and had this patent fact been grasped by the ruling classes in the eighteenth century, there need, perhaps, never have been an American Revolution.[1]

The settlers in the new world were therefore bound to be familiar with corporations, the characteristics of which are stated by Mr. Stewart Kyd, a contemporary of the framers of the Constitution, in his treatise on the law of corporations, published in 1793–4, shortly after the Constitution of the United States went into effect.   Mr. Kyd, dating the second of the two volumes from the Tower, to which he had been committed on a charge of high treason because of his liberal views — more unfashionable then than they are today — thus speaks of corporations:

Corpora-
tions

> Among the institutions of almost all the states of modern Europe, but among none more than those of England, many of these collective bodies of men, under the names of bodies politic, bodies corporate, or corporations, make a conspicuous figure.
>
> At their first introduction, they were little more than an improvement on the communities which had grown up imperceptibly, without any positive institution; and, for a considerable period, the shade which separated the one from the other, was of a touch so delicate as to require the most minute attention, and the most discerning eye, to distinguish.
>
> One essential characteristic of a corporation is an indefinite duration, by a continued accession of new members to supply the place of those who are removed by death, or other means, which, in the language of the law, is called perpetual succession: . . .

[1] Cawston and Keane, *The Early Chartered Companies*, pp. 198–9.

It is another characteristic of a corporation, that it is capable in its collective capacity of possessing property, and transmitting it in perpetual succession; . . .

A third characteristic of a corporation is, that the members of which it is composed, are subject to common burthens; . . .

Another characteristic of a corporation is, that it may sue and be sued in its collective capacity; . . .

And after stating what he calls the essentials, he continues:

A CORPORATION then, or a body politic, or body incorporate, is a collection of many individuals, united into one body, under a *special denomination,* having perpetual succession under an *artificial form,* and vested, by the policy of the law, with the capacity of acting, in several respects, as an *individual,* particularly of taking and granting property, of contracting obligations, and of suing and being sued, of enjoying privileges and immunities in *common,* and of exercising a variety of political rights, more or less extensive, according to the design of its institution, or the powers conferred upon it, either at the time of its creation, or at any subsequent period of its existence.[1]

The views which Mr. Kyd expressed and which were no doubt shared by American lawyers of his day were, it is believed, also the views of the early settlers; and these views were based upon reported cases decided by English Judges during the period of American colonization. Thus, Sir Henry Hobart, " a most learned, prudent, grave and religious Judge," Attorney General from 1606–13, when the early American charters were granted, and Chief Justice of the Court of Common Pleas from the latter date to his death in 1625, said in the case of *Norris* v. *Staps* (Hobart, 211), decided in 1617:

Now I am of opinion, that though power to make laws, is given by special clause in all incorporations, yet it is needless; for I hold it to be included   By-Laws
by law, in the very act of incorporating, as is also the power to sue, to purchase, and the like. For, as reason is given to the natural body for the governing of it, so the body corporate must have laws as a politick reason to govern it, but those laws must ever be subject to the general law of the realm as subordinate to it. And therefore though there be no proviso for that purpose, the law supplies it. And if the King in his letters patents of incorporation do make ordinances himself, as here it was (as aforesaid) yet they are also subject to the same rule of law.

In his treatise on the law of corporations Mr. Kyd laid it down that " not only all bye-laws must be reasonable and consistent with the general principles of the law of the land " for which Lord Hobart's authority is sufficient, but also " their reasonableness and legality must be determined by the Judges in the Superior Courts when they are properly before them "; for which statement the learned author invoked the authority of the *Master and Company of Framework-Knitters* v. *Green* (1 Lord Raymond, 114), decided in 1695, in which it was said by the Justices that " members of corporations are not bound

[1] Stewart Kyd, *A Treatise on The Law of Corporations,* 1793, Vol. i, pp. 2, 3–4, 7, 10, 13.

to perform by-laws unless they are reasonable, and the reasonableness of them is examinable by the Judges."

Finally, for present purposes, another quotation may be made from Kyd, as it is material to the subject in hand.   Thus he says:

> When the corporate body has a jurisdiction over certain limits, a bye-law made by them for the public good, and whose object is general without being limited to people of any particular description, binds every body coming within the limits of the jurisdiction, whether strangers or members of the corporate body [Brownl. and Goulds, 179]; for every man, says Holt, who comes within the limits of the local jurisdiction of a corporation, must take notice of their bye-laws at his peril [Per Holt, Skin. 35].[1]

The charter granted territory within which the trading companies should operate.   It incorporated certain persons, making of them and their successors a body politic, providing for a governor or treasurer, whom we today would call a president or chairman; for a general court, council, or assistants, whom we today would call a board of directors; and a more numerous body of persons declared to be " free of the company," whom we would today call stockholders in a company engaged in a common venture upon a joint capital, but who would be tradesmen in a trading company, where each member acted individually, not jointly.

The nature of this process, its development and its consequences are thus stated by Messrs. Cawston and Keane in their work on *The Early Chartered Companies:*

Development of Trading Companies

> The trading associations that were now springing up and clamouring for the aegis of 'the most high, mightie and magnificent Empresse Elizabeth' were constituted on two distinct principles.   First in the natural and actual order came the so-called *Regulated Companies,* which were suitable to the first efforts of the nation to acquire a share of the world's trade, but destined eventually to be superseded by the far more powerful and efficient *Joint-Stock Companies.*   For a long time all belonged to the first category, and even so late as the end of the seventeenth century there existed in England only three founded on the joint-stock principle, although these three — the *East India,* the *Royal African,* and the *Hudson Bay* — were perhaps more important than all the rest put together.
>
> In the 'regulated' companies, at that time chiefly represented by the *Russia,* the *Turkey,* and the *Eastland,* every member or 'freeman' traded solely on his own account, subject only to the 'regulations' of the association.   In fact, they may be regarded as growing out of the trade guilds, modified to meet the requirements of their more enlarged sphere of action.   In the guilds each member purchased a license to ply his trade in his own district at his personal risk, the guild itself being irresponsible for his liabilities in case of failure.   On the other hand, he enjoyed all the advantages of membership in an incorporated trade, which could not be exercised by outsiders, even though residents in the district.   In the same way no subject of the Crown could trade in any foreign 'district' where a regulated company was established without first acquiring membership by the payment of a fee.[2]

[1] Kyd, *A Treatise on the Law of Corporations,* Vol. ii, p. 104.
[2] Cawston and Keane, *Early Chartered Companies,* pp. 9–10.

It is thus seen that in the very elements of their constitution the regulated companies were merely a development of the local guilds adapted for trading purposes beyond the seas. The reasons which caused the scales to tip on the side of the joint-stock companies are thus stated by the same learned authors:

> Then came the time when, with the growth of wealth and experience, these pioneer traders in foreign lands acquired a deeper consciousness of their latent powers, a greater sense of their higher destinies, and especially that mutual confidence in each other which was needed for the adoption of the joint-stock principle. As in the regulated associations each member retained his personal independence, and mainly acted on his own account —'traded on his own bottom,' as was the phrase — so in the ' joint ' concerns the individual was largely merged in the corporate body, all working together primarily for the common good rather than for their direct personal advantage. . . .
>
> It was by the general adoption of this principle that the great chartered companies acquired their enormous expansion, and in some memorable instances were by the force of circumstances gradually transformed from mere commercial associations of Adventurers into powerful political organizations.[1]

On December 31, 1600, Queen Elizabeth granted to George, Earl of Cumberland, and to two hundred fifteen Knights, Aldermen, and Merchants a charter whose terms are thus stated in Anderson's *Origin of Commerce:*

> That, at their own costs and charges,— they might set forth one or more voyages to the East Indians, in the country and parts of Asia and Africa, and to the islands thereabouts,— divers of which countries, islands, &c. have long sithence been discovered by others of our subjects;— to be one body politic and corporate, by the name of, *The Governor and Company of Merchants of London trading to the East Indies;* — to have succession; — to purchase lands (without limitation;) — to have one Governor, and twenty-four persons, to be elected annually, who shall be called Committees, jointly to have the direction of the voyages, the provision of the shipping and merchandize, also the sale of the merchandize, and the management of all other things belonging to the said Company.— Sir Thomas Smith, Alderman of London, was to be the first Governor, and a Deputy-Governor to be elected in a General Court; both the Governors and all the Committees to take the oath of fidelity.— As also, every member shall take an oath, before being admitted, to traffic as a freeman of this Company.— The Company . . . may . . . freely and solely trade, by such ways and passages as are already found out, or which shall hereafter be discovered . . . beyond the cape of Bona Speranza to the Streights of Magellan, where any traffic of merchandize may be used to and from every of them, in such manner as shall, from time to time, be limited and agreed on at any public assembly or general court of the Company; any statute, usage, diversity of religion or faith, or any matter, to the contrary notwithstanding; so as it be not to any country already possessed by any Christian potentate in amity with her Majesty, who shall declare the same to be against his or their good liking.— Either the Governor or Deputy Governor must always be one in general assemblies, when they may make all reasonable laws, constitutions, &c. agreeable to the laws of England, for

[1] Cawston and Keane, *Early Chartered Companies*, pp. 11–12, 13.

their good government, by plurality of voices, and may punish, by fines and imprisonment, the offenders against their laws . . . None of the Queen's subjects, but the Company, their servants, or assigns, shall resort to India, without being licensed by the Company, upon pain of forfeiting ships and cargoes, with imprisonment, till the offenders give one thousand pounds bond to the Company, not to trade thither again.— Nevertheless, for the encouragement of merchant-strangers and others to bring in commodities into the realm, the Queen gives power to the Company to grant licenses to trade to the East Indies; and she promises not to grant leave to any others to trade thither during the Company's term, without their consent. The majority of any general meeting of the Company may admit apprentices, servants, factors, &c. to the fellowship or freedom of the said Company. . . .[1]

Under this charter, the East India Company was formed which, after many vicissitudes, became in 1876, the Empire of India.

In other words the Company consisted of a governor, a deputy governor and a committee or council of twenty-four persons. The governor (the first being named in the charter) and all other officers were to be chosen in a general court or assembly of the whole company; and every member, upon admission, was required under oath " to traffic as a freeman of the Company." The general assembly, consisting of the governor, the council, and the members of the corporation sitting as a body, was presided over by the governor or deputy governor, and the assembly was authorized " to make all reasonable laws, constitutions, etc., agreeable to the laws of England for their good Government by a plurality of voices "; and also " to punish by fines and imprisonment the offenders against these laws."

It is to be observed, in the first place, that this charter for the Asiatic trade was granted before an English colony was permanently planted on the mainland of America; and, in the second place, that the company was a body politic and corporate, possessed of legislative, executive and judicial functions, although they are not stated separately and in detail. Upon the death of Queen Elizabeth in 1603, that great monarch was succeeded by James I of England and VI of Scotland, who granted his first charter of Virginia in 1606, six years after that of his predecessor to the East India Company, to the vast tract of land named in honor of the Virgin Queen, and " this charter, with its subsequent modifications," to quote Mr. Morey's illuminating paper on *The Genesis of a Written Constitution,* " may be said to form the beginning of the constitutional history of the United States." [2]

Spread to America

This charter, drawn in first instance by Sir John Popham, Chief Justice of the King's Bench, and in final form by Sir Edward Coke, then Attorney General, and Sir James Doderidge, Solicitor General, divided, as is well known, the North American coast into two parts, assigning the southern por-

---

[1] Adam Anderson, *Historical and Chronological Deduction of the Origin of Commerce,* Coombe ed., 1790, Vol. ii, pp. 261-2.
[2] *Annals of the American Academy of Political and Social Science,* 1891, Vol. i, p. 537.

tion, between the 34th and 41st degrees of latitude to the London Company, and the northern portion, between the 38th and 45th degrees, to the Plymouth Company. Each company was to have a council of thirteen members residing therein, to be appointed and removed by the Crown. For these two companies there was to be appointed in England a council of Virginia, consisting of thirteen persons, to be appointed by the Crown, and to pass upon and to control the actions of the colonies subject to the instructions of the Crown.

The colonists, whether born in England or in the plantations, were specifically endowed with " all Liberties, Franchises and Immunities within any of our other Dominions, to all Intents and Purposes, as if they had been abiding and born, within this our realm of *England,* or any other of our said Dominions." [1]

The two colonies overlapped. It was later provided in the charter that there should be a space of 100 miles between the colonies planted in accordance with the charter. The north and the south were thus to be separated geographically, as they have been historically. The southern colonies have, as a matter of fact, been modeled upon the charter and the institutions of Virginia. The northern colonies have been modeled upon the charter of New England and its institutions. In their broad lines the development of the two sections has been similar, although not identical.

It is also to be noted that this first charter of Virginia in 1606 is less liberal than that of the East India Company,— because James I was more of a believer in divine right and less of a statesman than Elizabeth,— in that it does not contain a grant of legislative power, and subjected the council in the colony and the council in England to the royal pleasure, as expressed in the King's instructions.

The settlements under this charter did not thrive. It was an experiment   A Second Charter
which, within less than three years, had proved defective. Larger powers and more specific privileges were requisite. The result therefore was a second charter, probably drawn in first instance by Sir Edward Sandys, and in final form by Sir Henry Hobart, Attorney, and Sir Francis Bacon, Solicitor General. Under this second charter the company or association is created a body politic, to be known, called and incorporated by the name of " The Treasurer and Company of Adventurers and Planters of the City of London, for the first Colony in Virginia." The council and treasurer, or any of them, should in the future be nominated and chosen " out of the Company of the said Adventurers, by the Voice of the greater part of the said Company and Adventurers, in their Assembly for that Purpose." The council, under the presidency of its treasurer or his deputy, was to appoint all " Governors, Officers, and Ministers . . . fit and needful to be . . . used for the Government of

[1] Thorpe, *Charters and Constitutions,* Vol. 7, p. 3788; Poore, pp. 1891-2.

the said Colony and Plantation;" and the council should hereafter likewise " make, ordain, and establish all Manner of Orders, Laws, Directions, Instructions, Forms and Ceremonies of Government and Magistracy, fit and necessary for and concerning the Government of the said Colony and Plantation." The Treasurer and Company " and such Governors, Officers, and Ministers " appointed by them for that purpose, should, within the precincts of Virginia, " have full and absolute Power and Authority to correct, punish, pardon, govern, and rule " the King's subjects residing within the Colony, " according to such Orders, Ordinances, Constitutions, Directions, and Instructions," established by the council, and " in Defect thereof in case of Necessity, according to the good Discretion of the said Governor and Officers respectively, as well in Cases capital and criminal, as civil, both Marine and other; So always as the said Statutes, Ordinances and Proceedings as near as conveniently may be, be agreeable to the Laws, Statutes, Government, and Policy of this our Realm of *England*." [1]

By this second charter the Company is created a body politic, with legislative, executive and judicial functions, and the council created by the first charter to reside within the colony is displaced by a governor and officers invested by the corporation with powers of supervision and control.

A Third Charter

Time and experience having shown the need of ampler powers, a third charter, likewise drafted in first instance by Sir Edward Sandys and finally by Sir Henry Hobart, Attorney, and Sir Francis Bacon, Solicitor General, was granted in 1612, by virtue of which the London Company received the authority requisite to plant, develop and cultivate the colony as the Crown had and the proprietor should possess.

Court and Assembly

Passing over minor matters, such as the grant of the Bermuda Island to the Company, the Treasurer and Company of Adventurers and Planters were empowered, once a week or oftener at their pleasure, to " hold, and keep a Court and Assembly for the better Order and Government of the said Plantation, and such Things as shall concern the same; And that any five Persons of our Council for the said first Colony in *Virginia,* for the Time being, of which Company the Treasure[r], or his Deputy, to be always one, and the Number of fifteen others, at the least, of the Generality of the said Company, assembled together in such Manner, as is and hath been heretofore used and accustomed, shall be said, taken, held, and reputed to be, and shall be a *sufficient Court* of the said Company, for the handling and ordering, and dispatching of all such casual and particular Occurrences, and accidental Matters, of less Consequence and Weight, as shall from Time to Time happen, touching and concerning the said Plantation." [2]   Here we have a corporation au-

[1] Thorpe, *Charters and Constitutions,* Vol. 7, pp. 3795, 3797, 3798, 3801; Poore, pp. 1893, 1898, 1899, 1901.
[2] Thorpe, *ibid.,* p. 3805; Poore, p. 1904.

thorized to hold weekly meetings of such members as happened to be present, under the presidency of its executive, provided not less than fifteen members of the company attend, for the transaction of ordinary matters.

But the affairs of the company beyond the seas were not ordinary matters, and they needed the attention, not of the few who might happen to attend, but of the many who should be present and take part in their settlement. Therefore, the charter provided for this eventuality in the passage of its text immediately succeeding that which has been quoted:

> And that nevertheless, for the handling, ordering, and disposing of Matters and Affairs of greater Weight and Importance, and such as shall or may, in any Sort, concern the Weal Publick and general Good of the said Company and Plantation, as namely, the Manner of Government from Time to Time to be used, the ordering and Disposing of the Lands and Possessions, and the settling and establishing of a Trade there, or such like, there shall be held and kept every Year, upon the last *Wednesday,* save one, of *Hillary* Term, *Easter, Trinity,* and *Michaelmas* Terms, for ever, one great, general, and solemn Assembly, which four Assemblies shall be stiled and called, *The four Great and General Courts of the Council and Company of Adventurers for Virginia;* In all and every of which said Great and General Courts, so assembled, our Will and Pleasure is, and we do, for Us, our Heirs and Successors, for ever, Give and Grant to the said Treasurer and Company, and their Successors for ever, by these Presents, that they, the said Treasurer and Company, or the greater Number of them, so assembled, shall and may have full Power and Authority, from Time to Time, and at all Times hereafter, to elect and chuse discreet Persons, to be of our said Council for the said first Colony in *Virginia,* and to nominate and appoint such Officers as they shall think fit and requisite, for the Government, managing, ordering, and dispatching of the Affairs of the said Company; And shall likewise have full Power and Authority, to ordain and make such Laws and Ordinances, for the Good and Welfare of the said Plantation, as to them from Time to Time, shall be thought requisite and meet: *So always,* as the same be not contrary to the Laws and Statutes of this our Realm of *England;* [1]

[margin note: Great and General Courts]

Bearing in mind the fact that the third charter confirmed the powers and privileges granted by the second, while adding to them in the respects quoted, we have at last reached, by three successive steps the charter of the East India Company, granted by Queen Elizabeth in 1600, created for profit, with the difference that, in addition to the profit from trade, the charter of Virginia contemplated the settlement of a plantation and the creation of a colony as well. For this purpose the Company was empowered to admit new members, who, when admitted, became entitled to the rights and privileges possessed by the other members, thus making it possible for the Company to include all persons who should become inhabitants of the colony. Thus, the full and general court, assembled as aforesaid, was authorized from time to time and for all time to " elect, choose and admit into their Company, and

---

[1] Thorpe, *Charters and Constitutions,* Vol. 7, p. 3805; Poore, pp. 1904–5.

Society, any Person or Persons, as well Strangers and Aliens born in any Part beyond the Seas wheresoever, being in Amity with us, as our natural Liege Subjects born in any our Realms and Dominions;" and that all such persons were thereupon entitled to "have, hold, and enjoy all and singular Freedoms, Liberties, Franchises, Privileges, Immunities, Benefits, Profits, and Commodities whatsoever, to the said Company in any Sort belonging or appertaining, as fully, freely and amply as any other Adventurers now being, or which hereafter at any Time shall be of the said Company, hath, have, shall, may, might, or ought to have and enjoy the same to all Intents and Purposes whatsoever." [1]

A Representative Assembly

The settlers scattered themselves throughout the little colony, so that, in 1619, they might be said to form eleven separate communities, impressed, apparently, with the desire to assemble, as is declared to be the wont of Englishmen. This they did under the authority of the governor of the colony, who himself was apparently authorized thereto by a commission executed by the Virginia Company in November, 1618, and on July 30, 1619 two members or burgesses from each of the eleven settlements met with the governor and council in the little church in Jamestown, forming the first representative assembly ever meeting in the New World.

A Forecast of American Liberty

Two years later, in July, 1621, this action of the governor and of the settlers was specifically confirmed in a formal ordinance, which apparently established in that part of America, now comprised within the United States, the American system of liberty, that is to say, the exercise of political power in accordance with and pursuant to the terms of a written document emanating from superior authority, whether that document be a charter, an ordinance, a statute, a constitution, or whether emanating from a company, the crown, or the people. This ordinance, which is appropriately called the Constitution of the Treasurer, Council and Company in England, created "two Supreme Councils in *Virginia,* for the better Government of the said Colony aforesaid," [2] for the reasons stated in what may be called the preamble to this constitution or instrument of government, and which should be given in their language of the first person, as they were doing it directly, not indirectly. In so doing the treasurer, council and company declared themselves as "taking into our careful Consideration the present State of the said Colony of *Virginia,* and intending, by the Divine Assistance, to settle such a Form of Government there, as may be to the greatest Benefit and Comfort of the People, and whereby all Injustice, Grievances, and Oppression may be prevented and kept off as much as possible from the said Colony, have thought

[1] Thorpe, *Charters and Constitutions,* Vol. 7, p. 3806; Poore, p. 1905.
[2] William Stith, *History of the First Discovery and Settlement of Virginia,* Sabin ed., 1865, App. iv, p. 32.

fit to make our Entrance, by ordering and establishing such Supreme Councils, as may not only be assisting to the Governor for the time being, in the Administration of Justice, and the Executing of other Duties to this Office belonging, but also, by their vigilant Care and Prudence, may provide, as well for a Remedy of all Inconveniences, growing from time to time, as also for the advancing of Increase, Strength, Stability, and Prosperity of the said Colony."

The first, to be called the Council of State, appointed by the Treasurer, Council and Company, consisted of the Governor and certain specified persons, who were directed to " bend their Care and Endeavours to assist the said Governor," and to be " always, or for the most Part, residing about or near the Governor." [1] The second and the more important body is thus described:

> The other Council, more generally to be called by the Governor, once Yearly, and no oftener, but for very extraordinary and important Occasions, shall consist, for the present, of the said Council of State, and of two Burgesses out of every Town, Hundred, or other particular Plantation, to be respectively chosen by the Inhabitants: Which Council shall be called The General Assembly, wherein (as also in the said Council of State) all Matters shall be decided, determined, and ordered, by the greater Part of the Voices then present; reserving to the Governor always a Negative Voice. And this General Assembly shall have free Power to treat, consult, and conclude, as well of all emergent Occasions concerning the Publick Weal of the said Colony and every Part thereof, as also to make, ordain, and enact such general Laws and Orders, for the Behoof of the said Colony, and the good Government thereof, as shall, from time to time, appear necessary or requisite; . . .

But as this was an agency of the company, possessed under its charter of certain enumerated powers, it could not make a grant to its agent of powers and authority greater than it itself possessed. Hence, the general laws and orders which should from time to time appear necessary or requisite in behalf of the Colony are to be in accordance with the terms of the charter, and accordingly the general assembly and the Council of State are required, in the succeeding passage, " to imitate and follow the Policy of the Form of Government, Laws, Customs, and Manner of Trial, and other Administration of Justice, used in the Realm of *England,* as near as may be, even as ourselves, by his Majesty's Letters Patent are required." [2] But as the possessors of limited or enumerated powers are wont to construe them so liberally in their own behalf as to exceed the grant, there must be some authority to pass upon the exercise of such powers and to keep them within the terms of the grant. Therefore, it Ratification Required was provided in the succeeding article of the ordinance, " that no Law or Ordinance, made in the said General Assembly, shall be or continue in Force or

[1] Stith, *History of Virginia,* App. iv, p. 33.
[2] *Ibid.,* pp. 33–34.

Validity, unless the same shall be solemnly ratified and confirmed, in a General Quarter Court of the said Company here in *England,* and so ratified, be returned to them under our Seal." And by an act of generosity, possible, indeed, in men of good will but not to be expected from the Crown or that artificial person we call the State, it was further provided that " no Orders of Court afterwards shall bind the said Colony, unless they be ratified in like Manner in the General Assemblies."

So true it is, as stated by Guizot in his *History of Civilization,* that, when there scarcely remained traces of national assemblies, the remembrance of them, of " the right of free men to join together, to deliberate and transact their business together, resided in the minds of men as a primitive tradition and a thing which might again come about." [1] Innocent as these early settlers were of the customs of the primitive Germans, as depicted by Tacitus, they were unconscious of the fact that, in meeting together, they were following the custom of the great assembly in England, known to them and to us by the name of Parliament, the Lords and Commons of which met together and transacted their business in a single house for a long period of time. In like manner so the governor, council and burgesses continued to meet together. However, in 1680, the then governor, " Lord *Colepepper,* taking Advantage of some Disputes among them," to quote the language of a Virginian historian of the day, " procur'd the Council to sit apart from the Assembly ; and so they became two distinct Houses, in Imitation of the two Houses of Parliament in *England,* the Lords and Commons ; and so is the Constitution at this [1705] Day." [2]

Two Houses

The powers of the company were resumed by the Crown in 1624. From this period until the Revolution the colony was governed under instructions from the Crown, as doubtless it would have been under a charter if one had again been granted. On this state of affairs Mr. Morey feels justified in saying in his own behalf, and vouching for the truth of it a distinguished English authority, who can not be considered as having a thesis to maintain:

> It will be seen that all the essential features of this constitution were a reproduction of the constitution of the London Company and of its prototype, the East India Company, namely: (1) The three elements of the government — the chief executive, the council, and the assembly; (2) the administrative and judicial functions of the governor and council; and (3) the legislative functions of the governor, council, and freemen united in a single body. The only important modifications — namely, the introduction of deputies and the granting of the veto power to the governor — were clearly the direct result of the peculiar circumstances in which the colony was placed; the one due simply to convenience, and the other to the desire on the part of the company to preserve as far as possible its control over the legal acts of the colony. [3]

[1] F. Guizot, *The History of Civilization,* 1858, Vol. iii, p. 199.
[2] Robert Beverly, *History of Virginia,* 1722, p. 203.
[3] *Annals of the American Academy,* 1891, Vol. i, pp. 542-3.

The authority invoked by Mr. Morey is that of George Chalmers, who, after mentioning the provisions of the ordinance, says in his *Introduction to the History of the American Colonies,* first published in 1780:

> " Thus we trace to a commercial company the source of those free systems of provincial government, that has distinguished the English colonies above all others for their regard for the rights of men.   In this famous ordinance, we behold the model from which every future provincial form was copied, though varied by difference of circumstance." [1]

While the experience of Virginia is repeated in all of the colonies, it is but natural that the southern colonies, including Maryland, should follow more closely in the steps of what is affectionately called the Old Dominion, taking as their basis a trading company and a political corporation, with the seat of authority in England, not in America.   The northern colonies, as was also natural, followed more closely the experience and the example of Massachusetts, in which the charter was that of a trading company and of a body politic, with the seat of authority in England.   The charter was, however, transferred to America by the grantees, then apparently possessing what has come to be known as Yankee shrewdness, by the simple expedient of appointing the governor and officers of the company from those who were about to settle and who actually did settle in the colony.   Thus in New England the colony and the trading company became one and the same.

Distinction Between North and South

It will be recalled that the charter of 1606, granted to the London Company, divided the territory in America to which the Crown of Great Britain laid claim into two sections, the southern, out of which the southern colonies, including Maryland, were primarily carved, and the northern section, within which the colonies of New England and what are now the Middle States were principally created.   The second charter, granted to the London Company in 1609, excluded the northern section and restricted itself to Virginia, which, extensive as it was, occupied but a part of the southern division.   In 1620 the Plymouth Company obtained also a second charter dealing only with the northern division, which, as stated, had been separated by the second charter to the London Company granted eleven years previously.

The second charter of the Plymouth Company is similar to although not identical with the second of the London Company.   It possesses in general the same powers and authority, which, however, are separately analyzed.   By this charter the Plymouth Company became the Council of Plymouth for New England, and the starting point for the colonies of New England, and for the Middle States which followed, as it were, in its wake.

After reciting the grant of the Virginia charter of 1606 and the subse-

[1] George Chalmers, *Introduction to the History of the Revolt of the American Colonies,* 1845, Vol. i, pp. 16–17.

quent separation of the London and Plymouth Companies under the charter of 1609, the patent vests in the members of the Company the territory from sea to sea lying between the 40th degree — which, it may be said, passes through the present city of Philadelphia — and the 48th degree of North Latitude; and the territory was henceforth to be known by the name of New England in America. For the better planting and governing of New England, a body politic and corporate was created in the English town of Plymouth in the county of Devon, to consist of forty persons and to be known by the name of the Council established in Plymouth in the County of Devon " for the planting, ruling, ordering, and governing of New-England, in America." The council was authorized to fill vacancies in its membership, to receive, hold and dispose of realty and personal property, and, as a body corporate, to sue and be sued, and to elect from their members a president, to hold office during their pleasure. The council was also authorized in its discretion to admit such persons as they should think fit " to be made free and enabled to trade . . . unto . . . New-England . . ., and unto every Part and Parcell thereof, or to have . . . any Lands or Hereditaments in New-England . . .," according to such rules and regulations as the council might be pleased to establish in pursuance of the powers contained in the patent. In addition, the charter specifically granted full power and authority to the council to " nominate, make, constitute, ordaine, and confirme by such Name or Names, Sale or Sales, as to them shall seeme Good; and likewise to revoke, discharge, change, and alter, as well all and singular, Governors, Officers, and Ministers, which hereafter shall be by them thought fitt and needful to be made or used, as well to attend the Business of the said Company here, as for the Government of the said Collony and Plantation, and also to make . . . all Manner of Orders, Laws, Directions, Instructions, Forms, and Ceremonies of Government and Magistracy fitt and necessary for and concerning the Government of the said Collony and Plantation, so always as the same be not contrary to the Laws and Statutes of this our Realme of England, and the same att all Times hereafter to abrogate, revoke, or change, not only within the Precincts of the said Collony, but also upon the Seas in going and coming to and from the said Collony, as they in their good Discretions shall thinke to be fittest for the good of the Adventurers and Inhabitants there." [1]   The governors, officers and ministers to be appointed by the council were authorized and empowered, and the council, governors, officers and ministers, appointed by the council, were authorized, according to the nature and limits of their offices " within the said Precincts of New-England . . . to correct, punish, pardon, governe, and rule all such . . . as shall from time to time adventure themselves in any Voyage thither, or that shall att any Time heerafter inhabit in the Precincts

The
Plymouth
Company

---

[1] Thorpe, *Charters and Constitutions,* Vol. 3, pp. 1831–33; Poore, p. 925.

or Territories of the said Collony as aforesaid, according to such Laws, Orders, Ordinances, Directions, and Instructions as by the said Councill aforesaid shall be established; and in Defect thereof, in Cases of Necessity, according to the good Discretions of the said Governors and Officers respectively, as well in Cases capitall and criminall, as civill, both marine and others, so allways as the said Statutes, Ordinances, and Proceedings, as near as conveniently may be, agreeable to the Laws, Statutes, Government and Policie of this our Realme of England." [1]   After providing that unauthorized persons should not enter upon and dwell within the precincts and territory of New England, and that if they so do they may be proceeded against and expelled therefrom, it was finally provided, insofar as material to the present purpose, that "all and every the Persons, beinge our Subjects, which shall goe and inhabitt within the said Collony and Plantation, and every of their Children and Posterity, which shall happen to be born within the Limitts thereof, shall have and enjoy all Liberties, and ffranchizes, and Immunities of free Denizens and naturall Subjects within any of our other Dominions, to all Intents and Purposes, as if they had been abidinge and born within this our Kingdome of England, or any other our Dominions." [2]

Within a few years after this patent, settlements were made in the territory adjoining Massachusetts Bay, and, desiring to regularize their condition and to set up for themselves, they obtained a grant for a land and trading company.   Wishing, however, to have their venture confirmed by the highest authority, they applied to the Crown to confirm their patent, to which were added powers of government by the royal charter of March 4, 1628–9.   This first charter of Massachusetts was the third royal charter for New England, just as the Virginia charter of 1611–12 was the third royal charter for that portion of America, and, like it, so similar in terms that a reference to the summary of that charter would suffice, were it not for the importance of the colony whereof it was the charter and of the group of colonies to the north of Maryland.

After a recital of the patent of 1620 to the Council of New England, and the grant by that Council to the Land and Trading Company of 1627–8, both of which were confirmed by the present charter, the grantees and "all such others as shall hereafter be admitted and made free of the Company and Society hereafter mencōed," were created "one Body corporate and politique in Fact and Name, by the Name of the Governor and Company of the Mattachusetts Bay in Newe-England," by which name they were to have perpetual succession, to plead and be impleaded, to sue and to be sued, and to maintain actions "of what kinde or nature soever," and authorized to "acquire . . .

[1] Thorpe, *Charters and Constitutions*, Vol. 3, p. 1832; Poore, pp. 925–6.
[2] Thorpe, *ibid.*, p. 1839; Poore, p. 930.

any Landes, Tenements, or Hereditaments, or any Goodes or Chattells," with power to dispose thereof "as other our liege People of this our Realme of England, or any other corporacon or Body politique of the same may lawfully doe." [1]

In order to effect the purpose for which the colony was created, "one Governor, one Deputy Governor, and eighteene Assistants . . ., to be from tyme to tyme . . . chosen out of the Freemen of the saide Company, for the tyme being," it was provided that the officers should "applie themselves to take Care for the best disposeing and ordering of the generall buysines and Affaires of . . . the saide Landes and Premisses . . ., and the Plantacion thereof, and the Government of the People there." The charter thereupon appointed and mentioned by name the first governor, the deputy governor, and the assistants, to hold office for such time and in such manner as subsequently specified in the charter, empowering the governor or deputy governor to call together the members of the company so assembled. After authorizing the governor or deputy governor to call together the company, the charter then provides that the governor, deputy governor and assistants "shall or maie once every Moneth, or oftener at their Pleasures, assemble and houlde and keepe a Courte or Assemblie of themselves, for the better ordering and directing of their Affaires." [2] Seven or more assistants, with the governor or deputy governor, were to constitute a sufficient court.

For the larger and more important matters, as in the case of the third charter of Virginia, a general assembly was to be held four times a year, to be styled "the foure greate and generall Courts of the saide Company," which assembly, to be composed of the governor, or in his absence of the deputy governor, and of the assistants and at least six assistants or the freemen present, or the greater part of them, "shall have full Power and authoritie to choose, nominate, and appointe, such and soe many others as they shall thinke fitt, and that shall be willing to accept the same, to be free of the said Company and Body . . . and to elect and constitute such Officers as they shall thinke fitt and requisite" for the transaction of the affairs of the governor and company. The assembly was to possess, in addition, the attribute of sovereignty "to make Lawes and Ordiñnces for the Good and Welfare of the saide Company, and for the Government and ordering of the saide Landes and Plantaçon and the People inhabiting and to inhabite the same, as to them from tyme to tyme shalbe thought meete, soe as such Lawes and Ordinances be not contrarie or repugnant to the Lawes and Statuts of this our Realme of England."

The charter thereupon provided that officers of the Company were to be

---

[1] Thorpe, *Charters and Constitutions,* Vol. 3, p. 1852; Poore, p. 936.
[2] Thorpe, *ibid.,* pp. 1852-53; Poore, p. 937.

elected annually in the meeting of the general court or assembly held at Easter, and authority is given to fill by a majority of voices vacancies caused either by death, resignation or removal for cause; that the officers so appointed were required, before undertaking their duties, to take an oath for their faithful performance; that oaths of supremacy and allegiance were to be taken by all prospective colonists; that the colonists and their children, whether born in England or in the colonies, were invested with all the liberties and immunities of subjects in any of the British dominions as if born within England.   Thereupon follows the specific authorization to the governor or deputy governor, assistants and freemen of the company assembled in one joint court

> or in any other Courtes to be specially sumoned and assembled for that Purpose, or the greater Parte of them . . . from tyme to tyme, to make, ordeine, and establishe all Manner of wholesome and reasonable Orders, Lawes, Statutes, and Ordiñnces, Direccons, and Instruccons not contrarie to the Lawes of this our Realme of England, aswell for setling of the Formes and Ceremonies of Governmᵗ and Magistracy, fitt and necessary for the said Plantačon, and the Inhabitants there, and for nameing and stiling of all sorts of Officers, both superior and inferior, which they shall finde needefull for that Governement and Plantacon, and the distinguishing and setting forth of the severall duties, Powers, and Lymytts of every such Office and Place, and the Formes of such Oathes warrantable by the Lawes and Statutes of this our Realme of England as shalbe respectivelie ministred vnto them for the Execucon of the said severall Offices and Places; as also, for the disposing and ordering of the Eleccons of such of the said Officers as shalbe annuall, and of such others as shalbe to succeede in Case of Death or Removeall, and ministring the said Oathes to the newe elected Officers, and for Imposicons of lawfull Fynes, Mulcts, Imprisonment, or other lawfull Correccon, according to the Course of other Corporacons in this our Realme of England, and for the directing, ruling, and disposeing of all other Matters and Thinges, whereby our said People, Inhabitants there, may be soe religiously, peaceablie, and civilly governed, as their good Life and orderlie Conversation maie wynn and incite the Natives of [that] Country to the Knowledg and Obedience of the onlie true God and Sauior of Mankinde, and the Christian Fayth, which in our Royall Intencon, and the Adventurers free Profession, is the principall Ende of this Plantacion.[1]

Inasmuch as the provisions of this charter speak for themselves, it does not seem necessary to comment upon them further than to say that the grant constitutes the grantees, and such persons as they should admit to the company, its representatives in legislative, executive and judicial matters, in accordance with the terms of the charter, with the usual provision that all action should be in conformity with the laws and customs of England.   Under this charter a local government, known as " London's Plantation in Massachusetts Bay in New England " was established at Salem under the direction of John Endicott.   Shortly thereafter, in 1630, the charter and government

[1] Thorpe, *Charters and Constitutions*, Vol. 3, p. 1857; Poore, p. 940.

of the colony were transferred to America, the local government was discontinued, and remained in effect until the charter was annulled in 1684, which, however, was replaced by a royal charter in 1691 after the expulsion of James II, granting substantially the same rights and privileges, with the exception that the governor was hereafter to be appointed by the Crown instead of elected by the Assembly, as under the previous charter.

Growth
of Repre-
sentative
Institutions

There is an interesting passage in Mr. Hutchinson's *History of the Colony of Massachusets-Bay* in which that devoted son of New England and accurate historian traces the origin and growth of representative institutions in the Bay Colony. "The people," he says, "began to grow uneasy, and the number of freemen being greatly multiplied, an alteration of the constitution seems to have been agreed upon or fallen into by a general consent of the towns, for at a general court for elections, in 1634, twenty-four of the principal inhabitants appeared as the representatives of the body of freemen, and before they proceeded to the election of magistrates, the people asserted their right to a greater share in the government than had hitherto been allowed them, and resolved, ' That none but the general court had power to make and establish laws or to elect and appoint officers, as governor, deputy governor, assistants, treasurer, secretary, captains, lieutenants, ensigns, or any of like moment, or to remove such upon misdemeanor, or to set out the duties and powers of these officers — That none but the general court hath power to raise monies and taxes, and to dispose of lands, viz. to give and confirm proprieties.' " [1] Mr. Hutchinson states that after these resolutions they proceeded to the election of magistrates and that they further determined " That there shall be four general courts held yearly, to be summoned by the governor for the time being, and not to be dissolved without the consent of the major part of the court — That it shall be lawful for the freemen of each plantation to chuse two or three before every general court, to confer of and prepare such business as by them shall be thought fit to consider of at the next court, and that such persons, as shall be hereafter so deputed by the freemen of the several plantations to deal in their behalf in the affairs of the commonwealth, shall have the full power and voices of all the said freemen derived to them for the making and establishing of laws, granting of lands, &c. and to deal in all other affairs of the commonwealth, wherein the freemen have to do, the matter of election of magistrates and other officers only excepted, wherein every freeman is to give his own voice." Mr. Hutchinson vouchsafes a further reason for this action on the part of the early settlers, saying: " The freemen were so increased, that it was impracticable to debate and determine matters in a body, it was besides unsafe, on account of the Indians, and prejudicial to their private affairs, to be so long absent from their families and business,

---

[1] Hutchinson, *History of the Colony of Massachusetts-Bay,* pp. 35–6.

so that this representative body was a thing of necessity, but no provision had been made for it in their charter." Anticipating Sir John Seeley's happy remark that it is in the nature of Englishmen to assemble, he comments on this incident, rightly connecting it with that of Virginia, for from the action of these two colonies representative government in the western world is to be dated: " Thus they settled the legislative body which, except an alteration of the number of general courts which were soon reduced to two only in a year, and other not very material circumstances, continued the same as long as the charter lasted. This I suppose was the second house of representatives in any of the colonies. There was, as has been observed, no express provision for it in the charter, they supposed the natural rights of Englishmen reserved to them, implied it. In Virginia, a house of burgesses met first in May 1620. The government in every colony like that of the colonies of old Rome may be considered as the *effigies parva* of the mother State." [1]

As in the case of Virginia for a period the two houses sat together, so in Massachusetts they were together for ten years, when a separation took place for the reasons and with the results stated by Mr. Hutchinson: " About this time there was another struggle for power between the assistants or magistrates, and the deputies. The latter could not bear their votes should lose their effect by the non-concurrence of the former who were so much fewer in number; but, by the firmness of Mr. Winthrop, the assistants maintained their right at this time, and (March 25, 1644) the deputies, not being able to prevail, moved that the two houses might sit apart, and from that time votes were sent in a parliamentary way from one house to the other, and the consent of both was necessary to an act of the court." [2]

Thus, the colony of Virginia, under the charter of a trading company with its governing body in the home country, and the colony of Massachusetts, under the charter of a trading company with its seat of government in the colony, provided the same course of development, the one serving as a model for what may be called the southern colonies, and the other for those which, in comparison, may be called the northern colonies. In each case a charter created a body politic, empowered to make laws for the government of the inhabitants, conforming as far as possible to the laws, customs and institutions of England. In each case a governor, supplied with a council or assistants, was the executive. A legislature in each came into being, sharing with the council the making of laws in common, and in each case separate but nevertheless sharing in the responsibilities of government. In each case the authorization was a written instrument, a charter or a constitution, within which the actions of the colony were lawful and beyond which their actions,

Virginia and Massachusetts Colonies Compared

[1] Hutchinson, *History of the Colony of Massachusets-Bay,* p. 37.
[2] *Ibid.,* p. 143.

whether executive, legislative or judicial were unlawful as in excess of the grant.[1]

We of today should say it was to be expected that the colonies would, when they had broken with the mother country, fashion their future according to their own desires, and that in so doing they would revert to written charters in which the rights of governors and governed were stated in clear and unmistakable terms.   This, with the exception of Connecticut and Rhode Island, the thirteen colonies did when they declared themselves to be independent States.   This the States did when they confederated for the first time, drafting Articles of Confederation in their Congress, to be binding upon all when ratified by each.   This representatives of the States did, assembled in the Federal Convention in Philadelphia in 1787, when they formed a more perfect Union than that of the Confederation, in that charter of the Union and of the States which we call the Constitution, defining the rights of the Union and of the States and of the peoples of the States, with courts of justice to pass upon the acts of each, holding them valid when within the grant, holding them invalid when beyond the grant, just as in colonization days acts in excess of the charter were declared to be null and void.

[1] This process is stated in very brief compass by Richard Frothingham in a note to page 18 of his *Rise of the Republic of the United States,* which is here reproduced:—

Bancroft (i. 250) remarks, that "popular assemblies burst everywhere into life with a consciousness of their importance and an immediate capacity for efficient legislation." These assemblies, in some cases, at first were composed of the whole body of freemen. The dates of the formation of representative assemblies to make laws in the colonies are as follows:—

Virginia, July 30, 1619.— The governor summoned two burgesses from three cities, three hundreds, three plantations, Argals' gift, and Kiccowtan.— Proceedings in New-York Hist. Soc., Coll. 2d ser. 111, communicated by Bancroft in 1856. The governor, council, and burgesses continued to meet together, Beverly says (Hist. Va. b. iv. 31), till 1680, when "Lord Colepepper, taking advantage of some disputes among them, procured the council to sit apart from the assembly; and so they became two distinct houses, in imitation of the two Houses of Parliament in England,— the Lords and Commons,— and so is the Constitution at this (1705) day."

Massachusetts, May 19, 1634.— To the surprise of the magistrates, twenty-five delegates, chosen by the freemen of the towns, of their own motion, appeared and claimed a share in making the laws. The claim was allowed, and their names appear on the records of the day, with the magistrates, as part of the General Court. They sat together for ten years. In 1644, the "Massachusetts Records" say (i. 58), on account "of divers inconveniences," of the magistrates and deputies sitting together, and "accounting it wisdom to follow the laudable practice of other States, who have laid groundworks for government," it was ordered — both sitting together — that each should sit apart; and they became co-ordinate and co-equal branches, the assent of both being necessary to make a law. Plymouth had a representative assembly in 1639. The charter of 1692 named twenty-eight persons as counsellors: afterwards they were chosen annually by a joint vote of a new House of Representatives and the old counsellors.

Connecticut, Jan. 14, 1639.— An agreement among the towns to be as "one public State or commonwealth," provided for a representative assembly, consisting of deputies chosen by the freemen, who, with a governor and council, composed the legislative power. They sat together. The charter of 1662 provided, that the governor, deputy-governor, and twelve magistrates should be chosen at a general election, and deputies should be chosen by the towns. All these officers sat together. In 1698, it was ordered that the governor or deputy-governor and magistrates should be called the upper house, and the deputies the lower house, that they should sit apart, and that no bill become a law without the consent of both.— Trumbull's Connecticut, i. 102, 399.

Maryland, February, 1639.— An assembly of the body of freemen made provision for a representative assembly (Chalmers' Annals, 213). The composition of this body was peculiar. Griffith (Maryland, 7) says, that, "upon writs being issued by the governor, delegates elected by the freemen were to sit as burgesses, one or two for each hundred, with the persons especially called by the governor, and such freemen as had not consented to the election of others, or any twelve or more of them, including always the governor and secretary." The burgesses (Chalmers, 219) desired, in 1642, to sit by themselves; and, in 1650 (Griffith, 13), the assembly passed an act dividing themselves into two houses; the governor and secretary and council to be the upper house, and the burgesses the lower house; and all bills assented to by the major part of either to be the laws.

Rhode Island, May, 1647.— Provision was made under the patent or charter, granted in 1644 by the Parliamentary Commission, for a representation from the towns, which discussed proposed laws before they were presented to a general assembly.— Arnold's Rhode Island, i. 203. By the charter of 1663, a governor, deputy-governor, and assistants were to be chosen annually at Newport; and deputies were to be chosen by each town. At first, all sat in one room. In 1666, there was an effort to have the deputies sit as a separate house; but the measure was not adopted till 1696.— Arnold, 327, 533. The governor and assistants, or magistrates, were the upper house; the deputies, the lower house.

North Carolina, 1667.— Settlers were invited into this colony by the promise of legislative freedom.— Williamson, i. 94. Hawks (i. 144) thinks there was an assembly in 1666; but the general assembly, under the charter, consisted of the governor, twelve councilors, and twelve delegates, chosen by the freeholders.— Chalmers, 524. At a later period, while under proprietary rule (Hawks, ii. 147), the general assembly was divided into two houses.

New Jersey, 1668.— This proprietary colony was divided at first into East Jersey and West Jersey, which had separate assemblies: the first held in East Jersey was on May 26, 1668, and in West Jersey, Nov. 25, 1681.— Gordon's New Jersey, 44–48. In 1702, the two parts were united, a royal government formed, and a general assembly provided for, consisting of the governor, a council of twelve nominated by the king, and a house of representatives chosen by the freemen of the counties and cities. They sat together. In 1738, the council was made a separate branch; the governor withdrew from it, and no longer was the presiding officer.— Mulford's New Jersey, 335.

South Carolina, 1674.— Settlers were promised a share in making the laws.— Ramsay's South Carolina, i. 30. In 1674, the freemen elected representatives, when, Ramsay says, there were (ib. i. 35) "the governor, and upper and lower houses of assembly; and these three branches took the name of parliament." The colony became, in 1720, a royal government; it was settled that the governor and council be appointed by the king, and the representatives be chosen by the people. The whole house was chosen at Charleston, where "there had been often great tumults."— Carroll, ii. 149. About 1716, the colony was divided into parishes; and it was provided that each parish should elect its representatives, "to be balloted for at the several parish churches, or some other convenient place mentioned in the writs, which were to be directed to the church-wardens, and they to make returns of the elected members; and of this act the people were very fond, finding it gave them a greater freedom of election."—Ib. ii. 149. In 1720, when the colony became a royal government, it was provided that the governor and council should be appointed by the king, and the representatives chosen by the people.— Ramsay, i. 95.

New Hampshire, March 16, 1680.— By the decision of the crown, New Hampshire was separated from Massachusetts, and a commission constituted a president and council "to govern the province;" and this commission authorized the qualified voters of the four towns to choose an assembly. It consisted of eleven deputies, and sat as a distinct body; the council having a negative on its acts. The king engaged to "continue the privilege of an assembly in the same manner and form, unless he should see cause to alter the same." A Royal Commission, in 1692, provided for a governor and council, and a house of representatives, to be elected by the towns; both meeting separately, and acting as co-ordinate branches.— Belknap, i. 139, 145.

Pennsylvania, 1682.— In this colony, provision was made for a representative assembly under the Frame of Government of 1682; and also under forms tried in 1683 and 1696. In 1701, the charter agreed upon provided for an annual assembly to consist of four delegates from each county, or a greater number, if the governor and assembly should agree to it. This assembly was to choose a speaker and other officers, "to be judges of the qualifications and elections of their own members, sit upon their own adjournments, appoint committees, prepare bills, impeach criminals, and redress grievances, with all other powers and privileges of assembly, according to the rights of the free-born subjects of England, and the customs in any of the Queen's plantations in America."— Franklin's Works, iii. 155. In this colony (Douglass's Summary, ii. 317), the council had no concern in the legislation otherwise than advising the governor. The legislature had but one branch.

Delaware, 1682.— This colony became a dependency on New York, but was purchased by William Penn. The three lower counties of the Delaware, New Castle, Kent, and Sussex, claimed, under the charter of 1681, a separate assembly, which they obtained, but had the same executive as Pennsylvania.

New York, Oct. 17, 1683.— The governor called an assembly, composed of seventeen delegates, who adopted a charter of liberties, apportioned the representatives to the counties, and claimed to be a free assembly.— Dunlap's New York, i. 134. In 1791, the first assembly convened after the Revolution, and consisted of seventeen delegates. The acts of this assembly are the first that were considered valid by the courts of law.— Smith's New York, 87. The assembly, down to the Revolution, did not exceed twenty-seven members.— Dunlap's New York, i. 212. The council consisted of twelve, nominated by the crown, as was the governor, and sat by themselves.

Georgia, 1754.— The first representative assembly was called by the governor under a form of government matured by the Board of Trade, and authorized by the king. It was composed of nineteen delegates from three districts, and (McCall's Georgia, i, 248) had power similar to other colonial assemblies.

V

FURTHER COLONIAL PRECEDENTS

To balance a large state or society, whether monarchical or republican, on general laws, is a work of so great difficulty, that no human genius, however comprehensive, is able, by the mere dint of reason and reflection, to effect it. The judgments of many must unite in this work: Experience must guide their labour: Time must bring it to perfection: And the feeling of inconveniences must correct the mistakes, which they inevitably fall into, in their first trials and experiments. (*David Hume, Of the Rise and Progress of the Arts and Sciences, Essays and Treatises, 1742, edition of 1825, Vol. I, p. 117.*)

To any one who had inhabited a colony governed under a charter the effect of which on the validity of a colonial law was certainly liable to be considered by the Privy Council, there was nothing startling in empowering the judiciary to pronounce in given cases upon the constitutionality of Acts passed by assemblies whose powers were limited by the Constitution, just as the authority of the colonial legislatures was limited by charter or by Act of Parliament. (*Albert Venn Dicey, Introduction to the Study of the Law of the Constitution, 1885, 8th edition, 1915, p. 160.*)

The free fruition of such liberties Immunities and priveledges as humanitie, Civilitie, and Christianitie call for as due to every man in his place and proportion without impeachment and Infringement hath ever bene and ever will be the tranquillitie and Stabilitie of Churches and Commonwealths. And the deniall or deprivall thereof, the disturbance if not the ruine of both.

We hould it therefore our dutie and safetie whilst we are about the further establishing of this Government to collect and expresse all such freedomes as for present we foresee may concerne us, and our posteritie after us, And to ratify them with our sollemne consent.

Wee doe therefore this day religiously and unanimously decree and confirme these following Rites, liberties and priveledges concerneing our Churches, and Civill State to be respectively impartiallie and inviolably enjoyed and observed throughout our Jurisdiction for ever.

1. No mans life shall be taken away, no mans honour or good name shall be stayned, no mans person shall be arrested, restrayned, banished, dismembred, nor any wayes punished, no man shall be deprived of his wife or children, no mans goods or estaite shall be taken away from him, nor any way indammaged under colour of law, or Countenance of Authoritie, unlesse it be by vertue or equitie of some expresse law of the Country waranting the same, established by a generall Court and sufficiently published, or in case of the defect of a law in any parteculer case by the word of God. And in Capitall cases, or in cases concerning dismembring or banishment according to that word to be judged by the Generall

2. Every person within this Jurisdiction, whether Inhabitant or forreiner shall enjoy the same justice and law, that is generall for the plantation, which we constitute and execute one towards another without partialitie or delay. (*The Liberties of the Massachusets Colonie in New England, 1641, Old South Leaflets, Vol. VII, No. 164, p. 261.*)

In appealing to the common law, as the standard of exposition, in all doubts as to the meaning of written instruments; there is safety, certainty, and authority. The institutions of the colonies were based upon it; it was their system of jurisprudence, with only local exceptions, to suit the condition of the colonists, who claimed it as their birth-right and inheritance, 9 Cr. 333, in its largest sense, as including the whole system of English jurisprudence, I Gall. 493; the inexhaustible fountain from which we draw our laws, 9 S. & R. 330, 39, 58. So it continued after the colonies became states, in most of which the common law was adopted by acts of assembly, which gave it the force of a statute, from the time of such adoption, and as it was then; so that in the language of this Court—"At the adoption of the constitution, there were no states in this Union, the basis of whose jurisprudence was not essentially, that of the common law in its widest meaning; and probably no states were contemplated, in which it would not exist." 3 Pet. 446, 8. It is also the basis on which the federal system of jurisprudence was erected by the constitution, the judiciary and process acts, which refer to "*cases in law and in equity,*" "*suits at common law,*"

" the common law, the principles and usages of law " as they had at the time been defined and settled in England; 5 Cr. 222; 3 Wh. 221; 4 Wh. 115, 16; 7 Wh. 45; 10 Wh. 29, 32, 56, 8; 1 Pet. 613; and were adopted as then understood by the old states. (*Mr. Justice Baldwin, A General View of the Origin and Nature of the Constitution and Government of the United States, 1837, pp. 3–4.*)

It is in the colonial charter that we find the germ of American constitutional law. Each of these, whether of the proprietary, provincial, or republican type, was the fundamental law of the jurisdiction, according to which its government was to be organized and administered. Except that it was not self-imposed, and that it was subject to revocation without the consent of those for whom it was made, it answered very nearly to our modern conception of what a Constitution should be. It was a brief document, laying down a general scheme of political organization, granting large powers of legislation and administration, and imposing a few, and but a few, fundamental restrictions. (*Simeon E. Baldwin, Constitutional Law, Two Centuries' Growth of American Law, 1701–1901, 1902, p. 11.*)

The supervising power of the crown resided nominally in the King in Council; really in a committee of the Council without the King. Certain members of the Privy Council were thus made a standing tribunal, by the name of the Lords of Trade and Plantations. By their authority any colonial statute could be set aside as unauthorized by the charter, and the judgments of the colonial courts re-examined and reversed. From 1718 down to the treaty of peace with the United States in 1783 they were provided with a special counsel of their own, besides being entitled to call on the Attorney-General and Solicitor-General for advice.

In one respect this royal prerogative, which was not infrequently exercised, was favorable to the development of American liberty and law. It secured a certain unity of movement in their growth. It produced symmetry of form. It built up a sentiment of common nationality. It promoted the study of legal institutions. It helped to rear an American bar, worthy of the name. (*Simeon E. Baldwin, Constitutional Law, Two Centuries' Growth of American Law 1701–1901, 1902, p. 12.*)

In order to prepare the way still further for the proposition to be set forth in this article, it is necessary to say that the Federal Constitution is not only not a fiat-constitution projected from the brain of the Fathers, nor a copy of the contemporary constitution of England; it is also not founded upon any previous body of institutions which existed merely in the form of customs. As it is itself primarily a body of written law, so it is based upon successive strata of written constitutional law. (*William C. Morey, The Genesis of a Written Constitution, Annals of American Academy of Political and Social Science, 1890–91, Vol. I, p. 533.*)

The law of corporations was the law of their being for the four original New England colonies. Of whatever else they might be ignorant, every man, woman, and child must know something of that. It governed all the relations of life. This was true, whether the government to which they were subject was set up under a charter from the crown or those who held a royal patent, or — as in New Haven — was a theocratic republic, owing its authority to the consent of the inhabitants. The one rested on the law of private corporations *de jure:* the other on that of public corporations *de facto*. (*Simeon E. Baldwin, Constitutional Law, Two Centuries' Growth of American Law 1701–1901, 1902, p. 261.*)

The proceedings of a legal character in which the colonies had always been most interested were those which took place in England concerning their own charters. . . .

All the earlier colonial charters were such as were appropriate for the regulation of a trading adventure, or land speculation. Those to whom they were granted occupied the relation of shareholders, and elected their boards of direction and government to sit in England. Long before 1701, these boards in most of the colonies had been replaced by local legislatures, meeting on American soil, and the authority of foreign proprietaries was soon to be withdrawn in all. . . .

It is not surprising that English and American lawyers should have been inclined to look at the powers of the colonial assemblies and courts in very different ways. The doings of the original companies, under which the British plantations here were made, were, of course, as they took place in England, fully subject to control by the English courts. . . .

The system of judicial appeals to the King in Council was worked out with more and more precision as the eighteenth century advanced. . . .

Some of the judgments rendered by the King in Council denied validity to colonial statutes which were of the first importance. Such was that in the case of Winthrop v. Lechmere, rendered in 1727, by which the rules of inheritance which had been followed in Connecticut for nearly a hundred years were set aside as contrary to the laws of England respecting primogeniture.

Certain political ideas were thus firmly embedded in the American mind. One was that every statute was subject to be set aside if its enactment transcended the powers conceded in the charter to the colonial legislature. Another was that there was a supreme law — the common law of England, modified in rare instances by Act of Parliament — which was one and the same for every colony, and that if any of their judicial tribunals failed to respect it, the judgments could be reversed by an imperial court of appeal.

The jurisdiction of the King in Council, maintained hardly more for the protection of the royal prerogative than to repress the development of any distinctively colonial and un-English jurisprudence, thus served directly to prepare the way for the American theory of constitutional law. It supplied some of the necessary conditions by familiarizing our people with the elementary conceptions, the institutional prerequisites, out of which it must grow. (*Simeon E. Baldwin, Constitutional Law, Two Centuries' Growth of American Law, 1701-1901, 1902, pp. 17-20.*)

As the colony was created by a royal charter that called into being a subordinate law-making body, that body could neither violate the terms nor transcend the powers of the instrument to which it owed its existence. In colonial times "questions sometimes arose . . . whether the statutes made by these assemblies were in excess of the powers conferred by the charter; and, if the statutes were found in excess, they were held invalid by the courts, that is to say, in the first instance by the colonial courts, or, if the matter was carried to England, by the Privy Council." (Bryce, *The American Commonwealth,* i, 243.) After the severance from the mother country, that power to annul a statute, originally vested in the Privy Council, was simply assumed by the supreme courts of the emancipated states. (*Hannis Taylor, The Origin and Growth of the American Constitution, 1911, pp. 103-4.*)

CHAPTER V

FURTHER COLONIAL PRECEDENTS

An examination of the various charters of the plantations which became, in the course of time, the thirteen United States of America, discloses that, with the single exception of Pennsylvania — which, in fact, however, was not an exception — they contained the express declaration that the colonists and their children inhabiting them were to be deemed natural born British subjects, and that, as such, they should enjoy all the privileges and immunities thereof. We should expect this to be so, even although it were not expressly stated, as the doctrine of indelible allegiance was then, and for many years thereafter, the cardinal principle of English law, shortly stated in the phrase with which

"Once an
Englishman
Always an
Englishman"

we of the present day are familiar, " Once an Englishman, always an Englishman;" from which it would seem to follow that such an one, owing the duties of an Englishman, would likewise possess all his rights and privileges.

It was, however, foreseen that the new and unknown conditions of the new and unknown world to which the colonists were transplanted and in which they took root, would require laws fitted to the new environment; but, being Englishmen, subordinated to the duties and possessing the rights thereof, it was provided, as an examination of the charter discloses, that such rules and regulations as they might frame should, negatively expressed since it was impossible to state positively their content, not be contrary or repugnant to or inconsistent with the laws of England.

Relation
of English
Law to
Colonies

We should expect that the settlers would assume the rights of Englishmen without giving the subject much thought, that they would think less of their duties and be inclined to test their legality and to question their applicability, even if they should be found to be grounded in the common or statute law of the old country. Especially we should expect the colonists to appeal to the common and statutory law of England guaranteeing the privileges of Englishmen if the mother country should attempt to deprive them of the rights and privileges of Englishmen guaranteed to them by the common law and by statutes passed before the settlement of the colonies. These they could properly claim to carry with them, and they could not unreasonably claim the benefits of statutes passed after the settlement of the colonies giving Englishmen at home greater rights than they possessed at the time of the exodus of the settlers.

In expressing an opinion on this matter, it is important to bear in mind Rights of Conquest v. Rights of Discovery the situation of the New World when the colonies were planted, for if the territories parcelled out to companies and forming the colonies of the new world should be considered as conquered or as ceded territories, the laws there obtaining at the time of such cession or conquest, unless changed by the new sovereign, would obtain and continue in force unless inconsistent with the political, religious and moral ideals of the new master. Whereas, if these territories were to be regarded as vacant lands, subject to discovery and occupation by Englishmen, there would be no laws by which settlers could be governed other than those which they carried with them as Englishmen. Under the first theory, the common law would not follow the settler but would have to be extended to the territories by express act; under the second, the common law accompanied the settler and did not need to be extended to the territories. Sir William Blackstone, whose *Commentaries* appeared on the eve of the Revolution and whose opinions had great weight with the colonists, was inclined to the opinion that the territories of the New World were properly to be regarded as acquired by conquest or treaty, saying expressly that " Our American plantations are principally of this latter sort, being obtained in the last century either by right of conquest and driving out the natives (with what natural justice I shall not at present enquire), or by treaties. And therefore the common law of England, as such, has no allowance or authority there; they being no part of the mother country, but distinct (though dependent) dominions." [1]

If the facts be as alleged by the illustrious commentator, his conclusions Blackstone's Interpretation follow as a matter of course, but it does not appear that any of the territory claimed by Great Britain, and out of which the American plantations were formed, was conquered territory. New York, conquered from the Dutch, it may be said, was ceded by treaty, but the conquest and the treaty were regarded merely as removing the obstacles to and as confirming the English claim based upon discovery. It is believed, therefore, that Blackstone's statement lacks the premises without which it can not be supported, and the theory which obtained in colonial times, and the theory in accord with the facts, was clearly and unequivocally stated by Chief Justice Marshall in his masterly opinion in *Johnson* v. *M'Intosh* (8 Wheaton, 543), decided in 1823, in which that eminent jurist, after a survey of the discovery and settlement of the New World, held that the title of European nations was acquired by discovery, recognizing in the native Indians a right to possession but not to ownership of the land, which passed to the discoverer upon discovery and subject to appropriation by the discoverer.

[1] Sir William Blackstone, *Commentaries on the Laws of England,* 1765, Vol 1, p. 105.

Looking upon the territory as acquired by discovery and not by conquest or cession, the second theory is to be accepted as true in fact, and an authority or two need only be cited in order to make clear that the common law of England and the statutes in force at that time followed the colonists.   This question arose in the case of *Blankard* v. *Galdy* (2 Salkeld, 411; 4 Modern, 222), decided by Lord Chief Justice Holt in 1693.

From the facts in this case it appeared that the defendant purchased the office of provost marshal general in Jamaica, relating to the administration of justice in that island, and that he gave bonds for the purchase price of the office.   In an action of debt upon the bond, the defendant pleaded the statute of Edward VI against buying offices concerning the administration of justice, that the statute applied to the island, and that therefore the condition upon which the bond was given was illegal and void.   In reply to this contention, the plaintiff stated that Jamaica was an island beyond the seas, conquered from the Indians and Spaniards in the time of Queen Elizabeth, and that the inhabitants thereof were governed by their own laws and not by the laws of England.   To this the defendant rejoined that, before the conquest, they were indeed governed by their own laws, but since then by the laws of England. On behalf of the plaintiff Shower argued, in terms that support the claims of the colonists at a later date, that " on a judgment in Jamaica, no writ of error lies here, but only on appeal to the Council; and as they are not represented in our parliament, so they are not bound by our statutes, unless specially named."   Pemberton, for the defendant, contended " that by the conquest of a nation, its liberties, rights, and properties are quite lost; that by consequence their laws are lost too, for the law is but the rule and guard of the other; those that conquer, cannot by their victory lose their laws, and become subject to others."   Chief Justice Holt, apparently delivering the unanimous opinion of his brethren, drew the distinction between the settlement of an uninhabited country and of a country acquired by conquest or cession.   On the first point he is made to say in the Salkeld report that " In case of an uninhabited country newly found out by English subjects, all laws in force in England are in force there; " on the second point that, " Jamaica being conquered, and not pleaded to be parcel of the kingdom of England, but part of the possessions and revenue of the Crown of England, the laws of England did not take place there, until declared so by the conqueror or his successors. . . .   That it was impossible the laws of this nation, by mere conquest, without more, should take place in a conquered country; because, for a time, there must want officers, without which our laws can have no force: That if our law did take place, yet they in Jamaica having power to make new laws, our general laws may be altered by theirs in particulars."   In another account of the same case (4 Modern, 222), the court is reported to have said,

" And therefore it was held, that Jamaica was not governed by the laws of England after the conquest thereof, till new laws were made; for they had neither sheriff or counties; they were only an assembly of people which are not bound by our laws, unless particularly mentioned." Judgment was accordingly entered for the plaintiff, because, being a conquered country and not a parcel of the kingdom of England but a part of the possessions of the Crown, the laws of England did not apply unless expressly extended.[1]

This case, which may justly be called the leading one, is of very great importance, as it is believed to state accurately the English law on the subject, and in accord with the law of nations. Looked at solely from the first standpoint, it will be observed that it draws a distinction between the kingdom of England, on the one hand, in which the common and statute law prevailed as of course; and the possessions of the Crown, or, as Sir William Blackstone puts it, dependent dominions. For the kingdom of England, the Parliament legislated, and its act bound English subjects within the kingdom. The dominions necessarily required law, regulation and supervision, and they were bound by act of Parliament specifically mentioning and applying to them, inasmuch as the act of Parliament was the act of the Crown, the lords spiritual and temporal and the House of Commons, that is to say, of the supreme legislative authority of Great Britain. In the absence of such a legislative act, the King himself in council could and did legislate for the territories subject to the Crown, but he did so by an act of prerogative, which could not be contrary to but must be in accordance with the law of the land, including therein acts of Parliament. He might, however, divest himself of the right

Common Law of England Followed Colonists

---

[1] The law of this subject has been admirably summarized and stated by Sir Joseph Jekyll, Master of the Rolls, as follows:

Anonymous, 2 Peere Williams, 75, decided in 1722.

An uninhabited country newly found out, and inhabited by the English, to be governed by the laws of England.— A conquered country to be governed by such laws as the conqueror will impose: but until the conqueror gives them new laws, they are to be governed by their own laws, unless where these laws are contrary to the laws of God, or totally silent.

Memorandum, 9th of August 1722, it was said by the Master of the Rolls to have been determined by the Lords of the privy council, upon an appeal to the King in council from the foreign plantations,

1st, That if there be a new and uninhabited country found out by English subjects, as the law is the birthright of every subject, so, wherever they go, they carry their laws with them, and therefore such new found country is to be governed by the laws of England; though, after such country is inhabited by the English, acts of parliament made in England, without naming the foreign plantations, will not bind them; for which reason, it has been determined that the statute of frauds and perjuries, which requires three witnesses, and that these should subscribe in the testator's presence, in the case of a devise of land, does not bind Barbadoes; but that,

2dly, Where the King of England conquers a country, it is a different consideration: for there the conqueror, by saving the lives of the people conquered, gains a right and property in such people; in consequence of which he may impose upon them what laws he pleases. But,

3dly, Until such laws given by the conquering prince, the laws and customs of the conquered country shall hold place; unless where these are contrary to our religion, or enact any thing that is *malum in se,* or are silent; for in all such cases the laws of the conquering country shall prevail.

See the case of *Blankard* v. *Galdy* (2 Salk., 411).

to exercise his prerogative, as held in the leading case of *Campbell* v. *Hall* (Cowper 204), decided by the Court of King's Bench in 1774, at the very eve of the Revolution.

By the treaty of 1763 between France and Great Britain the former ceded to the latter country the Island of Grenada, which had been conquered by British arms. By the King's proclamation of October 7, 1763, the governor of the colony was authorized and required to call a general assembly in the manner and form used in the other colonies and provinces of America, which assembly, together with the council and governor, was authorized, as stated by Lord Mansfield in delivering the unanimous opinion of the court, " to make, constitute, and ordain laws, statutes, and ordinances, for the public peace, welfare, and good government of our said colonies and the inhabitants thereof, as near as may be agreeable to the laws of England, and under such regulations and restrictions, as are used in our other colonies." On April 9, 1764, by letters patent under the great seal, the King appointed General Melville governor " with a power to summon an assembly as soon as the state and circumstances of the island would admit, and to make laws with consent of the governor and council, with reference to the manner of the other assemblies of the king's provinces in America." The governor, thus commissioned, arrived in Grenada on December 14, 1764, and before the end of the succeeding year an assembly actually met in the island.

But before the Governor, commissioned on the 9th of April, 1764, arrived in the island, letters patent under the great seal were issued on July 20, 1764, laying a duty or impost of four and a half per cent on certain commodities grown, produced, and exported from the island " in lieu of all customs and import duties, hitherto collected upon goods imported and exported into and out of the said island, under the authority of his most Christian Majesty." One Campbell, a British subject, paid this duty to one Hall, a collector of his Majesty's customs, and an action of money had and received was brought by Campbell against Hall on the ground " that the money was paid to the defendant without any consideration; the duty, for which, and in respect of which he received it, not having been imposed by lawful or sufficient authority to warrant the same." Judgment was entered for the plaintiff on the ground, among others, that, having in the proper exercise of his prerogative created an assembly in Grenada, with power to raise revenue and to make laws with the consent of the council and governor, the King had divested himself of the power to legislate, as he otherwise could have done for this dependent dominion, now forming a part of the kingdom of Great Britain, and that legislation to bind the colony should henceforth be by act of Parliament, not by the prerogative of the King in Council.

It is interesting to note in this connection, although dwelt upon in another place, that the court considered the question of an excess of power in so far as the rights of individuals was concerned as a judicial question, since the letters patent imposing the duty were in excess of the power properly lodged in the King, thus furnishing a precedent whereof the framers of the Constitution availed themselves for setting aside acts of authority inconsistent with the fundamental law.

After summarizing the law as laid down in *Calvin's Case* and in *Blankard* **v.** *Galdy*, already cited (although Lord Mansfield did not refer in express terms to the latter case), his Lordship said:

> That if the king (and when I say the king, I always mean the king without the concurrence of parliament,) has a power to alter the old and to introduce new laws in a conquered country, this legislation being subordinate, that is, subordinate to his own authority in parliament, he cannot make any new change contrary to fundamental principles: he cannot exempt an inhabitant from that particular dominion; as for instance, from the laws of trade, or from the power of parliament, or give him privileges exclusive of his other subjects; and so in many other instances which might be put.

In support of his views, he invoked two authorities, who, at the time of giving their opinions, were respectively Attorney and Solicitor General:

> In the year 1722, the assembly of Jamaica being refractory, it was referred to Sir Phillip Yorke and Sir Clement Wearge, to know "what could be done if the assembly should obstinately continue to withhold all the usual supplies." They reported thus: "If Jamaica was still to be considered as a conquered island, the king had a right to levy taxes upon the inhabitants; but if it was to be considered in the same light as the other colonies, no tax could be imposed on the inhabitants but by an assembly of the island, or by an act of parliament."

Continuing to draw for illustration upon the island of Jamaica, with whose history Lord Mansfield was familiar,— as he had examined it and had himself, as Attorney General, given an opinion to the Crown on the matter in hand,— he proceeded to say that " King Charles 2d by proclamation invited settlers there, he made grants of lands: he appointed at first a governor and council only: afterwards he granted a commission to the governor to call an assembly." The conclusions to be drawn from these premises he thus stated:

> The constitution of every province, immediately under the king, has arisen in the same manner; not from grants, but from commissions to call assemblies: and, therefore, all the Spaniards having left the island or been driven out, Jamaica from the first settling was an English colony, who under the authority of the king planted a vacant island, belonging to him in right of his crown; . . .

And from this state of affairs he draws the necessary conclusion that:

A maxim of constitutional law as declared by all the judges in *Calvin's Case* and which two such men, in modern times, as Sir Philip Yorke and Sir Clement Wearge, took for granted, will require some authorities to shake.

But, in addition to the authority of these two distinguished lawyers, Lord Mansfield stated positively that there was no authority for the contrary view, saying that, "on the other side, no book, no saying, no opinion has been cited; no instance in any period of history produced, where a doubt had been raised concerning it;" and "that before the letters patent of the 20th July, 1764, the king had precluded himself from the exercise of a legislative authority over the island of Grenada. . . . That by the two proclamations and the commission to Governor Melville, the king had immediately and irrecoverably granted to all who were or should become inhabitants, or who had, or should acquire property in the island of Grenada, or more generally to all whom it might concern, that the subordinate legislation over the island should be exercised by an assembly with the consent of the governor and council, in like manner as the other islands belonging to the king." Although, before July 20, 1764, the king might have legislated, after that date His Lordship said: "To use the words of Sir Philip Yorke and Sir Clement Wearge, 'it can only now be done, by the assembly of the island, or by an act of the parliament of Great Britain.'"

It may, however, be advisable, in this connection, to invoke again the authority of the same distinguished Attorney General, with whom a greater even than Wearge concurred, as it regards not merely the subject in hand but introduces and decides a different and a related phase of the subject which it is necessary to understand. In connection with the petition of the plaintiff in *Winthrop* v. *Lechmere,* decided by the Privy Council in 1728, the following questions among others arose: "whether the said colony [of Connecticut] have thereby any power vested in them of making laws which affect property, or whether that power is not confined to the making of by-laws only, and whether if they have not the power of making laws affecting property, they have not forfeited their charter by passing such laws." To this series of questions Sir Philip Yorke and Sir Charles Talbot, respectively Attorney and Solicitor General, replied, under date of August 1, 1730, "we have considered the said charter and memorial, and are of opinion, that by the said charter, the general assembly of the said province have a power of making laws which affect property; but it is a necessary qualification of all such laws, that they be reasonable in themselves and not contrary to the laws of England; and if any laws have been there made, repugnant to the laws of England, they are absolutely null and void." [1]

In an earlier opinion, rendered to the Lords Commissioners of Trade and

---

[1] George Chalmers, *Opinions of Eminent Lawyers on Various Points of English Jurisprudence*, American ed., 1858, pp. 341–2.

Plantations, Richard West, then Counsel to the Board and later Lord Chancellor of Ireland, stated, it is believed, the conclusion to be drawn from the wording of the charters, the holdings of the courts, and the opinions of the Attorneys and Solicitors General, and within the compass of a single sentence, that " The common law of England is the common law of the plantations, and all statutes, in affirmance of the common law, passed in England, antecedent to the settlement of any colony, are in force in that colony, unless there is some private act to the contrary; though no statutes made since those settlements are there in force, unless the colonies are particularly mentioned." [1]

It would be foreign to the present purpose to attempt to show in this Colonial
Statutes place the sense in which the colonists understood and exercised their right to make laws. Suffice it to say that new conditions produced new laws, and although each colony claimed the benefit of the common law when to its advantage, it legislated and insisted upon its right to legislate in its own interest in the absence of provisions of the customary and statute law, and at times in the very teeth of either or both. But, as will presently appear, laws in excess of the charter were either negatived by the governor in council, the active and vigilant miniature of the King in Council, or by the King himself in Council if the Governor had inadvertently approved a statute which his royal master was advised to disapprove, or by a judicial proceeding, by the Lords of Appeal in the Council, reversing a colonial judgment based upon a local law contrary to the laws of the realm, as in the case of *Winthrop* v. *Lechmere.* The result seems to be, however, that in every colony customs grew up, laws were passed, which created what might be called a local system, reasonable in the opinion of the colonies and not opposed to the law of the mother country as it should be interpreted in the circumstances.

In a letter of ex-President Jefferson dated September 27, 1810, and addressed to Albert Gallatin, then Secretary of the Treasury in James Madison's administration, the result was stated with respect to New England in terms which were applicable to the colonies as a whole, considering the individual conditions of each:

> Was there ever a profound common lawyer known in one of the Eastern States? There never was, nor never can be one from those States. The basis of their law is neither common nor civil; it is an original, if any compound can so be called. Its foundation seems to have been laid in the spirit and principles of Jewish law, incorporated with some words and phrases of common law and an abundance of notions of their own. This makes an *amalgam sui generis,* . . .[2]

And in a letter written two years later to John Tyler, Judge of the United

[1] *Ibid.,* p. 511.
[2] *Writings of Thomas Jefferson,* H. A. Washington ed., 1861, Vol. v, p. 550.

States District Court of Virginia, and father of the future President, Mr. Jefferson said:

> I deride with you the ordinary doctrine, that we brought with us from England the *common law rights*. This narrow notion was a favorite in the first moment of rallying to our rights against Great Britain. But it was that of men who felt their rights before they had thought of their explanation. The truth is, that we brought with us the *rights of men* — of expatriated men. On our arrival here, the question would at once arise, by what law will we govern ourselves? The resolution seems to have been, by that system with which we are familiar, to be altered by ourselves occasionally, and adapted to our new situation. . . . But the state of the English law, at the date of our emigration, constituted the system adopted here.[1]

Mr. Jefferson's remark seems to be in substantial accord with history. As a matter of fact the colonists were not familiar with the common or statutory law in force at the moment of their departure from the mother country. They were not lawyers; the Bar was not held in honor until many years later; there were very few books of authority in which they could find the common or statute law during the course of the 17th century, and still fewer of those books and the reports containing the decisions of the English courts interpreting the common and statutory law made their way to the colonies. It was only on the eve of the Revolution, when the relations between the colonies had become closer and the advocates of colonial rights and privileges found the common law as an arsenal, from which they could seize weapons to be used in their defense, that, in Jefferson's phrase, " they thought of their explanation." Thus, it is stated in the celebrated Declaration of Resolves of the First Continental Congress, dated October 14, 1774:

> That our ancestors, who first settled these colonies, were at the time of their emigration from the mother country, entitled to all the rights, liberties, and immunities of free and natural-born subjects, within the realm of England.
>
> That by such emigration they by no means forfeited, surrendered, or lost any of those rights, but that they were, and their descendants now are, entitled to the exercise and enjoyment of all such of them, as their local and other circumstances enable them to exercise and enjoy. . . .
>
> That the respective colonies are entitled to the common law of England, and more especially to the great and inestimable privilege of being tried by their peers of the vicinage, according to the course of that law.
>
> That they are entitled to the benefit of such of the English statutes as existed at the time of their colonization; and which they have, by experience, respectively found to be applicable to their several local and other circumstances.[2]

It is the most familiar of maxims that no man can be a judge in his own case, and to have allowed the colonies to determine for themselves whether

---

[1] Lyon Gardiner Tyler, *The Letters and Times of the Tylers,* Vol. i, p. 265.
[2] *Journals of the Continental Congress,* Vol. i, pp. 68–9.

their acts of legislation were within the charter or grant would have placed their future wholly within their own hands, and would have amounted to a renunciation on the part of Great Britain of its rights to the colonies. To have conceded to Great Britain the right to pass upon these questions would or might have been fatal to the colonies, as the mother country might fairly be counted upon, with the best of intentions, to interpret the laws in its own interest. There was thus a conflict of interests, and there was in the nature of things a difficulty arising from the conflict which neither, intent on its own interest, could appreciate in so far as it affected the other. Yet the solution of the difficulty by Great Britain was, if not free from fault, far from faulty, and familiarity with the difficulty and with the method of overcoming it enabled the United States, when the colonies had cut adrift and set up for themselves, to meet and to solve the difficulty which presented itself, and which must always present itself, in an empire with self-governing colonies, in a union of States conferring upon an agent the exercise of large sovereign powers, in the unconscious association of nations which we call the society of nations, the members whereof are indeed sovereign powers.

Conflict of Interests

For present purposes, the prerogatives of the Crown may be defined to be the original rights which the kings of England had claimed and exercised, and which had not in the course of time been vested in the Parliament, or in courts of justice, provided, however, that the prerogatives remaining with the Crown were not, as stated by Lord Mansfield in a passage already quoted from the case of *Campbell* v. *Hall,* inconsistent with the fundamental laws of the realm. These prerogatives the king exercised in his Privy Council on the advice of certain persons appointed by him, as he had formerly exercised these rights in the older and larger council of the realm before he had divested himself or been divested of them. Deprived of its functions as a legislature and a court for the realm, the Privy Council was confined to administrative and executive functions in the kingdom, retaining in the dependent dominions legislative, executive and judicial rights, which, however, could not be contrary to the fundamental constitution of the kingdom.

Prerogatives of the Crown

In so far as the exercise of these prerogatives had not been granted to the colonies they remained with the King in Council; when granted to the colonies they could not lawfully be exercised by the King in Council, as held by Lord Mansfield in the leading case of *Campbell* v. *Hall.* But even in such cases the King in Council exercised the right of supervision and administration; otherwise, the colonial interpretation might differ from the royal, and the system become one of inextricable confusion. The Council for the Government of Foreign Plantations established by Charles II was abolished in 1674. A permanent board was created, known as the Lords Commissioners of Trade and Plantations, composed of great dignitaries, who were members of

Lords Commissioners of Trade and Plantations

the Privy Council, and of some persons not members, but added to the Board to secure its efficiency. The chief purpose of the Lords Commissioners was to advance the trade of the Kingdom and also of the colonies, and in so doing, the interests of the empire would be advanced — although the chief interest was that of the mother country. The Lords Commissioners reported to the King in Council, and, upon approval of their recommendations, appropriate action was taken by them. They recommended, for example, instructions to be sent to the Governors, laws to be approved of or to be vetoed, and, in case of disputes between the colonies relating particularly to boundaries, they suggested the appointment of commissions composed of members from adjoining provinces, issued instructions to the commissioners, and recommended, favorably, or unfavorably, their awards or opinions to the King in Council.

Committee for Hearing Appeals

For matters of a judicial nature, there existed a Committee for Hearing Appeals from the Plantations, which appears to have been not a specially appointed committee of the council but to have been composed of such members of the council who attended and gave their attention to the appeals. This committee might, if it chose, consider and determine the matter itself, or refer it for investigation and report to the Lords Commissioners of Trade and Plantations, whose report it might or might not approve. Its action, however, was submitted to the King in Council who, in the period of the Stuarts, attended with more or less regularity, but who, in the time of the Hanoverians, appears to have been present only on formal occasions and to have given his assent to the recommendations of the Council without taking part in its proceedings.

Three Kinds of Appeals from Colonial Courts

Appeals from judgments of the colonial courts might be of three kinds. First. The appeal was from a colonial judgment, in which the appellant claimed that a principle of law was wrongly applied because of an irregularity in procedure, because of prejudice on the part of the judge, or because of the misapplication of a principle of law. In these circumstances the appellant and defendant would be heard by counsel, either by the Committee for Hearing Appeals or upon reference from that body by the Lords Commissioners of Trade and Plantation, and proceedings in either would be had in accordance with English justice. If the case were referred to the Lords Commissioners, their recommendation would be reported to the Committee for Hearing Appeals, which could approve it or modify it. Whereupon the original or amended recommendation was referred to the King in Council, upon whose approval it became a decree of the King in Council and established the law of the case. In ordinary cases this would not involve the setting aside of a colonial statute. It is to be supposed, and it was the fact, that colonies did not relish appeals from the decisions of their courts and were indisposed to allow appeals from the Governor in Council, often the final colonial court of appeal. But, however reluctant the colonies might be to allow appeals to be taken to the King in Council, the mother country was inexorable, declaring it to be the right of every English subject residing within the colonies to appeal to the King in Council; and although the colonies sought to prevent appeals which they must needs permit, by allowing them only where large sums were involved and where security was given by the appellant for costs and for the payment of the judgment in case the judgment should be affirmed on appeal, the Privy Council decided upon petition of the appellant, irrespective of the amount involved, whether it would or would not allow the appeal in the interest of justice and its uniform administration.

Second. It might happen, however, that the judgment appealed from was based upon the statute of the colony claimed to be contrary or repugnant to or inconsistent with the laws of the realm. In such a case the Privy Council would perforce examine the laws, and, if it found them to be as alleged, it declared them to be null, void and of no effect and reversed the decision of the court based upon them. In certain colonies, more especially in Connecticut and Rhode Island (for the charter of Rhode Island was similar to that of Connecticut), the repugnancy of colonial legislation to the laws of the realm could only arise in a judicial proceeding of this kind, inasmuch as neither of these colonies was required to submit its laws to the mother country for approval or disapproval. The leading case on this point is that of *Winthrop* v. *Lechmere,* which will be seen to be a direct precedent for the courts of the United States in declaring, in a judicial proceeding, laws of the United States or of the States, contrary to the Constitution, to be null, void and of no effect.

Precedent for the Power of the Supreme Court over Legislatures

Third. A dispute might exist between two colonies, as in the case of boundaries based upon an agreement reduced to writing and in a form to be passed upon by the courts, interpreted, and, in appropriate cases, specifically enforced by a court of equity. This was the case with the celebrated agreement of 1732 between the sons of William Penn, proprietors of Pennsylvania, on the one hand, and Lord Baltimore, proprietor of Maryland, on the other, regarding the boundary between the provinces. In such a case, the Court of Chancery having jurisdiction of the parties who resided in England could and actually did order them to enforce their agreement, although it affected title to two provinces beyond the jurisdiction of the Court and indeed beyond the seas.

In disputes between the colonies there might be a wrong without a remedy unless there were a resort to a common authority, for, while each of the colonies was equal and independent of the others, they were all dependent upon the Crown. Therefore, in a justiciable question, whether it be between the colonies or inhabitants of different colonies, resort was had to the King in Council, for the reasons quaintly stated in the petition dated July 17, 1678, of

Randall Holden and John Green in behalf of themselves and of his Majestys oppressed Subjects the Inhabitants of the Towne of Warwick, and of other adjacent Places belonging to his Majestys Colony of Road Island and Providence Plantation in New-England, Setting forth the great Miserys and Calamitys they have undergone as well from the Government of the Massachusets, As by the unjust Proceedings of the Commissioners chosen out of the Three United Colonys of New Plymouth, Massachuset and Connecticut, not only in granting and awarding to one William Harris of Patuxet the Lands bought and improved by the Petitioners but giving him great Damages, notwithstanding the Testimony of one Mr. Williams the first Indian Purchaser of those Lands and other Materiall Witnesses on the Petitioners Behalf as by the Petition more at large appears. . . .[1]

The petitioners, however, were not content to have justice done in their individual cases. They put the ax to the tree, and recommended what the framers of the Constitution of the States did a century subsequently, not merely for New England but for the original thirteen States and all others composing the more perfect Union under the Constitution. After praying that "a Stop may be put to the Proceedings of the said Commissioners," they specifically ask "that for determining this and the like Differences that may and will arise between Colony and Colony, and for avoyding chargable Appeals from those remote parts His Majesty would be pleased to settle his Royall Authority over the whole country of New England, and erect a supreme and indifferent Judicature there."

The case is a very interesting one in itself, and necessarily makes a strong appeal to a New Englander, inasmuch as it reminds him of the New England Confederation established in 1643, and then in effect. The Commissioners thereof appear to have passed adversely upon the case of the petitioners, so much to their annoyance that they carried their appeal to the Privy Council, not only in their own behalf, but in behalf of the other inhabitants of the town, against Massachusetts and the Commissioners of the New England Confederation, thus involving the three colonies of Massachusetts, Plymouth and Connecticut, of which the Confederation was then formed.

Suit of a Citizen v. a State

But the case has a larger interest and makes an appeal to Americans without distinction, for it seems to be a precedent for the extension of the judicial power of the United States to the suit of a citizen of a State against another State of the American Union, as intimated by Chief Justice White, in delivering the opinion of the Supreme Court in *Virginia* v. *West Virginia*, (246 U. S., 565), decided in 1918. Therefore, the facts and the proceedings of this interesting controversy are stated somewhat at length and in detail.

Holden and Green Petition

The petition of Messrs. Holden and Green, "Deputyes for the Towne of Warwick and Colony in Road Island," represented to His Majesty in council "that some Persons within the Corporation of the Massachusetts Bay had

[1] *Acts of the Privy Council, Colonial Series, 1613-1680*, Vol. i, p. 785, § 1224.

by a printed paper affixed in publique places in New England, layd Claime to a Tract of Land, called the Kings Province," which the petitioners claimed belonged to His Majesty, and was subject to the jurisdiction of Rhode Island. The said printed paper in question was read at the board, and a copy thereof was ordered to be sent to the agents for Massachusetts, who were directed to attend two days later, "to shew by what authority or Title Simon Bradstreete Deputy Governor, or other Inhabitants of that Colony have by a printed Paper called an Advertisement dated at Boston the 30th of July last, layd Clayme to the Land of Narragansett and Niantic Countreyes, called the Kings Province." [1]

From the record of the Privy Council in the case, dated December 13, 1678, it appears that the agents of Massachusetts complied with the direction, and declared "that the Government of the Massachusetts is not at all concerned in this clayme, but only some Inhabitants, who had purchased those Lands from the Indyan sachins."

From the testimony of Messrs. Holden and Green, it appears that they had inhabited the region in question for above forty years; that the sachems and Indians of Narragansett had voluntarily submitted, with their peoples, to the government of his late Majesty, Charles I, by a deed dated April 19, 1644, that the purchases made in 1659 by one Major Atherton and others of the Massachusetts Colony were null and void, and were declared to be so by His Majesty's Commissioners for settling the Royal authority in New England, who visited Rhode Island in 1665, and who ordered the purchasers to vacate the lands, and declared "that the Magistrates of Rhode Island should exercise the authority of Justices of the Peace in the Narragansett Country, by them called the Kings Province . . . untill his Majestyes pleasure should be farther knowne." [2]

Without losing ourselves in a wilderness of detail concerning these boundary disputes, it is sufficient to say that Connecticut claimed by its charter of 1662, that the territory in question, and indeed all of the present State of Rhode Island, as far east as the Narragansett River, "comonly called Norrogancett Bay, where the said River falleth into the Sea"; that Rhode Island, by virtue of its charter of 1663 claimed the land in question "to the middle or channel of a river there, commonly called and known by the name of Pawcatuck," thus making of that river the eastern boundary of Connecticut, and by an agreement of the agents of Connecticut and Rhode Island, who secured their respective charters, to harmonize the overlapping grants of their charters by providing in the Rhode Island charter "that the sayd Pawcatuck river shall bee alsoe called alias Norrogansett or Narrogansett river, and that that river in our late graunt to Connecticut Collony mentioned as the easterly bounds of

[1] *Ibid.,* pp. 790–1, §§ 1233, 1234.
[2] *Ibid.,* p. 791, § 1234.

that Collony;" that Atherton and his associates sought to obtain by purchase and by mortgage, the lands in question, to be held by them either in Connecticut or Massachusetts, both of which claimed the region, but not under Rhode Island; that the decree of the Commissioners set aside the claims of Atherton and his associates, and gave Rhode Island the advantage of possession, leaving the question of title to be adjusted with Connecticut, as it eventually was, by the decree of the Privy Council in 1727, and with Massachusetts by a decree of that body in 1746 and by a decision of the Supreme Court of the United States exactly a century later.

But to return to the complaints of Messrs. Holden and Green. On the last day of January, 1679, the Committee of the Privy Council for hearing appeals presented their report, from which it appeared that the trouble was " chiefly occasioned by the pretensions and proceedings of William Harris of Patuxet in New England, who by his Petition presented vnto Your Majestie in Councill on the 11th of June, 1675, did set forth, that he and twelue others neer Forty yeares since purchased of the Indian Princes a certain parcell of Land called Patuxet, which they enjoyed Peaceable for many Yeares, notwithstanding the Seuerall Claymes of the Towne of Providence and of the Massachuset Colony, vntill John Harrud and a Party with him forceably entred vpon part of those Lands vnder pretence of a purchase from other Indians." [1]

Holden in his petition further alleged that Harris and party retained possession of a part of the lands in question against the verdict and judgment of court, so that by reason of the contiguity of Patuxet to the several towns and provinces, Harris and his partners apprehended " no Small Danger of loosing their Rights by the encroachment of the Towne of Providence, Warwick, new Plymouth and the Massachusets Colony."

In this state of affairs, in August, 1675, the governors of Massachusetts, New Plymouth, Connecticut and Rhode Island were directed to appoint " some able honest and indifferent Persons to join with each other, and to cause the Differences and troubles arising to the Petitioner and his Partners, concerning the Lands of Patuxet to be brought to a fair Triall, and that by a just indifferent, and vpright Jury in like manner appointed, all might be finally determined according to Justice and without delay." [2]

It appears that the commission was duly issued and executed, although no report of the proceedings was transmitted to the Privy Council, inasmuch as the Committee for Hearing Appeals stated that the first knowledge they had of it was obtained through the petition of Messrs. Holden and Green, from which the Committee likewise obtained its knowledge of the facts and the proceedings under the commission. These two gentlemen, to whom the

---

[1] *Acts of the Privy Council, Colonial Series, 1613–1680*, p. 800, § 1244.
[2] *Ibid.*, p. 801.

territorial integrity of Rhode Island is very largely due, set forth in their petition that in pursuance of royal letters they attended the time and place appointed by the commissioners, the major part of whom " being elected out of their professed, and mortall Ennemies, and ouervoted those of Rhode Island, granting and awarding to the said Harris the Lands bought and improved by them, and also giuing great Damages, notwithstanding the Testimony of one Mr. [Roger] Williams the first Indian purchaser of those Lands, and other materials Witnesses in that behalf, wherby aboue five thousand acres of land and Meadows belonging to the Town of Warwick and parts of adjacent were taken away from them." [1]

It appears, further, that the Commissioners had refused to suspend their sentence at the request of Messrs. Holden and Green, whereupon, taking advantage of their charter, they appealed to His Majesty, and undertook their mission to England, " to supplicate your Majesties Royall interposition and settlement of their Country, which by reason of the said different lawes and formes of Government in the seuerall Colonies, would not otherwise be accomplished." [2]

The voyage to England apparently was noised abroad, because the Committee states that, on the 15th of October, 1678, several months after the filing of the Holden and Green petition, a letter was received " from Mr. Leverret Gouernor of your Majesties Colony of the Massachusets . . . enclosing a Return made vnto him by the Comissioners of the Court constituted by Virtue of your Majesties said Letters upon the Case of William Harris, which having been communicated vnto vs, Wee found it to contein the proceedings of the said Court."   From Governor Leverett's report it appears that " two Commissioners from each of the respective Gouernments of your Majesties four Colonies of New England," appeared at Providence Plantation in the Colony of Rhode Island on the 3d of October, 1677, who, to quote the record, " having Duely Chosen twelve Jury men, adjourned to the 17th of November following, that so there might be timely Summons given to such as the plantifs or Demandents Desired to Commence their Action against;" that the jury rendered several verdicts in favor of William Harris and two of his partners who had joined with him; that a verdict was given for Harris and Field against the town of Warwick and the purchasers " of the said Land called Warwick;" that the verdict was accepted by the court with allowance of costs; that the court ordered the town of Providence " to choose able men, to run such a Dividing lyne as might distinguish and mark out the Lands claimed by William Harris and Partners "; that on June 18, 1678, the draft of the line was presented to but not accepted by the court, inasmuch as it did not seem to

[1] *Ibid.*, p. 801.
[2] *Ibid.*

that body to be " according to the true meaning of the Verdict "; that, after much debate, the court, deeming it " most satisfactory that the former Jury themselves should explain their owne meaning in their Verdict," summoned them to appear at their next adjournment on the 1st of October following.[1]

At this stage an unexpected difficulty presented itself, inasmuch as, to quote the language of the record, " one of the Commissioners of the Colony of Connecticut absenting himself the next Day after, gaue occasion to the Commissioners of Rhode Island to with Draw themselves from the Court." This did not, however, daunt the rest of the commissioners, who, " notwith-standing continued their meeting, and the Gentlemen of the Jury likewise made their appearance, except the three appointed by Rhode Islande, who being Come the next Day refused to act as to the Explanation of their former Verdict, alleaging that they had with the rest of the Jury, given in their Verdict vpon Oath, which was accepted by the Court and they Dismist, And therefore would not concerne themselues farther about it."   The other jurymen, how-ever, not suffering from the scruples of their brethren from Rhode Island, whose land was in question, " gaue in, vnder their hands an explanation of what they intended in their former Verdict, which the Commissioners con-ceiued to be that lyne, which, according to Verdict of Jury and Justice ought to be run, and possession accordingly given vnto the Plantifs, at least vntil his Majesties pleasure should be further knowne."   The procedure, however, worried the members of the court, for the record continues:

> Yet, forasmuch as one of the Commissioners was absent, and two being present, Did oppose the said explanation, and one, or more hesitated about the granting Execution; The said Commissioners thought fit to leaue the finall Determination of this whole affair vnto your Majestie." [2]

Upon the receipt of the report from Governor Leverett, the Committee ordered a copy thereof to be delivered to Messrs. Holden and Green, who made the following pertinent observations upon it: 1st, that the complaint of William Harris concerned the lands of Patuxet, not the lands of Warwick, which were not part thereof, and that the court therefore had no power to determine the ownership of any other lands than those of Patuxet; 2d, that the town of Warwick publicly protested in open court against the proceedings of the Commissioners and claimed an appeal to His Majesty in council, which the majority of the commission refused to grant, " Saying it would be of ill Consequence to the Country to allow of any appeal to your Majestie;" 3d, that from the oath of Roger Williams, who purchased the lands from the Indians which Harris and his partners then possessed, it appeared " that the Lands claimed by Harris of the Town of Warwick were nither bought by him of

---

[1] *Acts of Privy Council, Colonial Series, 1613–1680*, p. 801.
[2] *Ibid.*, p. 803.

the Indian Sachims or by him sold vnto Harris or Partners, nor is there mention of those Lands in any Deed of Sale;" 4th, that the line run by the town of Providence, "whereof Harris, and Field are Inhabitants was accepted by the Commissioners and is according to Right;" and 5th, that the line run was not satisfactory to the Commissioners themselves who had run it, in that they had been obliged to submit the whole matter to his Majesty in council.[1]

Therefore, Messrs. Holden and Green prayed that the original line be confirmed, or that matters remain "in the first state" until Harris and his partners should show cause to the contrary to His Majesty. "In Consideration of the Complainants humble appeale vnto your Majestie for Justice (which your Majestie in like Cases will alwaies allow of and encourage) together with the reasons, and Euidences Offered by them in Justification of their Right, and present possessions which do not appear to be any part of the Lands of Patuxet, which only by your Majesties Commission were to be brought to a tryall," the Committee for Hearing Appeals recommended that "Your Majestie do therfore Signifie Your Royall Pleasure vnto William Harris, and all others whom it may concerne that the Inhabitants of the Towne of Warwick be not Disturbed in the quiet and peaceable enjoyment of the Lands claymed and possessed by them the Inhabitants of the Town of Warwick, And that all things relating therevnto remain in the same state they were in before the meeting of the said Commissioners vntill the said William Harris or Partners shall, in the Lawfull Defence of their Right before your Majestie in Councill make out a Sufficient title to the said Lands." [2]

The report of the Committee was, as usual in such cases, approved and orders given accordingly for the inhabitants of Warwick. As regards the claims of Harris to lands situated within Patuxet, concerning which he went to England to petition the Privy Council, "which only by his Majesties Commission were to be brought to a tryall," the commissioners made a favorable report, and it was therefore ordered that Harris and his partners be peaceably and quietly possessed thereof.

The order of the King affirming the report of the Committee was dated January 2, 1679, but the matter did not rest here, as it appears from the record of the Privy Council under date of July 2 of the same year:

> Whereas the said Holden and Green were no sooner departed, but the Petitioner William Harris hath made his Appearance, beseeching your Majesty to take such Course as might finally determine the Matters complayned of by him.[3]

The Committee was very naturally of the opinion "That by reason of the distance of Places and Absence of the Parties it wilbe a matter of too great

---

[1] *Ibid.*, pp. 803, 804.
[2] *Ibid.*, pp. 804–5.
[3] *Ibid.*, p. 849, § 1291.

difficulty for your Majesty to give such Judgment therein as may equally decide their respective pretensions," and suiting the action to the words, they recommended, for the reasons stated by them, the following procedure which in their opinion should be adopted as it was calculated to do justice towards the parties:

> And whereas the said Holden and Green did offer their Exceptions against the Colonies of the Massachusets and Conecticut upon divers past differences between them, And that on the other side the Petitioner William Harris thinks he has just cause to except against the Colony of Rhode Island as being particularly interessed in the present Controversy. Wee therefore humbly offer, That your Majestys Royall Commands be again sent to the Governor and Magistrates of your Colony of New Plymouth, Authorizing and requiring them to call before them the said Randall Holden and John Green, and other Persons in whose behalf they have lately appealed unto your Majesty And having in due manner examined the Pretensions of the said Harris unto the Lands possessed by them, do returne unto your Majesty a particular State thereof and their opinions thereupon with all convenient speed.
>
> And whereas your Majesty hath already thought fit to Order, That the said William Harris and Partners be peacably and quietly possessed of the Lands of Patuxet adjudged unto them by the first and Three last Verdicts given in pursuance of your Majestys late Commission, Wee further offer That the Governor and Magistrates of the Colony of Rhode Island, to whose Jurisdiction the said lands apperteyne be strictly charged and required to put the said William Harris and Partners into the quiet possession thereof, and to take care that Execution be given for their Dammage and Costs allowed by the said Verdicts and Judgments of Court, within the space of Three Moneths at furthest after the Receipt of your Majesty's Comands, And that in default thereof, sufficient Powers may be sent unto the Neighbouring Colony of New Plymouth to cause the same to be duly executed without delay.[1]

Harris returned to Rhode Island in September, 1679, and was victorious in the rehearing against Warwick.

Further Judicial Precedents

As far as we are concerned, the dispute may well end here, inasmuch as the present purpose is not so much to show the decision, but the method of reaching it, where representatives of different colonies claimed land within another, where representatives of one and the same colony claimed lands to which adjoining colonies laid claim, and where, finally, the claim of land within one colony is based upon title alleged to rest in another and different colony. For all of which disputes this case, in its different phases may be cited as a precedent for the jurisdiction in these matters conferred upon the Supreme Court of the United States by the framers of the Constitution of the more perfect Union. However, it may perhaps be permissible to conclude the analysis of this interesting law-suit with the statement that after obtaining judgment against Warwick, the litigious Harris set sail for England in a vessel very inappropriately called *The Unity,* in order to appear before the

---

[1] *Acts of the Privy Council, Colonial Series, 1613–1680,* pp. 849–50.

Privy Council not only *in propria persona* but as the agent of Connecticut and of Major Atherton and his associates in their various pretensions to the Narragansett region. On the voyage thither he was taken, in January, 1680, by an Algerian pirate and held in slavery for ransom. When he was eventually released upon its payment, he died in London within a few days after his arrival, leaving it to the Privy Council to decide in 1727 and 1746 the claims which he had espoused, adverse to his contentions and in favor of the stout little colony of Rhode Island, of which he was an unworthy resident.

Passing by the many cases of appeal from local courts to the Privy Council involving a denial or miscarriage of justice, which could and probably would be taken in ordinary course from a lower to a court of last resort, inasmuch as they neither furnished a precedent nor throw light upon the judicial power of the United States, the three categories of appeals will be considered, and in some little detail, as they are apparently the source of that jurisdiction conferred in first instance upon the Congress by the ninth of the Articles of Confederation and upon the Supreme Court of the United States by twelve of the original thirteen States in creating the more perfect Union.

First as to boundary disputes between the colonies in the absence of an enforcible agreement between them. Instead of discoursing in general and in the abstract upon the nature and jurisdiction of the Privy Council and the Lords Commissioners of Trade and Plantations, it is advisable to take a specific and concrete case, to follow it from the beginning to the end, and thus, as it were, let it tell its own story. For this purpose the long drawn out controversy between New York and New Jersey is chosen, not only because it is complete in itself, but because it states perhaps better than any other the ordinary course of procedure in such disputes. *(Boundary Dispute Between New York and New Jersey)*

On December 23, 1717, an Act of the Assembly of the Colony of New York called attention to the fact that: *(From Negotiation to Judicial Procedure)*

> "The Partition Lines between this Colony and the Colony of . . . *New-Jersey*, are necessary to be known and ascertained, in order that such of the Inhabitants of this Colony, whose Estates or Habitations are adjacent to, and border on the said Partition Lines, may peaceably, and without Molestation, enjoy the Fruits of their Industry; and that the Government may not be defrauded of the publick Taxes that may arise and become due from the said Inhabitants, by their pretending that they do not dwell within this Colony. . . ."[1]

For this purpose money was appropriated to "be applyed to defray that part of the Charge of Running, Surveying and ascertaining the Partition Line Limitt and Boundary between this Colony and the Colony of *New Jersey* which may be requisite for this Colony to pay . . . in such parts & propor-

[1] *Laws of New-York from the Year 1691, to 1751, inclusive* (1762), p. 125.

tions as shall be requisite for that Service, when the Survey ascertaining and Runing of the said Line Limitt and Boundary shall be began and Carryed on by the mutual Consent and agreement of his Excellency & Councill of this Province and the Proprietors of the soil of the said Province of *New Jersey* . . . which Lines being Run ascertained and agreed on by the Surveyors and Commissioners of each Colony, as afore said, shall forever thereafter be Deemed taken be and remain as the partition Line Limitt and Boundary of this Colony, and all bodys Corporate and Politick, and all other persons whatsoever within this Province, shall be forever Concluded thereby."

On March 27, 1719, the Province of New Jersey passed an Act " for running and ascertaining the Division Line betwixt this Province and the Province of New-York," and after stating the existence of disputes and controversies between the two colonies, as in the case of the New York Act, provided for the appointment of two or more commissioners with the Surveyor General of the Province of New Jersey, by the Governor of New Jersey, by and with the consent of the Council, " empowered by a Commission under the Great Seal of this Province, to join with such Commissioners and Surveyors as shall be appointed on the Part and Behalf of the Province of *New-York*," to " Run, Survey, Agree on and Ascertain the said Line, Limits and Boundaries betwixt this Province of *New-Jersey*, and the said Province of *New-York*, according to the true Limits thereof, as near as conveniently can be done." And it was further provided that the line drawn by the commissioners of the two provinces in accordance with their commissions was to be considered the boundary line between the two provinces " any Law, Usage, Custom or Pretence to the contrary in any wise notwithstanding." [1]

In 1719, pursuant to the Acts of New York and New Jersey, Governor Hunter of the former colony issued commissions to two commissioners and the Surveyor of the province to meet with the two commissioners and the Surveyor General of the province of New Jersey, " in Order to find out and Determine which of the Streams is the Northermost Branch of the River Delaware, And that then when such Branch is so Discovered that the said Surveyor or Surveyors Carefully According to the best of their Knowledg and understanding Discover and find out that Place of the said Northermost Branch of Delaware River that Lyes in the Latitude of fforty one Degrees and fforty Minutes which is the North Partition Point of New York and New Jersey," and to " Discover that part on the West side of Hudson's River that Lyes in the fforty One Degree of Latitude," and having fixed these two points, to run a straight line between them, " which line being so Run and Marked out is forever hereafter [according to the Acts of the two Colonies] to be

[1] *The Acts of the General Assembly of the Province of New Jersey* (1752), Vol. i, pp. 77–8.

Deemed taken be and Remaine as the Partition Line Limitt and Boundary between our said Provinces of New York and New Jersey." [1]

By an indenture of July 25, 1719,[2] the commissions appointed by the two colonies certified that the point of the Delaware had been located, but owing to disputes which arose between the colonies, the commission did not complete its work, and the question remained unsettled until it was taken up anew by an Act of New Jersey of February 18, 1748, by virtue whereof the boundary line between the two provinces was to be drawn in pursuance of the Acts of the two colonies, of 1717 and 1719, if New York consented thereto, and if not, by commissioners on the part of New Jersey.[3] Because of protests on the part of New York, this Act containing a suspending clause which required the approval of the Crown was disallowed by the King in Council upon the recommendation of the Lords of Trade and Plantation dated July 18, 1753.[4] This recommendation, setting forth the proceedings actually had in this case and those which should have been had, is as follows.

In the first place the Board of Trade states that two considerations arise upon the New Jersey act: First, " such as relate to the principles upon which it is founded "; second, " such as relate to the Transactions and Circumstances which accompany it." Under the first heading the Board calls attention to the fact that the act of New Jersey is the attempt of that province to secure the determination of a matter of specific interest to New York and of general interest to the Crown. Thus:

> AS to the first, it is an Act of the Province of New Jersey, interested in the Determination of the limits, and in the consequential Advantages to Arise from it.
>
> THE Province of New Jersey in its distinct and separate Capacity can neither make nor Establish for deciding differences between itself and other parties concerned in Interest.
>
> THE Established Limits of its Jurisdiction and Territory are such as the Grants under which it claims have assigned. If those Grants are doubtful and differences Arise upon the Construction or upon the matter of them, We humbly Apprehend that there are but two methods of deciding them, either by the concurrence of all parties Concerned in Interest or by the regular and legal Forms of Judicial proceedings, And it appears to us, that the legal method of proceeding must be derived from the Immediate Authority of the Crown itself, signified by a Commission from your Majesty under the Great Seal the Commission of subordinate officers and of derivative powers being neither Competent nor adequate to such purposes. To judge otherwise would be, as We humble conceive, to set up ex parte Determination and Incompetent Jurisdictions in the place of Justice and legal authority.

[1] *Report of the Regents of the New York University on the Boundaries of the State of New York,* prepared by D. J. Pratt, 1884, Vol. ii, pp. 608, 609.

[2] *Documents Relating to the Colonial History of New Jersey,* ed. Wm. A. Whitehead, 1882, Vol. iv, p. 394. Also, Pratt, *Boundaries,* Vol. ii, pp. 611–614.

[3] *New Jersey Laws* (Allinson's Compilation), p. 172.

[4] *Documents Relating to the Colonial History of New Jersey,* ed. Wm. A. Whitehead, 1882, Vol. iii, part 1, pp. 144–150. Also, Pratt, *Boundaries,* pp. 656–9.

IF THE ACT OF NEW JERSEY cannot conclude other parties, it cannot be Effectual to the Ends proposed: and that it would not be Effectual to Form an absolute Decision in this Case, the Legislature of that province seems Sensible, while it endeavours to leave to your Majestys Determination the Decision of one point relative to this matter and of considerable Importance to it, which proves your Majesty cannot derive from them, without their having the Power to Establish the thing itself without the Assistance of your Majesty.

And for the reasons stated, the Board concludes that "the present Act without the Concurrence of other parties concerned in Interest, is unwarrantable and ineffectual." [1]

Under the second heading, the Board of Trade calls attention to the fact that the Crown, on the one hand, and the provinces of New York and New Jersey, on the other, are interested parties, and, as is to be expected, the interest of the Crown is first stated. In the first place the Board mentions that the Crown was not a party to the negotiations and agreements between the two provinces for the settlement of their dispute, and, because of this lack of confirmation, holds that the proceedings are void. In the next place, the interests of the Crown are specifically set forth. Thus:

> With regard to the Transactions on the part of New York, We beg leave to observe, that whatever agreements have been made formerly between the two provinces for settling their Boundaries whatever Acts of Assembly have passed, and whatever Commissions have been issued by the respective Governors and Governments the proceedings under them have never been perfected, the work remains unfinished, and the Disputes between the two provinces Subsist with as much Contradiction as ever. But there is a Circumstance which appears to us to have still more weight, namely that those Transactions were never properly warranted on the part of the CROWN: The CROWN never participated in them, and therefore cannot be bound with respect to its Interests by proceedings so authorized. [2]

In disputes of this kind, the interests of the Crown are said to be threefold: First, of "Sovereignty respecting mere Government;" second, "of Seigneurie which respects Escheats and Quit Rents;" third, "of property as relative to the soil itself, which last Interest takes place in such Cases where either Your Majesty has never made any Grants of the Soil or where such Grants have by Actual Escheats reverted to Your Majesty." On this phase of the subject the Board says:

> WITH regard to the first of these Interests viz, that of Sovereignty, it has been alleged to Us in Support of the Act, that it is not materially Affected by the Question, as both provinces are under Your Majestys immediate direction and Government: But they stand in a very different light with respect to Your Majestys Interests in the Quit Rents and Escheats, in both which articles the Situation of the two provinces appears to us to make a very material alteration. For altho' the province of New Jersey is not under regulations of pro-

[1] *Documents Relating to the Colonial History of New Jersey*, Vol. viii, part 1, pp. 145-6.
[2] *Ibid.*, p. 146.

priety or Charter with respect to its Government, yet it is a proprietary province with respect to the Grant & Tenure of its Territory, and consequently as New York is not in that predicament, the Determination of the Boundary in prejudice to that province will affect your Majestys Interest with respect to the Tenure of such Lands as are concerned in this question, it being evident that whatever Districts are supposed to be Immediately held of Your Majesty in New York, by being Supposed to be Included in the Limits of New Jersey, will Immediately pass to the proprietors of that province and be held of them; by which means Your Majesty would be deprived of your Escheats and the Quit Rents would pass into other Hands.

TO obviate this objection it has been alledged that the Crown has already made absolute Grants of the whole Territory, that can possibly come in Question under the Determination of this Boundary, and reserved only trifling and Inconsiderable Quit Rents on these Grants. But this Argument does not seem to us to be conclusive, since it Admits an Interest in your Majesty, the Greatness or Smallness of which is merely accidental, and therefore does not affect the Essence of the Question, And we beg leave farther to observe, that in the Case of Exorbitant Grants with Inconsiderable Quit Rents and where consequently it may reasonably be Supposed that the Crown has been deceived in Such Grants by its Officers, Your Majestys Contingent Right of property in Vertue of your Seigneurie seems rather to be enlarged than diminished.[1]

Because of these interests of the Crown, the Board came to the conclusion which would seem to be inevitable in the premises, that neither province should have entered into an agreement with the other, much less have appointed a commission to determine the boundaries without permission in advance and without confirmation of their acts by the Crown. Taking up the question of confirmation the Board observed:

But it has been further urged that the Crown has since Confirmed these Transactions, either by previous Declarations or by Subsequent Acquiescence, and consequently participated in them so far as to conclude itself. We shall therefore in the next place beg leave to Consider the Circumstance Urged for this purpose.

IT has been alledged that the Crown, by giving Consent to the aforesaid Act passed in New York in 1717 for paying and discharging several Debts due from that Colony &c., included and bound itself with respect to the subsequent proceedings had under the Commission issued by Governor Hunter.

In this connection the Board states that the approval of the Act could not be said to be an approval of the commission, for which a small sum of money was appropriated, and the proceedings to be had under it, which could only derive their validity from specific approval in advance and confirmation after completion. It may be that the approval of the act, including this item, justified Governor Hunter in the belief that he was authorized to appoint the commission, inasmuch as the moneys had been appropriated for it, and to enter into negotiations with New Jersey on the basis of the commission. But an

[1] *Ibid.*, Vol. viii, part 1, pp. 147–8.

examination of the text of the act, which is a revenue bill of enormous length, in which this clause is an item as difficult to find as is a needle in a haystack, will assuredly cause anybody who consults it not to sit in judgment on the Board of Trade for what might otherwise be considered as an inadvertence, oversight or slip.

The Board then takes up and discusses the subsequent approval of an agreement entered into between New York and Connecticut for the settlement of their boundaries, which had been pressed upon its attention as a precedent justifying the present action, regarding which the Lords Commissioners say:

> WE further beg leave humbly to represent to Your Majesty, that the lines of partition and Division between Your Majestys province of New York and Colony of Connecticut having been run and Ascertained pursuant to the Directions of an Act passed at New York for that purpose in the Year 1719 and Confirmed by his late Majesty in 1723, the Transactions between the said province and Colony upon that occasion have been alledged to be Similar to, and urged as a precedent and even as an approbation of the matter now in Question. But we are humbly of opinion, that the two Cases are materially and essentially different. The Act passed in New York in 1719 for running and Ascertaining the Lines of partition and Division between that Colony and the Colony of Connecticut Recites, " That in the Year 1683 the Governor and " Council of New York and the Governor and Commissioners of Connecticut " did in Council conclude an Agreement concerning the Boundaries of the " two Provinces; that in Consequence of this Agreement Commissioners and " Surveyors were appointed on the part of each Government who did actually " agree, Determine and ascertain the Lines of partition, marked out a Certain " part of them and fixed the point from whence the remaining parts should " be run, that the several things agreed on and done by the said Commissioners " were ratified by the respective Governors, entered on Record in each Colony, " and in March 1700 approved and Confirmed by order of King William the " third in His privy Council and by his said Majestys Letter to his Governor " of New York."
>
> From this Recital it Appears to Us that those Transactions were not only carried on with the participation, but Confirmed by the Express Act and Authority of the Crown, and that Confirmation made the foundation of the Act passed by New York for Settling the Boundaries between the two provinces; of all which Authority and Foundation the Act we now lay before your Majesty appears to us to be entirely destitute.[1]

The New Jersey act, therefore, of 1747-8, was disallowed for the reasons set forth at length before this digression. But the dispute would not down, and, as the initiative of New Jersey had failed, New York passed an act on December 7, 1754,[2] by the terms of which the dispute was referred to the adjudication of the Crown, and, on June 12, 1755, the Lords of Trade in an opinion to the Lords Justices, acting as Regents in the absence of the King from England, recommended that this Act be disallowed for the objections stated in the following passage of their recommendation:

---

[1] *Documents Relating to the Colonial History of New Jersey*, Vol. viii, Part 1, pp. 149–150.
[2] *Laws of New-York from the 11th Nov. 1752, to 22d May 1762* (1762), Vol. ii, p. 41.

It is improper as the method of determination which it proposes is unusual and contrary to the constant practice in cases of the like nature: questions of disputed boundary, whereby private property may be affected, having never been determined by the Crown in the first instance but always by a Commission from his Maje^{ty} with liberty to all parties which shall think themselves aggrieved by the Judgement of the Commiss^{rs}, to appeal to His Maj^{ty} from their decision.   It is also improper, because, altho' the very object of the Act is to submit the matter in dispute, as far as private property is concerned, to the determination of His Maj^{ty} yet, it previously ascertains in some degree the limits of private Right and property, by declaring that certain patentees, therein mentioned shall not extend their claims beyond a limit therein described; and if it was not liable to these objections, yet it would be ineffectual, as the Proprietors of New Jersey, have not consented to the method of decision therein proposed. For all which reasons we humbly beg leave, to lay the said Act before your Excellencies, for your Excellencies disallowance.

We beg leave further to represent to your Excellencies, that it appears to us to be of the greatest importance to the peace and tranquility of the two Provinces, that some certain line of property and Jurisdiction should be speedily settled between them, which, as we conceive, can only be done by a Commission to be issued in the same manner and under the same regulations as that issued in the year 1737, for running the boundary between the Provinces of the Massachusetts Bay and New Hampshire, with liberty to either party who shall think themselves aggrieved, to appeal to His Majesty in his Privy Council. The Agent for the Proprietors of New Jersey declared himself willing to concur in this measure, and has offered to give ample security, that the said Proprietors shall and will defray one half of the expence of such a Commission, but the Agent of New York, not being authorised by his Constituents has declined entering into such an agreement. We would therefore humbly propose to your Excellencies, that an additional Instruction be given to His Maj^{ty's} Govr. of New York directing him to recommend it to the Assembly of that province to make provision for defraying one half of the expence of obtaining and executing such Commission, as aforesaid, whenever his Maj^{ty} shall be graciously pleased to issue it.[1]

Owing to the French and Indian War, the New York Assembly felt itself unable to bear its share of the expenses in running the line, and the moneys were not appropriated. However, when the French and Indian War had practically ended, New York gave its consent by Act of December 11, 1762,[2] to the adjustment of the boundary by Royal Commission or otherwise, and agreed to the payment of " one equal Half Part of the Joint Expence to accrue on the final Settlement of the said Controversy, and the Boundary Line between the said Colonies."

The Colony of New Jersey by Act of February 23, 1764,[3] a year after the Treaty of Peace, did likewise. A commission was substituted for the Crown on October 7, 1767, consisting of thirteen persons chosen from the different

---

[1] *Documents Relating to the Colonial History of New Jersey,* Vol. viii, Part 2, pp. 109–110. Pursuant to this recommendation the Lords Justices on June 24, 1755, disallowed the Act. *Ibid.,* pp. 114–5; see also *Documents Relating to Colonial History of New York,* Vol. vi, p. 952.

[2] Pratt, *Boundaries,* Vol. ii, pp. 747–9.

[3] *Ibid.,* pp. 750–2.

colonies, of whom any five could act.   Seven of the Commissioners, with John Jay as Clerk of the Commission, met in the City of New York on July 18, 1769.   They were Charles Stewart, Esq., Surveyor General of the Customs for the District of Quebec, President; Andrew Elliot, Esq., Receiver General of Quit Rents in the Province of New York; Samuel Holland, Esq., Surveyor General of Lands for the Northern District of America; Andrew Oliver, Esq., Secretary of the Province of Massachusetts Bay; Charles Morris, Esq., Surveyor of Lands and one of the Council of the Province of Nova Scotia; and Jared Ingersoll, Esq., of the Colony of Connecticut.   After hearing the evidence presented by the colonies in dispute, four of the commissioners, Messrs. Stewart, Oliver, Elliot and Ingersoll, present on October 7, 1769, rendered a majority opinion, and two thereof, Messrs. Holland and Morris, a minority opinion.   The text of the majority opinion is not uninteresting in itself, and may well serve as a model of proceedings of this kind:

THE AGENTS on the part of both Colonies, having offered to the Court all that they thought necessary or proper in Support of their respective Claims, and the Court having Considered the Same, DO FIND

THAT King Charles the Second by his Letters patent bearing date the twelfth day of March, 1664, did Grant and Convey to his Brother the Duke of York, All that Tract of Country and Territory now Called the Colonies of New York and New Jersey; and that the said Duke of York afterwards by his Deed of Lease and Release bearing Date the 23d and 24th days of June, 1665, did Grant and Convey to Lord Berkley of Stratton and Sir George Carteret, that part of the Aforesaid Tract of Land Called New Jersey.   The Northern Bounds of which in said Deed are described to be "to the northward as far as the Northernmost Branch of the said Bay or River of Delaware which is in 41 deg. 40 min. of Latitude and Crosseth thence in a Straight Line to Hudson's River in 41 deg. of Latitude."

We further find amoung the many Exhibits a Certain Map compiled by Nicholas John Vischer, and published not long before the aforesaid Grant from the Duke of York, which we have reason to believe was Esteemed the most Correct Map of that Country at the Time of the said Grant, on which Map is Laid down a Fork or Branching of the River then called Zuydt River or South River now Delaware River in the Latitude of 41 deg. and 40 min., which Branch we Cannot doubt was the Branch in the Deed from the Duke of York called the Northernmost Branch of the said River, and which in the Deed is said to lye in the Latitude of 41 deg. and 40 min.   And from a Carefull Comparison of the several Parts and Places Laid down on the said Map, some of which, more Especially towards the Sea Coast and on Hudson's River We have Reason to believe were at that time well Known.   The Distance of the said Branch from the Sea Shore on the South, and the Relative situation of the same with regard to other places and the Lines of Latitude as they appear to be laid down on the said Map at that and other places in the Inland County: We are of opinion that the said Branch so laid down on the said Map is the Fork or Branch formed by the Junction of the Stream or Water Called the Mahackamack with the River Called Delaware or Fishkill and that the same is the Branch Intended and referred to in the before mentioned Deed from the Duke of York, as the Northern Station at the River Delaware, which Fork or Branch We find by an observation taken by the Surveyors appointed by the Court, to be in the Latitude of 41 deg. 21 min. and 37 seconds.

We are further of opinion that the Northern Station at Hudson's River being by the Words of the Said Deed from the Duke of York, Expressly Limited to the Latitude of 41 deg. should be fixed in that Latitude, which Latitude we have caused to be taken in the best manner by the Surveyors appointed by the Court, and which falls at a Rock on the West Side of Hudson's River marked by the said surveyors, being 79 Chains and 27 Links to the Southward on a Meridian from Sneydon's House, formerly Corbet's.

IT IS THEREFORE the final Determination of the Court That the Boundary or Partition Line between the said Colonies of New York and New Jersey be a direct and straight Line from the said Fork at the Mouth of the River Mahackimack in the Latitude of forty-one Degrees twenty-one Minutes and thirty-seven Seconds to Hudson's River at the said Rock in the Latitude of forty-one degrees as above described.[1]

As to the subsequent proceedings, it is to be said that the New York assembly passed an act on February 16, 1771,[2] ratifying the judgment of the Commission, and that New Jersey on its part passed an act September 26, 1772, referring to the act of New York confirming the judgment of the Commission,[3] conditioning its acceptance upon the allowance of the New York Act by his Majesty in Council. Therefore on September 1, 1773, the King in Council decreed as follows:

Whereas the Governor of His Majesty's Colony of New York, with the Council and Assembly of the said Colony, did in February 1771, pass an act which hath been transmitted in the Words following — Viz[t].

" An Act for Establishing the Boundary or Partition Line between the Colonies of New York and Nova Caesarea or New Jersey and for Confirming Titles and Possessions." . . .

Which Act, together with a Representation from the Lords Commissioners for Trade and Plantations thereupon, having been referred to the Consideration of a Committee of the Lords of His Majesty's most Honorable Privy Council for Plantation Affairs, the said Lords of the Committee did this Day Report as their opinion to His Majesty, that the said Act was proper to be approved — His Majesty taking the same into Consideration, was pleased, with the advice of His privy Council, to Declare his approbation of the said act; and pursuant to His Majesty's Royal Pleasure thereupon Expressed, the said Act is hereby Confirmed, finally Enacted and Ratified accordingly — Whereof the Governor Lieutenant, Governor or Commander in Chief of His Majesty's said Colony of New York for the time being, and all others whom it may concern are to take Notice and Govern themselves accordingly.[4]

The case of *New York* v. *New Jersey,* the proceedings of which have been stated with considerable fulness, began in negotiation and, through the intervention of the Board of Trade, ended in what may be called judicial de-

---

[1] Pratt, *Boundaries,* Vol. ii, pp. 769–70.
[2] *Ibid.,* pp. 782–5.
[3] *Ibid.,* 786–7.
[4] *Ibid.,* 789.

cision.   There are, however, two cases, shorter and less detailed, and which, with slight changes in the caption and in the phraseology of the opinion, might properly appear as judgments of the Supreme Court of the United States in the series of cases to which Rhode Island is a party.

The first is that of *Rhode Island* v. *Connecticut*,[1] decided in 1727, in which the boundary between Rhode Island on the west and Connecticut, its more powerful neighbor, was decided; and the second is that of *Rhode Island* v. *Massachusetts*,[2] decided in 1746, in which the eastern boundary of Rhode Island was determined in its favor against its stronger and aggressive neighbor to the east.   And, without stopping to analyze these cases, models of their kind and of judicial settlement, it may be proper to premise that partisans of judicial settlement are deeply indebted to the litigious little State, not only for these cases but for the seven lawsuits with the State of Massachusetts, decided by the Supreme Court of the United States and to be found in the official reports of that Tribunal, by virtue of which the northern boundary of Rhode Island, and therefore the southern boundary of Massachusetts, was finally determined.   If the Atlantic Ocean had not been made the southern boundary of the little State by charter, it would no doubt have instituted a law suit to have that determined, as it did in the western, eastern and northern points of the compass.   It thus furnishes, it is believed, the unique example of a State having submitted all disputes concerning its boundary to judicial decision, and thus having its bounds settled and its existence preserved by decree of court.   Justice is indeed the shield and buckler of the smaller States, if they did but know it, for Rhode Island would, without the shadow of a doubt, have been swallowed up by Connecticut and Massachusetts had their land hunger not been stayed by the just hand of the judge.[3]

Debt to Litigious Rhode Island

Justice to the Small State

---

[1] *Acts of the Privy Council, Colonial Series*, Vol. vi, p. 159, § 344.

[2] *Ibid.*, p. 267, § 470.

[3] An accurate, industrious and well informed writer has this to say on the settlement of disputes of this kind between the colonies:

"Boundary disputes between the several colonies were of even more pressing importance than were those with foreign nations.   In 1700 none of the colonies had its limits so well defined that it was free from such controversies, and as time went on these questions had to be settled.   It was difficult for the interested parties to arrive at a satisfactory agreement without recourse to some outside party: consequently the Board of Trade was the body to which, as a last resort, all these controversies were referred. . . .

"As all settlements of a boundary controversy were, of necessity, ratified by laws passed by the colonial legislature, any such settlement could be invalidated by the action of the Board of Trade.   If private individuals were injured in their property interests, they had just grounds for a complaint to the king, and such a complaint would involve the boundary dispute and its settlement.   If, on the other hand, the interests of the crown were at stake, it had to be made a party to the settlement or it would refuse to recognize its validity.   Thus in either case the question would come before the crown for ratification. . . .

"The regular method of procedure in settling a dispute was to secure the appointment of a royal commission.   All the important boundary controversies, such as those between North Carolina and Virginia [The commissions for settling this boundary were joint tribunals, appointed partly by the crown and partly by the proprietaries.   See: North Carolina *Colonial Records*, vol. i, 703, 716, 735, 750, vol. iii, 12, 17.], North and South Carolina [*Ibid.* vol. iv, 28.], New York and Massachusetts [Proposed but not carried into execution.   See: Pratt's *Boundaries of New York* vol. ii, 88–225.], and the latter province and New Hampshire [Com-

Second, as to appeals from judicial decisions of a colony involving the Legal Controversies Over Colonial Laws setting aside of colonial laws and the reversal of decisions of colonial courts based upon such laws.

In 1699 the colony of Connecticut passed an act regulating the descent of estates of persons dying intestate, allowing the children of the deceased, females as well as males, to share in the distribution of the realty, reserving only to the eldest son a double portion instead of casting upon him the realty in its entirety, as in the common law of England.[1] The charter of Connecticut allowed the colony "from Time to Time to Make, Ordain and Establish all manner of wholesome, and reasonable Laws, Statutes, Ordinances, Directions, and Instructions, not Contrary to the Laws of this realm of *England*."[2] There was no reservation in the charter for the transmission of the laws to England, there to be approved by the Crown before they went into effect, or to go into effect subject to be set aside by the Crown within a certain period.

The colonial officials elected by the freemen of the colony were not anxious to awaken sleeping dogs, if that homely expression rather than lions be applied to the mother country, and laws claimed to be in excess

mission of 1737. See: New York *Colonial Documents,* vol. vi, pp. 823, 953.] and Rhode Island [The commissioners in this case were Cadwallader Colden, Abraham Vanhorn, Phillip Livingston, Archibald Kennedy, and James De Lancey of New York; John Hamilton, John Wells, John Reading, Cornelius Vanhorn, and William Provost of New Jersey; and William Skeene, William Shirreft, Henry Cope, Erasmus James Phillips, and Otho Haymilton of Nova Scotia. See: Board of Trade to Governor Clinton. *Ibid.,* 167–168.], were settled in this way. These commissioners were appointed by the Board of Trade upon the authority of an Order in Council, were composed of men selected from the neighboring colonies, and were usually paid by the two parties to the controversy. This method of payment required the consent of both parties, but it seldom happened that a colony refused to bear its share of the charges. [In regard to a commission for settling the boundary between Massachusetts and Rhode Island, the Board says the 'charges of which and the execution thereof the agents for the Massachusetts Bay and Rhode Island have agreed are reasonable equally to be bourne by both provinces.'— Letter to Clinton, August 1, 1740. *Ibid.,* 167–168.] In some cases the Board secured authority to pay the expenses of such commissions from the quit rents of the provinces concerned, as was done in settling the southern boundary of Virginia in 1711 and again in 1729 [North Carolina *Colonial Records,* vol. iii, 13, 17, vol. iv, 28.] . . .

"It is thus seen that the Board of Trade acted as a high court of arbitration for disputes as to territory or jurisdiction. It did not settle disputes on its own authority, but it provided a way by which such controversies could be determined by special commissions. These were in reality special courts of arbitration, which had power to settle the questions at issue, but from which an appeal would lie to the Board. [In form it was an appeal to the king, but as all such complaints and appeals were heard by the Board of Trade, it was in reality an appeal to that body.] If either party were dissatisfied with the decision of such a commission, it could prosecute a complaint in the usual manner; and if its work should appear irregular, another commission was issued to rehear the case. In all this there was an evident attempt to do justice to all parties concerned. . . . The clause in the Constitution regarding changes in state boundaries is but a recognition of the constant practice of the Board of Trade in settling disputes of this character. . . ." (Oliver Morton Dickerson, *American Colonial Government, 1696–1765,* pp. 287, 288, 290–91, 295).

The learned writer might have added that such action of the King in Council through the Board of Trade is the precedent for the 9th of the Articles of Confederation, and it would appear, of that large and beneficent jurisdiction with which the Supreme Court of these United States has been endowed by Article II, Section 2 of the Constitution thereof.—ED.

[1] *The Public Records of the Colony of Connecticut, [Vol. I] 1689 to 1706,* C. J. Hoadly ed., 1868, pp. 306–9.

[2] Thorpe, *Charters and Constitutions,* Vol. 1, p. 533; Poore, p. 255.

of this grant would reach the King in Council or the Board of Trade through private parties and upon private initiative if at all. In this case the transmitter was at hand in the person of John Winthrop, son of Wait Still Winthrop, Major General of Massachusetts and Chief Justice of its Superior Court, who died intestate in 1717 owning personalty and realty in Connecticut, in which colony he had himself been born a son of the Governor thereof but had preferred to grace Massachusetts by his presence. John Winthrop, of whom Carlyle's mother would doubtless have said, as she said of her son, "he was an ill man to live with," had a sister, Anne, who married a well connected but not too well to do person by the name of Lechmere, who resided at that time in Boston. On behalf of his wife, he claimed one portion of the realty of the father-in-law's Connecticut estate. Winthrop was appointed administrator by the Court of Probates for the County of New London, Colony of Connecticut, in which the realty was situated, and, contending that he was entitled to the real property according to the doctrine of primogeniture, obtaining in the common law of England, did not include the realty in his inventory, as he should have done according to the Connecticut act of 1699 for the settlement of intestate estates. The Court of Probates therefore rejected the inventory and Winthrop, as administrator, thereupon appealed to the Superior Court. Pending the appeal, Lechmere applied to the Court of Probates for new letters of administration, which, however, denied his motion. Thereupon, on appeal to the Superior Court, having the two appeals before it at one and the same time, it decided both of them against Winthrop. The General Assembly refused to intervene in his behalf or allow an appeal to the King in Council. The appeal, however, was made by Winthrop and allowed by the King in Council, and the case on appeal referred to the Committee for Hearing Appeals from the Plantations.

Before this Committee Sir Philip Yorke, then Attorney General and later Lord Chief Justice of the King's Bench and Lord High Chancellor, known to lawyers as Lord Hardwicke and to the English speaking world as the greatest of equity judges, and Sir Charles Talbot, then Solicitor General, later Lord Chancellor Talbot, less known perhaps but hardly less deserving than Hardwicke, who succeeded him in the Chancellorship, appeared on behalf of Winthrop. On behalf of Lechmere one Willes, supposed to be Sir John Willes, later Attorney General and Lord Chief Justice of the Common Pleas, and an English barrister by the name of Barton, appeared.

Without referring the appeal to the Board of Trade, as was usual in such cases, the Committee for Hearing Appeals from the Plantations heard counsel for plaintiff and defendant and, after argument, recommended that the Connecticut act of 1699 for the settlement of intestate estates, and subse-

Another
Precedent
for Granting
Power of
Supreme
Court to Declare
Legislative Acts
Unconstitutional

quent acts in the case, be declared null and void as contrary to the common law of England, and that the decisions of the Connecticut courts as against Winthrop's contention and in favor of Lechmere and his wife be reversed and set aside as based upon the Connecticut statutes contrary to the charter, or, as we should say, as unconstitutional.

As the decree of the King in Council approving the recommendation of the Lords of Appeal was well known to the colonists, extending the judicial power to acts of the legislature as well as to judgments of a colonial court, and is the great precedent for investing the Supreme Court of the United States with the power of pronouncing laws unconstitutional and reversing decisions of courts of justice, whether of the State or of the United States, based upon such acts of Congress or such provisions of State constitutions, the material portion of the report of the Lords of Appeal, confirmed by the King in Council, is given in its exact words:

> Their Lordships, upon due consideration of the whole matter, do agree humbly to report as their opinion to your Majesty, that the said act for the settlement of intestate estates should be declared null and void, being contrary to the laws of England in regard it makes lands of inheritance distributable as personal estates and is not warranted by the charter of that colony; and that the said . . . sentences . . . rejecting the inventory . . . because it did not contain the real as well as personal estate . . . may be all reversed and set aside; and that the said sentence vacating the said letters of administration to the said Thomas and Anne Lechmere should also be reversed and set aside.[1]

Commentary upon this case could only weaken its force and effect as the younger Pitt is reported to have said of Erskine's speech following that of Fox, that it only repeated and weakened the arguments of that right honorable gentleman.

By the charter of June 26, 1632, the second Lord Baltimore was granted the province, now the State of Maryland, bounded on the north by the 40th parallel of North Latitude, on the west and southwest by a line south of this parallel to the farthest sources of the Potomac, and thence the " further bank " of that river to Chesapeake Bay; on the south by a line across the Bay and peninsula to the Atlantic Ocean; and on the east by that Ocean and Delaware Bay and River.[2]

[1] Privy Council, 1728 (*Connecticut Colonial Records*, 1726–1735, pp. 571, 577). See also J. B. Scott, *Judicial Settlement of Controversies Between States of the American Union*, Vol. i, pp. 93–8.
[2] The portion of the charter relating to the boundaries of the colony is, in English translation, as follows:
"All that Part of the Peninsula, or Chersonese, lying in the Parts of America, between the Ocean on the East, and the Bay of Chesapeake on the West, divided from the Residue thereof by a Right Line drawn from the Promontory, or Head-Land, called Watkin's Point, situate upon the Bay aforesaid, near the River of Wigloo, on the West, unto the Main Ocean on the East; and between that Boundary on the South, unto that Part of the Bay of Delaware on the North, which lieth under the Fortieth Degree of North Latitude from the Equinoctial, where New England is terminated; And all that Tract of Land within the Metes

On March 14, 1681, a charter was granted to William Penn of the tract of territory now known as Pennsylvania in honor of its first proprietor, including, as claimed by Penn, the three lower counties now known as and forming the State of Delaware. The territory was, according to the charter, " bounded on the East by *Delaware River,* from twelve Miles Distance Northwards of *Newcastle* Town unto the three-and-fortieth Degree of Northern Latitude, if the said River doth extend so far Northward; but if the said River shall not extend so far Northward, then by the said River so far as it doth extend; and from the Head of the said River, the Eastern Bounds are to be determined by a Meridian Line, to be drawn from the Head of the said River unto the said Forty-third Degree. The said Land to extend Westward five Degrees in Longitude, to be computed from the said Eastern Bounds; and the said Lands to be bounded on the North by the Beginning of the Three-and-fortieth Degree of Northern Latitude, and on the South by a Circle drawn at twelve Miles Distance from *Newcastle* Northward, and Westward unto the Beginning of the Fortieth Degree of Northern Latitude, and then by a straight Line Westward to the Limits of Longitude, above-mentioned." [1]

It will be observed that this grant does not include the town of Newcastle but begins at a point twelve miles to the north thereof. It thus excluded the three lower counties, or, in short, the State of Delaware. William Penn's claim to Delaware is based upon subsequent transactions. On August 24, 1682, he purchased a quit claim from the Duke of York to the lands west of the Delaware River embraced in the grant of Charles II of March 12, 1664, to James, Duke of York, and the confirmation of that grant by letters patent dated June 29, 1674, from Charles II to his brother, the Duke of York.

To the· laymen it would appear that Pennsylvania could not extend below 40° North Latitude, inasmuch as the province of Maryland was declared by its charter of 1632 to extend to that point, and that degree of latitude was likewise declared to be its northern boundary. It is true that the grant of Charles II to his brother, the Duke of York, of " all the main land of New England . . . and all the land from the west side of Connecti-

---

underwritten (that is to say) passing from the said Bay, called Delaware Bay, in a right Line, by the Degree aforesaid, unto the true meridian of the first Fountain of the River of Pattowmack, thence verging towards the South, unto the further Bank of the said River, and following the same on the West and South, unto a certain Place called Cinquack, situate near the Mouth of the said River, where it disembogues into the aforesaid Bay of Chesapeake, and thence by the shortest Line unto the aforesaid Promontory or Place, called Watkin's Point; so that the whole tract of land, divided by the Line aforesaid, between the main Ocean and Watkin's Point, unto the Promontory called Cape Charles, and every the Appendages thereof, may entirely remain excepted for ever to US, our Heirs and Successors." F. N. Thorpe, *The Federal and State Constitutions, Colonial Laws, etc. of the United States,* 1909, Vol. iii, p. 1678.

[1] *The Charters and Acts of Assembly of the Province of Pennsylvania,* 1762, Vol. i, p. 1.

cut to ye east side of Delaware Bay, confirmed by the letters patent of 1674," included Delaware, or was claimed to do so.   Penn was anxious to secure the tract of land from his little city of Philadelphia on the Delaware River, and through which the fortieth degree of north latitude ran, to the mouth of the Delaware Bay, some ninety miles to the south, and he took care to purchase and acquire the title to this tract claimed by the Duke of York under the two grants in question.   On the other hand, the proprietor of Maryland was anxious to have his province extend to the fortieth degree of north latitude and be bounded on the north throughout its entire extent by that parallel of latitude.

Here was a dispute involving a vast domain, claimed by Lord Baltimore under a charter of 1632 granted by Charles I, to which William Penn laid claim under a charter granted by Charles II in 1664.   The title of the son was preferred to that of the father, contrary to the time honored maxim of the law, *prior in tempore, potior in jure.* Penn v. Lord Baltimore

The Duke of York appears to have doubted his title to the three lower counties, or at least thought it well to have whatever cloud there might be upon his title cleared up.   He therefore applied to his royal brother, Charles II, for the grant of the counties, which appears to have been made, and which would inure to Penn's benefit, although it might have been and was contended that the grant to the Duke of York subsequent to his sale and conveyance of the same territory to Penn was an evasion, that the title was not, at the time of the earlier transaction, in the Duke, and that therefore it could not pass to his grantee.

When the news of the proposed grant of the lower counties to the Duke of York became known to Lord Baltimore, he prayed that it should not be made, in that the territory in question was comprised within his province. Baltimore's petition was referred to the Lords Commissioners for Trade and Plantations, who, under date of November 13, 1685, reported that, " Having examined the matters in difference between the Lord Baltimore and William Penn, Esq., on behalf of His then Majesty, concerning a tract of land called Delaware, they found the land intended to be granted to Lord Baltimore was only lands uncultivated, and inhabited by savages; and that the tract of land then in dispute, was inhabited and planted by Christians at and before the date of the Lord Baltimore's patent, as it had ever been since, to that time, and continued as a distinct colony, from Maryland, so that their Lordships humbly offered their opinion, that for avoiding further differences, the tract of land lying between the river and the eastern sea, on the one side, and Chesapeake Bay on the other, be divided into equal parts, by a line from the latitude of Cape Henlopen to the 40th degree of northern latitude; and that one-half thereof, lying towards the bay of Delaware and the eastern sea, be adjudged to belong to his Majesty, and the other half to Lord Baltimore." [1]

This report His Majesty approved, it was also affirmed in 1709 by Queen Anne in Council, and by this interpretation of the grants in question Penn would acquire that part of the three counties bordering on the Delaware River and the ocean as far south as Cape Henlopen, and Lord Baltimore the western half thereof. The boundaries, however, would remain to be run and marked, and, after much delay, an agreement was entered into, dated May 10, 1732, between Penn's sons, on the one hand, and the then Lord Baltimore, on the other, providing for the determination of the line by commissioners on or before Christmas, 1733. The line, however, was not drawn before the expiration of this time. The Penns thereupon petitioned the Privy Council to have the agreement executed, but the Committee for Hearing Appeals from the Plantations recommended, on May 10, 1735, "that the Consideration of the said Report and Petitions should be adjourned until the end of Michaelmass Term next in Order to give an Opportunity to the said John Thomas and Richard Penn to proceed in a Court of Equity to obtain relief upon the said Articles of Agreement so insisted upon by them according as they shall be advised." [2] Therefore the Penns filed their bill in equity on June 21, 1731, for the specific performance of the articles of the agreement.

In 1745 Lord Chancellor Hardwicke, before whom the case was heard, thought the bill should be amended by making the Attorney General a party on behalf of the Crown. [3] As amended, the bill was heard and, in 1750, the specific performance of the articles of agreement was decreed by Lord Hardwicke. [4] For present purposes it is sufficient to say that the plea to the jurisdiction of the court taken by Lord Baltimore was overruled, and properly, for although the lands lay beyond the jurisdiction of the court, the parties plaintiff and defendant were before it, and as equity acts *in personem* they could properly be, and they were ordered in England to perform the act in America.

This is, however, a matter of equity practice and procedure. The important point for us is that the Privy Council refused to assume jurisdiction, and, by means of commissions, to determine the boundaries in dispute, since there was an agreement between the parties on the very question, enforcible in equity. There was no need to resort to the King in Council, because the parties had their day in court. The question was therefore settled, upon

[1] Chalmers, *Opinions of Eminent Lawyers,* pp. 86–7.
[2] *Acts of the Privy Council, Colonial Series,* Vol. iii, p. 336.
[3] *Penn. v. Lord Baltimore* (Ridgeway temp. Hardwicke, 332; Reprint, *English Reports,* Vol. 27, p. 1132).
[4] *Penn. v. Lord Baltimore* (1 Vesey Sr., 444).

great deliberation, by the first of English Chancellors, that boundaries between provinces as large as kingdoms did not need to be settled by force of arms; that disputes of this nature were susceptible of judicial determination, and that an agreement to settle the dispute and to draw the boundaries in a particular manner made the question judicial, to be passed upon in a court of justice, although it might have been considered political, in the absence of an agreement, and as such been passed upon by the King in Council.

The case of *Penn* v. *Lord Baltimore* was, therefore, a precedent for the framers of the Constitution, clearly pointing out that political questions would become justiciable by an agreement to settle them, which, when made, could be interpreted and carried into execution by a court of justice. It was quoted as such in the leading case of *Rhode Island* v. *Massachusetts* (12 Peters, 657), decided in 1838, in which decision the distinction here taken was announced, and the procedure before the King in Council recognized as a precedent for investing the Supreme Court with jurisdiction of controversies between States. More recently Chief Justice White, in delivering the opinion of the court in *Virginia* v. *West Virginia* (246 U. S., 565, 597),[1] decided in 1918, thus referred to the case of *Rhode Island* v. *Massachusetts* and the proceedings in the Privy Council as a precedent, and gave to each, as such, the stamp of his approval:

A Political Dispute May Become Justiciable

> Bound by a common allegiance and absolutely controlled in their exterior relations by the mother country, the colonies before the Revolution were yet as regards each other practically independent, that is, distinct one from the other. Their common intercourse, more or less frequent, the contiguity of their boundaries, their conflicting claims, in many instances, of authority over undefined and outlying territory, of necessity brought about conflicting contentions between them. As these contentions became more and more irritating, if not seriously acute, the necessity for the creation of some means of settling them became more and more urgent, if physical conflict was to be avoided. And for this reason, it is to be assumed, it early came to pass that differences between the colonies were taken to the Privy Council for settlement and were there considered and passed upon during a long period of years, the sanction afforded to the conclusions of that body being the entire power of the realm, whether exerted through the medium of a royal decree or legislation by Parliament. This power, it is undoubtedly true, was principally called into play in cases of disputed boundary, but that it was applied also to the complaint of an individual against a colony concerning the wrongful possession of property by the colony alleged to belong to him, is not disputed. This general situation as to the disputes between the colonies and the power to dispose of them by the Privy Council was stated in *Rhode Island* v. *Massachusetts,* 12 Pet. 657, 739, *et seq.,* and will be found reviewed in the authorities referred to in the margin.
>
> When the Revolution came and the relations with the mother country were severed, indisputably controversies between some of the colonies, of the greatest moment to them, had been submitted to the Privy Council and were

[1] Also Scott, *Judicial Settlement,* Vol. ii, pp. 1751–73.

undetermined. The necessity for their consideration and solution was obviously not obscured by the struggle for independence which ensued, for, by the Ninth of the Articles of Confederation, an attempt to provide for them as well as for future controversies was made. Without going into detail it suffices to say that that article in express terms declared the Congress to be the final arbiter of controversies between the States and provided machinery for bringing into play a tribunal which had power to decide the same. That these powers were exerted concerning controversies between the States of the most serious character again cannot be disputed. But the mechanism devised for their solution proved unavailing because of a want of power in Congress to enforce the findings of the body charged with their solution, a deficiency of power which was generic, because resulting from the limited authority over the States conferred by the Articles of Confederation on Congress as to every subject. That this absence of power to control the governmental attributes of the States, for the purpose of enforcing findings concerning disputes between them, gave rise to the most serious consequences, and brought the States to the very verge of physical struggle, and resulted in the shedding of blood and would, if it had not been for the adoption of the Constitution of the United States, it may be reasonably assumed, have rendered nugatory the great results of the Revolution, is known of all and will be found stated in the authoritative works on the history of the time.

The views of the Chief Justice can not be gainsaid. If, however, contemporary exposition is preferred, as to the nature, function and rôle of the Privy Council in the administration of justice and the maintenance of order upon the basis of law, it is at hand, for in the seventeenth article of the Constitution of Delaware, adopted on Friday, September 20, 1776, by the three lower counties of Pennsylvania, forming "The Delaware State," as it was then called, it is provided that: "There shall be an appeal from the supreme court of Delaware in matters of law and equity, to a court of seven persons, to consist of the president for the time being, who shall preside therein, and six others, to be appointed, three by the legislative council, and three by the house of assembly, who shall continue in office during good behaviour, and be commissioned by the president under the great seal; which court shall be stiled, *The Court of Appeals,* and have all the authority and powers heretofore given by law in the last resort to the king in council, under the old government." [1]

[1] *The Constitutions of the Several Independent States of America,* 1781, p. 111.

VI

ESTABLISHMENT OF STATE CONSTITUTIONS

In short, these legislators derive their power from the constitution, how then can they change it, without destroying the foundation of their authority? (*M. de Vattel, The Law of Nations; or Principles of the Law of Nature: Applied to the Conduct and Affairs of Nations and Sovereigns, 1758, Translated from the French Vol. I, 1760, Book I, Chapter III, § 34, p. 18.*)

To examine the Union before we have studied the State would be to adopt a method filled with obstacles. . . . The great political principles which now govern American society undoubtedly took their growth in the State. (*Alexis de Tocqueville, De la Démocratie en Amérique, 2 Vols., 1835, Vol. I, p. 80.*)

"At a meeting of the Inhabitants of the Town of Concord being free and Twenty-one years of age and upward, upon adjournment on the twentyfirst Day of October, 1776, Ephraim Wood Junr being Moderator, Voted unanimously that the Present House of Representatives is not a proper Body to form a Constitution for this State. And Voted to Chuse a Committee of five men to make answer to the Question Proposed by the House of Representatives of this State and to Give the Reasons why the Town thinks them not a suitable body for that Purpas, the persons following was Chosen the Committee above mentioned, viz, Ephraim Wood Junr, Mr. Nathan Bond, Col. James Barrett, Col. John Buttrick, and James Barrett esqr. And the Committee Reported the following Draft which being Read several times over for Consideration it then was Read Resolve by Resolve and accepted unanimously in a very full Town meeting — the Reasones are as followes —
"Resolved 1st, that this State being at Present destitute of a properly established form of Government, it is absolutely necessary that one should be immediately formed and established.
"Resolved secondly that the supreme Legislative, Either in their proper capacity or in Joint Committee are by no means a Body Proper to form & Establish a Constitution or form of Government for Reasones following, viz — first Because we conceive that Constitution in its proper Idea intends a system of principals established to secure the subject in the Possession of and enjoyment of their Rights & Privileges against any encrouchment of the Governing Part. Secondly Because the same Body that forms a Constitution have of Consequence a power to alter it — thirdly Because a Constitution alterable by the Supreme Legislative is no security at all to the subject against the encrouchment of the Governing part on any or on all their Rights and Privileges.
"Resolved thirdly that it appears to this Town highly expidient that a Convention or Congress be immediately chosen to form and establish a Constitution, by the Inhabitants of the Respective Towns in this State being free and Twentyone years and upward, in Proportion as the Representatives of this State were formerly chosen; the Convention or Congress not to consist of a greater number than the house of assembly of this State heretofore might consist of, except that Each Town & District shall have Liberty to send one Representative; or otherwise as shall appear meet to the Inhabitants of this State in General.
"Resolved 4ly. That when the Convention or Congress have formed a Constitution, they adjourn for a short time, and publish their Proposed Constitution for the Inspection and Remarks of the Inhabitants of this State.
"Resolved 5ly. That the Honble. House of assembly of this State be Desired to recommend it to the Inhabitants of this State to Proceed to Chuse a Convention or Congress for the Purpas above mentioned as soon as possible. Signed by order of the Committee Ephraim Wood Ju Chairman, and the meeting was Desolved by the Moderator."
(*Roger Sherman Hoar, The Invention of Constitutional Conventions, 1918, in The Constitutional Review, vol. 2, pp. 99–100.*)

The elements of the British constitution, which the American people claimed as their inheritance, were not so much the customary forms which entered into the structure of the British government as those chartered privileges which might serve to protect them from the supervision and interference of autocratic power. What they most desired was to be let alone and to work out their own political salvation. And it was precisely when and where they were least hampered by foreign control, and least influenced by foreign models, that they developed those political features which have become the most distinctive characteristics of the American constitutional system. (*William C. Morey, The First State Constitutions, Annals of the American Academy of Political and Social Science, 1893, Vol. 4, p. 232.*)

The American colonists inherited the instincts of the English race. But under new circumstances they were called upon to work out problems which were peculiar to their own political life; and as a consequence of this we find that the constitutional system which grew up on this continent was an American and not a European product. Even those institutions which seem to have a general similarity to those which are foreign have here acquired specific characteristics which distinguish them from those belonging to any foreign country. (*William C. Morey, The First State Constitutions, Annals of the American Academy of Political and Social Science, 1893, Vol. 4, pt. 1, p. 203.*)

The first State constitutions were in their main features the direct descendants of the colonial governments, modified to the extent necessary to bring them into harmony with the republican spirit of the people. Every State, either in a preamble or in a separate declaration of rights, prefaced its constitution by a statement of the chartered rights upon which it had always insisted; and many of them also declared in general terms the democratic principles which their experience and reason had taught them and which had been partly realized in their previous governments. (*William C. Morey, The First State Constitutions, Annals of the American Academy of Political and Social Science, 1893, Vol. 4, pt. 1, p. 219.*)

In a previous paper published in this journal it was claimed that the real continuity in the growth of American constitutional law could be seen only by tracing: first, how the charters of the English trading companies were transformed into the organic laws of the early colonies; second, how the organic laws of the colonies were translated into the constitutions of the original States; and, finally, how the original State constitutions contributed to the Constitution of the Federal Union. (*William C. Morey, The First State Constitutions, Annals of the American Academy of Political and Social Science, 1893, Vol. 4, p. 202.*)

In applying the historical method to the study of the American political system it is not enough to trace the origin and growth of the various branches of the federal government. The origin of the forms of the federal government presents no great historical difficulties to one who has carefully studied the constitutional history of the early States and colonies. He finds that the central government of the United States, in its general structure and its various branches, is scarcely more than a reproduction on a higher plane of the government forms existing in the previous States, and more remotely in the early colonies. (*William C. Morey, The Sources of American Federalism, American Academy of Political and Social Sciences, 1895, Vol. 6, p. 197.*)

" The powers of the states depend on their own constitution; the people of every state had the right to modify and restrain them according to their own views of policy or principle; and they remain unaltered and unimpaired, except so far as they were granted to the government of the United States. These deductions have been positively recognised by the tenth amendment." 1 Wh. 325. " The powers retained by the states, proceed not from the people of America, but from the people of the several states, and remain after the adoption of the constitution what they were before, except so far as they may be abridged by that instrument." 4 Wh. 193. S. P.; 5 Wh. 17, 54; 9 Wh. 203, 9. " In our system, the legislature of a state is the supreme power; in all cases where its action is not restrained by the constitution of the United States." 12 Wh. 347. " Its jurisdiction is coextensive with its territory, coextensive with its legislative power," 3. Wh. 387; " and subject to this grant of power, adheres to the territory as a portion of sovereignty not yet given away." The residuary powers of legislation are still in the state. Ib. 389. " The sovereignty of a state extends to every thing which exists by its own authority, or is introduced by its permission." 6 Wh. 429; 4 Pet. 564. (*Mr. Justice Baldwin. A General View of the Origin and Nature of the Constitution and Government of the United States, 1837, pp. 14–15.*)

CHAPTER VI

ESTABLISHMENT OF STATE CONSTITUTIONS

WHEN the members of the Second Continental Congress assembled in Philadelphia on May 10, 1775, the King's troops and the provincials had met at Lexington and Concord on April 19, 1775, with the result that the adventurous sons of liberty were thronging to the aid of Boston. Here on the 17th of June of that year, the British troops were worsted at Bunker Hill, only to reform and to carry the heights. Here they were hemmed in and held in check by the volunteers from different parts of the country, soon to be commanded and ultimately led to victory by George Washington, the first Commander in Chief of the American Armies. These events made a great impression upon the members of Congress, as little by little news from the north reached their ears. What there took place on a large scale was taking place on a smaller scale in the different colonies. Resistance was offered to the royal authority, its officials were driven out by local leaders, and legitimate government in the former sense of the term ceased to exist.

The colonies, soon to be States, were anxious as to the course they should take, and looked to the Congress for advice, as the one central, although a revolutionary body, which could keep in touch with the continent and suggest, if it could not command, what should be done by each in the interest of the whole. The far sighted foresaw independence, but the im- mediate problem before them was to replace the old by new authority, and to check anarchy, which often precedes as well as follows revolution, by local government. Feeling and fearing the absence of authority, New Hampshire asked permission of the Congress " to regulate its internal police," and on November 3rd that body recommended the provincial convention of New Hampshire " to call a full and free representation of the people, and that the representatives, if they think it necessary, establish such a form of government, as, in their judgment, will best produce the happiness of the people, and most effectually secure peace and good order in the province, during the continuance of the present dispute between G[reat] Britain and the colonies." [1] The next day the Congress gave similar advice to South Carolina, and, with or without advice, other colonies began to take action.[2]

But the approach of independence made general concerted action advis-

[1] *Journals of the Continental Congress,* Vol. iii, p. 319.
[2] *Ibid.,* pp. 326–7.

able, and therefore, on May 15, 1776, the Congress resolved "that it be recommended to the respective assemblies and conventions of the United Colonies, where no government sufficient to the exigencies of their affairs have been hitherto established, to adopt such government as shall, in the opinion of the representatives of the people, best conduce to the happiness and safety of their constituents in particular, and America in general." [1] Therefore the colonies which heretofore had not formed local governments now took steps to do so, transforming the charter of the colony into the constitution of the State in the light of their experience and according to the needs which that experience had disclosed. They were their own agents and had a free hand. They did not need to wrangle with the Crown about the terms, for the Crown was excluded from their deliberations. Nor did they need to conform to the views of the Congress as to the provisions of their constitutions, for the Congress, while it could recommend, could not command. The ideas, therefore, which had slowly taken shape in the colonies and which had approved themselves in practice, or which were thought to be advisable, were now incorporated in the constitutions of the States. For this reason the constitutions can be taken as the solemn and formal expression of their views on government during the decade between the Declaration of Independence and the meeting of the Annapolis Convention of representatives of five States, which recommended the Congress to call a convention of all the States to frame an instrument of government which should be a constitution for the States in union and a constitution for each of the States considered separately.

The leaders of opinion in each of the colonies preserved those provisions of the charters, or, in the absence of a charter, the royal instructions, which met with the approval of their constituents, together with the views generally obtaining, and transferred and incorporated them in the constitutions of each of the States. The leaders of opinion, who had either framed or had had a hand either in the framing or in the administration of these instruments of government, or who had lived under these constitutions and were therefore familiar with their provisions, were chosen to represent their States in the convention of the States called to meet in Philadelphia on the second Monday of May, 1787, to revise the Articles of Confederation. Because they drafted a constitution instead of contenting themselves with a revision of the Articles, their assembly is affectionately called the Constitutional Convention, although it would with equal propriety be called, as it often is, the Federal Convention, as, in view of the facts, it should be termed the international conference of the American States.

As in the State conventions so in the international conference, the leaders

---

[1] *Journals of the Continental Congress,* Vol. iv, p. 342, Session of May 10.

cil, acted as courts of appeal, and the upper house, partaker in legislative functions, and, in association with the governor, may be considered as participating in the executive power and the governor may be said to share in all three.

The need, however, of an express separation and a limitation of powers had made itself felt, and although it is not complete in all respects, if indeed it can ever be so, the principle of separation and of limitation is incorporated in the State constitutions. In the constitution of Virginia of July 5, 1776, drafted before the introduction but adopted the day after the Declaration of Independence, it is stated immediately after the preamble that:

> The legislative, executive and judiciary departments shall be separate and distinct, so that neither exercise the powers properly belonging to the other.[1]

And the reason for this separation has never been more clearly stated, it is believed, than in the following classic paragraph from the thirtieth article of the Declaration of Rights prefixed to the first and present constitution of the commonwealth of Massachusetts:

> In the government of this commonwealth, the legislative department shall never exercise the executive and judicial powers, or either of them: The executive shall never exercise the legislative and judicial powers, or either of them: The judicial shall never exercise the legislative and executive powers, or either of them: to the end, it may be a government of laws, and not of men.[2]

Therefore, according to these principles, which pervaded the States of America, there was to be, and in fact there was a government of each of the States consisting of three branches, each more or less separate and distinct. The constitution was to be made by the representatives of the people met in convention for that purpose, or to be drafted by the legislature on behalf of the people, inasmuch as the sovereignty which had formerly vested in the Crown, the lords spiritual and temporal of Great Britain, was, by the Declaration of Independence, vested in the people of each of the States. But whether it was exercised in convention by representatives specially chosen to frame a constitution or by members of the legislature, the act of one or the other was only valid if within the scope of the agency: and convention and legislature were alike responsible to the people as the ultimate source of authority.

Sovereignty Vested in the People

The constitution was thus not a grant from above to the people below but a grant from the people to its agents, who apparently regarded the constitution as in the nature of a compact, in which the people as a whole contracted with each citizen, and each citizen with the whole people to observe its terms; and the goverment of the body politic was regarded as created not

[1] *The Constitutions of the Several Independent States of America,* 1781, p. 140.
[2] *Ibid.,* p. 14.

merely by or with the consent of the citizens but by their direct act or by their authorized agents for this purpose. The organization is a social compact as far as the association of the citizens forming it is concerned, and a political compact as far as the government of the body politic is concerned. Because of this action on their part they are bound by the compact, although on this theory it is difficult to see how their descendants are to be bound. The act which they committed, the association which they formed and the compact which they believed they created are perhaps most clearly stated in the preamble to " a constitution or frame of government, agreed upon by the delegates of the people of the State of Massachusetts Bay, in convention, begun and held at Cambridge, on the fifth of September, 1779, and continued by adjournments, to the second of March, 1780," which preamble, still prefixed to the constitution of that commonwealth, reads as follows:

A Social
and a Political
Compact

> The end of the institution, maintenance and administration of government, is to secure the existence of the body-politic, to protect it, and to furnish the individuals who compose it, with the power of enjoying, in safety and tranquillity, their natural right, and the blessings of life: And whenever these great objects are not obtained, the people have a right to alter the government, and to take measures necessary for their safety, prosperity and happiness.
>
> The body-politic is formed by a voluntary association of individuals; it is a social compact, by which the whole people covenants with each citizen, and each citizen with the whole people, that all shall be governed by certain laws for the common good. It is the duty of the people, therefore, in framing a constitution of government, to provide for an equitable mode of making laws, as well as for an impartial interpretation, and a faithful execution of them; that every man may, at all times, find his security in them.
>
> We, therefore, the people of Massachusetts, acknowledging, with grateful hearts, the goodness of the Great Legislator of the Universe, in affording us, in the course of his providence, an opportunity, deliberately, and peaceably, without fraud, violence, or surprize, of entering into an original, explicit, and solemn compact with each other; and of forming a new constitution of civil government, for ourselves and posterity; and devoutly imploring his direction in so interesting a design, DO agree upon, ordain, and establish, the following *Declaration of Rights,* and *Frame of Government,* as the CONSTITUTION OF THE COMMONWEALTH OF MASSACHUSETTS.[1]

The provisions of this social compact were not matters of theory with the good people of those days; they were principles of the constitution to be observed, a fact thus stated by the eighteenth article of the Declaration of Rights of Massachusetts:

> A frequent recurrence to the fundamental principles of the constitution, and a constant adherence to those of piety, justice, moderation, temperance, industry, and frugality, are absolutely necessary, to preserve the advantages of liberty, and to maintain a free government. The people ought, conse-

[1] *The Constitutions of the Several Independent States,* 1781, pp. 7-8.

quently, to have a particular attention to all those principles, in the choice of their officers and representatives: And they have a right to require of their lawgivers and magistrates, an exact and constant observance of them, in the formation and execution of all laws necessary for the good administration of the commonwealth.[1]

The same ideas are found expressed in the Bill of Rights adopted at the convention held at Williamsburg, Virginia, drafted by George Mason and adopted June 12, 1776, within five days after the motion made by Richard Henry Lee, on behalf of Virginia, for the Declaration of Independence, and several weeks before the adoption of the Declaration, drafted by Thomas Jefferson, likewise of Virginia. Thus:

> Section 1. That all men are by nature equally free and independent, and have certain inherent rights of which, when they enter into a state of society, they cannot, by any compact, deprive or divest their posterity; namely, the enjoyment of life and liberty, with the means of acquiring and possessing property, and pursuing and obtaining happiness and safety.
> Sec. 2. That all power is vested in, and consequently derived from, the people; that magistrates are their trustees and servants, and at all times amenable to them.
> Sec. 3. That government is, or ought to be, instituted for the common benefit, protection, and security of the people, nation or community; of all the various modes and forms of government, that is best which is capable of producing the greatest degree of happiness and safety, and is most effectually secured against the danger of maladministration; and that, when any government shall be found inadequate or contrary to these purposes, a majority of the community hath an indubitable, inalienable, and indefeasible right to reform, alter, or abolish it, in such manner as shall be judged most conducive to the public weal.
> Sec. 4. That no man, or set of men, are entitled to exclusive or separate emoluments or privileges from the community, but in consideration of public services; which, not being descendible, neither ought the offices of magistrate, legislator, or judge to be hereditary.[2]

In pursuance of this right to choose their form of government and to make it adequate to the purposes for which it was instituted, the constitutions were to be retained as long as they met the needs of the people, and to be changed whenever they failed to do so. Therefore, provisions were made for their amendment. Conventions were to be called for this purpose, or amendments were to be proposed in one session of the legislature and considered at a subsequent session or by a larger majority in the legislature; for, the constitution being a compact between the people on the one hand and each of the citizens of the State on the other, was a fundamental law. It was not an act of the legislature, to be withdrawn or modified by the simple majority of a deliberative assembly, as would be the case of an ordinary statute.

Compact a Fundamental Law

---

[1] *Ibid.*, pp. 12-13.
[2] Thorpe, *Charters and Constitutions*, Vol. 7, p. 3813; Poore, pp. 1908–9.

Each of the thirteen States had the threefold separation of powers, and each had a legislative branch, which, with the exception of Pennsylvania, consisted of two houses. Each had a single executive, called president or governor, and each had a judiciary, separate and distinct from both of these powers, but on appeal the judicial power was in some cases exercised in conjunction with one or both. In colonial times the legislative power had been exercised in an assembly composed of two branches, and this method was retained, but each branch, however, was henceforth elected by the people, rejecting the principle of appointment of the upper branch. In Pennsylvania, due apparently to the influence of Benjamin Franklin, there was but one chamber, and Vermont, being without experience, as it had not been a colony under the Crown nor a State under the Articles of Confederation, adopted the single house from Pennsylvania, and indeed its entire constitution. Each body could propose laws, but the approval of both was necessary to the statute, as was the approval of the governor.

Revenue Bills

The colonists, like the people of England, had learned that the power that held the purse would control the sword, and as the lower house was elected by the people and the upper house in most cases appointed by the governor or Crown, acting for the Crown, the colonists insisted that revenue bills should not only originate in the lower house, but that they could not be controlled by the upper house, consisting of the governor and appointed members. Having in mind this experience, the constitutions of the States provided that revenue bills should originate in the lower not in the upper house, although some allowed them to be amended in the upper house while others withheld this power from the second chamber.

Governor's Signature

The law, whether it be an ordinary statute or a revenue bill, in most cases required the approval of the governor, which is either a deviation from the principle of separation or is the cooperation recognized as separate and distinct in their nature. It was, however, appreciated that the governor might improperly or mistakenly withhold his approval, and that it would interfere with the legislature and be a detriment to this system of government if he were thus allowed to block the course of legislation. Therefore, a method was devised to overcome the deadlock between these two branches of government, the principle of which appears to be best stated in Article 3 of "the Constitution of the State of New York, established by the Convention authorized and empowered for that purpose April 20, 1777 " — the model of provisions in other States and the source of proposals made in the Constitutional Convention and the direct source of the principle ultimately adopted. Thus:

> And whereas, laws inconsistent with the spirit of this constitution, or with the public good, may be hastily and unadvisedly passed; be it ordained that the governor for the time being, the chancellor, and the judges of the supreme

court, or any two of them, together with the governor, shall be, and hereby are, constituted a council to revise all bills about to be passed into laws by the legislature, and for that purpose shall assemble themselves, from time to time, when the legislature shall be convened; for which, nevertheless, they shall not receive any salary or consideration, under any pretence whatever. And that all bills, which have passed the senate and assembly, shall, before they become laws, be presented to the said council for their revisal and consideration; and if upon such revision and consideration, it should appear improper to the said council, or a majority of them, that the said bill should become a law of this state, that they return the same, together with their objections thereto in writing, to the senate or house of assembly, in which so ever the same shall have originated, who shall enter the objections sent down by the council, at large, in their minutes, and proceed to reconsider the said bill. But if after such reconsideration, two-thirds of the said senate or house of assembly, shall, notwithstanding the said objections, agree to pass the same, it shall, together with the objections, be sent to the other branch of the legislature, where it shall also be reconsidered, and if approved by two-thirds of the members present, shall be a law.

And in order to prevent any unnecessary delays, be it further ordained, that if any bill shall not be returned by the council within ten days after it shall have been presented, the same shall be a law, unless the legislature shall, by their adjournment, render a return of the said bill within ten days impracticable; in which case the bill shall be returned on the first day of the meeting of the legislature, after the expiration of the said ten days.[1]

The grant of power to the legislature was contained in the constitution and was presumed to be complete, unless restricted. If it was deemed necessary or expedient in the opinion of the framers of the constitution to withhold power from the legislature, this was likewise done in the constitution, and the declarations of rights prefixed to the State constitutions are to be considered as limitations upon the legislative body. Therefore the powers to be enjoyed by the legislative branch of the States did not need to be enumerated in specific terms as in the case of the Articles of Confederation, or in specific and general terms as in the case of the Constitution of the United States, inasmuch as all powers of the State vested in the people of the State, and only such powers, could be exercised by the union of the States as should be granted expressly or by necessary implication. Nevertheless, the people of the States were so accustomed to a declaration of rights that they objected to its absence from the Federal Constitution, and although no power could be exercised by the government thereunder unless expressly or impliedly granted, they insisted upon amendments to the Constitution, of which twelve were proposed by the first congress of the more perfect Union and ten adopted by the States. These amendments, presumed to express the views of the framers of the Constitution, were so contemporaneous with that instrument as to be in fact, although not in form, a declaration of rights appended instead of being prefixed to it.

Legislative Powers

[1] *The Constitutions of the Several Independent States*, 1781, pp. 63-4.

The executive power was vested in the governor or president, as he is called in some of the constitutions, and he exercised, either alone or in conjunction with a smaller body, the executive power of the State. He was the Captain-General or the Commander-in-Chief of the land and naval forces of the State, and his duty was to obey its laws, to secure their universal observance, and to exercise in his discretion the rights vested in him as executive. He was elected, in some cases directly by the people, in others by the legislature. He appointed officers, in some cases by the advice and consent of the legislature or of one of the branches thereof, although in some States the officials, especially the judges, were elected by the legislature. The practice varied, and because of this variation, difficulty was experienced in hitting upon an acceptable method of choosing the judges in the Federal Convention; and because of the election of the executive, either by the people of the State or by the legislatures of the different States, there were differences of opinion in the Federal Convention difficult to reconcile because of diverse practice and a lack of experience in the case of the election of a president of the United States instead of an executive within each of the States. In the case of the colonies the governor was appointed by the proprietor, as in the case of the proprietary provinces of Maryland and of Pennsylvania, or appointed by the Crown, as in the colonies generally, or elected by the people, as in the case of Rhode Island and Connecticut, in the same manner as a Mayor in a Corporation in England. Because of lack of experience in the colonies as well as in the States, the method of selecting the president, devised by the framers of the Constitution, broke down within a few years after the institution of government under the Constitution, and has been twice amended.

In the matter of the judiciary it is sufficient to say in this connection that courts were organized and existed in each of the colonies, that they were appointed by the proprietors in Maryland and in Pennsylvania, that they were appointed by the Crown generally to serve during the pleasure of the Crown, although there was a determined attempt on the part of the colonies to have them hold office during good behavior, as in the case of the English judges, appointed after and in pursuance of the Bill of Rights of 1689, or they were appointed or elected by the colonial authorities, as in the case of Connecticut and Rhode Island. The final court of appeal was during the colonial period the King in Council, just as the laws of the colonies, with the exception of Connecticut and Rhode Island, were subject to veto under prescribed conditions, by the King in Council.

Under the constitutions of the States there was, as has been stated a judiciary, whose judges were ordinarily elected by the legislature, or, as in the case of Massachusetts, appointed by the governor with the advice and consent of the Senate, and, because of colonial experience, they held office during good behavior.

There were inferior courts, such as those presided over by justices of the peace; there were county courts, there were superior courts, there were courts of appeal, and there were courts of chancery, in most although not in all, and appeal lay from the lower to the higher courts. The Senate of New York was the ultimate court of appeal, following the English practice in which the House of Lords decides in final resort; the governor and three members of each house forming the court of appeals in Delaware and invested with the jurisdiction of the King in Council. Whether the officer was a legislator, executive or judge, he was responsible to some higher authority according to the principles of the constitutions, subject to impeachment by the legislature and, after trial either by the lower house or separate tribunal, removable from office. The governments under the constitutions were to be governments of law, not of men, in a larger and a more perfect sense than under the charters. The law was the constitution, to be observed by all and to be administered by agents, chosen directly or indirectly by the people of each of the States possessing the right of suffrage, which in most cases was limited, not universal. This law was indeed subject to amendment, but until amended it was binding upon the people who created it and the officials chosen to administer and to observe its provisions. The law of the constitution was superior to the act of the legislature, inasmuch as the creature of the moment was regarded as inferior to the provisions of the constitution in accordance with which the legislature was created and adopted. The constitution itself was in a more restricted sense the creature of the moment and was itself inferior to the creator of all political power.

It was to be expected that the States would, in the matter of a constitution *Source of Law* for their union, consider themselves as the source of law, that the instrument of government for the union would prescribe in explicit terms that law, whereof the people of the States were the source and the origin, that it would derive its power from the people of the States, either in convention created for that purpose or by legislatures of the States representing the people thereof, and that the form of government for the States would be based upon the form of government drafted by the States themselves. It was further to be expected that sovereign powers would be transferred from the States and conferred upon the government of the union for the common benefit of the States; that in all other cases the States would reserve to themselves the sovereign powers which they should consider necessary for their local interests and concerns, and that if this distribution of sovereign powers did not seem to safeguard sufficiently their local rights and interests and concerns, they would insist upon its amendment; for both by the State constitutions and by the Declaration of Independence of the United States, government derives its just powers from the consent of the governed.

As Mr. Justice Matthews has finely, truly, and impressively said in delivering the opinion of the Supreme Court in *Yick Wo* v. *Hopkins* (118 U. S., 356, 369), decided in 1886:

When we consider the nature and theory of our institutions of government, the principles upon which they are supposed to rest, and review the history of their development, we are constrained to conclude that they do not mean to leave room for the play and action of purely personal and arbitrary power. Sovereignty itself, is, of course, not subject to law, for it is the author and source of law; but in our system, while sovereign powers are delegated to the agencies of government, sovereignty itself remains with the people, by whom and for whom all government exists and acts. And the law is the definition and limitation of power. It is, indeed, quite true, that there must always be lodged somewhere, and in some person or body, the authority of final decision; and in many cases of mere administration the responsibility is purely political, no appeal lying except to the ultimate tribunal of the public judgment, exercised either in the pressure of opinion or by means of the suffrage. But the fundamental rights to life, liberty, and the pursuit of happiness, considered as individual possessions, are secured by those maxims of constitutional law which are the monuments showing the victorious progress of the race in securing to men the blessings of civilization under the reign of just and equal laws, so that, in the famous language of the Massachusetts Bill of Rights, the government of the Commonwealth " may be a government of laws and not of men." For the very idea that one man may be compelled to hold his life, or the means of living, or any material right essential to the enjoyment of life, at the mere will of another, seems to be intolerable in any country where freedom prevails, as being the essence of slavery itself.

VII

THE FEDERAL CONVENTION: AN INTERNATIONAL CONFERENCE

Philadᵃ. Oct. 22 — 1787.

I send you enclos'd the propos'd new Federal Constitution for these States. I was engag'd 4 Months of the last Summer in the Convention that form'd it. It is now sent by Congress to the several States for their Confirmation. If it succeeds, I do not see why you might not in Europe carry the Project of good Henry the 4th into Execution, by forming a Federal Union and One Grand Republick of all its different States & Kingdoms; by means of a like Convention; for we had many Interests to reconcile. (*Extract from letter of Benjamin Franklin to Ferdinand Grand, Documentary History, Vol. IV, pp. 341–342.*)

There is no difficulty in defining a state or nation. It is a body politic, a political community, formed by the people within certain boundaries; who, being separated from all others, adopt certain rules for their own government, with which no people without their limits can interfere. The power of each terminates at the line of separation; each is necessarily supreme within its own limits: of consequence, neither can have any jurisdiction within the limits of another, without its consent. The name given to such community, whether state, nation, power, people, or commonwealth, is only to denote its locality, as a self-governing body of men united for their own internal purposes, if two or more think proper to unite for common purposes, and to authorize the exertion of any power over themselves, by a body composed of delegates or ambassadors of each, they confederate. Each has the undoubted right of deciding, what portion of its own power, it will authorize to be exerted in a meeting, assembly, or congress, of all; what it will restrain, prohibit, or qualify. If this can be done by common consent, the terms of their union are defined, and according to their nature, they form a mere confederacy of states, or a federal government; the purposes and powers of which depend on the instrument agreed upon. If they cannot agree, then each state instructs its delegates according to its own will, and sends them to the body in which all the states are assembled by their deputies: each state is considered as present, and its will expressed by the vote of its delegates. The congress of states are left, in such case, to perform such duties as are enjoined, and execute such powers as are given to them, by their respective and varying instructions: the extent of which is testified in the credentials of the separate delegations, as before the confederation of 1781. (*Mr. Justice Baldwin, A General View of the Origin and Nature of the Constitution and Government of the United States, 1837, p. 16.*)

His Excellency Thomas Collins, Esquire, President, Captain General, and Commander in Chief of the Delaware State; To all to whom these Presents (Seal) shall come, Greeting. Know Ye, that among the Laws of the said State, passed by the General Assembly of the same, on the third day of February, in the Year of our Lord One thousand seven hundred and Eighty seven, it is thus inrolled.

In the Eleventh Year of the Independence of the Delaware State

An Act appointing Deputies from this State to the Convention proposed to be held in the City of Philadelphia for the Purpose of revising the Federal Constitution.

Whereas the General Assembly of this State are fully convinced of the Necessity of revising the Federal Constitution, and adding thereto such further Provisions, as may render the same more adequate to the Exigencies of the Union; And Whereas the Legislature of Virginia have already passed an Act of that Commonwealth, appointing and authorizing certain Commissioners to meet, at the City of Philadelphia, in May next, a Convention of Commissioners or Deputies from the different States: And this State being willing and desirous of co-operating with the Commonwealth of Virginia, and the other States in the Confederation, in so useful a design.

Be it therefore enacted by the General Assembly of Delaware, that George Read, Gunning Bedford, John Dickinson, Robert Bassett and Jacob Broom, Esquires, are hereby appointed Deputies from this State to meet in the Convention of the Deputies of other States, to be held at the City of Philadelphia on the Second day of May next: And the said George Read, Gunning Bedford, John Dickinson, Richard Bassett and Jacob Broom, Esquires, or any three of them, are hereby constituted and appointed Deputies from this State, with Powers to meet such Deputies as may be appointed and authorized by the other States to assemble in the said Convention at the City aforesaid, and to join with them in devising, deliberating on, and discussing, such Alterations and further Provisions as may be necessary to render the Fœderal Constitution adequate to the Exigencies of the Union; and in reporting such Act or Acts for that purpose to the United States in Congress Assembled, as when agreed to by them, and duly confirmed by the several States, may effectually provide for the same: So always and Provided, that such Alterations or further Provisions, or any of them, do not extend to that part of the Fifth Article of the Confederation of the said States, finally ratified on the first day of March, in the Year One thousand seven hundred and eighty one, which declares that "In determining Questions in the United States in Congress Assembled each State shall have one Vote."

And be it enacted, that in Case any of the said Deputies hereby nominated, shall happen to die, or to resign his or their Appointment, the President or Commander in Chief with the Advice of the Privy Council, in the Recess of the General Assembly, is hereby authorized to supply such Vacancies

Passed at Dover,   }   Signed by Order of the House of Assembly,
February 3ᵈ. 1787.   }   JOHN COOK, Speaker
                        }   Signed by Order of the Council
                              GEO CRAGHEAD, Speaker.

All and singular which Premises by the Tenor of these Presents, I have caused to be Exemplified. In Testimony whereof I have hereunto subscribed my Name, and caused the Great-Seal of the said State to be affixed to these Presents, at New Castle the Second day of April in the Year of our Lord One thousand seven hundred and eighty seven, and in the Eleventh Year of the Independence of the United States of America

THOˢ COLLINS

Attest
   JA BOOTH, Secʸ.

(Instructions of Delaware State to its Delegates in the Philadelphia Federal Convention of 1787, Documentary History of the United States, 1786–1870, Vol. I, 1894, pp. 23–25.)

DEPARTMENT OF STATE,
Washington, April 18, 1899.

Gentlemen: You have been appointed by the President to constitute a commission to represent him at an international conference called by His Imperial Majesty the Emperor of Russia to meet at The Hague, at a time to be indicated by the Government of the Netherlands, for the purpose of discussing the most efficacious means of assuring to all peoples the "benefits of a real and durable peace."

Upon your arrival at The Hague you will effect an organization of your commission, whose records will be kept by your secretary, Hon. Frederick W. Holls. All reports and communications will be made through this Department, according to its customary forms, for preservation in the archives.

The programme of topics suggested by the Russian minister of foreign affairs for discussion at the conference in his circular of December 30, 1898, is as follows: . . .

I am, etc.,

JOHN HAY.

(Instructions to the American Delegates at the First Hague Peace Conference, 1899, Papers Relating to the Foreign Relations of the United States, 1899, pp. 511, 513.)

DEPARTMENT OF STATE,
Washington, May 31, 1907.

Gentlemen: You have been appointed delegates plenipotentiary to represent the United States at a Second Peace Conference which is to meet at The Hague on the 15th of June, 1907. . . .

Following the precedent established by the commission to the First Conference, all your reports and communications to this Government will be made to the Department of State for proper consideration and eventual preservation in the archives. The records of your commission will be kept by your secretary, Mr. Chandler Hale. Should you be in doubt at any time regarding the meaning or effect of these instructions, or should you consider at any time that there is occasion for special instructions, you will communicate freely with the Department of State by telegraph. It is the President's earnest wish that you may contribute materially to the effective work of the conference and that its

deliberations may result in making international justice more certain and international peace
more secure.

I am, gentlemen, your obedient servant,

ELIHU ROOT.

(*Instructions to the American Delegates of the United States to the Hague Peace Conference of 1907, Foreign Relations of the United States, 1907, part 2, pp. 1128, 1139.*)

M^r. King objected to one of the rules in the Report authorising any member to call for
the yeas & nays and have them entered on the minutes. He urged that as the acts of the
Convention were not to bind the Constituents it was unnecessary to exhibit this evidence of
the votes; and improper as changes of opinion would be frequent in the course of the business & would fill the minutes with contradictions. . . .

The proposed rule was rejected nem. contradicente. (*Madison's Notes of Debates in
the Federal Convention, Session of Monday, May 28, 1787, Documentary History of the
Constitution of the United States of America, 1786–1870, Vol. III, 1900, pp. 10–12.*)

As is the rule in plenary sessions, each State shall have only one vote in each Commission.
(*Rule of the First Hague Peace Conference. Conférence internationale de la paix, La
Haye 18 mai–29 juillet 1899, procès-verbaux, part 1, p. 14.*)

Each delegation has a right to only one vote.

The vote is taken by roll call according to the alphabetical order of the Powers represented. (*Regulations of the Second Hague Peace Conference, Deuxième conférence internationale de la paix, La Haye 15 juin–18 octobre 1907. Actes et documents, p. 56.*)

The Ratification of the Conventions of nine States, shall be sufficient for the Establishment of this Constitution between the States so ratifying the Same.

Done in Convention by the Unanimous Consent of the States present the Seventeenth
Day of September in the Year of our Lord one thousand seven hundred and Eighty seven,
and of the Independence of the United States of America the Twelfth. In Witness whereof
We have hereunto subscribed our Names. (*The Constitution of the United States, Article
VII.*)

Article 52. The present Convention shall be ratified and the ratifications shall be deposited at The Hague as soon as all the Powers mentioned in Article 15 and in the table
annexed are in a position to do so.

The deposit of the ratifications shall take place, in any case, on the 30th June, 1909,
if the Powers which are ready to ratify furnish nine judges and nine deputy judges to
the Court, qualified to validly constitute a Court. If not, the deposit shall be postponed
until this condition is fulfilled. . . .

Article 54. The present Convention shall come into force six months from the deposit
of the ratifications contemplated in Article 52, paragraphs 1 and 2. . . . (*Convention No. XII
relating to the creation of an International Prize Court, October 18, 1907, adopted by
the Second Hague Peace Conference.*)

Two requisites seem necessary to constitute a Federal Government in this its most
perfect form. On the one hand, each of the members of the Union must be wholly independent in those matters which concern each member only. On the other hand, all must
be subject to a common power in those matters which concern the whole body of members
collectively. Thus each member will fix for itself the laws of its criminal jurisprudence,
and even the details of its political constitution. And it will do this, not as a matter of
privilege or concession from any higher power, but as a matter of absolute right, by virtue
of its inherent powers as an independent commonwealth. But in all matters which concern
the general body, the sovereignty of the several members will cease. Each member is
perfectly independent within its own sphere; but there is another sphere in which its independence, or rather its separate existence, vanishes. It is invested with every right of
sovereignty on one class of subjects, but there is another class of subjects on which it is
as incapable of separate political action as any province or city of a monarchy or of an
indivisible republic. The making of peace and war, the sending and receiving of ambassadors, generally all that comes within the department of International Law, will be
reserved wholly to the central power. Indeed, the very existence of the several members
of the Union will be diplomatically unknown to foreign nations, which will never be called
upon to deal with any power except the Central Government. A Federal Union, in short,
will form one State in relation to other powers, but many States as regards its internal

administration. This complete division of sovereignty we may look upon as essential to the absolute perfection of the Federal ideal. (*Edward A. Freeman, History of Federal Government, from the foundation of the Achaian League to the disruption of the United States, Vol. I, 1863, pp. 3–4.*)

The distribution of powers is an essential feature of federalism. The object for which a federal state is formed involves a division of authority between the national government and the separate States. The powers given to the nation form in effect so many limitations upon the authority of the separate States, and as it is not intended that the central government should have the opportunity of encroaching upon the rights retained by the States, its sphere of action necessarily becomes the object of rigorous definition. The Constitution, for instance, of the United States delegates special and closely defined powers to the executive, to the legislature, and to the judiciary of the Union, or in effect to the Union itself, whilst it provides that the powers "not delegated to the United States by the Constitution nor prohibited by it to the States are reserved to the States respectively or to the people."

This is all the amount of division which is essential to a federal constitution. But the principle of definiton and limitation of powers harmonises so well with the federal spirit that it is generally carried much farther than is dictated by the mere logic of the constitution. Thus the authority assigned to the United States under the Constitution is not concentrated in any single official or body of officials. The President has definite rights, upon which neither Congress nor the judicial department can encroach. Congress has but a limited, indeed a very limited, power of legislation, for it can make laws upon eighteen topics only; yet within its own sphere it is independent both of the President and of the Federal Courts. So, lastly, the judiciary have their own powers. They stand on a level both with the President and with Congress, and their authority (being directly derived from the constitution) cannot, without a distinct violation of law, be trenched upon either by the executive or by the legislature. (*Albert Venn Dicey, Introduction to the Study of the Law of the Constitution, 1885, 8th edition, 1915, pp. 147–149.*)

It is impossible to imagine liberty in its fulness, if the people as a totality, the country, the nation, whatever name may be preferred, or its government, is not independent on foreign interference. The country must have what the Greeks called autonomy. This implies, that the country must have the right, and, of course, the power, of establishing that government which it considers best, without interference from without or pressure from above. No foreigner must dictate; no extra-governmental principle, no divine right or "principle of legitimacy" must act in the choice and foundation of the government; no claim superior to that of the people's, that is, national sovereignty must be allowed. This independence or national self-government farther implies that, the civil government of free choice or free acquiescence being established, no influence from without, besides that of freely acknowledged justice, fairness, and morality, must be admitted. There must then be the requisite strength to resist when necessary. (*Francis Lieber, On Civil Liberty and Self-Government, 1853, Vol. I, p. 73.*)

The tendency plainly is towards a more centralized government by a freer interpretation of the United States Constitution. The dangers which menace us from this tendency, and from what may be called democratic abstraction, are met by such a book as this, which teaches that there is no safe liberty but one under checks and guarantees, one which is articulated, one which by institutions of local self-government educates the whole people and moderates the force of administrations, one which sets up the check of state power within certain well-defined limits against United States power, one which draws a broad line between the unorganized masses of men calling themselves the people and the people formed into bodies, "joined together and compacted" by constitutions and institutions. (*Theodore D. Woolsey, Introduction to Third Edition of Francis Lieber, On Civil Liberty and Self-Government, 1874, p. 10.*)

We know no reason in the nature of things why a state should be any the better for being large, and because throughout the greater part of history very large states have usually been states of a low type. (*Sir John Robert Seeley, Expansion of England, 1883, American edition, p. 294.*)

CHAPTER VII

THE FEDERAL CONVENTION: AN INTERNATIONAL CONFERENCE

IT was foreseen, as has already been pointed out, that amendments to the Articles of Confederation would need to be made, inasmuch as the Union, of which the Articles formed the instrument of government, was to be perpetual, and no instrument could, even in the opinion of its framers, be looked upon as so perfect as not to be susceptible of modifications under changing conditions. The Articles were, as a matter of fact, defective, or were thought to be so by large bodies of people in all the States. At any rate, their provisions were not observed, and it was apparent that modifications would have to be made in the framework of government even if it were possible to preserve the Articles as thus amended. " Every state " was, to quote the language of Article 13, to " abide by the determinations of the united states in congress assembled, on all questions which by this confederation are submitted to them." [1] This unfortunately was not done. It was next provided that the Articles of Confederation should " be inviolably observed by every state," that the union should be perpetual, and that no alteration should " at any time hereafter be made in any of them; unless such alteration be agreed to in a congress of the united states, and be afterwards confirmed by the legislatures of every state."

The requirement of unanimity, natural enough and indeed proper in a *Demands of Commerce and Navigation* diplomatic document, and to be understood unless there be a stipulation to the contrary, rendered an amendment of the Articles very difficult, as the experience of well nigh ten years had amply shown, and yet the consent of all must be had to a change affecting all, if that change were to take place and become effective. Without recounting the steps taken to invigorate the government, whose outward weakness was more apparent than its inner strength, it is sufficient to recall that Virginia, under the wise direction of Madison, took advantage of the meeting of delegates of that State and of Maryland concerning the freedom of navigation of the Potomac and of the Chesapeake to call a conference of all the States for this purpose, to meet at Annapolis the first Monday in September, 1786.

An agreement about commerce and navigation would have been a mere patch upon the Articles, which would otherwise remain as they were. The crying need of the Confederation was such a modification of the Articles as

[1] *The Constitutions of the Several Independent States,* 1781, pp. 201-2.

145

would vest the general government with power to regulate commerce and navigation, and by means thereof or by other means to acquire a revenue for the purposes of government. A revision limited to a part of the field might have enabled the Confederation to continue as thus modified until a more favorable occasion should present itself for a revision of the scheme of government as a whole.

Of the thirteen States invited, nine accepted the invitation and appointed delegates, but of the nine only the delegates of five arrived, and the representatives of Virginia, Maryland, New Jersey, Delaware and New York properly concluded that it would serve no useful purpose to draft a plan to be accepted by all when only five of the States were sufficiently interested to have their delegates take part in the convention. Therefore they wisely limited their report presented to the States and likewise to the Congress, to a statement of the needs of revision, and they recommended a conference of delegates of all the States, to meet in Philadelphia the second Monday of May in 1787, "to take into consideration the situation of the United States, to devise such further provisions as shall appear to them necessary to render the constitution of the Federal Government adequate to the exigencies of the Union; and to report such an act for that purpose to the United States in Congress assembled, as, when agreed to by them, and afterward confirmed by the Legislatures of every State, will effectually provide for the same." [1]

As the initiative came from the States, it was natural that those States most interested in the revision of the Articles should take action, even before the Congress should recommend the States so to do. It was perhaps necessary to do this in order that the Congress should see the advisability of action on its part, lest it might seem to be forced to move, and thus to lose the credit of directing what its members could not seemingly prevent. Therefore, after the State of Virginia (October 16, 1786), the State of New Jersey (November 23, 1786), the State of Pennsylvania (December 30, 1786), the State of North Carolina (January 6, 1787), the State of New Hampshire (January 17, 1787), the State of Delaware (February 3, 1787), and the State of Georgia (February 10, 1787) had complied with the recommendation of the Annapolis Convention and had appointed their delegates to the meeting in Philadelphia, the Congress, on February 21, 1787, passed the following resolution:

> Whereas there is provision in the Articles of Confederation & perpetual Union for making alterations therein by the Assent of a Congress of the United States and of the legislatures of the several States; And whereas experience hath evinced that there are defects in the present Confederation, as a mean to remedy which several of the States and particularly the State of New York by express instructions to their delegates in Congress have suggested a convention for the purposes expressed in the following resolution and

---

[1] Elliot's *Debates*, Vol. i, p. 118.

such Convention appearing to be the most probable mean of establishing in these states a firm national government.

Resolved that in the opinion of Congress it is expedient that on the second Monday in May next a Convention of delegates who shall have been appointed by the several states be held at Philadelphia for the sole and express purpose of revising the Articles of Confederation and reporting to Congress and the several legislatures such alterations and provisions therein as shall when agreed to in Congress and confirmed by the states render the federal constitution adequate to the exigencies of Government & the preservation of the Union.[1]

In consequence of this action of the Congress, the State of New York (February 28, 1787), the State of South Carolina (March 8, 1787), the State of Massachusetts (April 9, 1787), the State of Connecticut (May 2, 1787), and the State of Maryland (May 26, 1787) acted favorably upon the recommendation and appointed delegates to the conference of the States in Philadelphia, thus accounting for all the States with the exception of the State of Rhode Island, which, in its sovereign pleasure, or perhaps it may be more accurate to say, displeasure, refused to cast its lot with its sister States, although the better elements of the State, if their own testimony is to be taken, had attempted to line up the little Commonwealth with its equals, if not its betters.

May, 1787

The second Monday of May came, but the delegates did not. On the 14th day of the month, the Virginian delegation, with George Washington at its head, arrived at Philadelphia on time, where they were met by the Pennsylvanian delegates, who would have found it difficult to be elsewhere. A majority of the States was obtained for the first time on May 25, 1787. On that day the conference held the first of its sessions, which was not to revise the Articles of Confederation and to make them adequate for the purposes of union, but to create a more perfect Union, the model, as many think, of organization for the society of nations.

In the interval between these two periods the Virginian delegation met some two or three hours a day to consider the questions to come before the convention and to put their views in the form of resolutions which might serve, in the absence of others better, as a basis of discussion and of the future instrument of government. They also met and exchanged views with the delegates of the other States as they arrived, and especially, it would seem, entered into friendly and confidential relations with the Pennsylvanian members. An incident which happened before the opening of the conference is recorded by Mr. Madison, a member of the Virginian delegation destined to be the reporter of the conference and to be regarded as the father of the Constitution, just as General Washington, another Virginian delegate, was and is the father of the country. Interesting in itself, the incident has a permanent value in

[1] *Documentary History of the Constitution of the United States of America,* Vol. iv, p. 78.

that it shows the attitude of some of the delegates of the larger States which, it is believed, was shared consciously or unconsciously by that class of representatives.   It also discloses their attitude in advance and explains their purpose in the course of proceedings.

Large and
Small States

It appears that Gouverneur Morris, with the support of Robert Morris and of others from Pennsylvania, opposed " as unreasonable " the concession of an equal vote to the little States, on the ground that, armed with equality, the delegates of the smaller States would be enabled " to negative every good system of government " which the delegates of the larger States might propose, which, in the opinion of such delegates " must in the nature of things be founded on a violation of that equality."   The Virginian delegates, however, forecast the consequences of such action on the part of the larger States at the opening of the convention, as likely to " beget fatal altercations between the large and small States."   They felt that the attempt if made at this time would fail, whereas the smaller States might, in the course of debate, be prevailed upon " to give up their equality for the sake of an effective government."   They therefore, to quote James Madison's account of the incident, " discountenanced and stifled the project." [1]

It is, however, important to bear this incident in mind, as it shows the atmosphere of the convention, overcast before its opening and soon to be charged with electricity.   The opposition between the large and the small appears to be inherent in the nature of things and to come to the surface during the proceedings of an international conference.   The little States insist upon equality of representation, and upon their equality of right to present their views and to have them debated, even although if treated with courtesy and kindly consideration they are disposed to adopt the projects of the larger States if convinced that they are meant for the good of the whole.

Organization
of the Federal
Convention

On the 25th of May the delegates of seven States, being a majority of the original thirteen which had declared their independence of the mother country on July 4, 1776, and whose independence was recognized by the mother country on September 7, 1783, had arrived, and on that day they proceeded to the hall in which that independence had been proclaimed and, in conference, to hit upon a plan for its maintenance, collectively as well as individually.   As is the wont of international conferences, the leading member of the State in which the conference was held opened proceedings.   In the place of Benjamin Franklin, President of Pennsylvania, unavoidably absent, Robert Morris, a delegate from that State, to quote Mr. Madison's Notes, " informed the members assembled that by the instruction & in behalf of the deputation of Pen[a]. he proposed George Washington, Esq[r]., late Commander in chief for presi-

---

[1] *Madison Papers,* Gilpin ed., 1841, Vol. ii, p. 726 note.

dent of the Convention." [1]   As is also the wont of international conferences,
the delegate of another and a leading State seconded the nomination.   In
this instance it was John Rutledge of South Carolina who expressed, as is
ordinarily done on such occasions, his confidence that the choice would be
unanimous, observing with greater truth than is customary, " that the presence
of Genl. Washington forbade any observations on the occasion which might
otherwise be proper." [2]   On this transaction Mr. Madison makes the proper
comment that " the nomination came with particular grace from Penna, as
Doc^r. Franklin alone could have been thought of as a competitor.   The Doc^r.
was himself to have made the nomination of General Washington, but the
state of the weather and of his health confined him to his house." [3]   And it
may be said in this connection that Washington and Franklin were, by their
respective achievements, the two great personalities in the convention, in
which, according to the account of a contemporary, they moved with great
caution and circumspection.

As is not the wont, however, of international conferences, the election was
by ballot, which, in the case of Washington, could only result in a unanimous
election, after which he was conducted to the chair by Messrs. Morris and
Rutledge.   Thereupon, " in a very emphatic manner," to quote Mr. Madison,
" he thanked the Convention for the honor they had conferred on him, re-
minded them of the novelty of the scene of business in which he was to act,
lamented his want of better qualifications, and claimed the indulgence of the
House towards the involuntary errors which his inexperience might occasion." [4]   This language is also the language of international conferences,
but it was invariably Washington's attitude toward himself in private, and in
public, on the three great occasions in which he appeared before his countrymen, here, on accepting the chief command of the American armies, and on
being proposed and elected President of the United States.

As was also the wont of international conferences, a delegate from Pennsylvania, in this instance James Wilson, proposed the appointment of a secretary and nominated William Temple Franklin, whose selection would have
been agreeable to the authorities of Pennsylvania, inasmuch as he was the
grandson of its venerable chief executive.   But as the nomination was made
in a conference of the American States, accustomed to think and to act for
themselves and to choose those whom they really wanted, not those who were
imposed upon them, Mr. Franklin's nomination did not result in an election.
" Colonel," as Mr. Madison calls him, but as we should say today, Alexander

[1] *Documentary History of the Constitution,* Vol. iii, p. 8.
[2] *Ibid.*
[3] *Ibid.,* p. 9.
[4] *Ibid.,* pp. 8–9.

Hamilton, nominated Major Jackson, and upon ballot the major had five votes to the grandson's two.

The convention had a president and a secretary; it did not as yet have members. The credentials of those appointed by the States were presented and read, whereupon the deputies there assembled constituted the conference. As the members acted under instructions from their States, in accordance with the custom of international assemblies, it is desirable to give some attention to the form and content of their credentials. First of Virginia, to follow the order of the States accepting the recommendation of the Annapolis Convention, subsequently approved by the Congress.

Instructions
to
Delegates

The purpose is stated and the delegates are instructed " to meet such Deputies as may be appointed and authorized by other States to assemble in Convention at Philadelphia . . . and to join with them in devising and discussing all such Alterations and farther Provisions as may be necessary to render the Fœderal Constitution adequate to the Exigencies of the Union and in reporting such an Act for that purpose to the United States in Congress as when agreed to by them and duly confirmed by the several States will effectually provide for the same." [1]

The Pennsylvania delegates were constituted and appointed " with Powers to meet such Deputies as may be appointed and authorized by the other States . . . and to join with them in devising, deliberating on, and discussing, all such alterations and further Provisions, as may be necessary to render the fœderal Constitution fully adequate to the exigencies of the Union." [2]

The State of North Carolina authorized its deputies " to meet and confer with such Deputies as may be appointed by the other States for similar purposes, and with them to discuss and decide upon the most effectual means to remove the defects of our Fœderal Union, and to procure the enlarged Purposes which it was intended to effect, and that they report such an Act to the General Assembly of this State, as when agreed to by them, will effectually provide for the same." [3]

The delegates of New Hampshire were appointed and authorized " to discuss and decide upon the most effectual means to remedy the defects of our federal Union." [4]

The instructions to the delegates of Delaware contained a clause which showed the intention of that little commonwealth to maintain not only the independence but the equality which it had gained for itself, in conjunction with the other States, through a conflict of seven years. Thus, the deputies of the smallest of the States attending the Convention,— for Rhode Island,

[1] *Documentary History*, Vol. i, p. 28.
[2] *Ibid.*, p. 20.
[3] *Ibid.*, p. 35.
[4] *Ibid.*, p. 10.

as previously stated, failed to appear, — were appointed and authorized to meet the deputies appointed and authorized by the other States, " and to join with them in devising, deliberating on, and discussing, such Alterations and further Provisions as may be necessary to render the Fœderal Constitution adequate to the Exigencies of the Union. . . : So always and Provided, that such Alterations or further Provisions, or any of them, do not extend to that part of the Fifth Article of the Confederation of the said States, finally ratified on the first day of March, in the Year One thousand seven hundred and eighty one, which declares that ' In determining Questions in the United States in Congress Assembled each State shall have one vote.' " [1]

The reason for this action on behalf of Delaware is clearly stated in a letter dated New Castle, January 17, 1787, from George Read, soon to be head of the Delaware delegation, to John Dickinson, soon to be its leading member, as he already was a leading citizen of the United States, from which the following passages are quoted by way of comment:

> Finding that Virginia hath again taken the lead in the proposed convention at Philadelphia in May, as recommended in our report when at Annapolis, . . . it occurred to me, as a prudent measure on the part of our State, that its Legislature should, in the act of appointment, so far restrain the powers of the commissioners, whom they shall name on this service, as that they may not extend to any alteration in that part of the fifth article of the present Confederation, . . . that is, that such clause shall be preserved or inserted, for the like purpose, in any revision that shall be made and agreed to in the proposed convention.[2]

The reason for this suggestion, inuring to the benefit of the small States generally as well as to Delaware, and which John Dickinson, perhaps more than any other man, made a reality, is thus stated by Mr. Read, who, curiously enough, in the Convention went over to the larger States:

> I conceive our existence as a State will depend upon our preserving such rights, for I consider the acts of Congress hitherto, as to the ungranted lands in most of the larger States, as sacrificing the just claims of the smaller and bounded States to a proportional share therein, for the purpose of discharging the national debt incurred during the war; and such is my jealousy of most of the larger States, that I would trust nothing to their candor, generosity, or ideas of public justice in behalf of this State, from what has heretofore happened, and which, I presume, hath not escaped your notice. . . .
> Persuaded I am, from what I have seen occasionally in the public prints and heard in private conversations, that the voice of the States will be one of the subjects of revision, and in a meeting where there will be so great an interested majority, I suspect the argument or oratory of the smaller State commissioners will avail little. In such circumstances I conceive it will relieve the commissioners of the State from disagreeable argumentation, as well as prevent the downfall of the State, which would at once become a

---

[1] Farrand, *Records of the Federal Convention*, Vol. iii, p. 575.
[2] W. T. Read, *Life and Correspondence of George Read*, pp. 438–9.

cypher in the union, and have no chance of an accession of district, or even citizens. . . .

The clause in the instructions to the Delaware delegates, inserted upon the suggestion of Mr. Read, was not lost upon the delegates in the convention, as appears from the testimony of Mr. Madison, who says in his Notes that " on reading the credentials of the deputies it was noticed that those from Delaware were prohibited from changing the Article in the Confederation establishing an equality of votes among the States." [1]   This was the cloud no larger than a man's hand which portended approaching storm.

The instructions to the delegates from Georgia contained the usual authorization, with, however, the statement following the date of the year " of our Sovereignty and Independence the Eleventh." [2]   And the instructions of New York were similar, omitting the " year of our Lord " and substituting " this Ninth day of May in the Eleventh Year of the Independence of the said State." [3]

The instructions from the State of South Carolina did not differ materially from those of the other States, except that the delegates were to " join with such Deputies or Commissioners (they being duly authorized and empowered) in devising and discussing all such Alterations, Clauses, Articles and Provisions, as may be thought necessary to render the Fœderal Constitution entirely adequate to the actual Situation and future good Government of the confederated States." [4]

The Commonwealth of Massachusetts contented itself in its instructions with quoting the resolution of Congress and authorizing its representatives " to meet such Delegates as may be appointed by the other or any of the other States in the Union to meet in Convention at Philadelphia at the time and for the purposes aforesaid." [5]

The instructions to the Connecticut delegates, William Samuel Johnson, Roger Sherman, and Oliver Ellsworth, to whose efforts on crucial occasions the Constitution is largely due, provide that the three delegates to the convention, or any one of them in case of sickness or accident, are authorized and empowered " to Represent this State therein, and to confer with such Delegates appointed by the several States, for the purposes mentioned in the said Act of Congress that may be present and duly empowered to act in said Convention, and to discuss upon such Alterations and Provisions agreeable to the general Principles of Republican Government as they shall think proper to render the federal Constitution adequate to the exigencies of Government and, the preservation of the Union." [6]

---

[1] *Documentary History,* Vol. iii, p. 9.
[2] *Ibid.,* Vol. i, p. 44.
[3] *Ibid.,* p. 14.
[4] *Ibid.,* p. 38.
[5] *Ibid.,* p. 11.
[6] *Ibid.,* p. 13.

And finally, the Maryland delegates are instructed to join with the other delegates " in considering such Alterations and further Provisions as may be necessary to render the Fœderal Constitution adequate to the Exigencies of the Union and in reporting such an Act for that purpose to the United States in Congress Assembled as when agreed to by them, and duly confirmed by the several States will effectually provide for the same, and the said Deputies or such of them as shall attend the said Convention shall have full Power to represent this State for the Purposes aforesaid, and the said Deputies are hereby directed to report the Proceedings of the said Convention, and any Act agreed to therein, to the next session of the General Assembly of this State." [1]

It is apparent from these instructions that the convention in Philadelphia was a conference of the twelve States, continental if not international in the strict sense of the word; that the delegates represented the States in attendance and, as delegates, acted in accordance with specific instructions; that the action of the convention, in whatever form its proceedings might be couched, was a recommendation to the Congress and to the States; and that it derived whatever validity it would possess by the ratification of each of the States attending the conference or, as in the case of Rhode Island, adhering to its recommendation, as is the custom of States invited to but not actually participating in an international gathering. The clause concerning equality in the instructions to the delegates of Delaware was a warning to the larger and a rallying point for the delegates of the smaller States, when it appeared to them that the larger States were intent on swallowing them up or merging them in a common union in which the larger States would hold the whip hand.

With the reading of the credentials and the seating of the persons whose names were contained in them, there were present members appointed by the States for the convention. To act in an expeditious and orderly manner, and to accomplish the purpose for which it was called, it was necessary to have a system of rules and procedure. Therefore the next step was, to quote Mr. Madison's Notes, " the appointment of a committee . . . to prepare standing rules & orders." [2] The Convention therefore adjourned on Friday the 25th to Monday the 28th, in order to give the committee time to get to work, and at the meeting of the latter date the rules as reported were taken up and adopted, with an amendment striking out the call for yeas and nays and having them entered on the minutes at the request of any member. This procedure would have been proper enough in a parliamentary assembly, where each member represented himself, but improper

Committee on Rules and Orders

[1] *Ibid.*, pp. 25–6.
[2] *Ibid.*, Vol. iii, p. 9.

in an international conference, where the member represented the State. The reasons, differing in form though not in effect from the one already given, were thus stated by Mr. King of Massachusetts, who moved the amendment:

> As the acts of the Convention were not to bind the Constituents, it was unnecessary to exhibit this evidence of the votes; and improper as changes of opinion would be frequent in the course of the business & would fill the minutes with contradictions.

To which Mr. Mason of Virginia added:

> That such a record of the opinions of members would be an obstacle to a change of them on conviction; and in case of its being hereafter promulged must furnish handles to the adversaries of the Result of the Meeting.

The standing rules and orders as amended in this particular are thus worded:

> A House to do business shall consist of the Deputies of not less than seven States; and all questions shall be decided by the greater number of these which shall be fully represented; but a less number than seven may adjourn from day to day.
>
> Immediately after the President shall have taken the chair, and the members their seats, the minutes of the preceding day shall be read by the Secretary.
>
> Every member, rising to speak, shall address the President; and whilst he shall be speaking, none shall pass between them, or hold discourse with another, or read a book, pamphlet or paper, printed or manuscript — and of two members rising at the same time, the President shall name him who shall be first heard.
>
> A member shall not speak oftener than twice, without special leave, upon the same question; and not the second time, before every other, who had been silent, shall have been heard, if he choose to speak upon the subject.
>
> A motion made and seconded, shall be repeated, and if written, as it shall be when any member shall so require, read aloud by the Secretary, before it shall be debated; and may be withdrawn at any time, before the vote upon it shall have been declared.
>
> Orders of the day shall be read next after the minutes, and either discussed or postponed, before any other business shall be introduced.
>
> When a debate shall arise upon a question, no motion, other than to amend the question, to commit it, or to postpone the debate shall be received.
>
> A question which is complicated, shall, at the request of any member, be divided, and put separately on the propositions of which it is compounded.
>
> The determination of a question, altho' fully debated, shall be postponed, if the deputies of any State desire it until the next day.
>
> A writing which contains any matter brought on to be considered, shall be read once throughout for information, then by paragraphs be debated, and again, with the amendments, if any, made on the second reading; and afterwards the question shall be put on the whole, amended, or approved in its original form, as the case shall be.
>
> Committees shall be appointed by ballot; and the members who have the

greatest number of ballots, altho' not a majority of the votes present, shall be the Committee — When two or more members have an equal number of votes, the member standing first on the list in the order of taking down the ballots, shall be preferred.

A member may be called to order by any other member, as well as by the President; and may be allowed to explain his conduct or expressions supposed to be reprehensible. And all questions of order shall be decided by the President without appeal or debate.

Upon a question to adjourn for the day, which may be made at any time, if it be seconded, the question shall be put without a debate.

When the House shall adjourn, every member shall stand in his place, until the President pass him.[1]

It occurred to Mr. Pierce Butler, of South Carolina, that it would be advisable to provide against " interruption of business by absence of members, and against licentious publications of their proceedings." To this motion Mr. Richard Dobbs Spaight, of North Carolina, moved a provision " that on the one hand the House might not be precluded by a vote upon any question, from revising the subject matter of it, When they see cause, nor, on the other hand, be led too hastily to rescind a decision, which was the result of mature discussion." [2] These two motions were referred to the committee on standing rules, which, by its chairman, reported the next day the following additional rules, which were adopted and thus completed the standing rules and orders:

That no member be absent from the House, so as to interrupt the representation of the State, without leave.

That Committees do not sit whilst the House shall be or ought to be, sitting.

That no copy be taken of any entry on the journal during the sitting of the House without leave of the House.

That members only be permitted to inspect the journal.

That nothing spoken in the House be printed, or otherwise published or communicated without leave.

That a motion to reconsider a matter which had been determined by a majority, may be made, with leave unanimously given, on the same day on which the vote passed; but otherwise not without one day's previous notice: in which last case, if the House agree to the reconsideration, some future day shall be assigned for that purpose.[3]

From an inspection of the credentials of the members and the procedure adopted for its conduct it is evident that the Federal Convention was a conference in the international sense. It is clear that the States were represented as States, and they voted as States; that a method of procedure was devised calculated to put the project in its entirety and in its several parts before the convention, to diffuse understanding of it before debate, to furnish

International Aspects of the Convention

[1] *Documentary History,* Vol. iii, pp. 10–12.
[2] *Ibid.,* p. 13.
[3] *Ibid.,* pp. 14–15.

an opportunity for discussion upon each of its parts as well as upon the project as it should appear after debate and amendment for the approval of the convention; that committees should not be appointed by the president, even although that president was the impartial Washington, but their membership determined by ballot, which excluded favoritism on the part of the chair and secured the judgment of the States upon membership without disclosing the vote of the individual delegates; that members could not absent themselves without leave of the conference, in order that business should not be interrupted by their absence; that, to give all members an opportunity to keep in touch with the proceedings, no committee should sit while the convention itself was in session; and that, for their better information, they might indeed inspect the *Journal,* but, to secure the secrecy necessary to the success of the conference, only the members might do so, and nothing spoken in debate should be printed or published or communicated without leave.

As these standing rules and orders enabled a free and a fair exchange of views in the conference which drafted the agreement of the States, which is today the oldest existing written instrument of government, if the Constitution of Massachusetts be excluded, they are worthy of consideration for an international conference which shall draft and recommend projects to the States forming the society of nations, when the nations meet again in conference and may be inclined to provide the Society with some form of organization. It is to be borne in mind that each State is the equal in law, though not necessarily in influence, of all others represented in conference. Because of this, the rule of unanimity may be thought to be requisite, yet inasmuch as, then as now, the State is only bound by its own consent, and as the acts of the convention or conference do not of themselves bind the constituents, all questions may, in some future conference, as in the Federal Convention at Philadelphia, "be decided by the greater number of those which shall be fully represented."

Immediately after the additions to the standing rules and the rejection of the motion that a committee be appointed to superintend the minutes, which would have been wise in view of the careless manner in which they were kept by the secretary, Mr. Randolph, to quote Mr. Madison's Notes, "then opened the main business," and after expressing regret, as is the wont of public speakers, that the duty of opening proceedings should have fallen to one without greater experience,— he had been attorney general and was then governor of the State of Virginia, and destined to be attorney general and secretary of state of the United States,— he adverted to the fact that the convention, having originated from Virginia, some proposition would be expected to emanate from the delegation of that State, and that the duty

Opening of the Convention

of laying the proposition of his colleagues before the convention and of explaining its terms had devolved upon him.   In the course of what may be considered his introduction, he observed that, in revising the federal system, inquiry should be made into the properties which such a government ought to possess, the defects of the Confederation, the danger of the situation in which they found themselves, and the remedy.   On the first point he said:

> The character of such a government ought to secure 1. against foreign invasion: 2. against dissensions between members of the Union, or seditions in particular States: 3. to procure to the several States various blessings, of which an isolated situation was incapable: 4. to be able to defend itself against encroachment: & 5, to be paramount to the state constitutions.[1]

The defects of the Confederation he attributed somewhat condescendingly to " the then infancy of the science, of constitutions, & of confederacies," and to the further fact that the framers of the Articles had not then the benefit of experience, but he graciously concluded that perhaps nothing better could be obtained from the jealousy of the States with regard to their sovereignty.

Enumerating what he considered the defects of the Articles, he said:

> 1. that the confederation produced no security against foreign invasion; congress not being permitted to prevent a war nor to support it by their own authority — . . . that they could not cause infractions of treaties or of the law of nations to be punished: that particular states might by their conduct provoke war without controul; and that neither militia nor draughts being fit for defence on such occasions, enlistments only could be successful, and these could not be executed without money.
> 2. that the federal government could not check the quarrels between states, nor a rebellion in any, not having constitutional power Nor means to interpose according to the exigency.
> 3. that there were many advantages, . . . which were not attainable under the confederation — such as a productive impost — counteraction of the commercial regulations of other nations — pushing of commerce ad libitum — &c &c.
> 4. that the fœderal government could not defend itself against the encroachments from the states.
> 5. that it was not even paramount to the state constitutions, ratified as it was in many of the states.[2]

After referring to the danger of the situation and the prospect of anarchy, due to the general laxity of government, he then proceeded to point out the remedy, " the basis of which he said must be the republican principle."

It has been thought advisable to state somewhat fully Mr. Randolph's views on the first and second points of his address, in order that the reader

[1] *Documentary History,* Vol. iii, p. 15.
[2] *Ibid.,* pp. 15–16.

may, as far as possible, be in the position of his auditors, and be better able to appreciate the remedy which, Mr. Randolph was careful to say, should be of a republican nature, and which he laid before the convention with appropriate explanations, which unfortunately have not been preserved.

The Virginian or the Randolph plan, as it is indiscriminately called, consisted of fifteen resolutions. They were the basis of discussion from the day of their presentation, and are to be considered as embodying the general principles which expanded, systematized in the form of articles, form the more perfect Union of the United States and their constitution.

The first proposes that the Articles of Confederation be corrected and enlarged in the interest of " common defense, security of liberty, and general welfare."

The second, that suffrage in the National Legislature be proportioned " to the Quotas of Contribution, or to the number of free inhabitants."

The third, that the National Legislature consist of two branches.

The fourth, that " the members of the first branch of the National Legislature " be elected by the people of the several States for a term of years, that they be of a certain age, that they receive compensation for their services, and that they do not hold any office under the State or the United States incompatible with their position.

The fifth, that " the members of the second branch of the National Legislature " be elected by the first branch of the legislature from a list of nominees of the State legislatures, to hold office under approximately the same conditions as those of the first branch.

The sixth, that each branch originate legislation, that the National Legislature enjoy the rights vested in Congress by the Confederation, and such other rights for which the separate States are " incompetent," or in which the harmony of the United States is interrupted by State legislatures; that it possess in addition the right " to negative all laws passed by the several States contravening in the opinion of the National Legislature the articles of Union; and to call forth the force of the Union agst. any member of the Union failing to fulfill its duty under the articles thereof."

The seventh, that a National Executive, ineligible for a second term, chosen by the National Legislature for a term of years, be instituted, to receive a salary not subject to increase or diminution for his services, to execute the national laws and to enjoy " the Executive rights vested in Congress by the Confederation."

The eighth, that a Council of Revision of " the Executive and a convenient number of the National Judiciary " be created, with authority to examine the acts of the National and of each State Legislature and to reject them under certain contingencies.

The ninth, that a National Judiciary, consisting or one or more supreme and of inferior tribunals, be chosen by the National Legislature, composed of judges holding office during good behavior, receiving a salary not subject to increase or diminution during their term of office; that the inferior tribunals decide in first instance and the supreme tribunal in *dernier ressort* national and international questions, such as piracies and felonies committed on the high seas, captures made from an enemy, cases affecting foreigners or citizens of other States, the National revenue, impeachment of National officers, and, finally, "questions which may involve the national peace and harmony."

The tenth, that new States be admitted to the Union formed of territory within the limits of the United States, without requiring a unanimous vote in the National Legislature.

The eleventh, that a Republican government and the territory belonging to each State be guaranteed by the United States, "except in the instance of a voluntary junction of Government & territory."

The twelfth, that provision be made to continue the existing government and its obligations until "a given day after the reform of the articles of Union."

The thirteenth, that provision be made for amendment of "the Articles of Union," without requiring the assent of the National Legislature.

The fourteenth, that the officers of the several States be bound by oath to support "the articles of Union."

The fifteenth, and last, that the amendments offered to the Confederation by the convention be, with the approbation of Congress, submitted to conventions within the several States chosen by the people "to consider & decide thereon." [1]

It will be observed that Mr. Randolph's resolutions fall into four groups, based upon the theory and the practice of the separation of powers to be found, with more or less completeness, in every one of the constitutions of the thirteen States constituting the Confederation; that, leaving out the first resolution, to the effect that the Articles of Confederation should be corrected and enlarged in order to secure "the common defence, security of liberty, and general welfare," the second to the sixth, inclusive, deal with the legislative branch of government, the seventh and eighth with the executive department, the ninth with the judiciary (as did the ninth of the Articles of Confederation), and the remaining six with matters of a general nature, falling within the scope of the proposed government but of a general nature in the sense that no one of them belonged exclusively to any one of the three

The Four Groups

---

[1] *Documentary History,* Vol. iii, pp. 17–20.

branches into which the government of the more perfect Union was to be divided.

With the text of the Articles of Confederation before our eyes, it would appear that, grafting these resolutions upon the Articles was very like pouring new wine into old bottles, with the result to be expected of such a process. For the strongest advocate of the Articles of Confederation would not suggest that they provided for the threefold division of government, in the sense in which each of the States had done. The Congress under the Confederation did indeed possess the power of recommending, rather than of legislating, and the right, if not the power, in all cases of executing recommendations approved by the States, or its own acts in so far as the States did not interpose. If the Congress is to be considered as an executive, it was a numerous body, not a single person. The judicial power, in so far as it was contained in the Articles, consisted of the right to create a court for the trial of piracies and felonies committed on the high seas, which was never created, of a right to create a court of appeals in cases of capture, which was indeed created, but whose decisions depended upon the mere pleasure of the States for their enforcement; and finally, a power to call into being temporary tribunals, courts or commissions for the settlement of disputes and differences between two or more States concerning boundary, jurisdiction or any other matter of a justiciable nature.

It is true that the States under the Articles of Confederation renounced the exercise of certain rights, such as negotiating with foreign countries or concluding treaties of alliance with themselves, or going to war either with foreign countries or with one another, but there was apparently no power lodged in the Congress to make any of these rights effective.

Change of Purpose

The Convention was called by the Congress for the sole and exclusive purpose of revising the Articles of Confederation and of rendering them more effective. A strict and literal construction of this mandate would have suggested, if it did not require, the reading of the Articles as a whole, the discussion of each one of them in detail and its adoption as amended, and a vote upon the completed instrument as a whole as thus corrected and enlarged. This was not the method proposed by the Virginian plan, and a proposition to make the Articles of Confederation the basis of discussion was rejected by the Convention, which wisely preferred, in accordance with the procedure obtaining in international conferences, to invite the presentation of projects, to make one or more of them the basis of discussion, to refer, in original or amended form, those which met with approval to a drafting committee, called by the Federal Convention the Committee of Detail, to be inserted in their proper places in the treaty or convention under amendment, or to form a separate treaty or convention if the original one was displaced or if one did not exist. The result was also in accord with the practice of international conferences, from which, as a man well versed in their affairs has wittily said, we may expect anything except the procedure outlined in the program.

It is frequently stated in works of authority that the convention should have revised the Articles as its call was limited to their revision, and that failing to do so their proceedings were revolutionary. The charge was made on more than one occasion in the convention itself, but the answer then advanced was conclusive, at least it appeared so to the members; that it was proper for the convention to submit a draft of a more perfect Union which in their opinion was calculated to effect the purposes which lay behind the call of the conference, inasmuch as the labor of their hands would only be a recommendation to the Congress, and that in any event the form of government, if approved by the Congress, would be submitted to the States for their approval or rejection and would derive all its power and effect from the approval of the States. Or, as more elegantly expressed by the illustrious Washington, in speaking of the conference, that they should " raise a standard to which the wise and the honest can repair."

It will be observed that Mr. Randolph's resolutions speak of a national legislature, a national executive, a national judiciary, from which the consequence is often drawn that the framers intended to and actually did create a nation in which the States were merged and their identity lost, instead of a Union of the States, the government whereof was vested with the exercise of certain sovereign powers, expressly enumerated in the Constitution or arising by necessary implication from the grant of specific powers which the States made to the Union, renouncing at the same time, in behalf of the Union, certain sovereign powers expressly enumerated or arising from necessary implication. In the course of the proceedings, to be specific on June 20th, the term " national " in its relation to the legislature was stricken upon the motion of Oliver Ellsworth, of Connecticut, substituting " government of the United States " for " national legislature." [1] But it is believed that this amendment is immaterial, inasmuch as the term " national " was used as opposed to the federal form of government then existing, and that, in the language of the period, the term " consolidated " was employed where we of today would properly use national. The framers of the Constitution were more intent upon things than words.

We do not, however, need to resort to speculation, inasmuch as Mr. Madison has himself explained the sense in which the term " national " was to be understood in the Virginian resolutions. Thus, in a letter dated March 25, 1826, to Mr. Andrew Stevenson, a fellow Virginian, member of Con-

A Union of Free States

---

[1] Robert Yates, *Secret Proceedings and Debates of the Convention,* 1821, p. 142.

gress, later Speaker of that body and Minister to England, Mr. Madison said:

> Will you pardon me for pointing out an error of fact into which you have fallen, as others have done, by supposing that the term, *national* applied to the contemplated Government, in the early stage of the Convention, particularly in the propositions of Mr. Randolph, was equivalent to *unlimited* or consolidated. This was not the case. The term was used, not in contradistinction to a limited, but to a *federal* Government. As the latter operated within the extent of its authority thro' requisitions on the Confederated States, and rested on the sanction of State Legislatures, the Government to take its place, was to operate within the extent of its powers directly & coercively on individuals, and to receive the higher sanction of the people of the States. And there being no technical or appropriate denomination applicable to the new and unique System, the term national was used, with a confidence that it would not be taken in a wrong sense, especially as a right one could be readily suggested if not sufficiently implied by some of the propositions themselves. Certain it is that not more than two or three members of the Body and they rather theoretically than practically, were in favor of an unlimited Govt. founded on a consolidation of the States; and that neither Mr. Randolph, nor any one of his colleagues was of the number. His propositions were the result of a meeting of the whole Deputation, and concurred or acquiesced in unanimously, merely as a general introduction of the business; such as might be expected from the part Virginia had in bringing about the Convention, and as might be detailed, and defined in the progress of the work. The Journal shews that this was done.[1]

Again he wrote, in a letter dated December 26, 1826, addressed to Thomas Cooper:

> With respect to the term "National" as contradistinguished from the term "federal," it was not meant to express the *extent* of power, but the *mode* of *its operation,* which was to be not like the power of the old Confederation operating on *States;* but like that of ordinary Governments operating on individuals; & the substitution of "United States" for "National" noted in the journal, was not designed to change the meaning of the latter, but to guard agt. a mistake or misrepresentation of what was intended. The term "National" was used in the original propositions offered on the part of the Virga. Deputies, not one of whom attached to it any other meaning than that here explained. Mr. Randolph himself the organ of the Deputation, on the occasion, was a strenuous advocate for the federal quality of limited & specified powers; & finally refused to sign the constitution because its powers were not sufficiently limited & defined.[2]

And in a letter written in December, 1831, to Mr. N. P. Trist, Mr. Madison recurred to this question and thus elaborated his views:

> The whole course of proceedings on those Resolutions ought to have satisfied him [one Col. Taylor, whose views Madison was combating] that the term *National* as contradistinguished from *Federal,* was not meant to express

[1] *Documentary History,* Vol. v, pp. 332–3.
[2] *Ibid.,* p. 339.

more than that the powers to be vested in the new Gov[t]. were to operate as in a Nat[l]. Gov[t]. directly on the people, & not as in the Old Confed[cy]. on the States only.   The extent of the powers to be vested, also tho' expressed in loose terms, evidently had reference to limitations & definitions, to be made in the progress of the work, distinguishing it from a plenary & Consolidated Gov[t].

It ought to have occurred that the Gov[t]. of the U. S being a novelty & a compound, had no technical terms or phrases appropriate to it; and that old terms were to be used in new senses, explained by the context or by the facts of the case.

Some exulting inferences have been drawn from the change noted in the Journal of the Convention, of the word *National* into *"United States."* The change may be accounted for by a desire to avoid a misconception of the former, the latter being preferred as a familiar caption. That the change could have no effect on the real character of the Gov[t]. was & is obvious; this being necessarily deduced from the actual structure of the Gov[t]. and the quantum of its powers.[1]

The convention, it appears, met for the second time on May 29th at ten o'clock,— at least it had adjourned to that hour.   Some time was taken up by the discussion of amendments to the standing rules.   Mr. Randolph's address, opening "the main business," must have been an elaborate one, and his comments upon his fifteen resolutions "which he explained one by one," must have consumed much time; and the House must have been ready to adjourn at the conclusion of his remarks, for immediately thereafter it was resolved, to quote Mr. Madison's Notes, "That the House will tomorrow resolve itself into a Committee of the whole House to consider of the state of the American Union — and that the propositions moved by M[r]. Randolph be referred to the said Committee." [2]   It appears, however, from the entry immediately following in Mr. Madison's Notes, that "Mr. Charles Pinckney **Other** laid before the House the draft of a federal Government which he had pre- **"Plans"** pared, to be agreed upon between the free and independent States of America." Probably due to the lateness of the hour, Mr. Pinckney contented himself with laying his plan before the convention, accompanying it with some few remarks instead of by an elaborate speech, as Mr. Madison does not give a summary of an address.   It is said in *The Secret Proceedings of the Federal Convention,* consisting of notes made by Robert Yates, a delegate from New York, while he remained in attendance after an account of the Randolph resolutions, that "Mr. C. Pinckney, a member from South Carolina, then added, that he had reduced his ideas of a new government to a system, which he read, and confessed it was grounded on the same principle as of the above resolutions." [3]   Mr. Pinckney's plan, of which the text is not contained in any contemporary account, was likewise referred to the Committee of the Whole, and the Convention adjourned for the day.

At a later period a plan was laid before the convention by Mr. Patter-

[1] *Ibid.,* pp. 377–8.   [2] *Ibid.,* Vol. iii, p. 14.
                        [3] Yates, *Secret Proceedings,* p. 97.

son of New Jersey, and called indifferently the Patterson or the New Jersey plan. This proposed a revision of the Articles of Confederation in accordance with the recommendation of Congress, but it did not meet with favor and was, after discussion and debate, rejected in favor of Mr. Randolph's resolutions, although, as will appear, it had a decided influence on the course of proceedings, and was referred, with the Randolph resolutions, as amended and enlarged, and with Mr. Pinckney's plan, to the Committee of Detail to prepare a draft of the Constitution.

These were the only plans laid before the convention at any time, although Alexander Hamilton felt called upon, as did Mr. Pinckney, to express his personal views to the convention. They were, in the language of the day, "high toned," that is to say, they looked to a consolidated form of government, consisting of a threefold distribution of powers, in which the States were allowed to exist but reduced practically to the level of provinces, in which the executive was to hold office during good behavior, and, among other powers, was to appoint governors of the States, to hold office during his pleasure. This project fell flat, meeting, as far as known, only with the approval of George Read of Delaware, and its distinguished author did not feel encouraged to present a draft of a constitution in accordance with his views, although he did hand one to Mr. Madison at a much later period before the adjournment of the Convention. It was not laid before the Committee of Detail and, so far as known, Mr. Hamilton's views had no influence with that committee or in the convention, although his influence later brought about the ratification of the Constitution by the State of New York.[1] To secure this object and to turn the tide of public opinion in favor of the Constitution, he proposed and, with the large cooperation of James Madison and some help from Mr. Jay, wrote and published in the press a series of some eighty-six articles which, known in their collected form as *The Federalist,* are universally regarded as the classic exposition of the Constitution.

National v. Federal Government

Before passing to a consideration of the main subdivisions of Mr. Randolph's resolutions, it is advisable to call attention to Mr. Madison's distinction between a national government, on the one hand, operating upon individuals, and a purely federal government on the other hand, operating upon States, a distinction which arose early in the course of debate. It did not appear clearly in the text of Mr. Randolph's resolutions, although it may have been in the minds of the Virginia members who stood sponsor for the plan. In any event, the national legislature was empowered by the sixth reso-

[1] In his *Memoirs,* under date of November 19, 1818, John Quincy Adams records Major William Jackson, of Philadelphia, who had called upon him, as saying, "He told me how he had been chosen Secretary to the Convention . . . and said that by far the most efficient member of the Convention was Mr. Madison; that Mr. Hamilton took no active part in it, and made only one remarkable speech." *The Records of the Federal Convention,* Max Farrand, Editor. Vol. III (1911), p. 426.

lution " to call forth the force of the Union ag^{st}. any member of the Union failing to fulfil its duty under the articles thereof." [1]   On the very next day Mr. Mason observed, as reported by Mr. Madison, "that the present confederation was not only deficient in not providing for coercion & punishment ag^{st}. delinquent States; but argued very cogently that punishment could not in the nature of things be executed on the States collectively, and therefore that such a Gov^t. was necessary as could directly operate on individuals, and would punish those only whose guilt required it." [2]   The day following, when this clause of the sixth resolution came up for consideration, Mr. Madison himself observed, as stated in his Notes, " that the more he reflected on the use of force, the more he doubted, the practicability, the justice and the efficacy of it when applied to people collectively and not individually.— A union of the States containing such an ingredient seemed to provide for its own destruction.   The use of force ag^{st}. a State, would look more like a declaration of war, than an infliction of punishment, and would probably be considered by the party attacked as a dissolution of all previous compacts by which it might be bound.   He hoped that such a system would be framed as might render this recourse unnecessary, and moved that the clause be postponed,"— a motion which was " agreed to nem. con." [3]

Coercion of States

There was no opposition to the general plan, as the States were familiar with the threefold division of power and their delegates were apparently willing to provide the Union with a government of this kind.   Indeed, the threefold division seemed to disarm opposition and to lead the delegates to invest the government with greater power than would otherwise have been the case, and Mr. Madison quotes Mr. Butler of South Carolina as saying, in the session of May 30, 1787, on the very threshold of the debates, " that he had opposed the grant of powers to Cong^s. heretofore, because the whole power was vested in one body.   The proposed distribution of the powers into different bodies changed the case, and would induce him to go great lengths." [4]

Enumeration of General Powers

In a constitution meant to endure,— and the delegates of the Federal Convention hoped they were doing no vain thing,— it was impossible to foresee every contingency and to provide against it by a specific enumeration of powers.   The convention therefore wisely contented itself with the enumeration of what may be called general powers which a government adequate to the exigencies of the Union should possess, powers which could be better exercised by the Union of the States than by any one State.   Too long to quote, it is difficult to summarize these powers, inasmuch as the

[1] *Documentary History*, Vol. iii, p. 18.
[2] *Ibid.*, p. 22.
[3] *Ibid.*, pp. 33–4.
[4] *Ibid.*, p. 21.

language of the Constitution is so familiar as at times to defy paraphrase and so concise as to make a summary seem longer than the original. Without attempting the impossible, it may be observed that the great defect of the Articles of Confederation was met and overcome by empowering the Congress " to lay and collect taxes, duties and imposts," with the wise and indeed necessary proviso that they should be uniform throughout the United States. This would enable the more perfect Union to pay the debts already contracted and those which should be incurred in the future, and to do what the League of Friendship under the Articles of Confederation had never been able to do, namely, to " provide for the common defence and general welfare of the United States." It was foreseen that the government of the Union might need to borrow money, therefore it was specifically authorized to do this.

The second great defect of the Articles was the chaotic condition of commerce and the inability of the Confederation to regulate it. All attempts to amend the Articles in this sense had failed, but they were not fruitless, inasmuch as the Annapolis Convention called for this purpose brought about the Federal Convention of 1787, which accomplished it. Hence the Congress was given power to regulate commerce with foreign nations, the several States, and the Indian tribes.

The Confederation was, according to its critics, largely a bankrupt concern. It therefore had very special reasons to recognize the need of uniform laws on the subject and invested Congress with the power to make them. It was necessary to have money, therefore Congress was empowered to coin money, to regulate its value and that of foreign coin, and in the interest of trade and commerce to fix the standard of weights and measures. And to make these clauses effective, the Congress was authorized to punish counterfeiting of the securities and current coin of the United States. Allied with this phase of the subject, although not necessarily connected with it, was the progress of science and useful arts, therefore the Congress was given authority to make laws securing to authors and inventors copyrights and patents for " their respective writings and discoveries."

As it was recognized that a vast Union could not be held together for any length of time without means of communication, the Congress was authorized to establish post offices and post roads. Vast indeed the territory was, although but a fraction of that now subject to the laws of the Union. It was sparsely settled, but it was anticipated that large numbers of persons would forsake the old to find fortune and happiness in the new world. Accordingly the Congress was given the power " to establish an uniform Rule of Naturalization " that the new might enjoy the rights of the old.

The government was to be one of laws, not of men, therefore there was to be a Supreme Court which would interpret the laws and apply them to the concrete cases as they arose between States as well as their citizens, and likewise inferior tribunals. But the law was not merely to be the law of the States or of the Union; it was to be a law of the seas as well, and the Congress was given the power to punish piracies and felonies committed on the high seas beyond the jurisdiction of the States and of the United States. Wisely the Congress was vested with the power to define and punish "offences against the Law of Nations," a mere clause, yet introducing the whole body of international law, making it a part of the Constitution of the United States and of each State of the Union, for every citizen and inhabitant thereof. The Law of Nations of that day recognized letters of marque and reprisal, as it still does captures on land and water. Congress could therefore have enacted laws on these subjects without a specific authorization, yet the experience of the Confederation doubtless suggested the advisability of specific mention. They were then and are now incident to war, and on this point the framers of the Constitution, intent upon a government of laws not of men, were unwilling to trust any person to declare war, even the august president of the convention, General Washington himself, already designated in the minds and hearts of his countrymen to be the first of a line of presidents of the Union. Therefore only the Congress was to declare war, a body whose lower house was composed of representatives of the people of each State chosen by the people themselves divided into districts, and whose upper house was composed of two representatives from all States, large and small, representing the States. Representatives of the people and of the States do indeed declare war upon occasion, but not as easily and readily as members of a family owing their position and prestige to war and too often anxious to perpetuate them by the same means.

The Congress has so far been given the power to raise, borrow, and coin money, to regulate commerce, to establish means of communication, and to protect what may be called intellectual property, to establish inferior tribunals to administer within the States, to accept jurisdiction and punish violations of the Law of Nations, and to declare war. Consequently the Congress was vested with the powers incidental to the declaration of war, the power to raise and support land and naval forces and to make rules for their government. The war of course was to be carried on by the United States, not by any one of the States, inasmuch as each had by the Constitution renounced the right to wage war unless attacked. The president was indeed to be Commander-in-Chief of the army and navy, but Congress was to raise and support the armies, to provide and maintain a navy, and to make the rules of their government, as well as to declare war. And

International Law in the Constitution

to make the rights of Congress secure in the premises, no appropriation of money for these purposes was to be for "a longer Term than two Years." War was thus to be declared by civilians, armies and navies were to be raised and supported by civilians, the rules for their government were to be made by civilians, the army and navy in the war were to be commanded by a civilian, to the end that this may be a government of laws and not of men.

Government of Laws and Not of Men

While the States as such were not to wage war, it was clearly understood that they might have need of an armed force to protect them and their peoples, therefore each was to have a militia to be raised and officered by them, to be commanded by them in times of peace, but in time of war to be called into the service of the States as a whole instead of the individual States. Therefore the Congress was given the power to call forth "the Militia to execute the Laws of the Union, suppress Insurrections and repel Invasions." Because of this eventual service, the Congress was authorized to provide for "organizing, arming, and disciplining, the Militia, and for governing" the part of it taken into the service of the Union, the States reserving, however, the appointment of officers and the right of training the militia according to the discipline prescribed by Congress.

Seat of Government

Thus far we have a government without a habitat, for the Union was a Union of the States, and the territory to the west of the States belonged to the States. There was not a foot of American soil belonging to the Union as such. In this Union the States were to be equals. There was to be no *primus inter pares*. No State was to be vested with any prerogative, privilege or function not possessed by all. Therefore the Congress was authorized to accept and exercise exclusive jurisdiction within a district not exceeding ten miles square as particular States might cede, to become "the Seat of the Government of the United States," and the Congress was similarly authorized to exercise a like authority "over all places purchased by the Consent of the Legislature of the State in which the Same shall be, for the Erection of Forts, Magazines, Arsenals, dock-Yards, and other needful Buildings."

Government of Limited Powers

This was indeed a government of limited powers and limited extent, the seat of government itself ten miles square, to be ceded by the States if they should choose to do so, and any property acquired within the States to be purchased by the Congress with the consent of the legislature of the State involved. The enumeration of these powers necessarily carried with it the right to make such laws as should be necessary and proper to carry them into execution, but it was well to say so in order to remove doubt or misunderstanding, as also to authorize the Congress, as was done by the final paragraph of the eighth section of the first article, to carry into execution "all other Powers vested by this Constitution in the Government of the United States, or in any Department or Officer thereof."

VIII

CREATION OF THE FEDERAL LEGISLATURE

All states have three elements, and the good law-giver has to regard what is expedient for each state. When they are well-ordered, the state is well-ordered, and as they differ from one another, constitutions differ. What is the element first (1) which deliberates about public affairs; secondly (2) which is concerned with the magistrates and determines what they should be, over whom they should exercise authority, and what should be the mode of electing them; and thirdly (3) which has judicial power? (*The Politics of Aristotle, English translation by Benjamin Jowett, 1885, Vol. I, Book IV, Ch. 14, p. 133.*)

They saw that to live by one man's will became the cause of all men's misery. This constrained them to come unto laws, wherein all men might see their duties beforehand, and know the penalties of transgressing them. (*Richard Hooker, Of the Laws of Ecclesiastical Polity, 1594, Church edition, 1868, Book I, Section 10, p. 56.*)

The government of the United States has been emphatically termed a government of laws, and not of men. It will certainly cease to deserve this high appellation, if the laws furnish no remedy for the violation of a vested legal right. (*Mr. Chief Justice Marshall in Marbury v. Madison, 1 Cranch 137, 163, decided in 1803.*)

Relation being had to these two times, Government (to define it *de jure,* or according to antient Prudence) is an Art whereby a Civil Society of Men is instituted and preserv'd upon the Foundation of common Right or Interest; or (to follow Aristotle and Livy) It is the Empire of Laws, and not of Men.

And Government (to define it *de facto,* or according to modern Prudence) is an Art whereby some man, or some few men, subject a City or a Nation, and rule it according to his or their private Interest: which, because the Laws in such cases are made according to the interest of a man, or of some few Families, may be said to be the Empire of Men, and not of Laws. (*James Harrington, The Common-wealth of Oceana, 1656, Toland edition, 1737, Part I, The Preliminaries, Shewing the Principles of Government, p. 37.*)

But it is plain that where the Law is made by one Man, there it may be unmade by one man; so that the Man is not govern'd by the Law, but the Law by the Man; which amounts to the Government of the Man, and not of the Law: Whereas the Law being not to be made but by the Many, no man is govern'd by another man, but by that only which is the common interest; by which means this amounts to a Government of Laws, and not of Men. (*James Harrington, The Art of Law-giving, 1659, Toland edition, 1737, Preface, p. 386.*)

Where the People are not over-balanc'd by one Man, or by the Few, they are not capable of any other Superstructures of Government, or of any other just and quiet settlement whatsoever, than of such only as consists of a Senate as their Counsillors, of themselves or their Representatives as Sovereign Lords, and of a Magistracy answerable to the People, as distributers and executioners of the Laws made by the People. And thus much is of absolute necessity to any or every Government, that is or can be properly call'd a Common-wealth, whether it be well or ill order'd.

But the necessary definition of a Common-wealth, any thing well order'd, is, That it is a Government consisting of the Senate proposing, the People resolving, and the Magistracy executing.

Magistracy is a stile proper to the executive part: yet because in a Discourse of this kind it is hardly avoidable, but that such as are of the proposing or resolving Assemblies, will be sometimes compriz'd under this name or stile, it shall be enough for excuse to say, that Magistracy may be esteem'd of two kinds; the one proper or Executive, the other improper or Legislative. (*James Harrington, The Art of Law-giving, 1659, Toland edition, 1737, Ch. VI, p. 393.*)

Thirdly. I know what is said by the several admirers of *monarchy, aristocracy* and *democracy,* which are the rule of one, a few, and many, and are the three common ideas of government, when men discourse on the subject. But I chuse to solve the controversy with this small distinction, and it belongs to all three: *Any government is free to the people under it* (whatever be the frame) *where the laws rule, and the people are a party to those laws,* and more than this is tyranny, oligarchy, or confusion. (*William Penn's Preface to the Frame of Government of Pennsylvania, 1682, Ben. Perley Poore, The Federal and State Constitutions, Colonial Charters, and other Organic Laws of the United States, Part II, 1877, p. 1519.*)

The great end of Mens entring into Society, being the Enjoyment of their Properties in Peace and Safety, and the great instrument and means of that being the Laws establish'd in that Society; the *first and fundamental positive Law* of all Commonwealths, *is the establishing of the Legislative* Power; as the *first and fundamental natural Law,* which is to govern even the Legislative itself, *is the preservation of the Society,* and (as far as will consist with the publick good) of every person in it. (*John Locke, Two Treatises of Government, 1690, Book II, Ch. XI, section 134, Works, Edition of 1714, Vol. II.*)

The *Supream Power cannot take* from any Man any part of his *Property* without his own Consent. . . . This is not much to be fear'd in Governments where the *Legislative* consists, wholly or in part, in Assemblies which are variable, whose Members upon the dissolution of the Assembly, are Subjects under the common Laws of their Country, equally with the rest. (*John Locke, Two Treatises of Government, 1690, Book II, Ch. XI, section 138, Works, Edition of 1714, Vol. II.*)

When the legislative and executive powers are united in the same person, or in the same body of magistrates, there can be no liberty; because apprehensions may arise, lest the same monarch or senate should enact tyrannical laws, to execute them in a tyrannical manner.

Again there is no liberty, if the power of judging be not separated from the legislative and executive powers. Were it joined with the legislative, the life and liberty of the subject would be exposed to arbitrary controul; for the judge would then be the legislator. Were it joined to the executive power, the judge might behave with all the violence of an oppressor.

There would be an end of every thing, were the same man, or the same body, whether of the nobles or of the people, to exercise those three powers, that of enacting laws, and that of executing the public resolutions, and that of judging the crimes or differences of individuals. (*M. de Montesquieu, L'Esprit des Lois, 2 Vols., 1748, English translation of 1756, Vol. I, Book XI, Chap. VI, p. 165.*)

In the government of this commonwealth, the legislative department shall never exercise the executive and judicial powers, or either of them; the executive shall never exercise the legislative and judicial powers, or either of them; the judicial shall never exercise the legislative and executive powers, or either of them; to the end it may be a government of laws, and not of men. (*Declaration of Rights of the Inhabitants of the Commonwealth of Massachusetts, 1780, Ben: Perley Poore, The Federal and State Constitutions, Colonial Charters, and other Organic Laws of the United States, Part I, 1877, p. 960, Article XXX.*)

"Sir," said Rufus Choate, in the Massachusetts Convention of 1853, for revising the Constitution of the State (1 Debates, 120), "that same Bill of Rights, which so solicitously separates executive, judicial, and legislative powers from each other, 'to the end,'— in the fine and noble expression of Harrington, borrowed from the 'ancient prudence,' one of those historical phrases of the old glorious school of liberty of which this Bill of Rights is so full,— and which phrases I entreat the good taste of my accomplished friends in my eye, to whom it is committed, to spare in their very rust, as they would spare the general English of the Bible,—'to the end it may be a government of laws, and not of men'; that same Bill of Rights separates the people, with the same solicitude, and for the same reason, from every part of their actual government,—'to the end it may be a government of laws and not of men.'" (*James Bradley Thayer, Cases on Constitutional Law, 1895, Vol. I, foot-note, pp. 384–385.*)

The idea of an actual representation of all classes of the people by persons of each class is altogether visionary. Unless it were expressly provided in the Constitution that each different occupation should send one or more members, the thing would never take place in practice. (*Alexander Hamilton, The Federalist, No. 35 [33], 1788, Ford, Editor, 1898, p. 216.*)

The door ought to be equally open to all, (*Alexander Hamilton, The Federalist, No. 36 [34], 1788, Ford, Editor, 1898, p. 220.*)

The system of representation which grew up in the early colonies under no legal authority of the English crown (with the exception of Maryland, where it was only authorized and not directed), came to be recognized and ratified by subsequent charters. It was ratified in Connecticut by the charter of 1662; in Rhode Island by the charter of 1663, and later in Massachusetts by the charter of 1692. In the colonies established after the Restoration in 1660 it became usual for the English king to grant to the proprietor permission to give to the freemen the right to a share in legislation, either in person or by deputies. It thus seems evident that the representative system in America had its origin in the peculiar circumstances in which the early colonies were placed. It was the product of the practical instinct of the Teutonic race, which had given birth to a form of representation even before the time of Henry III. or Edward I. It was not established by any charter of the English king, and did not receive a chartered sanction until it had become an established institution in the colonies. It had its own peculiar features in America, which were evidently not patterned after any existing model. It was rather a reversion to an earlier type than a reproduction of an existing one; and was, in fact, more truly representative of the whole body of the people than was the contemporary English House of Commons. (*William C. Morey, The First State Constitutions, Annals of the American Academy of Political and Social Science, 1893, Vol. 4, p. 210.*)

The enlargement of population must always be attended either by the decay of democratic institutions, or else by the adoption of some form of representation. The special form which representation will assume in any people, which possesses the political sagacity to solve the problems growing out of its own social life, will be determined by the circumstances of time and place. It will be seen that the form of representation which grew up in the American colonies was not a reproduction of the elaborate and comparatively mature system which then existed in England, but was the outgrowth of the simple life of the colonists themselves, and was moreover marked by those inchoate features which distinguish a primitive from a well-developed institution. The need of representation was felt by the colonists as soon as their population became scattered and unable to meet in a single assembly. The system arose from the requirements of the colonists themselves, and was fully established before it was recognized by the English crown. (*William C. Morey, The First State Constitutions, Annals of the American Academy of Political and Social Science, 1893, Vol. 4, p. 205.*)

A federal state requires for its formation two conditions.

There must exist, in the first place, a body of countries such as the Cantons of Switzerland, the Colonies of America, or the Provinces of Canada, so closely connected by locality, by history, by race, or the like, as to be capable of bearing, in the eyes of their inhabitants, an impress of common nationality. . . .

A second condition absolutely essential to the founding of a federal system is the existence of a very peculiar state of sentiment among the inhabitants of the countries which it is proposed to unite. They must desire union, and must not desire unity. (*Albert Venn Dicey, Introduction to the Study of the Law of the Constitution, 1885, 8th edition, 1915, pp. 136-7.*)

A federal state is a political contrivance intended to reconcile national unity and power with the maintenance of " state rights." The end aimed at fixes the essential character of federalism. For the method by which Federalism attempts to reconcile the apparently inconsistent claims of national sovereignty and of state sovereignty consists of the formation of a Constitution under which the ordinary powers of sovereignty are elaborately divided between the common or national government and the separate states. The details of this division vary under every different federal constitution, but the general principle on which it should rest is obvious. Whatever concerns the nation as a whole should be placed under the control of the national government. All matters which are not primarily of common interest should remain in the hands of the several States. . . .

From the notion that national unity can be reconciled with state independence by a division of powers under a common constitution between the nation on the one hand and the individual States on the other, flow the three leading characteristics of completely developed federalism,— the supremacy of the constitution — the distribution among bodies with limited and co-ordinate authority of the different powers of government — the authority of the Courts to act as interpreters of the constitution. (*Albert Venn Dicey, Introduction to the Study of the Law of the Constitution, 1885, 8th edition, 1915, pp. 139-140.*)

CHAPTER VIII

CREATION OF THE FEDERAL LEGISLATURE

The
Spirit of
Compromise
IN Mr. Randolph's resolutions the legislative power precedes the executive and the judiciary, and therefore was the first to be taken up; and the
very first resolution of the group dealing with legislative power raised the
issues which divided the delegates of the large and the small States into
hostile camps. But the difference was adjusted by a concession of the extreme views of each, resulting in a compromise which made the Constitution a possibility; and indeed it may be stated in this connection, as it will
be illustrated in the course of this narrative, that agreement was only possible on that principle of give and take obtaining in international conferences, and that the Constitution itself is the very creature of compromise and
concession. The necessary spirit of concession was perhaps best stated by
Mr. John Langdon of New Hampshire, whom, apropos of the Militia clause
in the proposed Constitution, Mr. Madison reports as follows:

> M[r]. Langdon said He could not understand the jealousy expressed by some
> Gentleman. The General & State Gov[ts]. were not enemies to each other, but
> different institutions for the good of the people of America. As one of the
> people he could say, the National Gov[t]. is mine, the State Gov[t]. is mine —
> In transferring power from one to the other — I only take out of my left
> hand what it cannot so well use, and put it into my right hand where it can
> be better used.[1]

The Two
Branches
of the
Legislature
The plan provided for a national legislature of two houses, the first and
the second, which, in the completed instrument appear as the Congress, consisting of a House of Representatives and a Senate, the first representing
the people of the States according to their population, the second the States
or the people within the States, and in which each is represented by two
Senators, voting as individuals, not as delegates casting their vote under direct
and specific instructions of the State or the citizens thereof. There was
practically no objection to the bicameral system, although Pennsylvania, apparently influenced by Dr. Franklin's preference for a single chamber, proposed it, only to have it rejected.[2]

Nor was there any great opposition to the powers with which each of

---

[1] *Documentary History of the Constitution,* Vol. iii, p. 597.
[2] "The 3d Resolution 'that the national Legislature ought to consist of two branches'
was agreed to without debate or dissent, except that of Pennsylvania, given probably from
complaisance to Doc[r]. Franklin who was understood to be partial to a single House of Legislation." *Ibid.,* p. 26.

these branches was to be vested. These were indeed important matters, but they were rather questions of detail, after agreement upon the principle, and until that principle was accepted, a Constitution of the kind proposed by the Virginian plan was impossible. This principle was that the first branch should not merely be elected by the people of the several States but that the right of suffrage in the national legislature ought "to be proportioned to the quotas of contribution or to the number of free inhabitants." It was provided in the fifth resolution that the members of the second branch "ought to be elected by those of the first, out of a proper number of persons nominated by the individual Legislatures." [1]

There was little or no opposition to the election of the first branch by the people of each and every State, and after no great discussion Mr. Dickinson's motion was accepted on June 7th,[2] that the members of the second branch should be elected by the legislatures of the respective States, thus providing the basis for the compromise that the first branch should represent the people of the States as such, the second branch the States. The instructions of the State of Delaware, however, blocked the way, for although they did not prevent a double chamber, if the convention should think such a system desirable, they forbade the delegates of that State from accepting a system in which the States should not have an equal vote. This opposition was brought to a head by Mr. Madison, who moved, on May 30th, the first session in which the plan was discussed, "that the equality of suffrage established by the articles of Confederation ought not to prevail in the National legislature, and that an equitable ratio of representation ought to be substituted." [3]

It does not need to be recalled that Mr. Madison represented the large State of Virginia. In view of the discussion of the matter of equality between members of that delegation and of Pennsylvania before the opening of the convention, it was to be expected that Mr. Madison would be seconded by a member of that delegation, and it was, very appropriately by Gouverneur Morris, who had raised the question. Mr. Madison, commenting upon his motion, says that it was "generally relished" and that it "would have been agreed to; when,

Questions of Representation

> Mr. Reed moved that the whole clause relating to the point of Representation be postponed; reminding the Com^e. that the deputies from Delaware were restrained by their comission from assenting to any change of the rule of suffrage, and in case such a change should be fixed on, it might become their duty to retire from the Convention.[4]

[1] *Documentary History,* Vol. iii, p. 17.
[2] *Ibid.,* p. 87.
[3] *Ibid.,* p. 24.
[4] *Ibid.*

After some observations of a general nature, Mr. Read's motion to postpone prevailed, it being understood, according to Mr. Madison, that at most the State of Delaware would withdraw if this provision of the Virginian plan were agreed to.

Large and
Small States

It is to be feared that Mr. Madison, as a representative of the large States, was oversanguine in this, as the experience of the convention, as well as of other international conferences, shows that, although little States may not carry their points against the large ones, they can by uniting their forces nevertheless prevent the larger States from working their will to the detriment of the smaller.

It is not material to the present purpose to state in detail the arguments advanced by the delegates of the larger States in support of proportional representation, or to describe the generous sentiments in which they abounded, and the expressions of belief on their part that the rights of the smaller States would be sufficiently safeguarded by such an arrangement. Nor is it material to summarize the views of the small States, insisting upon an equality of right arising from the fact that they were States and from their suffering in a common cause, in which they had contributed their mite, in any case their all. Mr. Madison himself, in an elaborate argument on June 19th, stated it all in a nut-shell when he said that " The great difficulty lies in the affair of Representation; and if this could be adjusted, all others would be surmountable. It was admitted by both the gentlemen from N. Jersey (Mr. Brearly and Mr. Patterson) that it would not be *just to allow Virg*ᵃ. which was 16 times as large as Delaware an equal vote only. Their language was that it would not be *safe for Delaware* to allow Virgᵃ. 16 times as many votes. The expedient proposed by them was that all the States should be thrown into one mass and a new partition be made into 13 equal parts." [1]

The fear of the small States to be absorbed into the larger or deprived of their influence, and the unwillingness of the large States to be reduced to an equality, as proposed by the small " fry," led to a readjustment of the views of both, and it is desirable to consider the steps by which this compromise was reached. The dissatisfaction of the delegates of the smaller States with the national plan was evident from the moment of its introduction, but, as in international conferences, they allowed themselves to be rushed along until, after conference among themselves, they might hit upon a plan of their own, which would unite them in opposition to the resolutions sought to be imposed upon them. In this particular case there was a reason for delay not ordinarily present in international conferences, in that the delegates of all the States had not appeared, including some from the lesser

---

[1] *Documentary History,* Vol. iii, pp. 160–1.

States who could be counted upon.   Two States were not represented at all in the earlier sessions, and it was felt that, if New Hampshire and Rhode Island should appear, they could, as small States, be relied upon as members of the opposition.   It was bruited abroad that New Hampshire would be rep-resented.   On June 27th its delegates were appointed, although they attended for the first time nearly a month later, on July 23d.   So certain were the small States of New Hampshire, that, during the session of June 30th, in the heat of debate on the question of equality, Mr. Brearly of New Jersey moved, according to Mr. Madison, " that the Presid^t. write to the Executive of N. Hamshire, informing it that the business depending before the Convention was of such a nature as to require the immediate attendance of the deputies of that State.   In support of his motion he observed that the difficulties of the subject and the diversity of opinions called for all the assistance we could possibly obtain." [1]   This apparently was the reason advanced by Mr. Brearly.   The reason undoubtedly uppermost in his mind is thus added by Mr. Madison in parenthesis by way of comment:

> It was well understood that the object was to add N. Hamshire to the n^o. of States opposed to the doctrine of proportional representation, which it was presumed from her relative size she must be adverse to.

Mr. Patterson of New Jersey, the proposer of the small State plan, seconded the motion.   Mr. Rutledge of South Carolina, which ranged itself with the large States, " could see neither the necessity nor propriety of such a measure.   They are not unapprized of the meeting, and can attend if they choose.   Rho. Island might as well be urged to appoint & send deputies.   Are we to suspend the business until the deputies arrive? if we proceed he hoped all the great points would be adjusted before the letter could produce its effect."   Mr. King, then of Massachusetts and later of New York, Senator of that State, Minister to England and candidate of the Federalist party for President, said " he had written more than once as a private correspondent, & the answers gave him every reason to expect that State would be represented very shortly, if it sh^d. be so at all.   Circumstances of a personal nature had hitherto prevented it.   A letter c^d. have no effect."   Mr. Wilson of Pennsylvania, likewise one of the large States, " wished to know whether it would be consistent with the rule or reason of secrecy, to communicate to N. Hampshire that the business was of such a nature as the motion described.   It w^d. spread a great alarm.   Besides he doubted the propriety of soliciting any State on the subject; the meeting being merely voluntary."

Admitting that these reasons were well taken, it is to be observed that

[1] *Documentary History,* Vol. iii, p. 247.

the motion was made by a delegate of the State of New Jersey and seconded by a delegate of that State, and that all objections to the proposed course of action were made by delegates of the larger States, who hoped, as Mr. Rutledge bluntly put it, that "all the great points would be adjusted before the letter could produce its effect." Rhode Island, which undoubtedly would have voted with the smaller States, was not represented, and on June 11th, Abraham Baldwin of Georgia, which State usually voted with the larger ones, arrived. And it is worth while mentioning that he was a native of Connecticut, as was Oliver Ellsworth, a member of the convention from that State, who preferred to call it a middle rather than a small State. It is also noteworthy that Luther Martin of Maryland was, like Mr. Ellsworth, a graduate of Princeton College, and that both were partisans of equality. For whatever reason, Mr. Baldwin's vote on July 2d in favor of equality neutralized the vote of his colleague against it.[1] With Georgia thus eliminated as a State, since it voted neither in favor of nor against equality, the convention divided, five States for and five States against, which fact inclined the minds of the large States to compromise.

Other members had privately done as Mr. King said he had done, and on the 9th of June, when Luther Martin, the champion of equality, took his seat, Mr. Brearly, Chief Justice of New Jersey, wrote to Jonathan Dayton, urging his presence, saying that "We have been in a Committee of the Whole for some time, and have under consideration a number of very *important* propositions, none of which, however, have as yet been reported. My colleagues, as well as myself, are very desirous that you should join us immediately. The importance of the business really demands it." And it did.[2]

On the 13th the Committee of the Whole reported the Randolph plan, amending and expanding the original fifteen to nineteen articles. The convention was ready to take them up and would doubtless have done so on the morrow had not the smaller States then felt themselves sufficiently strong to take the initiative. Therefore, when the convention met on June 14, 1787, Mr. Patterson of New Jersey, to quote Mr. Madison's Notes, observed

---

[1] "It was Georgia that had changed. Her vote, hitherto regularly given to the majority, was this time divided. It was, in fact, one man only that had changed, and that man was Abraham Baldwin, a native of Connecticut, a graduate and sometime tutor of Yale, and but recently become a citizen of the state which he now sat for. The facts countenance a conjecture that the personal influence of the three leading men of his native state may have helped to turn him; but he may also have felt, as Georgia was the last state to vote, and had but two representatives, that he and his colleague had to decide whether the convention should continue in existence. He had said that he thought the second branch ought to be an aristocratic body, and his votes, both before and after this particular division, show that he was favorable to the national view. The chances are that to save the convention he had for the time being sacrificed his own opinions." W. G. Brown, *The Life of Oliver Ellsworth,* p. 144.

[2] J. F. Jameson, Studies in the History of the Federal Convention, in the *Annual Report of the American Historical Association* for 1902, p. 98.

" that it was the wish of several deputations, particularly that of N. Jersey, that further time might be allowed them to contemplate the plan reported from the Committee of the Whole, and to digest one purely federal, and contra-distinguished from the reported plan. He said they hoped to have such an one ready by tomorrow to be laid before the Convention: and the Convention adjourned that leisure might be given for the purpose." [1] Mr. Madison in later years added a comment to his notes, stating that " The eagerness displayed by the members opposed to a Nat^l. Gov^t. from these different motives began now to produce serious anxiety for the result of the Convention. M^r. Dickenson said to M^r. Madison You see the consequence of pushing things too far. Some of the members from the small States wish for two branches in the General Legislature, and are friends to a good National Government; but we would sooner submit to foreign power, than submit to be deprived of an equality of suffrage in both branches of the legislature, and thereby be thrown under the domination of the large States." [2]

On the 15th Mr. Patterson presented his plan, which, he said, " several of the deputations wished to be substituted in place of that proposed by Mr. Randolph." After discussion it was decided that it should be laid before the Committee of the Whole, that Mr. Randolph's plan should be recommitted in order that the two should be compared, and the convention likewise decided that it should not go into the Committee of the Whole until the day following, in order that the friends of the Patterson plan should be the better prepared to explain and support it and the members of the convention have the opportunity of providing themselves with copies. Thereupon, Mr. Patterson moved nine resolutions, proposing

1. That the Articles of Confederation be " revised, corrected & enlarged," *The New Jersey Plan* in order to render them " adequate to the exigencies of Government, & the preservation of the Union."

2. That in addition to the powers already possessed, the United States in Congress assembled be authorized to raise revenue and to expend it for federal purposes by duties imposed on imports, stamps upon paper and letters and packages passing through the general post-office; to regulate commerce with foreign nations and with the States; also that suits for the violation of any such regulations be brought in the State courts with an appeal in law and fact to " the Judiciary of the U. States."

3. That requisitions upon the States be made in proportion to the number of white and other free citizens, including inhabitants bound to servitude for a term of years and " three fifths of all other persons . . . except Indians

[1] *Documentary History*, Vol. iii, p. 123.
[2] *The Journal of the Debates*, Gaillard Hunt ed., Vol. i, p. 138 note.

not paying taxes "; provided, however, that the consent of   States be required for the exercise and enforcement of these powers.

4. That a federal Executive be elected to consist of   persons for a single term of   years, to receive compensation for services not to be increased or diminished during the term of office, and subject to removal; that this Executive be authorized to carry out federal acts, to appoint federal officers not otherwise provided for, and to direct military operations, without, however, commanding the army or navy.

5. That a federal Judiciary be established to consist of a supreme tribunal composed of judges ineligible for other positions during service, appointed by the Executive to serve during good behavior, receiving fixed compensation not subject to increase or diminution, possessing the jurisdiction in first instance of cases of impeachment of federal officers, and in *dernier ressort* of appeals in international matters affecting ambassadors, captures from the enemy, piracies and felonies committed on the high seas, cases involving foreigners, and the construction of treaties, " or which may arise on any of the Acts for regulation of trade, or the collection of the federal Revenue."

6. That the acts of the Congress in accordance with the original and revised Articles of Confederation, and treaties made and ratified under the authority of the United States, be the supreme law of all the States, insofar as such acts or treaties relate to the citizens of the States, that the Judiciaries be bound thereby " any thing in the respective laws of the individual States to the contrary notwithstanding," and that the federal Executive be authorized to use the power of the States " to enforce and compel an Obedience to such Acts, or an observance of such Treaties."

7. That " provision be made for the admission of new States into the Union."

8. That naturalization be uniform in every State.

9, and last.   That offenses committed in one State be tryable in any other State of the Union.[1]

It will be observed that this plan, although recognizing the threefold division of powers, is nevertheless to be looked upon as a revision of the Articles of Confederation, with important additions, not as a substitute for them. It was vigorously debated but it found little favor with the partisans of the national plan, or indeed with those desiring to provide the Union with an adequate government, while preserving the rights of the States.[2]   On the

---

[1] *Documentary History,* Vol. iii, pp. 125–8.

[2] In the session of August 23d the question of granting power to negative State legislation was revived by a motion of Mr. Pinckney. The diverging views of two delegates, as reported by Mr. Madison, are of interest:

Mr. Wilson considered this as the keystone wanted to compleat the wide arch of Government we are raising. The power of self-defence had been urged as necessary for

19th of June it was moved by M[r]. King of Massachusetts "whether the Comittee should rise & M[r]. Randolphs propositions be re-reported without alteration, which," as Mr. Madison says, "was in fact a question whether M[r]. R's should be adhered to as preferable to those of M[r]. Patterson "; [1] on which question the States divided as follows: Massachusetts, aye; Connecticut, aye; New York, no; New Jersey, no; Pennsylvania, aye; Delaware, no; Maryland, divided; Virginia, aye; North Carolina, aye; South Carolina, aye; Georgia, aye.

The Randolph plan, as amended and altered in the committee, was therefore reported to the convention and served as the basis of future discussion. The New Jersey plan, however, had served its turn. It had united the advocates of the States and made it clear that either Mr. Randolph's plan would prevail or that a compromise would have to be reached on middle ground. The attitude of the smaller States was accurately but somewhat brutally put by Mr. Pinckney, who is made by Mr. Madison to say that " the whole comes to this, as he conceived. Give N. Jersey an equal vote, and she will dismiss her scruples, and concur in the Nati[l]. system." [2]

The Patterson plan as a whole out of the way, the discussion turned on the Randolph resolutions as modified in such a way as to give the States an equal representation in the second branch. The foundation had already been laid for this compromise by John Dickinson of Delaware, the possibility of such a solution adverted to by Roger Sherman of Connecticut, and without attributing either the origin or the success of the project to the representatives of any State or any one person, the delegation of the State of Connecticut, which Oliver Ellsworth declared to be not a small but a middle State, seems to have occupied what may be called the strategic position. The conciliatory attitude of its members seemed inclined to produce conciliation, and from here on until the acceptance of the principle of equality Mr. Ellsworth seems to have played the leading rôle. Certain it is that the members of the Connecticut delegation not only assumed leadership and stated their views in such a way as to court concession from the larger States by showing themselves prepared to yield proportional representation in the first branch, but Mr. Ellsworth's motion of the 29th of June " that the rule of suffrage in the 2[d]. branch be the same with that established by the articles of confederation," [3] divided the States equally in the session of

The Connecticut Proposal

---

the State Governments — It was equally necessary for the General Government. The firmness of Judges is not of itself sufficient. . . . It will be better to prevent the passage of an improper law, than to declare it void when passed.

Mr. Rutlidge. If nothing else, this alone would damn and ought to damn the Constitution. Will any State ever agree to be bound hand & foot in this manner. It is worse than making mere corporations of them whose bye laws would not be subject to this shackle. *Documentary History*, Vol. iii, p. 602.

[1] *Ibid.*, p. 162.
[2] *Ibid.*, p. 136.   [3] *Ibid.*, p. 245.

July 2d, leading to the appointment of a committee of one from each State to find a way out.   This Committee of the States reported on July 5th the compromise ultimately adopted, that the principle of proportional representation should prevail in the first branch; that, in the second, each State should have an equal vote, with the further provision that revenue bills should originate in the first branch and should not be altered or amended in the second, which latter provision was changed in the course of debate by permitting the Senate to alter but not to originate money bills.   Or, as stated more at length in the report of Mr. Gerry, on behalf of the Committee:

> That the subsequent propositions be recommended to the Convention on condition that both shall be generally adopted.   I. that in the 1st branch of the Legislature each of the States now in the Union shall be allowed 1 member for every 40,000 inhabitants of the description reported in the 7th Resolution of the Come. of the whole House: that each State not containing that number shall be allowed 1 member: that all bills for raising or appropriating money, and for fixing the Salaries of the officers of the Govern. of the U. States shall originate in the 1st branch of the Legislature, and shall not be altered or amended by the 2d branch: and that no money shall be drawn from the public Treasury, but in pursuance of appropriations to be originated in the 1st branch   II. That in the 2d branch each State shall have an equal vote.[1]

In the session of the 25th of June, Mr. Ellsworth urged " the necessity of maintaining the existence & agency of the States.   Without their co-operation it would be impossible to support a Republican Govt. over so great an extent of Country." [2]   Dr. Johnson of Connecticut likewise urged " the necessity of preserving the State Govts.— which would be at the mercy of the Genl. Govt. on Mr. Wilson's plan "; and on the question to agree " that the members of the 2d branch be chosen by the individual Legislatures," nine States voted in its favor, with Pennsylvania and Virginia in the negative.

Thus, Mr. Dickinson's original motion, which laid the basis for the compromise, was reaffirmed for the reason stated by Mr. Madison in a note that " the largest States particularly Pennsylvania & Virginia always considered the choice of the 2d Branch by the State Legislatures as opposed to a proportional representation to which they were attached as a fundamental principle of just Government.   The smaller States who had opposite views, were reinforced by the members from the large States most anxious to secure the importance of the State Governments." [3]

In reply to an elaborate and somewhat theoretical disquisition on government by Mr. Madison in the session of the 28th, Mr. Sherman of Connecticut curtly and correctly said:

> The question is not what rights naturally belong to men; but how they

[1] *Documentary History*, Vol, iii, p. 270.
[2] *Ibid.*, p. 210.
[3] *Journal of Debates*, Hunt ed., Vol. i, p. 236 note.

may be most equally & effectually guarded in Society. And if some give up Diversity of Views more than others in order to obtain this end, there can be no room for complaint. To do otherwise, to require an equal concession from all, if it would create danger to the rights of some, would be sacrificing the end to the means. The rich man who enters into Society along with the poor man, gives up more than the poor man, yet with an equal vote he is equally safe. Were he to have more votes than the poor man in proportion to his superior stake the rights of the poor man would immediately cease to be secure. This consideration prevailed when the articles of Confederation were formed.[1]

Matters had come to such a pass that Dr. Franklin, immediately after Mr. Sherman's remarks, proposed that hereafter the session should open with prayer. On the 29th, Dr. Johnson carried the matter a step nearer agreement by a series of timely and well balanced remarks:

> The controversy must be endless whilst Gentlemen differ in the grounds of their arguments; Those on one side considering the States as districts of people composing one political Society; those on the other considering them as so many political societies. The fact is the States do exist as political Societies, and a Gov^t. is to be formed for them in their political capacity, as well as for the individuals composing them. Does it not seem to follow, that if the States as such are to exist they must be armed with some power of self-defence. . . . On the whole he thought that as in some respects the States are to be considered in their political capacity, and in others as districts of individual citizens, the two ideas embraced on different sides, instead of being opposed to each other, ought to be combined; that in *one* branch the *people,* ought to be represented, in the *other* the *States*.[2]

Later, in the same session, Dr. Johnson's colleague, Mr. Ellsworth, moved the proposition previously quoted, for equality of suffrage in the second branch, in accordance with the Articles of Confederation, and in support of his motion he is reported by Mr. Madison to have said:

> He was not sorry on the whole he said that the vote just passed, had determined against this rule in the first branch. He hoped it would become a ground of compromise with regard to the 2^d. branch. We were partly national; partly federal. The proportional representation in the first branch was conformable to the national principle & would secure the large States agst. the small. An equality of voices was conformable to the federal principle and was necessary to secure the Small States agst. the large. He trusted that on this middle ground a compromise would take place. He did not see that it could on any other. And if no compromise should take place, our meeting would not only be in vain but worse than in vain. To the Eastward he was sure Mass^{ts}. was the only State that would listen to a proposition for excluding the States as equal political Societies, from an equal voice in both branches. The others would risk every consequence rather than part with so dear a right. An attempt to deprive them of it, was at once cutting the body of America in two, and as he supposed would be the case, somewhere about this part of it. The large States he conceived would notwithstanding

[1] *Documentary History,* Vol. iii, p. 233.
[2] *Ibid.,* p. 237.

the equality of votes, have an influence that would maintain their superiority. . . . The power of self defence was essential to the small States. Nature had given it to the smallest insect of the creation. He could never admit that there was no danger of combinations among the large States. They will like individuals find out and avail themselves of the advantage to be gained by it. . . . Let a strong Executive, a Judiciary & Legislative power be created; but Let not too much be attempted; by which all may be lost. He was not in general a half-way man, yet he preferred doing half the good we could, rather than do nothing at all. The other half may be added, when the necessity shall be more fully experienced.[1]

On the 30th, Mr. Ellsworth's motion being under discussion, its mover thus replied to Mr. Wilson's "capital objection" that the minority would rule the majority:

> The power is given to the few to save them from being destroyed by the many. If an equality of votes had been given to them in both branches, the objection might have had weight. Is it a novel thing that the few should have a check on the many? . . . No instance of a Confederacy has existed in which an equality of voices has not been exercised by the members of it. We are running from one extreme to another. We are razing the foundations of the building. When we need only repair the roof. No salutary measure has been lost for want of a *majority of the States,* to favor it. If security be all that the great States wish for the 1st. branch secures them. The danger of combinations among them is not imaginary. . . .[2]

After illustrating the possibility of this he appealed, again to quote Mr. Madison, "to the obligations of the federal pact which was still in force, and which had been entered into with so much solemnity, persuading himself that some regard would still be paid to the plighted faith under which each State, small as well as great, held an equal right of suffrage in the general Councils. His remarks were not the result of particular or local views. The State he represented (Connecticut) held a middle rank."[3]

In the course of this debate, which was largely between Messrs. Ellsworth and Madison, Dr. Franklin interposed, saying:

> The diversity of opinions turns on two points. If a proportional representation takes place, the small States contend that their liberties will be in danger. If an equality of votes is to be put in its place, the large States say that their money will be in danger. When a broad table is to be made, and the edges of planks do not fit, the artist takes a little from both, and makes a good joint. In like manner here both sides must part with some of their demands, in order that they may join in some accommodating proposition.[4]

This was indeed an olive branch from a large State, and the necessity for a compromise, which Dr. Franklin suggested, was made evident by the re-

---

[1] *Documentary History,* Vol. iii, pp. 245–7.
[2] *Ibid.,* pp. 251–2.
[3] *Ibid.,* p. 252.
[4] *Ibid.,* p. 257.

marks of Mr. Bedford of Delaware, who, to quote Mr. Madison's report, " contended that there was no middle way between a perfect consolidation and a mere confederacy of the States.   The first is out of the question, and in the latter they must continue if not perfectly, yet equally sovereign.   If political Societies possess ambition, avarice, and all the other passions which render them formidable to each other, ought we not to view them in this light here?   Will not the same motives operate in America as elsewhere?   If any gentleman doubts it let him look at the votes.   Have they not been dictated by interest, by ambition?   Are not the large States evidently seeking to aggrandize themselves at the expense of the small?   They think no doubt that they have right on their side, but interest had blinded their eyes.   Look at Georgia.   Though a small State at present, she is actuated by the prospect of soon being a great one.   S. Carolina is actuated both by present interest & future prospects.   She hopes too to see the other States cut down to her own dimensions.   N. Carolina has the same motives of present & future interest.   Virg^a. follows.   Mary^d. is not on that side of the Question.   Pen^a. has a direct and future interest.   Mass^{ts}. has a decided and palpable interest in the part she takes.   Can it be expected that the small States will act from pure disinterestedness." [1]   After appealing to experience, Mr. Bedford·thus continued:

> Give the opportunity, and ambition will not fail to abuse it.   The whole History of mankind proves it.   The three large States have a common interest to bind them together in commerce.   But whether combination as we suppose, or a competition as others suppose, shall take place among them, in either case, the smaller States must be ruined.   We must like Solon make such a Govern^t. as the people will approve.   Will the smaller States ever agree to the proposed degradation of them.

After calling attention to the fact that all were agreed that the powers of Congress should be enlarged in order that it could meet its obligations, and after adding that the little States were willing to comply with their engagements, but only if the principle of equality be observed, he proceeded in language which caused no little commotion among the delegations on behalf of the large as well as of the small States:

> We have been told with a dictatorial air that this is the last moment for a fair trial in favor of a Good Governm^t.   It will be the last indeed if the propositions reported from the Committee go forth to the people.   He was under no apprehensions.   The Large States dare not dissolve the confederation.   If they do the small ones will find some foreign ally of more honor and good faith, who will take them by the hand and do them justice.   He did not mean by this to intimidate or alarm.   It was a natural consequence; which ought to be avoided by enlarging the federal powers not annihilating the federal

[1] *Documentary History,* Vol. iii, pp. 259–260.

system. This is what the people expect. All agree in the necessity of a more efficient Gov^t. and why not make such an one; as they desire.

Whereupon Mr. Ellsworth, in a more conciliatory and persuasive, yet hardly less decided way, said:

> Under a National Gov^t. he should participate in the National Security, as remarked by (Mr. King) but that was all. What he wanted was domestic happiness. The Nat^l. Gov^t. could not descend to the local objects on which this depended. It could not embrace objects of a general nature. He turned his eyes therefore for the preservation of his rights to the State Gov^{ts}. From these alone he could derive the greatest happiness he expects in this life. His happiness depends on their existence, as much as a new-born infant on its mother for nourishment. If this reasoning was not satisfactory, he had nothing to add that could be so.[1]

Under these circumstances, the convention adjourned on Saturday, June 30th, and after an interval of a day in which to reflect, met on July 2d. The Sunday was indeed a godsend to the small States, for when the Convention adjourned on Monday, July 2d, the vote upon Mr. Ellsworth's motion was had, resulting in a tie, Massachusetts, Pennsylvania, Virginia, North Carolina, and South Carolina voting against, Connecticut, New York (then considered one of the smaller States), New Jersey, Delaware, and Maryland voting for, with Georgia divided. Mr. Ellsworth's friendship with Mr. Baldwin had borne its fruit. Whereupon, General Charles Cotesworth Pinckney, a man of large experience and of broad views, although as set upon the rights of his State as any man could be, said that " some compromise seemed to be necessary: the States being exactly divided on the question for an equality of votes in the 2^d. branch. He proposed that a Committee consisting of a member from each State should be appointed to devise & report some compromise." [2]

Doubtless General Pinckney's motion appealed to the good sense of his colleagues open to conviction, for, as Mr. Sherman said, the Convention was " now at a full stop, and nobody he supposed meant that we sh^d. break up without doing something. A Committee he thought most likely to hit on some expedient." [3] Dr. Williamson of North Carolina, whose State had voted against equality, added that " If we do not concede on both sides, our business must soon be at an end." He favored the commitment, " supposing that as the Com^e. w^d. be a smaller body, a compromise would be pursued with more coolness." [4] Mr. Gerry of Massachusetts, later to be Vice President with Mr. Madison as President of the United States, likewise was for the commitment, saying, " Something must be done, or we shall disap-

[1] *Documentary History,* Vol. iii, p. 261.
[2] *Ibid.,* p. 264.
[3] *Ibid.*
[4] *Ibid.,* p. 268.

point not only America, but the whole world." He suggested a consideration of the state " we should be thrown into by the failure of the Union. We should be without an Umpire to decide controversies and must be at the mercy of events. What too is to become of our treaties — what of our foreign debts, what of our domestic? We must make concessions on both sides. Without these the constitutions of the several States would never have been formed." [1]

So the question was debated, decided in the affirmative, and the committee, elected by ballot, consisted of Messrs. Gerry, Ellsworth, Yates, Patterson, Franklin, Bedford, Martin (of Maryland), Mason, Davie, Rutledge, and Baldwin. " That time might be given to the Comittee, and to such as chose to attend to the celebration on the anniversary of Independence, the Convention adjourned till Thursday." [2]

On Thursday, July 5th, the committee reported the compromise whose terms had properly been suggested by Dr. Franklin.[3] The report was debated from every point of view and amended in certain particulars that need not detain us; and on July 16, 1787, the convention adopted it as amended, including, as Mr. Madison says, " the equality of votes in the 2^d. branch," [4] Connecticut, New Jersey, Delaware, Maryland, North Carolina, voting for, Pennsylvania, Virginia, South Carolina and Georgia against, Massachusetts divided, New York absent and New Hampshire not as yet represented, both of which States would have voted for the compromise.

The irritation of the larger States upon the victory of the smaller was voiced by Mr. Randolph, who, stating that it would be " in vain to come to any final decision with a bare majority on either side," wished " the Convention might adjourn, that the large States might consider the steps proper to be taken in the present solemn crisis of the business, and that the small

Victory of the Smaller States

---

[1] *Documentary History,* Vol. iii, p. 269.
[2] *Ibid.,* pp. 269–270.
[3] *Ibid.,* p. 270.   "Tuesday, *July* 3, 1787.
" The *grand committee* met. Mr. Gerry was chosen chairman.
" The committee proceeded to consider in what manner they should discharge the business with which they were intrusted. By the proceedings in the Convention, they were so equally divided on the important question of *representation in the two branches,* that the idea of a conciliatory adjustment must have been in contemplation of the house in the appointment of this committee. But still, how to effect this salutary purpose was the question. Many of the members, impressed with the utility of a general government, connected with it the indispensable necessity of a representation from the states *according to their numbers and wealth;* while others, equally tenacious of the rights of the states, would admit of no other representation but such as *was strictly federal,* or, in other words, *equality of suffrage.* This brought on a discussion of the principles on which the house had divided, and a lengthy recapitulation of the arguments advanced in the house in support of these opposite propositions. As I had not openly explained my sentiments on any former occasion on this question, but constantly, in giving my vote, *showed my attachment to the national government on federal principles, I took this occasion to explain my motives.*
" These remarks gave rise to a motion of Dr. Franklin, which after some modification was agreed to, and made the basis of the following report of the Committee." Yates, *Secret Proceedings,* p. 205.
[4] *Documentary History,* Vol. iii, p. 343.

States might also deliberate on the means of conciliation." [1]   The smaller States, however, had carried their point, and while they were willing to adjourn they were in no disposition to reconsider.   Indeed, Mr. Patterson of New Jersey, as reported by Mr. Madison, "thought with M^r. R. that it was high time for the Convention to adjourn that the rule of secrecy ought to be rescinded, and that our Constituents should be consulted.   No conciliation could be admissible on the part of the smaller States on any other ground than that of an equality of votes in the 2^d. branch.   If M^r. Randolph would reduce to form his motion for an adjournment sine die, he would second it with all his heart."   Mr. Randolph explained that he did not mean to move adjournment *sine die*, but until the morrow " in order that some conciliatory experiment might if possible be devised, and that in case the smaller States should continue to hold back, the larger might then take such measures, he would not say what, as might be necessary."   Mr. Patterson, being in an obliging spirit, seconded the adjournment, " till to-morrow, as an opportunity seemed to be wished by the larger States to deliberate further on conciliatory expedients."   On the question of adjournment the States divided equally, and the convention adjourned; but before doing so, they tied once on the question, and the frame of mind of the convention as well as of the delegations from the larger States is perhaps to be gathered from the following remarks of Mr. Rutledge, who, according to Mr. Madison, " could see no need of an adjourn^t. because he could see no chance of a compromise.   The little States were fixt.   They had repeatedly & solemnly declared themselves to be so.   All that the large States then had to do, was to decide whether they would yield or not.   For his part he conceived that altho' we could not do what we thought best, in itself, we ought to do something.   Had we not better keep the Gov^t. up a little longer, hoping that another Convention will supply our omissions, than abandon every thing to hazard.   Our Constituents will be very little satisfied with us if we take the latter course." [2]

The members from the larger States were apparently in a sorry plight. They could not break up the Convention on the ground that they were unwilling to compromise, they could not admit that they were outgeneraled by the little States, they could not form a Confederation composed of themselves, because they were not contiguous, and even large bricks require mortar to hold together.   The situation is thus stated in a passage from Mr. Madison's Notes, interposed between the adjournment after the vote and before the meeting of the 17th:

On the morning following before the hour of the Convention a number of

---

[1] *Documentary History,* Vol. iii, pp. 345–6.
[2] *Ibid.,* p. 347.

the members from the larger States, by common agreement met for the pur- The First Great Compromise pose of consulting on the proper steps to be taken in consequence of the vote in favor of an equal Representation in the 2^d branch, and the apparent inflexibility of the smaller States on that point — Several members from the latter States also attended. The time was wasted in vague conversation on the subject, without any specific proposition or agreement. It appeared indeed that the opinions of the members who disliked the equality of votes differed so much as to the importance of that point, and as to the policy of risking a failure of any general act of the Convention by inflexibly opposing it. Several of them supposing that no good Governm^t. could or would be built on that foundation, and that as a division of the Convention into two opinions was unavoidable it would be better that the side comprising the principal States, and a majority of the people of America, should propose a scheme of Gov^t. to the States, than that a scheme should be proposed on the other side, would have concurred in a firm opposition to the smaller States, and in a separate recommendation, if eventually necessary. Others seemed inclined to yield to the smaller States, and to concur in such an Act however imperfect & exceptionable, as might be agreed on by the Convention as a body, tho' decided by a bare majority of States and by a minority of the people of the U. States. It is probable that the result of this consultation satisfied the smaller States that they had nothing to apprehend from a Union of the larger, in any plan whatever agst. the equality of votes in the 2^d. branch.[1]

So much for the first compromise, which made the proposed Constitu- The Second Compromise tion probable. Next, for the second compromise, which made it a fact. And it is interesting to note that the second, like the first, deals with the question of suffrage, although it is confined to the first branch, involving questions of interest to the States as such. The compromise involved one member of Congress for every forty thousand inhabitants of the State, divided into districts popularly called Congressional Districts. The southern States, in which slavery prevailed, insisted that the slaves should be counted among the inhabitants, Mr. Butler and General Pinckney of South Carolina going so far as to insist that they should be " included in the rule of Representation *equally* with the whites," [2] whereas, after much misgiving, the delegations of the other States were willing to allow five negroes to be counted as three for the purpose of votes in such States where slavery existed, on the ground that such a proportion had been approved by eleven of the States in the Congress of 1783.[3] Again, the southern States insisted upon the right to continue the slave trade, at least for a period of twenty years, which was very galling to the members of the States where slavery did not exist and distasteful to some of the members of the slave States.[4] It happened,

[1] *Documentary History,* Vol. iii, pp. 347–8.
[2] *Ibid.,* p. 308. Session of July 11th.
[3] *Ibid.,* p. 323. Session of July 12th.
[4] Mr. Madison expressed the following opinion:
　　Twenty years will produce all the mischief that can be apprehended from the liberty to import slaves. So long a term will be more dishonorable to the National character than to say nothing about it in the Constitution. *Ibid.,* p. 616.
During the same session (that of August 25th) Mr. Madison stated that he " thought it

and this is the ground for the second compromise, that the southern States, producing products for exportation, were anxious to prevent regulations of commerce which would enable the Congress to do so by a mere majority, wishing a two-thirds vote in such cases for their protection. The eastern States, under the lead of Massachusetts, were unwilling to consent to this, as they were commercial States and changes in the regulations proving desirable would be very difficult if a two-thirds vote were required.

The opposition of the States to a tax upon their exports was met by a provision that no tax or duty should be laid on articles exported from any State, but the commercial States were unwilling to be bound hand and foot, as they thought they would be, by a two-thirds vote on the part of the legislature to regulate commerce, Mr. Gorham of Massachusetts saying on this very question that " He desired it to be remembered that the Eastern States had no motive to Union but a commercial one. They were able to protect themselves. They were not afraid of external danger and did not need the aid of the South^n. States." [1]

Section 6, Article VII, of the draft of the Constitution as reported on August 6th, provided that, " No navigation act shall be passed without the assent of two thirds of the members present in each House." [2]   At the session of August 22d this clause was, together with that relating to the importation of slaves, referred to a committee composed of a member from every State, which recommended two days later that the importation of slaves, euphemistically called " such persons as the several States now existing shall think proper to admit," be not prohibited prior to the year 1800, but that a tax upon mere migration or importation might be laid, and that Section 6, requiring a two-thirds vote for a navigation act, be omitted.[3]   On August 29th the report of this committee on the question of navigation came up for discussion. When the report was presented, Mr. Pinckney of South Carolina moved to insert the two-thirds requirement, which had been omitted by the committee, and in support of this motion remarked, as reported by Mr. Madison, that there were five distinct commercial interests: " 1. the fisheries & W. India trade, which belonged to the N. England States. 2. the interest of N. York lay in a free trade. 3. Wheat & flour the Staples of the two middle States, (N. J. & Penn^a.)— 4. Tob^o, the staple of Mary^d. & Virginia & partly of N. Carolina. 5. Rice & Indigo, the staples of S. Carolina & Georgia. These different interests would be a source of oppressive regulations if no check to a bare majority should be provided. States pursue their interests with less scruple than individuals. The power of regulating commerce was a

wrong to admit in the Constitution the idea that there could be property in men." *Documentary History*, Vol. iii, p. 618.
  [1] *Ibid.*, p. 591. Session of August 22d.
  [2] *Ibid.*, p. 450.
  [3] *Ibid.*, p. 606.

pure concession on the part of the S. States. They did not need the protection of the N. States at present."[1] To this statement General Pinckney, likewise of South Carolina, added that "it was the true interest of the S. States to have no regulation of commerce; but considering the loss brought on the commerce of the Eastern States by the revolution, their liberal conduct towards the views of South Carolina, and the interest the weak South[n]. States had in being united with the strong Eastern States, he thought it proper that no fetters should be imposed on the power of making commercial regulations; and that his constituents though prejudiced against the Eastern States, would be reconciled to this liberality — He had himself, he said, prejudices ag[st]. the Eastern States before he came here, but would acknowledge that he had found them as liberal and candid as any man whatever." The liberality and candor of South Carolina to which General Pinckney referred are thus stated by Mr. Madison in a note of later date:

> He [General Pinckney] meant the permission to import slaves. An understanding on the two subjects of *navigation* and *slavery,* had taken place between those parts of the Union, which explains the vote on the Motion depending, as well as the language of Gen[l]. Pinkney & others.[2]

In the course of the very interesting debate which ensued, the delegates of the States supposed to be affected by the two-thirds requirement, or by a navigation law of any kind, laid the views of their States before the Convention with commendable frankness. Mr. Butler of South Carolina, for example, speaking for the southern States, said that "he considered the interests of these and of the Eastern States, to be as different as the interests of Russia and Turkey." But nevertheless, "desirous of conciliating the affections of the East: States," he said he should vote against the two-thirds requirement instead of a majority.[3] Mr. Mason of Virginia, bitterly opposed to slavery and its recognition in the Constitution, said:

> If the Gov[t]. is to be lasting, it must be founded in the confidence & affections of the people, and must be so constructed as to obtain these. The *Majority* will be governed by their interests. The Southern States are the *minority* in both Houses. Is it to be expected that they will deliver themselves bound hand & foot to the Eastern States, and enable them to exclaim, in the words of Cromwell on a certain occasion —"the lord hath delivered them into our hands."

So much for the views of the southern States, to which Mr. Gorham, who had already expressed himself on the subject, replied:

> If the Government is to be so fettered as to be unable to relieve the Eastern

---

[1] *Documentary History,* Vol. iii, pp. 636–7.
[2] *Ibid.,* p. 637.
[3] *Ibid.,* p. 639.

States what motive can they have to join it, and thereby tie their own hands from measures which they could otherwise take for themselves. The Eastern States were not led to strengthen the Union by fear for their own safety. He deprecated the consequences of disunion, but if it should take place it was the Southern part of the Continent that had the most reason to dread them. He urged the improbability of a combination against the interest of the Southern States, the different situations of the Northern & Middle States being a security against it. It was moreover certain that foreign ships would never be altogether excluded especially those of Nations in treaty with us.[1]

The question had become one of Union or no Union, the Constitution or no Constitution, and as the eastern and southern States had reached an understanding there appeared nothing for the delegates of the northern and middle States to do but to confirm that understanding, or to renounce the attempt to unite. Indeed, the delegates appear to have been so impressed with the necessity of this that the report of the committee eliminating the requirements of " two thirds of each House to pass a navigation act " was, as Mr. Madison says, " then agreed to, nem: con: "

As a result of these two compromises, which have been stated at some length, the obstacles in the way of a Constitution of the kind proposed in the Randolph resolutions were circumvented if they were not wholly removed; and the concessions upon which the compromises were based appear to have been not concessions of the members as such, nor of the people as such, but of the States, represented in their political capacity, in the matter of equality; and of the States in the second compromise, or of the interests of the people of the different States, to be affected, on the one hand, by slavery, and by navigation laws on the other.

Grant of Legislative Power

It will be observed that the question, and therefore the compromise, in each case related to the legislative branch of the proposed government. In comparison with these questions, the powers to be granted to the legislative department were matters of detail, for it was generally agreed that this department should possess the powers granted to the Congress by the Articles of Confederation and certain added powers in order to render the proposed government adequate to the exigencies of the Union. Two of these powers were admittedly those to impose taxes in order to raise a revenue, and to regulate commerce with foreign nations and among the States themselves.

Two points are to be observed in this connection, that the grant of legislative powers was not general, as in the case of the Judiciary, by virtue whereof the judicial power of the United States is vested in a Supreme and inferior courts, the Constitution saying, in regard to the legislature, that all legislative powers herein granted " shall be vested in the Congress

[1] *Documentary History,* Vol. iii, pp. 641–2.

of the United States," to consist of a Senate and House of Representatives. As, therefore, the Union did not exist of itself but had to be created, and as the government of this Union, composed of three branches, had likewise to be created by the States, which already existed, it follows that the legislative department could possess only such powers which the delegates of the States, subsequently confirmed by conventions of the States, granted either directly or by necessary implication to the legislative department of the government of the Union.

But the powers granted are wisely enumerated in general terms, leaving the Congress free to exercise its discretion in the choice of means to carry out the powers expressly or impliedly granted, and the legislature as well as the Supreme Court has never forgotten, the one in passing laws, the other in interpreting and applying them, that each was dealing with a Constitution.

The second observation is that the powers were to be exercised in such a way as, to quote the language of Section 8 of Article I of the completed Constitution, " to provide for the common defense and general welfare of the United States," and, within the express or implied grant of powers for this great purpose, " to make all laws which shall be necessary and proper for carrying into execution the foregoing powers, and all other powers vested in this Constitution in the government of the United States or any department or officer thereof."

IX

CREATION OF THE EXECUTIVE

But because the Laws, that are at once, and in a short time made, have a constant and lasting Force, and need a *perpetual Execution,* or an attendance thereunto: Therefore 'tis necessary there should be a *Power always in Being,* which should see to the *Execution* of the Laws that are made, and remain in Force. And thus the *Legislative* and *Executive Power* come often to be separated. (*John Locke, Two Treaties of Government, 1690, Book II, Ch. XII, Section 144, Works, edition of 1714, Vol. II.*)

Section 1. The executive Power shall be vested in a President of the United States of America. He shall hold his Office during the Term of four Years, and, together with the Vice President, chosen for the same Term, be elected, as follows . . .

Before he enter on the Execution of his Office, he shall take the following Oath or Affirmation:—" I do solemnly swear (or affirm) that I will faithfully execute the Office of President of the United States, and will to the best of my Ability, preserve, protect and defend the Constitution of the United States."

Section 2. . . .

He shall have Power, by and with the Advice and Consent of the Senate, to make Treaties, provided two thirds of the Senators present concur; and he shall nominate, and by and with the Advice and Consent of the Senate, shall appoint Ambassadors, other public Ministers and Consuls, Judges of the supreme Court, and all other Officers of the United States, whose Appointments are not herein otherwise provided for, and which shall be established by Law: but the Congress may by Law vest the Appointment of such inferior Officers, as they think proper, in the President alone, in the Courts of Law, or in the Heads of Departments. . . .

Section 3. He shall from time to time give to the Congress Information of the State of the Union, and recommend to their Consideration such Measures as he shall judge necessary and expedient; he may, on extraordinary Occasions, convene both Houses, or either of them, and in Case of Disagreement between them, with Respect to the Time of Adjournment, he may adjourn them to such Time as he shall think proper; he shall receive Ambassadors and other public Ministers; he shall take Care that the Laws be faithfully executed, and shall Commission all the Officers of the United States.

Section 4. The President, Vice President and all civil Officers of the United States, shall be removed from Office on Impeachment for, and Conviction of, Treason, Bribery, or other high Crimes and Misdemeanors. (*Constitution of the United States, Article II.*)

Soon after the adjournment of the federal Convention some one said to Benjamin Franklin, "Well, Doctor, have you given us a republic or a monarchy?" Franklin replied, "A republic, if you can keep it." (*Andrew C. McLaughlin, The Courts, The Constitution and Parties, 1912, p. 151.*)

By the constitution of the United States, the President is invested with certain important political powers, in the exercise of which he is to use his own discretion, and is accountable only to his country in his political character, and to his own conscience. . . . The subjects are political. They respect the nation, not individual rights, and being entrusted to the executive, the decision of the executive is conclusive. . . .

The province of the court is, solely, to decide on the rights of individuals not to enquire how the executive, or executive officers, perform duties in which they have a discretion. Questions, in their nature political, or which are, by the constitution and laws, submitted to the executive, can never be made in this court. (*Chief Justice Marshall in Marbury v. Madison, 1 Cranch, 137, 165–166, 170, decided in 1803.*)

These orders, given by the executive, under the construction of the act of congress made by the department to which its execution was assigned, enjoin the seizure of American vessels sailing from a French port. Is the officer who obeys them liable for damages sustained by this misconstruction of the act, or will his orders excuse him? If his instructions afford him no protection, then the law must take its course, and he must pay such damages as are legally awarded against him; . . .

. . . I was strongly inclined to think, that where, in consequence of orders from the legitimate authority, a vessel is seized, with pure intention, the claim of the injured party for damages would be against that government from which the orders proceeded, and would be a proper subject for negotiation. But I have been convinced that I was mistaken, and I have receded from this first opinion. I acquiesce in that of my brethren, which, is, that the instructions cannot change the nature of the transaction, nor legalize an act which, without those instructions, would have been a plain trespass. (*Chief Justice Marshall in The Flying Fish, 2 Cranch, 170, 178, 179, decided in 1804.*)

There is another feature common to both governments. In England the king has his constitutional counsellors and councils. The *peers of the realm* are, by their birth, hereditary counsellors of the crown; and may be called together by the king to impart their advice, [4 Bl. Com.] 227. *The judges* are a council for law matters, 229. But the principal council is *the privy council,* and by way of eminence is called the *council,* 229. So the president has his *councils.* "He may require the opinion in writing of the principal officer at the head of each of the executive departments," &c. 2 Sec. 2 Art, Clause 2, Const. This is called a *cabinet council;* it is a *privy council,* in which the president is present, as the king is in person in his. 4 Bl. Com. 231. The *senate* is the *council* in making treaties, in *advising* and *consenting* to appointments to office. *Senators* are not, ex officio, counsellors individually; but the president "may convene both houses, *or either* of them." (*Mr. Justice Baldwin, A General View of the Origin and Nature of the Constitution and Government of the United States, 1837, p. 56.*)

It is believed to be one of the chief merits of the American system of written constitutional law, that all the powers intrusted to government, whether State or national, are divided into the three grand departments, the executive, the legislative, and the judicial. That the functions appropriate to each of these branches of government shall be vested in a separate body of public servants, and that the perfection of the system requires that the lines which separate and divide these departments shall be broadly and clearly defined. It is also essential to the successful working of this system that the persons intrusted with power in any one of these branches shall not be permitted to encroach upon the powers confided to the others, but that each shall by the law of its creation be limited to the exercise of the powers appropriate to its own department and no other. To these general propositions there are in the Constitution of the United States some important exceptions. One of these is, that the President is so far made a part of the legislative power, that his assent is required to the enactment of all statutes and resolutions of Congress.

This, however, is so only to a limited extent, for a bill may become a law notwithstanding the refusal of the President to approve it, by a vote of two-thirds of each House of Congress.

So, also, the Senate is made a partaker in the functions of appointing officers and making treaties, which are supposed to be properly executive, by requiring its consent to the appointment of such officers and the ratification of treaties. The Senate also exercises the judicial power of trying impeachments, and the House of preferring articles of impeachment.

In the main, however, that instrument, the model on which are constructed the fundamental laws of the States, has blocked out with singular precision, and in bold lines, in its three primary articles, the allotment of power to the executive, the legislative, and the judicial departments of the government. It also remains true, as a general rule, that the powers confided by the Constitution to one of these departments cannot be exercised by another.

It may be said that these are truisms which need no repetition here to give them force. But while the experience of almost a century has in general shown a wise and commendable forbearance in each of these branches from encroachments upon the others, it is not to be denied that such attempts have been made, and it is believed not always without success. The increase in the number of States, in their population and wealth, and in the amount of power, if not in its nature to be exercised by the Federal government, presents powerful and growing temptations to those to whom that exercise is intrusted, to overstep the just boundaries of their own department, and enter upon the domain of one of the others, or to assume powers not intrusted to either of them. (*Mr. Justice Miller in Kilbourn v. Thompson, 103 United States Reports, 168, 190, 192, decided in 1880.*)

But the principle of definition and limitation of powers harmonises so well with the federal spirit that it is generally carried much farther than is dictated by the mere logic of the constitution. Thus the authority assigned to the United States under the Constitution is not concentrated in any single official or body of officials. The President has definite rights, upon which neither Congress nor the judicial department can encroach. (*Albert Venn Dicey, Introduction to the Study of the Law of the Constitution, 1885, 8th edition, 1915, pp. 148–149.*)

CHAPTER IX

CREATION OF THE EXECUTIVE

It was not by chance that Mr. Randolph's resolutions began with the legislative department and it need occasion no surprise that the question of powers to be granted to this department of the proposed Government was the subject of prolonged debate and the grant itself the result of concession and compromise. The lack of power on the part of Congress to raise revenue, to maintain the government under the Articles of Confederation, and to regulate commerce with foreign nations and among the States was the cause of the convention, and this part of the plan would have been discussed and decided, as it was, if Mr. Randolph's resolutions had ended instead of beginning with the legislative department. But the fundamental question at issue was the definition of power. In comparison, the exercise of this power by an executive and indeed even the interpretation of the power were minor matters. Without the grant there could be no exercise of the power, there could be no interpretation, there could be no Constitution.

However a second branch of the proposed government was, according to the theory of the division of powers, the executive. Mr. Randolph's propositions contained in the seventh and eighth of his resolutions, provide respectively:

> 7. Res^d. that a National Executive be instituted; to be chosen by the National Legislature for the term of   years, to receive punctually at stated times, a fixed compensation for the services rendered, in which no increase or diminution shall be made so as to affect the Magistracy, existing at the time of increase or diminution, and to be ineligible a second time; and that besides a general authority to execute the national laws, it ought to enjoy the Executive rights vested in Congress by the Confederation.
>
> 8. Res^d. that the Executive and a convenient number of the National Judiciary, ought to compose a Council of revision with authority to examine every act of the National Legislature before it shall operate, & every act of a particular Legislature before a Negative thereon shall be final; and that the dissent of the said Council shall amount to a rejection, unless the Act of the National Legislature be again passed, or that of a particular Legislature be again negatived by   of the members of each branch.[1]

There appears to have been no objection on the part of any member to

---

[1] *Documentary History of the Constitution,* Vol. iii, pp. 18–19. Session of May 29th.

the institution of an executive department which should possess at least the rights " vested in Congress by the Confederation." A difference of opinion existed, however, as to whether the executive should consist of one person or a number; as to the period during which the executive should hold office; the eligibility of the incumbent to reelection; the method of choice and the powers which the executive should possess.

It would seem that Mr. Randolph, who stood sponsor for the resolutions which bear his name, although the authorship thereof is popularly accredited to Mr. Madison, was in favor of a plural executive representing the different sections of the Union. The New Jersey plan laid before the convention on June 15th specified " a federal Executive to consist of   persons." [1] The convention, however, decided, and wisely, in favor of a single executive. *A Single Executive*

It will be observed that in each plan the executive was to be elected by the national legislature. The first draft of the Constitution as reported on August 6th, provided, in the first section of its tenth article that, " the Executive Power of the United States shall be vested in a single person. His stile shall be ' The President of the United States of America '; and his title shall be, ' His Excellency.' He shall be elected by ballot by the Legislature. He shall hold his office during the term of seven years; but shall not be elected a second time." [2]

Although every other clause of the section was modified, the convention stood fast by the single executive, as the great desire of the delegates was to maintain, as a cardinal principle of the proposed scheme of government, a separation of powers, and therefore to make the president independent of the other departments of government. It was understood that the president was to be an elective officer; and as far as known, there was not made at any time a proposition for an hereditary executive. It was felt by some members that he should be elected for a fixed number of years and be ineligible to reelection. Those favoring his election by the national legislature were, as a rule, opposed to reelection and in favor of a longer term in order that his dependence upon the legislature might not be too close or too apparent. Those opposing the choice by the legislature appear to have favored a short term with the possibility of reelection. It is thus seen that these questions were interrelated not separate and distinct. Without pausing to trace the steps by which an agreement was reached upon the presidency, it will suffice to say that the term was fixed at a period of four years, subject to reelection. There is no provision in the Constitution preventing a president from being reelected for periods of four years throughout his natural lifetime. General Washington's refusal to stand a third time set a precedent followed by Messrs. Jefferson and *Term of Office*

[1] *Documentary History,* Vol. iii, p. 126.
[2] *Ibid.,* p. 453.

Jackson, who might have been elected for a third term, and has established a custom hitherto unbroken. Finally, as the result of much discussion, and of many propositions made only to be rejected, it was agreed that the president should be elected neither by the legislature, by the Congress, by the people, nor by the States, and yet that he should be elected by a method which suggests each of these. Thus, a number of persons called electors, equal to the number of senators and representatives to which each State was entitled in Congress, were to be appointed in such manner as the legislature of each of the States should determine. The electors thus chosen were to meet within their respective States, and to vote by ballot for two persons, only one of whom could be a citizen of the same State with themselves. The person having the greatest number of votes was to be president, provided he received a majority of the whole number of electors appointed. If more than one received a majority and had an equal number of votes, the House of Representatives would choose by ballot one of them for president. If no person received a majority, then the president was to be chosen from the five highest on the list. In such a case the House of Representatives voted by States, each of which was to possess one vote. For this purpose a quorum of the House was to consist of two-thirds of the States, and a majority of the States was necessary for a choice. In any event, the person having the greatest number of votes of electors was to be vice president, and if there remained two with equal votes, the Senate was, by ballot, to choose one, who thereupon became the vice president. All of these features were in the plan agreed to.

It is apparent, from this brief account of the method ultimately adopted, that the electors could be chosen by popular vote within a State if the legislature thereof cared so to do; or the legislature, if it preferred, might itself appoint them. The States might participate directly in the election in case no one voted for by the electors had received a majority of the votes cast. It was believed by the framers that this might frequently happen, inuring to the advantage of the smaller States, just as the selection by election would inure to the advantage of the larger ones. The election of the vice president under like circumstances would inure to the advantage of the small States equally represented by two senators in the upper house.

The members of the convention were without experience in this matter, and the work of their hands was faulty. It has twice been amended, and within the memory of men still living its application gave rise to a disputed election which tested the forbearance and the capacity of the American people for self-government. The precedent for the use of electors chosen in this way seems to have been taken from the Constitution of the State of Maryland, in which the senators were chosen by persons called electors chosen from each of the counties of the State, who, meeting in the city of Annapolis on a specified date, elected by ballot " either out of their own body, or the people at large, fifteen senators (nine of whom to be residents on the western, and six to be residents on the eastern shore) men of the most wisdom, experience and virtue. . . ." [1]

The great duty imposed upon the president appears to be that prescribed in the oath or affirmation taken before entering upon the execution of his high office, that he will to the best of his ability " preserve, protect and defend the Constitution of the United States." That he may be held to strict accountability both for the performance of his duties and the exercise of his rights, both he and the vice president, who succeeds him in case of death or disability, are, to quote the exact language of the fourth section of the second article of the Constitution, to " be removed from Office on Impeachment for, and conviction of, Treason, Bribery or other high Crimes and Misdemeanors." President's Oath of Office

It has often been stated that the president possesses greater power than any constitutional monarch, in that he is *ex officio* commander in chief of the army and navy in any event, and of the militia of the several States when called into the actual service of the United States. This is indeed a great power; but it is one with which the framers of the Constitution were familiar, and which they were therefore willing to entrust to an executive officer of their own choice, inasmuch as the several States had entrusted such powers to their chief executives, termed indifferently president or governor, and designated indifferently captain-general or commander-in-chief. The framers of the Constitution foresaw that it would be but natural that he would request the opinion of the principal officers of the various executive departments not created by but contemplated in the Constitution. It was neither unnatural that he should be authorized to grant reprieves and pardons for offenses against the United States; nor that he should be denied power, in cases of impeachment, lest he might be tempted to exercise it in behalf of one whom he himself had appointed and in whose offense he might have participated. His Great Powers

The convention was much disturbed as to the appointing power and as to its location. This was to be expected, both from the difficulty inherent in the subject and from the lack of any uniform rule in or experience had with the constitutions of the States, where various methods had been tried without the development of any one which commended itself as perfect or markedly superior to the others.

That the president should negotiate treaties in the first instance was seen to be inevitable from the outset; that he should conclude them and bind the States and their citizens and inhabitants without check or cooperation on the part of the legislative department was felt to be far from desirable. The solution in this case, however, was a very happy one, in that the president represents Treaties

[1] *The Constitutions of the Several Independent States,* 1781, p. 128, Article 15.

the States — and only States, not the citizens or inhabitants thereof, could conclude treaties.   Thus it seemed necessary to the members of the convention that the legislative branch should participate in the exercise of this power, inasmuch as treaties very frequently if not generally require legislation to carry them into effect.   The cooperation of both branches of the legislature might therefore have been required, the more especially so, as by the great compromise, revenue bills could only originate in the House subject to amendment or modification in the Senate.   The lower house therefore could have claimed a hand in the transaction, as it might be as unwilling to pass an appropriation to carry a treaty into effect, although approved or modified by the Senate, as if the president alone, without the concurrence of the Senate, had negotiated the treaty.[1]

There were other views of this question which weighed heavily with the members.   The Senate, as expected, would always be a small body in comparison with the House of Representatives, and matters of great delicacy, such as foreign affairs, could, it was felt, be best determined in a body of restricted membership, especially as it was to possess advisory as well as ratifying qualities.   Again, the States were expressly renouncing the right to conclude treaties and conventions with foreign powers, which, as free, sovereign and independent States, they had possessed.   By a happy device the president, the general agent of the States, now conducts the negotiations with foreign powers, and the Senate, as the representative of the States, acts as an advisory body and as a check upon his action.   That the advisability of the transaction

---

[1] " Mr. Madison observed that the Senate represented the States alone, and that for this as well as other obvious reasons it was proper that the President should be an agent in Treaties." *Documentary History*, Vol. iii, p. 604. Session of August 23d.

The following extracts, which are reprinted from Sydney George Fisher's *Evolution of the Constitution*, 1897, pp. 306-7, indicate the successive steps that led to the treaty-making plan finally adopted in the Constitution:

" That the president-general, with the advice of the grand council, hold or direct all Indian treaties in which the general interest or welfare of the colonies may be concerned." (Franklin's Plan of 1754.)

" That the president, by the advice of the council, may hold and manage all Indian treaties in which the general interest or welfare of the colonies may be concerned." (Hutchinson's Plan, 1754.)

" That the power and duty of congress shall extend to entering into alliances." (Franklin's Articles of Confederation, 1775.)

" That the president and commander-in-chief shall have no power to make war or peace, or enter into any final treaty, without the consent of the general assembly and legislative council." (South Carolina Constitution of 1776.)

" The United States, in congress assembled, shall have the sole and exclusive right and power of entering into treaties and alliances, provided that no treaty of commerce shall be made whereby the legislative power of the respective states shall be restrained from imposing such imposts and duties on foreigners as their own people are subjected to, or from prohibiting the exportation or importation of any species of goods or commodities whatsoever." (Articles of Confederation, 1778.)

" The congress shall have the sole power of entering into and concluding treaties and alliances with foreign powers." (Drayton's Articles of Confederation, 1778.)

" The senate shall have the sole and exclusive power to make treaties." (Pinckney's Plan, 1787.)

" He [the President] shall have power, by and with the advice and consent of the senate, to make treaties, provided two-thirds of the senators present concur." (The Constitution.)

be beyond question and that mere majorities should not control, the approval of two-thirds of the senators present was required for approval of the treaty or convention submitted.

The president, however, does not ordinarily negotiate directly with foreign countries, but indirectly by means of officers of the United States. The question naturally and inevitably arose as to the appointment of officers both to aid the president and to carry out the provisions of the Constitution in this and in other respects. At one time it was proposed that they be chosen by the Senate; but ultimately the convention, while reserving the right on the part of the legislature to determine the mode of appointment, other than those thought to be essential and therefore specified in the Constitution, vested their appointment in the president in the first instance, subject to confirmation in the Senate, as it seemed appropriate that persons to act as officers of the United States should be passed upon and confirmed by the branch of the government representing the States. The convention, in vesting the appointment of officers in the president subject to confirmation by the Senate, seems to have had in mind the practice of Massachusetts, a practice which was specifically called to its attention by Mr. Gorham, with the result that the power was happily at hand and in the following manner:

> He shall nominate, and by and with the Advice and Consent of the Senate, shall appoint Ambassadors, other public Ministers and Consuls, Judges of the supreme Court, and all other Officers of the United States, whose Appointments are not herein otherwise provided for, and which shall be established by Law: but the Congress may by Law vest the Appointment of such inferior Officers, as they think proper, in the President alone, in the Courts of Law, or in the Heads of Departments.[1]

It was natural, under these circumstances, that he should be empowered to commission all officers of the United States, that he should receive ambassadors and other public ministers, inasmuch as he himself was charged with the conduct of foreign relations; that he should from time to time give to the Congress "information of the state of the Union, and recommend to their consideration such measures as he shall judge necessary and expedient;" and, in view of the experience of the colonies and the provisions to be found in the constitutions of the States, that he should "on extraordinary occasions, convene both houses, or either of them, and in case of disagreement between them, with respect to the time of adjournment, he may adjourn them to such time as he shall think proper." As executive of the United States it was highly desirable that he should, in the language of the Constitution, "take care that the laws be faithfully executed."

If this were all, the eighth of Mr. Randolph's resolutions would have been

---

[1] Article II, Section 2, of the Constitution.

overlooked, although the president would indeed enjoy a general authority to execute the national laws, "enjoy the executive rights vested in Congress by the Confederation," in addition to others which could not well exist because of a defect of power in the Congress under the Articles of Confederation. And it may perhaps be said that the eighth resolution was one of the most difficult which confronted the convention, and one which, at the same time, was not the least successfully met and solved.

A Check
upon the
Legislature

The necessity was felt on all sides to have some check upon the legislative, just as there was a check upon the executive.   Wise laws and unwise statutes could be passed by the national legislature as well as by the legislatures of the States, opposed to the Constitution.   This the eighth and fourteenth of Mr. Randolph's resolutions (which can be called the large State plan), as well as the sixth of Mr. Patterson's resolutions (which may be called the small State plan), sought to obviate.   The colonies had had experience in both these matters.   The King in Council had passed upon acts of the colonies in some cases before they became law; in other cases rejected them within a prescribed period, and set aside decisions of courts of justice based upon alleged laws of the colonies in excess of the grant of power contained in the charter, or in instructions from the Crown.   This power of the King in Council must on the whole have been reasonably exercised, inasmuch as the members of the convention frequently referred to it without criticism or disapproval. Indeed the local statesmen of the day retained this right or prerogative in various forms in the constitutions of the several States when they became independent political communities.   Projects of the large and the small States containing provisions to the same effect can be taken as an opinion amounting to a conviction that some expedient or device of this kind was felt to be essential to the execution of the proposed Constitution, just as it was to the constitutions of the States and to the colonies under charter or governed directly by instructions from the Crown.   The idea was an especial favorite with Mr. Madison and those of his school of thought.   The eighth of Mr. Randolph's resolutions could be safely ascribed to Mr. Madison on the evidence of authorship contained in his correspondence with Mr. Randolph and with General Washington in the months preceding the Convention.[1]   The principle was sound but the method was faulty.

Admitting the necessity of some check upon the legislature, there were strong reasons for lodging it in the hands of the executive.   This would indeed be cooperation with the legislature in the framing of laws, violating to a certain degree the separation of functions which had been adopted as a fundamental principle of the proposed Constitution.   It would be a further viola-

---

[1] See letter to Edmund Randolph, April 8, 1787, *The Writings of James Madison*, Hunt ed., Vol. ii, pp. 336–340; and to George Washington, April 16, 1787, *Ibid.*, pp. 344–352.

tion, and indeed a very serious one, if the judiciary, charged with the interpretation of the laws, should be required to participate with the legislature and executive in their making. Therefore, after much discussion, debate and heart-burning on the part of Messrs. Madison and Wilson, the president was given a veto upon the proposed legislation of Congress, separate and distinct from the judiciary. Article 3 of the Constitution of the State of New York, eliminating therefrom the cooperation of the judiciary, had furnished a precedent which Massachusetts adopted, freed from the cooperation of the judges, in Section I, Article II of the Constitution of that commonwealth. The New York expedient was to have even a larger influence and application. Substituting the president for the council, the Federal Convention literally took this provision from the following passage of Article 3 of the Constitution of the State of New York of April 20, 1777:

> And that all bills, which have passed the senate and assembly, shall, before they become laws, be presented to the said council for their revisal and consideration; and if upon such revision and consideration, it should appear improper to the said council, or a majority of them, that the said bill should become a law of this state, that they return the same, together with their objections thereto in writing, to the senate or house of assembly, in whichsoever the same shall have originated, who shall enter the objections sent down by the council, at large, in their minutes, and proceed to reconsider the said bill. But if after such reconsideration, two-thirds of the said senate or house of assembly, shall, notwithstanding the said objections, agree to pass the same, it shall, together with the objections, be sent to the other branch of the legislature, where it shall also be reconsidered, and if approved by two-thirds of the members present, shall be a law.
>
> And in order to prevent any unnecessary delays, be it further ordained, that if any bill shall not be returned by the council within ten days after it shall have been presented, the same shall be a law, unless the legislature shall, by their adjournment, render a return of the said bill within ten days impracticable; in which case the bill shall be returned on the first day of the meeting of the legislature, after the expiration of the said ten days.[1]

So much for the act of Congress, which the president may deem unwise or inconsistent with the terms of the Constitution.

A more delicate and difficult question arose in the case of an act of a State legislature, which might be unwise and, in addition, inconsistent with the terms of the Constitution or an act of Congress or a treaty of the United States. The view which ultimately prevailed was stated in the session of August 23, 1787, by Mr. Sherman, who thought a negative unnecessary, "the laws of the General Government being Supreme & paramount to the State laws according to the plan as it now stands."[2] Mr. Wilson, as set as Mr. Madison upon the council of revision as a check upon the States, is

[1] *The Constitutions of the Several Independent States,* 1781, pp. 63-4.
[2] *Documentary History,* Vol. iii, pp. 601-2.

reported by the latter to the effect that he " considered this as the key-stone wanted to compleat the wide arch of Government we are raising.   The power of self-defence had been urged as necessary for the State Governments — It was equally necessary for the General Government.   The firmness of Judges is not of itself sufficient — Something further is requisite — It will be better to prevent the passage of an improper law, than to declare it void when passed." [1]   To which Mr. Rutledge of South Carolina replied, apparently with some heat, for he was not of an uncholeric disposition, that " If nothing else, this alone would damn and ought to damn the Constitution.   Will any State ever agree to be bound hand & foot in this manner.   It is worse than making mere corporations of them whose bye laws would not be subject to this shackle."

Executive and Judicial Vetoes   The way out was contained in the sixth of Mr. Patterson's resolutions, providing " that all Acts of the U. States in Cong^s., . . . and all Treaties made & ratified under the authority of the U. States shall be the supreme law of the respective States so far forth as those Acts or Treaties shall relate to the said States or their Citizens, and that the Judiciary of the several States shall be bound thereby in their decisions, any thing in the respective laws of the Individual States to the contrary notwithstanding." [2]   With slight modifications this clause became Article VI of the perfected Constitution, leaving with the president what may be called an executive veto of the acts of Congress and with the judiciary a judicial veto of the acts of the Congress and of the States inconsistent with the Constitution of the Union, whether embodied in the State constitutions or in their ordinary laws.

Laws Operate on Individuals   The President, it will be recalled, is charged with the execution of the laws of the United States, and it does not require argument that these should be executed, otherwise their enactment would be worse than futile.   It is, however, to be borne in mind that the government created by the Constitution was one without precedent, and that a principle was fortunately found which was meant to prevent the impracticable method of execution by force against a State, by having the laws operate directly on the individual, by virtue whereof a private citizen violating the law could be arrested and punished, and an official, national or State, violating the law could be restrained under a government of laws, not of men.   Indeed, Mr. Madison based the distinction between a national and a federal government on the fact that the former operated upon individuals, whereas the latter operated upon the States, and although this distinction did not appear clearly in the text of Mr. Randolph's resolutions, it may well have been in the minds of the Virginian members who stood sponsor for them.

[1] *Documentary History*, Vol. iii, p. 602.
[2] *Ibid.*, pp. 127–8.

In the plan of the Virginian delegation which Mr. Randolph laid before the convention on May 29th, the last clause of the sixth resolution authorized the national legislature " to call forth the force of the Union agst. any member of the Union failing to fulfill its duty under the articles thereof," [1] a proposition likewise contained in the New Jersey plan, introduced on June 15th by William Patterson of that State, authorizing the federal government " to call forth ye power of the Confederated States, or so much thereof as may be necessary to enforce and compel an obedience to such Acts, or an Observance of such Treaties." [2]

On the 30th of May, that is to say the very next day after Mr. Randolph's resolutions were introduced, Mr. Mason of Virginia observed, as reported by Mr. Madison, " that the present confederation was not only deficient in not providing for coercion & punishment agst. delinquent States; but argued very cogently that punishment could not in the nature of things be executed on the States collectively, and therefore that such a Gov^t. was necessary as could directly operate on individuals, and would punish those only whose guilt required it." [3]

A very little experience of the temper of the Convention convinced Mr. Madison of the impracticability of this provision, although he himself is credited with the authorship of the Virginian plan, so that on May 31st, but two days after the introduction of the resolution, he changed his mind, as appears from the following extract from the debates: *The Use of Force Against a State*

> The last clause of Resolution 6 authorizing an exertion of the force of the whole agst. a delinquent State came next into consideration.
> M^r. Madison observed that the more he reflected on the use of force, the more he doubted the practicability, the justice and efficacy of it when applied to people collectively and not individually,— a Union of the States containing such an ingredient seemed to provide for its own destruction. The use of force agst. a State, would look more like a declaration of war, than an infliction of punishment, and would probably be considered by the party attacked as a dissolution of all previous compacts by which it might be bound. He hoped that such a system would be framed as might render this recourse unnecessary, and moved that the clause be postponed." [4]

Mr. Madison informs us that " this motion was agreed to nem. con."   It does not figure in the Constitution for the reasons disclosed and set forth in the debates.

A few days later, to be specific on June 8th, Mr. Madison recurred to the subject and confirmed his recantation of the use of force against a State. Thus:

[1] *Documentary History,* Vol. iii, p. 18.
[2] *Ibid.,* p. 128.
[3] *Ibid.,* p. 22.
[4] *Ibid.,* pp. 33–4.

Could the national resources, if exerted to the utmost enforce a national decree agst. Mass^{ts}. abetted perhaps by several of her neighbours? It w^d. not be possible. A small proportion of the Community in a compact situation, acting on the defensive, and at one of its extremities might at any time bid defiance to the National authority. Any Gov^t. for the U. States formed on the supposed practicability of using force agst. the unconstitutional proceedings of the States, w^d. prove as visionary & fallacious as the Gov^t. of Cong^s." [1]

The views thus expressed by Mr. Madison survived the convention in which they were formed and stated, as appears from the following extract from a letter dated October 24, 1787, written after its adjournment to his friend Thomas Jefferson:

A *voluntary* observance of the Federal law by all the members could never be hoped for. A *compulsive* one could evidently never be reduced to practice, and if it could, involved equal calamities to the innocent & the guilty, the necessity of a military force both obnoxious & dangerous, and in general a scene resembling much more a civil war than the administration of a regular Government.

Hence was embraced the alternative of a Government which instead of operating, on the States, should operate without their intervention on the individuals composing them; and hence the change in the principle and proportion of representation. [2]

So much for the Father of the Constitution. Next, as to its classic expounder. In introducing on June 18th his plan of a national and highly centralized form of government, Alexander Hamilton enumerated "the great and essential principles necessary for the support of Government." Among these "great and essential principles" he mentioned force, of which he said:

Force by which may be understood a *coertion of laws* or *coertion of arms*. Cong^s. have not the former except in few cases. In particular States, this coercion is nearly sufficient; tho' he held it in most cases, not entirely so. A certain portion of military force is absolutely necessary in large communities. Mass^{ts}. is now feeling this necessity & making provision for it. But how can this force be exerted on the States collectively. It is impossible. It amounts to a war between the parties. Foreign powers also will not be idle spectators. They will interpose, the confusion will increase, and a dissolution of the Union ensue. [3]

Colonel Hamilton, as in the case of Mr. Madison, clung to the views which he had expressed in the convention, and expressed them with peculiar and convincing force in *The Federalist,* written to justify the Constitution, which is, as is well known, the joint product of the minds and hands of Messrs. Ham-

---

[1] *Documentary History,* Vol. iii, p. 89.
[2] *Writings of Madison,* Hunt ed., Vol. v, p. 19.
[3] *Documentary History,* Vol. iii, p. 141.

ilton, Madison and Jay. In the following passage from *The Federalist,* the Colonel pays his respects to force:

> Whoever considers the populousness and strength of several of these states singly at the present juncture, and looks forward to what they will become, even at the distance of half a century, will at once dismiss as idle and visionary any scheme, which aims at regulating their movements by laws, to operate upon them in their collective capacities, and to be executed by a coercion applicable to them in the same capacities. A project of this kind is little less romantic than the monster-taming spirit, attributed to the fabulous heroes and demi-gods of antiquity.
>
> Even in those confederacies which have been composed by members smaller than many of our counties, the principle of legislation for sovereign states, supported by military coercion, has never been found effectual. It has rarely been attempted to be employed, but against the weaker members; and in most instances attempts to coerce the refractory and disobedient, have been the signals of bloody wars; in which one half of the confederacy has displayed its banners against the other.[1]

And on a third occasion, when converting to the proposed Constitution a hostile majority of the New York Convention, by force of argument, not by force of arms, Alexander Hamilton restated his views on this interesting subject. In the first place, he declared it impossible to coerce States. Thus:

> If you make requisitions, and they are not complied with, what is to be done? It has been observed, to coerce the states is one of the maddest projects that was ever devised. A failure of compliance will never be confined to a single state. This being the case, can we suppose it wise to hazard a civil war?[2]

In the next place, he expressed the opinion that the States themselves would not agree to coerce others. Thus:

> But can we believe that one state will ever suffer itself to be used as an instrument of coercion? The thing is a dream; it is impossible.[3]

To the same effect is the language of George Mason, the bitterest opponent of the Constitution, as Messrs. Madison and Hamilton were its strongest advocates. On the matter of force, the opponents and the advocates agreed. Thus, Mr. Mason said on June 20th:

> It was acknowledged by Mr. Patterson that his plan could not be enforced without military coertion. Does he consider the force of this concession. The most jarring elements of nature; fire & water themselves are not more incompatible tha[n] such a mixture of civil liberty and military execution. Will the militia march from one State to another, in order to collect the arrears of taxes from the delinquent members of the Republic? Will they

---

[1] *The Federalist,* 1802, Vol. i, p. 102. Paper, No. xvi.
[2] Jonathan Elliot, *Debates in the Several State Conventions,* 1836, Vol. ii, pp. 232-3.
[3] *Ibid.,* p. 233.

maintain an army for this purpose? Will not the citizens of the invaded State assist one another till they rise as one Man, and shake off the Union altogether? Rebellion is the only case in which the military force of the State can be properly exerted agst. its Citizens.[1]

Finally, lest the views of the statesmen of the Revolution, the founders of the Republic, and the framers of the Constitution, become wearisome, but one further quotation is made. In advocating the ratification of the Constitution by the Connecticut Convention, Oliver Ellsworth, with that fine poise and balance of mind characteristic of the senator and of the Chief Justice of the Supreme Court of the United States, pointed out that nothing would prevent the States from falling out if they so desired, saying on this point:

> If the United States and the individual states will quarrel, if they want to fight, they may do it, and no frame of government can possibly prevent it.[2]

In advocating the need of a coercive principle, he added:

> We all see and feel this necessity. The only question is, Shall it be a coercion of law, or a coercion of arms? There is no other possible alternative. Where will those who oppose a coercion of law come out? Where will they end? A necessary consequence of their principles is a war of the states one against the other. I am for coercion by law — that coercion which acts only upon delinquent individuals. This Constitution does not attempt to coerce sovereign bodies, states, in their political capacity. No coercion is applicable to such bodies, but that of an armed force. If we should attempt to execute the laws of the Union by sending an armed force against a delinquent state, it would involve the good and bad, the innocent and guilty, in the same calamity.[3]

It was foreseen that force might be necessary to execute the laws of the Union, and therefore Congress was specifically empowered by a clause of the eighth section of the first article " to provide for calling forth the militia to execute the laws of the Union, suppress insurrections and repel invasions." But force is to be used, in accordance with the views previously set forth, against individuals, whether they act singly or in small groups, as a mob or in organized masses as insurgents. The individual, not the State, suffers; the individual, not the State, is coerced. At least this seems to have been the view of the framers of the Constitution and it has been the practice of the government of the more perfect Union of the North American States. In the session of the Federal Convention of July 14, 1787, Mr. Madison, adverting to this peculiarity of the proposed government for the union of the States, " called for a single instance in which the Genl. Gov^t. was not to operate on the people individually," and continued, without an answer having been interposed to his

---

[1] *Documentary History*, Vol. iii, pp. 171–2.
[2] Elliot, *Debates*, Vol. ii, p. 196.
[3] *Ibid.*, p. 197.

question, "The practicability of making laws, with coercive sanctions, for the States as political bodies has been exploded on all hands." [1]

[1] *Documentary History,* Vol. iii, p. 340.

X

THE FIRST PERMANENT TRIBUNAL OF THE STATES

Should not a court be established by authority of Congress, to take cognizance of prizes made by the Continental vessels? Whatever the mode is, which they are pleased to adopt, there is an absolute necessity of its being speedily determined on; for I cannot spare time from military affairs, to give proper attention to these matters. (*Extract from a letter of General Washington from Camp at Cambridge, to the President of Congress, November 11, 1775. Worthington Chauncey Ford, Editor, The Writings of George Washington, Vol. III, 1889, pp. 213–214.*)

Resolved, That a committee be appointed, to take into consideration so much of said letter as relates to the disposal of such vessels and cargoes belonging to the enemy, as shall fall into the hands of, or be taken by, the inhabitants of the United Colonies.

That the Committee consist of 7. (*Journals of the Continental Congress, Session of November 17, 1775, Library of Congress edition, Vol. III, 1905, pp. 357–358.*)

4. That it be and is hereby recommended to the several legislatures in the United Colonies, as soon as possible, to erect courts of Justice, or give jurisdiction to the courts now in being for the purpose of determining concerning the captures to be made as aforesaid, and to provide that all trials in such case be had by a jury under such qualifications, as to the respective legislatures shall seem expedient.

5. That all prosecutions shall be commenced in the court of that colony, in which the captures shall be made, but if no such court be at that time erected in the said colony, or if the capture be made on open sea, then the prosecution shall be in the court of such colony as the captor may find most convenient, provided that nothing contained in this resolution shall be construed so as to enable the captor to remove his prize from any colony competent to determine concerning the seizure, after he shall have carried the vessel so seized within any harbour of the same.

6. That in all cases an appeal shall be allowed to the Congress, or such person or persons as they shall appoint for the trial of appeals, provided the appeal be demanded within five days after definitive sentence, and such appeal be lodged with the secretary of Congress within forty days afterwards, and provided the party appealing shall give security to prosecute the said appeal to effect, and in case of the death of the secretary during the recess of Congress, then the said appeal to be lodged in Congress within 20 days after the meeting thereof. (*Journals of the Continental Congress, Session of November 25, 1775, Library of Congress edition, Vol. III, 1905, pp. 373–374.*)

The resolves relative to captures made by Continental armed vessels only want a court established for trial, to make them complete. This, I hope, will be soon done, as I have taken the liberty to urge it often to the Congress. (*Extract from a letter of General Washington, from Cambridge, to the President of the Congress, December 14, 1775. Worthington Chauncey Ford, Editor, The Writings of George Washington, Vol. III, 1889, p. 274.*)

Resolved, That a standing committee, to consist of five members, be appointed to hear and determine upon appeals brought against sentences passed on libels in the courts of Admiralty in the respective states, agreeable to the resolutions of Congress; and that the several appeals, when lodged with the secretary, be by him delivered to them for their final determination: . . . (*Journals of the Continental Congress, Session of January 30, 1777, Library of Congress edition, Vol. VII, 1907, p. 75.*)

Article IX. The United States in Congress assembled, shall have the sole and exclusive right and power . . . of establishing rules for deciding in all cases, what captures on land or water shall be legal, and in what manner prizes taken by land or naval forces in the service of the United States shall be divided or appropriated . . . and establishing courts for receiving and determining finally appeals in all cases of captures, provided that no member of Congress shall be appointed a judge of any of the said courts. (*The Articles of Confederation agreed to by the Congress, November 15, 1777, Revised Statutes of the United States, 1878, p. 9.*)

Resolved, That a court be established for the trial of all appeals from the courts of admiralty in these United States, in cases of capture, to consist of three judges, appointed and commissioned by Congress, either two of whom, in the absence of the other, to hold the said court for the despatch of business:

That the said court appoint their own register:

That the trials therein be according to the usage of nations and not by jury: . . .
(*Journals of the Continental Congress, Session of January 15, 1780, Library of Congress edition, Vol. XVI, 1910, p. 61.*)

Resolved, That the stile of the Court of Appeals appointed by Congress, be, "The Court of Appeals in Cases of Capture." . . .

Resolved, That appeals from the courts of admiralty in the respective states, be, as heretofore, demanded within five days after definitive sentence; and in future such appeals be lodged with the register of the Court of Appeals in cases of capture within forty days thereafter, provided the party appealing shall give security to prosecute such appeal to effect.

Resolved, That all matters respecting appeals in cases of capture, now depending before Congress, or the commissioners of appeals, consisting of members of Congress, be referred to the newly erected Court of Appeals, to be there adjudged and determined according to law; and that all papers touching appeals in cases of capture, lodged in the office of the secretary of Congress, be delivered to and lodged with the register of the Court of Appeals. (*Journals of the Continental Congress, Session of May 24, 1780, Library of Congress edition, Vol. XVII, 1910, pp. 458, 459.*)

Section 8. The Congress shall have Power . . . To declare War, grant Letters of Marque and Reprisal, and make Rules concerning Captures on Land and Water; . . . (*Constitution of the United States, Article I.*)

Section 2. The judicial Power shall extend . . . to all Cases of admiralty and maritime Jurisdiction. . . . (*Constitution of the United States, Article III.*)

The district courts of the United States are courts of prize; and have power to carry into effect the sentences of the old continental courts of appeals in prize causes. (*Per Mr. Chief Justice Marshall in Jennings v. Carson, 4 Cranch, 2, decided in 1807.*)

CHAPTER X

THE FIRST PERMANENT TRIBUNAL OF THE STATES

An examination of that part of the ninth of the Articles of Confederation relating to controversies and their settlement shows that it deals with three situations or conditions: first, prizes taken by land or naval forces; second, the trial of piracies and felonies committed on the high seas; third, controversies of all kinds between the States, sovereign, free and independent, forming the Confederation, styled in Article I, The United States of America.

Voluntary Self-denials — Including Disarmament

The members of the Congress understood, or their experience had taught them by 1777, when the Articles of Confederation were adopted by them for ratification by the States, that, although " each State retains its sovereignty, freedom, and independence, and every power, jurisdiction, and right which is not by this Confederation expressly delegated to the United States in Congress assembled," it was nevertheless necessary to provide for certain things if they were to hold together during the war against the mother country. They might agree to use force against Great Britain, and, indeed, their union was formed for this purpose; but they were unwilling, as are all sovereign, free and independent States, to have force used against themselves. They had practically disqualified themselves from settling disputes arising between them by direct negotiations, because in Article VI they had provided that " no two or more States shall enter into any treaty, confederation or alliance whatever between them, without the consent of the United States in Congress assembled." In the same article they had practically agreed to such a limitation of their forces as to amount to disarmament, providing that neither vessels of war nor armed forces should " be kept up in time of peace by any State, except such number only, as shall be deemed necessary by the United States in Congress assembled, for the defence of such State, or its trade." And they drew the logical conclusion from this provision, that no State should engage in war without the consent of the Congress, unless it was actually invaded by enemies or was menaced by such invasion.

Diplomatic and Military Settlements

The time-honored method of settling controversies between States sovereign, free and independent, has been and still is either by diplomatic negotiation or by armed conflict; and the Revolutionary statesmen were intelligent enough to recognize that, if diplomacy could not effect a settlement, and if an appeal to arms were excluded, there must be a resort to some method of settlement which was neither diplomatic nor military.   They interposed, therefore, between the two, the judicial method, recognizing, although not appealing to Aristotle in confirmation thereof, that " justice is the bond of men in States, and the administration of justice, which is the determination of what is just, is the principle of order in political society."   They had in mind a court of justice, and they so said.   They recognized that the court, to have jurisdiction over the States and to bind their actions, could only be created by them directly, or by their agent for this purpose, as they had no superior.   They therefore invested Congress with the power, a Congress in which each sovereign, free and independent State of the Confederacy had an equal vote, although each might, according to its pleasure, send an unequal number of representatives.

Another Kind of Settlement

After having defined the matters which, in the interest of the States, had to be settled with those countries which they considered foreign and those which they considered, by virtue of the Confederation, as domestic, the Confederated States authorized the Congress as their agent, or rather their own delegates in Congress assembled, to appoint " courts for the trial of piracies and felonies committed on the high seas; " to establish " courts for receiving and determining finally appeals in all cases of captures; " and, in the matter of disputes between the States themselves, to appoint " commissioners or judges to constitute a court for hearing and determining the matter in question." [1]

Courts of the Confederated States

It is to be observed that these are likewise considered judicial questions by the Constitution, which succeeded the Confederation, and that they are either referred to courts by the Constitution or by act of Congress passed in pursuance of authority vested in that body by the Constitution.   Therefore, in Section 8 of Article I of the Constitution, vesting all the legislative power in Congress which the States cared to grant to the United States, it is said that " Congress shall have Power . . . To define and punish Piracies and Felonies committed on the high Seas."   Going a step further, the framers of the Constitution added " and Offenses against the Law of Nations; " and, in the clause immediately following, the Congress is invested with the power " to make Rules concerning Captures on Land and Water."   In Article III of the Constitution it is declared that " the judicial Power of the United States, shall be vested in one supreme Court, and in such inferior Courts as the Congress may from time to time ordain and establish," in accordance with the clause in Section 8 of Article I, authorizing Congress " to constitute Tribunals inferior to the supreme Court."

After providing in the 1st section of Article III for the creation of a

[1] For the text of the Articles of Confederation and the Constitution, see *Appendix,* pp. 494–513.

International
Questions

Supreme Court and of inferior courts, the Constitution vests the judiciary with the express power to pass upon and to decide all cases affecting ambassadors and other public ministers, and consuls, all cases of admiralty and maritime jurisdiction, controversies to which the United States shall be a party, controversies between two or more States, and controversies between a State and foreign States, citizens or subjects.   It should further be said in this connection that certain judicial questions were deemed to be of such importance that the Supreme Court was vested with original jurisdiction thereof, whereas of other questions the Supreme Court was to exercise appellate jurisdiction.   Thus in Article III, Section 2, of the Constitution:

> In all cases affecting Ambassadors, other public Ministers and Consuls, and those in which a State shall be Party, the supreme Court shall have original Jurisdiction.

It will be seen that the first category consists of international questions, cases affecting ambassadors, public ministers and consuls, and suits between States of the American Union, which, by the 10th Amendment to the Constitution, are regarded as possessing the powers not delegated to the United States in the Constitution.   As in the case of the Confederation, the States renounced the right to enter into direct negotiations or to engage in war by two clauses of the 10th section of Article I, providing that " No State shall enter into any Treaty, Alliance, or Confederation;" that "no State shall, without the Consent of Congress . . . keep Troops, or Ships of War in time of Peace, enter into any Agreement or Compact with another State, or with a foreign Power, or engage in War, unless actually invaded or in such imminent Danger as will not admit of delay."   In other words, in the relations of the States with foreign nations, they invested the United States with their conduct and adjustment.   In questions between and among themselves they created another agency of their own, by which and through which these questions should be settled.   They showed their belief in the efficacy of judicial settlement by investing their Supreme Court with original jurisdiction in questions concerning ambassadors, ministers, and consuls, in the hope that disputes concerning these matters would be settled by judicial process, just as the disputes between themselves were to be settled by judicial process.

International
Implications
of the
Confederate
Judiciary

But as the nations of the world had not renounced direct negotiations or a resort to arms, as the States themselves had done in the exercise of their wisdom and discretion, the United States as their agent was invested by the Articles of Confederation with the right to conduct diplomatic negotiations and to resort to war if need be, thus confessing their faith in judicial settlement and manifesting, it would seem, their willingness to have the disputes of the Union, like the disputes of the States in matters of law and equity,

THE FIRST PERMANENT TRIBUNAL OF THE STATES 213

settled by decisions of courts, if the United States, like the States in their wisdom and discretion, should interpose the judicial remedy between the breakdown of diplomacy and the resort to arms. Because of the novelty and of the interest of the provisions of the Confederation in these respects, it is of importance to dwell upon them, since they are as capable of application to the sovereign, free and independent States forming the society of nations as they were to the sovereign, free and independent States forming the Confederation. Because of their retention in the Constitution and of their development into agencies which have justified themselves for a hundred years and more in the settlement of disputes between the States of the Union it is more evident to us today than it was to them that these agencies are likewise applicable to disputes between and among the members of the society of nations.

There is an added interest in such an examination, because the imperfect procedure of the Confederation became the perfected procedure of the Constitution. By the determination of what is just, exactly as set forth in the teachings of Aristotle, the principle of order in that political society which we call the United States can be and will be the principle of order in the political society which we call the society of nations unless the nations, like Saturn, are always to devour their offspring.

It was natural that the framers of the Constitution should confess their faith in judicial settlement, because there were courts in all the States and a Supreme Court in every State. They had had experience with felonies and piracies committed on the high seas; they had been parties to the wars of Great Britain — indeed, the Seven Years War, called by us the French and Indian War, began in the western world — and they felt the necessity of rules for the capture and disposition of prizes. Vice admiralty courts had been established in the colonies with appeals to Great Britain, and on the eve of the Revolution these admiralty courts had come very prominently to their attention, in that they had recently been invested with the trial of political offenses without the intervention of a jury, as a court of admiralty is a court of civil, not of common, law. They had had experience with disputes not only with the mother country concerning the correct interpretation of their charters; but with other colonies on the same and other matters. The King in Council had been the court of appeal in such cases; the King in Council exercised a large control over the colonies as well as in the settlement of their disputes; and the King in Council is today, through the instrumentality of the judicial committee thereof, the court of appeal from the colonies and of greater Britain. It was therefore natural that, brought together by what they regarded the oppression of the mother country, they should settle these matters in the way with which they were familiar, preferring the old rut to the new road whenever possible.

Lessons of the State Courts

Therefore, under the Articles of Confederation the Congress, with its powerless president, was substituted for the Council, with its powerful king. In the exercise of this jurisdiction, the Congress endeavored to avail itself of the institutions and agencies of the States, without attempting to create its own as to which it felt a lack of authority. Therefore, in the beginning the Congress contented itself with requesting the States to assume jurisdiction where their agencies could be made use of; but, in the end, Congress felt itself obliged to create an agency of its own, notwithstanding the existence of local institutions. It refrained from doing so until the Articles of Confederation had been adopted by the Congress and approved by the majority of the States, although not by all of them. In the case of disputes between the States, the Congress appears to have followed the practice of the King in Council in accepting jurisdiction before referring the matters to judicial determination by a commission or committee.[1]

Let us now take up the provisions of the ninth of the Articles of Confederation in each of these matters, and in the order in which they are set forth therein. "The United States, in Congress assembled, shall have the sole and exclusive right and power of . . . appointing courts for the trial of piracies and felonies committed on the high seas." Under this heading, the Congress contented itself with utilizing the machinery of the States. Thus, by an ordinance of April 5, 1781, it was provided that persons charged with such offenses should be " enquired of, tried and adjudged by grand and petit juries, according to the course of the common law, in like manner as if the piracy or felony were committed upon the land, and within some county, district or precinct in one of these United States." [2]

Trial of Piracies and Felonies

Having thus provided for the law, Congress determined the court in which the law should be administered. Thus, " the justices of the supreme or superior courts of judicature, and judge of the Court of Admiralty of the several and respective states, or any two or more of them, are hereby constituted and appointed judges for hearing and trying such offenders." In some of the States there was more than one Admiralty judge. Therefore, the Congress met this contingency by providing that " if there shall be more than one judge of the admiralty in any of the United States, that then, and in such case, the supreme executive power of such State may and shall commissionate one of them exclusively to join in performing the duties required by this ordinance."

---

[1] The following account is based upon an admirable and learned article entitled *Federal Courts Prior to the Adoption of the Constitution*, by the Honorable J. C. Bancroft Davis, Reporter to the Supreme Court of the United States (131 U. S., *App.* xix–lxiii), and *The Predecessor of the Supreme Court*, by Professor J. Franklin Jameson, in the volume entitled *Essays in the Constitutional History of the United States in the Formative Period, 1775–1789* (1889), pp. 1–45. Where not directly quoted, the texts of these remarkable essays have been paraphrased. A valuable account of this matter will be found in Chapters iv, v, and vi of Hampton L. Carson's *History of the Supreme Court of the United States*, Vol. i.

[2] *Journals of the Continental Congress*, Vol. xix, pp. 354–6.

As this ordinance was amended on March 4, 1783,[1] in matters of form rather than of substance, it is not necessary to quote it, and, following the example of Judge Davis in this very matter, " I have not thought that any good purpose would be served by hunting up and printing a list of the persons tried under these ordinances." [2]

The important fact for the matter in hand is that the States represented in Congress felt the need of some provision for the trial of piracies and felonies committed on the high seas, and the mere statement of this fact is sufficient as showing that, in their opinion, a judicial body was required for this purpose. As they were to be tried by a law common to the States, with which the States were familiar and which they had administered, the agencies of the States were used.

" The United States in Congress assembled shall have the sole and exclusive right and power of . . . establishing courts for receiving and determining finally appeals in all cases of captures, provided that no member of Congress shall be appointed a judge of any of the said courts." The power vested in Congress was exercised not merely, as in the case of piracies and felonies, at the end of the Revolution, but at the very beginning. The State machinery which was first employed was found inadequate, and the Congress established a court of its own, finally known as the Court of Appeals in Cases of Capture. This is the first instance of a federal tribunal created within the United States, and is considered as the immediate predecessor of the Supreme Court thereof; although, as will be seen later, it shares this exalted honor with the commissions under the ninth article appointed for the trial of controversies between the States. It is therefore necessary to define the nature and to consider the origin and development of this tribunal in some detail.

The First Federal Tribunal

The necessity of prize procedure was evident from the beginning of the Revolution, indeed before the Declaration of Independence, and the experience had in the matter of prizes forced Congress, somewhat reluctantly, to exercise the power of appointing a court for this purpose before the Articles of Confederation had been adopted by the last of the States on March 1, 1781, thus investing the Congress with the power legally so to do. It was inevitable that enterprising merchantmen of the different States would waylay British commerce upon the high seas, and it was clear to discerning minds that vessels belonging to different States and commanded by citizens thereof would fall out among themselves as to the shares of the prize to which they thought themselves entitled, involve the States in controversies and, by lawless conduct, draw the United States into controversy, perhaps into conflict, with foreign States.

[1] *Journals of the American Congress from 1774 to 1788* (1823), Vol. iv, p. 170.
[2] 131 U. S., *App.,* p. xiv.

The Revolution broke out in Massachusetts. It was therefore in Massachusetts that the first prize court was established. In June, 1775, Elbridge Gerry, then beginning a long and distinguished political career, moved the Provincial Congress of that Colony to encourage the fitting out of armed vessels and to establish a court for the trial and condemnation of prizes. On November 10, 1775, an act was passed which has been stated to be " the first actual avowal of offensive hostilities against the mother country, which is to be found in the annals of the revolution," [1] and which John Adams, then at the bar when not upon the hustings, considered to be one of the " boldest, most dangerous, and most important measures and epochas in the history of the new world, the commencement of an independent national establishment of a new maritime and naval military power." [2]   General Washington, then in command of the Continental army in and about Boston, which he had besieged and hemmed in, recognized the importance of this action. He also felt the necessity of uniform regulations and practice to prevent the States from quarreling among themselves, to secure uniformity of decision in matters of prize, which was in the interest alike of the States and of the United States in their relations with foreign countries. Therefore, on November 11, 1775, the day after the passage of the Massachusetts act, he thus wrote to John Hancock, President of the Continental Congress:

> Enclosed you have a copy of an act passed this session, by the honorable Council and House of Representatives of this province. It respects such captures as may be made by vessels fitted out by the province, or by individuals thereof. As the armed vessels, fitted out at the Continental expense, do not come under this law, I would have it submitted to the consideration of Congress, to point out a more summary way of proceeding, to determine the property and mode of condemnation of such prizes as have been or hereafter may be made, than is specified in this act.
>
> Should not a court be established by authority of Congress, to take cognizance of prizes made by the Continental vessels? Whatever the mode is, which they are pleased to adopt, there is an absolute necessity of its being speedily determined on. . . . [3]

Fearing that Congress had not taken action, he again wrote to its president on December 4th of the same year:

> It is some time since I recommended to the Congress, that they would institute a court for the trial of prizes made by the Continental armed vessels, which I hope they have ere now taken into their consideration; otherwise I should again take the liberty of urging it in the most pressing manner. [4]

And, as showing the importance which the General rightly attached to this

---

[1] James T. Austin, *The Life of Elbridge Gerry,* 1828, Vol. i, p. 94.
[2] *Ibid.,* p. 96.
[3] Ford, *Writings of George Washington,* Vol. iii, p. 213; Sparks, Vol. iii, pp. 154-5.
[4] Ford, *ibid.,* p. 257; Sparks, p. 184.

matter, a further quotation may be made from a letter addressed to his fellow-Virginian, Richard Henry Lee, who, a few months later, on June 7, 1776, was to move the momentous resolutions in Congress " that these United Colonies are and of right ought to be free and independent States." [1]   Thus, on December 26th, he wrote to Mr. Lee:

> . . . I must beg of you, my good Sir, to use your influence in having a court of admiralty, or some power appointed to hear and determine all matters relative to captures; you cannot conceive how I am plagued on this head, and how impossible it is for me to hear and determine upon matters of this sort, when the facts, perhaps, are only to be ascertained at ports, forty, fifty, or more miles distant, without bringing the parties here at great trouble and expense.   At any rate, my time will not allow me to be a competent judge of this business.[2]

The Congress, however, had not been remiss, and immediately upon the receipt of General Washington's first letter it took action.   On November 17th it was " *Resolved,* That a committee be appointed to take into consideration so much of said letter as relates to the disposal of such vessels and cargoes belonging to the enemy, as shall fall into the hands of, or be taken by, the inhabitants of the United Colonies." [3]   On November 23d, the committee to which the letter was referred brought in its report.   It was ordered to lie upon the table " for the perusal of the members;" it was " debated by paragraphs " on the 24th and 25th of the same month, and adopted on November 25, 1775.[4]   The resolutions authorized the capture of prizes upon the high seas and legalized those which had alread been made.   They determined the shares of the captors in the prize and the distribution of the money. They provided, as later in the case of piracies and felonies committed on the high seas, that the trial should take place in the colonial courts (because at this time the Declaration of Independence had not been proclaimed), and that an appeal should lie to the Congress.   The section dealing with procedure on appeal thus reads:

> 6. That in all cases an appeal shall be allowed to the Congress, or such person or persons as they shall appoint for the trial of appeals, provided the appeal be demanded within five days after definitive sentence, and such appeal be lodged with the secretary of Congress within forty days afterwards, and provided the party appealing shall give security to prosecute the said appeal to effect, and in case of the death of the secretary during the recess of Congress, then the said appeal to be lodged in Congress within 20 days after the meeting thereof.[5]

The passage of this resolution was pleasing to " the General," and, with a

---

[1] *Journals of the Continental Congress,* Vol. v, p. 425.
[2] Ford, *Writings of George Washington,* Vol. iii, p. 274; Sparks, Vol. iii, p. 217.
[3] *Journals of the Continental Congress,* Vol. iii, pp. 357–8.
[4] *Ibid.,* pp. 371–5.
[5] *Ibid.,* p. 374.

clearness of vision and a tenacity of purpose, recognized by his countrymen and with which a grateful posterity credits him, he pointed out the one thing needed to perfect the action of Congress in a passage from a letter to its president, dated December 14, 1775:

> The resolves relative to captures made by Continental armed vessels only want a court established for trial, to make them complete. This, I hope, will be soon done, as I have taken the liberty to urge it often to the Congress.[1]

In the end, the Congress was forced to take the action which the far-sighted Washington had recommended in the beginning; but it was only taken after great hesitation, with much reluctance, and when a very bitter experience had convinced its members of the absolute necessity of a court.

Before stating this incident, it should be mentioned that an Admiralty Court, generally requiring trial by jury, was organized in each of the colonies or States in accordance with the recommendation of the Congress that this be done, as it will be observed that Congress contented itself for the present with an appeal from the local jurisdictions, which were regarded as courts of first instance in prize matters. The intent of Congress seems to have been misunderstood, as on January 31st and February 27, 1776, two cases which had not been passed upon by the colonial courts were referred direct to the Congress by the petitioners, and in each case, in accordance with its understanding of its resolutions, the Congress referred the applicants to the colonial courts. However, a few weeks later (April 4, 1776), the Congress took original jurisdiction in the matter of a prize vessel which had been run ashore,[2] directed that it be sold, and decreed the distribution of the proceeds arising from the sale. This appears, however, to have been the only instance in which the Congress took original jurisdiction. Therefore, it only acted in cases of appeal, at first directly, shortly thereafter through committees, and finally by means of an appellate court established in accordance with General Washington's recommendation.

First Case of Appeal

The first case of appeal was that of the schooner *Thistle*,[3] which was laid before Congress on August 5, 1776, a month after the Declaration of Independence. Congress attempted to hear the appeal as a body but eventually referred it to a special committee, and the earlier cases were referred to special committees until, in the beginning of 1777, Congress felt the necessity of and therefore created a standing committee on appeals, to consider such cases as should be laid before it in accordance with its resolution of November 25, 1775. This important action was taken on January 30, 1777, when it was

Congressional Committee on Appeals

---

[1] Ford, *Writings of Washington*, Vol. iii, p. 274; Sparks, Vol. iii, pp. 196–7.
[2] *Journals of the Continental Congress*, Vol. iv, p. 256.
[3] *Ibid.*, Vol. v, p. 631.

"*Resolved,* That a standing committee to consist of five members, be appointed to hear and determine upon appeals brought against sentences passed on libels in the courts of Admiralty in the respective states, agreeable to the resolutions of Congress; and that the several appeals, when lodged with the secretary, be by him delivered to them for their final determination." [1]   The members of the committee were frequently changed, but the method was continued until a court was established.   The defects of a changing personnel, even although forming a permanent committee, were pointed out by the merchants and citizens of Philadelphia, with the approval of the Pennsylvanian authorities, in the petition to Congress of May, 1779, which is susceptible of a larger application:

> The success of the American privateers exceeded for a time the most sanguine expectation, and in all probability had still continued, if certain causes had not arisen to interrupt it.   What these Causes are, we do not mean to enumerate.   We shall only suggest one, and leave it to your honors to say what influence it may have had, and to provide a remedy against it in future.
>
> Certainty in the Laws is the great Source of the people's Security, and an adherence to prior adjudication is the principal means of attaining that certainty.   But the Court of Appeals in its present State is continually fluctuating, the same Judges seldom acting for more than a few months.   In a Court where there is this Constant change and succession of Judges, it is impossible that fixed principles can be established, or the doctrine of precedents ever take place.
>
> Every obstacle that creates unnecessary delay in the administration of Justice, should be carefully removed, but when the seeds of this delay are sown in the very Constitution of the Court, the People, rather than have recourse to a Tribunal of that kind, will be induced to give up their right. This we apprehend to be the nature of the Court of Appeals. . . .
>
> Impressed with these Considerations and others that might be mentioned, [we venture] to point out the propriety of nominating Judges of Appeal, who, not being members of Congress, would have more leisure for the discharge of their employment.   We shall only observe that we trust to the Wisdom of Congress to establish the Court of Appeal on a lasting and solid Foundation, and to remove by proper regulations the imperfections that are at present so generally the ground of Complaint. [2]

The merchants and citizens of Philadelphia were peculiarly qualified for discovering, and were interested in pointing out, the defects of the judgments obtained by a standing committee on appeal in prizes with a shifting membership, for events had taken place under their very eyes which filled them with apprehension, not only as to their own affairs but as to the state of the Union, if Union it could be called.   The case of the *Active,* for it is to this that reference is made, called attention to another great defect of the existing system, because, although a State decree was reversed by the committee on

---

[1] *Journals of the Continental Congress,* Vol. vii, p. 75.
[2] Jameson, *Essays in the Constitutional History of the United States,* pp. 24–26.

appeal, the State court did not feel itself obliged to give effect to the reversal of its judgment and to recognize by proper action the rights of property acquired under federal appeal.

The
Case of
the *Active*

The facts of this case are very interesting, and should be stated in this connection, as it was one of the cases which led to the organization of a court of appeal, and, indirectly, to the establishment of the Supreme Court itself. One Gideon Olmstead and three other citizens of Connecticut were captured by the British and carried to Jamaica, where they were put on board the sloop *Active,* laden with a cargo of supplies for New York, then in possession of the British. They were obliged to assist in its navigation, which they were unwilling to do. They therefore rose against the master and crew, took possession of the sloop, and made for the port of Egg Harbor, in New Jersey; but, before reaching this port, the *Active,* under their control, was captured by one Houston in command of the Pennsylvanian armed brig *Convention.* The *Active* was taken into the port of Philadelphia and libeled as prize of the *Convention.* The case was further complicated by the fact that the officers of a privateer, cruising in company with the *Convention,* claimed to have taken part in the capture, and therefore made claim to a part of the proceeds. Olmstead and his companions, claiming the sloop *Active,* in which they were in control when taken, put in a claim to the whole of the proceeds. In the admiralty court of Pennsylvania a trial was had by jury, the verdict of which was as follows:

> One-fourth of the net proceeds of the sloop *Active* and her cargo to the first claimants, three-fourths of the net proceeds of the said sloop and her cargo to the libellant and the second claimant, as per agreement between them.[1]

Judgment was entered upon the verdict, from which an appeal was taken by Olmstead and others to the Congressional committee of appeal. On December 15, 1778, the commissioners reversed the decision of the State court and rendered judgment in favor of Olmstead and others, directing the court below to sell the sloop and cargo and to pay the remainder to the appellants after deducting costs, charges and expenses. The judge of the Pennsylvania Court of Admiralty recognized the validity of the decision reversing the decree of his court, but, insisting that he could not set aside the verdict of the jury, issued an order that the sloop and cargo be sold and the proceeds brought into court. On December 28, 1778, the appellants moved the committee that process might issue to the Admiralty Court of Pennsylvania commanding the marshal to execute the decree of the committee. The committee accordingly directed the marshal to hold the money subject to their order, but he disregarded this order and paid the money to the Admiralty Judge; whereupon the committee de-

[1] *Journals of the Continental Congress,* Vol. xiii, p. 282.

clared that "this Court, being unwilling to enter into any proceedings for Contempt, lest Consequences might ensue at this Juncture dangerous to the public Peace of the United States, will not proceed farther in this affair, nor hear any Appeal, until the Authority of this Court shall be so settled as to give full Efficacy to their Decrees and Process."[1]   At the same time the committee laid the proceedings before Congress, which approved their action in an elaborate series of resolutions, which are so important, because of their larger bearing upon the relation of the States, or indeed of any nation to foreign countries, that they are quoted in full:

> *Resolved,* That Congress, or such person or persons as they appoint to hear and determine appeals from the courts of admiralty, have necessarily the power to examine as well into decisions on facts as decisions on the law, and to decree finally thereon, and that no finding of a jury in any court of admiralty, or court for determining the legality of captures on the high seas can or ought to destroy the right of appeal and the re-examination of the facts reserved to Congress;
>
> That no act of any one State can or ought to destroy the right of appeals to Congress in the sense above declared:
>
> That Congress is by these United States invested with the supreme sovereign power of war and peace:
>
> That the power of executing the law of nations is essential to the sovereign supreme power of war and peace:
>
> That the legality of all captures on the high seas must be determined by the law of nations:
>
> That the authority ultimately and finally to decide on all matters and questions touching the law of nations, does reside and is vested in the sovereign supreme power of war and peace:
>
> That a controul by appeal is necessary, in order to compel a just and uniform execution of the naw of nations:
>
> That the said controul must extend as well over the decisions of juries as judges in courts for determining the legality of captures on the sea; otherwise the juries would be possessed of the ultimate supreme power of executing the law of nations in all cases of captures, and might at any time exercise the same in such manner as to prevent a possibility of being controuled; a construction which involves many inconveniences and absurdities, destroys an essential part of the power of war and peace entrusted to Congress, and would disable the Congress of the United States from giving satisfaction to foreign nations complaining of a violation of neutralities, of treaties or other breaches of the law of nations, and would enable a jury in any one State to involve the United States in hostilities; a construction which for these and many other reasons is inadmissible:
>
> That this power of controuling by appeal the several admiralty jurisdictions of the states, has hitherto been exercised by Congress by the medium of a committee of their own members:
>
> *Resolved,* That the committee before whom was determined the appeal from the court of admiralty for the State of Pennsylvania, in the case of the sloop *Active,* was duly constituted and authorized to determine the same.[2]

Congressional Resolutions — the Relation of States

[1] Jameson, *Essays,* p. 20.
[2] *Journals of the Continental Congress,* Vol. xiii, pp. 283–4. Session of March 6, 1779.

The legislature of Pennsylvania, on March 8, 1780, repealed the statute authorizing juries to decide admiralty causes, but the case of the *Active* was not settled during the period of the Confederation, nor indeed for many years after the demise. The moneys had been deposited with one David Rittenhouse, the distinguished astronomer, at that time treasurer of the State, after whose death Olmstead and others sued his executrices for them in 1802 in the United States district court for Pennsylvania. Judge Peters decreed for the plaintiffs; but the legislature of Pennsylvania, apparently desirous of keeping the money within their jurisdiction, passed an act directing its attorney general to sue the executrices for the money and directing the governor to protect them from federal process. In 1809 the case came before the Supreme Court of the United States,[1] which had superseded the committee of appeals of the Confederation, and before Chief Justice Marshall, who sat in the seat of the commissioners, where the decision of the committee was finally affirmed, and execution of the judgment of the district court decreed. Even then the Pennsylvanian authorities were minded to resist. Pennsylvanian troops surrounded the house of the executrices to prevent the service of the writ, but in the end the federal marshal, " with some firmness, much composure, and great address," succeeded, as Professor Jameson says, in entering the house, afterward humorously called Fort Rittenhouse, and serving the process.[2]

It is easy to decry the weakness of the Confederation because of its failure to execute its judgment in the case of the *Active,* but it should be borne in mind that the Congress was a Congress of sovereign, free and independent States, which are loath to allow the use of force against themselves, even in the administration of justice — which appears also to be a characteristic of the American States composing the American Union; for, in the procedure and practice of the Supreme Court, States of the American Union have not been forced before the court as defendants to take part in the trial of a case, nor has the execution of a judgment of that august tribunal against them been compelled by force.

The moral of the *Active* was not lost upon the Congress, nor did the petition of the Philadelphian merchants and citizens fall upon deaf ears. On

---

[1] See *The United States* v. *Judge Peters,* 5 Cranch, 115.

[2] When the District Court proceeded to execute this mandate, the Governor issued orders to General Bright, " directing him to call out a portion of the militia in order to protect the persons and property of the representatives of Rittenhouse against any process issued by the District Court of the United States in pursuance of this *mandamus.* At first the marshal was prevented from serving the process by soldiers under the command of Bright, but subsequently, eluding their vigilance, he succeeded in taking into custody one of the defendants. A writ of *habeas corpus,* sued out on behalf of the prisoner, was, however, discharged by Chief Justice Tilghman, and subsequently General Bright with others were indicted in the Circuit Court of the United States for obstructing the process of the District Court. Mr. Justice Washington presided at the trial, which resulted in a verdict of guilty. The prisoners were sentenced to be imprisoned, and to pay a fine; but were immediately pardoned by the President of the United States. *Olmsted's Case,* Brightly's Rep., 1.

" This appears to have been the first case in which the supremacy of the Constitution was enforced by judicial tribunals against the assertion of State authority." (Mr. Justice Stanley Matthew's Address before the Yale Law School, June 26, 1888, pp. 19-20.)

May 22, 1779, the very day on which the petition had been read, a resolution was introduced, recommending " that each state pass an act empowering Congress, in advance of the ratification of the Articles of Confederation, to erect a permanent court of appeals; but the resolution does not appear to have passed," for the reason, suggested by Professor Jameson, from whom the above passage is quoted, that " probably Congress felt that they would be taking a stronger position if they assumed the existence of such power, as derived from their ' supreme sovereign power of war and peace,' in much the same way as the power to hear such appeals by committee of Congress had been; probably also it despaired of securing such action on the part of all thirteen of the states." [1]

But indeed, even earlier, the advisability of a court had been agitated, for on August 5, 1777, it was " *Resolved,* That Thursday next be assigned to take into consideration the propriety of establishing the Court of Appeals." Thursday came, but the court did not. The matter was postponed. In December of 1779, following the Philadelphian petition, an ordinance was drafted for a permanent court. As amended, it was passed on January 15, 1780, in the following form, a year in advance of the definitive adoption of the Articles of Confederation:

> *Resolved,* That a court be established for the trial of all appeals from the Courts of Admiralty in these United States, in cases of capture, to consist of three judges appointed and commissioned by Congress, either two of whom, in the absence of the other, to hold the said court for the despatch of business; that the said court appoint their own register; that the trials therein be according to the usage of nations, and not by jury.[2]

It was also resolved:

> That the said judges hold their first session as soon as may be at Philadelphia, and afterwards at such times and places as they shall judge most conducive to the public good, so that they do not at any time sit further eastward than Hartford in Connecticut, or southward than Williamsburg in Virginia.[3]

On January 22d the Congress chose as the three judges of the court, George Wythe of Virginia, William Paca of Maryland, and Titus Hosmer of Connecticut — an admirable personnel. Mr. Wythe declining, Cyrus Griffin of Virginia was elected in his place on April 28th. Mr. Paca accepted on the 9th of February, Mr. Hosmer and Mr. Griffin on the 4th of May.[4]

The act of January 15, 1780, creating the court, did not provide for the transfer to it of the cases pending before the committee. On May 9th the case of *Bragg* v. *The Sloop Dove* [5] was brought on appeal before Congress.

[1] Jameson, *Essays,* p. 27.
[2] 131 U. S., *App.,* p. xxv.
[3] *Ibid.*
[4] *Ibid.,* pp. xxv–xxvi.
[5] *Ibid.,* p. xliv.

It was referred to the new court and on May 24th Congress resolved "that the stile of the Court of Appeals appointed by Congress be 'the Court of Appeals in cases of capture;' that appeals from the Courts of Admiralty in the respective States be, as heretofore, demanded within five days after definitive sentence, and in future such appeals be lodged with the register of the Court of Appeals in cases of capture within forty days thereafter;" and " that all matters respecting Appeals in cases of capture now depending before Congress, or the Commissioners of Appeals, be referred to the newly erected Court of Appeals, to be there adjudged and determined according to law; and that all papers touching appeals in cases of capture lodged in the office of the Secretary of Congress, be delivered to and lodged with the register of the Court of Appeals." [1]   Thus the first permanent tribunal of these United States was established.

Mr. Davis, whose article entitled *The Federal Courts Prior to the Adoption of the Constitution* has largely served as, the basis for the above remarks, gives the following analysis of the work of the committees and of the court of appeals:

> Sixty-four cases in all were submitted to the committees of Congress, of which forty-nine were decided by them, four seem to have disappeared, and eleven went over to the Court of Appeals for decision. Fifty-six cases in all, including the eleven which went over, were submitted to the Court of Appeals, and all were disposed of. Appeals were heard from every maritime State except New York. None came from that State; doubtless because its maritime counties were occupied by the enemy from the autumn of 1776 to the end of the war. [2]

After examining the records of the committee and of the court of appeals, and enumerating the cases in which the court of appeals filed written opinions, Mr. Davis thus closes his account of the cases [3] determined on appeal by the Congress, its permanent committee, and the federal Court of Appeals:

> They were properly placed in the volumes which contain the commencement of the series of Reports of the Supreme Court of the United States; for the court from which they proceeded was in its day the highest court in the country, and the only appellate tribunal with jurisdiction over the whole United States. [4]

---

[1] 131 U. S., *App.*, p. xxvi.

[2] *Ibid.*, p. xxxiv.

[3] So far as appears by these papers, no written reports in the nature of opinions were made by the committees. The Court of Appeals filed only eight opinions, all of which are reported in 2 Dall. 1–42, under the general title of " Federal Court of Appeals." These opinions were delivered in, (1) *The Resolution*, p. 1; and (2) *S. C.*, on rehearing, p. 19; date of lodgment not known; final decree January 24, 1782;—(3) *The Erstern*, p. 33; lodged January 11, 1781; final decree February 5, 1782:—(4) *The Gloucester*, p. 36; date of lodgment not known; final decree February 5, 1782:—(5) *The Squirrel*, p. 40, see No. 90 *post* in table:—(6) *The Speedwell*, p. 40; lodged June 17, 1783; decided May 24, 1784:—(7) *Luke* v. *Hulbert*, p. 41; no papers on file:—(8) *The Experiment* v. *The Chester*, p. 41; referred by Congress by the resolution of July 24, 1786, already spoken of; decided May 1, 1787. (Davis' note, p. xxxv.)

[4] *Ibid.*, p. xxxv.

As to the influence of the Court of Appeals, which went out of existence two days after the meeting of the memorable convention, which, as Professor Jameson says, " provided the United States with a more comprehensive and more effective judiciary," and its importance in the development of a permanent judiciary Professor Jameson writes:

However this may be, it can not be doubted that the Court of Appeals, though, as remarked by counsel in Jennings v. Carson, " unpopular in those states which were attached to trial by jury," had an educative influence in bringing the people of the United States to consent to the establishment of such a successor. It could hardly be that one hundred and eighteen cases, though all in one restricted branch of judicature, should be brought by appeal from state courts to a federal tribunal, without familiarizing the public mind with the complete idea of a superior judicature, in federal matters, exercised by federal courts. The Court of Appeals in Cases of Capture may therefore be justly regarded, not simply as the predecessor, but as one of the origins, of the Supreme Court of the United States.[1]

[1] J. Franklin Jameson, *Essays*, pp. 43–4.

XI

TEMPORARY JUDICIAL COMMISSIONS

Difficulties and disputes that may arise between the subjects of the King and the inhabitants of the Swiss Cantons, shall be settled by the judgment of four men of standing, two of whom shall be named by each party; which four arbitrators shall hear, in an appointed place, the parties or their attorneys; and, if they shall be divided in opinion, there shall be chosen from the neighboring countries an unbiassed man of ability, who shall join with the arbitrators in determining the question. If the matter in dispute is between a subject of the Cantons and Leagues and the King of France, the Cantons will examine the demand, and, if it is well founded, they will present it to the King; but, if the King is not satisfied with it, they may call the King before the arbitrators, who shall be selected from among impartial judges of the countries of Coire or of Valois, and whatever shall be decided by the aforesaid judges, by a judicial or amicable sentence, shall be inviolably observed without any revocation. (*Treaty of Perpetual Peace between France and the Swiss Cantons and their Allies, November 29, 1516, M. de Flassan, Histoire Générale et Raisonnée de la Diplomatie Française, Depuis la fondation de la monarchie, jusqu'à la fin du règne de Louis XVI, Vol. I, 1809, pp. 307-308, English translation by John Bassett Moore, History and Digest of the International Arbitrations to which the United States has been a Party, Vol. V, 1898, p. 4830.*)

Arbitration is a method very reasonable, and very conformable to the law of nature, in determining all differences that do not directly interest the safety of the nation. Though the strict right may be mistaken by the arbitrator, it is still more to be feared that it will be overwhelmed by the fate of arms. The Swiss have had the precaution, in all their alliances among themselves, and even in those they have contracted with the neighbouring powers, to agree before-hand, on the manner in which their disputes were to be submitted to arbitrators, in case they could not adjust them in an amicable manner. This wise precaution has not a little contributed to maintain the Helvetic Republic in that flourishing state which secures its liberty, and renders it respectable throughout Europe. (*M. de Vattel, The Law of Nations; or Principles of the Law of Nature: Applied to the Conduct and Affairs of Nations and Sovereigns, 1758, Translated from the French, Vol. I, 1760, pp. 244-245.*)

XXVIII. Recites a seisure and detainer of English effects in the dominions of the King of Denmark, since the 18th of May, 1652. The States hereby oblige themselves to make the same good to the owners, to pay 5000 pounds English, to answer the expence of a proper enquiry, and 20,000 rixdollars to whom his Highness shall nominate immediately; which are to be deducted out of the gross sum to be awarded, and to enter into bonds of arbitration, in the penalty of 140,000, by proper persons in London, to answer the award.

XXX. That four commissioners shall be named on both sides to meet at London, the 19th of May next, who will be authorised to examine the injuries and losses in the year 1611, and after to the 18th of May 1652, as in the East Indies, Greenland, Muscovy, Brasil, &c. That if the said differences be not adjusted in three months, to be computed from the said 18th day of May, in such case the same shall be submitted to the arbitration of the Swiss Cantons, who shall delegate commissioners for that purpose, and shall give judgment within six months; within which time whatever the majority of such commissioners determine shall be binding to both parties, and duly performed. (*Treaty of Peace and Union between Oliver Cromwell, as Protector of England, and the United Provinces of the Netherlands, at Westminster, April 5th, 1645, Charles Jenkinson, A Collection of all the Treaties of Peace, Alliance, and Commerce, between Great-Britain and other Powers, from the Treaty signed at Munster in 1648, to the Treaties signed at Paris in 1783, Vol. I, 1785, pp. 47-48.*)

XXIV. That the debts due to the English from the King, on account of the previous sequestration of their effects, shall be discharged within two years, And the recognizances made to the King or any of his subjects by the English shall be cancelled and rescinded.

XXV. The adjusting of all matters in dispute shall be referred to the arbitration of Dr. Walter Walker, John Crowther, Dr. Jeronimus a Silva, secretary of the embassy, and Francis Ferreira Rabello, agent thereof, who shall sit at London the 20th of July next, O. S. who shall deliver their sentence on or before the first day of September next. And the same being then undetermined, shall afterwards be referred entirely to the Protector's consul, whose award shall be final and decisive: and what shall on their decree be found justly due, shall be paid by an allowance or remittance of one moiety of the duties usually paid until the sum awarded be fully satisfied.

The three last articles are general confirmations of the previous particulars, and limits the ratification to six months. (*Treaty of Peace and Alliance between* Oliver Cromwell, *Protector of* England, *and* John IV. *King of* Portugal, *made at* Westminster, July 10, 1654, *Charles Jenkinson, A Collection of all the Treaties of Peace, Alliance, and Commerce, between Great-Britain and other Powers, From the Treaty signed at Munster in 1648, to the Treaties signed at Paris in 1783, Vol. I, 1785, pp. 74-75.*)

XXIV. Whereas since the year 1640 many prizes have been taken on both sides, commissioners shall be appointed to settle the same at London, and if they do not determine in six months and a fortnight, the city of Hamburg shall be desired to delegate commissioners, whose arbitration shall be final, and their award made within four months; but if neither shall make an award, no force shall be used on either side until after the expiration of four months more.

XXV. The right of either to the three forts of Pentacost, St. John, and Port Royal in America, shall be determined by the same commissioners. (*Treaty of Peace between* Louis XIV. *King of* France *and* Navarre, *and the Lord Protector of the Republic of* England, Scotland, *and* Ireland, *at* Westminster, November 3, 1655, *Charles Jenkinson, A Collection of all the Treaties of Peace, Alliance, and Commerce, between Great-Britain and Other Powers, from the Treaty signed at Munster in 1648, to the Treaties signed at Paris in 1783, Vol. I, 1785, pp. 84-85.*)

VII. Relates to the manner of adjusting differences and captures of either side, according to the tenor of the XIIIth article of the treaty of Upsal, and is only a repetition thereof, and an agreement, in case of the same not being affected for a future convention. (*Treaty between* Charles Gustavus, *King of* Sweden, *and* Oliver Cromwell, *Protector of* England, *whereby the Treaty of Alliance made between the said States,* April 11, 1654, *is confirmed and explained. Done at* Westminster, July 15th, *and the Convention annexed* July 17, 1656. *Charles Jenkinson, A Collection of all the Treaties of Peace, Alliance, and Commerce between Great-Britain and other Powers, from the Treaty signed at Munster in 1648, to the Treaties signed at Paris in 1783, Vol. I, 1785, p. 99.*)

The United States in Congress assembled shall also be the last resort on appeal in all disputes and differences now subsisting or that hereafter may arise between two or more States concerning boundary, jurisdiction or any other cause whatever; which authority shall always be exercised in the manner following. Whenever the legislative or executive authority or lawful agent of any State in controversy with another shall present a petition to Congress, stating the matter in question and praying for a hearing, notice thereof shall be given by order of Congress to the legislative or executive authority of the other State in controversy, and a day assigned for the appearance of the parties by their lawful agents, who shall then be directed to appoint by joint consent, commissioners or judges to constitute a court for hearing and determining the matter in question: but if they can not agree, Congress shall name three persons out of each of the United States, and from the list of such persons each party shall alternately strike out one, the petitioners beginning, until the numbers shall be reduced to thirteen; and from that number not less than seven, nor more than nine names as Congress shall direct, shall in the presence of Congress be drawn out by lot, and the persons whose names shall be so drawn or any five of them, shall be commissioners or judges, to hear and finally determine the controversy, so always as a major part of the judges who shall hear the cause shall agree in the determination: and if either party shall neglect to attend at the day appointed, without showing reasons, which Congress shall judge sufficient, or being present shall refuse to strike, the Congress shall proceed to nominate three persons out of each State, and the Secretary of Congress shall strike in behalf of such party absent or refusing; and the judgment and sentence of the court to be appointed, in the manner before prescribed, shall be final and conclusive; and if any of the parties shall refuse to submit to the authority of such court, or to appear or defend their claim or cause, the court shall nevertheless proceed to pronounce sentence, or judgment, which shall in like manner be final and decisive, the judgment or sentence and other proceedings being in either case transmitted to Congress, and lodged among the acts of Congress for the security of the parties concerned: provided that every commissioner, before he sits in judgment, shall take an oath to be administered by one of the judges of the supreme or superior court of the State where the cause shall be tried, " well and truly to hear and determine the matter in question, according to the best of his judgment, without favour, affection or hope of reward: " provided also that no State shall be deprived of territory for the benefit of the United States.

All controversies concerning the private right of soil claimed under different grants of two or more States, whose jurisdiction as they may respect such lands, and the States which passed such grants are adjusted, the said grants or either of them being at the same time claimed to have originated antecedent to such settlement of jurisdiction, shall on the petition of either party to the Congress of the United States, be finally determined as near as may be in the same manner as is before prescribed for deciding disputes respecting territorial jurisdiction between different States. (*Articles of Confederation, 1777, Article IX, paragraph 2. Revised Statutes of the United States, 1878, pp. 9-10.*)

The agents attending, the Court pronounced the following sentence or judgment:
This cause has been well argued by the learned counsel on both sides.
The court are now to pronounce their sentence or judgment.
We are unanimously of opinion, that the state of Connecticut has no right to the lands in controversy.
We are also unanimously of opinion, that the jurisdiction and pre-emption of all the territory lying within the charter boundary of Pennsylvania, and now claimed by the state of Connecticut, do of right belong to the state of Pennsylvania. (*State of Pennsylvania v. State of Connecticut, Court of Commissioners Under 9th of Articles of Confederation, Journals of the American Congress, edition of 1823, Vol. IV, p. 140, decided December 30, 1782.*)

The great cause between Connecticut and Pennsylvania has been decided in favor of the latter. It is a singular event. There are few instances of independent states submitting their cause to a court of justice. The day will come when all disputes in the great republic of Europe will be tried in the same way, and America be quoted to exemplify the wisdom of the measure. (*Extract from letter of Robert R. Livingston, Secretary of Foreign Affairs, to La Fayette, January 10, 1783. Francis Wharton, The Revolutionary Diplomatic Correspondence of the United States, Vol. VI, 1889, p. 202.*)

CHAPTER XI

TEMPORARY JUDICIAL COMMISSIONS

BUT the Court of Prize was neither the most interesting nor the most important judicial organization, either for the people of the United States or for the world at large. But it was one of the origins of the Supreme Court. The other origin which is likely to prove further that the Revolutionary statesmen, as well as the fathers of the Constitution, were benefactors of their kind, was the machinery devised for the adjustment of quarrels between the States by means of temporary commissions:

> The United States in Congress assembled shall also be the last resort on appeal in all disputes and differences now subsisting or that hereafter may arise between two or more States concerning boundary, jurisdiction or any other cause whatsoever; . . .
>
> All controversies concerning the private right of soil claimed under different grants of two or more States, whose jurisdictions as they may respect such lands, and the States which passed such grants are adjusted, the said grants or either of them being at the same time claimed to have originated antecedent to such settlement of jurisdiction, shall on the petition of either party to the Congress of the United States, be finally determined as near as may be in the same manner as is before prescribed for deciding disputes respecting territorial jurisdiction between different States.[1]

Nature of the Commissions

The Articles of Confederation apparently considered the Congress as the successor of the King in Council. They authorized it therefore to direct the agents of the States in controversy to appoint commissioners or judges to constitute a court for hearing and determining the matter in question. Failing their agreement, Congress was authorized to "name three persons out of each of the United States," that is to say, thirty-nine in all, from which list the agents of the parties, beginning with the defendant, should alternately strike a name until thirteen were left, from which seven or nine, in the direction of Congress, should be drawn by lot, of whom the persons whose names were drawn, or any five of them, should be commissioners or judges of the commission charged with the determination of the dispute. Upon the absence of one or the other party, or the refusal of one of the parties present " to strike," the secretary of the Congress was to strike in lieu thereof and the commissioners were thereupon to be selected in the manner above

[1] Article IX, Articles of Confederation, 1777.

described.   The commissioners thus appointed formed the court which was to assume jurisdiction of the dispute, even although one party or the other might refuse to submit the case or appear or defend the claim.   The court thus constituted was to proceed to pronounce final sentence or judgment, which, together with the other proceedings, was to be transmitted to the Congress and by it filed for the security of the parties concerned.   Each commissioner was to take an oath before a court of record in the State in which the cause was to be tried, to decide the controversy " according to the best of his judgment, without favor, affection, or hope of reward."   And no State was to be " deprived of territory for the benefit of the United States."

It was natural that the States which, as has been pointed out, had renounced the right to enter into compacts and to conclude agreements, which maintained armaments merely for defensive purposes, and which had renounced the right to resort to war against one another, should have found it necessary to devise a method of settling the disputes which had frequently arisen between and among them, and which were certain to arise again in the matter of boundaries. It was also natural that the Congress should take advantage of this certainty to provide a method for settling boundary disputes which might arise between the States.   It was further natural that they should adopt the method of the Privy Council, which either settled the disputes itself or referred them to committees or to courts, as the case might be, and that the States should adapt the machinery at hand to their own circumstances and needs. Professor Jameson has called attention to the striking resemblance between the method of the Articles of Confederation and that devised by Grenville's Act of 1770 for the trial of disputed elections.   His language is so in point, and is so capable of a larger application, that it is quoted in full:

Influence of Privy Council

> It seems obvious that we have here a reproduction of the machinery provided by Mr. Grenville's famous Act of 1770 for the trial of disputed elections to the House of Commons.   Up to that time, disputed elections had for nearly a century been passed upon by the whole House.   The natural result of such a procedure was a scandalous disregard of justice, those contestants who belonged to the majority party being uniformly admitted, their competitors as uniformly rejected.   To remedy this abuse, Mr. Grenville's act provided that forty-nine members should be chosen by ballot, and that from this list the petitioner and the sitting member should strike out names alternately until the number was reduced to thirteen,— a process which later became known, in the slang of the House, as " knocking out the brains of the committee," each contestant excluding any able man likely to assist the cause of his opponent.   These thirteen, with an additional member nominated by each contestant, constituted the authoritative tribunal.   The act, celebrated at the time, was of course perfectly well known to lawyers in America six years after its passage.   It seems plain that, with the natural substitution of thirty-nine for forty-nine, we have, in this peculiar process established shortly before in England, the model on which Congress framed its scheme for con-

stituting temporarily a judiciary body when one was required for land disputes.[1]

The history of the proceedings under this portion of the ninth Article of Confederation is quickly told. One commission or court was constituted by the agents of the parties under the article, and this commission decided the one case which the article has to its credit. A temporary tribunal was formed in three additional instances, in one of which the agents of the parties were unable to agree upon the personnel, and resort was therefore had to the method of striking provided by the article.[2] In these three instances the cases were settled out of court by the parties themselves. Petitions to form tribunals were presented to Congress in other cases, but no courts were created, and upon the dissolution of the Confederation some eleven boundary disputes were outstanding and unsettled.[3] The one cause actually decided by commissioners or judges in the manner provided by the ninth article, is, however, a very famous case, in which blood had flowed, which of itself was sufficient to show the disadvantages of the old method, or rather of no method, and the possibilities of the new system.

Upon the signature of the Articles of Confederation by Maryland on the 1st day of March, 1781, they became the law of the land, and shortly thereafter Pennsylvania took advantage of the ninth of the articles in order to settle a dispute with Connecticut concerning a large strip of territory on the east bank of the Susquehanna River, and which today forms the County of Luzerne in the State of Pennsylvania. As the matter is thus important, and the details of the procedure interesting, some relevant passages are quoted from the documents in this case. The *Journal of Congress* on November 3, 1781, contains the following entry:

Pennsylvania v. Connecticut

> A petition from the supreme executive council of the Commonwealth of Pensylvania was read, stating a matter of dispute between the said State and the State of Connecticut, respecting sundry lands lying on the east branch of the River Susquehanna, and praying a hearing in the premises, agreeably to the 9th article of the Confederation.[4]

On the 14th of the same month, Congress assigned the fourth Monday in the following June for the appearance of the States by their lawful agents, and issued notice thereof in the following form to the States in controversy:

To the legislative authority of the State of Connecticut [Pennsylvania]:

[1] J. Franklin Jameson, *Essays in the Constitutional History of the United States*, pp. 44-5.

[2] J. C. Bancroft Davis, *Federal Courts Prior to the Adoption of the Constitution*, 131 U. S., *Appendix*, p. lxiii.

[3] *Ibid.*, p. xxxiv.

[4] *Journals of the Continental Congress*, Vol. xxi, p. 1092.

It is hereby made known, that pursuant to the ninth article of the Confederation, the supreme executive council of the State of Pensylvania, have presented a petition to Congress, stating that a controversy has long subsisted between the said State of Pensylvania, and the State of Connecticut, respecting sundry lands lying within the northern boundary of the said State of Pensylvania, and praying for a hearing in pursuance of the ninth article of the Confederation; and that the 4th Monday in June next, is assigned for the appearance of the said States of Pensylvania and Connecticut, by their lawful agents, at the place in which Congress shall then sit, to proceed in the premises as by the said Confederation is directed.[1]

On the appointed day the States appeared by their agents: for Pennsylvania, Messrs. William Bradford, Joseph Reed, James Wilson and Jonathan Dickinson Sergeant, and their credentials were spread upon the Journal.[2] For Connecticut, Eliphalet Dyer appeared and presented credentials, likewise spread upon the Journal, showing the appointment as duly accredited agents of that State, Messrs. Eliphalet Dyer, William Samuel Johnson and Jesse Root.[3] On June 27th Connecticut moved to postpone the proceedings until "after the termination of the present war."[4] This motion was denied. On the 16th of July the agents of the two States were directed "to appoint, by joint consent, commissioners or judges to constitute a court for hearing and determining the matter in question, agreeably to the 9th Article of the Confederation."[5] The agents complied with this direction and, on August 12th, Congress was informed by a paper signed by the agents of the contending States, and spread upon the Journal, that they had agreed upon William Whipple of New Hampshire, Major General Nathaniel Greene of Rhode Island, David Brearley and William Churchill Houston of New Jersey, Cyrus Griffin and Joseph Jones of Virginia, and John Rutledge of South Carolina, any five or more of whom were to constitute the court and to have authority to proceed and to determine the matter and difference between the States.[6] It was further agreed by and between the agents of the litigating States that the court should assemble at Trenton, N. J., on the 12th day of November.[7] On August 23, 1782, the agents reported to Congress that General Greene could not attend, that Mr. Rutledge had declined, and that they had therefore chosen Thomas Neilson of Virginia and Welcome Arnold of Rhode Island in their stead. Congress thereupon directed commissions to issue to the judges according to the amended list, and on the 28th of the same month the form of commission was settled and spread upon the Journal.[8]

[1] *Journals of the Continental Congress,* Vol. xxi, p. 1116.
[2] *Ibid.,* Vol. xxii, p. 345. Session of June 24, 1782.
[3] *Ibid.,* p. 347.
[4] *Ibid.,* p. 355.
[5] *Ibid.,* p. 392.
[6] *Ibid.,* Vol. xxiii, p. 461.
[7] *Ibid.,* p. 529. Session of August 23, 1782.
[8] *Ibid.,* p. 533.

It was finally agreed by and between the parties litigant that the court should assemble at Trenton, N. J., on the 12th of November of the same year. The court convened on the day assigned, November 12th, at Trenton, with only Messrs. Brearley and Houston present.[1] They adjourned from day to day to the 18th, when enough members being present, the court was organized, with Messrs. Whipple, Arnold, Brearley, Houston and Griffin in attendance as members. On the 22d of the month the agents on each side put in a written brief, showing the claims of their respective States, based in each case upon charters from the mother country. We have the word of the commissioners that the case was equally well argued on both sides, and we have their unanimous opinion in behalf of the State of Pennsylvania — for the commissioners had agreed that the minority should yield to the majority, so that the decision might be unanimous, and in framing their view they apparently heeded the sage advice of my Lord Mansfield to a lawyer turned judge and not very well grounded in the law, to abstain from reasons for his judgment. The award of the court follows in full:

The court met — Present as before.

The agents attending, the Court pronounced the following sentence or judgment:

This cause has been well argued by the learned counsel on both sides.

The court are now to pronounce their sentence or judgment.

We are unanimously of opinion, that the state of Connecticut has no right to the lands in controversy.

We are also unanimously of opinion, that the jurisdiction and pre-emption of all the territory lying within the charter boundary of Pennsylvania, and now claimed by the State of Connecticut, do of right belong to the state of Pennsylvania.[2]

The commissioners were of the opinion, as stated in a communication dated December 31, 1782, addressed to John Dickinson, then President of Pennsylvania, that the question for them to decide, and actually decided by them, was the right of Pennsylvania to the soil in its title of sovereign, and that the claims of individuals to the soil whether based upon grants from Connecticut or from Pennsylvania were unaffected by the decision. The Honorable Cyrus Griffin, the fifth member of the court, made a similar statement in a letter dated September 15, 1796, and vouchsafed the following interesting information concerning the procedure of the commissioners in the trial and disposition of the case:

Before the commissioners determined that important contest between Pennsylvania and Connecticut, it was agreed:

1st. That the reasons for the determination should never be given.

[1] Davis, *Federal Courts*, 131 U. S., *Appendix*, p. lv.
[2] *Journals of the American Congress*, 1823, Vol. IV, p. 140.

2nd. That the minority should concede the determination as the unanimous opinion of the court.

No doubt sufficient reasons appeared to us to adopt these preliminary points. . . .

But I can assure you, sir, that the commissioners were *unanimously of opinion* that the *private right of soil should not be affected by the decision.* The decision was *not to reach the question of property in soil.*[1]

The international significance of the strange and novel experience of a State appearing against a State in a tribunal of justice was not lost upon the public men of the day. No less a personage than Robert R. Livingston, then Secretary for Foreign Affairs of the Confederation, thought it of sufficient moment to refer to it in a letter dated January 10, 1783, addressed to the Marquis of Lafayette, in which he felt justified in saying:

The great cause between Connecticut and Pennsylvania has been decided in favor of the latter. It is a singular event. There are few instances of independent states submitting their cause to a court of justice. The day will come, when all disputes in the great republic of Europe will be tried in the same way, and America be quoted to exemplify the wisdom of the measure.[2]

Two
Other
Cases

The cases of *Massachusetts* v. *New York*[3] and *South Carolina* v. *Georgia*[4] were disputes in which commissioners were appointed and courts constituted for the trial of the causes in accordance with the ninth of the Articles of Confederation, and although the cases never came to trial, as the disputes were settled out of court, they are interesting, inasmuch as the case of *Massachusetts* v. *New York* is the only one in which a court had been appointed by agreement of the agents which did not come to trial; and the case of *South Carolina* v. *Georgia* is interesting and important in that it is the only case or controversy between the States under the ninth article in which the agents were unable to agree upon the members to form the court, and therefore the only one in which resort was had to the method of striking provided by the ninth article. The facts and procedure in these cases will therefore be briefly stated.

On June 3, 1784, Congress received the report of the committee to which it had referred " a petition from the legislature of the Commonwealth of Massachusetts, praying that a Federal Court may be appointed by Congress to decide a dispute between the said Commonwealth and the State of New York," [5] and the Congress resolved " that the first Monday in December next

---

[1] Henry M. Hoyt, *Brief of a Title in the Seventeen Townships of the County of Luzerne, a Syllabus of the Controversy between Connecticut and Pennsylvania*, 1879, pp. 45, 46.

[2] Francis Wharton, *Diplomatic Correspondence of the American Revolution*, Vol. 6, p. 202. See also Jared Sparks, *The Diplomatic Correspondence of the American Revolution* (1830), Vol. x, p. 21.

[3] 131 U. S., *Appendix*, p. lxi.

[4] *Ibid.*, p. lxii.

[5] *Ibid.*, p. lxi.

be assigned for the appearance of the said States of Massachusetts and New York by their lawful agents, at the place at which Congress shall then be sitting." [1]

From the petition of the State of Massachusetts, it appeared that this State claimed the tract of land between 42° 2' N. and 44° 15' N., which extended westwardly, in accordance with the terms of its charter, to the " Southern Ocean," which contention was denied by the State of New York as inconsistent with its charter. Therefore, on December 8, 1784, the litigating States appeared by their agents and presented their credentials, which were spread upon the Journal. The credentials of each were, by direction of Congress, examined by the agents of the two States and found to be without objection, whereupon, on December 10th, the agents were " directed to appoint, by joint consent, commissioners or judges to constitute a court for hearing and determining the matter in question, agreeable to the 9th of the articles of confederation and perpetual union." [2] The agents complied with the direction of Congress, and on June 9, 1785, the agents of the two States, namely, John Jay, Robert R. Livingston and Walter Livingston, on behalf of New York, and John Lowell, James Sullivan, Theophilus Parsons, Rufus King and S. Holton, on behalf of Massachusetts, informed Congress, in a paper to which they affixed their signatures, that they had selected as judges, Thomas Johnson, George Wythe, George Reed, James Monroe, Isaac Smith, William Patterson, Samuel Johnson, William Fleming and John Sitgreaves. [3] The agents requested that commissions might be issued to the judges and that they be notified to meet at Williamsburg, Va., on the third Tuesday of November next, to hear and determine the controversy. The court, however, did not meet, as appears from the following resolution of the Congress of October 8, 1787:

> Whereas it appears by the journals of Congress that a federal court has been instituted pursuant to the articles of confederation and perpetual union, to hear and determine a controversy respecting territory between the states of Massachusetts and New York; and whereas it appears by the representations of the delegates of the said states in Congress that the said controversy has ceased, and the same has been settled and determined by an agreement entered into on the 16th day of December last, by the agents of the said States, and any further proceedings in or relative to the aforesaid court having become unnecessary.
>
> _Resolved,_ That all further proceedings in and relative to the said federal court, as also the commissions of the judges thereof, cease and determine. [4]

The agreement between the two States was spread at length upon the Journal

[1] _Ibid.,_ p. lxi.
[2] _Journals of the American Congress,_ Vol. iv, p. 453.
[3] _Ibid.,_ p. 536.
[4] _Ibid.,_ p. 787.

of the Congress, in accordance with the provisions of the ninth article, that "the judgment or sentence and other proceedings being in either case transmitted to Congress, and lodged among the acts of Congress for the security of the parties concerned."

Almost a year to the date, namely, on June 1, 1785, after the case of *Massachusetts* v. *New York* had been brought before the Congress, that body resolved that "the second Monday in May next be assigned for the appearance of the states of South-Carolina and Georgia, by their lawful agents; and that notice thereof, and of the petition of the legislature of the state of South-Carolina, be given by the secretary of Congress, to the legislative authority of the state of Georgia." [1] As in the case of *Massachusetts* v. *New York,* the form of notice contained a copy of South Carolina's petition, from which it appeared that South Carolina claimed certain lands lying between North Carolina and a line to be run due west to a certain spot said to be the head of the Savannah River, a contention denied by Georgia, which insisted that the source of the Keowee River is to be considered as the head of the Savannah. [2] South Carolina also claimed the lands between a line drawn from the head of St. Mary River, the head of the Altamaha, the Mississippi and Florida, alleging that such lands were within the limits of its charter, and that they were not annexed to Georgia by the proclamation of the King of Great Britain, a contention denied by Georgia, which claimed the lands by virtue of such proclamation.

The agents who were to appear in the month of May did not do so, because the time had been extended. They appeared, however, on September 4, 1786, the date agreed upon, at which time they produced their credentials, which were spread in full upon the Journal. They were then directed by the Congress, as in the other cases, "to appoint, by joint consent, commissioners or judges to constitute a court for hearing and determining the matter in question, agreeable to the 9th of the articles of confederation and perpetual union." [3] The agents were less fortunate than in the case of *Pennsylvania* v. *Connecticut* and *Massachusetts* v. *New York,* in that they were unable to agree upon the members of the court. They therefore prayed Congress to proceed to strike a court agreeable to the Articles of Confederation. The Congress complied with this request, and on the 13th the agents of the States attended. On motion of the delegates of Georgia it was thereupon "*Resolved,* That Congress proceed to strike a court in the manner pointed out by the confederation." [4] Three persons were thus named from each of the States, and from the list of persons thus named each party alternately struck until the number

[1] *Journals of the American Congress,* Vol. iv, p. 529.
[2] 131 U. S., *App.,* p. lxii.
[3] *Journals of the American Congress,* Vol. iv, p. 693.
[4] *Ibid.,* p. 696.

was reduced to thirteen. After this, upon motion from the delegates of South Carolina, the thirteen names were put in a box and the following nine were drawn out in the presence of Congress: Alexander Contee Hanson, James Madison, Robert Goldsborough, James Duane, Philemon Dickinson, John Dickinson, Thomas McKean, Egbert Benson and William Pynchon.[1] The next day the delegates of Georgia moved that the court be held at the City of New York on the first Monday of May, 1787. The delegates from South Carolina proposed to substitute for this date the third Monday of November of the current year. The amendment failed, and the court was therefore directed to meet as proposed by the State of Georgia.[2]

The membership of this court was certainly such as to satisfy the most exacting requirements. It contained, as did the court in the case of *Massachusetts* v. *New York,* the name of a future president, and the gentleman who can in all probability be considered as the father of the Constitution, James Madison; John Dickinson, a member of the Continental Congress, who had refused to sign the Declaration of Independence because he believed it was inexpedient at the time and under the circumstances, but who enlisted and served as a private in the army after the Declaration had been proclaimed, who drafted the Articles of Confederation under which the proceeding was to take place, and who later was an influential member of the Constitutional Convention; Thomas McKean, Chief Justice of the Supreme Court of Pennsylvania and Governor of that State; Egbert Benson, Attorney General of New York, later a Justice of the Supreme Court of the State and a judge of the Circuit Court of the United States. The court, however, seems not to have met, and the difference was settled by compact between the States dated February 24, 1787, as appears from the first and second articles thereof, to be found in the case of *South Carolina* v. *Georgia,* recorded in 93 United States Reports, pp. 5–6.

These are, so far as known, the only cases of dispute between the States which were submitted, or prepared for submission, to temporary tribunals appointed according to the provisions of the ninth of the Articles of Confederation. In the first case, that of *Pennsylvania* v. *Connecticut,* the court was appointed by consent of the parties and rendered judgment. In the second, that of *Massachusetts* v. *New York,* a court was indeed appointed by consent of the parties, in accordance with the provisions of the ninth article, but the controversy was settled out of court. In the case of *South Carolina* v. *Georgia* a court was also appointed under the ninth article, but as the agents were unable to agree upon the commissioners or judges, they were chosen by the method

[1] *Ibid.,* p. 696.
[2] *Ibid.,* p. 697.

of the ninth article, devised to enable a court to be constituted when the States in controversy were unable to agree upon its composition. We thus have, in these three cases, a demonstration of the possibilities of peaceable settlement: first, where the parties agree upon the court, which actually renders a decision; second, where the parties, knowing that the controversy is to be settled by the court, reach an agreement, which appears to have been impossible without the existence of the court; and third, where the court has been constituted without the agreement of the parties, according to a method known in advance and, as in the previous case, an agreement is reached because of the existence of the tribunal and without recourse to its judgment.

Significance
of the
Temporary
Tribunals

Other
Appeals to
Congress

In three other cases the action of Congress was invoked, namely, the controversy between New Hampshire and Vermont, New York and Vermont, and Massachusetts and Vermont,[1] arising out of the so-called New Hampshire grants; the case of *Pennsylvania* v. *Virginia*[2] and the case of *New Jersey* v. *Virginia*.[3] In no one of these was a court appointed, but as they are interesting because of the reference to Congress, they will be briefly mentioned, in order that all known cases under the ninth article may be noted.

Dispute
Involving
the Existence
of a State

The case of the New Hampshire grants is very complicated, and it is referred to largely as showing the solicitude of the Congress, as the successor of the King in Council, that a dispute involving three States and a claimant to statehood should be peaceably settled. It is also referred to, as showing the impracticability if not futility of supposing that a community would submit to the arbitrament of a temporary tribunal the question of its existence or right to exist, for the statehood of Vermont hung in the balance.

New York claimed to the Connecticut River. In 1750, as recorded by the historian Bancroft, " New York carried its claims to the Connecticut river; France, which had command of Lake Champlain, extended her pretensions to the crest of the Green Mountains; while Wentworth, the only royal governor in New England, began to convey the soil between the Connecticut and Lake Champlain by grants under the seal of New Hampshire." [4] These grants are therefore known as the New Hampshire grants. In 1764 the King in Council, according to the same historian, " dismembered New Hampshire, and annexed to New York the country north of Massachusetts and west of Connecticut river. The decision was declaratory of the boundary; and it was therefore held by the royalists that the grants made under the sanction of the royal governor of New Hampshire were annulled." [5] However, the towns and villages in dispute were settled largely by New Englanders

[1] 131 U. S., *Appendix*, p. 1.
[2] *Ibid.*, p. liii.
[3] *Ibid.*, p. lviii.
[4] George Bancroft, *History of the United States of America*, 1883 ed., Vol. ii, p. 361.
[5] *Ibid.*, Vol. iii, p. 87.

under the New Hampshire grants. In 1775, again to quote Bancroft, " the court of common pleas was to be opened by the royal judges in what was called the New York county of Cumberland, at Westminster, in the New Hampshire Grants, on the eastern side of the Green Mountains. To prevent this assertion of the jurisdiction of New York and of the authority of the king, a body of young men from the neighboring farms on the thirteenth of March took possession of the court-house. The royal sheriff, who, against the wish of the judges, had raised sixty men armed with guns and bludgeons, demanded possession of the building; and, after reading the riot act and refusing to concede terms, late in the night ordered his party to fire. . . . The act closed the supremacy of the king and of New York to the east of Lake Champlain." [1]

The settlers of the Green Mountains organized themselves as a State, under the name of Vermont, and in convention on the 15th day of January, 1777,[2] declared their independence of New York. In the following July a convention assembled at Windsor, adopted a constitution, which was accepted by the legislature and declared to be a part of the laws of the State.[3]

It is clear from this brief statement that Massachusetts was not vitally interested, as the land lay to the north of its territory under the charter. It is clear that New York was vitally interested, as, if its contention were allowed, it would receive a very considerable extension of desirable territory. It is also evident that New Hampshire was even more interested because, if the contention of New York were granted, or if the settlers in Vermont had their way, the authorities of New Hampshire would lose title to a territory which they had possessed and which they naturally sought to retain. Finally, the settlers of Vermont were or were not a State, according as the case turned out.

A secret agreement between New York and New Hampshire to divide the territory in dispute did not result as anticipated by the two conspirators, owing to the resistance and the determination of " the Green Mountain boys," who showed their mettle by the defeat of the Hessians belonging to Burgoyne's army at the battle of Bennington. Unable to reach a settlement by direct negotiation, or even by secret agreement providing for dismemberment, New York bethought itself of the Congress, doubtless hoping that from the successor of the King in Council it would obtain a confirmation of title to the territory it had acquired by the decision of the King in Council in 1764.[4] On May 22, 1779, the day on which the petition from the merchants and citizens of Philadelphia had been read to provide a court of appeals in prize cases, the delegates of New York in the Congress moved a series of resolutions

[1] *Ibid.*, Vol. iv, p. 142.
[2] *Ibid.*, Vol. v, p. 157.
[3] *Ibid.*, p. 161.
[4] *Acts of the Privy Council, Colonial Series*, Vol. iv, pp. 673–4.

relating to the controversy.[1] On September 24th of that year it was "*Resolved, unanimously,* That it be, and hereby is, most earnestly recommended to the states of New Hampshire, Massachusetts Bay, and New York, forthwith to pass laws expressly authorizing Congress to hear and determine all differences between them relative to their respective boundaries, in the mode prescribed by the articles of confederation, so that Congress may proceed thereon by the first day of February next at the farthest: and further, that the said states of New Hampshire, Massachusetts Bay, and New York, do, by express laws for the purpose, refer to the decision of Congress all differences or disputes relative to jurisdiction, which they may respectively have with the people of the district aforesaid, so that Congress may proceed thereon on the first day of February next." [2] It was necessary for Congress to proffer such a request, inasmuch as it did not possess the authority to form a committee by "striking," at the request of the State of New York, because the Articles of Confederation were not then the law of the land. If they had been in effect, the situation would have been wholly different.

On October 2, 1779, the States were again urged "to authorize Congress to proceed to hear and determine all disputes subsisting between the grantees of the several states aforesaid, with one another, or with either of the said states, respecting title to lands lying in the said district, to be heard and determined by 'commissioners or judges,' to be appointed in the mode prescribed by the ninth article." [3] New York, having everything to gain, and New Hampshire, hoping to regain what would be lost either to New York or the people of Vermont if its contention were not sustained, enacted the necessary legislation.[4] Massachusetts, as above stated, had no real interest in the question, but the people of Vermont had to be reckoned with, and having organized themselves as a State, they were unwilling to have what they considered their lands voted away by acts of the legislatures of the claimant States, or by act of Congress. Their opposition undoubtedly prevented the appointment of a court, for none was constituted, and although, in the month of September, 1780, agents of New York laid their case before Congress,[5] claiming that from 1764 to 1777 the people of the territory in dispute were represented in the legislature of New York and submitted to its authority, although the agents of New Hampshire, in the same month, presented its case to the Congress,[6] maintaining that the tract lay within the limits of New Hampshire and that

---

[1] *Journals of the Continental Congress,* Vol. xiv, pp. 631–3.
[2] *Ibid.,* Vol. xv, pp. 1096–7.
[3] *Ibid.,* p. 1135.
[4] Act of New York, Oct. 21, 1779. *Papers of the Continental Congress,* No. 40, I; folio 269; Act of New Hampshire, November, 1779, folio 563.
[5] *Journals,* Vol. xviii, pp. 841, 843. Sessions of September 19 and 20, 1780.
[6] *Ibid.,* p. 868. Session of September 27, 1780.

the people inhabiting it had no right to a separate and independent existence, the Congress did not, because it could not, take action. The case had ceased, by the action of the settlers of Vermont, to be one of law, it had become one of force; it was no longer a matter for the courts; it had become a political instead of a judicial question.

The only solution compatible with peaceful settlement was apparently the recognition of the independent statehood of the settlers. This Massachusetts and New Hampshire did in 1781 and New York in 1790, and the controversy was settled in the end, as it should have been and was foredoomed to be settled in the beginning, by the admission of Vermont as a State of the American Union on February 18, 1791.[1] While the reasons for the failure of the Congress to appoint a court can be deduced from the mere statement of the facts, we nevertheless have them stated by a contemporary, whose word carries great weight. Thus, Alexander Hamilton wrote in *The Federalist*:

> Those who had an opportunity of seeing the inside of the transactions, which attended the progress of the controversy between this state [New York] and the district of Vermont, can vouch the opposition we experienced, as well from states not interested, as from those which were interested in the claim; and can attest the danger to which the peace of the confederacy might have been exposed, had this state attempted to assert its rights by force. . . . New-Jersy and Rode-Island, upon all occasions, discovered a warm zeal for the independence of Vermont; and Maryland, until alarmed by the appearance of a connection between Canada and that place, entered deeply into the same views.[2]

On December 27, 1779, the following entry in the *Journals of Congress* shows that a dispute had arisen between Pennsylvania and Virginia, and the action which the Congress, as the apparent successor of the King in Council thought should be taken: *Pennsylvania v. Virginia*

> Whereas it appears to Congress, from the representation of the delegates of the State of Pensylvania, that disputes have arisen between the states of Pensylvania and Virginia, relative to the extent of their boundaries, which may probably be productive of serious evils to both states, and tend to lessen their exertions in the common cause: therefore,
>
> *Resolved,* That it be recommended to the contending parties not to grant any part of the disputed land, or to disturb the possession of any persons living thereon, and to avoid every appearance of force until the dispute can be amicably settled by both states, or brought to a just decision by the intervention of Congress; that possessions forcibly taken be restored to the original possessors, and things placed in the situation in which they were at the commencement of the present war, without prejudice to the claims of either party.[3]

[1] 1 *Stat.*, 191.
[2] *The Federalist*, 1802 ed., Vol. i, pp. 36–7. Paper vii.
[3] *Journals of the Continental Congress*, Vol. xv, p. 1411.

The Congress was naturally desirous, as appears from the resolution, that the dispute be amicably settled by both States or brought to a just decision by the intervention of Congress, and, in order to render this possible, recommended the maintenance of the *status quo* pending settlement.   The States in controversy, interested in the common cause, seem to have acted in accordance with the desires of Congress, although it does not appear how and to what extent its advice was followed, as there is no further reference to the case in the records of that body.   An agreement for settlement was made in Baltimore on August 31, 1779,[1] in pursuance of which commissioners were appointed on the part of Pennsylvania and Virginia.   In consequence of this action on the part of the States, " the line commonly called Mason and Dixon's line " was " extended due west five degrees of longitude," " from the river Delaware for the southern boundary of Pennsylvania," and " a meridian line drawn from the western extremity thereof to the northern line of the State " became the western boundary.   On the 23d of August, 1784, the commission reported that the Ohio River was reached.[2]

The cession to the United States, dated March 1, 1784,[3] by Virginia of its claims to all territory from the northern bank of the Ohio lessened the interest which the Old Dominion, as Virginia is affectionately called by its citizens, might otherwise have had, not only in the prolongation of the line but in the prolongation of the controversy.

Congress Refuses to Appoint a Court

The last case coming before the Congress in which a request was made, and the only one in which the Congress refused the petition to appoint a court in accordance with the ninth article, was a controversy between New Jersey and Virginia.[4]   The dispute was ended, if indeed it can properly be said to have begun, by the cession of Virginia's claims to the Northwest Territory on the 1st of March, 1784.   The facts of the case, however, are interesting, as showing the magnitude of the cases referred to the Congress, because the territory in question was a large tract of land called Indiana, located between the Little Kennawa, the Monongahela and the southern boundary of Pennsylvania.   A memorial was presented to Congress on September 14, 1779,[5] by one George Morgan, as agent for the proprietors of this tract, claiming that his principals had acquired the tract of land by purchase from the Six Nations and other Indians, that after the purchase of the lands they had been withdrawn from the jurisdiction of Virginia by the King in Council, but that Virginia, having resumed jurisdiction thereof, was about to order sales to be made within the district in question.   The memorial prayed that, as in the

[1] 131 U. S., *Appendix*, p. liii.
[2] *Ibid.*, p. liv.
[3] Bancroft, *History of the United States*, Vol. vi, pp. 115-6.
[4] 131 U. S., *Appendix*, p. lviii.
[5] *Journals of the Continental Congress*, Vol. xv, pp. 1063-4.

case of *Pennsylvania* v. *Virginia,* the sales might be restrained and the *status quo* preserved until the matter could be heard by Congress. Leaving out various petitions to the Congress, it is sufficient for present purposes to say that a petition of Colonel George Morgan, as agent for the State of New Jersey, was presented to, read and considered by Congress while that body had before it, but before it had adopted the territorial cession of Virginia, whose acceptance by the Congress on behalf of the United States would end the controversy in so far as Virginia was concerned. The petition is interesting as it was an attempt on the part of a State to enable its citizens to present a claim to the Congress and to have a court appointed for the determination of land not claimed as belonging to the State of New Jersey as such, but to land acquired by some of its citizens whose cause New Jersey espoused by virtue of their citizenship. In view, therefore, of these facts and of this action of the State of New Jersey, which is capable of a larger application, the material portion of the petition is here set forth:

To the United States of America, in Congress assembled,

The petition of Colonel George Morgan, agent for the State of New Jersey respectfully sheweth; that a controversy now subsists between the said State and the Commonwealth of Virginia respecting a tract of land called Indiana, lying on the river Ohio, and being within the United States: That your petitioner and others, owners of the said tract of land, labor under grievances from the said Commonwealth of Virginia, whose legislature has set up pretensions thereto: That in consequence of instructions from the legislature of New Jersey to their delegates in Congress, anno 1781, and the petitions of Indiana proprietors, anno 1779, 1780 and 1781, a hearing was obtained before a very respectable committee of Congress, who, after a full and patient examination of the matter, did unanimously report . . . that the purchase of the Indiana Company was made *bona fide* for a valuable consideration, according to the then usage and custom of purchasing lands from the Indians, with the knowledge, consent and approbation of the Crown of Great Britain and the then governments of New York and Virginia: That notwithstanding this report, the State of Virginia still continues to claim the lands in question, to the great injury of your petitioner and others: That your petitioner, on behalf of himself and the other proprietors of the said tract of land, applied to the said State of New Jersey, of which some of them are citizens, for its protection: That the legislature of the said State thereupon nominated and appointed your petitioner the lawful agent of the said State, for the express purpose of preparing and presenting to Congress a memorial or petition on the part and behalf of the said State, representing the matter of the complaint aforesaid, to pray for a hearing, and to prosecute the said hearing to issue, in the mode pointed out by the Articles of Confederation: That the said legislature ordered that a commission should be issued by the executive authority of the said State, to your petitioner, for the purposes aforesaid: That a commission was accordingly issued to your petitioner by the executive authority of the said State, a copy whereof accompanies this petition. . . . Wherefore your petitioner, as lawful agent of the said State of New Jersey, prays for a hearing in the premises, agreeably to the 9th Article of Confederation and Perpetual Union between the United States of America.[1]

A motion to commit the petition and also a motion to consider and prepare an answer to it were lost, after which the Congress accepted the deed of cession from Virginia, as it had previously, in 1781, accepted a cession of the claims that New York had to the territory northwest of the Ohio. It was therefore unnecessary for the Congress to take further action on this petition in the form in which it was presented, as the claim of Messrs. Morgan and his principals was thereafter against the United States, not Virginia.

Doubtless the court of appeals in cases of capture inclined the hearts and the understanding of the good people of the Confederation to the establishment of a judiciary which could pass upon questions in which the States had assumed jurisdiction, and thus create uniformity where diversity would otherwise have existed and prejudice the Confederation as such in its relations with foreign nations. But prize cases had been for centuries submitted to prize courts, tribunals or commissions. The novelty of the procedure was to establish one court of appeal from thirteen States, a great incentive not only to the establishment of a Supreme Court but also to the establishment of an international court of prize. Controversies between States claiming to be sovereign, free and independent, and in their instrument of confederation stating and having their sovereignty, freedom and independence recognized, had not hitherto been submitted as a matter of course to courts, tribunals, and commissions. The statesmen of the American Revolution had put new wine into old bottles. They had hit upon a procedure as wise as it was novel in devising a method of settling international disputes without a resort to force, between the breakdown of diplomacy and the outbreak of war; and in the short space of ten years they had completed the long road between self-redress and arbitration to judicial settlement by the establishment of the permanent international judiciary known as the Supreme Court of the United States.

[1] 131 U. S., *Appendix*, p. lx.

XII

CREATION OF THE SUPREME COURT

The Americans form but one people in relation to their Federal government; but in the bosom of this people divers political bodies have been allowed to subsist, which are dependent on the national government in a few points, and independent in all the rest,—which have all a distinct origin, maxims peculiar to themselves, and special means of carrying on their affairs. To intrust the execution of the laws of the Union to tribunals instituted by these political bodies, would be to allow foreign judges to preside over the nation. Nay, more; not only is each State foreign to the Union at large, but it is a perpetual adversary, since whatever authority the Union loses turns to the advantage of the States. Thus, to enforce the laws of the Union by means of the State tribunals would be to allow not only foreign, but partial, judges to preside over the nation.

But the number, still more than the mere character, of the State tribunals, made them unfit for the service of the nation. When the Federal Constitution was formed, there were already thirteen courts of justice in the United States, which decided causes without appeal. That number is now increased to twenty-four [forty-eight]. To suppose that a state can subsist, when its fundamental laws are subjected to four-and-twenty different interpretations at the same time, is to advance a proposition alike contrary to reason and to experience. (*Alexis de Tocqueville, De la Démocratie en Amérique, 2 vols., 1835. Translation of Francis Bowen, Vol. I, 1862, pp. 177-178.*)

Section 1. The judicial Power of the United States, shall be vested in one supreme Court, and in such inferior Courts as the Congress may from time to time ordain and establish. The Judges, both of the supreme and inferior Courts, shall hold their Offices during good Behaviour, and shall, at stated Times, receive for their Services, a Compensation, which shall not be diminished during their Continuance in Office.

Section 2. The judicial Power shall extend to all Cases, in Law and Equity, arising under this Constitution, the Laws of the United States, and Treaties made, or which shall be made, under their Authority;—to all Cases affecting Ambassadors, other public Ministers and Consuls;—to all Cases of admiralty and maritime Jurisdiction;—to Controversies to which the United States shall be a Party;—to Controversies between two or more States;—between a State and Citizens of another State;—between Citizens of different States,—between Citizens of the same State claiming Lands under Grants of different States, and between a State, or the Citizens thereof, and foreign States, Citizens or Subjects.

In all Cases affecting Ambassadors, other public Ministers and Consuls, and those in which a State shall be Party, the supreme Court shall have original Jurisdiction. In all the other Cases before mentioned, the supreme Court shall have appellate Jurisdiction, both as to Law and Fact, with such Exceptions, and under such Regulations as the Congress shall make. . . . (*Constitution of the United States, Article III.*)

This Constitution defines the extent of the powers of the general government. If the general legislature should at any time overleap their limits, the judicial department is a constitutional check. If the United States go beyond their powers, if they make a law which the Constitution does not authorize, it is void; and the judicial power, the national judges, who, to secure their impartiality, are to be made independent, will declare it to be void. On the other hand, if the states go beyond their limits, if they make a law which is a usurpation upon the general government, the law is void; and upright, independent judges will declare it to be so. Still, however, if the United States and the individual states will quarrel, if they want to fight, they may do it, and no frame of government can possibly prevent it. It is sufficient for this Constitution, that, so far from laying them under a necessity of contending, it provides every reasonable check against it. (*Oliver Ellsworth in the Connecticut Convention, January 7, 1788, Jonathan Elliot, The Debates in the Several State Conventions on the Adoption of the Federal Constitution, Vol. II, 1836; second edition, Vol. II, 1891, p. 196.*)

That a federal system again can flourish only among communities imbued with a legal spirit and trained to reverence the law is as certain as can be any conclusion of political speculation. Federalism substitutes litigation for legislation, and none but a law-fearing people will be inclined to regard the decision of a suit as equivalent to the enactment of a law. The main reason why the United States has carried out the federal system with unequalled success is that the people of the Union are more thoroughly imbued with legal ideas than any other existing nation. Constitutional questions arising out of either the constitutions of the separate States or the articles of the federal Constitution are of daily occurrence and constantly occupy the Courts. Hence the citizens become a people of constitutionalists, and matters which excite the strongest popular feeling, as, for instance, the right of Chinese to settle in the country, are determined by the judicial Bench, and the decision of the Bench is acquiesced in by the people. This acquiescence or submission is due to the Americans inheriting the legal notions of the common law, *i. e.* of the "most legal system of law" (if the expression may be allowed) in the world. Tocqueville long ago remarked that the Swiss fell far short of the Americans in reverence for law and justice. The events of the last sixty years suggest that he perhaps underrated Swiss submission to law. But the law to which Switzerland is accustomed recognises wide discretionary power on the part of the executive, and has never fully severed the functions of the judge from those of the government. (*Albert Venn Dicey, Introduction to the Study of the Law of the Constitution, 1885, 8th edition, 1915, pp. 175-176.*)

We live under a peculiar Government, due to its dual character and limited power. We have to determine in this country not only what we ought to do, but what we can do, because we have a Government limited both as to which sovereignty shall exercise the power and limited also as to what matters can be dealt with at all. The one important original idea contained in the Constitution of the United States is the supremacy that is given to the judiciary. The thing that makes our Constitution unique from every one in the world is the fact that the Supreme Court of the United States is given power to say if the other branches of the Government have exceeded their power; has the right to declare null and void an act of the Legislature of the National Government; has the right to have disregarded the action of the Executive when it is beyond his power; and has the further right to say when the States have exceeded their sovereign powers. That is the greatest power ever given to a tribunal, and it is, as I have said, the one great characteristic of the American Constitution, and to it we owe more of the stability and grandeur of this country than to any other provision in that instrument.

Those who have read the history of America know that the real law of America is what finally exists after the statutes have been construed and passed upon by the courts of the land, that what passes Congress does not necessarily become the law of the land. Through the decisions of the Supreme Court the Constitution, open to many constructions, was so interpreted as to create a nation with power over matters of national importance and at the same time to preserve the sovereign States and their sovereignty over those matters peculiarly pertaining to the respective States and not to the nation at large. There have been times when the decisions of this court in the performance of its great functions have aroused great excitement and at times great indignation; but with the exception of the Dred Scott case [19 Howard, 393, decided in 1856] nearly every decision of that court undertaking to lay down the limits of national and State power has met with the final approval of the American people; and today it may not be inappropriate, when it has become the fashion of some of those in high places to criticise the judiciary, to call attention to these facts. Certainly, no man from my section of the country should ever care to utter a condemnation of the judiciary, for when passion ran riot, when men had lost their judgment, when the results of four years of bitter war produced legislation aimed not at justice, but frequently at punishment, it was the Supreme Court that stood between the citizen and his liberties and the passion of the hour. And I trust the day will never come when the American people will not be willing to submit respectfully and gladly to the decrees of that august tribunal. Temporarily they may seem to thwart the will of the people, but in their final analysis they will make, as they have made, for orderly government, for a government of laws and not of men, and we may be sure that the Supreme Court in the pure atmosphere of judicial inquiry that has always surrounded it will arrive at a better interpretation of the powers of both State and National Governments than can be possibly hoped for in a forum like this, where popular prejudice and the passions of the hour affect all of us, whether we will or no. (*Speech of the Honorable Swagar Sherley, of Kentucky, in the House of Representatives, January 10, 1908, the Congressional Record, Sixtieth Congress, First Session, Vol. XLII, 1908, p. 589.*)

CHAPTER XII

CREATION OF THE SUPREME COURT

WHEN the convention assembled in Philadelphia in the month of May, 1787, to eliminate the weaknesses of the Confederation and to correct its faults, it was evident that an agency of a judicial nature would be created, invested with the right and the duty to pass upon questions of an international nature, in order that the department of the government responsible for foreign affairs should not be embarrassed by what might be called a luxury of judicial decision, because the holdings of thirteen courts of the States on one and the same international question whereof they might take jurisdiction would embarrass the government, whatever its form might be, and prevent foreign nations from entering into relations with this government when the relations might be interpreted by one of the contracting parties in some thirteen different ways. It was also evident that this agency of a judicial nature, for like reasons, would be entrusted with the interpretation of the laws of the Union, because the right assumed and exercised by one State to interpret the meaning of a federal law meant the possibility of thirteen different interpretations, since if one State had the right to interpret such a law, all the States would possess this right; for, whatever form the Union might take, they would at least insist upon their sovereignty and equality in their relations one with another. The necessity of some kind of judicial agency of a confederate character had been recognized and had been partially met in the 9th of the Articles of Confederation, vesting the United States in Congress assembled with the right to appoint courts for the trial of piracies and felonies committed upon the high seas; for the trial and disposition of cases of capture on land and sea, and for the trial and disposition of disputes between the sovereign, free and equal States forming the Confederation.

The lack of an adequate agency of a judicial nature was one of the admitted weaknesses and faults of the perpetual Union created by the Articles of Confederation. Indeed a very keen observer and one whose opinion is law in this matter declared that the want of an adequate judicial power was its greatest defect. Thus, Alexander Hamilton felt himself justified in saying in *The Federalist:*

> A circumstance, which crowns the defects of the confederation, remains yet to be mentioned—the want of a judiciary power. Laws are a dead letter, without courts to expound and define their true meaning and opera-

247

tion. The treaties of the United States, to have any force at all, must be considered as part of the law of the land. Their true import, as far as respects individuals, must, like all other laws, be ascertained by judicial determinations. To produce uniformity in these determinations, they ought to be submitted in the last resort, to one SUPREME TRIBUNAL. And this tribunal ought to be instituted under the same authority which forms the treaties themselves. These ingredients are both indispensable. If there is in each state a court of final jurisdiction, there may be as many different final determinations on the same point, as there are courts. There are endless diversities in the opinions of men. We often see not only different courts, but the judges of the same court, differing from each other. To avoid the confusion which would unavoidably result from the contradictory decisions of a number of independent judicatories, all nations have found it necessary to establish one tribunal paramount to the rest, possessing a general superintendance, and authorized to settle and declare in the last resort an uniform rule of civil justice.

This is the more necessary where the frame of the government is so compounded, that the laws of the whole are in danger of being contravened by the laws of the parts. In this case, if the particular tribunals are invested with a right of ultimate decision, besides the contradictions to be expected from difference of opinion, there will be much to fear from the bias of local views and prejudices, and from the interference of local regulations. As often as such an interference should happen, there would be reason to apprehend, that the provisions of the particular laws might be preferred to those of the general laws, from the deference with which men in office naturally look up to that authority to which they owe their official existence. The treaties of the United States, under the present constitution, are liable to the infractions of thirteen different legislatures, and as many different courts of final jurisdiction, acting under the authority of those legislatures. The faith, the reputation, the peace of the whole union, are thus continually at the mercy of the prejudices, the passions, and the interests of every member of which these are composed. Is it possible that foreign nations can either respect or confide in such a government? Is it possible that the people of America will longer consent to trust their honour, their happiness, their safety, on so precarious a foundation?[1]

The members of the Confederation were thus faced with the problem of devising an agent of a judicial nature which, while adequate for the purposes of the Union in its international aspect, would meet the approval of the thirteen States, holding themselves to be sovereign, free and independent. The problem was complicated by the existence of this sovereignty whereof each State considered itself to be possessed, as, in the words of Hamilton,

Problem of Sovereignty

---

[1] *The Federalist*, 1802, Vol. I, pp. 145–6. Paper xxii.

In a later paper of *The Federalist* the principle involved in uniform determinations is thus expressed:

If there are such things as political axioms, the propriety of the judicial power of a government being co-extensive with its legislative, may be ranked among the number. The mere necessity of uniformity in the interpretation of the national laws decides the question. Thirteen independent courts of final jurisdiction over the same cause arising upon the same laws, is a hydra in government, from which nothing but contradiction and confusion can proceed. (Vol. II, p. 224, Paper lxxx.)

again expressed in *The Federalist,* " It is inherent in the nature of sovereignty, not to be amenable to the suit of an individual *without its consent."* In this passage he was doubtless making a concession against his personal convictions, and lest he might seem to be renouncing in *The Federalist* views which he had expressed on other public occasions, he hastened to add:

> This is the general sense, and the general practice of mankind; and the exemption, as one of the attributes of sovereignty, is now enjoyed by the government of every state in the Union. Unless, therefore, there is a surrender of this immunity in the plan of the convention it will remain with the states. . . .[1]

The men who met in conference in Philadelphia during the summer months of 1787 appreciated this crowning weakness of the Confederation, and their wisdom and ingenuity met and overcame the difficulties involved in the creation of a Supreme Court of a Union composed of States retaining the powers which they did not expressly grant to the Government of the new Union, or whose exercise would not be incompatible with the powers vested in the Union, by necessary implication, or of which they had not themselves consented to renounce the exercise. The framers of the Constitution followed the example of Solon, the renowned law-giver of antiquity, who, as stated by one of the members of the Convention in the course of debate, " gave the Athenians not the best Govt. he could devise; but the best they wd. receive." [2]

There appears to have been not merely substantial but general agreement that there should be an adequate judicial agency of the States, and there seems also to have been no opposition to its creation. There was much *Differences of Opinion* debate and difference of opinion as to whether the judiciary should have original or whether it should only have appellate jurisdiction, whether it should consist of one supreme court to which appeals should be made from the State judiciaries, or whether courts inferior to the Supreme Court should be established and vested with jurisdiction of matters of an interest to the States as a whole. There was also much difference of opinion as to the appointment of the members of the judiciary, some advocating their appointment by the legislature, others by the executive; still others, the executive in cooperation therewith. When, however, it was resolved to constitute a court for the existing States and such others as might later join or be added to the Union, the problem was solved in principle, and all other questions, however important in themselves, became matters of detail.

As has been seen, there were two great plans laid before the Convention: *The Two Plans*

[1] *Ibid.,* p. 238. Paper lxxxi.
[2] *Documentary History of the Constitution,* Vol. III, p. 68. Mr. Butler, session of June 5, 1787.

one, the Virginian plan, which the small States regarded as conceived in the interest of the large States; and the other, known as the New Jersey plan, expressly conceived in the interest of the smaller States. In the matter of the judiciary there was likewise a difference between the Virginian and the New Jersey plan, but both plans advocated the creation of a judiciary.

The Virginian Plan

The Journal of the Convention states, in its entry of May 29, 1787, that " Mr. Randolph, one of the deputies of Virginia, laid before the house, for their consideration, sundry propositions, in writing, concerning the American confederation, and the establishment of a national government," [1] and it was ordered that, on the morrow, " the propositions this day laid before the house, for their consideration, by Mr. Randolph," be referred to the said Committee of the whole House to consider the state of the American Union.[2] James Madison's Notes, the chief source of our knowledge of the proceedings of the Convention, give a summary of these resolutions, which must be regarded as their most authentic text, as unfortunately the original text which Mr. Randolph laid before the Convention has not been preserved other than in Mr. Madison's handwriting. According to this draft it was to be resolved " that the articles of Confederation ought to be so corrected & enlarged as to accomplish the objects proposed by their institution; namely, ' common defence, security of liberty and general welfare.' " [3] To effect these objects, a national legislature, consisting of two branches, was to be formed, a national executive to be instituted, and a national judiciary to be established.

It is to be observed, in this connection, that the very first draft of the new instrument of government provided for the threefold division into a legislative, executive and judicial department thereof, a principle borrowed, it would appear, from Montesquieu, and regarded as a matter of faith by Americans, then as now. The article on the judiciary, as given by Madison, reads:

> 9. Res[d]. that a National Judiciary be established to consist of one or more supreme tribunals, and of inferior tribunals to be chosen by the National Legislature, to hold their offices during good behaviour; and to receive punctually at stated times fixed compensation for their services, in which no increase or diminution shall be made so as to affect the persons actually in office at the time of such increase or diminution. that the jurisdiction of the inferior tribunals shall be to hear & determine in the first instance, and of the supreme tribunal to hear and determine in the dernier resort, all piracies & felonies on the high seas, captures from an enemy; cases in which foreigners or citizens of other States applying to such jurisdictions may be interested, or which respect the collection of the National

---

[1] *Journal, Acts and Proceedings of the Convention*, 1787, (1819), p. 66.
[2] *Ibid.*, pp. 70-1.
[3] *Documentary History of the Constitution*, Vol. III, p. 17.

revenue; impeachments of any National officers, and questions which may involve the national peace and harmony.[1]

On the same day the Journal contains the following entry:

> Mr. Charles Pinckney, one of the deputies of South Carolina, laid before the house for their consideration, the draught of a federal government to be agreed upon between the free and independent states of America.[2]

Unfortunately, the text of Mr. Pinckney's draft is not preserved in the Journal of the Convention in original or summary form. It was presented after Mr. Randolph's propositions, themselves preceded by a lengthy address of their proposer. It was doubtless late in the day, so that Mr. Pinckney did not have time to accompany them with an address, although he is reported by Robert Yates, in his notes of that day, as saying that " he had reduced his ideas of a new government to a system, which he read, and confessed it was grounded on the same principle as of the above resolutions." [3] In any event, the text of Mr. Pinckney's plan did not seem to impress the members present, as it was apparently not deemed of sufficient importance, then or later, to be abstracted by Mr. Madison. It is not referred to in the accounts of Mr. McHenry or Mr. Patterson, both of whom were present and made careful summaries of Mr. Randolph's proposals. It was not adopted or considered in the Conference, other than to be referred, apparently as a compliment, to the Committee of Detail along with Mr. Randolph's resolutions, in the form in which they had been amended, and the New Jersey resolutions, presented by Mr. Patterson for such consideration as the members of the Committee might care to give to them.

As in the case of Mr. Randolph's original propositions, it was ordered " that the said draught be referred to the committee of the whole house appointed to consider of the state of the American union." [4] On the following day, Mr. Randolph's resolution in favor of a national government, consisting of a legislative, judicial and executive department, was taken up, on which there is the following record in the Journal:

> Resolved, That a national government ought to be established, consisting of a supreme legislative, judiciary, and executive.[5]

On June 4th the Convention took up the discussion of the ninth article of Mr. Randolph's propositions, which, like the ninth article of the Confederation, dealt with a judiciary, and on this point the Journal reads:

---

[1] *Ibid.*, p. 19.
[2] *Journal of the Convention*, p. 71.
[3] Robert Yates, *Secret Proceedings and Debates of the Convention*, 1821, p. 97.
[4] *Journal of the Convention*, p. 81.
[5] *Ibid.*, p. 82.

When, on motion to agree to the first clause, namely,
"Resolved, That a national judiciary be established,"
It passed in the affirmative.
It was then moved and seconded to add these words to the first clause
of the ninth resolution, namely,
"To consist of one supreme tribunal, and of one or more inferior tri-
bunals."
And on the question to agree to the same.
It passed in the affirmative.[1]

On the 5th of June the Committee of the Whole further considered Mr.
Randolph's ninth resolution, and in the matter of inferior tribunals struck
out the words "one or more."[2] In the same connection, the phrase "the
national legislature" was stricken, leaving the question of selecting the
judges to be decided later; so that the ninth resolution, as then approved by
the Committee, read:

> Resolved, That a national judiciary be established to consist of one
> supreme tribunal, and of one or more inferior tribunals, to be appointed
> by   ; to hold their offices during good behaviour; and to
> receive punctually, at stated times, a fixed compensation for their services,
> in which no increase or diminution shall be made, so as to affect the per-
> sons actually in office, at the time of such increase or diminution.

Further consideration of the resolution was postponed.
Later in the day the Convention returned to the ninth article, and on
motion of John Rutledge, later Chief Justice of the United States, seconded
by Roger Sherman of Connecticut, who has the unique distinction of having
signed the Declaration of Independence, the Articles of Confederation and
the Constitution of the United States, that portion of Mr. Randolph's resolution relating to inferior tribunals was rejected and the following additional
clause was added to the resolution:

> That the national legislature be empowered to appoint inferior tribunals.[3]

The proposition to limit the judicial power of the United States to one
supreme tribunal, without inferior courts as proposed by Mr. Rutledge, and
accepted for the time being by the Convention, was a matter of great importance and was justly considered as such. James Madison, a future president, and James Wilson, a future justice of the Supreme Court, took issue,
and with the support of John Dickinson and Rufus King eventually carried the point against Messrs. Rutledge and Sherman. Mr. Madison's

[1] *Journal of the Convention*, p. 98.
[2] *Ibid.*, p. 99.
[3] *Ibid.*, p. 102.

Notes fortunately give, although very briefly, the views of the different members. Thus, John Rutledge argued:

> That the State Tribunals might and ought to be left in all cases to decide in the first instance the right of appeal to the supreme national tribunal being sufficient to secure the national rights & uniformity of Judgm^ts. that it was making an unnecessary encroachment on the jurisdiction of the States, and creating unnecessary obstacles to their adoption of the new system.[1]

Upon this, Mr. Madison, to quote his Notes again,

> observed that unless inferior tribunals were dispersed throughout the Republic with final jurisdiction in many cases, appeals would be multiplied to a most oppressive degree; that besides, an appeal would not in many cases be a remedy. What was to be done after improper Verdicts in State tribunals obtained under the biased directions of a dependent Judge, or the local prejudices of an undirected jury? To remand the cause for a new trial would answer no purpose. To order a new trial at the supreme bar would oblige the parties to bring up their witnesses, tho' ever so distant from the seat of the Court. An effective Judiciary establishment commensurate to the legislative authority, was essential. A Government without a proper Executive & Judiciary would be the mere trunk of a body without arms or legs to act or move.[2]

The difficulty was real and serious, yet capable of solution, for the power might be granted, leaving it to the future to determine whether it should be exercised or not. This solution appears to have been suggested by Mr. Dickinson, who is represented by Mr. Madison as contending " strongly that if there was to be a National Legislature, there ought to be a national Judiciary, and that the former ought to have authority to institute the latter." [3]

Upon the passing of Mr. Rutledge's motion to strike out " inferior tribunals," Messrs. Wilson and Madison " then moved, in pursuance of the idea expressed above by Mr. Dickinson,"

> to add to Resol: 9. the words following " that the National Legislature be empowered to institute inferior tribunals." They observed that there was a distinction between establishing such tribunals absolutely, and giving a discretion to the Legislature to establish or not establish them. They repeated the necessity of some such provision.[4]

This motion was carried, which did not direct but, what would of necessity amount to the same thing in the course of time, empowered the legislature to institute inferior tribunals.

[1] *Documentary History,* Vol. III, p. 67.
[2] *Ibid.*
[3] *Ibid.,* p. 68.
[4] *Ibid.*

On June 12th the matter of the judiciary was again taken up, and on the day following Mr. Randolph's ninth resolution was approved in the form which it had assumed as the result of discussion and debate in the Committee of the Whole.[1] On the first of these days the resolution fared very badly. The proceedings on June 12th were negatived; not merely were the leaves plucked from the branches, but the branches themselves were torn from the trunk, reminding one very much of Dr. Franklin's famous anecdote anent "John Thompson, *Hatter, makes* and *sells hats* for ready money," which simple sign, when revised, had lost the statement that John Thompson sold hats and made hats, and left the sign with but a picture of a hat to indicate what manner of man he was and what calling John Thompson followed.[2] Thus, to quote Madison's Notes, which are usually fuller than on this occasion:

> It was moved & 2[ded]. to alter Resol: 9. so as to read "that the jurisdiction of the supreme tribunal shall be to hear & determine in the dernier resort, all piracies, felonies, &c"
> It was moved & 2[ded]. to strike out "all piracies & felonies on the high seas," which was agreed to.
> It was moved & agreed to strike out "all captures from an enemy."
> It was moved and agreed to strike out "other States" and insert "two distinct States of the Union."
> It was moved & agreed to postpone the consideration of Resolution 9. relating to the Judiciary:[3]

After this, it is no wonder that, to quote the concluding line of Mr. Madison's entry for the day, "The Com[e]. then rose & the House adjourned."

This does not mean, however, that there was opposition to the court or to its jurisdiction, but that the Convention was pursuing the course of international conferences and of large bodies, in which broad principles are proposed and debated to advantage and matters of detail are referred to a smaller body for consideration and report. The first entry in Mr. Madison's Notes for the next day, June 13th, shows that the leaders of the Convention had come to this conclusion, for, the consideration of the ninth resolution being resumed, "the latter parts of the clause relating to the jurisdiction of the Nat[l]. tribunals was struck out nem. con in order to leave full room for their organization."[4] We do not need to speculate as to the reason for this motion on behalf of its sponsors, as it is specifically stated in Robert Yates' notes of the 13th, which on this point are more elaborate than usual and more satisfactory than Mr. Madison's. Thus, according to Mr. Yates:

---

[1] *Documentary History*, Vol. III, p. 122.
[2] A. H. Smyth, *The Writings of Benjamin Franklin*, Vol. I. pp. 38–9.
[3] *Documentary History*, Vol. III, p. 117.
[4] *Ibid.*

Gov. Randolph observed the difficulty in establishing the powers of the judiciary — the object however at present is to establish this principle, to wit, the security of foreigners where treaties are in their favor, and to preserve the harmony of states and that of the citizens thereof. This being once established, it will be the business of a sub-committee to detail it; and therefore moved to obliterate such parts of the resolve so as only to establish the principle, to wit, *that the jurisdiction of the national judiciary shall extend to all cases of national revenue, impeachment of national officers, and questions which involve the national peace or harmony.* Agreed to unanimously.[1]

The indefatigable Mr. Pinckney and the experienced Mr. Sherman thereupon moved that the judges of this supreme tribunal should be appointed by the national legislature. Mr. Madison, as recorded in his Notes,

objected to an app^t. by the whole Legislature. Many of them were incompetent Judges of the requisite qualifications. They were too much influended by their partialities. The candidate who was present, who had displayed a talent for business in the legislative field, who had perhaps assisted ignorant members in business of their own, or of their Constituents, or used other winning means, would without any of the essential qualifications for an expositor of the laws prevail over a competitor not having these recommendations, but possessed of every necessary accomplishment. He proposed that the appointment should be made by the Senate, which as a less numerous & more select body, would be more competent judges, and which was sufficiently numerous to justify such a confidence in them.[2]

Messrs. Pinckney and Sherman were convinced by this statement, as was also the Convention, which approved for the moment the appointment by the Senate. At this session, on the 13th of June, the Committee of the Whole reported on Mr. Randolph's propositions as approved by it, of which the portions concerning the matter in hand are as follows:

11. Resol^d that a Nat^l Judiciary be established, to consist of one supreme tribunal, the Judges of which to be appointed by the 2^d. branch of the Nat^l. Legislature, to hold their offices during good behaviour, & to receive punctually at stated times a fixed compensation for their services, in which no increase or diminution shall be made, so as to affect the persons actually in office at the time of such increase or diminution.

12. Resol^d. that the Nat^l. Legislature be empowered to appoint inferior Tribunals.

Res^d. that the jurisdiction of the Nat^l. Judiciary shall extend to all cases which respect the collection of the Nat^l. revenue, impeachments of any Nat^l. Officers, and questions which involve the national peace & harmony.[3]

So matters stood when the smaller States, which had remained in the background and contented themselves with amending the propositions of the

---

[1] *Secret Proceedings and Debates*, pp. 119, 120.
[2] *Documentary History*, Vol. III, p. 118.
[3] *Ibid.*, p. 122.

larger States, began not only to gather confidence and to play a larger part in the proceedings, but to present a plan, conceived in their interests, as they believed the Virginian plan to be conceived in the interests of the larger States. The Virginian plan, as originally submitted and amended in the Committee of the Whole, did not please the delegates of the smaller States, of which Mr. William Patterson, later a Senator from New Jersey and a Justice of the Supreme Court under the Constitution, may be considered the mouthpiece, and who, after conference with friends who shared his views, and in their behalf, presented on the 15th day of June what is generally called the New Jersey plan. This plan admitted the defects of the Confederation and recognized that the Articles thereof could and, as expressed in the first proposition of the New Jersey plan, " ought to be so revised, corrected & enlarged, as to render the federal Constitution adequate to the exigencies of Government, & the preservation of the Union." [1] The Congress was to be authorized " to pass Acts for the regulation of trade & commerce as well with foreign nations as with each other: provided that all punishments, fines, forfeitures & penalties to be incurred for contravening such acts rules and regulations shall be adjudged by the Common law Judiciarys of the State in which any offence contrary to the true intent & meaning of such Acts rules & regulations shall have been committed or perpetrated, with liberty of commencing in the first instance all suits & prosecutions for that purpose in the superior Common law Judiciary in such State, subject nevertheless, for the correction of all errors, both in law & fact in rendering judgment, to an appeal to the Judiciary of the U. States." [2]

The
New Jersey
Plan

According to this plan, the Government of the Union was to avail itself of the courts of the States composing it, not to create agencies of its own in the shape of inferior courts, from which an appeal would naturally lie to the supreme federal tribunal. This supreme court, called in the plan " tribunal," its nature, the extent of its jurisdiction and the qualifications for its judges are defined in the 5th article, which reads:

> Res^d. that a federal Judiciary be established to consist of a supreme Tribunal the Judges of which to be appointed by the Executive, & to hold their offices during good behaviour, to receive punctually at stated times a fixed compensation for their services in which no increase or diminution shall be made, so as to affect the persons actually in office at the time of such increase or diminution; that the Judiciary so established shall have authority to hear & determine in the first instance on all impeachments of federal officers, & by way of appeal in the dernier resort in all cases touching the rights of Ambassadors, in all cases of captures from an enemy, in all cases of piracies & felonies on the high seas, in all cases in which

[1] *Documentary History*, Vol. III, p. 125.
[2] *Ibid.*, pp. 125–6.

foreigners may be interested, in the construction of any treaty or treaties, or which may arise on any of the Acts for regulation of trade, or the collection of the federal Revenue; that none of the Judiciary shall during the time they remain in Office be capable of receiving or holding any other office or appointment during their time of service, or for there-after.[1]

But this was not all. The sixth article contained a very fruitful suggestion, which was destined to replace the proposal of a negative on the laws of the State or on the laws of Congress, either by the National Legislature or a Council of Revision, and, acting upon individuals, makes a resort to force against the States, contained in the last clause of the Article, unnecessary as it was always inexpedient, although originally espoused by such a man as Mr. Madison. Thus:

> 6. Res^d. that all Acts of the U. States in Cong^s. made by virtue & in in pursuance of the powers hereby & by the articles of confederation vested in them, and all Treaties made & ratified under the authority of the U. States shall be the supreme law of the respective States so far forth as those Acts or Treaties shall relate to the said States or their Citizens, and that the Judiciary of the several States shall be bound thereby in their decisions, any thing in the respective laws of the Individual States to the contrary notwithstanding; and that if any State, or any body of men in any State shall oppose or prevent y^e. carrying into execution such acts or treaties, the federal Executive shall be authorized to call forth ye power of the Confederated States, or so much thereof as may be necessary to enforce and compel an obedience to such Acts, or an Observance of such Treaties.[2]

It was recognized that these propositions could not be rejected off-hand, even although a majority of the Convention favored the Virginian plan. It was therefore agreed that the propositions which Mr. Patterson had introduced as a substitute for Mr. Randolph's should be referred to a Committee of the Whole, and the Randolph plan was likewise recommitted " in order to place the two plans in due comparison." [3]

On July 18th the Convention took up the question of the judiciary and considered the eleventh, twelfth and thirteenth resolutions of Mr. Randolph's plan, as modified by the Committee of the Whole, in preference to Mr. Patterson's plan, which, however, had been very carefully considered in the meantime. There was no dissent to the formation of a national judiciary or to the proposition that this judiciary should consist of one supreme tribunal, but the debate turned upon the appointment of the judges, an embarrassing, difficult and delicate matter. The views on this point were divergent, some

Question of Appointment of Judges

---

[1] *Ibid.*, p. 127.
[2] *Ibid.*, pp. 127–8.
[3] *Ibid.*, p. 124.

members advocating appointment by the legislature, others by the second house, some by the executive and still others preferring Mr. Gorham's suggestion that the " Judges be appointed by the Execu^ve. with the advice & consent of the 2^d branch, in the mode prescribed by the constitution of Mas^ts." [1] Mr. Gorham stated as a fact that " this mode had been long practiced in that country, & was found to answer perfectly well." It has since been practiced in the United States and has likewise been found to answer equally well.

After much debate without reaching an agreement, and the rejection of Mr. Wilson's motion leaving the appointment of the judges to the executive instead of to the second branch, Mr. Gorham moved " that the Judges be nominated and appointed by the Executive, by & with the advice & consent of the 2^d branch & every such nomination shall be made at least   days prior to such appointment." [2] " This mode," he said, according to Mr. Madison's Notes, " had been ratified by the experience of 140 years in Massachusetts. If the app^t. should be left to either branch of the Legislature, it will be a mere piece of jobbing."

The Convention tied on Mr. Gorham's motion, thereby defeating it, [3] whereupon Mr. Madison moved that " the Judges should be nominated by the Executive, & such nomination should become an appointment if not disagreed to within   days by ⅔ of the 2^d branch." On the 21st of the month it was considered in a slightly amended form and in its stead a motion was adopted that " the judges of which shall be appointed by the second branch of the national legislature." [4] An agreement on this vexed question was therefore very difficult.

The clause of the eleventh resolution, that the judges " hold their office during good behaviour " was unanimously adopted, as was also the clause concerning the punctual payment of their salaries. It will be recalled that, as worded, this clause prevented an increase or diminution of the salaries of the judges during their tenure of office. After much discussion and no little misgiving it was decided, and wisely, by a vote of 6 to 2, to strike out the provision against the increase of salaries, and as thus amended this portion of the resolution passed unanimously. [5]

The framers of the Constitution had decided upon a division of power within the Government of the Union, and, for the protection of the judiciary as well as for the impartial administration of justice, they were anxious that the judges, when and however selected, should be independent of the

[1] Documentary History, Vol. III, p. 363.
[2] Ibid., p. 366.
[3] Ibid., p. 367.
[4] Journal of the Convention, p. 196.
[5] Documentary History, Vol. III, pp. 363–8. Session of July 18.

appointing power. Therefore, they were to hold office during good behavior and during their tenure of office they were to receive salaries which assuredly should not be decreased, if indeed they might be increased, during their tenure of office, even although they might depend upon the pleasure or discretion of one or the other branch of the Government for their appointment. The experience of colonial days had shown them the wisdom if not the necessity of this action on their part; but if they had forgotten it, they had an object lesson before their very eyes, for in the preceding year the judges of Rhode Island, who had declared a law of that State to be unconstitutional in the case of *Trevett* v. *Weeden,* were summoned before the Assembly "to render their reasons for adjudging an act of the General Assembly to be unconstitutional and so void." [1] Although no action was taken against them they were not reelected by the Legislature at the expiration of their terms in the spring of the very year in which the Federal Convention met in Philadelphia.

The 12th resolution, empowering Congress to institute inferior tribunals, was equally fortunate, although it was objected to, Mr. Sherman saying that he was "willing to give the power to the Legislature but wished them to make use of the State Tribunals whenever it could be done with safety to the general interest." [2] But the views tersely expressed by George Mason apparently carried conviction, that "many circumstances might arise not now to be foreseen, which might render such a power absolutely necessary." [3]

The clause in the 13th resolution, relating to the impeachment of national officers, was struck out, and "several criticisms," to quote Mr. Madison's Notes, "having been made on the definitions" of the jurisdiction of the national judiciary, it was, with the approval of the Convention, recast by Mr. Madison so as to read, "that the jurisdiction shall extend to all cases arising under the Nat^l. laws: And to such other questions as may involve the Nat^l. peace & harmony." [4]

There seems to have been a tacit understanding that, although the general principles of the Constitution should be considered in the Committee of

---

[1] Brinton Coxe, *Judicial Power and Unconstitutional Legislation,* 1893, p. 246.

In the session of July 17th of the Federal Convention of 1787, Mr. Madison said, with direct reference to the case of *Trevett* v. *Weeden,*

Confidence cannot be put in the State Tribunals as guardians of the National authority and interests. In all the States these are more or less dependt. on the Legislatures. In Georgia they are appointed annually by the Legislature. In R. Island the Judges who refused to execute an unconstitutional law were displaced, and others substituted, by the Legislature who would be willing instruments of the wicked & arbitrary plans of their masters. *Documentary History,* Vol. III, p. 352. Also, J. B. Scott, *Judicial Settlement of Controversies between States,* Vol. I, pp. 101–3.

[2] *Documentary History,* Vol. III, p. 369.

[3] *Ibid.*

[4] *Ibid.*

the Whole, where the discussion was more informal than in the Convention itself, and although the Convention should formally pass upon each clause of the Constitution, it would be necessary to refer the resolutions agreed upon to some committee which should elaborate them, devise the framework of the Constitution, and insert them in the form of articles in the order which they might properly assume in an instrument of that kind. Therefore, on July 23rd, a motion was made and unanimously agreed to that " the proceedings of the Convention for the establishment of a Nat[l]. Gov[t]. except the part relating to the Executive), be referred to a Committee to prepare & report a Constitution conformable thereto." [1]   This motion was unanimously agreed to, and, recognizing from their own experience in the Convention that a small committee was more effective than a large one, it was unanimously resolved that the committee should consist of five members, to be appointed on the morrow.   Therefore, on the 24th, the five members

Committee of Detail

to compose the committee to report a constitution were elected by ballot: Messrs. Rutledge, Randolph, Gorham, Ellsworth, and Wilson.   It was likewise felt that the committee should have before it the projects relating to a constitution which had been presented by Mr. Pinckney in his own behalf and by Mr. Patterson on behalf of the smaller States.   They were therefore referred to this committee, henceforth known as the Committee of Detail.[2]

Inasmuch as the motion to refer the resolutions agreed upon was passed on the 23d, and as it was desirable that the committee should have before it any resolutions agreed to since that date, it was decided on the 26th to refer these as well to the Committee of Detail, and, in order to give its members an opportunity to consider the projects and to report a draft of a constitution, the Convention adjourned to August 6th.

In the very short period of ten days, between the 26th of July and the 6th of August, the committee was able to report an instrument which bears very strong resemblance to the present Constitution of the United States. On that day the Convention met and each member was provided with a printed draft which, amended and improved in many ways, became the actual Constitution.   We do not know just what took place in the Committee of Detail during the intervening ten days, other than that the Committee complied with the directions of the Convention to prepare and to report a draft " conformable to the resolutions passed by the Convention."   A very careful and critical examination of the papers and documents which have been preserved in various ways, and which have come to light in the course of the last few years, has enabled students of the Constitution to divine, where

---

[1] *Documentary History*, Vol. III, pp. 413–14.
[2] *Ibid.*, p. 423.

they can not actually describe, the method of procedure.[1] Among the papers of George Mason, a member of the Convention, there was found a paper in Mr. Randolph's handwriting, of which certain parts have been identified as the handwriting of John Rutledge. Among the papers in the possession of James Wilson, a member of the Committee of Detail, there were various documents, one of which is a draft of the Constitution in Wilson's handwriting, which seems to have incorporated in it certain portions of the Pinckney draft and of the New Jersey plan. It has been concluded that the Committee of Detail, under Mr. Rutledge's chairmanship, took up the resolutions of the Convention as referred; that, after discussion and debate, and agreement upon a general plan, the resolutions were referred to Mr. Randolph, the sponsor of the Virginian plan although he is not to be credited with its authorship; that Mr. Randolph prepared the instrument in his handwriting, which is found to be the first draft of the Constitution, together with suggestions and criticisms; that this draft was laid before the Committee of Detail, considered by it, and modifications thereof inserted in the document in the handwriting of Mr. Rutledge, its chairman; that at a later stage, James Wilson, with the amended Randolph draft before him and the Pinckney and Patterson propositions, prepared an enlarged and revised draft. This, called the Wilson draft, was likewise amended by the committee and the changes incorporated in it appear to be in the handwriting of Mr. Rutledge, its chairman.

Be this as it may, the printed report of the committee was laid before the Convention, and a printed copy of the report was at the same time furnished to each member.

The articles of the draft concerning the judiciary, the Supreme Court and inferior courts are as follows:

Draft
Proposals

VII

Sect. 1. The Legislature of the United States shall have the power . . .
To constitute tribunals inferior to the Supreme Court; . . .

VIII

The Acts of the Legislature of the United States made in pursuance of this Constitution, and all treaties made under the authority of the United States shall be the supreme law of the several States, and of their citizens and inhabitants; and the judges in the several States shall be bound thereby in their decisions; anything in the Constitutions or laws of the several States to the contrary notwithstanding.

[1] See Max Farrand, *The Framing of the Constitution of the United States*, Chapters IX and X; also, J. Franklin Jameson, Studies in the History of the Federal Convention of 1787, in *Annual Report of the American Historical Association*, 1902, Vol. I, pp. 89–167.

IX

Sect. 1. The Senate of the United States shall have power . . . . to appoint . . . . Judges of the supreme Court.

Sect. 2. In all disputes and controversies now subsisting, or that may hereafter subsist between two or more States, respecting jurisdiction or territory, the Senate shall possess the following powers. Whenever the Legislature, or the Executive authority, or lawful Agent of any State, in controversy with another, shall by memorial to the Senate, state the matter in question, and apply for a hearing; notice of such memorial and application shall be given by order of the Senate, to the Legislature or the Executive authority of the other State in Controversy. The Senate shall also assign a day for the appearance of the parties, by their agents, before the House. The Agents shall be directed to appoint, by joint consent, commissioners or judges to constitute a Court for hearing and determining the matter in question. But if the Agents cannot agree, the Senate shall name three persons out of each of the several States; and from the list of such persons each party shall alternately strike out one, until the number shall be reduced to thirteen; and from that number not less than seven nor more than nine names, as the Senate shall direct, shall in their presence, be drawn out by lot; and the persons whose names shall be so drawn, or any five of them shall be commissioners or Judges to hear and finally determine the controversy; provided a majority of the Judges, who shall hear the cause, agree in the determination. If either party shall neglect to attend at the day assigned, without shewing sufficient reasons for not attending, or being present shall refuse to strike, the Senate shall proceed to nominate three persons out of each State, and the Clerk of the Senate shall strike in behalf of the party absent or refusing. If any of the parties shall refuse to submit to the authority of such Court; or shall not appear to prosecute or defend their claim or cause, the Court shall nevertheless proceed to pronounce judgment. The judgment shall be final and conclusive. The proceedings shall be transmitted to the President of the Senate, and shall be lodged among the public records, for the security of the parties concerned. Every Commissioner shall, before he sit in judgment, take an oath, to be administered by one of the Judges of the Supreme or Superior Court of the State where the cause shall be tried, " well and truly to hear and determine the matter in question according to the best of his judgment, without favor, affection, or hope of reward."

XI

Sect. 1. The Judicial Power of the United States shall be vested in one Supreme Court, and in such inferior Courts as shall, when necessary, from time to time, be constituted by the Legislature of the United States.

Sect. 2. The Judges of the Supreme Court, and of the Inferior Courts, shall hold their offices during good behavior. They shall, at stated times, receive for their services, a compensation, which shall not be diminished during their continuance in office.

Sect. 3. The Jurisdiction of the Supreme Court shall extend to all cases arising under laws passed by the Legislature of the United States; to all cases affecting Ambassadors, other Public Ministers and Consuls; to the trial of impeachments of Officers of the United States; to all cases of Admiralty and maritime jurisdiction; to controversies between two or more States, (except such as shall regard Territory or Jurisdiction) between a State and Citizens of another State, between Citizens of different States, and between a State or the Citizens thereof and foreign States, citizens or subjects. In cases of impeachment, cases affecting Ambassadors, other Public Ministers and Consuls, and those in which a State shall be party, this jurisdiction shall be original. In all the other cases before mentioned, it shall be appellate, with such exceptions and under such regulations as the Legislature shall make. The Legislature may assign any part of the jurisdiction above mentioned (except the trial of the President of the United States) in the manner, and under the limitations which it shall think proper, to such Inferior Courts, as it shall constitute from time to time.

XVI

Full faith shall be given in each State to the acts of the Legislatures, and to the records and judicial proceedings of the Courts and Magistrates of every State.

XX

The members of the Legislatures, and the Executive and Judicial officers of the United States, and of the several States, shall be bound by oath to support this Constitution.[1]

The articles concerning the judiciary were taken up on August 27th, when Dr. Johnson proposed to extend the judicial power of the United States to cases involving law and equity. After discussion this was agreed to, and the phrase "both in law and equity" was inserted immediately after "the United States,"[2] thus making the first part of the section read

The judicial power of the United States, both in law and equity, shall be vested in one Supreme Court.

At a later date, namely, on September 15th, the Convention struck out the phrase concerning law and equity inserted in this part of the articles, because it was included in Sec. 2, and therefore did not need to be repeated.[3] The matter of the tenure of judges was taken up, and it was proposed by Mr. Dickinson, that "after the words 'good behaviour' the words 'provided that they may be removed by the Executive on the application by the Senate and House of Representatives'" be inserted.[4] Gouverneur Morris thought that it was a contradiction in terms to say "that the Judges should hold their offices during good behavior, and yet be removable without a trial," and Mr. Rutledge called attention to what he considered to be an insuperable objection to the motion, in that the Supreme Court was to judge between the United States and particular States. The motion was therefore rejected,[5] and with

[1] *Documentary History*, Vol. III, pp. 449–57.
[2] *Ibid.*, p. 623.
[3] *Journal of the Convention*, p. 384.
[4] *Documentary History*, Vol. III, pp. 623-4. Session of August 27th.
[5] *Ibid.*

modifications of form suggested by the Committee of Style, the article was adopted substantially as reported by the Committee of Detail, and in the Constitution as finally signed the two sections are thus merged:

Article III.

Section 1. The judicial Power of the United States, shall be vested in one supreme Court, and in such inferior Courts as the Congress may from time to time ordain and establish. The Judges, both of the supreme and inferior Courts, shall hold their Offices during good Behaviour, and shall, at stated Times, receive for their Services, a Compensation, which shall not be diminished during their Continuance in Office.

Section 3 of the 11th Article reported by the Committee of Detail dealt with the subject matter of the 2d Section of the present Constitution, and in addition with some other matters which will be referred to later. On August 27th, Mr. Madison and Gouverneur Morris, as stated in Madison's Notes, "moved to insert after the word 'controversies' the words 'to which the U— S— shall be a party,'" [1] which had the effect of investing the Supreme Court with jurisdiction in cases affecting the United States, and of subordinating the United States to the law as interpreted by the tribunal. This amendment gave effect to one of several proposals which Charles Pinckney had made on August 20th, as follows:

The Jurisdiction of the supreme Court shall be extended to all controversies between the U. S. and an individual State, or the U. S. and the Citizens of an individual State.[2]

Dr. Johnson moved to amend the first clause of the article as reported by the Committee of Detail by inserting before the word " laws " in the first clause thereof, the expression " this Constitution and the," [3] which would have the effect of extending the jurisdiction of the Supreme Court to all cases both in law and equity arising under " this Constitution and the laws of the United States," etc.

This raised a very important question, which was at any rate seen by Mr. Madison and called to the attention of the Convention, for, to quote his Notes, he " doubted whether it was not going too far to extend the jurisdiction of the Court generally to cases arising Under the Constitution, & whether it ought not to be limited to cases of a Judiciary Nature. The right of expounding the Constitution in cases not of this nature though not to be given to that Department." [4] That is to say, the court was to be a court of law

---

[1] *Documentary History,* Vol. III, p. 626.
[2] *Ibid.,* p. 566.
[3] *Ibid.,* p. 626.
[4] *Ibid.*

and equity; it was not to be a diplomatic body passing upon political questions.

There appears to have been no action taken on the question raised by Mr. Madison. Dr. Johnson's motion was agreed to " nem. con.," it being generally supposed, as Mr. Madison says, that the jurisdiction was constructively limited to cases of a judicial nature.[1]

This was not the only amendment to the clause, and one moved by Mr. Rutledge gave effect to one of the purposes for which the Convention had been called, namely, to enable the United States to have its international obligations passed upon by a tribunal of the Union instead of by tribunals of the individual States, with the possibility of inconsistent and jarring interpretations. Immediately after the expression " United States," contained in this clause, Mr. Rutledge moved to insert " and treaties made or which shall be made under their authority." He further moved the omission of the phrase " passed by the Legislature," and both his amendments carried.[2] The amendment, however, was due to Mr. Madison, upon whose motion it had been debated two days previously and in a different connection, as will presently appear.[3]

Without dwelling further upon these matters at this time, and leaving aside other and special phases of the Judiciary which will be discussed later, it is evident that the members of the Constitutional Convention were intent upon a Supreme Court of the more perfect Union in the technical sense of the word; that it should not pass upon all provisions of the Constitution, but only upon those of a judicial nature; that the Congress should have the power, to be exercised in its discretion, of appointing inferior tribunals from which an appeal should lie to the Supreme Court; that for uniformity of decision appeals should lie from State tribunals when national or international questions were concerned; and that in any event the provisions of the Constitution of a non-political character, the acts of Congress passed in pursuance of the Constitution, and treaties made or to be made by the United States, should be determined by the Supreme Court of the States, not finally determined even by the Supreme Courts of the several States. In a word, every national and every international act was in ultimate resort to be determined by the final judicial authority of the Union.

The framers of the Constitution, however, did not content themselves with a narrow and technical definition of judicial power. They extended it, wisely as we now know, to controversies between the States, making the Supreme Court an international tribunal and showing the possibility of an international court of justice for the Society of Nations.

[1] *Ibid.*, p. 626.
[2] *Ibid.*
[3] *Ibid.*, p. 619. Session of August 25th.

XIII

PROTOTYPE OF A COURT OF INTERNATIONAL JUSTICE

The usual remedies between nations, war and diplomacy, being precluded by the federal union, it is necessary that a judicial remedy should supply their place. The Supreme Court of the Federation dispenses international law, and is the first great example of what is now one of the most prominent wants of civilized society, a real International Tribunal. (*John Stuart Mill, Considerations on Representative Government, 1861, pp. 305–306.*)

Sitting, as it were, as an international, as well as a domestic tribunal, we apply Federal law, state law, and international law, as the exigencies of the particular case may demand. . . . (*Chief Justice Fuller in Kansas v. Colorado, 185 United States, 125, 146-147, decided in 1902.*)

The importance which the framers of the Constitution attached to such a tribunal, for the purpose of preserving internal tranquillity, is strikingly manifested by the clause which gives this court jurisdiction over the sovereign States which compose this Union, when a controversy arises between them. Instead of reserving the right to seek redress for injustice from another State by their sovereign powers, they have bound themselves to submit to the decision of this court, and to abide by its judgment. And it is not out of place to say, here, that experience has demonstrated that this power was not unwisely surrendered by the States; for in the time that has already elapsed since this Government came into existence, several irritating and angry controversies have taken place between adjoining States, in relation to their respective boundaries, and which have sometimes threatened to end in force and violence, but for the power vested in this court to hear them and decide between them. (*Chief Justice Taney in Ableman v. Booth, 21 Howard, 506, 519, decided in 1858.*)

Those states, in their highest sovereign capacity, in the convention of the people thereof; on whom, by the revolution, the prerogative of the crown, and the transcendent power of parliament devolved, in a plenitude unimpaired by any act, and controllable by no authority, adopted the constitution, by which they respectively made to the United States a grant of judicial power over controversies between two or more states. (*Mr. Justice Baldwin in Rhode Island v. Massachusetts, 12 Peters, 657, 720, decided in 1838.*)

So that the practice seems to be well settled, that in suits against a state, if the state shall refuse or neglect to appear, upon due service of process, no coercive measures will be taken to compel appearance; but the complainant, or plaintiff, will be allowed to proceed ex parte. (*Mr. Justice Thompson in Massachusetts v. Rhode Island, 12 Peters, 755, 761, decided in 1838.*)

From the character of the parties, and the nature of the controversy, we cannot, without committing great injustice, apply to this case the rules as to time, which govern Courts of Equity in suits between individuals. . . . But a case like this, and one too of so many years standing, the parties, in the nature of things, must be incapable of acting with the promptness of an individual. Agents must be employed, and much time may be required to search for historical documents, and to arrange and collate them, for the purpose of presenting to the Court the true grounds of the defence. (*Chief Justice Taney in Rhode Island v. Massachusetts, 13 Peters, 23, 24, decided in 1839.*)

The case to be determined is one of peculiar character, and altogether unknown in the ordinary course of judicial proceedings. It is a question of boundary between two sovereign states, litigated in a Court of Justice, and we have no precedents to guide us in the forms and modes of proceedings, by which a controversy of this description can most conveniently, and with justice to the parties, be brought to a final hearing. The subject was however fully considered at January term, 1838. . . . It was then decided, that the rules and practice of the Court of Chancery should govern in conducting this suit to a final issue. . . .

Yet, in a controversy where two sovereign states are contesting the boundary between them, it will be the duty of the Court to mould the rules of Chancery practice and pleading, in such a manner as to bring this case to a final hearing on its real merits. It is too important in its character, and the interests concerned are too great, to be decided upon the mere technical principles of Chancery pleading. (*Chief Justice Taney in Rhode Island v. Massachusetts, 14 Peters, 210, 256-7, decided in 1840.*)

And it would seem that when the Constitution was framed, and when this law was passed, it was confidently believed that a sense of justice and of mutual interest would insure a faithful execution of this constitutional provision by the Executive of every State, for every State had an equal interest in the execution of a compact absolutely essential to their peace and well being in their internal concerns, as well as members of the Union. Hence, the use of the words ordinarily employed when an undoubted obligation is required to be performed, " it shall be his duty."

But if the Governor of Ohio refuses to discharge this duty, there is no power delegated to the General Government, either through the Judicial Department or any other department, to use any coercive means to compel him. (*Chief Justice Taney in Kentucky v. Dennison, Governor of Ohio, 24 Howard, 66, 109-10, decided in 1860.*)

The opinions referred to will make it clear that both States were afforded the amplest opportunity to be heard and that all the propositions of law and fact urged were given the most solicitous consideration. Indeed, it is also true that in the course of the controversy, as demonstrated by the opinions cited, controlled by great consideration for the character of the parties, no technical rules were permitted to frustrate the right of both of the States to urge the very merits of every subject deemed by them to be material.

And, controlled by a like purpose, before coming to discharge our duty in the matter now before us, we have searched the record in vain for any indication that the assumed existence of any error committed has operated to prevent the discharge by West Virginia of the obligations resulting from the judgment and hence has led to the proceeding to enforce the judgment which is now before us. (*Chief Justice White in Virginia v. West Virginia, 246 United States, 565, 590, decided in 1918.*)

That judicial power essentially involves the right to enforce the results of its exertion is elementary. . . . And that this applies to the exertion of such power in controversies between States as the result of the exercise of original jurisdiction conferred upon this court by the Constitution is therefore certain. The many cases in which such controversies between States have been decided in the exercise of original jurisdiction make this truth manifest. Nor is there room for contending to the contrary because, in all the cases cited, the States against which judgments were rendered, conformably to their duty under the Constitution, voluntarily respected and gave effect to the same. This must be unless it can be said that, because a doctrine has been universally recognized as being beyond dispute and has hence hitherto, in every case from the foundation of the Government, been accepted and applied, it has by that fact alone now become a fit subject for dispute. (*Chief Justice White in Virginia v. West Virginia, 246 United States, 565, 591-2, decided in 1918.*)

The complainant, the Commonwealth of Virginia, now comes and informs the Court that the decree entered by the Court in this cause on the 14th of June, 1915, in favor of the complainant and against the defendant, for the sum of $12,393,929.50, with interest thereon from July 1st, 1915, until paid at the rate of five per centum per annum, together with one-half of the costs, has been fully satisfied and paid by the defendant in the manner provided in, and in accordance with the terms of the Act of the Legislature of the State of West Virginia approved April 1st, 1919, entitled " An Act providing for the payment of West Virginia's part of the public debt of the commonwealth of Virginia prior to the first day of January, one thousand eight hundred and sixty-one, as ascertained by the judgment of the Supreme Court of the United States and adjusted by the two States, and to provide for the issuance of bonds and the raising and appropriation of money for the payment of said judgment." (*Acknowledgment of Satisfaction of Decree filed in the Supreme Court of the United States, March 1, 1920, in the case of State of Virginia v. State of West Virginia, 238 United States, 202, decided in 1915.*)

CHAPTER XIII

PROTOTYPE OF A COURT OF INTERNATIONAL JUSTICE

Questions
Arising
Under
Treaties

THE effect of Mr. Rutledge's motion to have the judicial power of the United States extended to treaties made or to be made under their authority was to endow the Supreme Court with the power and the duty to pass upon the question of treaties and to ascertain and fix the obligation of the general government and of the States by judicial decision of the Supreme Court. A minor but not unimportant improvement of the draft of August 6th should be mentioned, which was made in the busy and fruitful session of August 27th. By an inspection of the draft it will appear that, by the first section of Article 11, "the Judicial Power of the United States shall be vested in one Supreme Court;" and in section 3 thereof, "the jurisdiction of the Supreme Court" is very naturally and properly defined.[1] This slight variation of language, which might be supposed to affect the meaning, was not lost upon Mr. Madison. He suggested, with the unanimous approval of the Convention, that the wording should be the same in each case, and therefore "the Judicial Power" of the United States was substituted for "the jurisdiction of the Supreme Court."[2]

There was an added reason for the change which could be advanced if any justification be needed, in that the first section expressly, and the second section impliedly, spoke of inferior courts to which the judicial power of the United States was to extend. Therefore this expression was really more accurate than the former. It will also be observed from the draft of the Committee of Detail that, while the jurisdiction of the Supreme Court, or, as amended, the judicial power of the United States, is extended to controversies between two or more States, controversies regarding "territory or jurisdiction" are excepted from the jurisdiction of the Supreme Court. It was intended, however, that they should be subject to the judicial power, although the procedure to be followed was different.

The reason for the exception is not difficult to find, for, in this as in other matters, the members of the Convention had in mind, and indeed under their very eyes, the Articles of Confederation, which they retained in spirit if not in letter whenever it seemed possible or advisable to do so. The ninth of these articles declared that "the United States in Congress assem-

---

[1] *Documentary History of the Constitution*, Vol. III, p. 454. Session of August 6th.
[2] *Ibid.*, p. 627.

bled shall also be the last resort on appeal in all disputes and differences now subsisting or that hereafter may arise between two or more States concerning boundary, jurisdiction, or any other cause whatever," and provided that they should be settled by means of temporary commissions to be appointed by the Congress upon the general consent of the agents of the States in controversy, or, in default of their agreement, from a list made up of three persons from each of the thirteen States represented in the Congress. The Committee of Detail had preserved this procedure, restricting it, however, to disputes and controversies " respecting jurisdiction or territory," and substituting the Senate of the Constitution for the Congress of the Confederation. In substance and in spirit the ninth article of the Confederation was preserved, as in the Senate the States were to be equally represented, as they had been under the Confederation; so that the representatives of the States as such were to take the necessary steps for the settlement of disputes and differences. The long section of the articles and of the proposed Constitution was replaced by the very simple provision that " the judicial power shall extend . . . to controversies between two or more States." In this change lies the promise of an international judiciary, for controversies involving questions of law and equity between two or more States of the American Union were to be decided by judges, not compromised by arbiters, just as controversies between members of the society of nations can and one day will be so decided involving " the principles of equity and right on which are based the security of States and the welfare of peoples," to quote the preamble to the Hague Convention for the pacific settlement of international disputes.[1]

As this point is so interesting and so important, and as the Supreme Court is the prototype of an international tribunal, the discussion of the matter in the Convention is set forth in full as found in Mr. Madison's Notes under date of August 24th:

> Sect: 2 & 3 of art: IX being taken up.
> M[r]. Rutledge said this provision for deciding controversies between the States was necessary under the Confederation, but will be rendered unnecessary by the National Judiciary now to be established, and moved to strike it out.
> Doc[r]. Johnson 2[ded]. the Motion.
> M[r]. Sherman concurred: so did M[r]. Dayton.
> M[r]. Williamson was for postponing instead of striking out, in order to consider whether this might not be a good provision, in cases where the Judiciary were interested or too closely connected with the parties—
> M[r]. Ghorum had doubts as to striking out, The Judges might be connected with the States being parties—He was inclined to think the mode

---

[1] *Statutes at Large,* 36: 2201.

proposed in the clause would be more satisfactory than to refer such cases to the Judiciary—

On the Question for postponing the 2^d. and 3^d. Section, in passed in the negative.

N. H. ay. Mas^{ts}. no. Con^t. no. N. J. no. Pen^a. abs^t. Del. no. M^d. no. V^a. no. N. C. ay. S- C no. Geo. ay.

Mr. Wilson urged the striking out, the Judiciary being a better provision.

On Question for striking out 2 & 3 Sections Art: IX.

N. H. ay. Mas: ay. C^t. ay. N. J– ay. P^a. abs^t. Del– ay. M^d. ay. V^a. ay. N. C. no. S. C. ay—Geo. no.[1]

How Political Questions Become Judicial

We are indeed fortunate to have even this brief account of one of the silent revolutions in the thought and therefore in the practice of mankind, for, with the lessons of history before them and with no exact precedent for their action, the members of the Convention recognized that the submission of a dispute between nations to a judicial tribunal makes of it a juridical question, and therefore a proper subject of judicial power, as pointed out by the agent of their creation in the controversy between Rhode Island and Massachusetts (12 Peters, 755) decided in 1838.

It is to be observed, in the first place, that the Convention regarded some method as "necessary" for settling the disputes between the States. Without a court some such provision as that of the Articles of Confederation was "necessary;" but the establishment of the court made the provision of the articles "unnecessary," as pointed out by Mr. Rutledge, in that there would be an agency ready and apt to decide the disputes without the delay involved in creating one for the case when it arose and which, as a temporary tribunal, would go out of being when the dispute had been settled. The provision of the articles was therefore unnecessary, and the gospel of the new dispensation was, as Mr. Wilson urged, "a better provision."

Arbitration Considered

It is further to be observed that the motion in this case was made by a distinguished lawyer, later to be Chief Justice of the Supreme Court of the United States, and that the recommendation for the judicial method came from Mr. Wilson, then a leader of the Pennsylvania bar and destined to be a Justice of the Supreme Court. It appeared to these men to go without argument that controversies of a legal and equitable nature between States could, and therefore should, be decided by a court, which for purposes of justice was to be the agent created by the States in which they consented to be sued, not an agency of government superior to the States and imposed upon them from above. It will also be observed that some of the delegates felt that the method of arbitration could still profitably be resorted to, as it was later to be pointed out by a distinguished French statesman at the Second Hague Peace Conference, that nations, while willing to submit their

[1] *Documentary History of the Constitution*, Vol. III, pp. 607-8.

controversies of a judicial nature to an international court, might prefer to submit their disputes of a different nature, or in which the judicial was slight in comparison to the political element, to arbitration.[1]

If the matter had stopped here, only a part of the jurisdiction exercised by the United States in Congress assembled under the ninth of the Articles of Confederation would have been vested in the Supreme Court. The ninth article submitted to the Congress " all controversies concerning the private right of soil claimed under different grants of two or more States " to " be finally determined as near as may be in the same manner . . . for deciding disputes respecting territorial jurisdiction between different States." This clause, forming the third section of the ninth of the Articles of Confederation, was retained in the proposed draft of the Constitution, which likewise formed the third section of the ninth article, with the substitution of the Senate, with its equal representation of the States, for the Congress, and is thus worded in the latter document:

> All controversies concerning lands claimed under different grants of two or more States, whose jurisdictions, as they respect such lands shall have been decided or adjusted subsequent to such grants, or any of them, shall, on application to the Senate, be finally determined, as near as may be, in the same manner as is before prescribed for deciding controversies between different States.[2]

Therefore, in the session of the 27th, three days after the Supreme Court was vested with jurisdiction of controversies between the States, Mr. Sherman proposed a further extension of judicial power by investing the court with the exercise of the power contained in the ninth of the Articles of Confederation, carried over to the ninth article of the proposed Constitution. As recorded by Mr. Madison, " Mr. Sherman moved to insert after the words ' between Citizens of different States ' the words, ' between Citizens of the same State claiming lands under grants of different States '— according to the provision in the ninth art: of the Confederation—which was agreed to nem: con: " [3] As thus modified, this section of the ninth article is embodied in the Constitution.

A further and not the least interesting modification of the proposed Constitution was likewise made in the session of the 27th, in which the Supreme Court was vested with the jurisdiction which the Congress had possessed

---

[1] " Thus it is seen that the cases for which the permanent tribunal is possible are the same as those in which compulsory arbitration is acceptable, being, generally speaking, cases of legal nature. Whereas political cases, in which the nations should be allowed freedom to resort to arbitration, are the very ones in which arbitrators are necessary rather than judges, that is, arbitrators chosen at the time the controversy arises." Discourse of M. Léon Bourgeois. James Brown Scott, *The Reports to the Hague Conferences of 1899 and 1907,* (1918), pp. 239–40.

[2] *Documentary History,* Vol. iii, p. 452. Session of August 6th.

[3] *Ibid.,* p. 627.

under the Confederation. A step in advance of this was taken by the Convention upon Mr. Madison's suggestion " agreed to nem. con.," that after the words " controversies between the States," the clause should be inserted " to which the U- S- shall be a party." [1] The Supreme Court was the appropriate court in which the United States should appear as a litigant, and it was natural that the right of the Government to avail itself of this tribunal should be expressly stated; although it might have been plausibly contended that the United States, as such, would be included within the clause extending the judicial power " to controversies between two or more States." The Convention either did not consider the United States as a State within the meaning of this clause, or deemed it preferable to separate the united from the individual States. Had it not done so, and if the United States were not included within the clause, it would have followed that the United States could be sued in the Supreme Court as well as appear as a plaintiff in a controversy with a State to which it was a party, whereas the United States would or would not be a party defendant under Mr. Madison's motion as the Supreme Court should interpret the clause when a case involving it was presented for its consideration. In any event, it is important to note the difference of language used with respect to the United States and to the States as such in these two clauses, as the Supreme Court has held that, by virtue of this wording, a State may be made defendant at the instance of a State because of the consent by them given in the Constitution, whereas the United States, by the clause in question, is authorized to make use of the Supreme Court in a controversy to which it is a party, but not to be made a defendant without its special consent, as the terms of the clause imply authorization, not consent.

Original and Appellate Jurisdiction

The second clause of the second section of the third article of the Constitution as finally adopted is designed to give effect to the grant of judicial power and to assign some of the subjects, by reason of their importance, to the original jurisdiction of the Supreme Court, and, in all other matters included in the article, to give the Supreme Court appellate jurisdiction " with such Exceptions, and under such Regulations as the Congress shall make " in order that there may be one law for the United States, one for the States, and one for the citizens thereof, in as far as what may be called federal questions are concerned. The impeachment of officers of the United

Impeachment

States fell within the original jurisdiction of the Supreme Court in the draft of the Committee of Detail as reported on August 6th.[2] This question was, however, ultimately removed from the judicial to the legislative branch of the Government of the Union. The requirement that the Chief Justice

[1] *Documentary History*, Vol. iii, p. 626.
[2] *Ibid.*, p. 454. Article XI, Sec. 3.

of the Supreme Court should preside in the Senate during the trial of persons impeached by the House of Representatives shows that, although removed from the court, the procedure was nevertheless to be judicial, making of the Senate, when so sitting, a high court of impeachment. With this further exception, the grant of original jurisdiction in the Constitution stands as reported by the Committee of Detail, with slight changes of language later made by the Committee on Style.

The balance of the clause, however, was changed in substance as well as in form by the Convention. Doubt having arisen in the mind of Gouverneur Morris as to whether the appellate jurisdiction of the Supreme Court already extended to matters of fact as well as law and to cases of common as well as civil law, Mr. Wilson, speaking for the Committee, of which he was a member, said:

> The Committee he believed meant facts as well as law & Common as well as Civil law. The jurisdiction of the federal Court of Appeals had he said been so construed.[1]

In order to clear up all doubt on this point, Mr. Dickinson moved, and his motion was unanimously agreed to, " to add after the word ' appellate ' the words ' both as to law & fact,' "[2] and on the following day, the 28th, to improve the English, the phrase " supreme Court " was substituted for the expression " it " before " appellate jurisdiction."[3] As thus amended, the appellate jurisdiction of what we should today call the federal courts was agreed upon in the session of the 27th of August, with the exception of certain formal changes proposed by the Committee on Style.

How were the judges to be appointed for the Supreme Court and the inferior courts which Congress might be minded to establish? In the first section of Article IX of the draft as reported by the Committee of Detail, it was provided that " the Senate of the United States shall have power to make treaties, and to appoint Ambassadors, and Judges of the supreme Court."[4] But in the discussions on the appointment of the judges, which have already been set forth, the method suggested by Mr. Gorham, although then defeated, was eventually adopted and applied to appointments generally, by virtue whereof they are made by the executive, by and with the consent of the second branch, that is to say, the Senate.

On the 23d of August the clause relating to the appointment of Ambassadors and judges came before the Convention, but no agreement was

[1] *Ibid.*, p. 627.
[2] *Ibid.*
[3] *Ibid.*, p. 628.
[4] *Ibid.*, p. 451.

reached, other than to refer the matter again to the Committee of Detail. This body did not, however, present a report; therefore the question went over to the Committee on Unfinished Portions, which considered the whole subject of appointments as properly before it and reported the following method, approved by the Convention on the 4th of September with the addition of "Consuls" after the word "Ministers":

> The President by and with the advice and Consent of the Senate, shall have power to make Treaties; and he shall nominate and by and with the advice and consent of the Senate shall appoint ambassadors, and other public Ministers, Judges of the Supreme Court, and all other Officers of the U- S-, whose appointments are not otherwise herein provided for. But no treaty shall be made without the consent of two thirds of the members present.[1]

The framers of the Constitution were much worried as to the method of appointing judges and as to the tenure of the judges when appointed. They were creating the judiciary equal in rank and dignity to the legislative and executive, and as we think of even greater importance, for great as are the powers of the other departments they are nevertheless defined and interpreted by the judiciary, and in cases of excess of the Constitutional grant they are declared by the men of the law to be null and void. To do this, they should be independent of the legislative and executive, " to the end," to cite again the Constitution of Massachusetts, " it may be a government of laws, and not of men." Fortunately for the administration of justice and the prevalence of law in these United States, their efforts were crowned with complete success.

Powers of
the Court

But the judiciary would not have stood out as the most prominent feature of the American system, and the judges could not have rendered the great services which they have to the American people, were it not for the second clause of the sixth article of the Constitution, which defined the sense in which the judicial power, extended by the third article to all cases in law and equity arising under the Constitution, the laws and treaties of the United States, was to be understood. It is therefore necessary to state the action upon Article VIII of the draft of the Constitution reported by the Committee of Detail, inasmuch as it declared the Constitution, the acts of Congress made in pursuance of the Constitution, and the treaties negotiated under the authority of the United States, the supreme law of the land, binding as of course the governments, Federal and State, and all officers, State and Federal, political or judicial.

It was clearly the intention of the large States, as indicated in the Vir-

[1] *Documentary History*, Vol. III, pp. 669-70.

ginian plan, and of the smaller States, as set forth in the New Jersey plan, to make the laws of the new Union within the grant of power superior to the laws of the States as such. As amended by the Committee, the sixth article of the Virginian plan included treaties as well. Thus:

> The Nat^l. Legislature ought to be empowered . . . to negative all laws passed by the several States contravening in the opinion of the National Legislature, the articles of Union, or any treaties subsisting under the authority of the Union.[1]

This was even more explicitly stated in the sixth article of the New Jersey plan, reading as follows:

> Res^d. that all Acts of the U. States in Cong^s. made by virtue & in pursuance of the powers hereby & by the articles of confederation vested in them, and all Treaties made & ratified under the authority of the U. States shall be the supreme law of the respective States so far forth as those Acts or Treaties shall relate to the said States or their Citizens, and that the Judiciary of the several States shall be bound thereby in their decisions, any thing in the respective laws of the Individual States to the contrary notwithstanding; and if any State, or any body of men in any State shall oppose or prevent y^e. carrying into execution such acts or treaties, the federal Executive shall be authorized to call forth ye power of the Confederated States, or so much thereof as may be necessary to enforce and compel an obedience to such Acts, or an Observance of such Treaties.[2]

The Convention, however, did not approve this article. On July 17th the following proposal was before the Convention:

> To negative all laws passed by the several States contravening in the opinion of the Nat: Legislature, the articles of Union, or any treaties subsisting under the authority of ye Union.[3]

After much debate and discussion, this proposition was adopted by a vote of seven to three of the States. Immediately thereupon, and without a break in the proceedings, Luther Martin of Maryland moved the following resolution, which was unanimously agreed to although it closely followed the New Jersey plan which had been rejected in all its parts:

> That the Legislative acts of the U. S. made by virtue & in pursuance of the articles of Union, and all treaties made & ratified under the authority of the U. S. shall be the supreme law of the respective States, as far as those acts or treaties shall relate to the said States, or their Citizens and inhabitants—& that the Judiciaries of the several States shall be bound thereby in their decisions, any thing in the respective laws of the individual States to the contrary notwithstanding.[4]

[1] *Ibid.*, p. 121. Session of June 13th.
[2] *Ibid.*, pp. 127–8. Session of June 15th.
[3] *Ibid.*, p. 351.
[4] *Ibid.*, p. 353.

The resolution proposed by Mr. Martin and adopted by the Convention was referred to the Committee of Detail, which reported its Article VIII of the proposed Constitution. On August 23 the Convention took up this article as reported by the Committee of Detail, and, upon Mr. Rutledge's motion, it was amended and unanimously adopted in the following form:

> This Constitution & the laws of the U. S. made in pursuance thereof, and all Treaties made under the authority of the U. S. shall be the supreme law of the several States and of their citizens and inhabitants; and the Judges in the several States shall be bound thereby in their decisions, any thing in the Constitutions or laws of the several States, to the contrary notwithstanding.[1]

The Supreme Law of the Land

Mr. Martin's resolution made acts of Congress within the grant of the Constitution and the treaties negotiated by the United States not merely the laws of the United States but of each State of the Union, in so far as the acts or treaties relate to the States. Mr. Rutledge's amendment added the "Constitution" and struck out the qualifying clause regarding the States, with the result that the Constitution, the laws of the United States made in pursuance of the Constitution, and the treaties of the United States likewise made in pursuance of the Constitution became the supreme law of each of the States to the same extent as if the Constitution had been drafted by Conventions held within the States instead of ratified by Conventions specially called for such purpose within the States.

But the article as amended, while it no doubt pleased Mr. Madison, in that the Constitution, laws and treaties of the United States became the laws of the States as if each had been made in each instance by each of the States, did not please him in the matter of treaties, as he was set upon making the clause so clear, its language so precise and its meaning so unmistakable, as to give to the treaty paramount effect, in order to enable British creditors to recover their debts in accordance with the treaty of 1783 with Great Britain recognizing the independence of the United States. In a letter written to Mr. Randolph, dated April 4, 1787, a month and more before the meeting of the Convention, he had said:

> But does the establishment of the treaty as a law provide certainly for the recovery of debts? Ought it not [to] be paramount to law; or at least to be one of those laws which are, in my opinion, beyond repeal, from being combined with a compact?[2]

---

[1] *Documentary History*, Vol. iii, p. 600.
[2] M. D. Conway, *Omitted Chapters of History Disclosed in the Life and Papers of Edmund Randolph*, 1888, p. 72.

Therefore, on August 25th, two days after the adoption of Mr. Rutledge's amendment, Mr. Madison, seconded by Gouverneur Morris, proposed to insert after " all treaties made " the phrase " or which shall be made," with the following result:

> And all treaties made, or which shall be made, under the authority of the United States, shall be the supreme law of the land.

In view of the letter to Mr. Randolph, written before the meeting of the Convention, we can understand the purpose which Mr. Madison had in mind; but it was not enough that Mr. Randolph knew it, it was necessary that the members of the Convention should know it and share it. Therefore, in proposing the amendment, he said, as he records in his Notes:

> This insertion was meant to obviate all doubt concerning the force of treaties preexisting, by making the words " all treaties made " to refer to them, as the words inserted would refer to future treaties.[1]

As thus amended, the article was referred to the Committee on Style,[2] which reported it back to the Convention in its present form, making the Constitution, the acts of Congress made in pursuance thereof, and treaties of the United States " the supreme law of the land " instead of " the supreme law of the respective States,"—an expression which no doubt seemed to them to be a difference of form but not of substance. It appears that this particular phrase was one with which the men of affairs of the day were familiar, inasmuch as eight Constitutions of the States referred to " the law of the land," a ninth to " the laws of the land "; and that the Articles of Confederation were considered part of " the law of the land " of each State. It further appears that the treaty with Great Britain recognizing the independence of the States and its provisions were stated to be part of the " laws of the land of each of the States " in resolutions unanimously passed by the Congress of the Confederation on March 21, 1787, on the eve of the Convention, and in the Federal letter addressed by the Congress on April 13, 1787, advocating the repeal of acts of the State inconsistent with the terms of that treaty.[3] These details, unimportant in themselves, have an added interest if it be borne in mind that four of the five members of the Committee on Style, to which the Constitution was referred for its finishing touches, were members of the Congress which had adopted the resolutions and addressed the Federal letter to the States. Indeed the content of the

---

[1] *Documentary History,* Vol. III, p. 619.
[2] This Committee was composed of Messrs. Johnson, Hamilton, Morris, Madison, and King.
[3] *Journals of the American Congress,* 1823, Vol. IV, pp. 735-8.

resolutions may have been responsible for the form of the clause. It is at least in conformity with the relation created between the Government of the Union, on the one hand, and the States, on the other, in the matter of treaties. The resolutions are therefore quoted:

> *Resolved,* That the legislatures of the several states cannot of right pass any act or acts, for interpreting, explaining, or construing a national treaty or any part or clause of it; nor for restraining, limiting, or in any manner impeding, retarding, or counteracting the operation and execution of the same, for that on being constitutionally made, ratified and published, they become in virtue of the confederation, part of the law of the land, and are not only independent of the will and power of such legislatures, but also binding and obligatory on them.
>
> *Resolved,* That all such acts or parts of acts as may be now existing in any of the states, repugnant to the treaty of peace, ought to be forthwith repealed, as well to prevent their continuing to be regarded as violations of that treaty, as to avoid the disagreeable necessity there might otherwise be of raising and discussing questions touching their validity and obligation.
>
> *Resolved,* That it be recommended to the several states to make such repeal rather by describing than reciting the said acts, and for that purpose to pass an act declaring in general terms, that all such acts and parts of acts, repugnant to the treaty of peace between the United States and his Britannic majesty, or any article thereof, shall be, and thereby are repealed, and that the courts of law and equity in all causes and questions cognizable by them respectively, and arising from or touching the said treaty, shall decide and adjudge according to the true intent and meaning of the same, any thing in the said acts or parts of acts to the contrary thereof in any wise notwithstanding.[1]

This is not the place to consider the origin, nature and the duty of judges to declare acts of Congress, constitutions and statutes of the States null and void in so far as they are contrary to the Constitution of the United States, which is also the Constitution of each of the States and therefore their fundamental law. It is nevertheless advisable to mention the way in which the judicial power of the United States, extended to cases in law and equity arising under the Constitution, acts of Congress and treaties, taken in connection with the clause of the Constitution under consideration, operates and renders the use of force against the States a stranger to the American system.

It was admitted on all sides that the authority of the United States within the sphere of its grant by the States should prevail within the States, because the grant made it the law of each of the States. That, however, was not enough, because it would not, on that account, take precedence of another or subsequent law of the State. By making the Constitution, the

---

[1] *Journals of the American Congress,* 1823, Vol. vi, pp. 729-30. Session of March 21st.

acts of Congress passed in pursuance thereof, and the treaties of the United States negotiated in accordance with its terms, the supreme law of the land of each of the States, the Constitution, the acts of Congress, and the treaties became laws of each of the States, just as if they had originated in each and had been made for each and by each for itself.

Admitting this to be so, what was to be done to the United States if a State framed a constitution or passed a law inconsistent with the Constitution? The national legislature ought to possess the power " to negative all laws," said Mr. Madison, supposing him to have been the author of the Virginian plan, " passed by the several States, contravening in the opinion of the National Legislature the articles of Union; and to call forth the force of the Union agst. any member of the Union failing to fulfil its duty under the articles thereof." [1] But a little reflection caused him to renounce the plan of coercing the States, which he did on the floor of the Convention within two days of its first session,[2] ultimately and with much misgiving relying upon the intervention of the courts to prevent a difficulty which he foresaw might present itself. Again, what was to be done with an act of Congress itself contrary to the terms of the Constitution? Have it passed upon by a council of revision, of which judges of the Supreme Court should be members, said Mr. Madison, and he and his friends clung to each of these proposals with dogged pertinacity.

The Question of Sanction

But the Convention was wiser than any of its members, including even the father of the Constitution. Admitting the necessity of coercion, the enlightened body preferred the coercion of law to the coercion of force, and in entrusting the interpretation of the laws to the courts and, in last resort, to the Supreme Court of the United States. As a step toward the desired goal, the judicial power of the United States was extended to all cases in law and equity arising under the Constitution, acts of Congress passed in pursuance thereof, and treaties made according to its terms. These were declared not merely the law of each of the States but the supreme law of the States, and this extension of the judicial power enabled any person in any State of the Union injured in his person or property to test the validity of the interpretation given to the Constitution, the validity of the law or of the treaty in a court of justice as a case in law or equity, as it arose under one or the other heading. In the course of the trial the Constitution would necessarily be interpreted and applied by the court. The act of Congress or treaty would be declared to be either in accord with the Constitution or contrary to it. In the latter case the act or treaty would be held null and void, and the transaction whereof the litigant complained would be illegal

Coercion of Law v. Coercion of Force

---

[1] *Documentary History*, Vol. III, p. 18. Session of May 29th.
[2] *Ibid.*, pp. 33–4. Session of May 31st.

and the injury to person and property redressed. The incorrect interpreta-tion of the Constitution of the Union or of the States, the treaty itself, and the statute of Congress or of the States, would be set aside in the sense that it would not be regarded by the court as a justification for the act committed under its cover. Repeated acts of a like nature would be declared illegal by the courts, so that, to all intents and purposes, the interpretation of the Constitution of the United States, upon which reliance was based, would be disapproved, and the act or treaty involved declared to be to all intents and purposes invalid. The purposes which Mr. Madison and his friends had in mind would be accomplished without the intervention of force and the State itself would not be involved, inasmuch as the suit was against an individual of the State claiming under its authority as a defense for his action. This process and its results have never been more adequately or more happily described than by Sir Henry Maine in the following passage, to be found in his essay on the Constitution of the United States:

> The Supreme Court of the United States, which is the American Fed-eral institution next claiming our attention, is not only a most interesting but a virtually unique creation of the founders of the Constitution. The functions which the Judges of this Court have to discharge under provi-sions of the Constitution arise primarily from its very nature. The Execu-tive and Legislative authorities of the United States have no powers, except such as are expressly conferred on them by the Constitution itself; and, on the other hand, the several States are forbidden by the Constitution to do certain acts and to pass certain laws. What then is to be done if these limitations of power are transgressed by any State, or by the United States? The duty of annulling such usurpations is confided by the Third Article of the Constitution to the Supreme Court, and to such inferior Courts as Congress may from time to time ordain and establish. But this remarkable power is capable only of indirect exercise; it is called into activity by "cases," by actual controversies, to which individuals, or States, or the United States, are parties. The point of unconstitutionality is raised by the arguments in such controversies; and the decision of the Court fol-lows the view which it takes of the Constitution. A declaration of uncon-stitutionality, not provoked by a definite dispute, is unknown to the Supreme Court.
>
> The success of this experiment has blinded men to its novelty. There is no exact precedent for it, either in the ancient or in the modern world. The builders of Constitutions have of course foreseen the violation of con-stitutional rules, but they have generally sought for an exclusive remedy, not in the civil, but in the criminal law, through the impeachment of the offender. And, in popular governments, fear or jealousy of an authority not directly delegated by the people has too often caused the difficulty to be left for settlement to chance or to the arbitrament of arms. "Je ne pense pas," wrote De Tocqueville, in his "Démocratie en Amérique," "que jusqu' à présent aucune nation du monde ait constitué le pouvoir judiciaire de la même manière que les Américains." [1]

[1] Maine, *Popular Government*, 1886, pp. 217–8.

The coercion of law was consciously preferred to the coercion of force, and the members of the Convention were themselves aware of the success of their labors. Thus, Mr. Madison, in a letter already quoted to his friend Thomas Jefferson after the close of the Convention, said:

> A *voluntary* observance of the federal law by all the members could never be hoped for. A *compulsive* one could evidently never be reduced to practice, and if it could, involved equal calamities to the innocent and the guilty, the necessity of a military force, both obnoxious and dangerous, and, in general, a scene resembling much more a civil war than the administration of a regular Government. Hence was embraced the alternative of a Government which, instead of operating on the States, should operate without their intervention on the individuals composing them.[1]

But the most notable and far-reaching statement is that likewise previously quoted of Mr. Oliver Ellsworth, a delegate from Connecticut, soon to be a Senator under the Constitution which he had helped to frame and Chief Justice of the Supreme Court of the United States. In the convention of Connecticut, called to ratify the Constitution, Mr. Ellsworth used, it may appropriately be said, the language of advocate and of statesman, of commentator and of prophet:

> This Constitution defines the extent of the powers of the general government. If the general legislature should at any time overleap their limits, the judicial department is a constitutional check. If the United States go beyond their powers, if they make a law which the Constitution does not authorize, it is void; and the judicial power, the national judges, who, to secure their impartiality, are to be made independent, will declare it to be void. On the other hand, if the states go beyond their limits, if they make a law which is a usurpation upon the general government the law is void; and upright, independent judges will declare it to be so. Still, however, if the United States and the individual states will quarrel, if they want to fight, they may do it, and no frame of government can possibly prevent it. It is sufficient for this Constitution, that, so far from laying them under a necessity of contending, it provides every reasonable check against it. But perhaps, at some time or other, there will be a contest; the states may rise against the general government. If this do take place, if all the states combine, if all oppose, the whole will not eat up the members, but the measure which is opposed to the sense of the people will prove abortive. . . .
> Hence we see how necessary for the Union is a coercive principle. No man pretends the contrary: we all see and feel this necessity. The only question is, Shall it be a coercion of law, or a coercion of arms? There is no other possible alternative. Where will those who oppose a coercion of law come out? Where will they end? A necessary consequence of their principles is a war of the states one against the other. I am for coercion by law—that coercion which acts only upon delinquent individuals. This Constitution does not attempt to coerce sovereign bodies, states, in their

---

[1] *The Writings of James Madison,* Hunt ed., Vol. V, p. 19. Letter of October 24, 1787.

political capacity. No coercion is applicable to such bodies, but that of an armed force. If we should attempt to execute the laws of the Union by sending an armed force against a delinquent state, it would involve the good and the bad, the innocent and guilty, in the same calamity.

But this legal coercion singles out the guilty individual, and punishes him for breaking the laws of the Union.[1]

It is obvious that the Society of Nations will be confronted with problems similar to if not identical with the problems which faced the framers of the American Constitution when they set about to create a Supreme Court of the Union which they were rendering more perfect. The Convention creating the closer union of the Society, like the Constitution creating the more perfect union of American States, will need to be interpreted, and the experience of the United States shows that this can best be done by a permanent court of the union.

General conventions or special treaties to which States of the Society of Nations are parties, will need to be interpreted; but, here again, the experience of the American Union, with its tribunal, should be enlightening.

A court of the Society will necessarily be a court of limited jurisdiction; but, with the growth of confidence in that tribunal, its jurisdiction will be enlarged in the way pointed out by the Supreme Court itself; that is to say, by an agreement to submit to the tribunal questions hitherto considered political, questions which, by the very act of submission, become judicial.

Gradually, as the result of experience, the usefulness of the court will be thus enhanced. The possibility of the substitution of law for physical force may dawn upon the statesmen of the modern world just as it dawned upon the framers of the American Union, and the conduct of nations, like the conduct of States of the American Union, be guided and eventually controlled by the principles of justice.

Coercion there must be, for nations, as shown by experience, are even less inclined than individuals to brook control; but the choice is, and it is believed the choice must always be, either for the coercion of law, or for the coercion of arms.

[1] Elliot, *Debates*, Vol. II, pp. 196-7.

XIV

THE ADMISSION OF NEW STATES

No principle of general law is more universally acknowledged, than the perfect equality of nations. Russia and Geneva have equal rights. It results from this equality, that no one can rightfully impose a rule on another. Each legislates for itself, but its legislation can operate on itself alone. A right, then, which is vested in all, by the consent of all, can be divested only by consent; and this trade, in which all have participated, must remain lawful to those who cannot be induced to relinquish it. As no nation can prescribe a rule for others, none can make a law of nations; and this traffic remains lawful to those whose governments have not forbidden it. (*Chief Justice Marshall in The Antelope, 10 Wheaton, 66, 122, decided in 1825.*)

Section 13. And for extending the fundamental principles of civil and religious liberty, which form the basis whereon these republics, their laws and constitutions, are erected; to fix and establish those principles as the basis of all laws, constitutions, and governments, which forever hereafter shall be formed in the said territory; to provide, also, for the establishment of States, and permanent government therein, and for their admission to a share in the Federal councils on an equal footing with the original States, at as early periods as may be consistent with the general interest:

Section 14. It is hereby ordained and declared, by the authority aforesaid, that the following articles shall be considered as articles of compact, between the original States and the people and States in the said territory, and forever remain unalterable, unless by common consent, to wit:

Article I. No person, demeaning himself in a peaceable and orderly manner, shall ever be molested on account of his mode of worship, or religious sentiments, in the said territories.

Article II. The inhabitants of the said territory shall always be entitled to the benefits of the writs of *habeas corpus,* and of the trial by jury; of a proportionate representation of the people in the legislature, and of judicial proceedings according to the course of the common law. All persons shall be bailable, unless for capital offences, where the proof shall be evident, or the presumption great. All fines shall be moderate; and no cruel or unusual punishments shall be inflicted. No man shall be deprived of his liberty or property, but by the judgment of his peers, or the law of the land, and should the public exigencies make it necessary, for the common preservation, to take any person's property, or to demand his particular services, full compensation shall be made for the same. And, in the just preservation of rights and property, it is understood and declared, that no law ought ever to be made, or have force in the said territory, that shall, in any manner whatever, interfere with or affect private contracts, or engagements, *bona fide,* and without fraud previously formed.

Article III. Religion, morality, and knowledge being necessary to good government and the happiness of mankind, schools and the means of education shall forever be encouraged. . . .

Article IV. The said territory, and the States which may be formed therein, shall forever remain a part of this confederacy of the United States of America, subject to the Articles of Confederation, and to such alterations therein as shall be constitutionally made; and to all the acts and ordinances of the United States in Congress assembled, conformable thereto. . . .

Article V. There shall be formed in the said territory not less than three nor more than five States; and the boundaries of the States, as soon as Virginia shall alter her act of cession and consent to the same, shall become fixed and established as follows, to wit: . . .

And whenever any of the said States shall have sixty thousand free inhabitants therein, such State shall be admitted, by its delegates, into the Congress of the United States, on an equal footing with the original States, in all respects whatever; and shall be at liberty to form a permanent constitution and State government: *Provided,* The constitution and government, so to be formed, shall be republican, and in conformity to the principles contained in these articles, and, so far as it can be consistent with the general interest of the confederacy, such admission shall be allowed at an earlier period, and when there may be a less number of free inhabitants in the State than sixty thousand.

Article VI. There shall be neither slavery nor involuntary servitude in the said territory, otherwise than in the punishment of crimes, whereof the party shall have been duly convicted; *Provided always,* That any person escaping into the same, from whom labor or service is lawfully claimed in any one of the original States, such fugitive may be lawfully reclaimed, and conveyed to the person claiming his or her labor or service as aforesaid. (*An Ordinance for the government of the territory of the United States northwest of the river Ohio, July 13, 1787, Revised Statutes of the United States, 1878, pp. 15 -16.*)

Section 3. New States may be admitted by the Congress into this Union; but no new State shall be formed or erected within the jurisdiction of any other State; nor any State be formed by the junction of two or more States, or Parts of States, without the Consent of the Legislatures of the States concerned as well as of the Congress.

The Congress shall have Power to dispose of and make all needful Rules and Regulations respecting the Territory or other Property belonging to the United States; and nothing in this Constitution shall be so construed as to Prejudice any Claims of the United States, or of any particular State.

Section 4. The United States shall guarantee to every State in this Union a Republican Form of Government, and shall protect each of them against Invasion; and on Application of the Legislature, or of the Executive (when the Legislature cannot be convened) against domestic Violence. (*Constitution of the United States, Article IV.*)

So far as this court has found occasion to advert to the effect of enabling acts as affirmative legislation affecting the power of new States after admission, there is to be found no sanction for the contention that any State may be deprived of any of the power constitutionally possessed by other States, as States, by reason of the terms in which the acts admitting them to the Union have been framed. . . .

The plain deduction from this case [*Pollard's Lessee* v. *Hagan,* 3 Howard, 212, decided in 1845] is that when a new State is admitted into the Union, it is so admitted with all of the powers of sovereignty and jurisdiction which pertain to the original States, and that such powers may not be constitutionally diminished, impaired or shorn away by any conditions, compacts or stipulations embraced in the act under which the new State came into the Union, which would not be valid and effectual if the subject of congressional legislation after admission. . . .

Has Oklahoma been admitted upon an equal footing with the original States? If she has, she by virtue of her jurisdictional sovereignty as such a State may determine for her own people the proper location of the local seat of government. She is not equal in power to them if she cannot.

In *Texas* v. *White,* 7 Wall. 700, 725, Chief Justice Chase said in strong and memorable language that, "the Constitution, in all of its provisions looks to an undestructible Union, composed of indestructible States."

In *Lane County* v. *Oregon,* 7 Wall. 76, he said:

"The people of the United States constitute one nation, under one government, and this government, within the scope of the powers with which it is invested, is supreme. On the other hand, the people of each State compose a State, having its own government, and endowed with all the functions essential to separate and independent existence. The States disunited might continue to exist. Without the States in union there could be no such political body as the United States."

To this we may add that the constitutional equality of the States is essential to the harmonious operation of the scheme upon which the Republic was organized. When that equality disappears we may remain a free people, but the Union will not be the Union of the Constitution. (*Mr. Justice Lurton in Coyle v. Smith, 221 United States Reports, 559, 570, 573, 579-580, decided in 1911.*)

So the Constitution operated to incorporate such of the old states as ratified it: so it did as new states have been admitted: so it must operate in future. It was a cession, by nine states, of so much of their separate power as was necessary for federal purposes, to the body politic, called the United States, the "American Confederacy," "Republic," or "Empire"; as a term of designation, including states and territories. The constitution was the charter of this federal corporation, as those of the different states were the charters of their state corporations of government; each with power to legislate according to the terms of their respective charters, subject only to that charter which had been made supreme for its designated purposes. (*Mr. Justice Baldwin, A General View of the Origin and Nature of the Constitution and Government of the United States, 1837, p. 84.*)

CHAPTER XIV

THE ADMISSION OF NEW STATES

The
Northwest
Ordinance

As throwing very great light upon the views of public men at the time of the Constitution, the Act of Congress of July 13, 1787, commonly called the Northwest Ordinance,[1] should receive careful attention, because it was passed at the very time when the Federal Convention was in session. Indeed some of the members of the Convention were obliged to absent themselves in order to take part in the Congress then meeting in New York.

It is also important to note in this connection that the ordinance was approved by the Act of August 7, 1789, passed by the first Congress held under the Constitution, which continued it in effect.[2] The ordinance therefore has the double advantage in its favor, of being drafted and promulgated during the session of the Federal Convention, and of being approved by the government installed under the Constitution.

The purpose of the Act is stated in its title, "An Ordinance for the Government of the Territory of the United States north-west of the river Ohio," that vast tract of territory ceded to the United States March 1, 1784, by the Virginian delegates in Congress, pursuant to the authorization of the General Assembly of that great State, December 20, 1783, by which the struggling Confederation became possessed of an imperial domain, so that if Virginia can be, as it has been called, the mother of Presidents, it can, with equal propriety, be called the mother of States.

The ordinance consists practically of two parts, the first of thirteen sections dealing with the organization of a government for the territory and with the details of that government; the second of six articles appended to the fourteenth section in the nature of a bill of rights, termed in the Act itself, "articles of compact, between the original states and the people and states in the said territory," and to "remain unalterable, unless by common consent."

For purposes of government, this vast tract was to be considered as a single district, to be subject to future division by Congress. A governor, to reside in the district, was to be appointed by the Congress for a period of three years "unless sooner revoked by Congress." There was to be a General Assembly or a Legislature, and there was to be a court. We thus

[1] *Journals of the American Congress*, Vol. IV, pp. 752-4.
[2] *U. S. Statutes at Large*, vol. 15, p. 50.

have the three branches of government, beginning, however, with the executive, instead of the legislative, as in the Constitution, apparently because the executive was to prepare the way for the other branches.

As the judges were to cooperate with him in this task, the judiciary is mentioned before the creation of the legislature, and the determination of its functions. Thus it is stated in Section 4 that " There shall also be appointed a court to consist of three judges, any two of whom to form a court, who shall have a common law jurisdiction, and reside in the district . . . and their commissions shall continue in force during good behaviour."

The first need of a district was order, and this was to be brought about through law. Therefore it was provided in Section 5 that " The governor and judges, or a majority of them, shall adopt and publish in the district such laws of the original states, criminal and civil, as may be necessary, and best suited to the circumstances of the district, and report them to Congress, from time to time." These laws were to be in force, unless disapproved by Congress, until the organization of the General Assembly, and subject to that body when it should come into being.

The governor was to be commander-in-chief of the militia, to appoint and commission all below the rank of general officers, who were to be appointed and commissioned by Congress. And the governor, prior to the meeting of the General Assembly, was to appoint magistrates and other civil officers in each county or township, and indeed, to appoint all magistrates and other civil officers, not otherwise provided for, during the continuance of the temporary government, the duties and powers whereof were to be fixed by the General Assembly when organized. It was also the duty of the governor to see to the execution of the laws, and to execute civil and criminal processes.

Whenever there were in the district five thousand free male inhabitants of full age, a General Assembly was to be established, with one representative for every five hundred such inhabitants until the number of representatives should increase to twenty-five, after which the proportion of representatives was to be regulated by the legislature, and the representatives themselves were to be elected for a period of two years. The provisions contained in Section 11 concerning the General Assembly are of especial interest, inasmuch as they show the Congress drawing upon the experience of the colonists, as was to be expected, and which, indeed, could hardly be obviated. Thus, the General Assembly or Legislature was to consist of " the governor, legislative council, and a house of representatives." The council was to consist of five members to serve for a period of five years, unless sooner removed by Congress, and any three of them were to constitute a quorum. The legislature was to present the name of ten persons to the Congress, from whom that body should choose five, and upon a vacancy, two names, from which the Congress should choose one. This process was apparently to be repeated four months before the expiration of the five year term.

The governor, appointed by the Congress, the legislative council, likewise appointed by the Congress, and the house of representatives elected by the inhabitants having the necessary qualifications, were vested with the authority to "make laws, in all cases, for the good government of the district, not repugnant to the principles and articles in this ordinance established and declared." And it was further provided that "all bills having passed by a majority in the house, and by a majority in the council" were to be referred to the governor for his assent, and that "no bill or legislative act whatever, shall be of any force without his assent."

Here we have the colonial governor, the governor's council, and the assembly with the power of veto of the governor, who was, in addition, to possess the power "to convene, prorogue and dissolve the general assembly" when in his opinion it should be expedient.

Inasmuch as the colonists maintained that taxation without representation was tyranny, the council and house in joint session and by joint ballot were to elect a delegate to the Congress who should have a seat therein "with the right of debating, but not of voting during this temporary government." The members of Congress recognized the gravity of the step they were taking, and the necessity of putting into practice the doctrine they had preached. They therefore prefixed to the declaration of rights which they expressly termed a "compact between the original states, and the people and states in the said territory," what may be called a preamble "for extending the fundamental principles of civil and religious liberty, which form the basis whereon these republics [apparently the thirteen original States], their laws and constitutions are erected; to fix and establish those principles as the basis of all laws, constitutions and governments, which forever hereafter shall be formed in the said territory; to provide also for the establishment of states, and permanent government therein, and for their admission to a share in the federal councils on an equal footing with the original states, at as early periods as may be consistent with the general interest."

The first two Articles are thus worded:

Art. 1st. No person, demeaning himself in a peaceable and orderly manner, shall ever be molested on account of his mode of worship or religious sentiments, in the said territory.

Art. 2d. The inhabitants of the said territory, shall always be entitled to the benefits of the writ of *habeas corpus,* and of the trial by jury; of

Compact
Between
People of
States and
Northwestern
Territory

a proportionate representation of the people in the legislature, and of judicial proceedings according to the course of the common law. All persons shall be bailable, unless for capital offences, where the proof shall be evident, or the presumption great. All fines shall be moderate; and no cruel or unusual punishments shall be inflicted. No man shall be deprived of his liberty or property, but by the judgment of his peers, or the law of the land, and should the public exigencies make it necessary, for the common preservation, to take any person's property, or to demand his particular services, full compensation shall be made for the same. And in the just preservation of rights and property, it is understood and declared, that no law ought ever to be made, or have force in the said territory, that shall, in any manner whatever, interfere with, or affect private contracts or engagements, *bona fide,* and without fraud previously formed.

The fourth Article is interesting, as it subjects the territory to the Articles of Confederation, the alterations made therein, " and to all the acts and ordinances of the United States in Congress assembled, conformable thereto."

This is clearly imperialism: the district subject to the realm; to acts made in accordance with its Constitution by the framers thereof. Nay more, the inhabitants and settlers within the territory were " to pay a part of the federal debts, contracted or to be contracted, and a proportional part of the expenses of government, to be apportioned on them by Congress, according to the same common rule and measure, by which apportionments thereof shall be made on the other states." The taxes, however, to meet these obligations, were to be raised by their own legislatures.

Out of this vast territory not less than three, nor more than five States were to be created, endowed with the right to form a permanent Constitution and state government whenever there were sixty thousand free inhabitants in any one thereof, and to be thereupon admitted into the Union upon an equality with the original States, " provided the constitution and government so to be formed, shall be republican, and in conformity to the principles contained in these articles." Indeed, they were to be admitted before they had sixty thousand inhabitants if this could conveniently be done.

And in every foot of this vast domain, it was specifically provided in the language of Article 6, to be later incorporated in the thirteenth amendment to the Constitution of the United States, that: " There shall be neither slavery nor involuntary servitude in the said territory, otherwise than in the punishment of crimes, whereof the party shall have been duly convicted."

Here we have the Congress sitting during the Federal Convention, giving its approval to the threefold distribution of power, providing for the government of a vast domain which should be broken up into territories and in the course of time admitted as States of the Union, specifying the fundamentals not merely of law and of order, but the principles which should enter into a bill of rights for the protection against the central government of the inhabitants of the district or districts into which the territory should be divided, and expressed in the form of a compact between the thirteen original States, whose representative the Congress was, with the peoples and political subdivisions of the Northwest Territory. The ordinance not only throws light upon the proceedings of the Federal Convention and upon the mental attitude of its members; it is the light, and it is the mental attitude.

The Constitution was devised primarily for the thirteen confederated States of America by official representatives of twelve of them. However, the statesmen who sat in the Federal Convention contemplated a Union composed of a larger number of States, for the Congress of the Confederation had, as has been said, pledged the faith of the United States to create States within the northwestern territory. Movements were elsewhere on foot, and indeed far advanced, to create States in the outlying portions of Virginia and of North Carolina which shortly resulted in the creation and admission to the Union of the States of Kentucky and Tennessee.

The good people of Vermont declined to be citizens of Massachusetts, of New Hampshire, of New York, although the latter two States were importunate. Vermont, however, stood to its guns in the literal sense of that term, resisting persuasion and refusing to yield to force. It considered itself to be a separate and distinct State, organized itself as such, provided a Constitution under which it governed itself, feeling itself to be an American State as free, as sovereign, and as independent as those of the Confederation of which it was not a member; ready and willing, however, to associate itself with them in the more perfect Union.

The Constitution would therefore have to provide for such contingencies, as questions of this kind were bound to arise and be decided in Convention. No plan could emanate from the Virginian delegation that did not contemplate it, because the cession of the claims of Virginia to the Northwestern Territory was conditioned upon the creation of States within that vast domain extending from the north of the Ohio to the Mississippi River. Indeed, the State of Kentucky was already taking form and shape within the territorial limits of Virginia. Therefore the tenth and in a less degree the eleventh of Mr. Randolph's resolutions dealt with this question. The tenth recommended that " provision ought to be made for the admission of States lawfully arising within the limits of the United States, whether from a voluntary junction of Government & Territory or otherwise, with the consent of a number of voices in the National Legislature less than the whole." [1] The eleventh resolution provided that " a Republican Government & the territory of each State, except in the instance of a voluntary junction of

---

[1] *Documentary History of the Constitution,* Vol. III, p. 19. Session of May 29th.

Government & territory, ought to be guaranteed by the United States to each State." Mr. Patterson's plan proposed, on behalf of the small States preferring a revision of the Articles of Confederation rather than a new scheme of government without reference to them, that "provision be made for the admission of new States into the Union." [1]

A feature thus appearing in the plans of the large and of the small States was one of general import which would require and receive settlement. In this matter the erstwhile colonies found themselves confronted with the problem that had faced the mother country in its relation with the colonies. And it must be said that some men of the large States looked at it rather from the standpoint of the imperialists on the other side of the water than as statesmen of the new world recognizing the equal rights of the parts of Empire as well as the rights of the Empire itself. The advocates of this school apparently wished to center all power in the Atlantic States and to place the new States not merely in an inferior position, but also to maintain them in continual tutelage. This attitude was perhaps most frankly and brutally expressed by Gouverneur Morris, a delegate from the large State of Pennsylvania. There were, however, notable exceptions to be found among the delegates of the larger States, especially George Mason and James Madison of Virginia, who were as outspoken in their views of the equality of western States as Gouverneur Morris was against it. *Attitude of Large States*

If the western boundaries of each of the existing States had been clear, definite and fixed, the question might have been as to whether the territory to the west of their boundaries was to be acquired by the Union or apportioned among the individual States as such. In the latter case, even if it had been possible, there would have been difficulty in allotting the territory to be obtained by each, as in the instance of a State situated as Rhode Island, cut off from all access to the west except through the territory of its neighbors. The question was complicated by the fact that only the western boundaries of New Hampshire, Rhode Island, New Jersey, Pennsylvania, Delaware and Maryland were definite, using that term in a generous sense, whereas the remaining States of Massachusetts, Connecticut, New York, Virginia, North Carolina, South Carolina and Georgia claimed by charter or irrespective of charter to extend indefinitely to the west. [2]

---

[1] *Documentary History of the Constitution*, Vol. iii, p. 128. Session of June 15th.

[2] The situation obtaining at this time is thus described in *American History Leaflets*, No. 22, "Documents Illustrating State Land Claims and Cessions, 1776–1802," ed. by Albert Bushnell Hart and Edward Channing, pp. 1–2:

"When the Revolution was impending, the boundaries between colonies had been for the most part adjusted; and by the Proclamation of 1763 no governors were to 'grant warrants of survey or pass patents for any lands beyond the heads or sources of any of the rivers which fall into the Atlantic Ocean from the west or northwest; or upon any lands whatever, which, not having been ceded to or purchased by us, as aforesaid, are reserved to the said Indians or any of them.'

The view of Maryland, concurred in by the States making no claim to the western territory, was that it ought " to be considered as a common property subject to be parcelled out by Congress into free, convenient and independent governments," inasmuch as it consisted of territory ceded by the treaty of Paris of 1763 to the British Crown and conquered from the mother country by the united efforts of the thirteen colonies. Maryland felt so strongly on this point that it refused to enter the Confederation unless and until the western domain was secured for the common benefit.

Against this action of its neighbor, Virginia protested, since it claimed not only the territory to the South of the Ohio, from which the State of Kentucky was carved, but also the territory to the northwest of the Ohio extending to the Mississippi River. The first step toward a compromise was taken by the State of New York, which, on February 19, 1780, empowered its delegates to concede for the common benefit a portion of the territory to which it laid claim.[1] On September 6th of the same year the Congress, encouraged by this action on the part of New York, advised the States to surrender a portion of their claims to the territory in question, inasmuch as without such action the Union under the Articles of Confederation essential " to our very existence as a free, sovereign and independent people " could not be established; and the States could not hope to preserve their claims, as to do so would endanger the Confederation, with the consequence that they would lose credit and confidence at home and prestige and reputation abroad.

On the 10th of October the Congress took a final step,[2] in as far as any

---

" The Revolution brought about several important changes in the territorial conditions of the former colonies. As soon as the English authority was extinguished, the States which had once had charters asserted that the territory embraced by such charters reverted to them. In the second place, the restriction to land east of the Appalachian water-shed and outside Indian tracts was held to have no more force. In the third place, several communities, notably Vermont, asserted that they were no longer included within the State of which they had been a part while it was still a colony. And in 1778 Virginia troops conquered the Northwest region, then a part of the English Province of Quebec. The result was confusion and clashing of interests. Western New York and Northern Pennsylvania were claimed by Massachusetts and Connecticut respectively; New York, Massachusetts, and Connecticut, and Virginia all claimed the same parcel of territory north of the Ohio River; and the States with strictly defined boundaries, especially Maryland, protested against the appropriation by individual States of lands gained by the common effort of the Revolutionary War.

" The controversy delayed the ratification of the Articles of Confederation and was finally adjusted by a series of agreements between the competing States, and a series of cessions to the Union, not completed until 1802."

[1] This deed of cession was authorized by Congress March 1, 1781. *Journals of the Continental Congress,* Vol. xix, pp. 211–13.

[2] The pledge of Congress took the following form:

Resolved, That the unappropriated lands that may be ceded or relinquished to the United States, by any particular states, pursuant to the recommendation of Congress of the 6 day of September last, shall be disposed of for the common benefit of the United States and be settled and formed into distinct republican states, which shall become members of the federal union, and have the same rights of sovereignty, freedom and independence, as the other states: that each state which shall be so formed shall contain a suitable measure taken by it could be final, resolving that the lands to which the States should cede their claims should be formed into republican States upon a footing of equality with those forming the Union which, by the second of the Articles of Confederation, was declared to be free, sovereign and independent.

The question had now become largely one between Virginia and Maryland. "Preferring the good of the country to every object of smaller importance," the State of Virginia sacrificed whatever claim it may have had to the west and the northwest by offering to cede it to the Union, thus removing from Maryland all ground for further delay in acceding to the Confederation. Yielding to the pressure of the States and to the desire of France that the Union be consummated in the interest of the common cause, the State of Maryland authorized, on February 2, 1781, its delegates to ratify the Articles. This was done on March 1, 1781. Pursuant to the agreement, Virginia authorized, by an act of December 20, 1783,[1] its delegates to execute a deed of cession to the territory in question to the United States, which was done on March 1, 1784, and on April 23d of the same year the Congress provided a temporary government for the ceded territory.[2]

It was evident that the United States in Congress assembled had earnestly sought to quiet title to the western territory, in order to open it to settlers upon what then was and now must be called equitable terms. The delegates of the States had pledged the Confederation to the admission of tracts to the west as States upon a footing of equality when the time should come for such action. The members of the Federal Convention who in some instances were, as has been stated, members of the very Congress which proposed the Northwest Ordinance during the sessions of the Convention, appeared to have taken it as a matter of course that the territory west of the mountains would be carved into States and admitted to the more perfect Union upon terms of equality. Therefore Article XVII of the first draft of the Constitution, reported on August 6, 1787, provided that new States should be admitted on the same terms with the original States. Mr. Gouverneur Morris moved to strike out this clause, saying that "he did not wish to bind down the Legislature to admit Western States on the terms here stated . . .

Virginia Relinquishes Claim

---

extent of territory, not less than one hundred nor more than one hundred and fifty miles square, or as near thereto as circumstances will admit:

That the necessary and reasonable expences which any particular state shall have incurred since the commencement of the present war, in subduing any of the British posts, or in maintaining forts or garrisons within and for the defence, or in acquiring any part of the territory that may be ceded or relinquished to the United States, shall be reimbursed;

That the said lands shall be granted and settled at such times and under such regulations as shall hereafter be agreed on by the United States in Congress assembled, or any nine or more of them. *Journals of the Continental Congress,* Vol. XVIII, p. 915.

[1] See *American History Leaflets,* No. 22, pp. 12–15.

[2] *Journals of the American Congress,* Vol. IV, pp. 379–80.

He did not wish however to throw the power into their hands." [1] Mr. Madison opposed this motion, " insisting that the Western States neither would nor ought to submit to a union which degraded them from an equal rank with the other States." Mr. Mason followed him, saying, " If it were possible by just means to prevent emigrations to the Western Country, it might be good policy. But go the people will as they find it for their interest, and the best policy is to treat them with that equality which will make them friends not enemies." But Roger Sherman of Connecticut had already put the matter on unassailable grounds, saying that he " thought there was no probability that the number of future States would exceed that of the Existing States. If the event should ever happen, it was too remote to be taken into consideration at this time. Besides We are providing for our posterity, for our children & our grand Children who would be as likely to be citizens of new Western States, as of the old States. On this consideration alone, we ought to make no such discrimination as was proposed by the motion." [2]

Because of the opposition of men of the school of Gouverneur Morris, the principle of equality was not consecrated in the Constitution, but as equality is the very life and breath of American institutions it has obtained in practice, and each new State is admitted to the Union upon a footing of equality. For, as stated by Mr. Justice Lurton in delivering the opinion of the Supreme Court in the case of *Coyle* v. *Smith* (221 U. S., 559, 580), decided in 1911:

> The constitutional equality of the States is essential to the harmonious operation of the scheme upon which the Republic was organized. When that equality disappears we may remain a free people, but the Union will not be the Union of the Constitution. [3]

The rights of the existing States, however, were safeguarded against partition or involuntary union with other States, which provisions inured to the benefit of all States. They are thus expressed in the third section of Article IV of the perfected Constitution:

> No new State shall be formed or erected within the Jurisdiction of any other State; nor any State be formed by the Junction of two or more States or Parts of States, without the Consent of the Legislatures of the States concerned as well as of the Congress.

It will be observed that the consent of Congress is required even when the States themselves might be willing, inasmuch as the question is one concerning the Union as a whole as well as of the States thought to be more closely involved.

[1] *Documentary History*, Vol. iii, pp. 642–3. Session of August 29th.
[2] *Ibid.*, pp. 332–3. Session of July 14th.
[3] J. B. Scott, *Judicial Settlement of Controversies between States*, Vol. i, p. 64.

A further passage of this section may be quoted as showing how easily despotism in others is the exercise of just rights in ourselves, for in the next succeeding clause it is provided that "the Congress shall have Power to dispose of and make all needful Rules and Regulations respecting the Territory or other Property belonging to the United States." And this clause has been interpreted by the Supreme Court to vest in the Congress, as to it shall seem expedient, the unquestioned and indeed unquestionable right to govern the territories of the United States until their admission to the Union. As a matter of fact Congress has exercised this power in such a way that the governors of the territories, the judges of their courts created by act of Congress, are appointed by the President by and with the consent of the Senate, and that the acts of their legislatures, created by the Congress and invested with such powers as the Congress deems advisable, may be set aside by the Congress of the United States. A delegate from each territory, elected by the qualified voters thereof, does indeed sit in the House of Representatives, but he may not vote although he may participate in debate.

Government
of the
Territories

As pronounced a friend and advocate of the more perfect Union under the Constitution as Chancellor Kent feared that the evils of the old system would reappear in the new, saying in his *Commentaries on American Law,* first published in 1826:

> If, therefore, the government of the United States should carry into execution the project of colonizing the great valley of the Oregon to the west of the Rocky Mountains, it would afford a subject of grave consideration what would be the future civil and political destiny of that country. It would be a long time before it would be populous enough to be created into one or more independent states; and, in the meantime, upon the doctrine taught by the acts of congress, and even by the judicial decisions of the Supreme Court, the colonists would be in a state of the most complete subordination, and as dependent upon the will of congress as the people of this country would have been upon the king and parliament of Great Britain, if they could have sustained their claim to bind us in all cases whatsoever. Such a state of absolute sovereignty on the one hand, and of absolute dependence on the other, is not at all congenial with the free and independent spirit of our native institutions; and the establishment of distant territorial governments, ruled according to will and pleasure, would have a very natural tendency, as all proconsular governments have had, to abuse and oppression.[1]

But the Congress has exercised its powers in wisdom, and the territories have been rapidly, indeed some think too rapidly, admitted to statehood. In Milton's conception, Presbyterian might indeed be " old priest writ large," but the Congress of the United States is not another form or name for that imperious Parliament whose powers it exercises in the New World.

[1] James Kent, *Commentaries,* 1826, Vol. I, pp. 360–1.

XV

AMENDMENTS AND RATIFICATIONS

It must be recollected that the Constitution was proposed to the people of the States as a *whole,* and unanimously adopted as a *whole,* it being a part of the Constitution that not less than ¾ should be competent to make any alteration in what had been unanimously agreed to. So great is the caution on this point, that in two cases where peculiar interests were at stake a majority even of ¾ are distrusted and a unanimity required to make any change affecting those cases.

When the Constitution was adopted as a whole, it is certain that there are many of its parts which if proposed by themselves would have been promptly rejected. It is far from impossible that every part of a whole would be rejected by a majority and yet the whole be unanimously accepted. Constitutions will rarely, probably never be formed without mutual concessions, without articles conditioned on & balancing each other. Is there a Constitution of a single State out of the 24 that would bear the experiment of having its component parts submitted to the people separately, and decided on according to their insulated merits. (*Extract from letter of James Madison to Robert Y. Hayne, United States Senator from South Carolina, dated April 3/4, 1830, Gaillard Hunt, Editor, The Writings of James Madison, Vol. IX, 1910, p. 392, note.*)

But it is universally understood, it is a part of the history of the day, that the great revolution which established the constitution of the United States, was not effected without immense opposition. Serious fears were extensively entertained, that those powers which the patriot statesmen, who then watched over the interests of our country, deemed essential to union, and to the attainment of those invaluable objects for which union was sought, might be exercised in a manner dangerous to liberty. In almost every convention by which the constitution was adopted, amendments to guard against the abuse of power were recommended. These amendments demanded security against the apprehended encroachments of the general government—not against those of the local governments. In compliance with a sentiment thus generally expressed, to quiet fears thus extensively entertained, amendments were proposed by the required majority in congress, and adopted by the states. These amendments contain no expression indicating an intention to apply them to the state governments. This court cannot so apply them. (*Chief Justice Marshall in Barron v. The Mayor and City of Baltimore, 7 Peters, 243, 250, decided in 1833.*)

The prohibition alluded to as contained in the amendments to the constitution, as well as others with which it is associated in those articles, were not designed as limits upon the State governments in reference to their own citizens. They are exclusively restrictions upon federal power, intended to prevent interference with the rights of the States, and of their citizens. Such has been the interpretation given to those amendments by this court, in the case of *Barron* v. *The Mayor and City Council of Baltimore,* 7 Pet., 243; and such indeed is the only rational and intelligible interpretation which those amendments can bear, since it is neither probable nor credible that the States should have anxiously insisted to ingraft upon the federal constitution restrictions upon their own authority,—restrictions which some of the States regarded as the *sine qua non* of its adoption by them. (*Mr. Justice Daniel in Fox v. The State of Ohio, 5 Howard, 410, 434-435, decided in 1847.*)

"This *term* United States, designates the whole American empire." It is the *name* given to *our great republic,* composed of states and territories; 5 Wh. 514; "constituent parts of one great empire;" 6 Wh. 414; "who have formed a confederated government;" 12 Wh. 334; 2 Pet. 590, 1; by the act of *the people* of the "great empire," the "great republic," the "American empire," *the United States.* "The people of *America,*" "the American people," "the people of the *United States,*" are but terms and names, to designate the grantor of the *thing,* which was thus formed, by the people, of the constituent parts; the thing, the *power* which formed it, by a thing, *this constitution, established* by the ratifications of nine things, conventions of *nine states,* by the people of each as *a state*. (*Mr. Justice Baldwin, A General View of the Origin and Nature of the Constitution and Government of the United States, 1837, p. 14.*)

Twelve states met in convention by their separate delegations, to digest, reduce to form, and submit to a congress of the states, a frame of government for such of the states, as should, in conventions of the state, ratify it as their act: the frame was made, it proposed the institution of a government between the states who should adopt it, nine of whom were declared competent. These separate conventions were not to be like the general convention, composed of members appointed by *state legislatures*, with power only to propose an act to them as *their* constituents, and through them to the *people* of the state. To the proposed act was prefaced a declaration, that it was to be the act of *the people*, and a *constitution* for a government, such as it delineated. So it was submitted to Congress, and by them to each state legislature, who called conventions of delegates elected by *the people of each state;* nine of these conventions separately ratified the act, in the name of the people who had authorized it; and thus the proposed frame of government was established as a constitution for those nine states, who then composed " The United States of America;" and between themselves only. The declaration, in its front, therefore, necessarily refers, not to the time when it was proposed, but when it was ordained and established, by "the ratification of the conventions of nine states," as this was done by the people of those states; so the act declares, " We the people of the United States, (which have ratified) do ordain (by our separate ratifications) this constitution," for (the states, and between the states so ratifying the same, who are thereby.) "The United States of America." (*Mr. Justice Baldwin, A General View of the Origin and Nature of the Constitution and Government of the United States, 1837, p. 18.*)

There never has been, or can be any difference of opinion as to the meaning of the ordaining parts of the constitution in the terms, "*the people of the several states;*" "*the several states which may be included in this union;*" "*each state;*" for they do not admit of two meanings. They refer to those states which, having ratified the constitution, are each a constituent part of the United States, composing, by their union, *the United States of America;* and to the people of each state, as *the people of these United States.* When terms are so definite in the body of an instrument, and one less definite is used in the preamble, which can be made equally definite by reference, the established maxim applies— "*id certum est quod certum reddi potest.*" (*Mr. Justice Baldwin, A General View of the Origin and Nature of the Constitution and Government of the United States, 1837, p. 30.*)

I have only to add one other consideration, to illustrate the meaning of the preamble. All agree that the constitution was to be established by *the people* of the United States, whenever the conventions of nine states should ratify it; all must agree, that when it was proposed for adoption in 1787, it could not be foreseen which of the states would so ratify it; the states therefore could not be named till their separate ratifications were given. It provided for the admission of new states, but no one could divine their names or locality; states could be "formed by the junction of two or more states," but none could say of which. The constitution was intended for posterity, through all time; and for "the land," the whole territory, and all the states, old and new; as one law, speaking in the same words, and with the same intention, at the time it was proposed, and at each period when any state ratified it, and thus became one of "the United States of America," by the act of the people of the states respectively.

When the terms "we, the people," "of the United States," are thus applied, they seem to me not only appropriate to the instrument, but the only terms that would be so; it uses terms in all its parts, yet we find no definitions or explanations; it was not intended for a code; and the term "people," was a mere designation of the power by which the constitution was made, as "the states" were designated by their separate ratifications. Hence it referred, in 1789, to eleven only, then to the old thirteen states, and now refers to the thirteen new states: and when others shall be admitted into the Union, it will refer to them as it did to the old, and now does to the new. "The people" "of the several states, which may be included within this Union," as the constituent power of the federal government. (*Mr. Justice Baldwin, A General View of the Origin and Nature of the Constitution and Government of the United States, 1837, p. 97.*)

Each state still has two constitutions of government, one for state, the other for federal purposes; both ordained by the same people, and in the same manner, in a convention of their representatives, elected by the electors of the states, for the special object, whereby in the simple, impressive, instructive, and strictly constitutional language of this Court,

" The national and state systems are to be regarded as one whole." 6 Wh. 419. " The powers of government are divided between the government of the Union, and those of the states." " They are each sovereign, with respect to the objects committed to it; and neither sovereign, with respect to the objects committed to the other." 4 Wh. 410 (*Mr. Justice Baldwin, A General View of the Origin and Nature of the Constitution and Government of the United States, 1837, p. 91.*)

Art. 7. " The ratifications of the conventions of nine states shall be sufficient for the establishment of this constitution, between the states so ratifying the same."

It is then, by the separate action of the states, in conventions of nine states, (not of a convention of nine states) that the grant was made; the act of eight produced no result; but when the ninth acted, the great work was effected as between the nine. Until the other four so acted, they were no part of the United States; nor were the people of the non-ratifying states, any part of the people of the United States, who ordained and established it.

That the term, conventions of states, meant conventions of delegates, elected by the people of the several states, for the express purpose of assenting or dissenting, to their adoption of the proposed constitution, is admitted by all; as also, that no general convention of the whole people was ever convened for any purpose: and that the members of the convention which framed it, met, and acted as states, consented to, and signed it for and in behalf of the states, whom they respectively represented, appears on its face. It was proposed to the people of each state separately, and was so ratified; it existed only between those states, whose people had so accepted it. It would, therefore, most strangely contradict itself, throughout all its provisions, to so construe the preamble, as to make it a declaration, that it was ordained by any other power than that of the people of the several states, as distinct bodies politic, over whom no external power could be exerted, but by their own consent.

These are not only the necessary conclusions, which flow from the plain language and definite provisions of the constitution itself, but their settled interpretation by this Court. " From these conventions the constitution derives its whole authority. The government proceeds directly from the people, and is ordained and established in the name of the people." 4 Wh. 403.

If it is asked what people; the answer is at hand, "*A convention of delegates chosen in each state, by the people thereof, assembled in their several states.*" Ib. sup. (*Mr. Justice Baldwin, A General View of the Origin and Nature of the Constitution and Government of the United States, 1837, p. 35.*)

CHAPTER XV

AMENDMENTS AND RATIFICATIONS

THE members of the Convention were too wise not to foresee that, however perfect they might themselves consider their work, it would suffer revision at other hands. They were indeed ostensibly engaged in revising one instrument of government, and while attempting to correct the obvious defects in the Articles of Confederation which experience had disclosed, they could not, nor did they attempt, to forecast events in such a way as to exclude the possibility of change in the fundamental charter of the Union. They wisely left the future to " posterity." Indeed they were so convinced of the necessity of revision that they facilitated it by rejecting the requirement that it could only be brought about by the unanimous consent of the States.

The thirteenth of Mr. Randolph's resolutions stated that " provision ought to be made for the amendment of the Articles of Union whensoever it shall seem necessary, and that the assent of the National Legislature ought not to be required thereto." This was indefinite, and purposely so, inasmuch as the question was difficult in itself and depended upon the adoption of a satisfactory form of government by the States in Convention assembled. *Provisions for Amendment*

Without entering into details, it is sufficient to note in this connection that the unanimous consent required by the thirteenth of the Articles of Confederation was rejected, as it had been found impracticable if not impossible to obtain the consent of each of the States to a modification of the Articles when, rightly or wrongly, the interest of any State was supposed to be unfavorably affected by the amendment; and it is not too much to say that the Articles of Confederation failed and were discarded largely because of the practical if not the theoretical lack of power of amendment.

As in so many other parts of the Constitution, the fifth Article, which states the final views of the Convention on this subject, was the result of concession and compromise. Thus, the States themselves conceded that all might be bound by the decision of a lesser number, eventually fixed at three-fourths. But the parties which had stood for their interests and had secured their recognition were unwilling to lose the fruits of victory through amendment. For example, the States in which slavery existed and appeared to be profitable, or at least was the basis of their economic system, insisted that the slave trade, guaranteed by Article I, Section 9 of the Constitution, should

Representation
of Small States
Not Subject to
Amendment

not be lost.   Therefore, it was provided that "no Amendment which may be made prior to the Year One thousand eight hundred and eight shall in any manner affect the first and fourth Clauses in the Ninth Section of the first Article."   Indeed, after the Constitution was a completed instrument, the right of the small States to equality was, in the session of September 15, 1787, safeguarded for all time against amendment; for although the Constitution may be amended in every other particular, it may not, according to its terms, be legally amended in this respect.   A motion was put to that effect by a delegate of one of the large States, and curiously enough by that very delegate who, in conference with the Virginian delegates before the opening of the Convention, had proposed to deprive the little States of equality.   "M^r. Govr. Morris," to quote Mr. Madison's Notes, "moved to annex a further proviso — 'that no State, without its consent shall be deprived of its equal suffrage in the Senate.'"   And Mr. Madison, perhaps not without a smile, for he possessed a keen sense of humor, continued, "This motion being dictated by the circulating murmurs of the small States was agreed to without debate, no one opposing it, or on the question, saying no." [1]   This provision appropriately forms the last and final clause of the fifth Article dealing with amendment.

Admitting therefore that the Constitution was to be amended, that certain interests were so important that they should not be affected, one for the period of twenty years, the other for all time, the question of amendment, accepted in principle, became a matter of detail.   Extreme advocates of the rights of the States, such as Mr. Luther Martin of Maryland, would insist that no modification should be made in the instrument of government without the consent of all the States.   The advocates of a consolidated government could not propose less than a majority.   Neither of these views could prevail.   The matter was plainly one for compromise, and a compromise was effected.

It will be recalled that, in the matter of amendment, Mr. Randolph's resolution on the subject proposed "the assent of the national Legislature ought not to be required thereto," a proposal made, no doubt, because of the difficulty in getting Congress to move; but the Congress of the more perfect Union was to be different from the Congress of the Confederation.   It was in any event a central authority, and it might appropriately be used as an agent for this purpose, provided, however, that it was only an agent, not a principal and that the States might take the initiative in the matter if they so desired.   By concession and compromise, it therefore resulted that two-thirds of both houses or the legislatures of two-thirds of the several States were to propose amendments, but their ratification was in no event to depend

Methods
of Amendment

[1] *Documentary History of the Constitution*, Vol. III, p. 758.

upon the Congress, which is after all only the agent of the States for certain defined legislative purposes, but upon the States or their citizens, who are the source of power.

The amendments thus proposed were to be submitted by the Congress. Whether they were proposed by the Congress or by a convention called by the Congress upon the initiative of the States, the proposals themselves were to be " ratified by the Legislatures of three fourths of the several States, or by Conventions in three fourths thereof," as the one or the other mode of ratification may be proposed by the Congress. Whereupon the amendments thus approved are " valid to all Intents and Purposes, as Part of this Constitution." It will be observed that the ratification by the legislature or special convention of a State is regarded as of equal force and effect, whereas Article VII of the Constitution provides that " the Ratification of the Conventions of nine States, shall be sufficient for the Establishment of this Constitution between the States so ratifying the same." It is also to be noted that, in the letter of the President of the Convention transmitting on its behalf the Constitution to the Congress, it is " Resolved, That the preceding Constitution be laid before the United States in Congress assembled, and that it is the Opinion of this Convention, that it should afterwards be submitted to a Convention of Delegates, chosen in each State by the People thereof, under the Recommendation of its Legislature, for their Assent and Ratification; and that each Convention assenting to, and ratifying the Same, should give Notice thereof to the United States in Congress assembled." [1]

The question may arise as to the difference of procedure in ratifying the Constitution and the amendments thereto, for the Constitution receives its validity only from the approval of conventions of the several States, whereas an amendment changing the Constitution is valid if made by the legislature or convention of the States. The question is not unimportant. The fifteenth of Mr. Randolph's resolutions provided " that the amendments which shall be offered to the Confederation, by the Convention ought at a proper time, or times, after the approbation of Congress to be submitted to an assembly or assemblies of Representatives, recommended by the several Legislatures to be expressly chosen by the people, to consider & decide thereon." The slightest familiarity with the proceedings of the Convention shows that the advocates of the more perfect Union regarded the ratification of the Constitution by conventions specially called within the States instead of the legislatures therein existing as both fundamental and essential to its success. To extreme advocates of the rights of the State, such as Mr. Luther Martin, the ratification by the State was sufficient, as the State was sovereign and it was immaterial whether it be by special assembly or by the legislature of the

[1] *Ibid.*, Vol. ii, p. 20.

State, as this was an internal matter. To the delegates of the small States ratification by the legislatures seemed adequate, inasmuch as the legislature represented the State, which was thus necessarily bound by its act. And it must be confessed that this view is reasonable, and that the difference seems to be one of form, not of substance, unless we look below the surface. If we do we see that the whole theory of the Constitution depends upon this conception, for the purpose of Mr. Madison, who may be considered as the exponent of this view, was not merely to have a constitution for the more perfect Union, but to have this constitution become, by means of its ratification by the people of each of the States, the constitution of the State as if it had originated within the State. In this event the constitution would be the constitution of the State and similar to an ordinary State constitution in that it referred to matters affecting the State and therefore properly determined by it. It differed, however, from the ordinary constitution in that it also affected the other States. It was therefore devised by delegates of the States and ratified by conventions of their people. In this way it became the constitution of all for general purposes, or for matters in common. The constitution framed in first instance and adopted by the people of the State deals with local or particular interests and not with interests held by the States in common. It begins and ends in the State in the sense that its provisions do not affect the States in general. It is confined to the State and is accordingly considered in the narrower sense the constitution of the State. In either case ratified by a Convention of the people of the State called for that purpose, it is the constitution of that State, just as the instrument of government, whether originating in the State, framed in convention and ratified by the voters of the State, is the constitution of that State. The purpose of the Convention was that each State should have two constitutions, one for general purposes, dealing with their interests in common, framed by their delegates in the Federal Convention submitted to and ratified by the Conventions of the States to be bound; the other for local purposes, confined to or not extending beyond the State, framed by its delegates in legislature or in convention and ratified by the people of the State according to their pleasure.

But this was not enough, for if the general and the special constitution were each ratified by the people of the States, each would have an equal validity and the later expression of the popular will would prevail. That is to say, if the State constitution were adopted subsequent to the ratification of the Federal Constitution the provisions of the State constitution would necessarily govern. Therefore, in order to prevent this, and by one act to make the Federal Constitution the supreme law of the State as well as the instrument of government of the Union, and irrevocable and not

A System
of Double
Constitu-
tions

subject to amendment except by the vote of three-fourths of the States, it was provided in the second clause of Article VI that " This Constitution, and the Laws of the United States which shall be made in Pursuance thereof; and all Treaties made, or which shall be made, under the Authority of the United States, shall be the supreme Law of the Land; and the Judges in every State shall be bound thereby, any Thing in the Constitution or the Laws of any State to the Contrary notwithstanding."

The meaning of this is clear: the Constitution, the acts of Congress passed in accordance with its terms and the treaties of the United States are to be " the supreme law of the land," an expression ultimately substituted by the Committee on Style and adopted by the Convention September 12, 1787, for " the supreme law of the several States, and of their citizens and inhabitants " (Article 8 of the first draft of the Constitution, submitted on August 6th).

There was to be one constitution of each State for general purposes. There could be as many State constitutions as the people thereof were minded to make, but the Constitution adopted by the delegates of the States, when ratified by the people of the State, was to be supreme, " any Thing in the Constitution or Laws of any State to the Contrary notwithstanding." [1]

It will be observed that the judges of each of the States are to be bound by the Constitution, the acts of Congress made in pursuance thereof and the treaties of the United States. This was naturally and properly so, because the Constitution of the United States was also the law of the land, that is to say, of each State. The act of Congress in pursuance of its terms was a law of the State. A treaty of the United States, being a law of the United States, was necessarily a law of each State. The judicial power of the State would necessarily extend to the provisions of the Constitution, acts of Congress and treaties of the United States. There would, however,

---

[1] The question as to what constitutes the government of a community seeking admission to the Union is a political rather than a judicial one, and the power of recognizing a State government was left in the hands of Congress. This was made clear in the case of *Luther* v. *Borden* (7 Howard, 1, 42), decided in 1849, in which the constitutionality of the accepted form of government in Rhode Island was disputed. Mr. Chief Justice Taney, in delivering the opinion of the court, said:

It rests with Congress to decide what government is the established one in a State. For as the United States guarantee to each State a republican government, Congress must necessarily decide what government is established in the State before it can determine whether it is republican or not.

A similar issue arose in the case of *Minor* v. *Happersett* (21 Wallace, 162), decided in 1874, and was settled in the following language:

The guarantee [for a republican form of government] necessarily implies a duty on the part of the States themselves to provide such a government. All the States had governments when the Constitution was adopted. In all, the people participated to some extent, through their representatives elected in the manner specially provided. These governments the Constitution did not change. They were accepted precisely as they were, and it is, therefore, to be presumed that they were such as it was the duty of the States to provide. Thus we have unmistakable evidence of what was republican in form, within the meaning of that term, as employed in the Constitution.

be a difference in the action of the Federal and of the State courts. An error of the State court in the interpretation of the Federal law would be corrected on appeal by the Supreme Court of the United States; whereas the constructions put upon the State Constitution and the laws of the State would be followed by the Supreme Court in so far as they were not inconsistent with the Federal Constitution, with acts of Congress made in pursuance thereof, or with treaties of the United States. In matters of general as distinguished from local jurisprudence, the Federal Court would be free to decide for itself, yet would be inclined to accept the decision of the State Court.

That there might be no doubt as to the supremacy of the Federal Constitution, the acts of Congress consistent with its terms and treaties of the United States, it was further and wisely provided that all officers of the States as well as of the United States should bind their consciences by oath or affirmation to support the Federal Constitution; thus making it not merely supreme on paper and of general application, but supreme in fact in the special and concrete case. Thus the clause of Article VI immediately following the one last quoted proceeds:

> The Senators and Representatives before mentioned, and the Members of the several State Legislatures, and all executive and judicial Officers, both of the United States and of the several States, shall be bound by Oath or Affirmation, to support this Constitution.

Finally, in this connection, it is to be noted that the Federal Constitution was, by these various provisions, made the supreme and fundamental law of each State of the Union and was adopted in its entirety by each of the States ratifying it. Article V, concerning amendments, was therefore necessarily adopted as an integral part of the Constitution, which, in providing for its amendment, made its ratification depend not merely upon the sovereign pleasure of any one State but upon the approval of three-fourths of the States of the Union. It was therefore beyond the power of any one State to change an iota of its fundamental constitution, except in conjunction with three-fourths of the States. An attempt to do so would be illegal and could only be looked upon as an attempt to amend this constitution in a method contrary to its provisions. It could not be done according to the law of the land. It could only be done by revolution. It was, after the formal ratification of the Constitution by conventions of the peoples within the State, immaterial whether the amendments were made by legislature or convention within the States, inasmuch as the supremacy of the Constitution had been established, and inasmuch as it could not be disestablished except by the votes of three-fourths of the States, in which event the will of three-fourths of the States,

The
Power
to Amend

whether expressed in legislature or in convention, would prevail in fact and should prevail in law.

In a letter addressed to Edmund Randolph, under date of April 8, 1787, Mr. Madison outlined the principles which he thought should be contained in the new Federal pact, and expressed the opinion that " to give the new system its proper energy, it will be desirable to have it ratified by the authority of the people, and not merely by that of the Legislatures." [1] This provision, therefore, appeared in the fifteenth of Mr. Randolph's resolutions, and it was debated at large and in detail in the Convention. In the session of June 5th it appears to have first been taken up, on which occasion Mr. Sherman " thought such a popular ratification unnecessary: the articles of Confederation providing for changes and alterations with the assent of Cong^s. and ratification of State Legislatures." Naturally, Mr. Madison, as the author of the clause, thought " this provision essential," saying in reply to Mr. Sherman that: Ratification

> The articles of Confed^n. themselves were defective in this respect, resting in many of the States on the Legislative sanction only. Hence in conflicts between acts of the States, and of Cong^s. especially where the former are of posterior date, and the decision is to be made by State Tribunals, an uncertainty must necessarily prevail, or rather perhaps a certain decision in favor of the State authority. He suggested also that as far as the articles of Union were to be considered as a Treaty only of a particular sort, among the Governments of Independent States, the doctrine might be set up that a breach of any one article, by any of the parties, absolved the other parties from the whole obligation. For these reasons as well as others he thought it indispensable that the new Constitution should be ratified in the most unexceptionable form, and by the supreme authority of the people themselves.[2]

After an exchange of views the question was postponed, but was passed on the 12th, Massachusetts, Pennsylvania, Virginia, North Carolina, South Carolina and Georgia voting for, Connecticut, New York and New Jersey against, and the delegations of Delaware and Maryland divided. On July 23d, three days before Mr. Randolph's resolutions as amended were referred to the Committee of Detail to report a draft of a Constitution, the question again came before the Convention and was very carefully and elaborately considered. ● Mr. Ellsworth of Connecticut moved that the Constitution be referred to the legislatures of the States for ratification and was appropriately seconded by Mr. Patterson of New Jersey. In the course of the debate Messrs. Mason and Madison argued strongly for the submission of the Constitution to conventions within the States; Mr. Ellsworth stood out for Discussion
of the
Mode of
Ratification

---

[1] *The Writings of James Madison*, Hunt ed., **Vol. II, p. 340.**
[2] *Documentary History*, Vol. III, pp. 65–6.

submission to the Legislatures, and the reasons pro and con were admirably stated. Thus,

> Col. Mason considered a reference of the plan to the authority of the people as one of the most important and essential of the Resolutions. The Legislatures have no power to ratify it. They are the mere creatures of the State Constitutions, and cannot be greater than their creators. And he knew of no power in any of the Constitutions, he knew there was no power in some of them, that could be competent to this object. Whither then must we resort? To the people with whom all power remains that has not been given up in the Constitutions derived from them. It was of great moment he observed that this doctrine should be cherished as the basis of free Government. Another strong reason was that admitting the Legislatures to have a competent authority, it would be wrong to refer the plan to them, because succeeding Legislatures having equal authority could undo the acts of their predecessors; and the National Gov^t. would stand in each State on the weak and tottering foundation of an Act of Assembly. There was a remaining consideration of some weight. In some of the States the Gov^{ts}. were not derived from the clear & undisputed authority of the people. This was the case in Virginia. Some of the best & wisest citizens considered the Constitution as established by an assumed authority. A National Constitution derived from such a source would be exposed to the severest criticisms.[1]

Mr. Madison, as sponsor for the proposition, added the weight of his authority to its adoption, saying, in his own summary of his views, that he

> thought it clear that the Legislatures were incompetent to the proposed changes. These changes would make essential inroads on the State Constitutions, and it would be a novel & dangerous doctrine that a Legislature could change the constitution under which it held its existence. There might indeed be some Constitutions within the Union, which had given a power to the Legislature to concur in alterations of the federal Compact. But there were certainly some which had not; and in the case of these, a ratification must of necessity be obtained from the people. He considered the difference between a system founded on the Legislatures only, and one founded on the people, to be the true difference between a *league* or *treaty*, and a *Constitution*. The former in point of *moral obligation* might be as inviolable as the later. In point of *political operation*, there were two important distinctions in favor of the latter.   1. A law violating a treaty ratified by a pre-existing law, might be respected by the Judges as a law, though an unwise & perfidious one. A law violating a constitution established by the people themselves, would be considered by the Judges as null & void. 2. The doctrine laid down by the law of Nations in the case of treaties is that a breach of any one article by any of the parties, frees the other parties from their engagements. In case of a union of people under one Constitution, the nature of the pact has always been understood to exclude such an interpretation. Comparing the two modes in point of expediency he thought all the considerations which recommended this Convention in preference to Congress for proposing the reform were in favor of State Conventions in preference to the Legislatures for examining and adopting it.[2]

[1] *Documentary History*, Vol. iii, p. 405.
[2] *Ibid.*, Vol. iii, pp. 410–11.

In the session of August 31, Mr. Madison recurred to this subject in connection with the difficulty which some of the States, particularly Maryland, alleged they would experience because the State constitutions did not provide for amendment and the officials of the States were bound by oath to obey the provisions thereof. Mr. Madison, according to his own report,

> considered it best to require Conventions; Among other reasons, for this, that the powers given to the Genl. Govt. being taken from the State Govts. the Legislatures would be more disinclined than conventions composed in part at least of other men; and if disinclined, they could devise modes apparently promoting, but really thwarting the ratification. . . . The people were in fact, the fountain of all power, and by resorting to them, all difficulties were got over. They could alter constitutions as they pleased. It was a principle in the Bills of rights, that first principles might be resorted to.[1]

In the session of July 23d, Mr. Ellsworth paid special attention to Mr. Mason's views, saying, in support of his motion that the Constitution be referred to the legislatures of the States for ratication:

> If there be any Legislatures who should find themselves incompetent to the ratification, he should be content to let them advise with their constituents and pursue such a mode as wd. be competent. He thought more was to be expected from the Legislatures than from the people. . . . It was said by Col. Mason 1. that the Legislatures have no authority in this case. 2. that their successors having equal authority could rescind their acts. As to the 2d. point he could not admit it to be well founded. An act to which the States by their Legislatures, make themselves parties, becomes a compact from which no one of the parties can recede of itself. As to the 1st. point, he observed that a new sett of ideas seemed to have crept in since the articles of Confederation were established. Conventions of the people, or with power derived expressly from the people, were not then thought of. The Legislatures were considered as competent. Their ratification has been asquiesced in without complaint.[2]

Mr. Ellsworth was correct in stating that "a new sett of ideas seemed to have crept in since the articles of Confederation were established," and the ratification by conventions in the States naturally sprang out of the new ideas by virtue of which the people were the source of all power, that therefore constitutions should not be conceded by a king, monarch, or legislature to the people, but that all power, emanating from the people, was, as far as they considered it safe or necessary, vested in branches of government created by them and to be exercised by officials responsible to them.

The new set of ideas to which Mr. Ellsworth referred are thus stated

[1] *Ibid.*, p. 656.
[2] *Ibid.*, p. 408.

in the Virginia bill of rights of June 12, 1776, drafted by Mr. Mason himself:

> That all power is vested in, and consequently derived from, the people; that magistrates are their trustees and servants, and at all times amenable to them.
>
> That government is, or ought to be, instituted for the common benefit, protection, and security of the people, nation, or community; . . . and that, when any government shall be found inadequate or contrary to these purposes, a majority of the community hath an indubitable, inalienable, and indefeasible right to reform, alter, or abolish it, in such manner as shall be judged most conducive to the public weal.[1]

And the new set of ideas was thus stated in the Declaration of Independence adopted by the Congress of the United States on July 4, 1776:

> We hold these truths to be self-evident, that all men are created equal, that they are endowed by their Creator with certain unalienable Rights, that among these are Life, Liberty and the pursuit of Happiness. That to secure these rights, Governments are instituted among Men, deriving their just powers from the consent of the governed, That whenever any Form of Government becomes destructive of these ends, it is the Right of the People to alter or to abolish it, and to institute new Government, laying its foundation on such principles and organizing its powers in such form, as to them shall seem most likely to effect their Safety and Happiness.

In accordance with these ideas the Constitution, to bind the people, should be ratified by the people as the source of power, not by the legislature as the agent thereof. This was the view of the Convention, expressed immediately after Mr. Madison's remarks of July 23d, New Hampshire, Massachusetts, Pennsylvania, Virginia, North Carolina, South Carolina, and Georgia voting against Mr. Ellsworth's motion to refer the Constitution to the legislatures of the States, and Connecticut, Delaware and Maryland voting for the motion. New York was not represented, and New Jersey took no part in the vote.

The letter of the President of the Convention transmitting the Constitution with its recommendation that it should be submitted for ratification to conventions of the States specially called for this purpose was received by the Congress; and, on September 28, 1787, it was " Resolved Unanimously that the said Report with the resolutions and letter accompanying the same be transmitted to the several legislatures in Order to be submitted to a convention of Delegates chosen in each state by the people thereof in conformity to the resolves of the Convention made and provided in that case." [2] This was done, and in the course of that and the ensuing year the Constitu-

---

[1] Thorpe, *Charters and Constitutions*, Vol. 7, p. 3813; Poore, pp. 1908-9.
[2] *Documentary History*, Vol. ii, p. 22.

tion was ratified by conventions held in the different States. There were two exceptions: North Carolina, which failed to ratify it at this time, although it did so on November 21, 1789, after the Constitution had gone into effect and the government thereunder organized; Rhode Island, which was not represented in the Convention but which, on May 29, 1790, adopted the Constitution, or " adhered to it " as we should say in international parlance.

Some of the States ratified the Constitution unanimously, without diffi-culty and without the suggestion of amendments. Other States ratified it by a close vote, with great difficulty, and in the belief that certain amend-ments to the Constitution would be proposed and submitted to the States in accordance with the provisions of Article V thereof relating to amendments. It is to be observed, however, that the Constitution was in every case accepted in its entirety; that it was absolutely, not conditionally, ratified, although at one time its advocates were so hard pressed as to consider this proposition. Colonel Hamilton, with the New York Convention on his hands, consulted Mr. Madison, with the Virginian Convention just off his hands. The latter ended whatever wavering the Colonel may have had by stating that a conditional ratification would be no ratification at all; but a rejection. Mr. Madison's exact language was:

> My opinion is that a reservation of a right to withdraw, if amendments be not decided on under the form of the Constitution within a certain time, is a *conditional* ratification; that it does not make N. York a member of the New Union, and consequently that that she could not be received on that plan.[1]

It is important to bear this statement in mind, inasmuch as it shows that, although desirous of having New York become a member of the more perfect Union, and although Mr. Madison was in a frame of mind to make concessions, as his attitude in the international conference and in the State convention abundantly showed, he nevertheless felt that a State should decide on the threshold whether it should or should not enter the Union, and that, if it decided to enter and actually did enter the Union, it could not withdraw. Mr. Madison's language is important for the further reason that, as the Constitution derives its validity solely from its ratification by the States, it was essential that it be ratified by them in its entirety and unconditionally in order to be susceptible of a universal interpretation and of a universal application.

Delaware, the smallest of the States represented in the Convention, was the first to act in favor of the Constitution, and its action was unanimous. New Jersey was the third in point of time, and its action was unanimous,

The
Spirit of
the
Ratifications

[1] *Ibid.*, vol. iv, p. 803.

which showed that the small States were satisfied with the compromise by virtue whereof their equality was maintained and safeguarded. The second State to ratify was the Commonwealth of Pennsylvania. It is to be noted however that while the Constitution was carried, there was a strong minority opposed to it. The variety of amendments suggested as reasonable by and acceptable to this minority appears to have won favor not only with the opponents of the Constitution in other States but are said to have been the basis of the amendments proposed by Mr. Madison on June 6, 1789, in the first session of the first Congress of the United States held under the Constitution.

Delaware ratified December 7, 1787; Pennsylvania, December 12, 1787; New Jersey, December 18, 1787; Georgia, January 2, 1788; and Connecticut, January 9, 1788, without amendments. As previously stated, the action of Delaware and New Jersey was unanimous. In Pennsylvania the friends of the Constitution had a comfortable majority, and a still larger majority in Connecticut.

One great State had declared itself. Massachusetts, the second of the great States, adopted the Constitution February 7, 1788, but only after a hard fought contest and the adoption of amendments. The adoption by this commonwealth grew out of a faith and confidence that amendments would be made to the Constitution and that the particular amendments which the Massachusetts Convention recommended would be laid before the Congress. Indeed its Senators and Representatives were instructed so to do, in accordance with the provision of the Constitution relating to amendments. This method of action seems to have satisfied the scruples of Mr. John Hancock, President of the Convention, and known to be not overfavorable to the Constitution. He had been President of the Continental Congress; and the large, bold hand in which he signed his name to the Declaration of Independence keeps his memory green among his countrymen. He was then in private life, with an eye, it is said, to the governorship of his State. Some ill-natured persons, enemies of the great man, thought that he aspired to the presidency, in the event that Virginia did not enter the more perfect Union. The method also satisfied Mr. Samuel Adams, the great Revolutionary leader and advocate of democracy, who was at first opposed to the Constitution, but who was won over to its support by the recommendation of amendments. The action of Massachusetts was important not merely because it was then one of the three great States, without whose support the Constitution could not well be put into effect, but because it provided the means of overcoming opposition in the other States, especially in the then third great State of Virginia, and in New York. The method of recommendations was indeed the bridge that carried the doubting Thomases and in some instances the opponents across to the other side. It is worthy of note that after the action of Massachusetts only one of the remaining States ratified without suggesting amendments.

It is appropriate to add that the following letter from General Washington, published in Virginia, in Pennsylvania and in a Massachusetts paper during the session of the Convention of that State, had a great effect upon the good people thereof and inclined them to conciliation, by showing them how to realize the improvements to the Constitution which they had in view and in strict accordance with its express provisions concerning amendment:

And clear I am, if another Foederal Convention is attempted, the sentiments of the members will be more discordant. . . . I am fully persuaded . . . that it [the Constitution] or disunion is before us. If the first is our choice, . . . a constitutional door is opened for amendments, and may be adopted in a peaceable manner without tumult or disorder.[1]

Maryland ratified without suggesting amendments April 28, 1788; South Carolina on May 23, 1788, and in view of the action subsequently taken by that State the material portion of its act of ratification is quoted:

And whereas it is essential to the preservation of the rights reserved to the several states, and the freedom of the people, under the operations of a general government, that the right of prescribing the manner, time, and places, of holding the elections to the federal legislature, should be forever inseparably annexed to the sovereignty of the several states,—This Convention doth declare, that the same ought to remain, to all posterity, a perpetual and fundamental right in the local, exclusive of the interference of the general government, except in cases where the legislatures of the states shall refuse or neglect to perform and fulfil the same, according to the tenor of the said Constitution.

This Convention doth also declare, that no section or paragraph of the said Constitution warrants a construction that the states do not retain every power not expressly relinquished by them, and vested in the general government of the Union.

Resolved, That the general government of the United States ought never to impose direct taxes, *but* where the moneys arising from the duties, imports, and excise, are insufficient for the public exigencies, *nor then until* Congress shall have made a requisition upon the states to assess, levy, and pay, their respective proportions of such requisitions; and in case any state shall neglect or refuse to pay its proportion, pursuant to such requisition, then Congress may assess and levy such state's proportion, together with interest thereon, at the rate of six per centum per annum, from the time of payment prescribed by such requisition.

Resolved, That the third section of the sixth article ought to be amended, by inserting the word " other " between the words " no " and " religious."

[1] *Documentary History,* vol. iv, pp. 406–7.

Resolved, That it be a standing instruction to all such delegates as may hereafter be elected to represent this state in the general government, to exert their utmost abilities and influence to effect an alteration of the Constitution, conformably to the aforegoing resolutions.[1]

South Carolina was the eighth of the States to ratify, but the Constitution made the ratification of nine a prerequisite to its going into effect. With the ratification of New Hampshire on June 21, 1788, the people of nine States had pledged their faith to the Constitution, and it had become the government of each of the nine and of the Union composed of the nine. The influence of Massachusetts, to which New Hampshire belonged for a long time, was very marked upon that State during the colonial period, and the influence of Massachusetts did not cease with the Revolution, as the adoption by New Hampshire of the State Constitution and of the Constitution of the United States amply disclosed. When the Convention met in New Hampshire in February, 1788, the opponents of adoption were in a slight majority. The friends of the new government, however, were able to adjourn until June, by which time the members were more favorably disposed, so that, after four days' debate, the Constitution was ratified by a vote of 57 to 47, with a series of amendments, as in the case of Massachusetts.

Difficulties of
Ratification

The action of New Hampshire inspired the supporters of the Constitution with confidence as well as hope, as it would be less difficult for the States in doubt as to the Constitution to join the more perfect Union when formed than to refuse to take part in its formation. It is, however, doubtful whether the Union would have been formed and the government under the Constitution have gone into effect in 1789 with chances of success unless New York, in a way the dividing line between the eastern and the middle States, and especially if Virginia, the great dominion to the South, had not decided for better or for worse to unite themselves with their sister States. Had the latter State not done so, the world might have lost the perfect type and model of a chief executive which the American people found in Washington, who, as a Virginian, could not have been President of the Union in which Virginia was not represented.

However, Virginia ratified the Constitution on June 26, 1788, but five days after the favorable action of New Hampshire, before the action of that State was known and while it appeared that Virginia, in addition to proposing the Constitution, had by its adherence to the Union made it operative.

The struggle in Virginia was a struggle of giants. The ratification was opposed by Patrick Henry, the most famous of American orators, who was appointed a member of the Federal Convention but who declined to accept, saying somewhat inelegantly but forcibly that he " smelt a rat."

[1] Elliot, *Debates,* Vol. I, p. 325.

It was also opposed by George Mason, a member of the Convention, who refused to sign, primarily because Congress was not restrained by a two-thirds vote in matters of navigation and because of a lack of a bill of rights, and of whom Mr. Madison said " that he possessed the greatest talents for debate of any man he had ever seen, or heard speak." [1] It was a herculean task for the quiet, studious and unimpressive Madison to stem and to over-come the tide of such opposition. He was supported without the Convention by General Washington and within the Convention by Edmund Randolph who had refused to sign the Constitution largely because he felt it should be submitted for revision to a second convention which he now saw to be impossible. Mr. Madison was also aided by John Marshall, a young and vigorous man of thirty-two, destined years later to expound the Constitution from the Bench and to make the more perfect Union even more perfect through a series of masterly decisions. Yet Mr. Madison, insisting that the Constitution be read in its entirety and that each clause be considered in relation to all of its parts instead of in isolation, was able to show that the Constitution did create a more perfect Union of States, just as we today believe that it has created the most perfect Union of States ever known.

The vote, however, on June 25, 1788, was close, 89 delegates voting for its ratification and 79 against. The ratification was accompanied by a bill of rights of twenty articles, and the bill itself by twenty other amendments, which were to be presented to the Congress for adoption as amendments to the Constitution. If George Mason could not bend to his will the delegates of the Philadelphia Convention and impose upon them in express terms a bill of rights, he was irresistible in Virginia, to which State he had given a bill of rights prefixed to its Constitution, which is today a model; and if the advocates of amendment to the Constitution, as it was ultimately framed in Philadelphia, failed to impress their fellow delegates with the justness of their views, the Convention of Virginia stood squarely for amendment. And in order that the spirit in which the Constitution was adopted might be known and understood by their countrymen, the Convention accompanied it with the following declaration, which may at least be taken as evidence that the Virginians had no intention of degrading the State into a province:

> We, the delegates of the people of Virginia, duly elected in pursuance of a recommendation from the General Assembly, and now met in Convention, having fully and freely investigated and discussed the proceedings of the Federal Convention, and being prepared as well as the most mature deliberation hath enabled us, to decide thereon,—Do, in the name and in behalf of the people of Virginia, declare and make known, that the powers granted under the Constitution, being derived from the people of the United States, may be resumed by them, whensoever the same shall be perverted to their injury or oppression, and that every power not granted

[1] John P. Kennedy, *Memoirs of the Life of William Wirt*, 1849, Vol. I, p. 354.

thereby remains with them, and at their will; that, therefore, no right, of any denomination, can be cancelled, abridged, restrained, or modified, by the Congress, by the Senate or House of Representatives, acting in any capacity, by the President, or any department or officer of the United States, except in those instances in which power is given by the Constitution for those purposes; and that, among other essential rights, the liberty of conscience, and of the press, cannot be cancelled, abridged, restrained, or modified, by any authority of the United States. With these impressions, with a solemn appeal to the Searcher of all hearts for the purity of our intentions, and under the conviction that whatsoever imperfections may exist in the Constitution ought rather to be examined in the mode prescribed therein, than to bring the Union into danger by a delay with a hope of obtaining amendments previous to the ratifications,—We, the said delegates, in the name and in behalf of the people of Virginia, do, by these presents, assent to and ratify the Constitution recommended, on the 17th day of September, 1787, by the Federal Convention, for the government of the United States, hereby announcing to all those whom it may concern, that the said Constitution is binding upon the said people, according to an authentic copy hereto annexed, in the words following. . . .[1]

Contest in
New York

The contest in New York was even more severe than in Virginia, and, indeed, than in any other State; for when the Convention met, the opponents of ratification were securely in the saddle under the presidency of George Clinton, Governor of the State, and under the leadership of Melancthon Smith, who, however, showed himself to be a man of principle and as such open to conviction. The friends of the Constitution, were, however, led in a masterly manner by Alexander Hamilton who, as is well known, took a rather insignificant part in the Philadelphia Convention, where he was outvoted by his two colleagues before they withdrew and where he apparently had little sympathy for any plan proposed by others and not much confidence in his own. Any constitution, however, was better to him than none. He loyally accepted the Constitution as drafted, as the best that could be got under the circumstances, and devoted his commanding abilities and his energy, which proved to be resistless, to its ratification by the State of which he was not a native but whereof he is today the most distinguished of a long line of distinguished citizens.

For Colonel Hamilton it was not enough to argue and debate, and by means thereof to produce conviction within the Convention. He felt the necessity of creating an atmosphere without, which should influence opinion within the Convention. For this purpose he planned a series of papers explaining and justifying the Constitution, to be issued at rapid intervals in the public press of the State. With him in the undertaking were associated John Jay, who contributed five articles, and Mr. Madison who wrote some twenty-nine. He himself wrote fifty-one of the eighty-five articles, which

[1] Elliot, *Debates*, Vol. I, p. 327.

taken together form *The Federalist,* then a journalistic venture, today the The Federalist classic exposition of the Constitution.

But even the ability of Alexander Hamilton, John Jay and Robert R. Livingston within the New York Convention, with the aid of James Madison without its doors, might have proved unavailing had the stars in their courses not fought for the Constitution. The first week of the session in New York showed that two-thirds were opposed to ratification, but the news, welcome to Hamilton although distasteful to the majority, that the ninth State, New Hampshire, had ratified the Constitution, decided that the experiment was to be tried. On July 3d the news of the ratification by Virginia reached the members of the New York Convention. Should New York fail to adopt the Constitution it would be surrounded by the New England States on the East and New Jersey and Pennsylvania to the South, and it would be so far separated from Rhode Island and North Carolina, which had not then ratified the Constitution, that it could not well form a union with them. In the end, Melancthon Smith, leader of the opposition, rose and stated that he would vote for the Constitution, and by a majority of three it was adopted by the Convention, " in confidence that the amendments which shall have been proposed to the said Constitution will receive an early and mature consideration," and " in full confidence " that a convention should be called and convened for proposing amendments.[1]

The amendments were very elaborate. Their character may be judged by the opening paragraphs of what may be considered the preamble to the act of ratification, in which it is stated:

> That all power is originally vested in, and consequently derived from, the people, and that government is instituted by them for their common interest, protection, and security.
> That the enjoyment of life, liberty, and the pursuit of happiness, are essential rights, which every government ought to respect and preserve.
> That the powers of government may be reassumed by the people whensoever it shall become necessary to their happiness; that every power, jurisdiction, and right, which is not by the said Constitution clearly delegated to the Congress of the United States, or the departments of the government thereof, remains to the people of the several states, or to their respective state governments, to whom they may have granted the same; and that those clauses in the said Constitution, which declare that Congress shall not have or exercise certain powers, do not imply that Congress is entitled to any powers not given by the said Constitution; but such clauses are to be construed either as exceptions to certain specified powers, or as inserted merely for greater caution.[2]

The adoption of the Constitution, however, even with express declarations and a series of recommendations, was a concrete victory for the cause

---

[1] *Ibid.,* Vol. i, p. 329.
[2] *Ibid.,* p. 327.

of union, inasmuch as it assured geographical unity and that the authority of the Government should extend from New Hampshire on the north to the south of Virginia. Rhode Island was on the outskirts and could not affect the Union; and North Carolina, between Virginia and South Carolina, could not resist propinquity, which affects even the union of States.

A Convention called in North Carolina adjourned August 4, 1788, without ratifying the Constitution, for the reasons stated in its resolution of August 1st of that month and year:

> *Resolved*, That a declaration of rights, asserting and securing from encroachments the great principles of civil and religious liberty, and the unalienable rights of the people, together with amendments to the most ambiguous and exceptionable parts of the said Constitution of government, ought to be laid before Congress, and the convention of the states that shall or may be called for the purpose of amending the said Constitution, for their consideration, previous to the ratification of the Constitution aforesaid, on the part of the State of North Carolina.[1]

It is proper to say in this connection that the declaration of rights proposed by North Carolina consisted of twenty Articles, the amendments of twenty-six. The ratification, however, of eleven of the thirteen States, the formation of the Union and its successful operation without North Carolina and Rhode Island, caused the good people of the former State to bethink themselves, with the result that, on November 21, 1789, the people of North Carolina, assembled in convention, adopted and ratified "the said Constitution and form of government." And on May 29, 1790, the people of Rhode Island, in convention assembled, likewise adopted the Constitution, with a series of declarations in the nature of a bill of rights and of amendments almost as large as the State, which by this time had come to the conclusion that the Union was more necessary to it than it was to the Union. Thus through the long and narrow way of amendments and ratifications, the course of the Constitution was finally fashioned. State and Union came to their own. Divergent interests, at first seemingly irreconcilable, merged. The way opened for the United States of America.

[1] Elliot, *Debates*, Vol. i, pp. 331-2.

XVI

GOVERNMENT SET UP: AMENDMENTS

Whilst the last members were signing it [the Constitution] Doct: Franklin looking towards the Presidents Chair, at the back of which a rising sun happened to be painted, observed to a few members near him, that Painters had found it difficult to distinguish in their art a rising from a setting sun. I have said he, often and often in the course of the Session, and the vicissitudes of my hopes and fears as to its issue, looked at that behind the President without being able to tell whether it was rising or setting: But now at length I have the happiness to know that it is a rising and not a setting Sun. (*Madison's Notes of Debates in the Federal Convention of 1787, Session of September 17, 1787, Documentary History of the Constitution of the United States of America, 1786-1870, Vol. III, 1900, p. 770.*)

It has hitherto been understood, that the supreme power, that is, the sovereignty of the people of the States, was in its nature divisible, and was in fact divided, according to the Constitution of the U. States, between the States in their united and the States in their individual capacities that as the States, in their highest sov. char., were competent to surrender the whole sovereignty and form themselves into a consolidated State, so they might surrender a part & retain, as they have done, the other part, forming a mixed Gov: with a division of its attributes as marked out in the Constitution. . . .
Certain it is that the constitutional compact of the U. S. has allotted the supreme power of Gov: partly to the United States by special grants, partly to the individual States by general reservations; and if sovereignty be in its nature divisible, the true question to be decided is, whether the allotment has been made by the competent authority, and this question is answered by the fact that it was an act of the *majority* of the people in each State in their highest sovereign capacity, equipollent to a *unanimous* act of the people composing the State in that capacity. (*James Madison on "Sovereignty," 1835, Gaillard Hunt, Editor, The Writings of James Madison, Vol. IX, 1910, pp. 568-9, 572.*)

"These states are constitutent parts of the United States. They are members of one great *empire*," ("members of the American *confederacy;*" 2 Pet. 312,) "for some purposes sovereign, for some purposes subordinate." 6 Wh. 414. The political character of the several states of this Union, in relation to each other, is this: "For all *national* purposes, the states and the citizens thereof, are one; united under the same sovereign authority, and governed by the same laws. In *all other* respects the states are necessarily *foreign* to and independent of each other. "They form a *confederated* government; yet the several states retain their individual sovereignties, and with respect to their municipal regulations, are to each other sovereign." 2 Pet. 590, 1; 10 Pet. 579. S. P.; 12 Wh. 334. "The national and state systems are to be regarded as *one whole*." 6 Wh. 419. "In America, the powers of sovereignty are divided between the government of the Union, and those of the states. They are each sovereign with respect to the objects committed to it; and neither sovereign with respect to the objects committed to the other." 4 Wh. 410. (*Mr. Justice Baldwin, A General View of the Origin and Nature of the Constitution and Government of the United States, 1837, p. 14.*)

The great and incurable defect of the confederation was, the dependence of congress on state laws to execute and to carry into effect their resolutions and requisitions: generally speaking, the jurisdiction of the old and new congress was the same, except as to the regulation of commerce and a judicial system. The states would not delegate the power of execution to operate directly on the subjects of its jurisdiction; the people of the states granted this power, by the constitution, by which alone the federal government became efficient and competent to the objects of its creation. (*Mr. Justice Baldwin, A General View of the Origin and Nature of the Constitution and Government of the United States, 1837, pp. 105-106.*)

317

In this outline of *our* old constitution of government, we see the pattern of our *new* one, though with a different distribution of powers; the most important of those which are in the king, by prerogative, in England, are granted to congress; the judicial power is vested in the courts of the United States, exclusively; and the executive power is as much defined by enumeration, as the legislative and judicial powers of the constitution are. Herein consists one great difference between the two governments; and from this there arises another, which is all important. The powers not delegated, or prohibited, being reserved to the states respectively, or the people; none can exist by prerogative, or inherent power, in any branch of the government. (*Mr. Justice Baldwin, A General View of the Origin and Nature of the Constitution and Government of the United States, 1837, pp. 54-55.*)

This change was effected by the constitution, which, in the language of this Court, is a *grant*. "The grant does not convey power, which might be beneficial to the grantor, if retained by himself, or which can move solely to the benefit of the grantee; but is an *investment* of power for the general advantage, in the hands of *agents*, selected for that purpose, which power can never be exercised by the people themselves, but must be placed in the hands of *agents* or lie dormant," 9. Wh. 189. The language of the constitution is the same. "All *legislative powers* herein *granted*, shall be vested in a congress of the United States," &c. "*The executive power* shall be *vested* in a president of the United States of America." "*The judicial power* of the United States shall be *vested* in one Supreme Court."
Here then, there is something visible to the judicial eye, tangible by judicial minds, reasoning, illustration, and analogy; intelligible by judicial rules and maxims, which, through all time, have prescribed its nature, effect, and meaning. It is a *grant, by a grantor, to a grantee,* of the *things granted;* which are, *legislative, executive,* and *judicial power, vested by a constituent,* in *agents,* for the enumerated purposes and objects of the grant. It declares the grantor and constituent, to be "*the people of the United States,*" who, for the purposes set forth, "ordained and established" it as a "constitution for the United States of America;" "the supreme law of the land;" creating what its framers unanimously named, "*the federal government of these states.*" Its frame was "done in convention, by the unanimous consent of the states present." The 7th article whereof declared that, "the ratification of the conventions of nine states, shall be sufficient for the establishment of this constitution, between the states so ratifying the same." And, to leave no doubt of their intention, as to what should be deemed a convention of a state, the members thereof, by the unanimous order of the convention, laid it before congress, with their opinions, that it should be submitted to a *convention of delegates* chosen *in each state, by the people thereof,* under the recommendation of its legislatures, for their assent and ratification. 1 Vol. Laws U. S. 70, 71. (*Mr. Justice Baldwin, A General View of the Origin and Nature of the Constitution and Government of the United States, 1837, pp. 11-12.*)

These colonies were not declared to be free and independent states, by substituting congress in the place of king and parliament; nor by the people of the states, transferring to *the United States,* that allegiance they had owed to the crown; or making with *the state,* or *nation,* of the United States, a political connection, similar to that which had existed with *the state* of Great Britain.
A state, to be free, must be exempt from all external control; on a "separate and equal station with the other powers of the earth;" within whose territorial limits, no state or nation can have any jurisdiction: this is of the essence of *freedom,* and being *free,* in the grant and exercise of legislative power at their pleasure, a *state,* and *the people thereof,* must have the absolute sovereignty, illimitable, save by the people themselves. Such was the situation of the states and people, from 1776 till 1781, when the several state legislatures made an act of federation, as *allied sovereigns,* which was only a league or alliance; and being utterly defective, was substituted by a new act of federation; a constitution, ordained by *the people of the several states,* in their primary inherent right and power, existing in themselves; before any portion of its sovereignty had been impaired by any act of federation, or any severance from its territorial boundary. (*Mr. Justice Baldwin, A General View of the Origin and Nature of the Constitution and Government of the United States, 1837, p. 29.*)

That a new government was necessary was the universal opinion; but the difficulty was, in agreeing what additional powers should be given to congress by the surrender of the states; no statesman or jurist pretended that this could be done in any other way than by the voluntary act of the separate states; in their sovereign capacity, by the people in conventions. . . .

The powers of the general government are made up of concessions from the several states; whatever is not expressly given to the former, the latter expressly reserves;" 7 Cr. 33; United States v. Hudson and Goodwin. (*Mr. Justice Baldwin, A General View of the Origin and Nature of the Constitution and Government of the United States, 1837, pp. 66-67.*)

On the other hand, if the government is admitted to be the work of the separate people of each state, there can be no pretext for nullification: the sovereign power of the state has made the grant; has declared it the law of the land, supreme in obligation over its own laws and constitution; has commanded its judges to obey it; has appointed a tribunal to expound it; and bound itself to abide by changes to be made by alterations or amendments. (*Mr. Justice Baldwin, A General View of the Origin and Nature of the Constitution and Government of the United States, 1837, p. 101.*)

I go further, and affirm that bills of rights, in the sense and to the extent in which they are contended for, are not only unnecessary in the proposed Constitution, but would even be dangerous. They would contain various exceptions to powers not granted; and, on this very account, would afford a colorable pretext to claim more than were granted. For why declare that things shall not be done which there is no power to do? Why, for instance, should it be said that the liberty of the press shall not be restrained, when no power is given by which restrictions may be imposed? . . . This may serve as a specimen of the numerous handles which would be given to the doctrine of constructive powers, by the indulgence of an injudicious zeal for bills of rights. . . .

There remains but one other view of this matter to conclude the point. The truth is, after all the declamations we have heard, that the Constitution is itself in every rational sense, and to every useful purpose, A BILL OF RIGHTS. The several bills of rights in Great Britain form its constitution, and conversely the constitution of each State is its bill of rights. And the proposed Constitution, if adopted, will be the bill of rights of the Union. (*Alexander Hamilton in The Federalist, No. 84, 1788, Paul Leicester Ford, Editor, 1898, pp. 573-575.*)

ARTICLES IN ADDITION TO, AND AMENDMENT OF, THE CONSTITUTION OF THE UNITED STATES OF AMERICA, PROPOSED BY CONGRESS (1789), AND RATIFIED BY THE LEGISLATURES OF THE SEVERAL STATES (1789-1791) PURSUANT TO THE FIFTH ARTICLE OF THE ORIGINAL CONSTITUTION.

ARTICLE I.

Congress shall make no law respecting an establishment of religion, or prohibiting the free exercise thereof; or abridging the freedom of speech, or of the press; or the right of the people peaceably to assemble, and to petition the Government for a redress of grievances.

ARTICLE II.

A well regulated Militia, being necessary to the security of a free State, the right of the people to keep and bear Arms, shall not be infringed.

ARTICLE III.

No Soldier shall, in time of peace be quartered in any house, without the consent of the Owner, nor in time of war, but in a manner to be prescribed by law.

ARTICLE IV.

The right of the people to be secure in their persons, houses, papers, and effects, against unreasonable searches and seizures, shall not be violated, and no Warrants shall issue, but upon probable cause, supported by Oath or affirmation, and particularly describing the place to be searched, and the persons or things to be seized.

ARTICLE V.

No person shall be held to answer for a capital, or otherwise infamous crime, unless on a presentment or indictment of a Grand Jury, except in cases arising in the land or naval forces, or in the Militia, when in actual service in time of War or public danger; nor shall any person be subject for the same offence to be twice put in jeopardy of life or limb; nor shall be compelled in any Criminal Case to be a witness against himself, nor be deprived of life, liberty, or property, without due process of law; nor shall private property be taken for public use, without just compensation.

ARTICLE VI.

In all criminal prosecutions, the accused shall enjoy the right to a speedy and public trial, by an impartial jury of the State and district wherein the crime shall have been committed, which district shall have been previously ascertained by law, and to be informed of the nature and cause of the accusation; to be confronted with the witnesses against him; to have compulsory process for obtaining Witnesses in his favor, and to have the Assistance of Counsel for his defence.

ARTICLE VII.

In suits at common law, where the value in controversy shall exceed twenty dollars, the right of trial by jury shall be preserved, and no fact tried by a jury shall be otherwise re-examined in any Court of the United States, than according to the rules of the common law.

ARTICLE VIII.

Excessive bail shall not be required, nor excessive fines imposed, nor cruel and unusual punishments inflicted.

ARTICLE IX.

The enumeration in the Constitution, of certain rights, shall not be construed to deny or disparage others retained by the people.

ARTICLE X.

The powers not delegated to the United States by the Constitution, nor prohibited by it to the States, are reserved to the States respectively, or to the people.

It has been said that the liberty which the Anglo-Saxon race everywhere enjoys is derived from the British Constitution as settled by the Revolution of 1688. All subsequent revolutions in Europe are not more plainly the offspring of the French Revolution than was ours of the Revolution of 1688. It was founded, like that, upon a breach of the fundamental law by the rulers. The language of the State Conventions at the time of the separation from England shows that the people universally regarded the liberties for which they were contending as an inheritance from their forefathers. When their independence was achieved, the object of the people was still to preserve under the new conditions these ancient liberties. "Upon that body and stock of inheritance," to adopt the language of Burke in reference to the Whig leaders of 1688, "they took care not to inoculate any scion alien to the nature of the original plant." Although the framers of our Constitution were without any grasp of the modern conception of the historical continuity of the race, they revered the ancient constitutional traditions of England. And thus it comes to pass that Magna Charta, the Acts of the Long Parliament, the Declaration of Right, the Declaration of Independence, and the Constitution of 1787 constitute the record of an evolution. (*W. T. Brantly, Of the Influence of European Speculation in the Formation of the Federal Constitution, 1880, the Southern Law Review, New Series, Vol. VI, 1881, pp. 351-352.*)

The first ten amendments were adopted immediately after the Constitution. Several States had ratified it upon the faith of the pledge given by the Federalists that such amendments would be made. They are in the nature of a Bill of Rights, the unwise omission of which from the Constitution was made the subject of loud complaint. These amendments recite the immemorial privileges of British subjects, and employ in some instances the very words of Magna Charta and the Declaration of Right. (*W. T. Brantly, Of the Influence of European Speculation in the Formation of the Federal Constitution, 1880, The Southern Law Review, New Series, Vol. VI, 1881, p. 366.*)

The several agreements in England for better securing the rights and liberties of the subjects, were the models for the "Bill of Rights," as distinguished in some state constitutions from the "Frame of Government." The more farsighted saw this distinction to be illusory, and justly observed that the constitution was itself a "Bill of Rights." (*James Harvey Robinson, The Original and Derived Features of the Constitution, 1890, Annals of the American Academy of Political and Social Science, 1890-1891, Vol. I, p. 209.*)

In its chief features, then, we find our Constitution to be a skillful synthesis of elements carefully selected from those entering into the composition of the then existing state governments. The Convention "was led astray by no theories of what *might* be good, but clave closely to what experience had demonstrated to be good." (*James Harvey Robinson, The Original and Derived Features of the Constitution, 1890, Annals of the American Academy of Political and Social Science, 1890-1891, Vol. I, p. 242.*)

CHAPTER XVI

GOVERNMENT SET UP: AMENDMENTS

I⊤ was foreseen by the members of the Convention that if a constitution *Per Interim* were to be formed which would meet the approval of the States, a period would necessarily elapse between its adoption and the organization of the government under its provisions. In the meantime the Congress of the Confederation would need to continue, and it would be required to take measures to institute the new government. The twelfth of Mr. Randolph's resolutions dealt in general terms with this question, to the effect that "provision ought to be made for the continuance of Congress and their authorities and privileges, until a given day after the reform of the articles of Union shall be adopted." The first draft of the Constitution prepared by the Committee of Detail and reported by it on August 6th went more into particulars, but not wholly to the satisfaction of the Convention, which slightly amended and adopted the twenty-third Article in the session of August 31st. It was, however, thought best that the Article, being of a temporary nature, be stricken from the Constitution, and be included in the formal letter of the President of the Convention transmitting the Constitution to the Congress, in which document it is thus worded:

> That it is the Opinion of this Convention, that as soon as the Conventions of nine States shall have ratified this Constitution, the United States in Congress assembled should fix a Day on which Electors should be appointed by the States which shall have ratified the same, and a Day on which the Electors should assemble to vote for the President, and the Time and Place for commencing Proceedings under this Constitution. That after such Publication the Electors should be appointed, and the Senators and Representatives elected: That the Electors should meet on the Day fixed for the Election of the President, and should transmit their Votes certified, signed, sealed and directed, as the Constitution requires, to the Secretary of the United States in Congress assembled, that the Senators and Representatives should convene at the Time and Place assigned; that the Senators should appoint a President of the Senate, for the sole Purpose of receiving, opening and counting the Votes for President; and, that after he shall be chosen, the Congress, together with the President, should, without Delay, proceed to execute this Constitution.[1]

Upon the ratification of the Constitution by the ninth of the States, the Congress, to which the Constitution had been transmitted, was in a position

[1] *Documentary History of the Constitution*, Vol. II, pp. 20–1.

to take the necessary action.   Therefore on July 2, 1788, it was, upon the suggestion of the President of that body, " Ordered, That the ratifications of the constitution of the United States transmitted to Congress be referred to a Com^{ee}. to examine the same and report an Act to Congress for putting the said constitution into operation in pursuance of the resolutions of the late federal Convention." [1]   The motion passing in the affirmative, the committee to which the ratifications were referred reported on July 14, 1788,— a year to a day before the storming of the Bastille, ushering in the new order of things in the Old World—an act for this purpose, which was adopted on September 13, 1788, in the following form:

> Whereas the Convention assembled in Philadelphia pursuant to the resolution of Congress of the 21st. of Feby. 1787 did on the 17th. of Sep^{t}. in the same year report to the United States in Congress assembled a constitution for the people of the United States, Whereupon Congress on the 28 of the same Sept. did resolve unanimously " That the said report with the resolutions & letter accompanying the same be transmitted to the several legislatures in order to be submitted to a convention of Delegates chosen in each state by the people thereof in conformity to the resolves of the convention made and provided in that case " And whereas the constitution so reported by the Convention and by Congress transmitted to the several legislatures has been ratified in the manner therein declared to be sufficient for the establishment of the same and such ratifications duly authenticated have been received by Congress and are filed in the Office of the Secretary therefore Resolved That the first Wednesday in Jany. next be the day for appointing Electors in the several states, which before the said day shall have ratified the said Constitution; that the first Wednesday in feb^{y}. next be the day for the electors to assemble in their respective states and vote for a president; And that the first Wednesday in March next be the time and the present seat of Congress the place for commencing proceedings under the said constitution.[2]

The New Government Begun

The elections were held in the States which had ratified the Constitution. On March 4, 1789, the government under the Constitution began in the city of New York, where on April 30, 1789, George Washington, the unanimous choice of the electors, was inaugurated President of the United States.

The great purpose for which the delegates had assembled in convention throughout the summer of 1787 was accomplished.   A Constitution creating a more perfect Union of the States had been formed, and the government thereunder organized.   But the apprehensions of the States which had ratified the Constitution with much difficulty and, in certain cases, with no little misgiving, remained to be satisfied.   If the declarations, explanations, and proposed amendments which accompanied the ratifications in some instances did not create a legal, they nevertheless raised a moral, obligation to propose

---

[1] *Documentary History*, Vol. II, p. 161.
[2] *Ibid.*, pp. 263–4.

amendments to the Constitution in accordance with its provisions in order to meet the expressed desires of States which might not have ratified the Constitution without assurances amounting to a moral certainty that appropriate steps would be taken to this end.

Accordingly, on June 8, 1789, in the first session of the first Congress held under the Constitution, Mr. Madison, then a member of the House of Representatives from Virginia, moved in that body, in accordance with notice to that effect of the 4th instant, the consideration of various amendments to the Constitution.   In support of the motion he said:

> this house is bound by every motive of prudence, not to let the first session pass over without proposing to the state legislatures some things to be incorporated into the constitution, as will render it as acceptable to the whole people of the United States, as it has been found acceptable to a majority of them. . . .
>
> It cannot be a secret to the gentlemen in this house, that, notwithstanding the ratification of this system of government by eleven of the thirteen United States, in some cases unanimously, in others by large majorities; yet still there is a great number of our constituents who are dissatisfied with it; among whom are many respectable for their talents, their patriotism, and respectable for the jealousy they have for their liberty, which, though mistaken in its object, is laudable in its motive. . . . We ought not to disregard their inclination, but, on principles of amity and moderation, conform to their wishes, and expressly declare the great rights of mankind secured under this constitution.[1]

Mr. Madison then alluded to the two States " that have not thought fit to throw themselves into the bosom of the confederacy," and, saying on this point that " it is a desirable thing, on our part as well as theirs, that a re-union should take place as soon as possible," he predicted if measures should be taken at that juncture which were both prudent and requisite, " that in a short time we should see that disposition prevailing in those states that are not come in, that we have seen prevailing in those states which are.[2]

After stating that all power is subject to abuse, and admitting that it was possible to guard more securely against possible abuse of the powers granted to the general government than had been done, he said that by so doing they had something to gain and nothing to lose.   While unwilling to offer amendments going to the whole structure of the government, he was nevertheless willing to propose such as seemed likely in his opinion to meet " with the concurrence of two-thirds of both houses, and the approbation of three-fourths of the state legislatures," assuring the House that he would not propose a single alteration which he did not wish to see made, and which in

---

[1] *The Congressional Register*, Vol. I, pp. 424-5.
[2] *Ibid.*, p. 425.

Amendments
Moved

his opinion was "intrinsically proper in itself, or proper because it is wished for by a respectable number" of his fellow citizens.

Passing to the objections which had been made against the Constitution, he said that they were of various kinds. "Some were levelled against its structure, because the president was without a council; because the senate, which is a legislative body, had judicial powers in trials on impeachments; and because the powers of that body were compounded in other respects, in a manner that did not correspond with a particular theory; because it grants more power than is supposed to be necessary for every good purpose, and controuls the ordinary powers of the state governments." [1]

Demand
for a Bill
of Rights

But Mr. Madison avowed his belief that "the great mass of the people who opposed it, disliked it because it did not contain effectual provision against the encroachments on particular rights, and those safeguards which they have been long accustomed to have interposed between them and the magistrate who exercised the sovereign power; nor ought we to consider them safe, while a great number of our fellow citizens think these securities necessary." That is to say, that while certain provisions of the Constitution were objected to, the great criticism directed against it, as a whole, was that it did not contain a bill of rights. Such a bill of rights was necessary for the protection of the people of the States against the abusive power on the part of the general government making it clear to them; although it seemed evident to Mr. Madison, that the powers not granted to the general government under the Constitution were reserved to the States, and therefore beyond the reach of the United States as such.

Mr. Madison further declared that he did not believe in the necessity of a bill of rights, but that he considered one neither improper nor altogether useless. Adverting to the bills of this nature passed by the States, he thus analyzed their content:

"In some instances they assert those rights which are exercised by the people in forming and establishing a plan of government. In other instances, they specify those rights which are retained when particular powers are given up to be exercised by the legislature. In other instances, they specify positive rights, which may seem to result from the nature of the compact. . . . In other instances, they lay down dogmatic maxims with respect to the construction of the government; declaring, that the legislative, executive, and judicial branches shall be kept separate and distinct. . . .

But whatever may be [the] form which the several states have adopted in making declarations in favor of particular rights, the great object in view is to limit and qualify the powers of government, by excepting out of the grant of power those cases in which the government ought not to act, or to act only in a particular mode. They point these exceptions sometimes against the abuse of the executive power, sometimes against the legislative,

[1] *The Congressional Register*, Vol. i, p. 426.

and, in some cases, against the community itself; or, in other words, against the majority in favor of the minority." [1]

Without enumerating the amendments which Mr. Madison proposed, which, for the most part were adopted in substance, if not in form, there is one matter upon which his exact language should be quoted, as it deals with the relation of the States to the Union and the powers which they apparently thought they reserved from the grant to the general government. On this point Mr. Madison said: Relation of States to the Union

"I find, from looking into the amendments proposed by the state conventions, that several are particularly anxious that it should be declared in the constitution, that the powers not therein delegated, should be reserved to the several states. Perhaps words which may define this more precisely, than the whole of the instrument now does, may be considered as superfluous. I admit they may be deemed unnecessary; but there can be no harm in making such a declaration, if gentlemen will allow that the fact is as stated, I am sure I understand it so, and do therefore propose it." [2]

After some discussion Mr. Madison's motion was referred to a Committee of the Whole on the state of the Union. On July 21st when he brought the question of amendments again to the attention of the House, it was ordered after debate, " that Mr. Madison's motion, stating certain specific amendments, proper to be proposed by congress to the legislatures of the states, to become, if ratified by three-fourths thereof, part of the constitution of the United States, together with the amendments to the said constitution as proposed by the several states, to be referred to a committee, to consist of a member from each state, with instruction to take the subject of amendments to the constitution of the United States, generally into their consideration, and to report thereupon to the house." [3]

On July 27th the Committee reported, and the report was ordered to lie on the table. On August 13th the House took up the report of the Committee and debated it continuously, during the course of which other amendments were proposed. On August 22nd an agreement was reached upon the amendments to be submitted, and on the 24th, a committee appointed for rearrangement of the articles of amendments to the Constitution as agreed to on the 21st, presented its report with the following resolution to be prefixed to them:

Resolved, by the senate and house of representatives of the United States of America in Congress assembled, two thirds of both houses deeming it necessary, that the following articles be proposed to the legislatures

[1] *Ibid.,* pp. 430-1.
[2] *Ibid.,* p. 436.
[3] *Ibid.,* Vol. ii, p. 111.

of the several states as amendments to the constitution of the United States, all of any of which articles, when ratified by three fourths of the said legislatures, to be valid to all intents and purposes as part of the said constitution.[1]

The House immediately transmitted the proposed amendments, seventeen in number, to the Senate for their consideration, where they were received on the 25th, and considered on September 2d, 4th, 7th, and 25th. The Senate as the result of conference concurred in the amendments proposed by the House of Representatives to the amendments of the Senate, and the following twelve were transmitted by the President of the United States to the Executives of the eleven States which had ratified the Constitution, and likewise to those of the States of Rhode Island and North Carolina.

Article the first. . . . After the first enumeration required by the first Article of the Constitution, there shall be one Representative for every thirty thousand, until the number shall amount to one hundred, after which, the proportion shall be so regulated by Congress, that there shall not be less than one hundred Representatives, nor less than one Representative for every forty thousand persons, until the number of Representatives shall amount to two hundred, after which the proportion shall be so regulated by Congress, that there shall not be less than two hundred Representatives, nor more than one Representative for every fifty thousand persons.

Article the second. . . . No law, varying the compensation for the services of the Senators and Representatives, shall take effect, until an election of Representatives shall have intervened.

Article the third. . . . Congress shall make no law respecting an establishment of religion, or prohibiting the free exercise thereof; or abridging the freedom of speech, or of the press; or the right of the people peaceably to assemble, and to petition the Government for a redress of grievances.

Article the fourth. . . . A well regulated Militia, being necessary to the security of a free State, the right of the people to keep and bear Arms, shall not be infringed.

Article the fifth. . . . No Soldier shall, in time of peace be quartered in any house, without the consent of the Owner, nor in time of war, but in a manner to be prescribed by law.

Article the sixth. . . . The right of the people to be secure in their persons, houses, papers, and effects, against unreasonable searches and seizures, shall not be violated, and no Warrants shall issue, but upon probable cause, supported by Oath or affirmation, and particularly describing the place to be searched, and the persons or things to be seized.

Article the seventh. . . . No person shall be held to answer for a capital, or otherwise infamous crime, unless on a presentment or indictment of a Grand Jury, except in cases arising in the land or naval forces, or in the Militia, when in actual service in time of War or public danger; nor shall any person be subject for the same offence to be twice put in jeopardy of life or limb; nor shall be compelled in any criminal case to be a witness against himself, nor be

---

[1] *Congressional Register*, Vol. II, p. 259.

deprived of life, liberty, or property, without due process of law; nor shall private property be taken for public use, without just compensation.

Article the eighth. . . . In all criminal prosecutions, the accused shall enjoy the right of a speedy and public trial, by an impartial jury of the State and district wherein the crime shall have been committed, which district shall have been previously ascertained by law, and to be informed of the nature and cause of the accusation; to be confronted with the witnesses against him; to have compulsory process for obtaining witnesses in his favor; and to have the Assistance of Counsel for his defence.

Article the ninth. . . . In Suits at common law, where the value in controversy shall exceed twenty dollars, the right of trial by jury shall be preserved, and no fact tried by a jury, shall be otherwise re-examined, in any Court of the United States, than according to the rules of the common law.

Article the tenth. . . . Excessive bail shall not be required, nor excessive fines imposed, nor cruel and unusual punishments inflicted.

Article the eleventh. . . . The enumeration in the Constitution, of certain rights, shall not be construed to deny or disparage others retained by the people.

Article the twelfth. . . . The powers not delegated to the United States by the Constitution, nor prohibited by it to the States, are reserved to the States respectively, or to the people.[1]

Mr. Madison, who is to be regarded not merely as the father of the Constitution but as the initiator of the amendments to that instrument, had proposed that the amendments themselves should not only modify the sense of the Constitution, but that they should be incorporated in the text in lieu of the rejected matter. But fortunately the view prevailed that the text of the instrument should be preserved inviolate, and that the amendments, in the form of articles, should be added to its text. It is perhaps also of interest to add that the amendments, reasonable and acceptable in themselves, proposed by the opponents of the Constitution but rejected by the majority of the Convention of Pennsylvania called to consider that instrument, are alleged to have been the source of Mr. Madison's propositions.[2]

Of the twelve amendments submitted to the States, the first two failed for lack of the required majority, but the remaining ten were adopted and form the first ten amendments to the Constitution of the United States. Submitted as they were by the first Congress under the Constitution and adopted within two years thereafter, they can be considered as the authoritative and contemporaneous interpretation of the States of the Union in the matter of their relation to the government of the Union, which the States had created by vesting it with certain powers whereof they divested them-

[1] *Documentary History,* Vol. II, pp. 321–4.

[2] They are fifteen in number, and are remarkable as containing the substance of the ten amendments afterwards added to the Constitution. Similarity so marked can not be accidental. There is much reason, therefore, to believe that when Mr. Madison, in 1789, drew up the amendments for the House of Representatives, he made use of those offered by the minority of the Convention of Pennsylvania. See *Pennsylvania and the Federal Constitution,* McMaster and Stone ed., 1888, p. 19. The text of the amendments is to be found on pp. 321–3 of that volume.

selves. The ten amendments are in their entirety limitations upon the general power of the Government. The ninth and tenth cannot be too often pondered by those who would understand the nature of the more perfect Union created by the Constitution, and who would like to see something of the kind obtain in the society of nations. They are therefore quoted:

> The enumeration in the Constitution, of certain rights, shall not be construed to deny or disparage others retained by the people. (Article IX.)
> The powers not delegated to the United States by the Constitution, nor prohibited by it to the States, are reserved to the States respectively, or to the people. (Article X.)

It is believed that there would have been little opposition within and without the Federal Convention to a bill of rights composed of the matters included within the first ten amendments, which are themselves in the nature of a bill of rights. It is not too much to say that, if such a course had been taken, opposition to the Constitution would have been largely disarmed, if not rendered wholly powerless. The truth of the matter seems to be that, as always happens in an international conference, the discussions moved in a leisurely way at the beginning; that, in the course of its sessions, propositions were made and discussed in such numbers as to impede progress; and that, in the closing days of the session, the members, in sheer desperation to do something to justify their calling and to adjourn within a reasonable period, became excited, not to say irascible; and that they rejected measures which they would otherwise have adopted, on the ground that they were unnecessary or that their adoption would unduly prolong the session, notwithstanding the fact that, if unnecessary, it would not hurt to adopt them, especially as their adoption would tranquilize the minds of their proposers.

Mr. Mason's proposal for a bill of rights,—and perhaps as the framer of the Virginian Bill of Rights he appeared to his colleagues a trifle obsessed with its importance,—received scant consideration, made, as it was, in the closing days. On September 12th Mr. Mason stated that " he wished the plan had been prefaced with a Bill of Rights, & would second a Motion if made for the purpose—It would give great quiet to the people; and with the aid of the State declarations, a bill might be prepared in a few hours." [1] The Convention, however, made short shrift of the proposal, and after other observations in the nature of remarks, the proposal made by Mr. Gerry of Massachusetts and seconded by Mr. Mason was negatived by ten of the eleven States, with Massachusetts abstaining.

The spirit of the Convention at this time is perhaps best shown by the

---

[1] *Documentary History*, Vol. III, p. 734.

action of the Convention on the 15th, when a proposal was made that an address should be prepared to the people to accompany the Constitution, inasmuch, as stated by its proposer, as " the people had been accustomed to such on great occasions, and would expect it on this." To this proposal Mr. Rutledge of South Carolina objected, " on account of the delay it would produce and the impropriety of addressing the people before it was known whether Congress would approve and support the plan." The motion was rejected by a vote of six States to four, with North Carolina abstaining.[1]

Many years after the adjournment of the Convention, Mr. Madison, speaking of the method of electing the President, said, in a letter dated August 23, 1823, addressed to Mr. George Hay:

> As the final arrangement of it took place in the latter stage of the Session, it was not exempt from a degree of the hurrying influence produced by fatigue and impatience in all such Bodies, tho' the degree was much less than usually prevails in them.[2]

The general view on the subject of a bill of rights, at least the view of the moderate reformers, is best expressed by Washington in a letter to Lafayette, dated April 28, 1788, in which he says:

> There was not a member of the convention, I believe, who had the least objection to what is contended for by the advocates for a *Bill of Rights* and *Trial by Jury*. The first, where the people evidently retained every thing, which they did not in express terms give up, was considered nugatory . . . and, as to the second, it was only the difficulty of establishing a mode, which should not interfere with the fixed modes of any of the States, that induced the convention to leave it as a matter of future adjustment.[3]

Writing many years after the event, Mr. Madison himself used the following language in a letter dated November 27, 1830, addressed to Mr. Andrew Stevenson, which states better than any amount of argument Mr. Mason's case:

> Besides the restrictive & explanatory amendments to the text of the Constitution it may be observed, that a long list was premised under the name and in the nature of " Declarations of Rights "; all of them indicating a jealousy of the federal powers, and an anxiety to multiply securities against a constructive enlargement of them. But the appeal is more particularly made to the number & nature of the amendments proposed to be made specific & integral parts of the Constitutional text.
>
> No less than seven States, it appears, concurred in adding to their rati-

---

[1] *Ibid.*, Vol. iii, p. 749.
[2] *The Writings of James Madison*, Hunt ed., Vol. ix, p. 147.
[3] Ford, *The Writings of George Washington*, Vol. ii, p. 256; Sparks, Vol. ix, pp. 357-8.

fications a series of amendments, wch. they deemed requisite. Of these amendments, *nine* were proposed by the Convention of Massachusetts, *five* by that of S. Carolina, *twelve* by that of N. Hampshire, *twenty* by that of Virginia, *thirty-three* by that of N. York, *twenty-six* by that of N. Carolina, *twenty-one* by that of R. Island.

Here are a majority of the States, proposing amendments, in one instance thirty-three by a single State; all of them intended to circumscribe the powers granted to the General Government, by explanations, restrictions or prohibitions.[1]

Value of
the
Amendments

Experience has shown that the amendments to the Constitution, in substance though not in form a Bill of Rights, were not useless. They have been frequently invoked on appropriate occasions, and they have been the subject of many appeals to the Supreme Court. They are, we believe universal truths and therefore susceptible of universal application; and indeed but yesterday they were weighed and found not wanting by a distinguished Secretary of War, who restated them with slight changes, and additions, and prescribed them for the government of the Philippines in 1900. Thus Mr. Root said in his instructions approved by the President on April 7, 1900:

It is evident that the most enlightened thought of the Philippine Islands fully appreciates the importance of these principles and rules, and they will inevitably within a short time command universal assent. Upon every division and branch of the government of the Philippines, therefore, must be imposed these inviolable rules:

That no person shall be deprived of life, liberty, or property without due process of law; that private property shall not be taken for public use without just compensation; that in all criminal prosecutions the accused shall enjoy the right to a speedy and public trial, to be informed of the nature and cause of the accusation, to be confronted with the witnesses against him, to have compulsory process for obtaining witnesses in his favor, and to have the assistance of counsel for his defense; that excessive bail shall not be required, nor excessive fines imposed, nor cruel and unusual punishment inflicted; that no person shall be put twice in jeopardy for the same offense, or be compelled in any criminal case to be a witness against himself; that the right to be secure against unreasonable searches and seizures shall not be violated; that neither slavery nor involuntary servitude shall exist except as a punishment for crime; that no bill of attainder or *ex post facto* law shall be passed; that no law shall be passed abridging the freedom of speech or of the press, or the rights of the people peaceably to assemble and petition the Government for a redress of grievances; that no law shall be made respecting an establishment of religion or prohibiting the free exercise thereof, and that the free exercise and enjoyment of religious profession and worship without discrimination or preference shall forever be allowed.[2]

---

[1] *Writings of Madison*, Vol. ix, pp. 421–2.
[2] Elihu Root, *The Military and Colonial Policy of the United States*, Robert Bacon and J. B. Scott ed., pp. 291–2.

And in the case of *Kepner* v. *United States* (195 U. S., 100, 123–4), decided by the Supreme Court in 1903, Mr. Justice Day, speaking of these instructions, thus comments upon them:

> These words are not strange to the American lawyer or student of constitutional history. They are the familiar language of the Bill of Rights, slightly changed in form, but not in substance, as found in the first nine amendments to the Constitution of the United States, with the omission of the provision preserving the right to trial by jury and the right of the people to bear arms, and adding the prohibition of the Thirteenth Amendment against slavery or involuntary servitude except as a punishment for crime, and that of Art. 1, § 9, to the passage of bills of attainder and *ex post facto* laws. These principles were not taken from the Spanish law; they were carefully collated from our own Constitution, and embody almost verbatim the safeguards of that instrument for the protection of life and liberty.

In interpreting the Constitution it must always be borne in mind that, while the intent of the framers of that instrument is important, as showing the meaning which they ascribed to it, the greatest weight must be given to the proceedings in the State Conventions ratifying the Constitution and to the first ten amendments which are, as already stated, in the nature of an authoritative and contemporaneous interpretation put upon the Constitution by three-fourths and more of the States in the exercise of their rights under the Constitution. It is believed that these principles of interpretation, constituting as they do a perfect canon of construction, have never been better stated than by Mr. Madison, who would have been supposed to be inclined to favor the views of the framers, because of his membership in the Convention and his authorship of the Notes in which their views are preserved, to the detriment of the authority of the State conventions. Thus, Mr. Madison said:

State Convention

The First Ten Amendments

> But, after all, whatever veneration might be entertained for the body of men who formed our Constitution, the sense of that body could never be regarded as the oracular guide in expounding the Constitution. As the instrument came from them it was nothing more than the draft of a plan, nothing but a dead letter, until life and validity were breathed into it by the voice of the people, speaking through the several State Conventions. If we were to look, therefore, for the meaning of the instrument beyond the face of the instrument, we must look for it, not in the General Convention, which proposed, but in the State Conventions, which accepted and ratified the Constitution.[1]
> As a guide in expounding and applying the provisions of the Constitution, the debates and incidental decisions of the Convention can have no authoritative character. However desirable it be that they should be pre-

---

[1] James Madison in the House of Representatives. *Annals of Congress*, Fourth Congress, First Session, p. 776.

served as a gratification to the laudable curiosity felt by every people to trace the origin and progress of their political Institutions, & as a source perhaps of some lights on the Science of Gov^t. the legitimate meaning of the Instrument must be derived from the text itself; or if a key is to be sought elsewhere, it must be not in the opinions or intentions of the Body which planned & proposed the Constitution, but in the sense attached to it by the people in their respective State Conventions where it rec^d. all the Authority which it possesses.[1]

I must say that the real measure of the powers meant to be granted to Congress by the Convention, as I understood and believe, is to be sought in the specifications, to be expounded indeed not with the strictness applied to an ordinary statute by a Court of Law; nor on the other hand with a latitude that under the name of means for carrying into execution a limited Government, would transform it into a Government without limits.[2]

And finally, in speaking of the difference of opinion between Colonel Hamilton, on the one side, and himself, on the other, Mr. Madison said, as reported by Mr. N. P. Trist in his Memoranda, under date of September 27, 1834, but two years before Mr. Madison's death:

> In a word, the divergence between us took place—from his wishing to *administration,* or rather to administer the Government (these were Mr. M.'s very words), into what he thought it ought to be; while, on my part, I endeavored to make it conform to the Constitution as understood by the Convention that produced and recommended it, and particularly by the State conventions that *adopted* it.[3]

Difficulties Overcome

Perhaps the difficulties of forming the more perfect Union under the Constitution and of the influence which it was foreseen it might have upon the society of nations have never been better stated than by the two great members of the Convention, whose presence alone would have rendered that conference of the States illustrious. Thus, George Washington said in a letter dated November 16, 1787, addressed to Mrs. Macaulay Graham:

> The various and opposite interests which were to be conciliated, the local prejudices which were to be subdued, the diversity of opinions and sentiments which were to be reconciled, and, in fine, the sacrifices which were necessary to be made on all sides for the general welfare, combined to make it a work of so intricate and difficult a nature, that I think it is much to be wondered at, that any thing could have been produced with such unanimity as the constitution proposed.[4]

Thus Benjamin Franklin wrote in a letter to Mr. Grand dated October 22, 1787:

[1] James Madison to Thomas Ritchie, September 15, 1821. *Writings of Madison,* Vol. ix, pp. 71-2, note.
[2] James Madison to M. L. Hurlbert, May, 1830. *Ibid.,* pp. 371-2.
[3] H. S. Randall, *Life of Thomas Jefferson,* Vol. iii, p. 595.
[4] Sparks, *The Writings of Washington,* Vol. ix, p. 283.

If it succeeds, I do not see why you might not in Europe carry the Project of good Henry the 4th into Execution, by forming a Federal Union and One Grand Republick of all its different States & Kingdoms, by means of a like Convention, for we had many Interests to reconcile.[1]

In an address on the United States Supreme Court and the sovereignty of the people, delivered in 1890, the late Mr. Edward John Phelps, a distinguished lawyer of the United States, its Minister Plenipotentiary and Envoy Extraordinary to Great Britain and leading counsel before the Behring Sea Commission of 1893, finely said: " American experience has made it an axiom in political science that no written constitution of government can hope to stand without a paramount and independent tribunal to determine its construction and to enforce its precepts in the last resort. This is the great and foremost duty cast by the Constitution, for the sake of the Constitution, upon the Supreme Court of the United States." [2]

The construction placed by the States of the Union upon the Constitution would seem to indicate to the unprejudiced mind that at that time they regarded themselves as States, not provinces, entering into union, granting all powers to the Union of their creation which it could exercise, and reserving to themselves the exercise of powers which they had not directly granted or which they had not granted by necessary implication, or whose exercise by themselves they had not renounced in the common good. The Supreme Court of the United States, which is the " paramount and independent tribunal," to quote Mr. Phelps' language, " to determine its construction," has repeatedly, in the hundred years and more following the institution of the Government under the Constitution, been called upon to interpret that charter of government in cases presented to it and properly involving its provisions, and it has, from its first to its last decision, spoken the uniform language of statesman and of jurist, irrespective of section or party. Thus, Mr. Justice Iredell said, in his dissenting opinion in the case of *Chisholm* v. *Georgia,* (2 Dallas, 419, 435), decided in 1793, an opinion approved by the 11th amendment to the Constitution of the United States: *The Sovereignty of the States*

Every State in the *Union,* in every instance where its sovereignty has not been delegated to the *United States,* I consider to be as compleatly sovereign, as the *United States* are in respect to the powers surrendered. The *United States* are sovereign as to all the powers of Government actually surrendered: Each State in the *Union* is sovereign as to all the powers reserved. It must necessarily be so, because the *United States* have no claim to any authority but *such as the States have surrendered to them:* Of course the part not surrendered must remain as it did before.

[1] A. H. Smyth, *The Writings of Benjamin Franklin,* Vol. ix, p. 619.
[2] Phelps, *Orations and Essays,* pp. 58–9.

To the same effect, Mr. Justice Story said, in delivering the opinion of the Supreme Court in *Martin* v. *Hunter* (1 Wheaton, 304, 325–6), decided in 1816:

> On the other hand, it is perfectly clear that the sovereign powers vested in the state governments, by their respective constitutions, remained unaltered and unimpaired, except so far as they were granted to the government of the United States.
>
> These deductions do not rest upon general reasoning, plain and obvious as they seem to be. They have been positively recognised by one of the articles in amendment of the constitution, which declares, that " the powers not delegated to the United States by the constitution, nor prohibited by it to the states, are reserved to the *states* respectively, or *to the people.*"
>
> The government, then, of the United States can claim no powers which are not granted to it by the constitution, and the powers actually granted, must be such as are expressly given, or given by necessary implication.

The great Chief Justice of the United States, John Marshall, said, in delivering the unanimous opinion of his brethren of the court in *McCulloch* v. *Maryland* (4 Wheaton, 316, 403, 410), decided in 1819:

The Division of Sovereign Powers

> No political dreamer was ever wild enough to think of breaking down the lines which separate the States, and of compounding the American people into one common mass. Of consequence, when they act, they act in their States. . . .
>
> In America, the powers of sovereignty are divided between the government of the Union, and those of the States. They are each sovereign, with respect to the objects committed to it, and neither sovereign with respect to the objects committed to the other.

In a very much later case, when the Civil War might have seemed to the partisan to have changed the relation of the States to the Union and of the Union to the States, Mr. Chief Justice Chase said, in delivering the opinion of the court in *Texas* v. *White* (7 Wallace, 700, 725), decided in 1868, and involving this very relationship:

> Under the Articles of Confederation each State retained its sovereignty, freedom, and independence, and every power, jurisdiction, and right not expressly delegated to the United States. Under the Constitution, though the powers of the States were much restricted, still, all powers not delegated to the United States, nor prohibited to the States, are reserved to the States respectively, or to the people. And we have already had occasion to remark at this term, that " the people of each State compose a State, having its own government, and endowed with all the functions essential to separate and independent existence," and that " without the States in union, there could be no such political body as the United States." Not only, therefore, can there be no loss of separate and independent autonomy to the States, through their union under the Constitution, but it may be not unreasonably said that the preservation of the States, and the maintenance of their governments, are as much within the design and care of the Constitution as the preservation of the Union and the maintenance of the Na-

tional Government. The Constitution, in all its provisions, looks to an indestructible Union, composed of indestructible States.

Two years later, in a case involving an act of Congress in excess of the Constitutional grant of power, affecting an official of one of the States of the Union, and therefore the State, Mr. Justice Nelson, speaking for the court, said, in *Collector* v. *Day* (11 Wallace, 113, 124), decided in 1870:

> The general government, and the States, although both exist within the same territorial limits, are separate and distinct sovereignties, acting separately and independently of each other, within their respective spheres. The former in its appropriate sphere is supreme; but the States within the limits of their powers not granted, or, in the language of the tenth amendment, "reserved," are as independent of the general government as that government within its sphere is independent of the States.

And finally, Mr. Justice Brewer said more recently, in delivering the opinion of the court in *South Carolina* v. *United States* (199 U. S., 437, 448), decided in 1905:

> We have in this Republic a dual system of government, National and state, each operating within the same territory and upon the same persons; and yet working without collision, because their functions are different. There are certain matters over which the National Government has absolute control and no action of the State can interfere therewith, and there are others in which the State is supreme, and in respect to them the National Government is powerless. To preserve the even balance between these two governments and hold each in its separate sphere is the peculiar duty of all courts, preëminently of this—a duty oftentimes of great delicacy and difficulty.

It is believed that the views of accredited publicists, and decisions of the Supreme Court, have been but as a gloss upon the views of Mr. Madison, expressed in a letter to Robert Y. Hayne, United States Senator from South Carolina, taking issue with the theory of the Constitution propounded by that gentleman.

In the draft of this admirable letter dated April 3/4, 1830, Mr. Madison, who would doubtless be called the Father of the Constitution if his modesty had not forbidden it,[1] who was, in any event, the best informed delegate in the Convention, and who afterward became a member of the Congress, Secretary of State, and President of the United States under the Constitution, wrote:

> It appears to me that in deciding on the character of the Constitution of the U. S. it is not sufficiently kept in view that being an unprecedented

[1] "Your letter of the 18th Ult. was duly received. You give me a credit to which I have no claim, in calling me '*the* writer of the Constitution of the U. S.' This was not, like the fabled Goddess of Wisdom, the offspring of a single brain. It ought to be regarded as the work of many heads & many hands." Extract from letter of James Madison to William Cogswell, March 10, 1834, from the Madison MSS. in the Library of Congress. See also, *The Writings of James Madison*, Hunt, Editor, Vol. IX (1910), pp. 533-534.

modification of the powers of Gov^t. it must not be looked at thro' the refracting medium either of a consolidated Government, or of a confederated Gov^t; that being essentially different from both, it must be its own interpreter according to its text and *the facts of the case*.

Its characteristic peculiarities are 1. the mode of its formation. 2. its division of the supreme powers of Gov^t. between the States in their united capacity, and the States in their individual capacities.

1. It was formed not by the Governments of the States as the Federal Government superseded by it was formed; nor by a majority of the people of the U. S. as a single Community, in the manner of a consolidated Government.

It was formed by the States, that is by the people of each State, acting in their highest sovereign capacity thro' Conventions representing them in that capacity, in like manner and by the same authority as the State Constitutions were formed; with this characteristic & essential difference that the Constitution of the U. S. being a compact among the States that is the people thereof making them the parties to the compact over one people for specified objects can not be revoked or changed at the will of any State within its limits as the Constitution of a State may be changed at the will of the State, that is the people who compose the State & are the parties to its constitution & retained their powers over it. The idea of a compact between the Governors & the Governed was exploded with the Royal doctrine that Government was held by some tenure independent of the people.

The Constitution of the U. S. is therefore within its prescribed sphere a Constitution in as strict a sense of the term as are the Constitutions of the individual States, within their respective spheres.

2. And that it divides the supreme powers of Gov^t between the two Governments is seen on the face of it; the powers of war & taxation, that is of the sword & the purse, of commerce of treaties &c. vested in the Gov^t of the U. S. being of as high a character as any of the powers reserved to the State Gov^{ts}.

If we advert to the Gov^t of the U. S. as created by the Constitution it is found also to be a Gov^t in as strict a sense of the term, within the sphere of its powers, as the Gov^{ts} created by the Constitutions of the States are within their respective spheres. It is like them organized into a Legislative, Executive & Judicial Dep^t It has, like them, acknowledged cases in which the powers of those Departments are to operate and the operation is to be the same in both; that is *directly* on the persons & things submitted to their power. The concurrent operation in certain cases is one of the features constituting the peculiarity of the system.

Between these two Constitutional Gov^{ts}, the one operating in all the States, the others operating in each respectively; with the aggregate powers of Gov^t divided between them, it could not escape attention, that controversies concerning the boundary of Jurisdiction would arise, and that without some adequate provision for deciding them, conflicts of physical force might ensue. A political system that does not provide for a peaceable & authoritative termination of occurring controversies, can be but the name & shadow of a Gov^t the very object and end of a real Gov^t being the substitution of law & order for uncertainty confusion & violence.

That a final decision of such controversies, if left to each of 13 State now 24 with a prospective increase, would make the Constitution & laws of the U. S. different in different States, was obvious; and equally obvious that this diversity of independent decisions must disorganize the Government of the Union, and even decompose the Union itself.

Against such fatal consequences the Constitution undertakes to guard 1. by declaring that the Constitution & laws of the States in their united capacity shall have effect, anything in the Constitution or laws of any State in its individual capacity to the contrary notwithstanding, by giving to the Judicial authority of the U. S. an appellate supremacy in all cases arising under the Constitution; & within the course of its functions, arrangements supposed to be justified by the necessity of the case; and by the agency of the people & Legislatures of the States in electing & appointing the Functionaries of the Common Gov.ᵗ whilst no corresponding relation existed between the latter and the Functionaries of the States.

2. Should these provisions be found notwithstanding the responsibility of the functionaries of the Gov.ᵗ of the U. S. to the Legislatures & people of the States not to secure the State Gov.ᵗˢ against usurpations of the Gov.ᵗ of the United States there remains within the purview of the Const.ⁿ an impeachment of the Executive & Judicial Functionaries, in case of their participation in the guilt, the prosecution to depend on the Representatives of the people in one branch, and the trial on the Representatives of the States in the other branch of the Gov.ᵗ of the U. S.

3. The last resort within the purview of the Const.ⁿ is the process of amendment provided for by itself and to be executed by the States.

Whether these provisions taken together be the best that might have been made; and if not, what are the improvements, that ought to be introduced, are questions altogether distinct from the object presented by your communication, which relates to the Constitution as it stands.

In the event of a failure of all these Constitutional resorts against usurpations and abuses of power and of an accumulation thereof rendering passive obedience & nonresistance a greater evil than resistance and revolution, there can remain but one resort, the last of all, the appeal from the cancelled obligation of the Constitutional compact to original rights and the law of self-preservation. This is the Ultima ratio, under all Governments, whether consolidated, confederated, or partaking of both those characters. Nor can it be doubted that in such an extremity a single State would have a right, tho' it would be a natural not a *constitutional* Right to make the appeal. The same may be said indeed of particular portions of any political community whatever so oppressed as to be driven to a choice between the alternative evils. . . .[1]

[1] *The Writings of James Madison,* Hunt ed., Vol. ix, pp. 383-7.

XVII

THE NATURE OF JUDICIAL POWER

What is judicial power? It will not do to answer that it is the power exercised by the courts, because one of the very things to be determined is what power they may exercise. It is, indeed, very difficult to find any exact definition made to hand. It is not to be found in any of the old treatises, or any of the old English authorities or judicial decisions, for a very obvious reason. While in a general way it may be true that they had this division between legislative and judicial power, yet their legislature was, nevertheless, in the habit of exercising a very large part of the latter. The House of Lords was often the Court of Appeals, and Parliament was in the habit of passing bills of attainder as well as enacting convictions for treason and other crimes.

Judicial power is, perhaps, better defined in some of the reports of our own courts than in any other place, and especially so in the Supreme Court of the United States, because it has more often been the subject of comment there, and its consideration more frequently necessary to the determination of questions arising in that court than anywhere else. It is the power of a court to decide and pronounce a judgment and carry it into effect between persons and parties who bring a case before it for decision. (*Mr. Justice Miller, Lectures on the Constitution of the United States, 1891, pp. 313-314.*)

As to what is meant by the phrase "judicial power," see *Callanan* v. *Judd*, 23 Wisconsin, 343, 349. Also charge of Judge Nelson to grand jury of the Circuit Court, 1851, that it is the power conferred upon courts in the strict sense of that term; courts that compose one of the great departments of the government; and not power judicial in its nature, or *quasi* judicial, invested from time to time in individuals, separately or collectively, for a particular purpose and limited time. 1 Blatchford, 635. *Gilbert* v. *Priest*, 65 Barb. 444, 448. (*Mr. Justice Miller, Lectures on the Constitution of the United States, 1891, p. 313, note.*)

It appears in our books, that in many cases, the common law will controul Acts of Parliament, and sometimes adjudge them to be utterly void: . . . (*Lord Chief Justice Coke, in Doctor Bonham's Case, 8 Co. Rep. 113b, 118a, decided in 1610, English Reports, Full Reprint, Vol. LXXVII, King's Bench Division, VI, 1907, p. 652.*)

Even an Act of Parliament, made against natural equity, as to make a man Judge in his own case, is void in it self, for jura naturæ sunt immutabilia, and they are leges legum. (*Lord Chief Justice Hobart in Day v. Savadge, Hobart 85, 87, decided in 1615, English Reports, Full Reprint, Vol. LXXX, King's Bench Division, IX, 1907, p. 237.*)

And what my Lord Coke says in *Dr. Bonham's case* in his 8 Co. is far from any extravagancy, for it is a very reasonable and true saying, that if an Act of Parliament should ordain that the same person should be party and Judge, or, which is the same thing, Judge in his own cause, it would be a void Act of Parliament; . . . (*Lord Chief Justice Holt, in The City of London v. Wood, 12 Mod. 669, 687-688, decided in 1702, English Reports, Full Reprint, Vol. LXXXVIII, King's Bench Division, XVII, 1908, p. 1602.*)

The great and *chief End* therefore, of Mens uniting into Commonwealths, and putting themselves under Government, *is the Preservation of their Property*. To which in the state of Nature there are many things wanting.

First, There wants an *establish'd*, settled, known *Law*, received and allowed by common Consent to be the Standard of right and wrong, and the common Measure to decide all Controversies between them. For though the Law of Nature be plain and intelligible to all rational Creatures; yet Men being biassed by their Interest, as well as ignorant for want of Study of it, are not apt to allow of it as a Law binding to them in the application of it to their particular Cases.

Secondly, In the state of Nature there wants *a known and indifferent Judge,* with Authority to determine all Differences according to the established Law. For every one in that State being both Judge and Executioner of the Law of Nature, Men being partial to themselves, Passion and Revenge is very apt to carry them too far, and with too much Heat, in their own Cases; as well as Negligence, and unconcernedness, to make them too remiss in others Mens.

Thirdly, In the state of Nature there often wants *Power* to back and support the Sentence when right, and to *give* it due *Execution.* They who by any Injustice offended, will seldom fail, where they are able, by Force to make good their Injustice; such Resistance many times makes the Punishment dangerous, and frequently destructive, to those who attempt it. (*John Locke, Two Treatises of Government, 1690, Book II, Ch. IX, Sections 124-126, Works, Edition of 1714, Vol. II.*)

This writ is against the fundamental principles of law. . . .

As to Acts of Parliament. An act against the Constitution is void; an act against natural equity is void; and if an act of Parliament should be made, in the very words of this petition, it would be void. The executive Courts must pass such acts into disuse.

8 Rep. 118 from Viner Reason of the common law to control an act of Parliament. Iron manufacture. Noble Lord's proposal, that we should send our horses to England to be shod. . . . (*Argument of James Otis in Paxton's Case on Writs of Assistance, 1761, Works of John Adams, Vol. 2, 1850, pp. 521-522.*)

The law was laid down in the same way, on the authority of the above cases, in Bacon's Abridgment, first published in 1735; in Viner's Abridgment, published 1741-51, from which *Otis* quoted it; and in Comyn's Digest, published 1762-7, but written more than twenty years before. And there are older authorities to the same effect. So that at the time of *Otis's* agreement his position appeared to be supported by some of the highest authorities in the English law.

The same doctrine was repeatedly asserted by *Otis,* and was a favorite in the Colonies before the Revolution. There are later *dicta* of many eminent judges to the effect that a statute may be void as exceeding the just limits of legislative power; but it is believed there is no instance, except one case in South Carolina, in which an act of the Legislature has been set aside by the courts, except for conflict with some written constitutional provision.

The reduction of the fundamental principles of government in the American States to the form of written constitutions, established by the people themselves, and beyond the control of their representatives, necessarily obliged the judicial department, in case of a conflict between a constitutional provision and a legislative act, to obey the Constitution as the fundamental law and disregard the statute. This duty was recognized, and unconstitutional acts set aside, by courts of justice, even before the adoption of the Constitution of the United States. Since the ratification of that Constitution the power of the courts to declare unconstitutional statutes void has become too well settled to require an accumulation of authorities. But as the office of the judiciary is to decide particular cases, and not to issue general edicts, only so much of a statute is to be declared void as is repugnant to the Constitution and covers the case before the court, unless the constitutional and unconstitutional provisions are so interwoven as to convince the court that the legislature would not have passed the one without the other. (*Mr. Justice Gray, Were the Writs of Assistance Legal, 1865, in Quincy, Massachusetts Reports, 1761-1772, Appendix I, pp. 526-530.*)

Judicial power, as contradistinguished from the power of the laws, has no existence. Courts are the mere instruments of the law, and can will nothing. When they are said to exercise a discretion, it is a mere legal discretion, a discretion to be exercised in discerning the course prescribed by law; and, when that is discerned, it is the duty of the court to follow it. Judicial power is never exercised for the purpose of giving effect to the will of the judge; always for the purpose of giving effect to the will of the legislature; or, in other words, to the will of the law. (*Chief Justice Marshall in Osborn v. United States Bank, 9 Wheaton, 738, 866, decided in 1824.*)

The judicial power mentioned in the constitution, and vested in the courts, means the power conferred upon courts ordained and established by and under the constitution, in the strict and appropriate sense of that term—courts that compose one of the three great departments of the government prescribed by the fundamental law, the same as the other two, the legislative and the executive. (*Mr. Justice Nelson on The Fugitive Slave Law, I Blatchford, Appendix, p. 644, decided in 1851.*)

The award of execution is a part, and an essential part of every judgment passed by a court exercising judicial power. It is no judgment, in the legal sense of the term, without it. Without such an award the judgment would be inoperative and nugatory, leaving the aggrieved party without a remedy. (*Chief Justice Taney in Gordon v. United States, 117 United States, 697, 702, decided in 1864.*)

In the Constitution are provisions in separate articles for the three great departments of government—legislative, executive and judicial. But there is this significant difference in the grants of powers to these departments: The first article, treating of legislative powers, does not make a general grant of legislative power. . . . By reason of the fact that there is no general grant of legislative power it has become an accepted constitutional rule that this is a government of enumerated powers. . . .

On the other hand, in Article III, which treats of the judicial department . . . we find that section 1 reads that "the judicial power of the United States, shall be vested in one Supreme Court, and in such inferior courts as the Congress may from time to time ordain and establish." By this is granted the entire judicial power of the Nation. . . .

Speaking generally, it may be observed that the judicial power of a nation extends to all controversies justiciable in their nature, the parties to which or the property involved in which may be reached by judicial process, and when the judicial power of the United States was vested in the Supreme and other courts all the judicial power which the Nation was capable of exercising was vested in those tribunals, and unless there be some limitations expressed in the Constitution it must be held to embrace all controversies of a justiciable nature arising within the territorial limits of the Nation, no matter who may be the parties thereto. (*Mr. Justice Brewer in Kansas v. Colorado, 206 United States, 46, 81-83, decided in 1907.*)

CHAPTER XVII

THE NATURE OF JUDICIAL POWER

As heretofore suggested, the statesmen of the Constitutional Convention The Influence of Montesquieu appear to have read and deeply pondered Montesquieu's *Spirit of the Laws,* and the great and conscious division of the more perfect Union into three departments appears to be due largely to Montesquieu's influence and to be traceable to the *Spirit of the Laws,* and more especially to the following passage:

> When the legislative and executive powers are united in the same person, or in the same body of magistrates, there can be no liberty; because apprehensions may arise, lest the same monarch or senate should enact tyrannical laws, to execute them in a tyrannical manner.
>
> Again, there is no liberty, if the power of judging be not separated from the legislative and executive powers. Were it joined with the legislative, the life and liberty of the subject would be exposed to arbitrary controul; for the judge would be then the legislator. Were it joined to the executive power, the judge might behave with all the violence of an oppressor.
>
> There would be an end of every thing, were the same man, or the same body, whether of the nobles or of the people, to exercise those three powers, that of enacting laws, that of executing the public resolutions, and that of judging the crimes or differences of individuals.[1]

The Articles of Confederation created a union intended to be perpetual; but it contented itself with an association of the States, without creating an agency to make that association effective, even for the specified purposes. The Congress was the legislative department, but its acts were in the nature of recommendations, rather than laws in the ordinary sense of the word. There was no executive department, unless the Congress is to be considered an executive, which, however, could not carry into effect the laws which it enacted. There was no Judiciary, although the ninth of the Articles of Confederation authorized and the Congress in fact did establish a Court of Appeal for prize cases, which, as we have seen in the famous case of *The Active,* overruled a decision of the Pennsylvania prize court, a form of judiciary which was, however, unable to carry its decision into effect. The same article, recognizing the necessity of judicial settlement of disputes between

[1] Montesquieu, *The Spirit of Laws,* English translation, 1756, Vol. I, Book XI, Chap VI, p. 165.

the States, provided a method by which temporary commissions should be created, coming into being for a special dispute and going out of existence with its decision. But of a real judiciary there was nothing.

The advocates of a more perfect Union foresaw that it could not be permanent, unless it was organized upon a broader basis, and unless the Union of the States was provided with appropriate agencies to carry into effect the sovereign powers, of which the States divested themselves in the common interest while reserving the exercise of all other sovereign powers which they did not grant to the agency they were creating, or otherwise divest themselves of.

Recognizing the need of the three departments of government, the necessity of their separation, as advocated by Montesquieu, and the necessity likewise of their equality, springing from their separation, the framers of the Constitution created a legislative, executive and judiciary department. As the Government of the United States was one of limited powers, it necessarily followed that the legislature would be limited, but nevertheless competent to carry into effect the powers directly or impliedly granted to the United States. The first article of the Constitution, while creating a Congress, does not vest it with legislative power in general, but with "all the legislative powers herein granted." In the same manner the executive power was vested in a President of the United States of America, whose powers were likewise limited, inasmuch as he could only execute the powers vested in the United States which were expressly or impliedly granted; and the origin, nature and source of the power and authority of the President are, as stated in the oath of office, to execute the office of President and, to the best of his ability, "preserve, protect, and defend the Constitution of the United States."

Limitation of Powers

The third article of the Constitution, for each of these divisions is covered by an article, and in this order, vests "the judicial power of the United States" in a Supreme Court and such inferior courts as Congress may from time to time ordain and establish. As in the previous cases, this can only mean the judicial power necessarily or impliedly granted to the United States, but since the Supreme Court was a new institution and as judicial power, in the sense in which it was here used, was and unfortunately still is a novelty in the older world, the Congress defined its extent, although it did not attempt to define its nature. The judiciary, while coextensive with the legislative and executive departments is, like each of them, limited in extent if not in nature. In the case of *Kilbourn* v. *Thompson* (103 U. S. 168, 190), decided in 1880, Mr. Justice Miller, speaking for the court said:

Congress defines Extent but not Nature of the Court's Power

> It is believed to be one of the chief merits of the American system of written constitutional law, that all the powers intrusted to government, whether State or national, are divided into the three grand departments, the

executive, the legislative, and the judicial. That the functions appropriate to each of these branches of government shall be vested in a separate body of public servants, and that the perfection of the system requires that the lines which separate and divide these departments shall be broadly and clearly defined. It is also essential to the successful working of this system that the persons intrusted with power in any one of these branches shall not be permitted to encroach upon the powers confided to the others, but that each shall by the law of its creation be limited to the exercise of the powers appropriate to its own department and no other.

What is judicial power? This question Mr. Justice Miller puts in his "Lectures on the Constitution of the United States;" and, after commenting upon its difficulty, proceeds to answer it by a reference to decisions of the Supreme Court of the United States. "It will not do," he says, "to answer that it is the power exercised by the courts, because one of the very things to be determined is what power they may exercise. It is, indeed, very difficult to find any exact definition made to hand. . . . .

Judicial Power defined by Court Itself

"Judicial power is, perhaps, better defined in some of the reports of our own courts than in any other place, and especially so in the Supreme Court of the United States, because it has more often been the subject of comment there, and its consideration more frequently necessary to the determination of questions arising in that court than anywhere else. It is the power of a court to decide and pronounce a judgment and carry it into effect between persons and parties who bring a case before it for decision." [1]

In this connection, however, we must not forget that the first English colonists brought with them the common law of England, that the British plantations in America were therefore familiar with the principles of the common law, and that the statesmen who framed the Constitution were born and bred in it. To the common law, therefore, we must look for the nature of judicial power, just as we look to the Constitution for its extent. It is common knowledge that the first Englishman to set his foot upon the New World brought with him the rights and privileges of Englishmen and the law by which they were defined, interpreted and protected, and it would be a cheap display of learning to quote authority for the position that the law in force in England before the Declaration of Independence was, in as far as it was applicable to the colonies, binding upon them as bodies politic and upon the colonists as English subjects. We should expect, therefore, to find that the settlers understood judicial power in the sense in which it was understood in the mother country and that the statesmen of the Revolution and the framers of the Constitution used the expression "judicial power" in the sense in which it was used in the jurisprudence of the old country, except in so far as the meaning attached to that expression in the English system was consciously modified or departed from.

Influence of English Common Law

[1] S. F. Miller, *Lectures on the Constitution of the United States,* 1893, pp. 313, 314.

It is therefore enlightening as well as instructive to examine a few English cases dealing with the nature of judicial power, for by so doing we not only obtain an insight into the subject and enable ourselves to understand the state of mind of the framers of the Constitution, but to comprehend how the Supreme Court of the United States, without the express and literal authority of the Constitution, has naturally and inevitably passed upon the constitutionality of federal as well as State legislation.

English
Cases
on the
Judicial
Power

A very interesting and early case, to be found in Professor Wambaugh's Cases on Constitutional Law (from which these examples are taken), was the subject of discussion in 1460 and is known as the Duke of York's claim to the Crown.[1] Without going into details, it is sufficient for present purposes to state that the Duke of York claimed the English Crown, and by his counsel presented his claim in writing to the Lord Chancellor, with the request that it be laid by him before the Lords spiritual and temporal of the then Parliament, and " that the said Duke might have brief and expedient answer thereof." The Lords spiritual and temporal were much troubled, and in the end they sent for the King's Justices " to have their advice and counsel in this behalf, and there delivered to them the writing of the claim of the said Duke, and in the King's name gave them strictly in commandment, sadly to take advisement therein, and to search and find all such objections as might be laid against the same, in fortifying the King's right." Apparently, the Justices were also much troubled by this request, for, when summoned before the Lords spiritual and temporal for answer, they said:

> That they were the Kyngs Justices, and have to determyne such maters as com before theym in the lawe, betwene partie and partie, and in such maters as been betwene partie and partie, they may not be of Counseill; and sith this mater was betwene the Kyng and the seid Duc of York as two parties, and also it hath not be accustumed to calle the Justices to Counseill in such maters . . . . they humble bysought all the Lordes, to have theym utterly excused of eny avyce or Counseill, by theym to be yeven in that matier.[2]

In *Clark's Case* (5 Coke's Reports, 64a), decided in 1596, it appeared that the town of St. Albans, with the assent of the plaintiff and other burgesses " did assess a sum on every inhabitant for the charges in erecting the courts there; and ordained, that if any should refuse to pay, &c. that he should be imprisoned." The Court of Common Pleas held, however, that the ordinance to this effect was null, as contrary to the Magna Charta, Chapter 29, providing that *nullus liber homo imprisonetur.* The court also held that the consent of the plaintiff could not enable it to take jurisdiction forbidden by

---

[1] Eugene Wambaugh, *A Selection of Cases on Constitutional Law,* 1914, Book i, pp. 1–3.
[2] 5 *Rotuli Parliamentorum,* 375–6.

law, and that, while the corporation of St. Albans could not impose imprisonment for a failure to pay the charge, as this was contrary to the statute, it
might very properly have imposed a penalty or a fine.

A few years later, in 1607, a very interesting case arose, entitled *Prohibitions Del Roy* (12 Coke's Reports, 63, 65), which involved the question
whether James I as King of England could himself administer justice between party and party, or whether law or justice, being the exercise of
judicial power, could only be administered by the court. The question was
one of such importance that all the Judges of England and Barons of Ex-
chequer were summoned before his Majesty, and Sir Edward Coke, then
Chief Justice of the Common Pleas, spoke on behalf and with the consent of
the judges, denying the claim of the King to dispense justice in the concrete
case. The question involved in this dispute between the King and the court is
so material to the functions of a court, and so clearly states the necessity of
independence on the part of judges, as to deserve quotation. After the statement of Lord Coke that, although justice is administered in the name of the
King, the judgment is nevertheless reached and delivered by the judges of the
court, sworn to execute justice according to the law and custom of England,
the King said, as reported by his Lordship, " He thought the law was
founded upon reason, and that he and others had reason, as well as the
Judges." To which the Chief Justice answered:

> True it was, that God had endowed his Majesty with excellent science,
> and great endowments of nature; but His Majesty was not learned in the
> laws of his realm of England, and causes which concern the life, or inherit-
> ance, or goods, or fortunes of his subjects, are not to be decided by natural
> reason but by the artificial reason and judgment of law, which law is an
> act which requires long study and experience, before that a man can attain to
> the cognizance of it: and that the law was the golden met-wand and measure
> to try the causes of the subjects; and which protected his Majesty in safety
> and peace: with which the King was greatly offended, and said, that then
> he should be under the law, which was treason to affirm, as he said; to
> which I said, that Bracton saith, *quod Rex non debet esse sub homine, sed
> sub Deo et lege.*

This solemn opinion of the judges, given under these trying circumstances,
denying the judicial power to the executive, was not a deterrent to a man of
King James' type, who not only claimed the power to interpret the law but to
make that law which he claimed the right to interpret. In the matter of
Proclamations (12 Coke's Reports, 74–6), which was argued before the Privy
Council in 1610, Lord Chief Justice Coke again came into collision with his
Majesty, who claimed the right to prohibit new buildings in and about London, and likewise by proclamation to prohibit the making of starch out of
wheat. As these acts on the part of his Majesty were regarded as grievances

and against law and justice, the King conferred with his Privy Council and his judges. Lord Coke again expressed his opinion as became a judge, saying squarely that "the King cannot change any part of the common law, nor create any offence by his proclamation, which was not an offence before, without Parliament." But, recognizing the importance of the question, Lord Coke asked " to have a time of consideration and conference " with his brethren, a request which was reluctantly granted. The result of the consideration and conference is thus reported by Coke himself:

> In the same term it was resolved by the two Chief Justices, Chief Baron, and Baron Altham, upon conference betwixt the Lords of the Privy Council and them, that the King by his proclamation cannot create any offence which was not an offence before, for then he may alter the law of the land by his proclamation in a high point; for if he may create an offence where none is, upon that ensues fine and imprisonment; also the law of England is divided into three parts, common law, statute law, and custom; but the King's proclamation is none of them.

It is believed that these cases, tried and decided before an English colony had been firmly planted in America, show that the conception of judicial power, as it was later to obtain in America, was already well understood in the mother country, and that, because of that fact, it was bound to prevail in the English speaking portion of the New World. Before considering the American cases dealing with this subject, it is advisable to refer to two further English cases, decided after the establishment of the American colonies, but before the Declaration of Independence.

The first case is *Rex* v. *Cutbush* (4 Burrow, 2204, 2208), decided by the King's Bench in 1768. This was upon what is called an information, in the nature of a *quo warranto,* brought against the defendant to show by what warrant he claimed to be a common councilman of Maidstone. It appears that Maidstone was incorporated in the twenty-first year of King George II, under the name of " the mayor, jurats, and commonalty of the King's town and parish of *Maidstone* in the county of *Kent*," the charter of incorporation providing that thirteen of the inhabitants should be chosen Jurats and one of the Jurats Mayor, and that forty of the remaining principal inhabitants should be chosen as the Common Council of the said town and parish. On the plea that the Commonalty of Maidstone was very numerous, and that an admission of them to vote in the election of a common councilman had been found by experience to occasion divers riots, disorders, and great popular confusion, the Mayor, Jurats and Common Council made a by-law providing that, in lieu of election by the Commonalty, the Common Councilmen should be elected by the present members thereof and sixty others, who, at the time of the election, should be the senior common freemen of the said town and parish of Maidstone as they should stand in order and place of seniority upon the books of admission of freemen of the said town and parish. The defendant, Cutbush, was elected a common councilman pursuant to this by-law. If the by-law was valid, he was properly elected; if the by-law was inconsistent with the charter of incorporation, he was then illegally elected and not entitled to hold the office. The court was unanimously of the opinion that the by-law was bad, that it was contrary to the intention of the charter, Lord Chief Justice Mansfield saying:

> It is made by a part of the corporation, to deprive the rest of their right to elect, without their consent. The charter gives this right to the whole body of the commonalty; the by-law confines it to a narrow compass of the sixty seniors only. This expressly contradicts the charter.

Mr. Justice Yates concurred with Lord Mansfield, and added that:

> Where a corporation is by charter, and the common-council is *created by the charter,* they ought (as being the *creature* of the charter) to be restrained from making any by-laws inconsistent with it, or counteracting the end, intentions and directions of it.

The second of these cases is *Campbell* v. *Hill* (Cowper, 204, 212, 213), decided by the King's Bench in 1774, upon the eve of the American Revolution. For present purposes, it is sufficient to say that the Island of Grenada had been captured from the French and ceded to Great Britain by the treaty of February 10, 1763; that by proclamations of King George III dated October 7, 1763, and April 9, 1764, the Crown empowered the Governor, as soon as the state of the Island should permit, to summon a General Assembly in the manner used in the colonies and provinces of America; and that such assemblies should make laws with the consent of the Governor and Council. After the issuance of the proclamation of October 7, 1763, the King issued a further proclamation, laying an export duty of 4½ per cent upon all of the commodities produced in the Island. The defendant collected the duties from the plaintiff, who sued in an action of money had and received, to recover the amount of the export duties which he had been obliged to pay. The question was whether the King could, by a later proclamation, lay an export tax upon the produce of the Island when, by the earlier proclamation of October 7, 1763, he had, to quote Lord Mansfield's language, " *precluded* himself from the exercise of a legislative authority over the island of *Grenada.*" On this point the court was unanimous, holding that " the King had immediately and *irrevocably* granted to all who were or should become inhabitants, or who had, or should acquire property in the Island of *Grenada,* or more generally *to all whom it might concern,* that the subordinate legislation over the island should be exercised by an assembly with the consent of the governor and council, in like manner as the other islands belonging to the king." As in the case of *Rex* v. *Cutbush,* where we have the judicial power declaring the by-law of the parish of Maidstone void as inconsistent with the charter of incorporation, that is to say, the judicial power setting aside an act of the legislature (in this case a corporation) inconsistent with the grant, so in the case of *Campbell* v. *Hall,* we have the judicial power taking jurisdiction of an act of the executive and declaring it inconsistent with the law of the land.

We are now prepared to consider a leading case of colonial times, in which the judicial power of the mother country set aside an act of the colonial legislature of Connecticut and a judgment of the Connecticut Court of Probate organized under the charter of the colony, as the act and the judgment were in excess of the power granted by the charter. The case of *Winthrop* v. *Lechmere* (7 Connecticut Colonial Records, 571), decided by the Privy Council in 1728, involved the validity of an act of the colonial legislature, providing that, in the case of a person dying intestate, the realty should descend to the male and female children of the deceased, and that the male should receive a double portion, contrary to the law of descent in England, which, in such a case, vested all the realty in the male to the exclusion of the female. From the decision of the Connecticut Court, distributing the property according to the colonial statute, the male child, one Winthrop, son of the deceased intestate, appealed to the King in Council to admit an appeal, which had been disallowed by the Connecticut authorities. The appeal was granted and the appeal was referred to the Committee for Hearing Appeals from the Plantations. The question was elaborately argued for the appellant by Sir Philip Yorke, then Attorney General, later Lord Chancellor Hardwicke, and Sir Charles Talbot, then Solicitor General and later Lord Chancellor Talbot, with the result that the Committee for Hearing Appeals from the Plantations advised his Majesty " that the said act for the settlement of Intestate Estates should be declared null and void, being contrary to the laws of England, in regard it makes lands of inheritances distributable as personal estates, and is not warranted by the charter of that Colony." We here have the act of a legislature of a body politic, a colony, and later to be a State of the American Union under this very charter, set aside as null and void by a committee exercising judicial powers.

We are justified in saying that, before the outbreak of the American Revolution, the lawyers and statesmen of England as well as of the colonies were familiar with that conception of judicial power, by virtue of which it refused, as in the case of the Duke of York's claim, to pass upon a political question; by virtue of which it denied to the executive the right to administer justice between parties litigant and the right to issue proclamations, decree prohibitions inconsistent with the law, or to make law; and by virtue of which a by-law of an incorporated town and an act of the legislature of a colony were held by the judicial power to be in excess of the grant of power contained in the charter.

These are English precedents, with which the lawyers of the colonies were familiar, or of which they were ignorant at their peril. We have, however, an American case, decided in 1780, one year before the Articles of Confederation creating the Confederacy went into operation, and by the Chief Justice of the court, a framer of the more perfect Union, participating in the trial and disposition of the case. In *Holmes* v. *Walton*,[1] for this is the case to which reference has been made, it appeared that one Walton, acting under a statute of the State of New Jersey passed October 8, 1778, seized goods in the possession of Holmes and Ketcham which had been brought into the American lines from a place in possession of the British, and, in conformity with the statute, Walton took the goods before a Justice of the Peace. And, still acting under the statute, which required the Justice to grant a jury of six men upon the demand of either party and forbade an appeal in case of verdict, a jury of six was appointed, a verdict thereof given in favor of Walton and judgment entered accordingly in his favor. Notwithstanding the inhibition of the statute, the defendant appealed to the Supreme Court of New Jersey, invoking in his behalf section XXII of the Constitution of New Jersey, adopted July 2, 1776, providing " that the inestimable right of trial by jury shall remain confirmed as a part of the law of this colony, without repeal forever," and calling attention to the fact that the verdict of the jury upon which judgment was rendered consisted of six men only, when, " by the laws of the land it should have consisted of twelve men." As a jury of six was unknown to the common law, the defendant insisted that the verdict be set aside. The case was one in which the feeling of the community was with the plaintiff below, who had seized goods found in possession of the British and brought them within the American lines. The court apparently was in doubt, so that it took time to consider, but on September 7, 1780, in the presence of all the judges (among them David Brearley, Chief Justice, and later a delegate of his State to the Constitutional Convention), the following mandate was entered:

> This cause having been argued several terms past and the court having taken time to consider the same, and being now ready to deliver their opinion, gave the same seriation for the plaintiffs *in certiorari*. And on motion of Boudinot for the plaintiffs, judgment is ordered for the plaintiffs, and that the judgment of the justice in the court below be reversed. . . .[2]

An American Case

Court Can Pass on Constitutionality of a Legislative Act

[1] *The American Historical Review*, Vol. IV, pp. 456–69 (April, 1899).
[2] Wambaugh, *Cases*, Book I, p. 22.

It was natural, therefore, that the framers of the Constitution should regard as a proper exercise of the judicial power a decree of a court setting aside an act of the Congress of the United States, or a provision of the constitution of a State, or an act of its legislature or of the executive department as inconsistent with the grant of power in the Constitution of the United States.

Continuing what may be called the general phase of the subject, there are instructive instances of an attempt to invest judges with the performance of other than judicial duties, which bring into prominence the essence of judicial power and of judicial duty under the constitutional grant. Shortly after the government was organized under the present Constitution, on March 4, 1789, an act of Congress was passed " to provide for the settlement of the Claims of Widows and Orphans barred by the limitations heretofore established, and to regulate the Claims to Invalid Pensions." [1]   The duty to determine these claims was assigned to the Circuit Courts of the United States, organized in pursuance of the judiciary act of September 25, 1789.   Each of the three Circuit Courts, into which the United States was divided, considered the question, and, although deeply interested in the purpose of the act and desirous of complying with it, insofar as the limits of judicial power would permit them to do so, the judges stated it to be their opinion that the duty imposed by the act was inconsistent with judicial power, and that therefore the court could not, and that the judges should not, comply with it.   The Circuit Court for the District of New York, consisting of Jay, Chief Justice, Cushing, Justice, and Duane, District Judge, stated that the judges of the Circuit were unanimously of the opinion:

> That by the Constitution of the United States, the government thereof is divided into *three* distinct and independent branches, and that it is the duty of each to abstain from, and to oppose, encroachments on either.
> That neither the *Legislative* nor the *Executive* branches, can constitutionally assign to the *Judicial* any duties, but such as are properly judicial, and to be performed in a judicial manner.
> That the duties assigned to the Circuit courts, by this act, are not of that description, and that the act itself does not appear to contemplate them as such; in as much as it subjects the decisions of these courts, made pursuant to those duties, first to the consideration and suspension of the Secretary at War, and then to the revision of the Legislature; whereas by the Constitution, neither the Secretary at War, nor any other Executive officer, nor even the Legislature, are authorized to sit as a court of errors on the judicial acts or opinions of this court.[2]

The Circuit Court for the District of Pennsylvania, consisting of Wilson and Blair, Justices, and Peters, District Judge, made the following repre-

---

[1] 1 Statutes at Large, 243.
[2] *Hayburn's Case,* 2 Dallas, 410, Note.

sentation to the President of the United States in a letter dated April 18, 1792:

> To you it officially belongs to "take care that the laws" of the United States "be faithfully executed." Before you, therefore, we think it our duty to lay the sentiments, which, on a late painful occasion, governed us with regard to an act passed by the legislature of the Union.
>
> The people of the United States have vested in Congress all *legislative* powers " granted in the constitution."
>
> They have vested in one Supreme court, and in such inferior courts as the Congress shall establish, " the *judicial* power of the United States." . . .
>
> This Constitution is "the Supreme Law of the Land." This supreme law " all judicial officers of the United States are bound, by oath or affirmation, to support."
>
> It is a principle important to freedom, that in government, the *judicial* should be distinct from, and independent of, the legislative department. To this important principle the people of the United States, in forming their Constitution, have manifested the highest regard.
>
> They have placed their *judicial* power not in Congress, but in "*courts.*" They have ordained that the " Judges of those courts shall hold their offices during good behaviour," and that " during their continuance in office, their salaries shall not be diminished."
>
> Congress have lately passed an act, to regulate, among other things, "the claims to invalid pensions."
>
> Upon due consideration, we have been unanimously of opinion, that, under this act, the Circuit court held for the Pennsylvania district could not proceed;
>
> 1st. Because the business directed by this act is not of a judicial nature. It forms no part of the power vested by the Constitution in the courts of the United States; the Circuit court must, consequently, have proceeded *without* constitutional authority.
>
> 2d. Because, if, upon that business, the court had proceeded, its *judgments* (for its *opinions* are its judgments) might, under the same act, have been revised and controuled by the legislature, and by an officer in the executive department. Such revision and controul we deemed radically inconsistent with the independence of that judicial power which is vested in the courts; and, consequently, with that important principle which is so strictly observed by the Constitution of the United States.[1]

The Circuit Court for the District of North Carolina, consisting of Iredell, Justice, and Sitgreaves, District Judge, thus addressed the President of the United States on June 8, 1792:

> 1. That the Legislative, Executive, and Judicial departments, are each formed in a separate and independent manner; and that the ultimate basis of each is the Constitution only, within the limits of which each department can alone justify any act of authority.
>
> 2. That the Legislature, among other important powers, unquestionably possess that of establishing courts in such a manner as to their wisdom

[1] 2 Dallas, 411, Note. For the facts of the " painful occasion " referred to above, see *post,* p. 365.

shall appear best, limited by the terms of the constitution only; and to whatever extent that power may be exercised, or however severe the duty they may think proper to require, the Judges, when appointed in virtue of any such establishment, owe implicit and unreserved obedience to it.

3. That at the same time such courts cannot be warranted, as we conceive, by virtue of that part of the Constitution delegating *Judicial power,* for the exercise of which any act of the legislature is provided, in exercising (even under the authority of another act) any power not in its nature *judicial,* or, if *judicial,* not provided for upon the terms the Constitution requires.

4. That whatever doubt may be suggested, whether the power in question is properly of a judicial nature, yet inasmuch as the decision of the court is not made final, but may be at least suspended in its operation by the Secretary at War, if he shall have cause to suspect imposition or mistake; this subjects the decision of the court to a mode of revision which we consider to be unwarranted by the Constitution; for, though Congress may certainly establish, in instances not yet provided for, courts of appellate jurisdiction, yet such courts must consist of judges appointed in the manner the Constitution requires, and holding their offices by no other tenure than that of their good behaviour, by which tenure the office of Secretary at War is not held. And we beg leave to add, with all due deference, that no decision of any court of the United States can, under any circumstances, in our opinion, agreeable to the Constitution, be liable to a reversion, or even suspension, by the Legislature itself, in whom no judicial power of any kind appears to be vested, but the important one relative to impeachments.[1]

The question as to whether the act of Congress conferred upon the Circuit Court a judicial function, and whether the Federal judges could act as commissioners if they could not act as judges, arose in 1792 in Hayburn's case (2 Dallas, 409). It was then, however, not decided by that august tribunal, as it took the question under advisement until the next term. But no decision was ever pronounced, as the sections of the act of 1792 under which action had been taken were in the meantime repealed, and, as the reporter informs us, the legislature at the intermediate session provided in another way for the relief of the pensioners. While it is correct to say, as is often done, that Hayburn's case did not decide the question, it was not left undecided, as it appears from a note by Mr. Chief Justice Taney, appended to the case of *United States* v. *Ferreira* (13 Howard, 40), decided in 1851, that the exact question was raised and decided in 1794 by the Supreme Court in the case of *United States* v. *Todd.*

An act of Congress was passed in 1793, directing the Secretary of War and the Attorney General to get the opinion of the Supreme Court upon the question, and the court, contrary to subsequent practice, assumed jurisdiction on the theory that the act in question gave it original jurisdiction. An agreed statement of facts was presented, setting forth that on May 3, 1792, one Yale

---

[1] 2 Dallas, 412, Note.

Todd appeared before the Circuit Court, composed of John Jay, Chief Justice, William Cushing, Justice, and Richard Law, District Judge, then sitting in New Haven and acting as commissioners under the act of 1792; that Todd submitted his claim under the act to the court, supporting it by evidence, and that the court delivered the opinion that Todd should be placed upon the pension list. A certificate of the proceedings and opinion of the court was, on May 8, 1792, transmitted to the Secretary of War, who, following the opinion of the court, placed Todd upon the pension list and paid over to him, in accordance with the opinion and on behalf of the United States, the sum of $150 for arrears and $22.91 for pension to be due in September. The United States, in order to test the question, sued Todd as defendant to recover payment of the sum of $172.91, it being agreed in this remarkable proceeding that if the judges of the Circuit Court " sitting as Commissioners, and not as a Circuit Court," had power to entertain and decide the case, judgment should be given for the defendant; whereas, if the Circuit Court, sitting as commissioners, was not authorized to have taken jurisdiction and to adjudge the original case, judgment should be entered against Todd for the sum of $172.91 and six cents costs. Todd appeared by distinguished counsel and the case was argued by the Attorney General on behalf of the United States. In the following passage from the note to *United States* v. *Ferreira,* giving the facts and the decision in the Todd case, Mr. Chief Justice Taney not only states the decision of the court but comments upon it:

Powers of Court Strictly Judicial

> Chief Justice Jay and Justice Cushing, Wilson, Blair, and Paterson, were present at the decision. No opinion was filed stating the grounds of the decision. Nor is any dissent from the judgment entered on the record. It would seem, therefore, to have been unanimous, and that Chief Justice Jay and Justice Cushing became satisfied, on further reflection, that the power given in the act of 1792 to the Circuit Court as a court, could not be construed to give it to the judges out of court as commissioners. It must be admitted that the justice of the claims and the meritorious character of the claimants would appear to have exercised some influence on their judgments in the first instance, and to have led them to give a construction to the law which its language would hardly justify upon the most liberal rules of interpretation.
>
> The result of the opinions expressed by the judges of the Supreme Court of that day in the note to Hayburn's case, and in the case of the United States *v.* Todd, is this:
>
> 1. That the power proposed to be conferred on the Circuit Courts of the United States by the act of 1792 was not judicial power within the meaning of the Constitution, and was, therefore, unconstitutional, and could not lawfully be exercised by the courts.
>
> 2. That as the act of Congress intended to confer the power on the courts as a judicial function, it could not be construed as an authority to the judges composing the court to exercise the power out of court in the character of commissioners.[1]

[1] 13 Howard, 52–3, Note.

It thus appears that the Supreme Court decided, within a very few years after its institution, as it has since held, that the Federal courts could only exercise judicial power; and the decision is all the more noteworthy, as the case was one in which the sympathy of the judges was deeply enlisted and in which some of them had acted as individuals, although they felt that they could not act officially as judges.

Further Distinction between Judicial and Other Powers

Two further cases, dealing with the general attributes of judicial as distinguished from legislative or executive power, deserve examination in this connection, in each of which the opinion was prepared by Chief Justice Taney, who worthily wore the mantle of the great Chief Justice. The first case to be considered is that of *United States* v. *Ferreira,* decided in 1851, to which *United States* v. *Todd* was appended as a note. This case grew out of the treaty of February 22, 1819, between the United States and Spain, by which the latter country ceded Florida to the United States, and two acts of Congress were passed in order to give effect to the following stipulation contained in that treaty:

> The United States shall cause satisfaction to be made for the injuries, if any, which by process of law shall be established to have been suffered by the Spanish officers and individual Spanish inhabitants by the late operations of the American army in Florida.[1]

By three acts of Congress of 1823, 1834 and 1849, the judge of the territorial court of Florida, and later the judge of the District Court of the United States for the northern district of Florida, was directed to receive, examine and adjudge all cases and claims for losses and to report his decisions in favor of the claimants, together with the evidence upon which they were based, to the Secretary of the Treasury, who was authorized to pay to the claimants the sum awarded to them, " on being satisfied that the same is just and equitable, within the provisions of the treaty."

It will be observed that the facts of the case bring it within the principle laid down in *United States* v. *Todd,* which has just been considered, a fact not lost upon the Chief Justice, who referred to Hayburn's case and the opinion of the judges who had allowed themselves to act under the law of Congress relating to pensions. But the court evidently considered the questions involved of such importance as to justify an examination of the case upon its merits without regard to precedent.

In the first place the Chief Justice, on behalf of the court, analyzed the acts which the judge was obliged to perform under the laws of Congress, and, after having done so, indulged in comment as valuable today as it was then. Thus:

[1] 13 Howard, 40.

It is manifest that this power to decide upon the validity of these claims, is not conferred on them as a judicial function, to be exercised in the ordinary forms of a court of justice. For there is to be no suit; no parties in the legal acceptance of the term, are to be made — no process to issue; and no one is authorized to appear on behalf of the United States, or to summon witnesses in the case. The proceeding is altogether *ex parte;* and all that the judge is required to do, is to receive the claim when the party presents it, and to adjust it upon such evidence as he may have before him, or be able himself to obtain. But neither the evidence nor his award, are to be filed in the court in which he presides, nor recorded there; but he is required to transmit, both the decision and the evidence upon which he decided, to the Secretary of the Treasury; and the claim is to be paid if the Secretary thinks it just and equitable, but not otherwise. It is to be a debt from the United States upon the decision of the Secretary, but not upon that of the judge.[1]

Upon these facts the Chief Justice thus commented:

It is too evident for argument on the subject, that such a tribunal is not a judicial one, and that the act of Congress did not intend to make it one. The authority conferred on the respective judges was nothing more than that of a commissioner to adjust certain claims against the United States; and the office of judges, and their respective jurisdictions, are referred to in the law, merely as a designation of the persons to whom the authority is confided, and the territorial limits to which it extends. The decision is not the judgment of a court of justice. It is the award of a commissioner. The act of 1834 calls it an award. And an appeal to this court from such a decision, by such an authority from the judgment of a court of record, would be an anomaly in the history of jurisprudence. An appeal might as well have been taken from the awards of the board of commissioners, under the Mexican treaty, which were recently sitting in this city.[2]

The Chief Justice was, of course, aware that the act was judicial, as opposed to a legislative, executive or ministerial act, as its successful performance involved legal principles and judicial discretion. But he was of the opinion that it was not an exercise of the judicial power of the United States, as that term is used in the Constitution, and as judicial power is to be exercised in courts organized in pursuance of the Constitution. Indeed, he himself said:

The powers conferred by these acts of Congress upon the judge as well as the Secretary, are, it is true, judicial in their nature. For judgment and discretion must be exercised by both of them. But it is nothing more than the power ordinarily given by law to a commissioner appointed to adjust claims to lands or money under a treaty; or special powers to inquire into or to decide any other particular class of controversies in which the public or individuals may be concerned. A power of this description may constitutionally be conferred on a Secretary as well as on a commissioner. But is

[1] 13 Howard, 46-7.
[2] *Ibid.,* 47.

not judicial in either case, in the sense in which judicial power is granted by the Constitution to the Courts of the United States.[1]

The second case to which reference has been made is that of *Gordon* v. *United States* (2 Wallace, 561), decided by the Supreme Court in 1864. Mr. Chief Justice Taney had prepared a very careful opinion on the question of jurisdiction involved in this case, but he died before the decision was announced, and the opinion which he had written and communicated to his brethren appears to have been mislaid by them; but a copy, later found among his papers, was, by direction of the court, printed as an appendix to 117 U. S. Reports, 696–706.[2] As Mr. Chief Justice Taney's opinion is on a subject with which he was peculiarly familiar, and inasmuch as it is commonly referred to as the authority on the subject, it seems advisable to consider the case at some length.

The plaintiff, Gordon, administrator of one Fisher, presented a petition in the Court of Claims of the United States for damages done to Fisher by troops of the United States in the war of 1812 with Great Britain. The Court of Claims decided against the claim and Gordon appealed to the Supreme Court. The question was similar to but not identical with that in the Ferreira case, as the judgment of the court did not determine the case finally but made the payment depend upon the inclusion of the claim in the Secretary's estimate and upon the appropriation of the estimated amount by the Congress. Under an act of Congress, an appeal could be taken to the Supreme Court from the Court of Claims, but Mr. Chief Justice Taney in his opinion, and the court in its judgment, held that an appeal would not lie from the Court of Claims in this instance, because that court had not exercised judicial power in the sense of the Constitution, and its opinion, therefore, was more in the nature of an award than a judgment upon which an appeal would lie to the Supreme Court; because, in either event, the Court of Claims or the Supreme Court would merely certify its opinion to the executive officer, whose action, not the opinion of either court, concluded the matter.

[1] 13 Howard, 48.

[2] This cause was submitted on the 18th December, 1863. On the 4th of April, 1864, the court ordered it to be argued on the second day of the following December Term. Mr. Chief Justice Taney had prepared an opinion expressing his views upon the question of jurisdiction. This he placed in the hands of the clerk in vacation, to be delivered to the judges on their reassembling in December. Before the judges met he died. The clerk complied with his request. It is the recollection of the surviving members of the court, that this paper was carefully considered by the members of the court in reaching the conclusion reported in 2 Wall. 561; and that it was proposed to make it the basis of the opinion, which, it appears by the report of the case, was to be subsequently prepared. The paper was not restored to the custody of the clerk, nor was the proposed opinion ever prepared. At the suggestion of the surviving members of the court, the reporter made efforts to find the missing paper, and, having succeeded in doing so, now prints it with their assent. (117 U. S., *Appendix*, 697.)

In speaking of the nature and functions of the Supreme Court and the action it should take in the present case, Mr. Chief Justice Taney said:

> But whether this Court can be required or authorized to hear an appeal from such a tribunal, and give an opinion upon it without the power of pronouncing a judgment, and issuing the appropriate judicial process to carry it into effect, is a very different question, and rests on principles altogether different. The Supreme Court does not owe its existence or its powers to the Legislative Department of the Government. It is created by the Constitution, and represents one of the three great divisions of power in the Government of the United States, to each of which the Constitution has assigned its appropriate duties and powers, and made each independent of the other in performing its appropriate functions. The power conferred on this court is exclusively judicial, and it cannot be required or authorized to exercise any other.[1]

After quoting the first section of Article III of the Constitution, vesting the judicial power of the United States in the Supreme Court, and the last clause of the same Article, providing that " The Supreme Court shall have appellate jurisdiction, both as to law and fact, with such exceptions and under such regulations as the Congress shall make," the Chief Justice thus continued, in language peculiarly appropriate to the purposes of the present essay:

Appellate Jurisdiction

> The existence of this Court is, therefore, as essential to the organization of the government established by the Constitution as the election of a president or members of Congress. It is the tribunal which is ultimately to decide all judicial questions confided to the Government of the United States. No appeal is given from its decisions, nor any power given to the legislative or executive departments to interfere with its judgments or process of execution. Its jurisdiction and powers and duties being defined in the organic law of the government, and being all strictly judicial, Congress cannot require or authorize the court to exercise any other jurisdiction or power, or perform any other duty. Chancellor Kent says: " The judicial power of the United States is in point of origin and title equal with the other powers of the government, and is as exclusively vested in the court created by or pursuant to the Constitution, as the legislative power is vested in Congress, or the Executive power in the President." I Kent. Com., 209–291, 6th ed. See also Story Const., pp. 449–450.[2]

After stating the elevated and indeed the unique position which the judicial power occupies in the American system of government, the Chief Justice proceeded to discuss the reason for the creation of this power. Thus:

> The reason for giving such unusual power to a judicial tribunal is obvious. It was necessary to give it from the complex character of the Government of the United States, which is in part National and in part

---

[1] 117 U. S., *Appendix,* 699–700.
[2] *Ibid.,* p. 700.

Federal: where two separate Governments exercise certain powers of sovereignty over the same territory, each independent of the other within its appropriate sphere of action, and where there was, therefore, an absolute necessity, in order to preserve internal tranquility, that there should be some tribunal to decide between the Government of the United States and the government of a State whenever any controversy should arise as to their relative and respective powers in the common territory. The Supreme Court was created for that purpose, and to insure its impartiality it was absolutely necessary to make it independent of the legislative power, and the influence direct or indirect of Congress and the Executive. Hence the care with which its jurisdiction, powers, and duties are defined in the Constitution, and its independence of the legislative branch of the government secured.[1]

The Chief Justice supports his contention by a passage from the 39th number of *The Federalist* written by James Madison, in which he says that the decision is to be made impartially and that every precaution is to be taken in order to secure this impartiality, because, to quote his exact language, " some such tribunal (as the Supreme Court) is clearly essential to prevent an appeal to the sword, and a dissolution of the compact." [2] Upon this statement, taking the passage quoted from Mr. Madison as a point of departure, the Chief Justice thus continues:

> It was to prevent an appeal to the sword and a dissolution of the compact that this Court, by the organic law, was made equal in origin and equal in title to the legislative and executive branches of the government: its powers defined, and limited, and made strictly judicial, and placed therefore beyond the reach of the powers delegated to the Legislative and Executive Departments. And it is upon the principle of the perfect independence of this Court, that in cases where the Constitution gives it original jurisdiction, the action of Congress has not been deemed necessary to regulate its exercise, or to prescribe the process to be used to bring the parties before the Court, or to carry its judgment into execution. The jurisdiction and judicial power being vested in the court, it proceeded to prescribe its process and regulate its proceedings according to its own judgment, and Congress has never attempted to control or interfere with the action of the court in this respect.[3]

Original
Jurisdiction

It will be observed that, in this passage, the Chief Justice refers to the original jurisdiction of the court, and that his remarks are strictly limited to this portion of its jurisdiction; for, while it is true that, in the exercise of its original jurisdiction, the Supreme Court does not compel a State to appear before it nor, hitherto at least, by force compel the execution of a judgment against a State, the Supreme Court can and does, in the exercise of appellate jurisdiction, compel the presence of individuals before it and

[1] 117 U. S., *Appendix*, pp. 700-1.
[2] *The Federalist*, 1802, Vol. i, p. 259.
[3] 117 U. S., *Appendix*, 701-2.

does likewise compel the execution of its judgment against individuals by the amount of force required to secure obedience to its mandates. After saying that an inferior court, in which the judicial power is vested but from which an appeal lies to the Supreme Court, can only be a judicial tribunal authorized to render a judgment, finally deciding the rights of parties litigant unless appealed from, and upon which execution may be issued to carry the judgment into effect, the Chief Justice goes on to say that " Congress cannot extend the appellate power of this Court beyond the limits prescribed by the Constitution, and can neither confer nor impose on it the authority or duty of hearing and determining an appeal from a Commissioner or Auditor, or any other tribunal exercising only special powers under an act of Congress; nor can Congress authorize or require this Court to express an opinion on a case where its judicial power could not be exercised, and where its judgment would not be final and conclusive upon the rights of the parties, and process of execution awarded to carry it into effect."

The Chief Justice finally insists that it is not only inherent in judicial power to decide a question finally, but also that execution shall issue to carry the judgment into effect, and that, if the holding of the court be not final in first instance, or upon appeal, and if it can not be executed, it is not an exercise of the judicial power in the sense of the Constitution. Thus, he says:

> The award of execution is a part, and an essential part of every judgment passed by a court exercising judicial power. It is no judgment, in the legal sense of the term, without it. Without such an award the judgment would be inoperative and nugatory, leaving the aggrieved party without a remedy. It would be merely an opinion, which would remain a dead letter, and without any operation upon the rights of the parties, unless Congress should at some future time sanction it, and pass a law authorizing the court to carry its opinion into effect. Such is not the judicial power confided to this Court, in the exercise of its appellate jurisdiction: yet it is the whole power that the Court is allowed to exercise under this act of Congress.[1]

In the concluding passage of this opinion, which can not be too often recommended and read, the Chief Justice calls attention to the fact that an attempt on the part of the Congress or of the government to invest the courts of the United States with the exercise of power not properly included in the grant of judicial power, would be an attempt on the part of the Government to infringe upon the sovereignty of the States creating the Union, which reserved to themselves and their people the powers not directly or indirectly delegated to the United States. Thus, Mr. Chief Justice Taney

[1] 117 U. S., *Appendix*, 702.

(marginal notes:) The Court may Compel Individuals but not States to Appear

Sovereignty of States Protected

said in the last opinion which he was destined to write as Chief Justice of the Court over which he presided:

> The Constitution of the United States delegates no judicial power to Congress. Its powers are confined to legislative duties, and restricted within certain prescribed limits. By the second section of Article VI., the laws of Congress are made the supreme law of the land only when they are made in pursuance of the legislative power specified in the Constitution; and by the Xth amendment the powers not delegated to the United States nor prohibited by it to the States, are reserved to the States respectively or to the people. The reservation to the States respectively can only mean the reservation of the rights of sovereignty which they respectively possessed before the adoption of the Constitution of the United States, and which they had not parted from by that instrument. And any legislation by Congress beyond the limits of the power delegated, would be trespassing upon the rights of the States or the people, and would not be the supreme law of the land, but null and void; and it would be the duty of the courts to declare it so. For whether an act of Congress is within the limits of its delegated power or not is a judicial question, to be decided by the courts, the Constitution having, in express terms, declared that the judicial power shall extend to all cases arising under the Constitution.[1]

Separation of Powers

After referring to the separation in England of the judicial power from the legislative and executive, he thus concludes:

> These cardinal principles of free government had not only been long established in England, but also in the United States from the time of their earliest colonization, and guided the American people in framing and adopting the present Constitution. And it is the duty of this Court to maintain it unimpaired as far as it may have the power. And while it executes firmly all the judicial powers entrusted to it, the Court will carefully abstain from exercising any power that is not strictly judicial in its character, and which is not clearly confided to it by the Constitution.[2]

In *In re* Sanborn (148 U. S., 222, 226), decided in 1893, the Supreme Court had occasion to recur to its holding in the Gordon case, and in so doing it referred with approval to Mr. Chief Justice Taney's opinion written for the court in that case. It is therefore unnecessary to state the facts in *In re* Sanborn, but a passage from the unanimous opinion of the Court is quoted as showing that that tribunal, upon reconsideration and

Finality of the Court's Decree

argument, insisted upon the finality of decision as essential to judicial power. Thus, Mr. Justice Shiras, in speaking for the court, said:

> Such a finding is not made obligatory on the department to which it is reported—certainly not so in terms,—and not so, as we think, by any necessary implication. We regard the function of the Court of Claims, in

---

[1] 117 U. S., *Appendix*, 705.
[2] *Ibid.*, 706.

such a case, as ancillary and advisory only.   The finding or conclusion reached by that court is not enforceable by any process of execution issuing from the court, nor is it made, by the statute, the final and indisputable basis of action either by the department or by congress.

In the leading case of *Marbury* v. *Madison* (1 Cranch, 137, 177), decided in 1803, which will later be considered at length, Mr. Chief Justice Marshall said: " It is emphatically the province and duty of the judicial department to say what the law is; " and to decide the conflict between competing rules of law is " of the very essence of judicial duty."   Some striking examples of the nature of judicial power have already been stated in the English cases on this subject, and, incidentally, in passages quoted from decisions of the Supreme Court. · As, however, the success of the great experiment—for the Supreme Court, without an exact model, was an experiment—was due to the fact that, in the exercise of judicial power, it has kept not merely departments of the General Government within the meed of power granted them by the Constitution, but also keeps the States of the Union themselves within their orbits, it is advisable in this connection to state the reason for and to show the process by which the Supreme Court of the United States, through the exercise of judicial power, necessarily restrains the acts of the departments of the General Government and of the States within those limits which the States themselves prescribed in the Constitution.

There are two passages from the Constitution to be considered in this connection.   The first, to be dealt with later, extends the judicial power to " all Cases, in Law and Equity, arising under this Constitution, the Laws of the United States, and Treaties made, or which shall be made, under their Authority." [1]   The second declares " this Constitution and the Laws of the United States," made as in the first passage, " the supreme Law of the Land; and the Judges in every State shall be bound thereby, any Thing in the Constitution or Laws of any State to the Contrary notwithstanding." [2] It will be observed that, while the Constitution is the supreme law of the land, the laws of the United States are only to be considered supreme and binding if they are made in pursuance of the Constitution, for it might be attempted to pass laws which were not in pursuance of that instrument.   In this latter case they are void, because the grant is to make laws in accordance with, not inconsistent with, the Constitution.   The intention of the framers to have the judicial power pass upon and determine these questions is evident in extending it to the Constitution, to the laws of the United States, and to the treaties, which are likewise laws, made under the authority of the United States, and by requiring judges in every State to be bound

[1] Art. III, Section 2, of the Constitution.
[2] Art. VI of the Constitution.

by the Constitution, laws of the United States made in pursuance of the Constitution and the treaties of the United States.

Experience shows that men can not safely be entrusted with interpreting, applying and executing the laws which they themselves have made, and no man can in reason be allowed to be suitor, judge and sheriff in his own case. There is indeed a presumption that the legislature, owing its existence to the Constitution, will restrain its acts within the grant of power, and there may also be a presumption that the executive will not knowingly exceed the grant of power. But if the legislative or executive department should determine this question for itself, there is reason to believe, and indeed to fear, that self-interest might enter into the determination. The case with the judiciary is different. The court does not make the law which it interprets and applies. The judge is not a party to the case. If he has any interest in it, he can be challenged and disqualified. And he does not himself execute the decision which he has rendered, as this is the duty of the executive branch of the government.

But the framers of the Constitution did not need to rely upon unaided reason, or even to be guided by the dangers suggested by experience. As colonists they had been kept by the King in Council, acting directly or indirectly through a committee, within the sphere of the grant of power contained in the colonial charters, and they were familiar with English cases declaring null and void by-laws of a corporation in excess of the grant. We would therefore expect that they would have invested the judiciary with this power, and although there is no express grant of this function or attribute of power in the Constitution other than the words which have been quoted, it is a fact that the framers of the Constitution stated in the debates, as reported by Mr. Madison, that the Supreme Court would exercise this power, and it is also a fact that statements of a like kind were made in the *Federalist,* which was written by Messrs. Hamilton, Madison and Jay for the purpose of securing the ratification of the Constitution of the United States and which is today regarded as the classical and contemporaneous exposition of the Constitution. It is further a fact that members of the State conventions, called for the express purpose of ratifying the Constitution, declared that the Supreme Court possessed such power under the constitutional grant. And it is, finally, a fact that the Chief Justice who first passed upon this question, and who rendered the classical decision in favor of the judicial power, expressly so said in the Virginia convention.

A well informed and accurate writer states that, among the fifty-five members of the Constitutional Convention, there were " twenty-five whose character, ability, diligence and regularity of attendance, separately or in combination, made them the dominant element in the Convention; " and that, of these twenty-five, "seventeen . . . declared, directly or indirectly, for judicial control."[1] To these are also to be added two members not included among the twenty-five, who expressed themselves in favor of judicial control by deed rather than by word of mouth; because David Brearly, a delegate from New Jersey and Chief Justice of its Supreme Court, had, it is believed, supplied an early if not the first instance in American annals of the judicial power declaring an act of the legislature unconstitutional, as inconsistent with the fundamental law of the land, in the case of *Holmes* v. *Walton,* decided in 1780. George Wythe, a delegate from Virginia and justice of the Court of Appeals of his State, appears to have said, two years later (1782), in the case of *Commonwealth* v. *Caton* (4 Call, 5), that an act of the legislature of Virginia was unconstitutional for a like reason. Elbridge Gerry, a delegate from Massachusetts, expressed himself strongly on this point on two occasions. In the matter of making judges members of the proposed council of revision, he doubted whether the judiciary ought to form a part of it " as they will have a sufficient check ag[st]. encroachments on their own department by their exposition of the laws, which involved a power of deciding on their Constitutionality. In some States the Judges had actually set aside laws as being ag[st]. the Constitution. This was done too with general approbation. It was quite foreign from the nature of y[e] office to make them judges of the policy of public measures."[2] On a second occasion he said:

> If the power of making declaratory acts really vests in Congress and the judges are bound by our decisions, we may alter that part of the Constitution which is secured from being amended by the 5th article; . . . The merchant does not construe the Constitution in the manner that we have done. He therefore institutes a suit and brings it before the supreme judicature of the United States for trial. The judges, who are bound by oath to support the Constitution, declare against this law; they would therefore give judgment in favor of the merchant.[3]

This latter statement of Mr. Gerry is especially noteworthy, as it recognized the power and method in which it is exercised at the suit of an individual who feels himself aggrieved in his property or in his person.

We would expect to have Alexander Hamilton state his views on this very important and, in the language of the day, interesting question, and we are not disappointed. In the 78th number of *The Federalist,* written to advocate the revision of the Constitution, Colonel Hamilton said:

> There is no position which depends on clearer principles, than that every act of a delegated authority, contrary to the tenor of the commission

[1] Charles A. Beard, *The Supreme Court and the Constitution,* 1912, pp. 17-18.
[2] *Documentary History,* Vol. iii, pp. 54-5. Session of June 4th.
[3] Elliot, *Debates,* Vol. iv, p. 393.

under which it is exercised, is void. No legislative act, therefore, contrary to the constitution, can be valid. To deny this, would be to affirm, that the deputy is greater than his principal; that the servant is above his master; that the representatives of the people are superior to the people themselves; that men, acting by virtue of powers, may do not only what their powers do not authorize, but what they forbid.[1]

And in a later passage from the same number, he says:

> The interpretation of the laws is the proper and peculiar province of the courts. A constitution is, in fact, and must be, regarded by the judges as a fundamental law. It must therefore belong to them to ascertain its meaning, as well as the meaning of any particular act proceeding from the legislative body. If there should happen to be an irreconcilable variance between the two, that which has the superior obligation and validity ought, of course, to be preferred; in other words, the constitution ought to be preferred to the statute, the intention of the people to the intention of their agents.[2]

In addition to these authoritative pronouncements, we have the expressions of opinion of two men made in the convention of their States, both destined to be Chief Justices of the Supreme Court of the United States. Thus, Oliver Ellsworth, who had been a member of the Philadelphia Convention, said:

> This Constitution defines the extent of the powers of the general government. If the general legislature should at any time overleap their limits, the judicial department is a constitutional check. If the United States go beyond their powers, if they make a law which the Constitution does not authorize, it is void; and the judicial power, the national judges, who, to secure their impartiality, are to be made independent, will declare it to be void.[3]

The other, John Marshall, a member of the Virginian, though not of the Constitutional, Convention, but destined to be the great expounder of the Constitution from the bench, said in the course of the debates in his State Convention:

> Has the government of the United States power to make laws on every subject? . . . Can they make laws affecting the mode of transferring property, or contracts, or claims, between citizens of the same state? Can they go beyond the delegated powers? If they were to make a law not warranted by any of the powers enumerated, it would be considered by the judges as an infringement of the Constitution which they are to guard. They would not consider such a law as coming under their jurisdiction. They would declare it void.[4]

[1] *The Federalist*, 1802, Vol. ii, p. 212.
[2] *Ibid.*, Vol. ii, pp. 212–13.
[3] Elliot, *Debates*, Vol. ii, p. 196.
[4] *Ibid.*, Vol. iii, p. 553.

These expressions of opinion before the Constitution went into effect, are of importance in that they foreshadow the actions of courts established under the Constitution in the interpretation and application of judicial power to cases brought before them involving the Constitution, laws of the United States made in pursuance thereof, and treaties concluded by the United States with foreign countries. It will be recalled that, in a letter addressed to the President under date of April 18, 1792, by Messrs. Wilson and Blair, Justices, and Judge Peters of the District Court of Pennsylvania, they referred to " the sentiments, which, on a late painful occasion, governed us, with regard to an act passed by the legislature of the union." [1]

This is conjectured and may be taken as established by Professor Farrand in an interesting note on the first Hayburn case to be the application of one William Hayburn to the Circuit Court of Pennsylvania for a pension under the act of Congress of 1792, and the decision of the court, just one week before the date of the letter, that such act was unconstitutional and that the judges could not therefore entertain and grant the application. The following further passage from the letter is thought by Professor Farrand to refer to this action of the Circuit Court:

> Upon due consideration, we have been unanimously of opinion, that, under this act, the circuit court, held for the Pennsylvania district, could not proceed; . . . Be assured, that, though it became necessary, it was far from being pleasant. To be obliged to act contrary either to the obvious directions of congress, or to a constitutional principle, in our judgment, equally obvious, excited feelings in us, which we hope never to experience again.[2]

The reader will now be prepared to appreciate the brief record copied from the docket of the Circuit Court, a discovery made known by Professor Farrand:

> At a Circuit Court of the United States in and for the Pennsylvania District, etc.
> 11th day of April, 1792, before Wilson, Blair and Peters.
> The petition of William Hayburn, was read and after due deliberation thereupon had it is considered by the Court that the same be not proceeded upon.[3]

Three years later, in 1795, the Circuit Court of the United States for the District of Pennsylvania, declared an act of that State to be null and void, as repugnant to the constitution of Pennsylvania, in *Van Horne's*

---

[1] See *ante*, p. 351.
[2] Max Farrand, The First Hayburn Case, 1792, *American Historical Review*, Vol. xiii, p. 283. (January, 1908.)
[3] *Ibid.*

Lessee v. *Dorrance* (2 Dallas, 304, 308, 309).   More fortunate than Messrs. Wilson and Blair in the Hayburn case, the opinion, or rather the charge, of Mr. Justice Patterson has been preserved, in accordance with which the jury rendered its verdict and the court its judgment.

In the course of his charge, Mr. Justice Patterson had occasion to refer to the origin and nature of a constitution and the relation to it of laws passed by a legislature under a constitutional grant of power, and his language is applicable to the constitution of any state where the American system prevails.   Thus, he said:

> The Constitution is the work or will of the People themselves, in their original, sovereign, and unlimited capacity.   Law is the work or will of the Legislature in their derivative and subordinate capacity.   The one is the work of the Creator, and the other of the Creature.   The Constitution fixes limits to the exercise of legislative authority, and prescribes the orbit within which it must move.   In short, gentlemen, the Constitution is the sun of the political system, around which all Legislative, Executive and Judicial bodies must revolve.   Whatever may be the case in other countries, yet in this there can be no doubt, that every act of the Legislature, repugnant to the Constitution, is absolutely void. . . .
> The Constitution of a State is stable and permanent, not to be worked upon by the temper of the times, nor to rise and fall with the tide of events: notwithstanding the competition of opposing interests, and the violence of contending parties, it remains firm and immoveable, as a mountain amidst the strife of storms, or a rock in the ocean amidst the raging of the waves.   I take it to be a clear position; that if a legislative act oppugns a constitutional principle, the former must give way, and be rejected on the score of repugnance.   I hold it to be a position equally clear and sound, that, in such case, it will be the duty of the Court to adhere to the Constitution, and to declare the act null and void.   The Constitution is the basis of legislative authority; it lies at the foundation of all law, and is a rule and commission by which both Legislators and Judges are to proceed.   It is an important principle, which, in the discussion of questions of the present kind, ought never to be lost sight of, that the Judiciary in this country is not a subordinate, but co-ordinate, branch of the government.[1]

Fifteen years later, that is to say, in 1803, after having his experience at the bar broadened by service in Congress, as Minister to France, as Secretary of War and as Secretary of State, John Marshall was called upon, as Chief Justice of the Supreme Court, to decide the very question in fact which he had decided in theory in the Constitutional Convention of his State.   In holding that the original jurisdiction of the Supreme Court as stated in the Constitution could neither be enlarged nor lessened by the Congress, he declared on behalf of the court, in the case of *Marbury* v. *Madison* (1 Cranch, 137), an act of Congress unconstitutional and as null

[1] 2 Dallas, 308-9.

and void, which attempted to enlarge its original jurisdiction. In the course
of his opinion he said:

> The question, whether an act, repugnant to the constitution, can become
> the law of the land, is a question deeply interesting to the United States;
> but, happily, not of an intricacy proportioned to its interest. It seems only
> necessary to recognise certain principles, supposed to have been long and
> well established, to decide it.
>
> That the people have an original right to establish, for their future gov-
> ernment, such principles as, in their opinion, shall most conduce to their
> own happiness is the basis on which the whole American fabric has been
> erected. The exercise of this original right is a very great exertion; nor
> can it, nor ought it, to be frequently repeated. The principles, therefore,
> so established, are deemed fundamental. And as the authority from which
> they proceed is supreme, and can seldom act, they are designed to be
> permanent.
>
> This original and supreme will organizes the government, and assigns
> to different departments their respective powers. It may either stop here,
> or establish certain limits not to be transcended by those departments.
>
> The government of the United States is of the latter description. The
> powers of the legislature are defined and limited; and that these limits may
> not be mistaken, or forgotten, the constitution is written. To what purpose
> are powers limited, and to what purpose is that limitation committed to
> writing, if these limits may, at any time, be passed by those intended to be
> restrained? The distinction between a government with limited and unlim-
> ited powers is abolished, if those limits do not confine the persons on whom
> they are imposed, and if acts prohibited and acts allowed, are of equal
> obligation. It is a proposition too plain to be contested, that the consti-
> tution controls any legislative act repugnant to it; or, that the legislature
> may alter the constitution by an ordinary act. . . .
>
> It is emphatically the province and duty of the judicial department to
> say what the law is. Those who apply the rule to particular cases, must
> of necessity expound and interpret that rule. If two laws conflict with
> each other, the courts must decide on the operation of each.
>
> So if a law be in opposition to the constitution; if both the law and the
> constitution apply to a particular case, so that the court must either decide
> that case conformably to the law, disregarding the constitution; or con-
> formably to the constitution, disregarding the law; the court must determine
> which of these conflicting rules governs the case. This is of the very
> essence of judicial duty.
>
> If, then, the courts are to regard the constitution, and the constitution
> is superior to any ordinary act of the legislature, the constitution, and not
> such ordinary act, must govern the case to which they both apply.
>
> Those, then, who controvert the principle that the constitution is to be
> considered, in court, as a paramount law, are reduced to the necessity of
> maintaining that courts must close their eyes on the constitution, and see
> only the law.
>
> This doctrine would subvert the very foundation of all written consti-
> tutions. It would declare that an act which, according to the principles and
> theory of our government, is entirely void, is yet, in practice, completely
> obligatory. It would declare that if the legislature shall do what is expressly
> forbidden, such act, notwithstanding the express prohibition, is in reality

effectual. It would be giving to the legislature a practical and real omnipotence, with the same breath which professes to restrict their powers within narrow limits. It is prescribing limits, and declaring that those limits may be passed at pleasure.

That it thus reduces to nothing what we have deemed the greatest improvement on political institutions—a written constitution—would of itself be sufficient, in America, where written constitutions have been viewed with so much reverence, for rejecting the construction. But the peculiar expressions of the constitution of the United States furnish additional arguments in favor of its rejection.

The judicial power of the United States is extended to all cases arising under the constitution.

Could it be the intention of those who gave this power, to say that in using it the constitution should not be looked into? That a case arising under the constitution should be decided without examining the instrument under which it arises?

This is too extravagant to be maintained.

In some cases, then, the constitution must be looked into by the judges. And if they can open it at all, what part of it are they forbidden to read or obey?[1]

Two further cases may be considered in this connection, *McCulloch* v. *Maryland* (4 Wheaton, 316), decided in 1819, and *Collector* v. *Day* (11 Wallace, 113), decided in 1870.

For present purposes, the facts in *McCulloch* v. *Maryland* may be stated as an attempt on the part of the State of Maryland, by act of its legislature, to impose a tax upon a branch of the bank of the United States establishment in that State. We are not concerned with the power of the United States to establish a bank, for, although the power to create a corporation was not given in express terms to the Congress by the Constitution, and while the Congress might not have been authorized to establish a corporation as such, without relation to powers expressly or impliedly granted, nevertheless the court found that a corporation could be created, such as a bank, as a financial or fiscal agent of the United States, under the authorization to Congress to make all laws which shall be necessary and proper for carrying into execution the powers vested in the Congress.

Admitting the power to create the bank as an agency of the government of the Union, the court held that a State of the Union could not tax an agency of the General Government, and that a law of Maryland attempting to do so was unconstitutional, and therefore null and void, inasmuch as the United States was sovereign and could therefore lawfully exercise sovereign powers within the limits of the Constitution. It was the opinion of the court that,

[1] 1 Cranch, 175-9.

In America, the powers of sovereignty are divided between the government of the Union, and those of the States. They are each sovereign, with respect to the objects committed to it, and neither sovereign with respect to the objects committed to the other.[1]

These were not idle words on the part of Mr. Chief Justice Marshall. He meant what he said, and, recognizing that " In America, the powers of sovereignty are divided between the government of the Union, and those of the States," the Supreme Court held the reverse to be true in the case of *Collector* v. *Day* (11 Wallace, 113), that the United States could not, under the Constitution, tax an agent of the States, in this particular instance a judicial officer of Massachusetts, and that an Act of Congress attempting to do so was unconstitutional, and therefore null and void. In delivering the opinion of the court, Mr. Justice Nelson referred throughout to *McCulloch* v. *Maryland,* saying:

It is conceded in the case of *McCulloch* v. *Maryland,* that the power of taxation by the States was not abridged by the grant of a similar power to the government of the Union; that it was retained by the States, and that the power is to be concurrently exercised by the two governments; and also that there is no express constitutional prohibition upon the States against taxing the means or instrumentalities of the general government. But, it was held, and, we agree properly held, to be prohibited by necessary implication; otherwise, the States might impose taxation to an extent that would impair, if not wholly defeat, the operations of the Federal authorities when acting in their appropriate sphere.[2]

That the United States could not tax an agency of the State would seem to be as clear as that the State could not tax an agency of the United States, and Mr. Justice Nelson, speaking for the court, so held for the following reasons:

It is a familiar rule of construction of the Constitution of the Union, that the sovereign powers vested in the State governments by their respective constitutions, remained unaltered and unimpaired, except so far as they were granted to the government of the United States. That the intention of the framers of the Constitution in this respect might not be misunderstood, this rule of interpretation is expressly declared in the tenth article of the amendments, namely: " The powers not delegated to the United States are reserved to the States respectively, or, to the people." The government of the United States, therefore, can claim no powers which are not granted to it by the Constitution, and the powers actually granted must be such as are expressly given, or given by necessary implication.

The general government, and the States, although both exist within the same territorial limits, are separate and distinct sovereignties, acting separately and independently of each other, within their respective spheres.

Court's
Relation
to the
Government
and to the
States

[1] 4 Wheaton, 410.
[2] 11 Wallace, 123–4.

The former in its appropriate sphere is supreme; but the States within the limits of their powers not granted, or, in the language of the tenth amendment, "reserved," are as independent of the general government as that government within its sphere is independent of the States.[1]

It is indeed, as Mr. Chief Justice Marshall said, "the province and duty of the judicial department to say what the law is" and that it is "of the very essence of judicial duty" to decide the conflict between competing rules of law. But the judicial power of the United States was not meant to be and is not the agency of the General Government, to maintain its supremacy at the expense of the States. It maintains the powers which the States, in their common interest, freely granted to the agency of their creation, which we call the United States, and protects it from assault by one of the States in its own interest. On the other hand, it maintains the rights of the States not granted by them to the Government of the Union, but, in the language of the 10th Amendment, "reserved to the States respectively, or to the people" against assault of that Government in the unconstitutional exercise of power. As Chief Justice Chase said in the great and leading case of *Texas* v. *White* (7 Wallace, 700, 725), decided in 1868, at a time when the existence of the States depended upon the correct interpretation of the judicial power of the United States:

> . . . "the people of each State compose a State, having its own government, and endowed with all the functions essential to separate and independent existence," and that "without the States in union, there could be no such political body as the United States." [County of Lane *v.* The State of Oregon, 7 Wall. 76.] Not only, therefore, can there be no loss of separate and independent autonomy to the States, through their union under the Constitution, but it may be not unreasonably said that the preservation of the States, and the maintenance of their governments, are as much within the design and care of the Constitution as the preservation of the Union and the maintenance of the National government. The Constitution, in all its provisions, looks to an indestructible Union, composed of indestructible States.

A difficulty standing in the creation of an international court of justice has been, and appears still to be, the difficulty of distinguishing judicial from political power. There appears to be a willingness to create an international judiciary, reserving, however, the right of each State in controversy, to determine whether the question involved is or is not political.

The experience of the United States shows that this question can properly be determined by a court, because in a long line of decisions the Supreme Court of the United States has not only been able to draw the line with precision, but also to the satisfaction of the litigating parties.

The nature of judicial power should, therefore, be clear to those who really care to unveil its mysteries.

[1] 11 Wallace, 124.

XVIII

POWERS OF THE SUPREME COURT

I directed this cause to stand over for judgment, not so much from any doubt of what was the justice of the case, as by reason of the nature of it, the great consequence and importance, and the great labour and ability of the argument on both sides; it being for the determination of the right and boundaries of two great provincial governments and three counties; of a nature worthy the judicature of a *Roman* senate rather than of a single judge: and my consolation is, that if I should err in my judgment, there is a judicature equal in dignity to a *Roman* senate that will correct it. . . .

The relief prayed must be admitted to be the common and ordinary equity dispensed by this court; the specific performance of agreements being one of the great heads of this court, and the most useful one, and better than damages at law, so far as relates to the thing in *specie;* and more useful in a case of this nature than in most others; because no damages in an action of covenant could be at all adequate to what is intended by the parties, and to the utility to arise from this agreement, *viz.* the settling and fixing these boundaries in peace, to prevent the disorder and mischief, which in remote countries, distant from the seat of government, are most likely to happen, and most mischievous. Therefore the remedy prayed by a specific performance is more necessary here than in other cases: provided it is proper in other respects: and the relief sought must prevail, unless sufficient objections are shewn by defendant; who has made many and various for that purpose. . . .

. . . This court therefore has no original jurisdiction on the direct question of the original right of the boundaries; and this bill does not stand in need of that. It is founded on articles executed in *England* under seal for mutual consideration; which gives jurisdiction to the King's courts both of law and equity, whatever be the subject matter. . . The conscience of the party was bound by this agreement; and being within the jurisdiction of this court (4 Inst. 213; 1 Ves. sen. 204, 255), which acts *in personam*, the court may properly decree it as an agreement, if a foundation for it. To go a step farther: as this court collaterally and in consequence of the agreement judges concerning matters not originally in its jurisdiction, it would decree a performance of articles of agreement to perform a sentence in the Ecclesiastical court, just as a court of law would maintain an action for damages in breach of covenant. (*Lord Chancellor Hardwicke in Penn v. Lord Baltimore, 1 Vesey, Sr., 444, 446-448, decided in 1750, English Reports, Full Reprint, Vol. XXVII, Chancery VII, 1903, pp. 1133-1135.*)

We are all satisfied, that the bill must be dismissed. It is a case of mutual treaty between persons acting in that instance as states independent of each other; and the circumstance, that the *East India* Company are mere subjects with relation to this country, has nothing to do with that. That treaty was entered into with them, not as subjects, but as a neighbouring independent state, and is the same, as if it was a treaty between two sovereigns; and consequently is not a subject of private, municipal, jurisdiction. (*Barclay v. Russell, 3 Ves. 424. Dolder v. Lord Huntingfield, 9 Ves. 283.*)

The Court considers the case totally independent of the judgment, the *Lord Chancellor* pronounced: for the case, upon which the Court proceeds, is introduced by the answer, which has added a great number of particulars to the case by introducing the other treaty, which explains the first; and shews, it was not mercantile in its nature, but political; and therefore this decision stands wholly clear of the judgment upon the plea. (*Lord Commissioner Eyre in Nabob of the Carnatic v. East India Company, 2 Vesey, Jr., 56, 60, decided in 1793, English Reports, Full Reprint, Vol. XXX, Chancery X, 1903, p. 523.*)

If the bill contains no averment of a right of soil in *New-York*, I think it must be defective, and lays no foundation for an injunction. To have the benefit of the agreement between the states, the defendants below (who are the settlers of *New-York*) must apply to a court of equity as well as the state herself; but, in no case, can a specific performance be decreed, unless there is a substantial right of soil, not a mere political jurisdiction, to be protected and enforced. (*Chief Justice Ellsworth in State of New York v. State of Connecticut, 4 Dallas, 3, 4, note, decided in 1799.*)

It is emphatically the province and duty of the judicial department to say what the law is. Those who apply the rule to particular cases, must of necessity expound and interpret that rule. If two laws conflict with each other, the courts must decide on the operation of each.

So if a law be in opposition to the constitution; if both the law and the constitution apply to a particular case, so that the court must either decide that case conformably to the law, disregarding the constitution; or conformably to the constitution, disregarding the law; the court must determine which of these conflicting rules governs the case. This is of the very essence of judicial duty. (*Chief Justice Marshall in Marbury v. Madison, 1 Cranch, 137, 177-178, decided in 1803.*)

A serious additional objection exists to the jurisdiction of the court. Is the matter of the bill the proper subject for judicial inquiry and decision? It seeks to restrain a state from the forcible exercise of legislative power over a neighbouring people, asserting their independence; their right to which the state denies. . .

. . . The bill requires us to control the legislature of Georgia, and to restrain the exertion of its physical force. The propriety of such an interposition by the court may be well questioned. It savours too much of the exercise of political power to be within the proper province of the judicial department. (*Chief Justice Marshall in Cherokee Nation v. State of Georgia, 5 Peters, 1, 20, decided in 1831.*)

In council, the king had no original judicial power, 1 Ves. sen. 447. He decided on appeals from the colonial courts, settled boundaries, in virtue of his prerogative, where there was no agreement; but if there is a disputed agreement, the king cannot decree on it, and therefore, the council remit it to be determined in another place, on the foot of the contract, 1 Ves. sen. 447. In virtue of his prerogative, where there was no agreement, 1 Ves. sen. 205, the king acts not as a judge, but as the sovereign acting by the advice of his counsel, the members whereof do not and cannot sit as judges. By the statute 20 E. 3, ch. 1, it is declared, that "the king hath delegated his whole judicial power to the judges, all matters of judicature according to the laws," 1 Ruff. 246; 4 Co. Inst. 70, 74; he had, therefore, none to exercise: and judges, though members of council, did not sit in judicature, but merely as his advisers. . .

If judicial authority is competent to settle what is the line between judicial and political power and questions, it appears from this view of the law, as administered in England and the courts of the United States, to have been done without any one decision to the contrary, from the time of Edward the Third. The statute referred to, operated like our constitution to make all questions judicial, which were submitted to judicial power, by the parliament of England, the people or legislature of these states, or congress; and when this has been done by the constitution, in reference to disputed boundaries, it will be a dead letter if we did not exercise it now, as this Court has done in the cases referred to. (*Mr. Justice Baldwin in State of Rhode Island v. State of Massachusetts, 12 Peters, 657, 739-748, decided in 1838.*)

A motion has been made by the counsel for the defendants to dismiss the bill for want of jurisdiction, for which a precedent is found in the case of *The State of Rhode Island* v. *The State of Massachusetts.* It is claimed that the court has no jurisdiction either over the subject-matter set forth in the bill or over the parties defendants. And, in support of the first ground, it is urged that the matters involved, and presented for adjudication, are political and not judicial, and, therefore, not the subject of judicial cognizance.

This distinction results from the organization of the government into the three great departments, executive, legislative, and judicial, and from the assignment and limitation of the powers of each by the Constitution.

The judicial power is vested in one supreme court, and in such inferior courts as Congress may ordain and establish: the political power of the government in the other two departments.

The distinction between judicial and political power is so generally acknowledged in the jurisprudence both of England and of this country, that we need do no more than refer to some of the authorities on the subject. They are all in one direction. Nabob of Carnatic *v.* The East India Co., 1 Vesey, Jr., 375-393, S. C., 2 Id. 56-60; Penn *v.* Lord Baltimore, 1 Vesey, 446-7; New York *v.* Connecticut, 4 Dallas, 4-6; The Cherokee Nation *v.* Georgia, 5 Peters, 1, 20, 29, 30, 51, 75; The State of Rhode Island *v.* The State of Massachusetts, 12 Ib., 657, 733, 734, 737, 738. (*Mr. Justice Nelson in Georgia v. Stanton, 6 Wallace, 50, 71, decided in 1867.*)

The position and rank, therefore, assigned to this Court in the Government of the United States, differ from that of the highest judicial power in England, which is subordinate to the legislative power, and bound to obey any law that Parliament may pass, although it may, in the opinion of the court, be in conflict with the principles of Magna Charta or the Petition of Rights.

The reason for giving such unusual power to a judicial tribunal is obvious. It was necessary to give it from the complex character of the Government of the United States, which is in part National and in part Federal: where two separate governments exercise certain powers of sovereignty over the same territory, each independent of the other within its appropriate sphere of action, and where there was, therefore, an absolute necessity, in order to preserve internal tranquillity, that there should be some tribunal to decide between the Government of the United States and the government of a State whenever any controversy should arise as to their relative and respective powers in the common territory. The Supreme Court was created for that purpose, and to insure its impartiality it was absolutely necessary to make it independent of the legislative power, and the influence direct or indirect of Congress and the Executive. Hence the care with which its jurisdiction, powers, and duties are defined in the Constitution, and its independence of the legislative branch of the government secured. (*Chief Justice Taney in Gordon v. United States, 117 United States, 697, 700-701, decided in 1864.*)

It was to prevent an appeal to the sword and a dissolution of the compact that this Court, by the organic law, was made equal in origin and equal in title to the legislative and executive branches of the government: its powers defined, and limited, and made strictly judicial, and placed therefore beyond the reach of the powers delegated to the Legislative and Executive Departments. (*Chief Justice Taney in Gordon v. United States, 117 United States, 697, 701, decided in 1864.*)

The legal supremacy of the constitution is essential to the existence of the state; the glory of the founders of the United States is to have devised or adopted arrangements under which the Constitution became in reality as well as name the supreme law of the land. This end they attained by adherence to a very obvious principle, and by the invention of appropriate machinery for carrying this principle into effect.

The principle is clearly expressed in the Constitution of the United States. "The Constitution," runs article 6, "and the laws of the United States which shall be made in pursuance thereof . . . shall be the supreme law of the land, and the judges in every State shall be bound thereby, anything in the constitution or laws of any State to the contrary notwithstanding." The import of these expressions is unmistakable. . .

To have laid down the principle with distinctness is much, but the great problem was how to ensure that the principle should be obeyed; for there existed a danger that judges depending on the federal government should wrest the Constitution in favour of the central power, and that judges created by the States should wrest it in favour of State rights or interests. This problem has been solved by the creation of the Supreme Court and of the Federal Judiciary. (*Albert Venn Dicey, Introduction to the Study of the Law of the Constitution, 1885, 8th edition, 1915, pp. 154-155.*)

CHAPTER XVIII

POWERS OF THE SUPREME COURT

IN settling the jurisdiction of the Supreme Court, the draft of the Constitution as it left the hands of the Committee of Detail provided—in the 3d section of its 11th article, that " the Jurisdiction of the Supreme Court shall extend to all cases arising under laws passed by the Legislature of the United States." That the court should possess and that it should only exercise judicial power was the intent of the framers of the Constitution, as plainly indicated by the following passage from Mr. Madison's Notes:

> Doc^r. Johnson moved to insert the words " this Constitution and the " before the word " laws."
>
> M^r. Madison doubted whether it was not going too far to extend the jurisdiction of the Court generally to cases arising Under the Constitution, & whether it ought not to be limited to cases of a Judiciary Nature. The right of expounding the Constitution in cases not of this nature ought not to be given to that Department.
>
> The motion of Doc^r. Johnson was agreed to nem: con: it being generally supposed that the jurisdiction given was constructively limited to cases of a Judiciary nature.

Determination of Constitutionality

And, that there might be no doubt on this point, Mr. Madison moved that the phrase " the jurisdiction of the Supreme Court " should be stricken and replaced by the words " Judicial power," which, as Mr. Madison records, " was agreed to nem: con:" [1]

The framers of the Constitution were clear in their minds as to the function of the Supreme Court. The Government of the Union as well as the Union itself, owes its existence to the Constitution, and that instrument is at once the source and measure of power which these United States can lawfully exercise. Laws in accordance with it are constitutional, laws inconsistent with it are unconstitutional, whether they be laws of the Congress, constitutions or laws of the States of the Union.

To determine these questions is important, often difficult, and as delicate as difficult. The power to do so must be lodged somewhere. The legislature can not decide whether its act is proper, because so to do would subordinate the Constitution to its creature. The executive can not decide

---

[1] *Documentary History of the Constitution*, Vol. III, pp. 626, 627. Session of August 27th.

374

finally, although he may exercise a veto upon legislation, because to do so would subordinate the Constitution to his will or pleasure. The framers of the Constitution, therefore, confided the determination of these questions to the judicial power by extending it " to all cases in law and equity arising under this Constitution, the laws of the United States and treaties made or which shall be made under their authority." And, that there might be no doubt upon this fundamental question, they provided, in Article 6, that " This Constitution and the laws of the United States which shall be made in pursuance thereof; and all treaties made, or which shall be made, under the authority of the United States, shall be the supreme law of the land; and the judges in every State shall be bound thereby, anything in the constitution or laws of any State to the contrary notwithstanding."

Upon this section two observations may be made at this time: first, the Constitution is supreme, an equality only shared by the laws of the United States made in pursuance thereof and by treaties of the United States; second, that the judges of the States, in interpreting laws, are to be bound by the supreme law of the land.

No authority need be cited for the statement that the interpretation of a written instrument is a judicial question. The colony was bound by its charter, and all acts of the colony or colonists in excess of the charter as authoritatively interpreted, were void. The Constitution was to be the charter of the erstwhile colonies, now States of the Union, and all acts in excess of the powers, directly or indirectly granted to the Government of the Union, were to be null and void. In the case of the colony, the King in Council decided; in the case of the Union, the Supreme Court of the States.

It was therefore essential that the judicial power should not be associated in the labors of the executive or legislative branch. The judges should not be members of the proposed but unadopted Council to revise the laws of the States, nor should they be members of an advisory council to the executive; for they could not be expected to pass upon the actions of one or the other in a spirit of detachment, if they had been directly, or, indeed, indirectly, concerned with either. Therefore, the judges should hold the scales of jus- *Powers Purely Judicial* tice firmly in their hands, lest the legislative or executive should tip the balance against the Constitution. The functions of the judges were to be and to remain judicial, and the judicial power, therefore, was to stand separate and apart from the legislative and the executive branches, which, in contradistinction to the judiciary, can be called the political branches of the Government.

In the exercise of their respective powers, the legislative and the executive could not be subject to the judiciary, because the exercise of a right depends upon the body possessing it. It may decide wisely or unwisely, but, having the power to decide, it necessarily must determine when it shall or shall not make a use of this power. The function of the judiciary can only be to determine, not the wisdom or the folly of the exercise of power, but whether the power exercised is or is not, in an appropriate case, within the power expressly or impliedly delegated by the Constitution to the Government of the Union.

If the question is political, the judicial power will not pass upon it, as the legislative and executive branches of the Government are vested with its exercise. If, however, it is claimed by the legislative or executive to be political, whereas in fact it is not, the judicial power extends to it, inasmuch as the legislative and executive departments of the Government can only exercise political, not judicial power; and even if the question be political, the judiciary must needs examine it in a proper and specific case, in order to determine whether it is within or without the grant of power. It was to be expected that cases of this nature would arise. They have frequently arisen, and can best be analyzed and defined by decisions of the Supreme Court of the United States.

Political
Contrasted
with
Judicial
Powers

We may accept in the abstract the separation of judicial from political functions; but it is only through the concrete case that the line of demarcation, existing in theory, is rendered visible in fact. A few, therefore, of the many cases involving this question, will be considered, in order that the reader may frame for himself the definition of political power and draw the line between judicial power, on the one hand, and legislative and executive power, on the other.

In *Foster* v. *Neilson* (2 Peters, 253), decided in 1829, the Supreme Court had occasion to consider the question of international relations, the conduct of which is confided by the Constitution to the President, with the advice and consent of the Senate. A treaty thus made is, by the Constitution, part of the supreme law of the land. As a law, the judicial power is extended to it, but only in the sense of interpreting it and applying it to a concrete case of a justiciable nature. The propriety of making the treaty depends upon the discretion of the President and of two-thirds of the Senators present during its consideration, in whom the treaty-making power is vested.

The facts in the case are very complicated, and for present purposes it may be said that the plaintiffs claimed a large tract of land lying in Louisiana, about thirty miles east of the Mississippi River and in the possession of the defendant under a grant of the Spanish Governor, confirmed by the King of Spain. The defendant, admitting the grant, claimed that it was null and void in that the land in question was situated in territory which, before the grant, had been ceded to France and by France to the

United States. From a judgment in favor of the defendant, had in the District Court of the United States for the Eastern District of Louisiana, the cause was heard before the Supreme Court upon a writ of error. Mr. Chief Justice Marshall thus stated the facts:

> The case presents this very intricate, and, at one time, very interesting question: To whom did the country between the Iberville and the Perdido rightfully belong, when the title now asserted by the plaintiffs was acquired?
>
> This question has been repeatedly discussed, with great talent and research, by the government of the United States and that of Spain. The United States have perseveringly and earnestly insisted, that by the treaty of St. Ildefonso, made on the 1st of October, in the year 1800, Spain ceded the disputed territory as part of Louisiana to France; and that France, by the treaty of Paris, signed on the 30th of April 1803, and ratified on the 21st of October, in the same year, ceded it to the United States. Spain has with equal perseverance and earnestness maintained that her cession to France comprehended that territory only which was at that time, denominated Louisiana, consisting of the island of New Orleans, and the country she received from France west of the Mississippi.[1]

In view of these circumstances, Mr. Chief Justice Marshall said, on behalf of the court:

> However this may be, it is, we think, incontestable, that the American construction of the article, if not entirely free from question, is supported by arguments of great strength, which cannot be easily confuted.
>
> In a controversy between two nations, concerning national boundary, it is scarcely possible, that the courts of either should refuse to abide by the measures adopted by its own government. There being no common tribunal to decide between them, each determines for itself on its own rights, and if they cannot adjust their differences peaceably, the right remains with the strongest. The judiciary is not that department of the government, to which the assertion of its interests against foreign powers is confided; and its duty commonly is to decide upon individual rights, according to those principles which the political departments of the nation have established. If the course of the nation has been a plain one, its courts would hesitate to pronounce it erroneous.
>
> We think, then, however individual judges might construe the treaty of St. Ildefonso, it is the province of the Court to conform its decisions to the will of the legislature, if that will has been clearly expressed. . . .
>
> After these acts of sovereign power over the territory in dispute, asserting the American construction of the treaty, by which the government claims it, to maintain the opposite construction in its own courts would certainly be an anomaly in the history and practice of nations. If those departments which are intrusted with the foreign intercourse of the nation, which assert and maintain its interests against foreign powers, have unequivocally asserted its rights of dominion over a country of which it is in possession, and which it claims under a treaty; if the legislature has acted on the construction thus asserted, it is not in its own courts that this construction is

---

[1] *Foster* v. *Neilson,* 2 Peters, 299.

to be denied. A question like this respecting the boundaries of nations, is, as has been truly said, more a political than a legal question, and in its discussion, the courts of every country must respect the pronounced will of the legislature.[1]

Judicial
Power as to
Treaties

If the court had stopped here, we should be perplexed to understand how the judicial power extends to treaties, or why, if it does, the court refused to exercise the judicial power. This was not overlooked by the great Chief Justice, who stated, in a subsequent portion of his opinion, both the nature of a treaty as a contract in the world at large, as a law in the United States, and the conditions under which the judicial power attaches to it. Thus:

> A treaty is, in its nature, a contract between two nations, not a legislative act. It does not generally effect, of itself, the object to be accomplished; especially so far as its operation is infra-territorial; but is carried into execution by the sovereign power of the respective parties to the instrument.
>
> In the United States, a different principle is established. Our constitution declares a treaty to be the law of the land. It is, consequently, to be regarded in courts of justice as equivalent to an act of the legislature, whenever it operates of itself without the aid of any legislative provision. But when the terms of the stipulation import a contract when either of the parties engages to perform a particular act, the treaty addresses itself to the political, not the judicial department; and the legislature must execute the contract, before it can become a rule for the court.[2]

The same question presented itself in a different form in *Williams* v. *Suffolk Insurance Co.* (13 Peters, 415), decided by the Supreme Court in 1839, in which it was held that the title of a foreign government to territory is a political question, to be decided by the political department, not by the judicial power of the United States. In delivering the opinion of the court, Mr. Justice McLean stated the facts involved, the rule of law, and the reason for the rule. First, as to the facts:

> As the fact is stated in the first point certified, that there is a controversy between this government and that of Buenos Ayres, whether the jurisdiction is rightful, which is assumed to be exercised over the Falkland Islands by the latter; and that this right is asserted on the one side and denied by the other, it will not be necessary to look into the correspondence between the two governments on the subject. To what sovereignty any island or country belongs, is a question which often arises before courts in the exercise of a maritime jurisdiction; and also in actions on policies of insurance.[3]

Next, as to the rule:

> And can there be any doubt, that when the executive branch of the government, which is charged with our foreign relations, shall, in its

[1] 2 Peters, 307, 309.
[2] *Ibid.,* 314.
[3] 13 Peters, 420.

correspondence with a foreign nation, assume a fact in regard to the sovereignty of any island or country, it is conclusive on the judicial department? And in this view, it is not material to inquire, nor is it the province of the court to determine, whether the executive be right or wrong. It is enough to know, that in the exercise of his constitutional functions, he had decided the question. Having done this, under the responsibilities which belong to him, it is obligatory on the people and government of the Union.[1]

Finally, as to the reason of the rule:

If this were not the rule, cases might often arise, in which, on the most important questions of foreign jurisdiction, there would be an irreconcilable difference between the executive and judicial departments. By one of these departments, a foreign island or country might be considered as at peace with the United States; whilst the other would consider it in a state of war. No well-regulated government has ever sanctioned a principle so unwise, and so destructive of national character. In the cases of *Foster* v. *Neilson,* 2 Pet. 253, 307, and *Garcia* v. *Lee,* 12 Ibid. 511, this court have laid down the rule, that the action of the political branches of the government in a matter that belongs to them, is conclusive. And we think, in the present case, as the executive, in his message, and in his correspondence with the government of Buenos Ayres, has denied the jurisdiction which it has assumed to exercise over the Falkland islands; the fact must be taken and acted on by this court as thus asserted and maintained.[2]

[1] *Ibid.*
[2] *Ibid.*
In cases involving the action of the political departments of the government, the judiciary is bound by such action. *Williams* v. *Suffolk Ins. Co.,* 13 Pet., 420; *Garcia* v. *Lee,* 12 Pet., 511; *Kennet* v. *Chambers,* 14 How., 38; *Foster* v. *Neilson,* 2 Pet., 253; *Nabob of the Carnatic* v. *The East Ind. Co.,* 2 Ves., Jr., 60; *Luther* v. *Borden,* 7 How., 1; *Rhode Island* v. *Massachusetts,* 12 Pet., 714.
The judiciary recognizes the condition of things with respect to the government of another country which once existed as still subsisting, unless the political department of its own government has decided otherwise. *Kennet* v. *Chambers,* 7 How., 38. (Mr. Justice Swayne in *Phillips* v. *Payne,* 92 U. S., 130, 132, decided in 1875.)
Who is the sovereign, *de jure* or *de facto,* of a territory is not a judicial, but a political question, the determination of which by the legislative and executive departments of any government conclusively binds the judges, as well as all other officers, citizens and subjects of that government. This principle has always been upheld by this court, and has been affirmed under a great variety of circumstances. (Mr. Justice Gray, in *Jones* v. *United States,* 137 U. S., 202, 212, decided in 1890.)
It appears that certain American citizens, asserting interests in the Isle of Pines, had contended that it belonged to the United States under the treaty, and the sixth clause of the Platt Amendment, while not asserting an absolute claim of title on our part, gave opportunity for an examination of the question of ownership and its settlement through a treaty with Cuba. The Republic of Cuba has been governing the isle since May 20, 1902—the present situation need not be discussed—and has made various improvements in administration at the suggestion of our Government, but Congress has taken no action to the contrary to Cuba's title as superior to ours.
It may be conceded that the action of both the political departments has not been sufficiently definite to furnish a conclusive interpretation of the treaty of peace as an original question, and as yet no agreement has been reached under the Platt Amendment. The Isle of Pines continues at least *de facto* under the jurisdiction of the government of the Republic of Cuba, and that settles the question before us. . . . It must be treated as foreign, for this Government has never taken, nor aimed to take, that possession in fact and in law which is essential to render it domestic. (Mr. Chief Justice Fuller in *Percy* v. *Stranahan,* 205 U. S., 257, 271–2, decided in 1907.)

The next case, entitled *Luther* v. *Borden* (7 Howard, 1), decided in 1849, is a very important one, holding that the recognition of a government of a State of the American Union is, as in States of the society of nations, a political question, and as such is to be passed upon by the political, not by the judicial, department of the United States. As, however, the facts of the case are interesting, and as Mr. Chief Justice Taney is a recognized authority on all questions pertaining to the judicial power, the facts of the case and the opinion of the court are briefly given. The facts and the holding of the court are thus stated in the head-note of the case:

> At the period of the American Revolution, Rhode Island did not, like the other States, adopt a new constitution, but continued the form of government established by the charter of Charles the Second, making only such alterations, by acts of the Legislature, as were necessary to adapt it to their condition and rights as an independent State. . . .
>
> In 1841 a portion of the people held meetings and formed associations, which resulted in the election of a convention to form a new constitution, to be submitted to the people for their adoption or rejection.
>
> This convention framed a constitution, directed a vote to be taken upon it, declared afterwards that it had been adopted and ratified by a majority of the people of the State, and was the paramount law and constitution of Rhode Island.
>
> Under it, elections were held for Governor, members of the Legislature, and other officers, who assembled together in May, 1842, and proceeded to organize the new government.
>
> But the charter government did not acquiesce in these proceedings. On the contrary, it passed stringent laws, and finally passed an act declaring the State under martial law.
>
> In May, 1843, a new constitution, which had been framed by a convention called together by the charter government, went into operation, and has continued ever since.
>
> The question which of the two opposing governments was the legitimate one, viz. the charter government, or the government established by the voluntary convention, has not heretofore been regarded as a judicial one in any of the State courts. The political department has always determined whether a proposed constitution or amendment was ratified or not by the people of the State, and the judicial power has followed its decision.

The framers of the Constitution found it necessary to guarantee the existence of the States, as those States had renounced their diplomacy and a resort to war, and they did so in the following manner by section 4 of Article IV of that instrument:

> The United States shall guarantee to every State in this Union a Republican Form of Government, and shall protect each of them against Invasion; and on Application of the Legislature, or of the Executive (when the Legislature cannot be convened) against domestic Violence.

Adverting to this state of affairs, Mr. Chief Justice Taney thus continues:

Under this article of the Constitution it rests with Congress to decide what government is the established one in a State. For as the United States guarantee to each State a republican government, Congress must necessarily decide what government is established in the State before it can determine whether it is republican or not. And when the senators and representatives of a State are admitted into the councils of the Union, the authority of the government under which they are appointed, as well as its republican character, is recognized by the proper constitutional authority. And its decision is binding on every other department of the government, and could not be questioned in a judicial tribunal. It is true that the contest in this case did not last long enough to bring the matter to this issue; and as no senators or representatives were elected under the authority of the government of which Mr. Dorr was the head, Congress was not called upon to decide the controversy. Yet the right to decide is placed there, and not in the courts.

So, too, as relates to the clause in the above-mentioned article of the Constitution, providing for cases of domestic violence. It rested with Congress, too, to determine upon the means proper to be adopted to fulfil this guarantee. They might, if they had deemed it most advisable to do so, have placed it in the power of a court to decide when the contingency had happened which required the federal government to interfere. But Congress thought otherwise, and no doubt wisely; and by the act of February 28, 1795, provided, that, " in case of an insurrection in any State against the government thereof, it shall be lawful for the President of the United States, on application of the legislature of such State or of the executive (when the legislature cannot be convened), to call forth such number of the militia of any other State or States, as may be applied for, as he may judge sufficient to suppress such insurrection."

By this act, the power of deciding whether the exigency had arisen upon which the government of the United States is bound to interfere, is given to the President.[1]

The attitude of the Supreme Court towards political questions, and the reserve which becomes it on such occasions, are admirably pointed out by the Chief Justice in the concluding passage of his opinion:

Much of the argument on the part of the plaintiff turned upon political rights and political questions, upon which the court has been urged to express an opinion. We decline doing so. The high power has been conferred on this court of passing judgment upon the acts of the State sovereignties, and of the legislative and executive branches of the federal government, and of determining whether they are beyond the limits of power marked out for them respectively by the Constitution of the United States. This tribunal, therefore, should be the last to overstep the boundaries which limit its own jurisdiction. And while it should always be ready to meet any question confided to it by the Constitution, it is equally its duty not to pass beyond its appropriate sphere of action, and to take care not to involve itself in discussions which properly belong to other forums. No one, we believe, has ever

[1] *Luther* v. *Borden,* 7 Howard, 42–3.

doubted the proposition, that, according to the institutions of this country, the sovereignty in every State resides in the people of the State, and that they may alter and change their form of government at their own pleasure. But whether they have changed it or not by abolishing an old government, and establishing a new one in its place, is a question to be settled by the political power. And when that power has decided, the courts are bound to take notice of its decision, and to follow it.[1]

In the Neilson case (*supra,* p. 376), the power, primarily lodged with the President, was shared with the Senate in its execution. In the Borden case (*supra,* p. 380), the power, primarily lodged in the Congress, is delegated to the President, who becomes the agent of the Congress in deciding the facts which justify intervention on behalf of the Government of the Union. In the Suffolk Ins. Co. Case (*supra,* p. 378), the power pertained to the President, as in the Prize Cases (2 Black, 635), decided by the Supreme Court in 1862.

The facts in these cases are peculiarly American, and the case has an interest of its own far exceeding that of *Luther* v. *Borden.* The States of the Union were at war. The ports of the Southern States had been blockaded by Mr. Lincoln, then President of the United States. If the blockade was legal, that is to say, if the President had the right to close the ports of the Southern States by blockade without an act of Congress declaring war, then certain vessels, violating this blockade, could be properly seized and confiscated; whereas, if a declaration of war by Congress was necessary, the proclamation would have been without binding effect, inasmuch as a blockade presupposes the existence of a state of war. The question, therefore, before the court was, as stated by Mr. Justice Grier, who delivered its opinion:

President's Rights under International Law

> Had the President a right to institute a blockade of ports in possession of persons in armed rebellion against the Government, on the principles of international law, as known and acknowledged among civilized States?[2]

It is to be observed that, by the Constitution, the law of nations is recognized and that, by repeated decisions of the Supreme Court, it is declared to be a part of the law of the land. By the law of nations, a proclamation of blockade recognizes the existence of war and confers upon the parties to it both the rights and duties of belligerents in a war between nations. On the very point in question, Mr. Justice Grier said:

> Whether the President in fulfilling his duties, as Commander-in-chief, in suppressing an insurrection, has met with such armed hostile resistance, and a civil war of such alarming proportions as will compel him to accord

[1] 7 Howard, 46-7.
[2] *The Prize Cases,* 2 Black, 665.

to them the character of belligerents, is a question to be decided *by him,* and this Court must be governed by the decisions and acts of the political department of the Government to which this power was entrusted. " He must determine what degree of force the crisis demands." The proclamation of blockade is itself official and conclusive evidence to the Court that a state of war existed which demanded and authorized a recourse to such a measure, under the circumstances peculiar to the case.[1]

If, however, the action of Congress was necessary in the case of a Civil War, which could not be declared as in the case of a war against a foreign nation, the learned Justice considered the acts of Congress relating to the war as a sufficient declaration of its existence. Speaking on behalf of the majority, he considered the act of Congress of 1861, " approving, legalizing, and making valid all the acts, proclamations, and orders of the President, &c., as if they had been *issued and done under the previous express authority* and direction of the Congress of the United States," as a ratification of the act of the President, if indeed one were needed. In this part of his opinion he relied upon the following statement of Mr. Justice Story in the case of *Brown* v. *United States* decided in 1814 (8 Cranch, 133) :

> I am perfectly satisfied . . . . . that no subject can legally commit hostilities, or capture property of an enemy, when . . . the sovereign . . . . . has prohibited it. But suppose, he does, I would ask, if the sovereign may not ratify his proceedings ; and thus, by a retroactive operation, give validity to them?

The court therefore concluded, in the language of Mr. Justice Grier :

> On this first question therefore we are of the opinion that the President had a right, *jure belli,* to institute a blockade of ports in possession of the States in rebellion, which neutrals are bound to regard.[2]

Further light is thrown upon this subject by three cases, in two of which the President of the United States is concerned; in the last, a State of the Union, in each of which the court refused to accept jurisdiction because the questions were political, and as such, beyond the scope of judicial power.

In *State of Mississippi* v. *Johnson,* (4 Wallace, 475), decided in 1866, Mr. Chief Justice Chase delivering the unanimous opinion of the court, stated the facts as follows :.

> A motion was made, some days since, in behalf of the State of Mississippi, for leave to file a bill in the name of the State, praying this court perpetually to enjoin and restrain Andrew Johnson, President of the United

[1] *Ibid.,* 670.
[2] *Ibid.,* 671.

States, and E. O. C. Ord, general commanding in the District of Mississippi and Arkansas, from executing, or in any manner carrying out, certain acts of Congress therein named.

The acts referred to are those of March 2d and March 23d, 1867, commonly known as the Reconstruction Acts.

The Attorney-General objected to the leave asked for, upon the ground that no bill which makes a President a defendant, and seeks an injunction against him to restrain the performance of his duties as President, should be allowed to be filed in this court.[1]

The case was elaborately argued by counsel for Mississippi and by the Attorney General on behalf of the President, the counsel for Mississippi maintaining that the duty cast upon the President by the Acts in question was ministerial and that the performance of a ministerial act could be compelled by mandamus or enjoined by injunction.

The case, as considered by the court was, as stated by the Chief Justice, "Can the President be restrained by injunction from carrying into effect an act of Congress alleged to be unconstitutional?"

The Chief Justice first defined a ministerial duty, then invoked adjudged cases in support of the definition, and finally distinguished the duty imposed upon the President by the Statute which, in his opinion and in the opinion of the court, required not merely discretion, but discretion of the highest possible degree. Thus:

> A ministerial duty, the performance of which may, in proper cases, be required of the head of a department, by judicial process, is one in respect to which nothing is left to discretion. It is a simple, definite duty, arising under conditions admitted or proved to exist, and imposed by law.

For this he vouched, in first instance, the case of *Marbury* v. *Madison,* (1 Cranch, 137) of which he said:

> A citizen had been nominated, confirmed, and appointed a justice of the peace for the District of Columbia, and his commission had been made out, signed, and sealed. Nothing remained to be done except delivery, and the duty of delivery was imposed by law on the Secretary of State. It was held that the performance of this duty might be enforced by *mandamus* issuing from a court having jurisdiction.[2]

And in the second, the case of *Kendal, Postmaster-General* v. *Stockton & Stokes,* (12 Peters, 527), the Chief Justice said:

> An act of Congress had directed the Postmaster-General to credit Stockton & Stokes with such sums as the Solicitor of the Treasury should find due to them; and that officer refused to credit them with certain sums, so

[1] 4 Wallace, 497–8.
[2] *Ibid.,* 498.

found due. It was held that the crediting of this money was a mere ministerial duty, the performance of which might be judicially enforced.[1]

After stating that in each of these cases nothing was left to discretion, that there was no room for the exercise of judgment, and that the law required the performance of a single specific act rightly compellable by mandamus, the Chief Justice thus distinguished the case before him:

> Very different is the duty of the President in the exercise of the power to see that the laws are faithfully executed, and among these laws the acts named in the bill. By the first of these acts he is required to assign generals to command in the several military districts, and to detail sufficient military force to enable such officers to discharge their duties under the law. By the supplementary act, other duties are imposed on the several commanding generals, and these duties must necessarily be performed under the supervision of the President as commander-in-chief. The duty thus imposed on the President is in no just sense ministerial. It is purely executive and political.
>
> An attempt on the part of the judicial department of the government to enforce the performance of such duties by the President might be justly characterized, in the language of Chief Justice Marshall, as " an absurd and excessive extravagance."
>
> It is true that in the instance before us the interposition of the court is not sought to enforce action by the Executive under constitutional legislation, but to restrain such action under legislation alleged to be unconstitutional. But we are unable to perceive that this circumstance takes the case out of the general principles which forbid judicial interference with the exercise of Executive discretion.

After declaring that the Congress is the Legislative Department of the Government, that the President is the Executive Department, that:

> Neither can be restrained in its action by the judicial department; though the acts of both, when performed, are, in proper cases, subject to its cognizance.

The Chief Justice thus stated the reason obtaining in this category of cases:

> The impropriety of such interference will be clearly seen upon consideration of its possible consequences.
>
> Suppose the bill filed and the injunction prayed for allowed. If the President refuse obedience, it is needless to observe that the court is without power to enforce its process. If, on the other hand, the President complies with the order of the court and refuses to execute the acts of Congress, is it not clear that a collision may occur between the executive and legislative departments of the government? May not the House of Representatives impeach the President for such refusal? And in that case could this court interfere, in behalf of the President, thus endangered by com-

[1] *Ibid.*, 499.

pliance with its mandate, and restrain by injunction the Senate of the United States from sitting as a court of impeachment? Would the strange spectacle be offered to the public world of an attempt by this court to arrest proceedings in that court?

These questions answer themselves.[1]

The State of Georgia presented practically the same question in a different form. If the President of the United States might not be enjoined why not the Secretary of War and the Commanding Officers of the Army from carrying into effect the provisions of the Reconstruction Acts? This counsel for Georgia attempted to do in the *State of Georgia* v. *Stanton,* (6 Wallace, 50), decided in the December term, 1867, adverse to the contention of Georgia, and in accordance with the opinion of the Court in the case of *Mississippi* v. *Johnson.*

Mr. Justice Nelson who delivered the opinion of the court first noted the objection that the questions presented for adjudication were " political and not judicial, and therefore, not the subject of judicial cognizance "; he next adverted to the importance of the objection, and continued:

> This distinction results from the organization of the government into the three great departments, executive, legislative, and judicial, and from the assignment and limitation of the powers of each by the Constitution.
>
> The judicial power is vested in one supreme court, and in such inferior courts as Congress may ordain and establish: the political power of the government in the other two departments.
>
> The distinction between judicial and political power is so generally acknowledged in the jurisprudence both of England and of this country, that we need do no more than refer to some of the authorities on the subject. They are all in one direction. (*Nabob of Carnatic* v. *The East India Co.,* 1 Vesey, Jr., 375–393, S. C., 2 Id. 56–60; *Penn* v. *Lord Baltimore,* 1 Vesey, 446–7; *New York* v. *Connecticut,* 4 Dallas, 4–6; *The Cherokee Nation* v. *Georgia,* 5 Peters, 1, 20, 29, 30, 51, 75; *The State of Rhode Island* v. *The State of Massachusetts,* 12 Ib., 657, 733, 734, 737, 738.)[2]

He then took up *The State of Rhode Island* v. *The State of Massachusetts,* which was regarded by counsel as an exception, and by an examination of the opinion of Mr. Justice Baldwin in that case, showed that the question was judicial in its nature, and that it was only political in the sense that the decision of the boundary between the two States involved sovereignty and political rights as incident to the ownership of the land. He quoted with approval the following statement from Mr. Justice Baldwin's opinion:

> Taking the case on the bill and plea, the question is, whether the stake set up on Wrentham Plain by Woodward and Saffrey, in 1842, is the true point from which to run an east and west line as the compact boundary

---

[1] 4 Wallace, 500–1.
[2] 6 Wallace, 71.

between the States. In the first aspect of the case it depends on a fact; in the second, on the law of equity, whether the agreement is void or valid; neither of which present a political controversy, but one of an ordinary judicial nature of frequent occurrence in suits between individuals.[1]

Having thus shown that a political question was not involved in *Rhode Island* v. *Massachusetts,* and that the court did not overstep the line separating the judicial from the political departments of the Government, Mr. Justice Nelson proceeded to quote, with the approval of the court, the portion of Mr. Justice Baldwin's opinion in which that learned Justice laid down in clear, precise, and unassailable terms, the distinction between judicial and political power:

> From the time of such submission the question ceases to be a political one, to be decided by the *sic volo, sic jubeo,* of political power. It comes to the court to be decided by its judgment, legal discretion, and solemn consideration of the rules of law, appropriate to its nature as a judicial question, depending on the exercise of judicial powers, as it is bound to act by known and settled principles of national or municipal jurisprudence, as the case requires.[2]

And in commenting upon this passage, he said:

> that the question thus submitted by the sovereign, or state, to a judicial determination, must be one appropriate for the exercise of judicial power; such as a question of boundary, or as in the case of *Penn* v. *Lord Baltimore,* a contract between the parties in respect to their boundary. Lord Hardwicke places his right in that case to entertain jurisdiction upon this ground.[3]

Mr. Justice Nelson, and the Court for which he spoke, considered as more, and indeed most in point, the case of *The Cherokee Nation* v. *The State of Georgia,* (5 Peters, 1), decided in 1831, seven years previous to that of *Rhode Island* v. *Massachusetts.* In that case, the Cherokee Nation then residing within the limits of Georgia prayed the Supreme Court that that State be enjoined from extending its laws over the Cherokee Nation whose existence as a separate and distinct political community had been recognized by the United States. The Court dismissed the bill on the ground that the Supreme Court could not take original jurisdiction of the case because the Cherokee Nation was neither a foreign State nor a member of the American Union, but a dependent domestic State which did not therefore have the right to file an original bill in the Supreme Court, as a foreign nation or State of the American Union possessed under the Constitution. There was, however, an added reason in the opinion of the majority of the Court why

[1] *Ibid.,* 72.
[2] *Ibid.*
[3] *Ibid.,* 73.

jurisdiction should not be asumed even if the Cherokee Nation could file its bill, which was thus stated by Mr. Chief Justice Marshall:

> That the part of the bill which respects the land occupied by the Indians, and prays the aid of the court to protect their possessions, may be more doubtful. The mere question of right might, perhaps, be decided by this court in a proper case with proper parties. But the court is asked to do more than decide on the title. The bill requires us to control the legislature of Georgia, and to restrain the exertions of its physical force. The propriety of such an interposition by the court may be well questioned. It savors too much of the exercise of political power, to be within the province of the judicial department.[1]

A concurring opinion was delivered by Mr. Justice Johnson, in which he doubted the propriety of considering the Cherokee Nation even as a domestic State, and an opinion by Mr. Justice Baldwin denying to them that equality.

A very elaborate dissenting opinion, delivered by Mr. Justice Thompson, in which Mr. Justice Story concurred, held that the Cherokee Nation was a nation in the sense of the Constitution and that the Court could take jurisdiction of the bill in so far as the parties to the controversy were concerned, but admitted that the remedy could only be granted in part, as the question was largely political. On this point, Mr. Justice Thompson said:

> For the purpose of guarding against any erroneous conclusions, it is proper I should state, that I do not claim for this court, the exercise of jurisdiction upon any matter properly falling under the denomination of political power. Relief to the full extent prayed for by the bill may be beyond the reach of this court. Much of the matters therein contained by way of complaint, would seem to depend for relief upon the exercise of political power; and, as such, appropriately devolving upon the executive, and not the judicial department of the government. This court can grant relief so far, only, as the rights of persons or property are drawn in question, and have been infringed.[2]

This and the following portion of his opinion in that case are quoted by Mr. Justice Nelson on behalf of the Court:

> I certainly do not claim, as belonging to the judiciary, the exercise of political power. That belongs to another branch of the Government. The protection and enforcement of many rights secured by treaties, most certainly do not belong to the judiciary. It is only where the rights of persons or property are involved, and when such rights can be presented under some judicial form of proceedings, that courts of justice can interpose relief. This court can have no right to pronounce an abstract opinion upon the constitutionality of a State law. Such law must be brought into actual, or

[1] 6 Wallace, 74.
[2] *Ibid.*, 74–5.

threatened operation upon rights properly falling under judicial cognizance, or a remedy is not to be had here.[1]

Mr. Justice Nelson thereupon stated that by the bill the Court is:

called upon to restrain the defendants, who represent the executive authority of the government, from carrying into execution certain acts of Congress, inasmuch as such execution would annul, and totally abolish the existing State government of Georgia, and establish another and different one in its place; in other words, would overthrow and destroy the corporate existence of the State, by depriving it of all the means and instrumentalities whereby its existence might, and, otherwise would, be maintained.[2]

Testing the prayer of the bill by the principles laid down in the previous cases, Mr. Justice Nelson thus continued and concluded:

That these matters, both as stated in the body of the bill, and, in the prayers for relief, call for the judgment of the court upon political questions, and, upon rights, not of persons or property, but of a political character, will hardly be denied. For the rights for the protection of which our authority is invoked, are the rights of sovereignty, of political jurisdiction, of government, of corporate existence as a State, with all its constitutional powers and privileges. No case of private rights or private property infringed, or in danger of actual or threatened infringement, is presented by the bill, in a judicial form, for the judgment of the court.

It is true, the bill, in setting forth the political rights of the State, and of its people to be protected, among other matters, avers, that Georgia owns certain real estate and buildings therein, State capitol, and executive mansion, and other real and personal property; and that putting the acts of Congress into execution, and destroying the State, would deprive it of the possession and enjoyment of its property. But, it is apparent, that this reference to property and statement concerning it, are only by way of showing one of the grievances resulting from the threatened destruction of the State, and in aggravation of it, not as a specific ground of relief. This matter of property is neither stated as an independent ground, nor is it noticed at all in the prayers for relief. Indeed the case, as made in the bill, would have stopped far short of the relief sought by the State, and its main purpose and design given up, by restraining its remedial effect, simply to the protection of the title and possession of its property. Such relief would have called for a very different bill from the one before us.

Having arrived at the conclusion that this court, for the reasons above stated, possesses no jurisdiction over the subject-matter presented in the bill for relief, it is unimportant to examine the question as it respects jurisdiction over the parties defendants.[3]

In the very recent case of *Pacific Telephone Company* v. *Oregon*, (223 U. S., 118) decided in 1912, a political question was again before the Supreme Court, in what may be considered a leading case, and the opinion of

[1] *Ibid.*, 75.
[2] *Ibid.*, 76.
[3] *Ibid.*, 77.

Mr. Chief Justice White, for a unanimous court, is a careful analysis of the elements which in that case formed the political question, because of which the court refused to entertain jurisdiction.

The facts in the case were, in so far as they are material to the present purpose, that the State of Oregon, in 1902, amended its Constitution, introducing what is called the Initiative and Referendum.

" As to the first," to quote the language of Chief Justice White in delivering the opinion of the Court, " the initiative, it suffices to say that a stated number of voters were given the right at any time to secure a submission to popular vote for approval of any matter which it was desired to have enacted into law, and providing that the proposition thus submitted when approved by popular vote should become the law of the State. The second, the referendum, provided for a reference to a popular vote, for approval or disapproval, of any law passed by the legislature, such reference to take place either as the result of the action of the legislature itself or of a petition filed for that purpose by a specified number of voters." [1] That is to say, the Initiative provided for direct legislation by the people, instead of by a select body of persons representing the people in the State Legislature, and the Referendum for a direct and specific confirmation or rejection by the people of acts of the Legislature, instead of the approval or disapproval of its measures by the slower process of defeating or reelecting members of the Legislature, whose conduct the people condemned or commended.

By resorting to the Initiative a law was submitted to and voted by the people in 1903, taxing certain classes of corporations, by virtue of which telephone and telegraph companies were taxed two per centum as an annual license, upon their gross revenue derived from business done within the State; and penalties were provided for non-payment in case of delinquency.

The Pacific Telephone and Telegraph Company, an Oregon corporation engaged in business in that State, made return of its gross receipts as required by the law, and was assessed two per centum upon the amount thereof. Upon failure to pay the tax, suit was brought by the State, to enforce payment and to recover the statutory penalties for delinquency.

The Company pleaded among other defenses, that government by Initiative and Referendum was not the Republican form of government under the Constitution, and that it was in conflict with the fourth section of Article IV thereof, providing that, " The United States shall guarantee to every State in this Union a Republican Form of Government."

Inasmuch as the legality of the Initiative and Referendum was the basis of the defense, the case reduced itself, to quote the language of the Chief Justice:

[1] 223 U. S., 134.

to the single issue whether the enforcement of that provision, because of its political character, is exclusively committed to Congress or is judicial in its character.[1]

After calling attention to the fact that the defense, if admitted, would not only affect the present Statute, but every other passed " in Oregon since the adoption of the initiative and referendum," the Chief Justice proceeded thus to examine the nature and the consequence of defendant's contention:

Let us briefly fix the inconceivable expansion of the judicial power and the ruinous destruction of legislative authority in matters purely political which would necessarily be occasioned by giving sanction to the doctrine which underlies and would be necessarily involved in sustaining the propositions contended for. First. That however perfect and absolute may be the establishment and dominion in fact of a state government, however complete may be its participation in and enjoyment of all its powers and rights as a member of the national Government, and however all the departments of that Government may recognize such state government, nevertheless every citizen of such State or person subject to taxation therein, or owing any duty to the established government, may be heard, for the purpose of defeating the payment of such taxes or avoiding the discharge of such duty, to assail in a court of justice the rightful existence of the State. Second. As a result, it becomes the duty of the courts of the United States, where such a claim is made, to examine as a justiciable issue the contention as to the illegal existence of a State and if such contention be thought well founded to disregard the existence in fact of the State, of its recognition by all the departments of the Federal Government, and practically award a decree absolving from all obligation to contribute to the support of or obey the laws of such established state government. And as a consequence of the existence of such judicial authority a power in the judiciary must be implied, unless it be that anarchy is to ensue, to build by judicial action upon the ruins of the previously established government a new one, a right which by its very terms also implies the power to control the legislative department of the Government of the United States in the recognition of such new government and the admission of representatives therefrom, as well as to strip the executive department of that government of its otherwise lawful and discretionary authority.[2]

Still further pursuing this phase of the subject the Chief Justice continued:

Do the provisions of § 4, Art. IV, bring about these strange, far-reaching and injurious results? That is to say, do the provisions of that Article obliterate the division between judicial authority and legislative power upon which the Constitution rests? In other words, do they authorize the judiciary to substitute its judgment as to a matter purely political for the judgment of Congress on a subject committed to it and thus overthrow the Constitu-

[1] *Ibid.*, 137.
[2] *Ibid.*, 141–2.

tion upon the ground that thereby the guarantee to the States of a government republican in form may be secured, a conception which after all rests upon the assumption that the States are to be guaranteed a government republican in form by destroying the very existence of a government republican in form in the Nation.

To state such consequences would seem to refute the premises upon which they were based, and from which they were drawn; and it was not necessary for the Chief Justice to answer theoretical arguments which had been rejected in the great and leading case of *Luther v. Borden,* (7 Howard, 1), decided in 1849, in which the question involved in the guarantee of republican government was conclusively shown to be political, not judicial. After an elaborate statement of the facts involved in the case, Mr. Chief Justice White quoted with approval the following language of Chief Justice Taney, in that case:

> Under this article of the constitution it rests with congress to decide what government is the established one in a State. For, as the United States guarantee to each State a republican government, congress must necessarily decide what government is established in the State before it can determine whether it is republican or not. And when the senators and representatives of a State are admitted into the councils of the Union, the authority of the government under which they are appointed, as well as its republican character, is recognized by the proper constitutional authority. And its decision is binding on every other department of the government, and could not be questioned in a judicial tribunal. It is true that the contest in this case did not last long enough to bring the matter to this issue; and as no senators or representatives were elected under the authority of the government of which Mr. Dorr was the head, Congress was not called upon to decide the controversy. Yet the right to decide is placed there, and not in the courts.[1]

Stating in agreement with Mr. Chief Justice Taney, that if the judicial power extended thus far it is "a guarantee of anarchy, and not of order," Mr. Chief Justice White thus concluded the opinion of the Court, which can well be taken as the last word on this difficult and perplexing subject:

> It is indeed a singular misconception of the nature and character of our constitutional system of government to suggest that the settled distinction which the doctrine just stated points out between judicial authority over justiciable controversies and legislative power as to purely political questions tends to destroy the duty of the judiciary in proper cases to enforce the Constitution. The suggestion but results from failing to distinguish between things which are widely different, that is, the legislative duty to determine the political questions involved in deciding whether a state government republican in form exists, and the judicial power and ever-present duty whenever it becomes necessary in a controversy properly submitted to

[1] 223 U. S., 147.

enforce and uphold the applicable provisions of the Constitution as to each and every exercise of governmental power.

How better can the broad lines which distinguish these two subjects be pointed out than by considering the character of the defense in this very case? The defendant company does not contend here that it could not have been required to pay a license tax. It does not assert that it was denied an opportunity to be heard as to the amount for which it was taxed, or that there was anything inhering in the tax or involved intrinsically in the law which violated any of its constitutional rights. If such questions had been raised they would have been justiciable, and therefore would have required the calling into operation of judicial power. Instead, however, of doing any of these things, the attack on the statute here made is of a wholly different character. Its essentially political nature is at once made manifest by understanding that the assault which the contention here advanced makes it not on the tax as a tax, but on the State as a State. It is addressed to the framework and political character of the government by which the statute levying the tax was passed. It is the government, the political entity, which (reducing the case to its essence) is called to the bar of this court, not for the purpose of testing judicially some exercise of power assailed, on the ground that its exertion has injuriously affected the rights of an individual because of repugnancy to some constitutional limitation, but to demand of the State that it establish its right to exist as a State, republican in form.

As the issues presented, in their very essence, are, and have long since by this court been, definitely determined to be political and governmental, and embraced within the scope of the powers conferred upon Congress, and not therefore within the reach of judicial power, it follows that the case presented is not within our jurisdiction, and the writ of error must therefore be, and it is, dismissed for want of jurisdiction.[1]

[1] *Ibid.*, 149–51.

XIX

EXTENT AND EXERCISE OF JUDICIAL POWER

This Constitution, and the Laws of the United States which shall be made in Pursuance thereof; and all Treaties made, or which shall be made, under the Authority of the United States, shall be the supreme Law of the Land; and the Judges in every State shall be bound thereby, any Thing in the Constitution or Laws of any State to the Contrary notwithstanding. (*Constitution of the United States, Article VI, paragraph 2.*)

The Judicial power of the United States shall not be construed to extend to any suit in law or equity, commenced or prosecuted against one of the United States by Citizens of another State, or by Citizens or Subjects of any Foreign State. (*Constitution of the United States, 11th Amendment, adopted 1798.*)

By the constitution, it was ordained that this judicial power, in cases where a state was a party, should be exercised by this Court as one of original jurisdiction. The states waived their exemption from judicial power, as sovereigns by original and inherent right, by their own grant of its exercise over themselves in such cases, but which they would not grant to any inferior tribunal. By this grant, this Court has acquired jurisdiction over the parties in this cause, by their own consent and delegated authority; as their agent for executing the judicial power of the United States in the cases specified. (*Mr. Justice Baldwin in Rhode Island v. Massachusetts, 12 Peters, 657, 720, decided in 1838.*)

Our next inquiry will be, whether we have jurisdiction of the subject matters of the suit, to hear and determine them.

That it is a controversy between two states, cannot be denied; and though the constitution does not, in terms, extend the judicial power to all controversies between two or more states, yet it in terms excludes none, whatever may be their nature or subject. It is, therefore, a question of construction, whether the controversy in the present case is within the grant of judicial power. (*Mr. Justice Baldwin in State of Rhode Island v. State of Massachusetts, 12 Peters, 657, 721, decided in 1838.*)

The founders of our government could not but know, what has ever been, and is familiar to every statesman and jurist, that all controversies between nations, are, in this sense, political, and not judicial, as none but the sovereign can settle them. . . . None can be settled without war or treaty, which is by political power; but under the old and new confederacy they could and can be settled by a court constituted by themselves, as their own substitutes, authorized to do that for states, which states alone could do before. We are thus pointed to the true boundary line between political and judicial power, and questions. A sovereign decides by his own will, which is the supreme law within his own boundary; 6 Peters, 714; 9 Peters, 748; a court, or judge, decides according to the law prescribed by the sovereign power, and that law is the rule for judgment. The submission by the sovereigns, or states, to a court of law or equity, of a controversy between them, without prescribing any rule of decision, gives power to decide according to the appropriate law of the case; 11 Ves. 294; which depends on the subject matter, the source and nature of the claims of the parties, and the law which governs them. From the time of such submission, the question ceases to be a political one, to be decided by the sic volo, sic jubeo, of political power; it comes to the court to be decided by its judgment, legal discretion, and solemn consideration of the rules of law appropriate to its nature as a judicial question, depending on the exercise of judicial power; as it is bound to act by known and settled principles of national or municipal jurisprudence, as the case requires.

It has never been contended that prize courts of admiralty jurisdiction, or questions before them, are not strictly judicial; they decide on questions of war and peace, the law of nations, treaties, and the municipal laws of the capturing nation, by which alone they are constituted; a fortiori, if such courts were constituted by a solemn treaty between the state under whose authority the capture was made, and the state whose citizens or subjects suffer by the capture. All nations submit to the jurisdiction of such courts over their subjects, and hold their final decrees conclusive on rights of property. 6 Cr. 284-5.

These considerations lead to the definition of political and judicial power and questions; the former is that which a sovereign or state exerts by his or its own authority, as reprisal and confiscation; 3 Ves. 429: the latter is that which is granted to a court or judicial tribunal. So of controversies between states; they are in their nature political, when the sovereign or state reserves to itself the right of deciding on it; makes it the "subject of a treaty, to be settled as between states independent," or "the foundation of representations from state to state." This is political equity, to be adjudged by the parties themselves, as contradistinguished from judicial equity, administered by a court of justice, decreeing the equum et bonum of the case, let who or what be the parties before them. (*Mr. Justice Baldwin in Rhode Island v. Massachusetts, 12 Peters, 657, 736-738, decided in 1838.*)

The grant of judicial power is not confined to the administration of laws passed in pursuance to the provisions of the Constitution, nor confined to the interpretation of such laws; but, by the very terms of the grant, the Constitution is under their view when any act of Congress is brought before them, and it is their duty to declare the law void, and refuse to execute it, if it is not pursuant to the legislative powers conferred upon Congress. And as the final appellate power in all such questions is given to this court, controversies as to the respective powers of the United States and the States, instead of being determined by military and physical force, are heard, investigated, and finally settled, with the calmness and deliberation of judicial inquiry. And no one can fail to see, that if such an arbiter had not been provided, in our complicated system of government, internal tranquillity could not have been preserved; and if such controversies were left to arbitrament of physical force, our Government, State and National, would soon cease to be Governments of laws, and revolutions by force of arms would take the place of courts of justice and judicial decisions.

In organizing such a tribunal, it is evident that every precaution was taken, which human wisdom could devise, to fit it for the high duty with which it was intrusted. . . . This tribunal, therefore, was erected, and the powers of which we have spoken conferred upon it, not by the Federal Government, but by the people of the States, who formed and adopted that Government, and conferred upon it all the powers, legislative, executive, and judicial, which it now possesses. And in order to secure its independence, and enable it faithfully and firmly to perform its duty, it engrafted it upon the Constitution itself, and declared that this court should have appellate power in all cases arising under the Constitution and laws of the United States. So long, therefore, as this Constitution shall endure, this tribunal must exist with it, deciding in the peaceful forms of judicial proceeding the angry and irritating controversies between sovereignties, which in other countries have been determined by the arbitrament of force. (*Chief Justice Taney in Ableman v. Booth, 21 Howard, 506, 520-521, decided in 1858.*)

A court is a tribunal presided over by one or more judges, for the exercise of such judicial power as has been conferred upon it by law. Blackstone, following Coke, defines it as "a place where justice is judicially administered" (3 Bl. Com. 23); but it is also essential that this place be designated by law, and that the person or persons authorized to administer justice be at that place for the purpose of administering justice at such times as may be also designated by law. The times fixed by law for the transaction of judicial business are called "terms," and the periods between the end of one term and the beginning of the next are called "vacations." These "terms" vary in different jurisdictions according to the statutes by which they are fixed, in some states ending at fixed dates and in others continuing until the commencement of a succeeding term. (*Mr. Justice Harrison in Von Schmidt v. Widber, 99 California, 511, 512, decided in 1893.*)

As jurisdiction is the first question which must arise in every cause, I have confined my examination of this, entirely to that point, and that branch of it which relates to the capacity of the plaintiffs to ask the interposition of this court. . . .

In my opinion there is no plaintiff in this suit; and this opinion precludes any examination into the merits of the bill, or the weight of any minor objections. My judgment stops me at the threshold, and forbids me to examine into the acts complained of. (*Mr. Justice Baldwin in Cherokee Nation v. State of Georgia, 5 Peters, 1, 31-32, decided in 1831.*)

The power to hear and determine a cause is jurisdiction; it is *"coram judice,"* whenever a case is presented which brings this power into action; if the petitioner states such a case in this petition, that on a demurrer, the court would render judgment in his favor, it is an undoubted case of jurisdiction; whether on an answer denying and putting in issue the allegations of the petition, the petitioner makes out his case, is the exercise of jurisdiction conferred by the filing of a petition containing all the requisites and in the manner prescribed by law. (*Mr. Justice Baldwin, in United States v. Arredondo, 6 Peters, 691, 709, decided in 1832.*)

The case is now before us for consideration, on a motion by the defendant, to dismiss the bill for want of jurisdiction in the cause.

However late this objection has been made, or may be made in any cause, in an inferior or appellate court of the United States, it must be considered and decided, before any court can move one further step in the cause; as any movement is necessarily the exercise of jurisdiction. Jurisdiction is the power to hear and determine the subject matter in controversy between parties to a suit, to adjudicate or exercise any judicial power over them; the question is, whether on the case before a court, their action is judicial or extra-judicial; with or without the authority of law, to render a judgment or decree upon the rights of the litigant parties. If the law confers the power to render a judgment or decree, then the court has jurisdiction; what shall be adjudged or decreed between the parties, and with which is the right of the case, is judicial action, by hearing and determining it. 6 Peters, 709; 4 Russell, 415; 3 Peters, 203-7.

A motion to dismiss a cause pending in the courts of the United States, is not analogous to a plea to the jurisdiction of a court of common law or equity in England; there the superior courts have a general jurisdiction over all persons within the realm, and all causes of action between them. It depends on the subject matter, whether the jurisdiction shall be exercised by a court of law or equity; but that court, to which it appropriately belongs, can act judicially upon the party and the subject of the suit; unless it shall be made apparent to the court that the judicial determination of the case has been withdrawn from the court of general jurisdiction, to an inferior and limited one. . . .

But as this Court is one of limited and special original jurisdiction, its action must be confined to the particular cases, controversies, and parties over which the constitution and laws have authorized it to act; any proceeding without the limits prescribed, is coram non judice, and its action a nullity. 10 Peters, 474; S. P. 4 Russ. 415. And whether the want or excess of power is objected by a party, or is apparent to the Court, it must surcease its action, or proceed extra-judicially.

Before we can proceed in this cause we must, therefore, inquire whether we can hear and determine the matters in controversy between the parties, who are two states of this Union, sovereign within their respective boundaries, save that portion of power which they have granted to the federal government, and foreign to each other for all but federal purposes. (*Mr. Justice Baldwin in State of Rhode Island v. State of Massachusetts, 12 Peters, 657, 718, 720, decided in 1838.*)

The power to hear and determine a cause is jurisdiction; and it is *coram judice* whenever a case is presented which brings this power into action. But before this power can be affirmed to exist, it must be made to appear that the law has given the tribunal capacity to entertain the complaint against the person or thing sought to be charged or affected; that such complaint has actually been preferred; and that such person or thing has been properly brought before the tribunal to answer the charge therein contained. When these appear, the jurisdiction has attached; the right to hear and determine is perfect; and the decision of every question thereafter arising is but the exercise of the jurisdiction thus conferred; and whether determined rightfully or wrongfully, correctly or erroneously, is alike immaterial to the validity, force, and effect of the final judgment, when brought collaterally in question. (*Mr. Justice Ranney in Sheldon v. Newton, 3 Ohio St. 494, 499, decided in 1854.*)

The cases in this court show that the framers of the Constitution did provide, by that instrument, for the judicial determination of all cases in law and equity between two or more States, including those involving questions of boundary. Did they omit to provide for the judicial determination of controversies arising between the United States and one or more of the States of the Union? This question is in effect answered by *United States v. North Carolina,* 136 U. S. 211. That was an action of debt brought in this court by the United States against the State of North Carolina, upon certain bonds issued by that State. The State appeared, the case was determined here upon its merits, and judgment was rendered for the State. It is true that no question was made as to the jurisdiction of this court, and nothing was therefore said in the opinion upon that subject. But it did not escape the attention of the court, and the judgment would not have been rendered except upon the theory that this court has original jurisdiction of a suit by the United States against a State. As, however, the question of jurisdiction is vital in this case, and is distinctly raised, it is proper to consider it upon its merits. (*Mr. Justice Harlan in United States v. State of Texas, 143 United States, 621, 642, decided in 1892.*)

We think these proceedings were instituted under a mistaken apprehension of the proper functions of the judiciary. Courts of justice are established to try questions pertaining to the rights of individuals. An action is the form of a suit given by law for the recovery of that which is one's due, or a legal demand of one's right. . . . But courts will not go out of their proper sphere to determine the constitutionality or unconstitutionality of a law. They will not declare a law unconstitutional or void in the abstract, for that would be interfering with the legislative power, which is separate and distinct . . . But unless some individual right directly affecting the parties litigant is thus brought in question, so that a judicial decision becomes necessary to settle the matters in controversy between them relative thereto, the courts have no jurisdiction; and it would be a perversion of the purposes for which they were instituted, and an assumption of functions that do not belong to them, to undertake to settle abstract questions of law, in whatever shape such questions may be presented. . . . Indeed, it is well settled, that courts will not take cognizance of fictitious suits, instituted merely to obtain judicial opinions upon points of law. . . . As we are distinctly informed by both parties that this is a fictitious suit, without enquiring into the grounds upon whch the judgment was rendered, as it was for the defendant and only for costs, the judgment below will be affirmed at the plaintiff's costs in this court. (*Mr. Justice Smith in Brewington v. Lowe, 1 Indiana, 79, 80-81, decided in 1848.*)

No consent of counsel can give jurisdiction. Appellate jurisdiction depends on the Constitution and the acts of Congress. When these do not confer it, courts of the United States cannot exercise it.

We cannot take cognizance of a case not brought before us in conformity with the law.

The case at bar, therefore, must be DISMISSED. (*Chief Justice Chase in The Lucy, 8 Wallace, 307, 309-310, decided in 1868.*)

Since men are naturally equal, and their rights and obligations are the same, as equally proceeding from nature, nations composed of men considered as so many free persons, living together in the state of nature, are naturally equal, and receive from nature the same obligations and rights. . . . A dwarf is as much a man as a giant; a small republic is as much a sovereign state as the most powerful kingdom. (*M. de Vattel, The Law of Nations; or Principles of the Law of Nature: Applied to the Conduct and Affairs of Nations and Sovereigns, 1758. Translated from the French, Vol. I, 1760, p. 6.*)

One cardinal rule, underlying all the relations of the States to each other, is that of equality of right. Each State stands on the same level with all the rest. It can impose its own legislation on no one of the others, and is bound to yield its own views to none. Yet, whenever, as in the case of *Missouri v. Illinois,* 180 U. S. 208, the action of one State reaches through the agency of natural laws into the territory of another State, the question of the extent and the limitations of the rights of the two States becomes a matter of justiciable dispute between them, and this court is called upon to settle that dispute in such a way as will recognize the equal rights of both and at the same time establish justice between them. In other words, through these successive disputes and decisions this court is practically building up what may not improperly be called interstate common law. (*Mr. Justice Brewer in Kansas v. Colorado, 206 United States, 46, 97-8, decided in 1907.*)

CHAPTER XIX

EXTENT AND EXERCISE OF JUDICIAL POWER

The
Question
of Extent

AFTER having considered at some length the nature of judicial power, and the powers of the Supreme Court under the Constitution, we are prepared to take up the question of the extent of judicial power and the manner in which it is to be exercised. The first part of this question need not long detain us, for the Constitution itself has determined the extent of the judicial power of the United States, which can only be enlarged, lessened, or modified by an amendment to the Constitution of the United States. In the second section of Article II it is said:

> The judicial Power shall extend to all Cases, in Law and Equity, arising under this Constitution, the Laws of the United States, and Treaties made, or which shall be made, under their Authority; — to all Cases affecting Ambassadors, other public Ministers and Consuls; — to all Cases of admiralty and maritime Jurisdiction; — to Controversies to which the United States shall be a Party; — to Controversies between two or more States; — between a State and Citizens of another State; — between Citizens of different States; — between Citizens of the same State claiming Lands under Grants of different States, and between a State, or the Citizens thereof, and foreign States, Citizens or Subjects.
>
> In all Cases affecting Ambassadors, other public Ministers and Consuls, and those in which a State shall be Party, the supreme Court shall have original Jurisdiction. In all the other Cases before mentioned, the supreme Court shall have appellate Jurisdiction, both as to Law and Fact, with such Exceptions, and under such Regulations as the Congress shall make.

It will be observed that, in the first of these two paragraphs, all of the cases are enumerated to which the judicial power of the United States shall extend, that in the second paragraph the distinction is drawn between original and appellate jurisdiction of the Supreme Court, leaving the Congress free to vest in the inferior courts which it may establish the other phases of the judicial power; but with the significant proviso that, in all the cases to which the judicial power of the United States extends, with the necessary exception of cases of original jurisdiction, the Supreme Court " shall have appellate Jurisdiction, both as to Law and Fact, with such Exceptions, and under such Regulations as the Congress shall make."

It is further to be observed that appellate jurisdiction is not confined to cases originating in the inferior courts " as Congress may from time to time ordain and establish," but that it extends to all cases specified in the grant of power, whether they be begun in a State or Federal court; and that, first and foremost among such cases, are those in law and equity "arising under this Constitution, the Laws of the United States, and Treaties made, or which shall be made, under their Authority." The Government of the Union is a government of enumerated powers, and therefore of limited jurisdiction; but within the extent of those powers it is supreme, and the propriety or impropriety of its action is to be determined, in the last resort, by the Supreme Court of the States, whose agent it is, not by the States themselves.

The judicial power of the United States is thus, in its entirety, vested in a Federal court, whether it be supreme or inferior. It was proposed and urged in the Federal Convention to vest the courts of the individual States with jurisdiction and to allow an appeal from the judgments of the State courts to the Supreme Court of the United States, in order to secure uniformity of decision by the use of existing agencies. But the framers of the Constitution decided, wisely, as experience shows, in favor of a judicial agency of the United States as a whole, in preference to the use of a court of any particular State as the common agency of the States.

By the first section of the third article of the Constitution, "The judicial Power of the United States, shall be vested in one Supreme Court, and in such inferior Courts" as may be established from time to time by the Congress. In the second section of the same Article this Supreme Court is invested with original jurisdiction "in all cases affecting Ambassadors, other public Ministers and Consuls, and those in which a State shall be a party." These were matters of supreme importance, and therefore confided to the Supreme Court if, as will be seen, the beneficiaries chose to consider its jurisdiction exclusive and availed themselves of the Supreme instead of an inferior tribunal. This does not mean that the other cases to which the judicial power was extended were not important, but that, in the opinion of the framers of the Constitution, they might arise and be decided in inferior tribunals of the State or of the United States, subject to appeal to the Supreme Court in order to correct error and to ensure uniformity of decision. As we are dealing with technical matters, it is well to be technical, and to define the sense in which these terms are used and understood in order to make for comprehension and clearness, even if the terms are so familiar that they seem to carry their own meaning with them.

In rendering the opinion of the court in the case of *White County Commissioners* v. *Gwin* (136 Indiana Reports, 562, 577), decided in 1893, Mr. Justice McCabe said, on behalf of his brethren:

Court
Defined

In modern times, and under our form of government, the judicial power is exercised by means of courts. A court is an instrumentality of government. It is a creation of the law, and in some respects it is an imaginary thing, that exists only in legal contemplation, very similar to a corporation. A time when, a place where, and the persons by whom judicial functions are to be exercised, are essential to complete the idea of a court. It is in its organized aspect, with all these constituent elements of time, place, and officers, that completes the idea of a court in the general legal acceptation of the term.

This is the language of a State court, but the idea pervades the United States as well as the States, and to show its universality the decision of a State has been chosen in preference to that of a Federal court.

The word
"Supreme"

For a like reason, the definition of a supreme court is taken from the opinion of Mr. Justice Dent in the case of *Koonce* v. *Doolittle* (48 W. Va. Rep., 592, 594), decided in 1900, who says:

The word "Supreme" meaning highest in the sense of final or last resort. Here all litigation must end, and when this Court has once finally determined a question it has no power to reopen it.

Finality

It will be noted that two elements are present and must coexist—finality as regards the litigant and finality as regards the court. That is to say, it is the last court to which the case can be carried, and, when that court has finally decided the case, it has exhausted the judicial power with which it is vested, and, because thereof, it has no power to reopen it.

Jurisdiction

But something more is needed to complete the idea of a court, whether it be a supreme or inferior tribunal. That idea is contained in the term "jurisdiction," which, like the other two, has been admirably defined by a State judge in the case of *Munday* v. *Vail* (34 N. J. Law Rep., 418, 422), decided in 1871, in which Mr. Chief Justice Beasley, speaking for his brethren, said:

Jurisdiction may be defined to be the right to adjudicate concerning the subject matter in the given case. To constitute this there are three essentials: First. The court must have cognizance of the class of cases to which the one to be adjudged belongs. Second. The proper parties must be present. And, Third. The point decided must be, in substance and effect, within the sphere, and that its action is void with respect to persons who are strangers to its proceedings, are propositions established by a multitude of authorities.

A matter of fundamental importance in this connection is that a court of limited jurisdiction, as are the Federal courts, Supreme as well as inferior, must, before it entertains a case, decide for itself whether it possesses jurisdiction, and whether it can lawfully assume and finally decide the case presented to it. In this regard the federal differ from courts of general jurisdictions, in which, it is to be presumed, unless the contrary be shown, that jurisdiction exists, with its necessary consequences. In the opening sentence of his opinion in *Cherokee Nation* v. *Georgia* (5 Peters, 1, 31), decided in 1831, Mr. Justice Baldwin said that he had confined his examination of the case to the point of jurisdiction, "as jurisdiction is the first question which must confront us in every case." And, delivering the opinion of the court in the great and leading case of *Rhode Island* v. *Massachusetts* (12 Peters, 657, 718), decided seven years later, he had occasion to consider the matter of jurisdiction in detail, inasmuch as Massachusetts objected to the jurisdiction of the Supreme Court in the bill against it filed by Rhode Island and to make clear the distinction, so important in federal courts, between tribunals of general and limited powers. On the first phase of the subject he said:

> However late this objection has been made, or may be made in any cause, in an inferior or appellate court of the United States, it must be considered and decided, before any court can move one further step in the cause; as any movement is necessarily the exercise of jurisdiction. Jurisdiction is the power to hear and determine the subject matter in controversy between parties to a suit, to adjudicate or exercise any judicial power over them; the question is, whether on the case before a court, their action is judicial or extra-judicial; with or without the authority of law, to render a judgment or decree upon the rights of the litigant parties. If the law confers the power to render a judgment or decree, then the court has jurisdiction; what shall be adjudged or decreed between the parties, and with which is the right of the case, is judicial action, by hearing and determining it.

On the second branch of the question, the learned Justice observed:

> A motion to dismiss a cause pending in the courts of the United States, is not analagous to a plea to the jurisdiction of a court of common law or equity in England; there the superior courts have a general jurisdiction over all persons within the realm, and all causes of action between them. It depends on the subject matter, whether the jurisdiction shall be exercised by a court of law or equity; but that court, to which it appropriately belongs, can act judicially upon the party and the subject of the suit; unless it shall be made apparent to the court that the judicial determination of the case has been withdrawn from the court of general jurisdiction. . . .
>
> As a denial of jurisdiction over the subject matter of a suit between parties within the realm, over which and whom the court has power to act, cannot be successful in an English court of general jurisdiction; a motion like the present could not be sustained consistently with the principles of its constitution. But as this Court is one of limited and special original jurisdiction, its action must be confined to the particular cases, controversies, and parties over which the constitution and laws have authorized it

to act; any proceeding without the limits prescribed, is coram non judice, and its action a nullity. . . . And whether the want or excess of power is objected by a party, or is apparent to the Court, it must surcease its action, or proceed extra-judicially.

Before we can proceed in this cause we must, therefore, inquire whether we can hear and determine the matters in controversy between the parties, who are two states of this Union, sovereign within their respective boundaries, save that portion of power which they have granted to the federal government, and foreign to each other for all but federal purposes.[1]

It will not have escaped attention that, after defining the original jurisdiction of the Supreme Court and limiting it to ambassadors, public ministers, consuls, and cases to which a State was a party, the Constitution declared that " the Supreme Court shall have appellate jurisdiction, both as to law and fact, with such exceptions and under such regulations as the Congress shall make." It is evident that the intervention of Congress was necessary, inasmuch as the appellate jurisdiction to be exercised by the courts was not to be defined by them but exercised according to a rule which the Congress should make. Until Congress had acted, the Supreme Court could exercise the original jurisdiction expressly conferred upon it by the Constitution, but could not sit as an appellate tribunal until inferior tribunals had been established, from whose judgments an appeal might be taken, or until the manner of appeal from State courts should have been determined.

" Judiciary
Act "

The first Congress accordingly proceeded to execute this power with which it was vested, pursuant to the authorization contained in Article I, Section 8, clause 18, " to make all Laws which shall be necessary and proper for carrying into Execution the foregoing Powers, and all other Powers vested by this Constitution in the Government of the United States, or in any Department or Officer thereof." The result of its labors, in so far as the courts are concerned, is embraced in the act to establish the judicial courts of the United States, approved September 24, 1789, providing, among other things, that the Supreme Court should consist of a Chief Justice and five Associate Justices; that the United States, for judicial purposes, should be divided into thirteen districts, with a district court in each, and three circuits for these districts; that the district and circuit courts should have original jurisdiction in some cases and concurrent jurisdiction in others with the courts of the States; that the Supreme Court should exercise the original jurisdiction in the cases mentioned in the Constitution. The act also defined and regulated appeals from the Federal and State courts to the Supreme Court of the Union and of the States. This remarkable statute was drafted by a committee of the Senate consisting of eight members, of

---

[1] 12 Peters, 718–20.

whom five,—including its chairman, Oliver Ellsworth, later to be Chief Justice,—had been members of the Federal Convention. Section 13 of the act, for which Mr. Ellsworth is deemed to have been chiefly responsible, provided:

> That the Supreme Court shall have exclusive jurisdiction of all controversies of a civil nature, where a state is a party, except between a state and its citizens; and except also between a state and citizens of other states, or aliens, in which latter case it shall have original but not exclusive jurisdiction. And shall have exclusively all such jurisdiction of suits or proceedings against ambassadors, or other public ministers, or their domestics, or domestic servants, as a court of law can have or exercise consistently with the law of nations; and original, but not exclusive jurisdiction of all suits brought by ambassadors, or other public ministers, or in which a consul, or vice consul, shall be a party. . . . The Supreme Court shall also have appellate jurisdiction from the circuit courts and courts of the several states, in the cases herein after specially provided for; and shall have power to issue writs of prohibition to the district courts, when proceeding as courts of admiralty and maritime jurisdiction, and writs of *mandamus,* in cases warranted by the principles and usages of law, to any courts appointed, or persons holding office, under the authority of the United States.[1]

Passing over the method of appeal from the district to the circuit, and from the circuit courts to the Supreme Court, Section 25 of the act deals with appeals from the courts of the several States, enacting:

> That a final judgment or decree in any suit, in the highest court of law or equity of a State in which a decision in the suit could be had, where is drawn in question the validity of a treaty or statute of, or an authority exercised under the United States, and the decision is against their validity; or where is drawn in question the validity of a statute of, or an authority exercised under any State, on the ground of their being repugnant to the constitution, treaties or laws of the United States, and the decision is in favour of such their validity, or where is drawn in question the construction of any clause of the constitution, or of a treaty, or statute of, or commission held under the United States, and the decision is against the title, right, privilege or exemption specially set up or claimed by either party, under such clause of the said Constitution, treaty, statute or commission, may be re-examined and reversed or affirmed in the Supreme Court of the United States upon a writ of error, the citation being signed by the chief justice, or judge or chancellor of the court rendering or passing the judgment or decree complained of, or by a justice of the Supreme Court of the United States, in the same manner and under the same regulations, and the writ shall have the same effect, as if the judgment or decree complained of had been rendered or passed in a circuit court, and the proceeding upon the reversal shall also be the same, except that the Supreme Court, instead of remanding the cause for a final decision as before provided, may at their discretion, if the cause shall have been once remanded before, proceed to a final decision of the same, and award execution. But

[1] 1 Statutes at Large, 80–1.

no other error shall be assigned or regarded as a ground of reversal in any such case as aforesaid, than such as appears on the face of the record, and immediately respects the before mentioned questions of validity or construction of the said constitution, treaties, statutes, commissions, or authorities in dispute.[1]

Without dwelling at this time upon the provisions of these sections of the judiciary act, as it is called, it will be observed that, as far as the judicial power of the United States is concerned, a decision of a State court is not subject to reexamination in the Supreme Court of the United States unless the judgment or decree is contrary to the Constitution, treaty or law of the United States; but it should also be observed that this section enabled the State court to decide the question involved in favor of the Constitution, treaty or law of the United States, although a Federal court might be of a different opinion if the case were presented to it.   To prevent this, and to enable the Federal courts to pass upon a question involving the Constitution, treaties or laws of the United States, whether the decision of the State court was in favor or against the Constitution, treaty or law of the United States, it was enacted by the Congress, approved December 23, 1914, that:

> " It shall be competent for the Supreme Court to require, by certiorari or otherwise, any such case to be certified to the Supreme Court for its review and determination, with the same power and authority in the case as if it had been carried by an appeal or writ of error to the Supreme Court, although the decision in such case may have been in favor of the validity of the treaty or statute or authority exercised under the United States or may have been against the validity of the State statute or authority claimed to be repugnant to the Constitution, treaties, or laws of the United States, or in favor of the title, right, privilege, or immunity claimed under the Constitution, treaty, statute, commission, or authority of the United States." [2]

As in the nature of judicial power, so in the matter of its extent, the decisions of the Supreme Court of the United States are the best, and in this instance the ultimate, authority to which to resort; and because of this, several leading decisions of this tribunal will be considered in turn and somewhat at length.

In *Martin* v. *Hunter* (1 Wheaton, 304), decided in 1816, the Supreme Court had occasion to consider the nature and extent of the appellate power of the United States in its relation to the " final judgment or decree in any suit in the highest court of law or equity of a state."   In this instance the

---

[1] 1 Statutes at Large, 85-7.
[2] 38 Statutes at Large, 790.

Court of Appeals of Virginia, which, on a mandate from the Supreme Court of the United States, rendered its judgment in the following terms:

> The court is unanimously of opinion that the appellate power of the supreme court of the United States does not extend to this court under a sound construction of the constitution of the United States; that so much of the 25th section of the act of congress, to establish the judicial courts of the United States, as extends the appellate jurisdiction of the supreme court to this court, is not in pursuance of the constitution of the United States. That the writ of error in this cause was improvidently allowed under the authority of that act; that the proceedings thereon in the supreme court were *coram non judice,* in relation to this court, and that obedience to its mandate be declined by the court.[1]

The question, therefore, presented by this case, was, stripped of technicalities, whether, under the Constitution, the Supreme Court could properly subject the decision of the highest State court to a re-examination and, in an appropriate case, reverse that judgment or decree. In other words, whether the Supreme Court of the United States or the court of final resort of one of the States was to interpret the Constitution of the United States; or, narrowing the issue, whether the nature and extent of the judicial power of the United States were to be determined by the court of all the States or by the court of any one of them. As was stated by Mr. Justice Baldwin, in the leading case of *Rhode Island* v. *Massachusetts* (12 Peters, 657, 722), decided in 1838, " the power of congress to make this provision for carrying into execution the judicial power . . ., taken in connection with the constitution, presents the great question in this cause, which is one of construction appropriate to judicial power, and exclusively of judicial cognizance, till the legislative power acts again upon it." `" Nature and Extent " Determined`

In the case of *Martin* v. *Hunter,* under consideration, Mr. Justice Story, recently appointed to the bench, delivered the opinion of the court, which has stood the test of criticism and re-examination. After explaining the nature of the more perfect Union of the States and of the two sovereignties created by the Constitution, and having quoted and analyzed the section of the Constitution dealing with judicial power, he continues, saying:

> The next consideration is as to the courts in which the judicial power shall be vested. It is manifest that a supreme court must be established; but whether it be equally obligatory to establish inferior courts, is a question of some difficulty. If congress may lawfully omit to establish inferior courts, it might follow, that in some of the enumerated cases the judicial power could nowhere exist. The supreme court can have original jurisdiction in two classes of cases only, viz. in cases affecting ambassadors, other public ministers and consuls, and in cases in which a state is a party. Congress cannot vest any portion of the judicial power of the United

[1] 1 Wheaton, 305–6.

States, except in courts ordained and established by itself; and if in any of the cases enumerated in the constitution, the state courts did not then possess jurisdiction, the appellate jurisdiction of the supreme court (admitting that it could act on state courts) could not reach those cases, and consequently, the injunction of the constitution, that the judicial power " *shall be vested*," would be disobeyed. It would seem, therefore, to follow, that congress are bound to create some inferior courts, in which to vest all that jurisdiction which, under the constitution, is *exclusively* vested in the United States, and of which the supreme court cannot take original cognisance. They might establish one or more inferior courts; they might parcel out the jurisdiction among such courts, from time to time, at their own pleasure. But the whole judicial power of the United States should be, at all times, vested either in an original or appellate form, in some courts created under its authority.[1]

After reenforcing the view which he had just expressed by an attentive examination of the second section of the third article, he thus states a further question, which naturally presented itself:

It being, then, established that the language of this clause is imperative, the next question is as the cases to which it shall apply. The answer is found in the constitution itself. The judicial power shall extend to all the cases enumerated in the constitution. As the mode is not limited, it may extend to all such cases, in any form, in which judicial power may be exercised. It may, therefore, extend to them in the shape of original or appellate jurisdiction, or both; for there is nothing in the nature of the cases which binds to the exercise of the one in preference to the other.[2]

The learned justice next asks the question, "In what cases (if any) is this judicial power exclusive, or exclusive at the election of congress" and, in regard to the States, he says:

At all events, whether the one construction or the other prevail, it is manifest that the judicial power of the United States is unavoidably, in some cases, exclusive of all state authority, and in all others, may be made so at the election of congress. No part of the criminal jurisdiction of the United States can, consistently with the constitution, be delegated to state tribunals. The admiralty and maritime jurisdiction is of the same exclusive cognisance; and it can only be in those cases where, previous to the constitution, state tribunals possessed jurisdiction independent of national authority, that they can now constitutionally exercise a concurrent jurisdiction. Congress, throughout the judicial act, and particularly in the 9th, 11th, and 13th sections, have legislated upon the supposition that in all the cases to which the judicial powers of the United States extended, they might rightfully vest exclusive jurisdiction in their own courts.[3]

After stating that the original jurisdiction of the Supreme Court is

[1] 1 Wheaton, 330–1.
[2] *Ibid.*, 333.
[3] *Ibid.*, 336–7.

limited, but that there are no terms of limitation upon the jurisdiction which it may assume upon appeal, in so far as the Constitution, the treaties and the laws of the United States are concerned, Mr. Justice Story comes to the specific question before him for decision. Thus:

> As, then, by the terms of the constitution, the appellate jurisdiction is not limited as to the supreme court, and as to this court it may be exercised in all other cases than those of which it has original cognisance, what is there to restrain its exercise over state tribunals, in the enumerated cases? [1]

And to this question he gives the following conclusive answer:

> The appellate power is not limited by the terms of the third article to any particular courts. The words are, "the judicial power (which includes appellate power) shall extend *to all cases,*" &c., and "in all other cases before mentioned the supreme court shall have appellate jurisdiction." It is the *case,* then, and not *the court,* that gives the jurisdiction. If the judicial power extends to the case, it will be in vain to search in the letter of the constitution for any qualification as to the tribunal where it depends. [2]

Examining this phase of the case more closely, he continued:

> On the other hand, if, as has been contended, a discretion be vested in congress to establish, or not to establish, inferior courts at their own pleasure, and congress should not establish such courts, the appellate jurisdiction of the supreme court would have nothing to act upon, unless it could act upon cases pending in the state courts. Under such circumstances it must be held that the appellate power would extend to state courts; for the constitution is peremptory that it shall extend to certain enumerated cases, which cases could exist in no other courts. [3]

There was, however, an argument stronger than that based upon the reason of the thing, which Mr. Justice Story thus states in the very next paragraph of his opinion:

> But it is plain that the framers of the constitution did contemplate that cases within the judicial cognizance of the United States not only might but would arise in the state courts, in the exercise of their ordinary jurisdiction. With this view the sixth article declares, that "this constitution, and the laws of the United States which shall be made in pursuance thereof, and all treaties made, or which shall be made, under the authority of the United States, shall be the supreme law of the land, and the judges in every state shall be bound thereby, any thing in the constitution or laws of any state to the contrary notwithstanding." It is obvious that this obligation is imperative upon the state judges in their official, and not merely in their private, capacities. From the very nature of their judicial duties they would be called upon to pronounce the law applicable to the case in judg-

[1] *Ibid.,* 338.
[2] *Ibid.*
[3] *Ibid.,* 339–40.

ment. They were not to decide merely according to the laws or constitution of the state, but according to the constitution, laws and treaties of the United States—"the supreme law of the land."

With this statement of the language of the judicial section and of the obligation imposed by the sixth article of the Constitution, Mr. Justice Story might have concluded this portion of his opinion, but he was unwilling to overlook two further reasons, which then, and now, after the experience of a century, are of importance.

> As to the first reason [to quote Mr. Justice Story's language]—admitting that the judges of the state courts are, and always will be, of as much learning, integrity, and wisdom, as those of the courts of the United States, (which we very cheerfully admit) it does not aid the argument. It is manifest that the constitution has proceeded upon a theory of its own, and given or withheld powers according to the judgment of the American people, by whom it was adopted. We can only construe its powers, and cannot inquire into the policy or principles which induced the grant of them. The constitution has presumed (whether rightly or wrongly we do not inquire), that state attachments, state prejudices, state jealousies, and state interests, might sometimes obstruct, or control, or be supposed to obstruct, or control, the regular administration of justice. Hence, in controversies between states; between citizens of different states; between citizens claiming grants under different states; between a state and its citizens, or foreigners, and between citizens and foreigners, it enables the parties, under the authority of congress, to have the controversies heard, tried, and determined before the national tribunals. No other reason than that which has been stated can be assigned, why some, at least, of those cases should not have been left to the cognizance of the state courts. In respect to the other enumerated cases—the cases arising under the constitution, laws, and treaties of the United States, cases affecting ambassadors and other public ministers, and cases of admiralty and maritime jurisdiction—reasons of a higher and more extensive nature, touching the safety, peace, and sovereignty of the nation, might well justify a grant of exclusive jurisdiction.[1]

So much for the first reason; as to the second, Mr. Justice Story said:

> A motive of another kind, perfectly compatible with the most sincere respect for state tribunals, might induce the grant of appellate power over their decisions. That motive is the importance, and even necessity of *uniformity* of decisions throughout the whole United States, upon all subjects within the purview of the constitution. Judges of equal learning and integrity, in different states, might differently interpret a statute, or a treaty of the United States, or even the constitution itself: If there were no revising authority to control these jarring and discordant judgments, and harmonize them into uniformity, the laws, the treaties, and the constitution of the United States would be different in different states, and might, perhaps, never have precisely the same construction, obligation, or efficacy, in any two states. The public mischiefs that would attend such a state of

---

[1] 1 Wheaton, 346–7.

things would be truly deplorable; and it cannot be believed that they could have escaped the enlightened convention which formed the constitution. What, indeed, might then have been only prophecy, has now become fact; and the appellate jurisdiction must continue to be the only adequate remedy for such evils.[1]

In *Cohens* v. *Virginia* (6 Wheaton, 264), decided in 1821, the same general question arose in a different way and was argued differently, but decided in accordance with the principle of *Martin* v. *Hunter,* although the *ratio decidendi* of the Cohens case differed from that of *Martin* v. *Hunter* in that Mr. Chief Justice Marshall instead of Mr. Justice Story delivered the opinion.

There was a statute of the State of Virginia forbidding the sale of lottery tickets within the State. There was an act of Congress of May 4, 1812, permitting the drawing of lotteries within the District of Columbia; and the question was, whether this act of Congress could be pleaded as a defense to the law of Virginia forbidding the sale of lottery tickets within the State. From the judgment of the highest court of the State having jurisdiction of the cause of action, the case was removed, by writ of error, to the Supreme Court of the United States, where counsel for defendant moved to dismiss the writ for want of jurisdiction, upon the ground that a State was a defendant, that a writ of error does not lie from the Supreme Court of the United States to a State court, and that the Supreme Court had no jurisdiction of the case because the judgment violated neither the Constitution nor any law of the United States.

On the important question as stated, Mr. Chief Justice Marshall said, in delivering the unanimous opinion of the court:

> The questions presented to the Court by the first two points made at the bar are of great magnitude, and may be truly said vitally to affect the Union. They exclude the inquiry whether the constitution and laws of the United States have been violated by the judgment which the plaintiffs in error seek to review; and maintain that, admitting such violation, it is not in the power of the government to apply a corrective. They maintain that the nation does not possess a department capable of restraining peaceably, and by authority of law, any attempts which may be made, by any part, against the legitimate powers of the whole; and that the government is reduced to the alternative of submitting to such attempts, or of resisting them by force. They maintain that the constitution of the United States has provided no tribunal for the final construction of itself, or of the laws or treaties of the nation; but that this power may be exercised in the last resort by the Courts of every State in the Union. That the constitution, laws, and treaties, may receive as many constructions as there are States; and that this is not a mischief, or, if a mischief, is irremediable.[2]

[1] *Ibid.,* 347–8.
[2] 6 Wheaton, 376–7.

After this statement, the Chief Justice proceeded to discuss the question in which the case before him was to be distinguished in form, though not in substance, from that of *Martin* v. *Hunter,* and the conclusion which he reached on this first point is deeply imbedded in the jurisprudence of the United States, and is hardly less familiar than the language of the Constitution, which it interprets.

After saying that "jurisdiction is given to the Courts of the Union in two classes of cases," he thus enumerates them:

> In the first, their jurisdiction depends on the character of the cause, whoever may be the parties. This class comprehends "all cases in law and equity arising under this constitution, the laws of the United States, and treaties made, or which shall be made, under their authority." This clause extends the jurisdiction of the Court to all the cases described, without making in its terms any exception whatever, and without any regard to the condition of the party. If there be any exception, it is to be implied against the express words of the article.
>
> In the second class, the jurisdiction depends entirely on the character of the parties. In this are comprehended "controversies between two or more States, between a State and citizens of another State," and "between a State and foreign States, citizens or subjects." If these be the parties, it is entirely unimportant what may be the subject of controversy. Be it what it may, these parties have a constitutional right to come into the Courts of the Union.[1]

The
Liability
of States

To break the force of this statement, counsel for defendant in error contended "that a sovereign, independent State is not suable except by its own consent." Upon which statement, the Chief Justice made the following comment:

> This general proposition will not be controverted. But its consent is not requisite in each particular case. It may be given in a general law. And if a state has surrendered any portion of its sovereignty, the question whether a liability to suit be a part of this portion, depends on the instrument by which the surrender is made. If, upon a just construction of that instrument, it shall appear that the State has submitted to be sued, then it has parted with the sovereign right of judging in every case on the justice of its own pretentions, and has entrusted that power to a tribunal in whose impartiality it confides.[2]

After quoting the express provision of the Constitution, extending the judicial power to controversies between two or more States, between citizens of a State and another State, and between citizens of a foreign State, citizens or subjects, the Chief Justice concludes that "the mere circumstance that a State is a party gives jurisdiction to the court," and that "the Con-

---

[1] 6 Wheaton, 378.
[2] *Ibid.,* 380.

stitution gave to every person having a claim upon a State a right to submit his case to the Court of the nation." To show the importance of having a case, even although a State be a party, passed upon by the Supreme Court when the Constitution, treaties or laws of the United States be drawn in question, and the decision opposed to the supreme law of the land, the Chief Justice thus reenforces the reasons already advanced by Mr. Justice Story, saying:

> What power of the government could be executed by its own means, in any State disposed to resist its execution by a course of legislation? The laws must be executed by individuals acting within the several States. If these individuals may be exposed to penalties, and if the Courts of the Union cannot correct the judgments by which these penalties may be enforced, the course of the government may be, at any time, arrested by the will of one of its members. Each member will possess a *veto* on the will of the whole.[1]

And again:

> Different States may entertain different opinions on the true construction of the constitutional powers of Congress. We know, that at one time, the assumption of the debts contracted by the several States, during the war of our revolution, was deemed unconstitutional by some of them. We know, too, that at other times, certain taxes, imposed by Congress, have been pronounced unconstitutional. Other laws have been questioned partially, while they were supported by the great majority of the American people. We have no assurance that we shall be less divided than we have been. States may legislate in conformity to their opinions, and may enforce those opinions by penalties. It would be hazarding too much to assert, that the judicatures of the States will be exempt from the prejudices by which the legislatures and people are influenced, and will constitute perfectly impartial tribunals. In many States the judges are dependent for office and for salary on the will of the legislature. The constitution of the United States furnishes no security against the universal adoption of this principle. When we observe the importance which that constitution attaches to the independence of judges, we are the less inclined to suppose that it can have intended to leave these constitutional questions to tribunals where this independence may not exist, in all cases where a State shall prosecute an individual who claims the protection of an act of Congress.[2]

Taking up another phase of the question involved in the contention, the Chief Justice said:

> It has been also urged, as an additional objection to the jurisdiction of the Court, that cases between a State and one of its own citizens, do not come within the general scope of the constitution; and were obviously never intended to be made cognizable in the federal Courts. . . .

[1] *Ibid.*, 385.
[2] *Ibid.*, 386-7.

This is very true, so far as the jurisdiction depends on the character of the parties; and the argument would have great force if urged to prove that this Court could not establish the demand of a citizen upon his State, but is not entitled to the same force when urged to prove that this Court cannot inquire whether the constitution or laws of the United States protect a citizen from a prosecution instituted against him by a State. If jurisdiction depended entirely on the character of the parties, and was not given where the parties have not an original right to come into Court, that part of the 2d section of the 3d article, which extends the judicial power to all cases arising under the constitution and laws of the United States, would be mere surplusage. It is to give jurisdiction where the character of the parties would not give it, that this very important part of the clause was inserted. . . . If the constitution or laws may be violated by proceedings instituted by a State against its own citizens, and if that violation may be such as essentially to affect the constitution and the laws, such as to arrest the progress of government in its constitutional course, why should these cases be excepted from that provision which expressly extends the judicial power of the Union to *all* cases arising under the constitution and laws?[1]

To this question, thus put, no satisfactory answer has as yet been made.

In some respects the case of *Osborn* v. *Bank of the United States* (9 Wheaton, 737), decided in 1824, is to be considered as an appeal from the decision of the Supreme Court in the case of *McCulloch* v. *Maryland* (4 Wheaton, 316), decided five years earlier, holding that a State law taxing a branch of the bank of the United States in that State is a tax upon an agency of the United States and is unconstitutional, null and void. The decision in the McCulloch case was re-examined and affirmed. In addition, the court held that a suit against officers of a State, enjoining them from proceeding against the bank, was not a suit against the State in the sense of the 11th Amendment, unless the State itself were a party to the record. While, however, the Osborn case is an authority for these views, for present purposes it is cited to show when and how a case arises in law and equity under the Constitution, treaties and laws of the United States.

How Cases
May Arise
in Law and
Equity

Counsel for the defendants had insisted that it was not such a case; counsel for the plaintiff that it was; and, meeting the issue as presented, the court examined the question and rejected the defendant's thesis. Speaking for the court, Mr. Chief Justice Marshall said:

> The appellants contend, that it does not, because several questions may arise in it, which depend on the general principles of the law, not on any act of Congress.
> If this were sufficient to withdraw a case from the jurisdiction of the federal Courts, almost every case, although involving the construction of a law, would be withdrawn; and a clause in the constitution, relating to a subject of vital importance to the government, and expressed in the most comprehensive terms, would be construed to mean almost nothing.[2]

[1] 6 Wheaton, 390–2.
[2] 9 Wheaton, 819–20.

The Chief Justice thereupon asks if jurisdiction is excluded because the case involves questions depending on general principles, and holds that it is not, saying and declaring the law on this point:

> A cause may depend on several questions of fact and law. Some of these may depend on the construction of a law of the United States; others on principles unconnected with that law. If it be a sufficient foundation for jurisdiction, that the title or right set up by the party, may be defeated by one construction of the constitution or law of the United States, and sustained by the opposite construction, provided the facts necessary to support the action be made out, then all the other questions must be decided as incidental to this, which gives that jurisdiction. Those other questions cannot arrest the proceedings. Under this construction, the judicial power of the Union extends effectively and beneficially to that most important class of cases, which depend on the character of the cause. On the opposite construction, the judicial power never can be extended to a whole case, as expressed by the constitution, but to those parts of cases only which present the particular question involving the construction of the constitution or the law. We say it never can be extended to the whole case, because, if the circumstance that other points are involved in it, shall disable Congress from authorizing the Courts of the Union to take jurisdiction of the original cause, it equally disables Congress from authorizing those Courts to take jurisdiction of the whole cause, on an appeal, and thus will be restricted to a single question in that cause; and words obviously intended to secure to those who claim rights under the constitution, laws, or treaties of the United States, a trial in the federal Courts, will be restricted to the insecure remedy of an appeal upon an insulated point, after it has received that shape which may be given to it by another tribunal, into which he is forced against his will.
>
> We think, then, that when a question to which the judicial power of the Union is extended by the constitution, forms an ingredient of the original cause, it is in the power of Congress to give the Circuit Courts jurisdiction of that cause, although other questions of fact or of law may be involved in it.[1]

It requires no comment to show the necessity of such a decision, as otherwise the purpose of the Constitution would be frustrated, in that cases in law and equity arising under the Constitution, treaties or laws of the United States would not be examined by the Supreme Court, either originally or upon appeal, and the Government of the States would be unable to defend itself in many cases against the acts of the States. Such a construction would not extend the judicial power of the United States but would withdraw such power from cases in law and equity arising under the Constitution, laws and treaties of the United States.

The question frequently arises whether the judicial power of the United States is concurrent with that of the States; or whether it is, in its nature, exclusive. Advocates of a highly centralized government insist that the

Is Judicial Power Concurrent or Exclusive?

[1] *Ibid.*, 821–3.

judicial power of the United States is exclusive wherever it attaches, whereas advocates of the States insist that the States retained the right to the exercise of judicial power in all cases where it has not been renounced, or where the Government of the Union, in pursuance of the Constitution, has not invested the judicial power exclusively in the courts of the Union. The framers of the Constitution, its classic expounders, the Congress and the Supreme Court, seem to belong to the latter class. As far as the framers of the Constitution and the Congress are concerned, it is only necessary to point to Section 9 of the judiciary act of September 24, 1789, which recognizes concurrent jurisdiction by declaring, among other things, that the district courts of the United States "shall also have cognizance, concurrent with the courts of the several States, or the circuit courts, as the case may be, of all causes where an alien sues for a tort only in violation of the law of nations or a treaty of the United States." [1]

Members of the committee framing this act had been members of the Federal Convention. The hand that drew it was Oliver Ellsworth, member of the Federal Convention, member of the State Convention of Connecticut for the ratification of the Constitution, first United States Senator from his State under the Constitution, and soon to be Chief Justice of the Supreme Court of the United States. Alexander Hamilton was no friend of the States. He wished to blot them out of existence. In the plan of the Constitution which he proposed to the Federal Convention they would have been little more than provinces, with governors appointed for life or during good behavior with a veto upon the laws of the State, and appointed by a President holding office for life or during good behavior. Yet he admitted freely, in *The Federalist*, that the States under the Constitution were to be considered as sovereign bodies, possessing the powers which they did not expressly or impliedly grant to the Government of the Union, or which they did not themselves renounce. In the 82d number of *The Federalist* he speaks of the Government as composed of distinct sovereignties, and, discussing the relation of the State to the Federal judiciary, he asks: "Is this to be exclusive or are those courts to possess a concurrent jurisdiction? If the latter, in what relation will they stand to the national tribunals?" These inquiries, which, he says, "we meet with in the mouths of men of sense," he thus answers:

> The principles established in a former paper teach us, that the states will retain all *pre-existing* authorities, which may not be exclusively delegated to the federal head; and that this exclusive delegation can only exist in one of three cases: where an exclusive authority is, in express terms, granted to the union; or where a particular authority is granted to the

[1] 1 Statutes at Large, 77.

union, and the exercise of a like authority is prohibited to the states; or, where an authority is granted to the union, with which a similar authority in the states would be utterly incompatible. Though these principles may not apply with the same force to the judiciary, as to the legislative power; yet I am inclined to think, that they are in the main, just with respect to the former, as well as the latter. And under this impression I shall lay it down as a rule, that the state courts will *retain* the jurisdiction they now have, unless it appears to be taken away in one of the enumerated modes.[1]

These are also the views of the Supreme Court, and indeed, in the case of *Clafflin* v. *Houseman* (93 U. S., 130), decided in 1876, Mr. Justice Bradley, speaking for a unanimous court, refers to this very number of *The Federalist* and appears to approve not merely the view which has been quoted, but Hamilton's entire conception and statement of the concurrent powers of the Federal and of the State courts. And the approval of the Supreme Court is not indirect, but express and direct, in that it thus quotes and approves the Hamiltonian conception:

> It was fully examined in the eighty-second number of " The Federalist," by Alexander Hamilton, with his usual analytical power and far-seeing genius; and hardly an argument or a suggestion has been made since which he did not anticipate. After showing that exclusive delegation of authority to the Federal government can arise only in one of three ways,—either by express grant of exclusive authority over a particular subject; or by a simple grant of authority, with a subsequent prohibition thereof to the States; or, lastly, where an authority granted to the Union would be utterly incompatible with a similar authority in the States,—he says, that these principles may also apply to the judiciary as well as the legislative power. Hence, he infers that the State courts will retain the jurisdiction they then had, unless taken away in one of the enumerated modes. But, as their previous jurisdiction could not by possibility extend to cases which might grow out of and be peculiar to the new constitution, he considered that, as to such cases, Congress might give the Federal courts sole jurisdiction. " I hold," says he, " that the State courts will be divested of no part of their primitive jurisdiction, further than may relate to an appeal; and I am even of opinion, that in every case in which they were not expressly excluded by the future acts of the national legislature, they will, of course, take cognizance of the causes to which those acts may give birth. This I infer from the nature of judiciary power, and from the general genius of the system. The judiciary power of every government looks beyond its own local or municipal laws, and, in civil cases, lays hold of all subjects of litigation between parties within its jurisdiction, though the causes of dispute are relative to the laws of the most distant part of the globe. . . . When, in addition to this, we consider the State governments and the national government, as they truly are, in the light of kindred systems, and as parts of ONE WHOLE, the inference seems to be conclusive, that the State courts would have concurrent jurisdiction in all cases arising under the laws of the Union, where it was not expressly prohibited."[2]

[1] *The Federalist*, 1802 ed., Vol. II, pp. 243–4.
[2] 93 U. S. 138.

After referring to the passage of the judiciary act, which has been quoted, and to the exact language of the Constitution, Mr. Justice Bradley next invokes the authority of the great Chief Justice himself. Thus:

> In *Cohens* v. *Virginia,* 6 Wheat. 415, Chief Justice Marshall demonstrates the necessity of an appellate power in the Federal judiciary to revise the decisions of State courts in cases arising under the Constitution and laws of the United States, in order that the constitutional grant of judicial power, extending it to all such cases, may have full effect. He says, " The propriety of intrusting the construction of the Constitution and laws, made in pursuance thereof, to the judiciary of the Union, has not, we believe, as yet, been drawn in question. It seems to be a corollary from this political axiom, that the Federal courts should either possess exclusive jurisdiction in such cases, or a power to revise the judgment rendered in them by the State tribunals. If the Federal and State courts have concurrent jurisdiction in all cases arising under the Constitution, laws, and treaties of the United States, and if a case of this description brought in a State court cannot be removed before judgment, nor revised after judgment, then the construction of the Constitution, laws, and treaties of the United States is not confided particularly to their judicial department, but is confided equally to that department and to the State courts, however they may be constituted.[1]

The Clafflin case was one to test the nature and extent of concurrent jurisdiction on the part of the State and Federal courts, inasmuch as it involved a question of bankruptcy, which, under the bankruptcy law of the United States, passed by Congress pursuant to Article I, Section 8, of the Constitution, invests Congress with the power " to establish . . . uniform Laws on the subject of Bankruptcies throughout the United States." Speaking for the court, Mr. Justice Bradley said and concluded:

> We hold that the assignee in bankruptcy, under the Bankrupt Act of 1867, as it stood before the revision, had authority to bring a suit in the State courts, wherever those courts were invested with appropriate jurisdiction, suited to the nature of the case.[2]

The last case to be considered in this connection is that of *Ames* v. *Kansas* (111 U. S., 449), decided in 1884, in which the court had occasion to consider the original and appellate jurisdiction of the United States, and to establish the principle that, even in those cases in which the Supreme Court has original jurisdiction by the Constitution, the term "original" is not necessarily exclusive.

After referring to the judicial clause of the Constitution, to the judiciary act of 1789, passed within six months after the inauguration of the Government under the Constitution, vesting suits against Ambassadors in the

---

[1] 93 U. S., 142.
[2] *Ibid.,* 143.

Supreme Court as could be brought against ambassadors, "and original, but not exclusive, jurisdiction of all suits brought by ambassadors, or other public ministers, or to which a consul, or vice-consul shall be a party," Mr. Chief Justice Waite, speaking for a unanimous court, said:

> It thus appears that the first Congress, in which were many who had been leading and influential members of the convention, and who were familiar with the discussions that preceded the adoption of the Constitution by the States and with the objections urged against it, did not understand that the original jurisdiction vested in the Supreme Court was necessarily exclusive. That jurisdiction included all cases affecting ambassadors, other public ministers and consuls, and those in which a State was a party. The evident purpose was to open and keep open the highest court of the nation for the determination, in the first instance, of suits involving a State or a diplomatic or commercial representative of a foreign government. So much was due to the rank and dignity of those for whom the provision was made; but to compel a State to resort to this one tribunal for the redress of all its grievances, or to deprive an ambassador, public minister or consul of the privilege of suing in any court he chose having jurisdiction of the parties and the subject matter of his action, would be, in many cases, to convert what was intended as a favor into a burden.[1]

The Chief Justice and his brethren were of opinion that the purpose of the framers of the Constitution would be subserved if the parties entitled to invoke the original jurisdiction of the Supreme Court could not be made defendants in another tribunal. Thus, the Chief Justice said:

> Acting on this construction of the Constitution, Congress took care to provide that no suit should be brought *against* an ambassador or other public minister except in the Supreme Court, but that he might sue in any court he chose that was open to him. As to consuls, the commercial representatives of foreign governments, the jurisdiction of the Supreme Court was made concurrent with the District Courts, and suits of a civil nature could be brought against them in either tribunal. . . . In this way States, ambassadors, and public ministers were protected from the compulsory process of any court other than one suited to their high positions, but were left free to seek redress for their own grievances in any court that had the requisite jurisdiction. No limits were set on their powers of choice in this particular. This, of course, did not prevent a State from allowing itself to be sued in its own courts or elsewhere in any way or to any extent it chose.[2]

After an examination of the precedents, Mr. Chief Justice Waite thus concluded the portion of the opinion material to the present purpose:

> In view of the practical construction put on this provision of the Constitution by Congress at the very moment of the organization of the gov-

[1] 111 U. S., 464.
[2] *Ibid.*, 464–5.

ernment, and of the significant fact that from 1789 until now no court of the United States has ever in its actual adjudications determined to the contrary, we are unable to say that it is not within the power of Congress to grant to the inferior courts of the United States jurisdiction in cases where the Supreme Court has been vested by the Constitution with original jurisdiction. It rests with the legislative department of the government to say to what extent such grants shall be made, and it may safely be assumed that nothing will ever be done to encroach upon the high privileges of those for whose protection the constitutional provision was intended. At any rate, we are unwilling to say that the power to make the grant does not exist.[1]

In the Federal Convention which adopted the Constitution, it was proposed to establish a council of revision to pass upon the acts of the State legislatures and upon those of the Congress, and, in appropriate cases, to negative the acts of each. Omitting details and the various forms which this proposition assumed, it is sufficient for present purposes to state that, in each instance, this body was to be composed in part of the national judiciary, thus investing its members with political functions. This proposition, in various forms and at various times, was urged upon the Convention by the ablest members, such as Messrs. Madison, Wilson, and Ellsworth. The Convention, however, wiser than its wisest members, insisted upon the separation of judicial and political powers, and, after much debate and deliberation, rejected the proposition, for the very substantial reasons contained in a few of the many passages which could be quoted from Mr. Madison's Notes of the debates.

Confusion over Political v. Judicial Questions

1.   Mr. Ghorum did not see the advantage of employing the Judges in this way. As Judges they are not to be presumed to possess any peculiar knowledge of the mere policy of public measures.
2.   Mr. Gerry did not expect to see this point which had undergone full discussion, again revived. . . . The motion was liable to strong objections. It was combining & mixing together the Legislative & the other departments. It was establishing an improper coalition between the Executive & Judiciary departments. It was making Statesmen of the Judges; and setting them up as the guardians of the Rights of the people. . . . It was making the Expositors of the Laws, the Legislators which ought never to be done.
3.   Mr. Strong thought with Mr. Gerry that the power of making ought to be kept distinct from that of expounding, the laws. No maxim was better established. The Judges in exercising the function of expositors might be influenced by the part they had taken, in framing the laws.
4.   Mr. L. Martin considered the association of the Judges with the Executive as a dangerous innovation; . . . A knowledge of Mankind, and of Legislative affairs cannot be presumed to belong in a higher degree to the Judges than to the Legislature. And as to the Constitutionality of the laws, that point will come before the Judges in their proper official charac-

[1] 111 U. S., 469.

ter. In this character they have a negative on the laws. Join them with the Executive in the Revision and they will have a double negative.

5.   M^r. Gerry had rather give the Executive an absolute negative for its own defence than thus to blend together the Judiciary & Executive departments. It will bind them together in an offensive and defensive alliance agst. the Legislature, and render the latter unwilling to enter into a contest with them.

6.   M^r. Ghorum. All agree that a check on the Legislature is necessary. But there are two objections agst. admitting the Judges to share in it which no observations on the other side seem to obviate. The 1st. is that the Judges ought to carry into the exposition of the laws no prepossessions with regard to them. 2^d. that as the Judges will outnumber the Executive, the revisionary check would be thrown entirely out of the Executive hands, and instead of enabling him to defend himself, would enable the Judges to sacrifice him.

7.   M^r. Rutlidge thought the Judges of all men the most unfit to be concerned in the revisionary Council. The Judges ought never to give their opinion on a law till it comes before them. He thought it equally unnecessary. The Executive could advise with the officers of State, as of war, finance &c. and avail himself of their information and opinions.[1]

8.   M^r. Sherman. Can one man be trusted better than all the others if they all agree? This was neither wise nor safe. He disapproved of Judges meddling in politics and parties.[2]

It was clearly the intention of the framers that the judiciary should not busy itself with politics, and repeated decisions of the Supreme Court have given effect to their intention, that the judicial power does not extend to political questions. Controversies between States were not justiciable before the Constitution of the United States. They were political questions, and as such they were not submitted, or were not regarded as capable of submission, to a court of justice. This fact was adverted to by Mr. Justice Bradley in *Hans* v. *Louisiana* (134 U. S., 1, 15), decided in 1889, who said, on behalf of the court:

> The truth is, that the cognizance of suits and actions unknown to the law, and forbidden by the law, was not contemplated by the Constitution when establishing the judicial power of the United States.

Had he stopped here, questions at that time considered political would have remained so, but he adds:

> Some things, undoubtedly, were made justiciable which were not known as such at the common law; such, for example, as controversies between States as to boundary lines, and other questions admitting of judicial solution.

[1] *Documentary History of the Constitution,* Vol. III, pp. 391–9. Session of July 21st.
[2] *Ibid.,* p. 539. Session of August 15th.

The distinction, therefore, is not hard and fast. Things political may become justiciable, and therefore submitted to a court for decision; and the question arises, how this transformation may be brought about. Fortunately, we do not need to indulge in speculative or theoretical reasoning, for we have on this very point the authority of the Supreme Court of the United States, showing (1) how political power, vested originally in the crown, became judicial by submission to courts of justice; (2) that controversies between the colonies, settled as such by the King in Council because they had no other common superior, became by the same process judicial when submitted to a court of justice; and (3), that the agreement by the States of the American Union to submit their controversies to courts of justice made them justiciable.

In *Rhode Island* v. *Massachusetts* (12 Peters, 657), decided in 1838, this whole question was examined, the distinction between judicial and political questions outlined and defined and the process by which questions, originally political, could become justiciable, and therefore judicial, stated and applied. In proof of the first of these contentions, Mr. Justice Baldwin, delivering the opinion of the court in this case, quotes an early English statute and Coke's Institutes, of hardly less authority. The learned Justice quotes the statute of 20 Edward III, Chapter I. The passages from Coke's Institutes, referring to and summarizing this among other statutes, are as follows:

First, where Bracton saith, *Habet rex plures curias in quibus diversae actiones terminantur;* Hereby, and in effect by Britton, and this conclusion followeth, that the King hath committed and distributed all his whole power of judicature to severall Courts of Justice, and therefore the judgement must be *ideo consideratum est per Curiam.* And herewith do agree divers Acts of parliament and Book cases, some whereof, for illustration, we will briefly remember; and leave the judicious reader to the rest. . . . .
8 H. 4. the King hath committed all his power judiciall, some in one Court, and some in another, so as if any would render himselfe to the judgement of a King in such case where the king hath committed all his power judiciall to others, such a render should be to no effect. An 8 H. 6. the king doth judge by his Judges (the king having distributed his power judiciall to several Courts) And the king hath wholly left matters of judicature according to his lawes to his Judges.[1]

Therefore, as the interpretation of an agreement is a judicial question, the compact between Penn and Lord Baltimore concerning the boundaries of Pennsylvania, Delaware and Maryland was referred to a court of justice, because it was an agreement, and to that particular court of justice called the High Court of Chancery, because that tribunal alone enforced the specific

[1] Sir Edward Coke, *The Fourth Part of the Institutes of the Laws of England,* 1644, pp. 70-71.

performance of an agreement, as prayed by Penn in that case. Where there was no agreement, the king in council took jurisdiction and decided by virtue of his political prerogative, with the advice of his members, who sat as advisers.

From the detailed and closely knit argument of Mr. Justice Baldwin the following passage may be quoted, as showing the process by which he reached his conclusion, as well as the conclusion itself:

> The king had no jurisdiction over boundary within the realm, without he had it in all his dominions, as the absolute owner of the territory, from whom all title and power must flow, 1 Bl. Com. 241; Co. Litt. 1; Hob. 322; 7 D. C. D. 76; Cowp. 205–11; 7 Co. 17, b., as the supreme legislator; save a limited power in parliament. He could make and unmake boundaries in any part of his dominions, except in proprietary provinces. He exercised this power by treaty, as in 1763, by limiting the colonies to the Mississippi, whose charters extended to the South sea; by proclamation, which was a supreme law, as in Florida and Georgia, 12 Wheat. 524; 1 Laws U. S. 443–51; by order in council, as between Massachusetts and New Hampshire, cited in the argument. But in all cases it was by his political power, which was competent to dismember royal, though it was not exercised on the chartered or proprietary provinces. M'Intosh v. Johnson, 8 Wheaton, 580. In council, the king had no original judicial power, 1 Ves. sen. 447. He decided on appeals from the colonial courts, settled boundaries, in virtue of his prerogative, where there was no agreement; but if there is a disputed agreement, the king cannot decree on it, and therefore, the council remit it to be determined in another place, on the foot of the contract, 1 Ves. sen. 447. In virtue of his prerogative, where there was no agreement, 1 Ves. sen. 205, the king acts not as a judge, but as the sovereign acting by the advice of his counsel, the members whereof do not and cannot sit as judges. By the statute 20 E. 3, ch. 1, it is declared, that " the king hath delegated his whole judicial power to the judges, all matters of judicature according to the laws," 1 Ruff. 246; 4 Co. Inst. 70, 74; he had, therefore, none to exercise: and judges, though members of council, did not sit in judicature, but merely as his advisers.[1]

And after an elaborate examination of English precedent and cases, including the judicial interpretation of compacts between nations, Mr. Justice Baldwin concluded:

> From this view of the law of England, the results are clear, that the settlement of boundaries by the king in council, is by his prerogative; which is political power acting on a political question between dependent corporations or proprietaries, in his dominions without the realm. When it is done in chancery, it is by its judicial power, in " judicature according to the law," and necessarily a judicial question, whether it relates to the boundary of provinces, according to an agreement between the owners, as Penn v. Baltimore [1 Ves. sen. 448]; the title to a feudal kingdom, in a suit appropriate

---

[1] 12 Peters, 739.

to equity, where the feudal king appears and pleads, as in the case of the Isle of Man; or on an agreement between a foreign sovereign and the East India Company, in their mere corporate capacity. But when the company assumed the character of a sovereign, assert the agreement to be a " federal treaty," between them and the plaintiff, as neighbouring sovereigns, each independent, and the subject matter to be peace and war, political in its nature, on which no municipal court can act by the law of nations, chancery has no jurisdiction but to dismiss the bill. Not because it is founded on a treaty, but because the defendant refused to submit it to judicial power; for, had the company not made the objection, by their answer, the court must have proceeded as in The King of Spain v. Machado [4 Russell, 225], and decreed on the validity, as well as the construction of the treaties. The court, in one case, could not force a sovereign defendant to submit the merits of the case to their cognizance; but in the other, when he was plaintiff, and a subject was a defendant, who appeared and plead, the whole subject matter of the pleadings was decided by judicial power, as a judicial question; and such has been, and is the settled course of equity in England.[1]

Armed with these precedents, Mr. Justice Baldwin turns his attention in the following passage to the colonies and States of the American Union:

In the colonies, there was no judicial tribunal which could settle boundaries between them; for the court of one could not adjudicate on the rights of another, unless as a plaintiff. The only power to do it remained in the king, where there was no agreement; and in chancery, where there was one, and the parties appeared; so that the question was partly political and partly judicial, and so remained till the declaration of independence. Then the states, being independent, reserved to themselves the power of settling their own boundaries, which was necessarily a purely political matter, and so continued until 1781. Then the states delegated the whole power over controverted boundaries to congress, to appoint and its court to decide, as judges, and give a final sentence and judgment upon it, as a judicial question, settled by specially appointed judicial power, as the substitute of the king in council, and the court of chancery in a proper case; before the one as a political, and the other as a judicial question.

Then came the constitution, which divided the power between the political and judicial departments, after incapacitating the states from settling their controversies upon any subject, by treaty, compact, or agreement; and completely reversed the long established course of the laws of England. Compacts and agreements were referred to the political, controversies to the judicial power. This presents this part of the case in a very simple and plain aspect. All the states have transferred the decision of their controversies to this Court; each had a right to demand of it the exercise of the power which they had made judicial by the confederation of 1781 and 1788; that we should do that which neither states or congress could do, settle the controversies between them. We should forget our high duty, to declare to litigant states that we have jurisdiction over judicial, but not the power to hear and determine political controversies; that boundary was of a political nature, and not a civil one; and dismiss the plaintiff's bill from our records, without even giving it judicial consideration. We should equally forget the

---

[1] 12 Peters, 742-3.

dictate of reason, the known rule drawn by fact and law; that from the nature of a controversy between kings or states, it cannot be judicial; that where they reserve to themselves the final decision, it is of necessity by their inherent political power; not that which has been delegated to the judges, as matters of judicature, according to the law.[1]

In another portion of his opinion, the learned Justice, speaking of the States of the American Union, says:

Those states, in their highest sovereign capacity, in the convention of the people thereof; on whom, by the revolution, the prerogative of the crown, and the transcendent power of parliament devolved, in a plenitude unimpaired by any act, and controllable by no authority, 6 Wheat. 651; 8 Wheat. 584, 88; adopted the constitution, by which they respectively made to the United States a grant of judicial power over controversies between two or more states. By the constitution, it was ordained that this judicial power, in cases where a state was a party, should be exercised by this Court as one of original jurisdiction. The states waived their exemption from judicial power, 6 Wheat. 378, 80, as sovereigns by original and inherent right, by their own grant of its exercise over themselves in such cases, but which they would not grant to any inferior tribunal. By this grant, this Court has acquired jurisdiction over the parties in this cause, by their own consent and delegated authority; as their agent for executing the judicial power of the United States in the cases specified.[2]

In a third and a final passage, for it is impossible to quote or to summarize the whole opinion, Mr. Justice Baldwin not only states the process, the reason for the process, but the procedure to be followed in the actual trial and disposition of controversies between States submitted to a court of justice:

The founders of our government could not but know, what has ever been, and is familiar to every statesman and jurist, that all controversies between nations, are, in this sense, political, and not judicial, as none but the sovereign can settle them. In the declaration of independence, the states assumed their equal station among the powers of the earth, and asserted that they could of right do, what other independent states could do; "declare war, make peace, contract alliances;" of consequence, to settle their controversies with a foreign power, or among themselves, which no state, and no power, could do for them. They did contract an alliance with France, in 1778; and with each other, in 1781: the object of both was to defend and secure their asserted rights as states; but they surrendered to congress, and its appointed Court, the right and power of settling their mutual controversies; thus making them judicial questions, whether they arose on "boundary, jurisdiction, or any other cause whatever." There is neither the authority of law or reason for the position, that boundary between nations or states, is, in its nature, any more a political question, than any other subject on which

[1] 12 Peters, 743–4.
[2] *Ibid.*, 720.

they may contend. None can be settled without war or treaty, which is by political power; but under the old and new confederacy they could and can be settled by a court constituted by themselves, as their own substitutes, authorized to do that for states, which states alone could do before. We are thus pointed to the true boundary line between political and judicial power, and questions. A sovereign decides by his own will, which is the supreme law within his own boundary; 6 Peters, 714; 9 Peters, 748; a court, or judge, decides according to the law prescribed by the sovereign power, and that law is the rule for judgment. The submission by the sovereigns, or states, to a court of law or equity, of a controversy between them, without prescribing any rule of decision, gives power to decide according to the appropriate law of the case; 11 Ves. 294; which depends on the subject matter, the source and nature of the claims of the parties, and the law which governs them. From the time of such submission, the question ceases to be a political one, to be decided by the sic volo, sic jubeo, of political power; it comes to the court to be decided by its judgment, legal discretion, and solemn consideration of the rules of law appropriate to its nature as a judicial question, depending on the exercise of judicial power; as it is bound to act by known and settled principles of national or municipal jurisprudence, as the case requires.

It has never been contended that prize courts of admiralty jurisdiction, or questions before them, are not strictly judicial; they decide on questions of war and peace, the law of nations, treaties, and the municipal laws of the capturing nation, by which alone they are constituted; a fortiori, if such courts were constituted by a solemn treaty between the state under whose authority the capture was made, and the state whose citizens or subjects suffer by the capture. All nations submit to the jurisdiction of such courts over their subjects, and hold their final decrees conclusive on rights of property. 6 Cr., 284–5.

These considerations lead to the definition of political and judicial power and questions; the former is that which a sovereign or state exerts by his or its own authority, as reprisal and confiscation; 3 Ves., 429; the latter is that which is granted to a court or judicial tribunal. So of controversies between states; they are in their nature political, when the sovereign or state reserves to itself the right of deciding on it; makes it the " subject of a treaty, to be settled as between states independent," or " the foundation of representations from state to state." This is political equity, to be adjudged by the parties themselves, as contradistinguished from judicial equity, administered by a court of justice, decreeing the equum et bonum of the case, let who or what be the parties before them.[1]

Application to Society of Nations

Questions political in their nature may thus become judicial by submission to a court of justice, to be decided in accordance with principles of law and equity, and we are justified in the belief that the States composing the society of nations can, if they will, agree by convention to submit their disputes to a tribunal of their own creation for the settlement of their controversies, just as the States composing the American Union agreed by constitution to submit their controversies to the Supreme Court of the States.

[1] 12 Peters, 736–8.

XX

CASE — CONTROVERSY — SUIT

The act of *Congress* more particularly mentions *civil* controversies, a qualification of the general word in the Constitution, which I do not doubt every reasonable man will think well warranted, for it cannot be presumed that the general word "controversies" was intended to include any proceedings that relate to criminal cases, which in all instances that respect the same Government, only, are uniformly considered of a local nature, and to be decided by its particular laws. (*Mr. Justice Iredell in Chisholm v. Georgia, 2 Dallas, 419, 431-432, decided in 1793.*)

A case in law or equity consists of the right of the one party, as well as of the other, and may truly be said to arise under the constitution or a law of the United States, whenever its correct decision depends on the construction of either. (*Chief Justice Marshall in Cohens v. Virginia, 6 Wheaton, 264, 379, decided in 1821.*)

The article does not extend the judicial power to every violation of the constitution which may possibly take place, but to "a case in law or equity," in which a right, under such law, is asserted in a Court of justice. If the question can not be brought into a Court, then there is no case in law or equity, and no jurisdiction is given by the words of the article. But if, in any controversy depending in a Court, the cause should depend on the validity of such a law, that would be a case arising under the constitution, to which the judicial power of the United States would extend. (*Chief Justice Marshall in Cohens v. Virginia, 6 Wheaton, 264, 405, decided in 1821.*)

That power is capable of acting only when the subject is submitted to it by a party who asserts his rights in the form prescribed by law. It then becomes a case, and the constitution declares, that the judicial power shall extend to all cases arising under the constitution, laws, and treaties of the United States. (*Chief Justice Marshall in Osborn v. Bank of the United States, 9 Wheaton, 738, 819, decided in 1824.*)

What then is to be done if these limitations of power are transgressed by any State, or by the United States? The duty of annulling such usurpations is confided by the Third Article of the Constitution to the Supreme Court, and to such inferior Courts as Congress may from time to time ordain and establish. But this remarkable power is capable only of indirect exercise; it is called into activity by "cases," by actual controversies, to which individuals, or States, or the United States, are parties. The point of unconstitutionality is raised by the arguments in such controversies; and the decision of the Court follows the view which it takes of the Constitution. A declaration of unconstitutionality, not provoked by a definite dispute, is unknown to the Supreme Court. (*Sir Henry Sumner Maine, Popular Government, 1886, pp. 217-218.*)

In order to entitle the party to the remedy a case must be presented appropriate for the exercise of judicial power; the rights in danger must be rights of persons or property; not merely political rights, which do not belong to the jurisdiction of a court, either in law or equity. *State of Georgia* v. *Stanton, 6 Wall. 50, 76.*

When a right is asserted by a party before a court in the manner prescribed by law, it then becomes a *case* to which the judicial power extends. This includes the right of both parties to the litigation; and the case may be said to *arise* whenever its correct decision is dependent upon the construction of the Constitution, laws, or treaties of the United States. (*Mr. Justice Miller, Lectures on the Constitution of the United States, 1891, p. 315, note.*)

The President of the United States of America and His Majesty the King of the United Kingdom of Great Britain and Ireland and of the British Dominions beyond the Seas, Emperor of India, desiring in pursuance of the principles set forth in Articles 15-19 of the Convention for the pacific settlement of international disputes, signed at The

Hague July 29, 1899, to enter into negotiations for the conclusion of an Arbitration Convention, have named as their Plenipotentiaries, to wit:

The President of the United States of America, Elihu Root, Secretary of State of the United States, and

His Majesty the King of the United Kingdom of Great Britain and Ireland and of the British Dominions beyond the Seas, Emperor of India, The Right Honorable James Bryce, O. M.,

who, after having communicated to one another their full powers, found in good and due form, have agreed upon the following articles:

ARTICLE I. Differences which may arise of a legal nature or relating to the interpretation of treaties existing between the two Contracting Parties and which it may not have been possible to settle by diplomacy, shall be referred to the Permanent Court of Arbitration established at The Hague by the Convention of the 29th of July, 1899, provided, nevertheless, that they do not affect the vital interests, the independence, or the honor of the two Contracting States, and do not concern the interests of third Parties.

ARTICLE II. In each individual case the High Contracting Parties, before appealing to the Permanent Court of Arbitration, shall conclude a special Agreement defining clearly the matter in dispute, the scope of the powers of the Arbitrators, and the periods to be fixed for the formation of the Arbitral Tribunal and the several stages of the procedure. It is understood that such special agreements on the part of the United States will be made by the President of the United States, by and with the advice and consent of the Senate thereof; His Majesty's Government reserving the right before concluding a special agreement in any matter affecting the interests of a self-governing Dominion of the British Empire to obtain the concurrence therein of the Government of that Dominion.

Such Agreements shall be binding only when confirmed by the two Governments by an Exchange of Notes.

ARTICLE III. The present Convention shall be ratified by the President of the United States of America by and with the advice and consent of the Senate thereof, and by His Britannic Majesty. The ratifications shall be exchanged at Washington as soon as possible, and the Convention shall take effect on the date of the exchange of its ratifications.

ARTICLE IV. The present Convention is concluded for a period of five years, dating from the day of the exchange of its ratifications.

Done in duplicate at the City of Washington, this fourth day of April, in the year 1908.

ELIHU ROOT [SEAL]
JAMES BRYCE [SEAL]

(*Arbitration Convention between the United States and Great Britain, Signed at Washington April 4, 1908. U. S. Statutes at Large, Vol. XXXV, pp. 1960-1961.*)

The high contracting powers agree to refer to the existing Permanent Court of Arbitration at The Hague, or to the Court of Arbitral Justice proposed at the Second Hague Conference when established, or to some other Arbitral Tribunal, all disputes between them (including those affecting honor and vital interests) which are of a justiciable character, and which the powers concerned have failed to settle by diplomatic methods. The powers so referring to arbitration agree to accept and give effect to the award of the Tribunal.

Disputes of a justiciable character are defined as disputes as to the interpretation of a treaty, as to any question of international law, as to the existence of any fact which if established would constitute a breach of any international obligation, or as to the nature and extent of the reparation to be made for any such breach.

Any question which may arise as to whether a dispute is of a justiciable character is to be referred for decision to the Court of Arbitral Justice when constituted, or, until it is constituted, to the existing Permanent Court of Arbitration at The Hague. (Article for an International Convention Defining Disputes of a Justiciable Character, proposed by Elihu Root, and printed in the *Proceedings of the American Society of International Law, 1919, p. 50, note 1.*)

CHAPTER XX

CASE — CONTROVERSY — SUIT

THE entire judicial power of the United States, created by the Constitution, is not only extended to all cases in law and equity arising under the Constitution, the laws of the United States, and treaties made or which shall be made under their authority; but its exercise depends on the nature of a case in law or equity of the kind specified, inasmuch as there is no way of obtaining the opinion of Federal courts and of their judges upon the Constitution, law or equity, unless a specific case comes before them in litigation by parties claiming a right under the provisions of one or other of these sources. The individual is protected against unlawful action on the part of a fellow-citizen, a State of the Union, or the Government of that Union; the rights of the individual States are guarded against the encroachment of the Government of the United States, or in controversies between themselves, by a case in law or equity begun in the courts. The Government of the United States is protected against the unlawful conduct of the individual and assaults of the States by a case in law or equity, submitted to the courts for their consideration and decision. The threefold division of power among the departments of that Government is maintained by the simple expedient of a case in law or equity, differing, indeed, in purpose; modified, it may be, in form, but identical in substance with the case in law or equity of a private suitor. For if jurisdiction depends upon a case, a suit or controversy, it is necessary to determine at the very threshold the sense in which the word *case, suit* or *controversy* is used in connection with the judicial power. For if the matter is not a case, suit or controversy, falling within the proper exercise of this power, there is nothing whereof the court can take jurisdiction, and there is nothing to be decided. If we are, as so often stated, a government of laws, not of men, it is the court which interprets the laws, passes upon the conduct of men, and stays the hand of government itself if only a case arise under the Constitution, the laws and treaties of the United States, and come before courts of justice in the ordinary form of case, suit, or controversy, in law or equity.

In the leading case of *Marbury* v. *Madison* (1 Cranch, 137), decided in 1803, in which John Marshall, as Chief Justice, first disclosed to the bench and bar his capacity as a judge, he defined a case to be a suit instituted according to the regular course of judicial procedure. In two later cases he

427

either had or took occasion to go into the details of a case, to analyze and to state its essentials in terms which his successors have been content to repeat and to follow. In *Cohens* v. *Virginia* (6 Wheaton, 264, 379), decided in 1821, the Chief Justice said:

> A case in law or equity consists of the right of the one party, as well as of the other, and may truly be said to arise under the constitution or a law of the United States, whenever its correct decision depends on the construction of either.

In a later passage of his opinion (405), he adds:

> The article does not extend the judicial power to every violation of the constitution which may possibly take place, but to "a case in law or equity," in which a right, under such law, is asserted in a court of justice. If the question cannot be brought into a court, then there is no case in law or equity, and no jurisdiction is given by the words of the article. But if, in any controversy depending in a court, the cause should depend on the validity of such a law, that would be a case arising under the constitution, to which the judicial power of the United States would extend.

And, immediately following this passage, the Chief Justice takes up and defines the term *suit,* used in the 11th Amendment apparently synonymous with *case,* stating not only the nature of a suit, but how and when it begins:

" Suit " Defined

> What is a suit? We understand it to be the prosecution or pursuit of some claim, demand or request; in law language, it is the prosecution of some demand in a Court of justice. The remedy for every species of wrong is, says Judge Blackstone, " the being put in possession of that right whereof the party injured is deprived." " The instruments whereby this remedy is obtained, are a diversity of suits and actions, which are defined by the Mirror, to be 'the lawful demand of one's right;' or, as Bracton and Fleta express it, in the words of Justinian, '*jus prosequendi in judicio quod alicui debetur.*'" Blackstone then proceeds to describe every species of remedy by suit; and they are all cases where the party suing claims to obtain something to which he has a right.
>
> To commence a suit is to demand something by the institution of process in a Court of justice; and to prosecute the suit, is, according to the common acceptation of language, to continue that demand. By a suit commenced by an individual against a State, we should understand process sued out by that individual against the State, for the purpose of establishing some claim against it by the judgment of a court; and the prosecution of that suit is its continuance. Whatever may be the stages of its progress, the actor is still the same.[1]

Finally, in *Osborn* v. *Bank of the United States* (9 Wheaton, 737, 819), decided in 1824, the same Chief Justice, recurring to this question, thus discussed it in its larger as well as in its technical bearings:

[1] 6 Wheaton, 407–8.

It is said, that the legislative, executive and judicial powers of every well-constructed government, are co-extensive with each other; that is, they are potentially co-extensive. The executive department may constitutionally execute every law which the legislature may constitutionally make, and the judicial department may receive from the legislature the power of construing every such law. All governments which are not extremely defective in their organization, must possess, within themselves, the means of expounding, as well as enforcing, their own laws. If we examine the constitution of the United States, we find, that its framers kept this great political principle in view. The 2d article vests the whole executive power in the president; and the 3d article declares, "that the judicial power shall extend to all cases in law and equity, arising under this constitution, the laws of the United States, and treaties made, or which shall be made, under their authority."

This clause enables the judicial department to receive jurisdiction to the full extent of the constitution, laws and treaties of the United States, when any question respecting them shall assume such a form that the judicial power is capable of acting on it. That power is capable of acting only when the subject is submitted to it, by a party who asserts his rights in the form prescribed by law. It then becomes a case, and the constitution declares, that the judicial power shall extend to all cases arising under the constitution, laws and treaties of the United States.[1]

So far, case or suit has been considered; but the Constitution extends the judicial power to controversies between two or more States, not to *all* controversies — inasmuch as some of them might be political in character, and therefore more fitted for treaty or compact than judicial decision — but to controversies of a justiciable nature, to which the judicial power can properly extend. This phase of the question arose in the case of *Chisholm* v. *Georgia* (2 Dallas, 419, 432), decided in 1793, in which Mr. Justice Iredell said, commenting upon the judiciary act of 1789, in an opinion which has commended itself to posterity:

The act of Congress more particularly mentions *civil* controversies, a qualification of the general word in the Constitution, which I do not doubt every reasonable man will think well warranted, for it cannot be presumed, that the general word "controversies" was intended to include any proceedings that relate to criminal cases, which in all instances that respect the same Government only, are uniformly considered of a local nature, and to be decided by its particular laws.

In *In re* Pacific Railway Commission (32 Fed. Rep., 241, 255), decided in 1887, Mr. Justice Field, sitting at circuit, had occasion to consider the terms *cases* and *controversies,* to be found in the second section of the third article of the Constitution, regarding which he said: **Cases and Controversies**

The judicial article of the constitution mentions cases and controversies. The term "controversies," if distinguishable at all from "cases," is

[1] 9 Wheaton, 818–19.

so in that it is less comprehensive than the latter, and includes only suits of a civil nature. *Chisholm* v. *Georgia,* 2 Dall. 431, 432; 1 Tuck. Bl. Comm. App. 420, 421. By cases and controversies are intended the claims of litigants brought before the courts for determination by such regular proceedings as are established by law or custom for the protection or enforcement of rights, or the prevention, redress, or punishment of wrongs. Whenever the claim of a party under the constitution, laws, or treaties of the United States takes such a form that the judicial power is capable of acting upon it, then it has become a case. The term implies the existence of present or possible adverse parties whose contentions are submitted to the court for adjudication.

In *Osborn* v. *U. S.,* 9 Wheat. 819, the supreme court, speaking by Chief Justice Marshall, after quoting the third article of the constitution declaring the extent of the judicial power of the United States, said:

> " This clause enables the judicial department to receive jurisdiction to the full extent of the constitution, laws, and treaties of the United States, when any question respecting them shall assume such a form that the judicial power is capable of acting on it. *That power is capable of acting only when the subject is submitted to it by a party who asserts his rights in the form prescribed by law.* It then becomes a case, and the constitution declares, that the judicial power shall extend to all cases arising under the constitution, laws, and treaties of the United States."

In his Commentaries on the Constitution, Mr. Justice Story says:

> " It is clear that the judicial department is authorized to exercise jurisdiction to the full extent of the constitution, laws, and treaties of the United States, whenever any question respecting them shall assume such a form that the judicial power is capable of acting upon it. *When it has assumed such a form, it then becomes a case; and then, and not till then, the judicial power attaches to it.* A case, then, in the sense of this clause of the constitution, arises when some subject touching the constitution, laws, or treaties of the United States is submitted to the courts by a party who asserts his rights in the form prescribed by law." [1]

And Mr. Justice Story refers in a note to the speech of Marshall on the case of Robbins, in the house of representatives, before he became chief justice, which contains a clear statement of the conditions upon which the judicial power of the United States can be exercised. His language was:

> " By extending the judicial power to all cases in law and equity, the constitution has never been understood to confer on that department any political power whatever. To come within this description, a question must assume a legal form for forensic litigation and judicial decision. There must be parties to come into court, who can be reached by its process, and bound by its power; whose rights admit of ultimate decision by a tribunal to which they are bound to submit." [1]

[1] 32 Federal Reporter, 256.

The distinction between controversies of a civil and criminal nature, first mentioned by Mr. Justice Iredell in the Chisholm case, and quoted with approval by Mr. Justice Field, was affirmed by the Supreme Court in the case of *Wisconsin* v. *Pelican Insurance Company* (127 U. S., 265), decided in 1888 by Mr. Justice Gray, speaking for a unanimous court.

But cases and controversies are apparently considered as synonymous, differing, if at all, in that the latter include only suits of a civil nature. But a case and a controversy are identical in nature and coextensive as far as they go, as was admirably pointed out by Putnam, Circuit Justice, who said, in the case of *King* v. *McLean Asylum* (64 Fed. Rep., 332, 335–6), decided in 1894:

> The appellees rely on a supposed distinction between the use of the word " cases " and the word " controversies " in the section of the consti- tution defining the federal judicial power. That section uses the word " cases " in the first three clauses, namely, " cases, in law and equity," aris- ing under the constitution and the laws and treaties of the United States, " cases affecting ambassadors, other public ministers and consuls," and " cases of admiralty and maritime jurisdiction." So far it has relation mainly, although not entirely, to the subject-matter of the litigation, and not to the parties involved. It then changes to the word " controversies," and uses this with reference to " controversies to which the United States shall be a party," " to controversies between two or more states," and then, without repeating the word, continues " between a state and citizens of another state; between citizens of different states; between citizens of the same state claiming lands under grants of different states, and between a state, or the citizens thereof, and foreign states, citizens or subjects." . . . The change under consideration, from the word " cases " to the word " con- troversies," will be found to have been a mere matter of style, and to have no relation to any limitation or extension of the class of questions to be adjudicated. As we have already said, so long as this section of the con- stitution speaks especially with reference to the nature of the questions involved, it uses the word " cases," but, when it considers more particularly proceedings having relation to the existence of parties, it uses the word " controversies," probably because, when parties are spoken of as arrayed against each other, literary style suggested the change.

The nature of a case was considered, not merely in its constitutional but in its international aspect, in *La Abra Silver Mining Co.* v. *United States* (175 U. S., 423, 457), decided in 1899, in which the Supreme Court was obliged to consider an award in behalf of a citizen of the United States, rendered in his favor by a mixed commission organized under the treaty of July 4, 1868, between the United States and Mexico, and which the latter country alleged to be vitiated by the fraud of the American claimant, which, to our shame be it said, proved to be only too true. The Congress, which might have determined the matter, referred it to the Court of Claims, in accordance with the observation of Mr. Justice Curtis, speaking for the

International "Case"

court in *Murray* v. *Hoboken* (18 Howard, 272, 284), decided in 1855, who, after saying that the Congress can neither "withdraw from judicial cognizance any matter which, from its nature, is the subject of a suit at the common law, or in equity, or admiralty; nor, on the other hand, can it bring under the judicial power a matter which, from its nature, is not a subject for judicial determination," stated, however, that "there are matters, involving public rights, which may be presented in such form that the judicial power is capable of acting on them, and which are susceptible of judicial determination, but which congress may or may not bring within the cognizance of the courts of the United States, as it may deem proper."

The objection taken by counsel for the Silver Mining Co. was "that the Court of Claims has no jurisdiction over this matter, because it is not a 'case' within the meaning of the Constitution, nor is it a 'controversy' to which the United States is a party." The question whether fraud entered into and vitiated a transaction is clearly a judicial question, in the sense that it can be investigated and decided by a court of justice, and therefore a question involving this is of necessity a suit or a controversy in the sense of the Constitution.

As previously stated, however, the government can not consult the court nor take the opinion of the justices at its discretion. It can only do so in a judicial proceeding, and not in a moot but in a controverted case. It was, therefore, necessary to show that the United States had such an interest in the award as to enable it to appear as a party and in its own behalf before the court.

The interest of the United States was manifest, in that it had espoused and presented the claim on behalf of its citizens to the mixed commission, which it should not have done if such claim lacked equity and was void in law; and in that the moneys awarded by the mixed commission passed to the United States and were only payable to the claimant to whom the Government is satisfied they are properly due. In the course of his opinion, Mr. Justice Harlan, speaking for a unanimous court, referred to the definition of *case* given in the decisions already quoted, and discussed the case of *Gordon* v. *United States* (2 Wallace, 561; 117 U. S., 697), decided in 1864, to the effect that finality of decision is essential to the exercise of judicial power. In the following passage from his opinion, he brings the question within the requirements of the Supreme Court in the matter of case, suit, or controversy:

> The act of 1892 is to be taken as a recognition, so far as the United States is concerned, of the legal right of the Company to receive the moneys in question unless it appeared upon judicial investigation that the United States was entitled, by reason of fraud practised in the interest of

that corporation, to withhold such moneys from it. Here then is a matter subjected to judicial investigation in respect of which the parties assert *rights* — the United States insisting upon its right under the principles of international comity to withhold moneys received by it under a treaty on account of a certain claim presented through it before the Commission organized under that treaty in the belief, superinduced by the claimant, that it was an honest demand; the claimant insisting upon its absolute legal right under the treaty and the award of the Commission, independently of any question of fraud, to receive the money and disputing the right of the United States upon any ground to withhold the sum awarded. We entertain no doubt these rights are susceptible of judicial determination within the meaning of the adjudged cases relating to the judicial power of the courts of the United States as distinguished from the powers committed to the Executive branch of the Government.[1]

But the case or controversy contemplated by the Constitution does not mean a moot or friendly case. It means one which has arisen under law or equity and in which the parties before the court as litigants would, in primitive times, have settled their dispute by force; for the court is a substitute for self-redress of litigants, whether those litigants are individuals or States. It is of the utmost importance to bear in mind this fact, because the judicial power of the United States is limited to cases involving a contest under law or equity, of which the courts can therefore take jurisdiction, and which it decided, thus withdrawing from them the power to act in an advisory capacity.

In the recent case of *Muskrat* v. *United States* (219 U. S., 346, 354), decided in 1911, the Supreme Court, per Mr. Justice Day, thus refers to the opinion of the judges of the Supreme Court taken extra-judicially, on the question of their advisory power:

In 1793, by direction of the President, Secretary of State Jefferson addressed to the Justices of the Supreme Court a communication soliciting their views upon the question whether their advice to the executive would be available in the solution of important questions of the construction of treaties, laws of nations and laws of the land, which the Secretary said were often presented under circumstances which "*do not give cognizance of them to the tribunals of the country.*" The answer to the question was postponed until the subsequent sitting of the Supreme Court, when Chief Justice Jay and his associates answered to President Washington that in consideration of the lines of separation drawn by the Constitution between the three departments of government, and being judges of a court of last resort, afforded strong arguments against the propriety of extrajudicially deciding the questions alluded to, and expressing the view that the power given by the Constitution to the President of calling on heads of departments for opinions "seems to have been purposely, as well as expressly, united to the executitve departments." Correspondence and Public Papers of John Jay, vol. 3, p. 486.

[1] *La Abra Co.* v. *U. S.,* 175 U. S., 460–1.

This action of the Justices seems to have settled the point, because, from that day to this, the Supreme Court has not acted in an advisory capacity. We have also an adjudged case that the judicial power of the Constitution does not extend to a moot or friendly case, for in *Chicago and Grand Trunk Railway Co.* v. *Wellman* (143 U. S., 339, 344), decided in 1891, the court had occasion to consider this matter. The Supreme Court of Michigan, from which the case was brought by writ of error to the Supreme Court, had said, per Mr. Justice Morse:

> It being evident from the record that this was a friendly suit between the plaintiff and the defendant to test the constitutionality of this legislation, the attorney general, when it was brought into this court upon writ of error, very properly interposed and secured counsel to represent the public interest. In the stipulation of facts or in the taking of testimony in the court below neither the attorney general nor any other person interested for or employed in behalf of the people of the State took any part. What difference there might have been in the record had the people been represented in the court below, however, under our view of the case, is not of material inquiry.

In the Supreme Court of the United States, Mr. Justice Brewer refers to this fact, and thus speaks on behalf of his brethren:

> Whenever, in pursuance of an honest and actual antagonistic assertion of rights by one individual against another, there is presented a question involving the validity of any act of any legislature, State or Federal, and the decision necessarily rests on the competency of the legislature to so enact, the court must, in the exercise of its solemn duties, determine whether the act be constitutional or not; but such an exercise of power is the ultimate and supreme function of courts. It is legitimate only in the last resort, and as a necessity in the determination of real, earnest and vital controversy between individuals. It never was the thought that, by means of a friendly suit, a party beaten in the legislature could transfer to the courts an inquiry as to the constitutionality of the legislative act.[1]

[1] 143 U. S., 345.

XXI

JUDICIAL POWERS AND THEIR RELATION TO LAW AND EQUITY, TO ADMIRALTY, MARITIME AND INTERNATIONAL LAW

In appealing to the common law, as the standard of exposition, in all doubts as to the meaning of written instruments; there is safety, certainty, and authority. The institutions of the colonies were based upon it; it was their system of jurisprudence, with only local exceptions, to suit the condition of the colonists, who claimed it as their birth-right and inheritance, 9 Cr. 333, in its largest sense, as including the whole system of English jurisprudence, 1 Gall. 493; the inexhaustible fountain from which we draw our laws, 9 S. & R. 330, 39, 58. So it continued after the colonies became states, in most of which the common law was adopted by acts of assembly, which gave it the force of a statute, from the time of such adoption, and as it was then; so that in the language of this Court—"At the adoption of the constitution, there were no states in this Union, the basis of whose jurisprudence was not essentially, that of the common law in its widest meaning; and probably no states were contemplated, in which it would not exist." 3 Pet. 446, 8. It is also the basis on which the federal system of jurisprudence was erected by the constitution, the judiciary and process acts, which refer to " *cases in law and in equity,*" " *suits at common law,*" " *the common law, the principles and usages of law,*" as they had at the time been defined and settled in England; 5 Cr. 222; 3 Wh. 221; 4 Wh. 115, 16; 7 Wh. 45; 10 Wh. 29, 32, 56, 8: 1 Pet. 613: and were adopted as then understood by the old states. (*Mr. Justice Baldwin, A General View of the Origin and Nature of the Constitution and Government of the United States, 1837, pp. 3-4.*)

But whatever may in England be the binding authority of the common law decisions upon this subject, in the United States we are at liberty to reexamine the doctrines, and to construe the jurisdiction of the admiralty upon enlarged and liberal principles. The constitution has delegated to the judicial power of the United States cognizance "of all cases of admiralty and maritime jurisdiction;" and the act of Congress (24 Sept. 1789, ch. 20, s. 9) has given to the District Court "cognizance of all civil causes of admiralty and maritime jurisdiction, including all seizures under laws of impost, navigation or trade, of the United States, where the seizures are made on waters navigable from the sea by vessels of ten or more tons burthen; within their respective districts, as well as upon the high seas." . . .

On the whole, I am, without the slightest hesitation, ready to pronounce, that the delegation of cognizance of "all civil cases of admiralty and maritime jurisdiction" to the courts of the United States comprehends all maritime contracts, torts, and injuries. The latter branch is necessarily bounded by locality; the former extends over all contracts, (wheresoever they may be made or executed, or whatsoever may be the form of the stipulations,) which relate to the navigation, business or commerce of the sea. (*Mr. Justice Story, in De Lovio v. Boit, 2 Gallison, 398, 467-468, 474-475, decided in 1815.*)

Judicial power, in all cases of admiralty and maritime jurisdiction, is delegated by the Constitution to the Federal Government in general terms, and courts of this character had then been established in all commercial and maritime nations, differing, however, materially in different countries in the powers and duties confided to them; the extent of the jurisdiction conferred depending very much upon the character of the government in which they were created; and this circumstance, with the general terms of the grant, rendered it difficult to define the exact limits of its power in the United States.

This difficulty was increased by the complex character of our Government, where separate and distinct specified powers of sovereignty are exercised by the United States and a State independently of each other within the same territorial limits. And the reports of the decisions of this court will show that the subject has often been before it, and carefully considered, without being able to fix with precision its definite boundaries; but cer-

435

tainly no State-law can enlarge it, nor can an act of Congress or rule of court make it broader than the judicial power may determine to be its true limits. And this boundary is to be ascertained by a reasonable and just construction of the words used in the Constitution, taken in connection with the whole instrument, and the purposes for which admiralty and maritime jurisdiction was granted to the Federal Government. (*Mr. Chief Justice Taney, in The Steamer St. Lawrence, 1 Black, 522, 526-527, decided in 1861.*)

Guided by these sound principles, this court has felt itself at liberty to recognize the admiralty jurisdiction as extending to localities and subjects which, by the jealousy of the common law, were prohibited to it in England, but which fairly belong to it on every ground of reason when applied to the peculiar circumstances of this country, with its extended territories, its inland seas, and its navigable rivers, especiallly as the narrow restrictions of the English law had never prevailed on this side of the Atlantic, even in colonial times. (*Mr. Justice Bradley in The Lottawanna, 21 Wallace, 558, 576, decided in 1874.*)

From all that has been said, these things would seem to be clear: *First,* that the maritime law, existing as it does by the common consent of nations, and, being a general law, cannot be changed or modified as to its general operation by any particular sovereignty; *second,* that it has force in any country only by its adoption, express or implied, by that country, and may be modified in its special operation in that jurisdiction at the will of that special sovereignty; *third,* that it is by such adoption part of the federal law of the United States, and incapable of modification by state enactment,—Congress having exclusive power, under the constitution, "to regulate commerce with foreign nations, and among the several states, and with the Indian tribes;" and the judicial power of the United States, "exclusive of the state courts," extending "to all cases of admiralty and maritime jurisdiction." (*Hughes, Circuit Judge, in The Manhasset, 18 Federal Reporter, 918, 922, decided 1884.*)

Now besides that law which simply concerneth men as men, and that which belongeth unto them as they are men linked with others in some form of politic society, there is a third kind of law which toucheth all such several bodies politic, so far forth as one of them hath public commerce with another. And this third is the *Law of Nations.* (*Richard Hooker, Of the Laws of Ecclesiastical Polity, 1594, Church edition, 1868, Book I, Section 10, p. 64.*)

I remember in a case before Lord Talbot, of *Buvot* v. *Barbut,* (1736) . . . Lord Talbot declared a clear opinion—"That the law of nations, in its full extent was part of the law of England."—"That the Act of Parliament was declaratory; and occasioned by a particular incident."—"That the law of nations was to be collected from the practice of different nations, and the authority of writers." Accordingly, he argued and determined from such instances, and the authority of Grotius, Barbeyrac, Binkershoek, Wiquefort, &c. there being no English writer of eminence, upon the subject.
I was counsel in this case; and have a full note of it. (*Lord Chief Justice Mansfield in Triquet v. Bath, 3 Burrow, 1478, 1480-1481, decided in 1764, English Reports, Full Reprint, Vol. XCVII, King's Bench Division, XXVI, 1909, pp. 937-938.*)

The Law of Nations, founded upon Justice, Equity, Convenience, and the Reason of the Thing, and confirmed by long Usage, . . . (*Report of the law officers of the Crown, dated January 18, 1753, signed Geo. Lee, G. Paul, D. Ryder, W. Murray [Lord Mansfield, to whom the definition is commonly attributed], printed in Sir Ernest Satow, The Silesian Loan and Frederick the Great, 1915, p. 82.*)

The law of nations is a system of rules, deducible by natural reason, and established by universal consent among the civilized inhabitants of the world; in order to decide all disputes, to regulate all ceremonies and civilities, and to insure the observance of justice and good faith, in that intercourse which must frequently occur between two or more independent states, and the individuals belonging to each. This general law is founded upon this principle, that different nations ought in time of peace to do one another all the good they can; and, in time of war, as little harm as possible, without prejudice to their own real interests. And, as none of these states will allow a superiority in the other, therefore neither can dictate or prescribe the rules of this law to the rest; but such rules must necessarily result from those principles of natural justice, in which all the learned of every nation agree; or they depend upon mutual compacts or treaties between the respective communities; in the construction of which there is also no judge to resort to, but the law of nature and reason, being the only one in which all the contracting parties are equally conversant, and to which they are equally subject.

In arbitrary states this law, wherever it contradicts or is not provided for by the municipal law of the country, is enforced by the royal power: but since in England no royal power can introduce a new law, or suspend the execution of the old, therefore the law of nations (wherever any question arises which is properly the object of it's jurisdiction) is here adopted in its full extent by the common law, and is held to be a part of the law of the land. And those acts of parliament, which have from time to time been made to enforce this universal law, or to facilitate the execution of it's decisions, are not to be considered as introductive of any new rule, but merely as declaratory of the old fundamental constitutions of the kingdom; without which it must cease to be a part of the civilized world. (*Sir William Blackstone, Commentaries on the Laws of England, Book IV, 1769, ch. 5, pp. 66-67.*)

It has also been observed, that an act of congress ought never to be construed to violate the law of nations, if any other possible construction remains, and consequently, can never be construed to violate neutral rights, or to affect neutral commerce, further than is warranted by the law of nations as understood in this country. These principles are believed to be correct, and they ought to be kept in view, in construing the act now under consideration. (*Chief Justice Marshall, in The Charming Betsy, 2 Cranch, 64, 118, decided in 1804.*)

Until such an act be passed, the court is bound by the law of nations, which is a part of the law of the land. (*Chief Justice Marshall in The Nereide, 9 Cranch, 388, 423, decided in 1815.*)

The law of nations is the great source from which we derive those rules, respecting belligerent and neutral rights, which are recognized by all civilized and commercial states throughout Europe and America. This law is in part unwritten, and in part conventional. To ascertain that which is unwritten, we resort to the great principles of reason and justice: but as these principles will be differently understood by different nations, under different circumstances, we consider them as being, in some degree, fixed and rendered stable by a series of judicial decisions. The decisions of the courts of every country, so far as they are founded upon a law common to every country, will be received, not as authority, but with respect. The decisions of the courts of every country show how the law of nations, in the given case, is understood in that country, and will be considered in adopting the rule which is to prevail in this.

Without taking a comparative view of the justice or fairness of the rules established in the British courts, and of those established in the courts of other nations, there are circumstances not to be excluded from consideration, which give to those rules a claim to our attention that we cannot entirely disregard. The United States having, at one time, formed a component part of the British empire, their prize law was our prize law. When we separated, it continued to be our prize law, so far as it was adapted to our circumstances, and was not varied by the power which was capable of changing it. (*Chief Justice Marshall, in Thirty Hogsheads of Sugar v. Boyle, 9 Cranch, 191, 198, decided in 1815.*)

International law is part of our law, and must be ascertained and administered by the courts of justice of appropriate jurisdiction, as often as questions of right depending upon it are duly presented for their determination. For this purpose, where there is no treaty, and no controlling executive or legislative act or judicial decision, resort must be had to the customs and usages of civilized nations; and, as evidence of these, to the works of jurists and commentators, who by years of labor, research and experience, have made themselves peculiarly well acquainted with the subjects of which they treat. Such works are resorted to by judicial tribunals, not for the speculations of their authors concerning what the law ought to be, but for trustworthy evidence of what the law really is. (*Mr. Justice Gray, in The Paquete Habana, 175 United States Reports, 677, 700, decided in 1900.*)

CHAPTER XXI

JUDICIAL POWERS AND THEIR RELATION TO LAW AND EQUITY, TO ADMIRALTY, MARITIME AND INTERNATIONAL LAW

Definition
of "Law"
and "Equity"

IT will be observed that the judicial power under the Constitution does not extend to all cases; but to cases of law and equity. The question arises as to the meaning to be attached to law and equity in this connection, as they affect the nature and extent of the case, to which alone it is to extend. The importance of precision in this matter and the consequences that would flow from a misconception, have never been better stated by the great Chief Justice from the bench than they were by him upon the floor of the House of Representatives in his speech on the Robbins case, delivered in 1800. In the course of a debate, to which the extradition of Jonathan Robbins gave rise, Representative Marshall said:

> A case in law or equity was a term well understood, and of limited significance. It was a controversy between parties which had taken a shape for judicial decision. If the Judicial power extended to every question under the Constitution, it would involve almost every subject proper for Legislative discussion and decision; if, to every question under the laws and treaties of the United States, it would involve almost every subject on which the Executive could act. The division of power which the gentleman had stated, could exist no longer, and the other departments would be swallowed up by the Judiciary. . . . By extending the Judicial power to all cases in law and equity, the Constitution had never been understood to confer on that department any political power whatever. To come within this description, a question must assume a legal form for forensic litigation and judicial decision. There must be parties to come into court, who can be reached by its process, and bound by its power; whose rights admit of ultimate decision by a tribunal to which they are bound to submit.[1]

Influence
of English
Terminology

It is common knowledge that technical terms employed in the Constitution are to be taken in the sense in which they were understood in English jurisprudence; because the law of England, no less assuredly than the language of England, in which the laws were expressed, accompanied the colonist as a matter of course. We have good authority for the assertion that the law of England was a favorite study of his successors, and that they were familiar with its principles. In Edmund Burke's speech on con-

---

[1] *Annals of Congress,* Vol. 10, p. 606. Session of March 7, 1800.

ciliation with America, delivered in the House of Commons on March 22, 1775, that great statesman and friend of the colonies said:

> In no country perhaps in the world is the law so general a study. The profession itself is numerous and powerful; and in most provinces it takes the lead. The greater number of the deputies sent to the congress were lawyers. But all who read, and most do read, endeavor to obtain some smattering in that science. I have been told by an eminent bookseller, that in no branch of his business, after tracts of popular devotion, were so many books as those on the law exported to the plantations. The colonists have now fallen into the way of printing them for their own use. I hear that they have sold nearly as many of Blackstone's Commentaries in America as in England.[1]

It is therefore to be expected that, when terms of municipal law are found in the Constitution, they are to be understood in the sense in which they were used in Blackstone's Commentaries; and, when the law of nations is referred to, that its principles are to be understood in the sense in which Vattel defined them. Blackstone and Vattel

On August 22, 1787, the question of an *ex post facto* law was before the Federal Convention, and there appearing to be some confusion as to its exact meaning, Mr. Madison reports in his notes that a week later "M^r. Dickenson mentioned to the House that on examining Blackstone's Commentaries, he found that the terms ' ex post facto ' related to criminal cases only." [2] And in Blackstone's sense the phrase is to be construed, as appears from the leading case of *Calder* v. *Bull,* (3 Dallas, 386), decided in 1798.

We have it on equally good authority that the colonists were not only interested in and familiar with municipal law, which they would prefer to call the common law of England, but that they regarded as indispensable, a knowledge of international law, which they would have called the law of nations, and which could with propriety be termed the common law of nations. In a letter dated Philadelphia, December 19, 1775, written to Charles W. F. Dumas, at The Hague, the venerable Dr. Franklin said: International Law the Common Law of Nations

> I am much obliged by the kind present you have made us of your edition of Vattel.[3] It came to us in good season, when the circumstances of a rising State make it necessary frequently to consult the Law of Nations.

---

[1] *The Works of Edmund Burke,* Boston, 1839, Vol. II, p. 36.

[2] *Documentary History of the Constitution,* Vol. III, p. 636. Session of August 29, 1787.

[3] The original edition of Vattel's "Law of Nations," in two quarto volumes, was printed at Neuchâtel in 1758, and part of the edition bears the imprint of Leyden and of London. An edition in three volumes, 12 mo. appeared in the same year. The title which Vattel gave to his work was *Le droit des gens, ou principes de la loi naturelle, appliqués à la conduite et aux affaires des nations et des souverains.* The edition for which Mr. Dumas was responsible appeared in Amsterdam in 1775, reproducing the original title with the addition of the following phrases: *Nouvelle édition augmentée, revue et corrigée. Avec quelques remarques de l'éditeur.*

Accordingly, that copy which I kept (after depositing one in our own public library here, and sending the other to the College of Massachusetts Bay, as you directed) has been continually in the hands of the members of our Congress now sitting, who are much pleased with your notes and preface, and have entertained a high and just esteem for their author.[1]

As to the common law of nations, we thus have Dr. Franklin's authority for the statement that the members of the Continental Congress referred to and accepted Vattel's famous treatise, as the measure and standard of the duties of the colonies, soon to become free and independent States.[2] We could, however, dispense with his authority, inasmuch as the common law of nations was then regarded as an intricate part of the common law of England, and adopted as a system by the adoption of the common law. For does not Blackstone inform us, in his Commentaries, that " the law of nations (whenever any question arises which is properly the object of its jurisdiction) is hereby adopted in its full extent by the common law, and is held to be a part of the law of the land." [3]

Law and
Equity

Let us now consider the phrase " law and equity," and determine the sense in which those terms were understood by the framers of the Constitution, and therefore are to be understood in the Constitution itself.

In the first place, it will be well to cite an authority to the effect that terms of art are to be accepted in the sense in which they were used in that system of law in which the framers of the Constitution were educated, and from which they borrowed. Of the many cases which might be cited for this purpose, that of *Robinson v. Campbell,* (3 Wheaton, 212, 221–3), decided in 1818, will suffice. In speaking for a unanimous court, of which Messrs. Marshall and Story were members, Mr. Justice Todd said:

> By the laws of the United States, the circuit courts have cognizance of all suits of a civil nature, at common law and in equity, in cases which fall within the limits prescribed by those laws. By the 34th section of the judiciary act of 1789, it is provided, that the laws of the several states, except where the constitution, treaties or statutes of the United States shall otherwise require or provide, shall be regarded as rules of decision,

[1] Francis Wharton, *Diplomatic Correspondence of the American Revolution,* 1889, Vol. ii, p. 64.

[2] It is interesting to note that in the debates of the Federal Convention, Luther Martin, delegate from Maryland, invoked Vattel's authority "in order to prove that individuals in a State of nature are equally free & independent," and he vouched the same great authority "to prove that the case is the same with States till they surrender their sovereignty." (Madison's Notes. *Documentary History,* Vol. iii, p. 225. Session of June 27th.)

[3] The question of distinction between suits of a civil nature and suits coming properly under the law of nations was raised in *In Re* Baiz (135 U. S., 403), decided in 1890. Although the petitioner claimed to be a public minister representing a foreign country, Mr. Chief Justice Fuller concluded that the District Court had jurisdiction, and denied the writs. For opinions in analogous cases, see J. B. Scott, *Judicial Settlement of Controversies Between States,* Vol. i, p. 388, Note.

in trials at common law, in the courts of the United States, in cases where they apply. The act of May, 1792, confirms the modes of proceeding then used in suits at common law, in the courts of the United States, and declares, that the modes of proceeding in suits of equity, shall be "according to the principles, rules and usages which belong to courts of equity, as contradistinguished from courts of common law," except so far as may have been provided for by the act to establish the judicial courts of the United States.

After a brief discussion of this question, the learned Justice continued and concluded:

> The court, therefore, think, that to effectuate the purposes of the legislature, the remedies in the courts of the United States are to be, at common law or in equity, not according to the practice of state courts, but according to the principles of common law and equity, as distinguished and defined in that country from which we derive our knowledge of those principles.

Accepting as we needs must, that by law, common law is meant, and by equity, the practice in chancery, we are obliged to probe beneath the surface, in order to ascertain the meaning to be assigned to these terms. In the first place, we must bear in mind that the United States, meaning thereby the more perfect union of the States, was a creation of the States meeting in conference at Philadelphia, and that the Union only possessed the powers expressly or impliedly granted by the delegates of the States and ratified by the State conventions. It was, therefore, a union without government and without law, except as government and law were provided by the Constitution and legislature in accordance with its terms. Each State had its government and had its law. The law of each State was common law and equity, although separate and distinct courts for the administration of the latter system did not exist in all the States.

In defining law in terms of common law, the law of crimes as well as the law in civil disputes might have been adopted. It was for some years supposed by such men as Chief Justice Jay and Chief Justice Ellsworth, that the common law adopted included the law of crimes. These views, however, are expressly repudiated by the Supreme Court in *United States* v. *Hudson* (7 Cranch 32, 33), decided in 1812, in which the court was called upon to determine "whether the circuit courts of the United States can exercise a common-law jurisdiction in criminal cases." In delivering the opinion of the court, Mr. Justice Johnson said that public opinion had long since decided the question, although it was now presented to the court for the first time. "The course of reasoning which leads to this conclusion," he continued, "is simple, obvious, and admits of but little illustra-

Common
Law
Limited to
Civil Cases

from the several states — whatever is not expressly given to the former, the latter expressly reserve. The judicial power of the United States is a constituent part of those concessions; that power is to be exercised by Courts organized for the purpose, and brought into existence by an effort of the legislative power of the Union." The question was not whether the courts could exercise jurisdiction in matters of crimes, but whether it had been conferred, as the court could not act without law. To the contention that such jurisdiction would be implied, Mr. Justice Johnson thus replied:

Common Law Applicable in Cases Covered by Special Legislative Act

The only ground on which it has ever been contended that this jurisdiction could be maintained is, that, upon the formation of any political body, an implied power to preserve its own existence and promote the end and object of its creation, necessarily results to it. But, without examining how far this consideration is applicable to the peculiar character of our constitution, it may be remarked, that it is a principle by no means peculiar to the common law. It is coeval, probably, with the first formation of a limited Government; belongs to a system of universal law, and may as well support the assumption of many other powers as those more peculiarly acknowledged by the common law of England.

But if admitted as applicable to the state of things in this country, the consequence would not result from it which is here contended for. If it may communicate certain implied powers to the general Government, it would not follow, that the Courts of that Government are vested with jurisdiction over any particular act done by an individual, in supposed violation of the peace and dignity of the sovereign power. The legislative authority of the Union must first make an act a crime, affix a punishment to it, and declare the Court that shall have jurisdiction of the offence.[1]

Such was the law as declared by the Supreme Court in 1812; and such is the law today, by virtue whereof such criminal jurisdiction as federal courts exercise has been created by Act of Congress making an act a crime, affixing a punishment to it, and specifying the court in which the offense shall be tried.

It had previously been suggested by Mr. Justice Iredell, in *Chisholm* v. *Georgia,* (2 Dallas, 419, 432), decided in 1792, that criminal cases were not included among the controversies between States to be passed upon by the Supreme Court. But it is equally well settled that technical expressions, terms, and phrases to be found in the Acts of Congress dealing with crimes are to be interpreted in the sense in which they were understood and used in the jurisprudence of the mother country.

Interpretation of Terms

In the case of *Kepner* v. *United States,* (195 U. S., 100), decided in 1904, the Supreme Court had occasion to pass upon the clause " that no person shall be put twice in jeopardy for the same offence " contained in

---

[1] *United States* v. *Hudson and Goodwin,* 7 Cranch, 33–4.

instructions to the Philippine Commission, drafted by a great Secretary of War, statesman and lawyer alike,[1] by virtue whereof the dependencies of the United States separated on the west by an ocean from the continent, were secured in life, liberty and property, which the British colonies in America, separated from the mother country by an eastern ocean, were denied by lawyers who were not statesmen.

Mr. Justice Day, after a careful reference to the authorities, said:

> In ascertaining the meaning of the phrase taken from the Bill of Rights [for such the Amendments to the Constitution are frequently called] it must be construed with reference to the common law from which it was taken.[2]

And in another portion of his judgment, he laid down a rule of interpretation and of construction which may be quoted in this connection, saying:

> How can it be successfully maintained that these expressions of fundamental rights, which have been the subject of frequent adjudication in the courts of this country, and the maintenance of which has been ever deemed essential to our Government, could be used by Congress in any other sense than that which has been placed upon them in construing the instrument from which they were taken?
>
> It is a well-settled rule of construction that language used in a statute which has a settled and well-known meaning, sanctioned by judicial decision, is presumed to be used in that sense by the legislative body.[3]

In support of this contention, and with more special reference to what may be called the civil side of the common law, other cases of the Supreme Court may be invoked. Thus, in *Smith* v. *Alabama,* (124 U. S., 465, 478–9), decided in 1888, Mr. Justice Matthews, speaking for a unanimous court, said:

> There is no common law of the United States, in the sense of a national customary law, distinct from the common law of England as adopted by the several States each for itself, applied as its local law, and subject to such alteration as may be provided by its own statutes. . . .
>
> There is, however, one clear exception to the statement that there is no national common law. The interpretation of the Constitution of the United States is necessarily influenced by the fact that its provisions are framed in the language of the English common law, and are to be read in the light of its history. The code of constitutional and statutory construction which, therefore, is gradually formed by the judgments of this court, in the application of the Constitution and the laws and treaties made in pursuance thereof, has for its basis so much of the common law as may be implied in the subject, and constitutes a common law resting on national authority.

[1] See Secretary Root's Instructions to the Philippine Commission, Report of the Secretary of War for 1900, pp. 72, *et seq.,* reprinted in Elihu Root, Military and Colonial Policy of the United States, pp. 287, *et seq.*

[2] *Kepner* v. *U. S.,* 195 U. S., 125.

[3] *Ibid.,* 124.

In support of these views, Mr. Justice Matthews refers to *Moore* v. *United States* (91 U. S., 270, 273–4), decided in 1875, in which Mr. Justice Bradley, speaking for a unanimous court, had said:

> The question is, By what law is the Court of Claims to be governed in this respect? May it adopt its own rules of evidence? or is it to be governed by some system of law? In our opinion, it must be governed by law; and we know of no system of law by which it should be governed other than the common law. That is the system from which our judicial ideas and legal definitions are derived. The language of the Constitution and of many acts of Congress could not be understood without reference to the common law.

In the later case of *United States* v. *Wong Kim Ark* (169 U. S., 649, 654), decided in 1898, Mr. Justice Gray, who may properly be called the very learned Justice, speaking for the court, said:

> The Constitution nowhere defines the meaning of these words, either by way of inclusion or of exclusion, except in so far as this is done by the affirmative declaration that " all persons born or naturalized in the United States, and subject to the jurisdiction thereof, are citizens of the United States." In this, as in other respects, it must be interpreted in the light of the common law, the principles and history of which were familiarly known to the framers of the Constitution. *Minor* v. *Happersett,* 21 Wall. 162; *Ex parte Wilson,* 114 U. S. 417, 422; *Boyd* v. *United States,* 116 U. S. 616, 624, 625; *Smith* v. *Alabama,* 124, U. S. 465. The language of the Constitution, as has been well said, could not be understood without reference to the common law. 1 Kent Com. 336; Bradley, J., in *Moore* v. *United States,* 91 U. S. 270, 274.

But common law in its criminal and civil sense, and equity, existed in the colonies forming the thirteen States. Common law and equity exist in the States formed since the creation of the more perfect union. It will therefore be well to consider these matters very briefly, before further considering the nature and content of the law in the sense of the Constitution.

In the very interesting and instructive case of *Ohio* v. *Lafferty,* (Tappan's Ohio Reports, 81) decided in 1817, Mr. Justice Tappan, speaking for the court of Common Pleas of the State of Ohio, had occasion to consider whether the common law was the rule of decision in that State. In the course of his opinion, he thus referred to the Act of the Congress of the United States, commonly called the Northwest Ordinance, passed July 13, 1787, during the very session of the Federal Convention of that year in Philadelphia, which made the Constitution of the more perfect union:

> The ordinance passed by the congress of the United States, on the 13th of July 1787, " for the government of the territory of the United States

North West of the river Ohio," is the earliest of our written laws. Possessing the North Western Territory in absolute sovereignty, the United States, by that instrument, provide for the temporary government of the people who may settle there; and, to use the language of that instrument, " for extending the fundamental principles of civil and religious liberty, which form the basis whereon these republics, their laws and constitutions, are erected; to fix and establish those principles as the basis of all laws; constitutions and governments, which forever hereafter shall be formed in the said territory; to provide also for the establishment of states and permanent government therein; and for their admission to a share in the federal councils, on an equal footing with the original states, at as early periods as may be consistent with the general interest," it was ordained and declared, " that the inhabitants of the said territory shall *always* be entitled to the benefits of the writ of habeas corpus, and of the trial by jury; of a proportionate representation of the people in the legislature, *and of judicial proceedings according to the course of the common law"* — as one of the articles of compact between the original states, and the people and states in the said territory, to remain forever unalterable unless by common consent.[1]

In a previous portion of his opinion the learned judge had referred to the common law as obtaining in the colonies, saying of the colonists that:

In their charters from the crown, they were careful to have it recognized as the foundation on which they were to erect their laws and governments; not more anxious was Æneas to secure from the burning ruins of Troy his household Gods, than were these first settlers of America to secure to themselves and their children the benefits of the common law of England. From thence, through every stage of the colonial governments, the common law was in force, so far as it was found necessary or useful. When the revolution commenced, and independent state governments were formed; in the midst of hostile collisions with the mother country, when the passions of men were inflamed, and a deep and general abhorrence of the tyranny of the British government was felt; the sages and patriots who commenced that revolution, and founded those state governments, recognized in the common law a guardian of liberty and social order. The common law of England has thus always been the common law of the colonies and states of North America; not indeed in its full extent, supporting a monarchy, aristocracy, and hierarchy, but so far as it was applicable to our more free and happy habits of government.[2]

As throwing further light upon the subject reference is made to two cases, the first taken from an older State of the Union, explaining the sense in which the common law is to be understood, and the second from one of the younger States, defining the sense in which it is to be accepted:

In *Commonwealth* v. *Chapman,* (13 Metcalf, 68), decided in 1848, Mr. Chief Justice Shaw of the Supreme Court of Massachusetts said:

We take it to be a well settled principle, acknowledged by all civilized states governed by law, that by means of a political revolution, by which

[1] Tappan, 83–4.
[2] *Ibid.,* 83.

the political organization is changed, the municipal laws, regulating their social relations, duties and rights, are not necessarily abrogated. They remain in force, except so far as they are repealed or modified by the new sovereign authority. Indeed, the existence of this body of laws, and the social and personal rights dependent upon them, from 1776, when the declaration of independence was made, and our political revolution took place, to 1780, when this constitution was adopted, depend on this principle.[1]

So much for the general principle; next for the colony of English origin:

When our ancestors [that very great and learned Chief Justice continues] first settled this country, they came here as English subjects; they settled on the land as English territory, constituting part of the realm of England, and of course governed by its laws; they accepted charters from the English government, conferring both political powers and civil privileges; and they never ceased to acknowledge themselves English subjects, and never ceased to claim the rights and privileges of English subjects, till the revolution. It is not therefore, perhaps, so accurate to say that they established the laws of England here, as to say, that they were subject to the laws of England. When they left one portion of its territory, they were alike subject, on their transit and when they arrived at another portion of the English territory; and therefore always, till the declaration of independence, they were governed and protected by the laws of England, so far as those laws were applicable to their state and condition. Under this category must come all municipal laws regulating and securing the rights of real and personal property, of person and personal liberty, of habitation, of reputation and character, and of peace. The laws designed for the protection of reputation and character, and to prevent private quarrels, affrays and breaches of peace, by punishing malicious libel, were as important and as applicable to the state and conditon of the colonists, as the law punishing violations of the rights of property, of person, or of habitation; that is, as laws for punishing larceny, assault and battery, or burglary. Being part of the common law of England, applicable to the state and condition of the colonists, they necessarily applied to all English subjects and territories, as well in America as in Great Britain, and so continued applicable till the declaration of independence.[2]

In the case of *Callanan* v. *Judd* (23 Wisconsin, 343), decided in 1868, Mr. Justice Paine thus spoke of law and equity, particularly of the latter:

In order to determine the meaning of the phrase "judicial power as to matters of law and equity," it is only necessary to recur to the system of jurisprudence established in this country and derived from England, in which the courts had certain well-defined powers in those two classes of action. In actions at law they had the power of determining questions of law, and were required to submit questions of fact to a jury. When the constitution, therefore, vested in certain courts judicial power in matters at law, this would be construed as vesting such power as the courts, under the English and American systems of jurisprudence, had always exer-

[1] 13 Metcalf, 71.
[2] *Ibid.*, 73–4.

cised in that class of actions. It would not import that they were to decide questions of fact, because such was not the judicial power in such actions. . . .

Under the old equity system, the chancellor might at any time refer questions of fact to a jury, but it was merely to inform his conscience. He might, if he saw fit, disregard their verdict, and take it upon himself to dispose of the questions of fact absolutely, as he could have done in the first instance.[1]

In considering judicial power in the sense of the Federal Convention held August 27, 1787, Mr. Gouverneur Morris asked whether the apparent jurisdiction " extended to matters of fact as well as law . . . and to cases of Common law as well as Civil law." [2] To this enquiry Mr. Wilson, on behalf of the Committee of Detail, of which he had been an industrious and perhaps the most valuable member, replied that " The Committee he believed meant facts as well as law & Common as well as Civil law." And he added, " The jurisdiction of the federal Court of Appeals had . . . been so construed." The question and the answer were not unimportant, as the framers of the Constitution were using terms which have a definite signification, and the law about which Mr. Gouverneur Morris inquired and which Mr. Wilson had in mind was the system of law obtaining in courts of admiralty and maritime jurisdiction to which the judicial power of the United States expressly extends by the second section of the third article of the Constitution. With this system of law the public men of that day were familiar, inasmuch as the civil law in its technical signification meant, as distinct from the common law of England, the principles of Roman law which had found their way into the practice and procedure of courts of admiralty. *Admiralty and Maritime Jurisdiction Included*

In view of the experience had with the Court of Federal Appeals, elsewhere considered; in view of the express language of the Constitution and leading decisions of the federal courts, which have given precision and refinement to admiralty procedure in the United States, it does not seem necessary to dwell upon this phase of the subject.[3]

It is however advisable to advert to the fact that the judicial power of the United States was held in the case of *Penhallow* v. *Doane,* (3 Dallas, 54), decided in 1795, to extend to cases which had already been decided by the Federal Court of Appeals under the Confederation, but whose judgments had not been executed, and to the decision of *The Betsey,* (3 Dallas, 6), decided the year before, in which the Supreme Court held that the District *An International Court of Prize*

[1] 23 Wisconsin, 349, 350.
[2] *Documentary History of the Constitution,* Vol. iii, p. 627.
[3] See on this subject the following three out of the many cases which might be cited: *De Lovio* v. *Boit* (2 Gallison, 398), 1815, by Mr. Justice Story on Circuit; *The Scotia,* (14 Wallace, 170), decided by the Supreme Court in 1871; *The Lottawanna* (21 Wallace, 558), decided in 1874.

Court of the United States was not merely a court of admiralty jurisdiction, but that it was a prize court without having to be specifically created as such.

In this latter court, as is well known, the law of nations, in so far as it deals with prize, is administered, which Sir William Blackstone held in his "Commentaries" to be a part of the common law, saying:

> the law of nations (whenever any question arises which is properly the object of its jurisdiction) is here adopted in its full extent by the common law, and is held to be a part of the law of the land.[1]

For this statement the learned commentator had the best of authority. Lord Chancellor Talbot had said in the case of *Buvot* v. *Barbut*, (Cases Tempore Talbot, 231), "That the law of nations in its full extent was part of the law of England." And Lord Mansfield himself, who had been of counsel in the case of *Buvot* v. *Barbut*, said in the case of *Triquet* v. *Bath* (3 Burrow, 1478, 1480), decided in 1764, that "this privilege of foreign ministers and their domestic servants depends upon the law of nations. The act of parliament of 7. *Ann, c.* 12, is *declaratory* of it." Three years later His Lordship further said in the leading case of *Heathfield* v. *Chilton*, (4 Burrow, 2015, 2016), that "the privileges of public ministers and their retinue depend upon the law of *nations,* which is *part* of the common law of *England,* And the act of Parliament of 7 *Ann c.* 12 did not *intend* to alter, nor *can* alter the law of nations." It was natural, therefore, that the statesmen of the Revolution should consider the law of nations as part of the common law. They had by ordinance of the Congress of December 4, 1781, relating to maritime captures professed obedience to the law of nations "according to the general usages of Europe." There was a very interesting case with which they must have been familiar, inasmuch as it happened in Philadelphia, then generally looked upon as the capital of the country, and *as* it involved the French minister plenipotentiary and the King of France it must have created a stir. In the case of *Respublica* v. *De Longchamps,* (1 Dallas, 111), decided in 1784, the defendant was indicted and convicted because, as stated in the indictment, on the 17th of May, "in the dwelling-house of his Excellency the French Minister Plenipotentiary, in the presence of *Francis Barbe Marbois,* unlawfully and insolently did threaten and menace bodily harm and violence to the person of the said *Francis Barbe Marbois,* he being Consul General of *France* to the *United States,* Consul for the state of *Pennsylvania,* Secretary of the French Legation, &c. resident in the house aforesaid, and under the protection of the law of nations and this Commonwealth."

The case was as interesting as it was novel. Mr. Chief Justice McKean,

---

[1] Sir William Blackstone, *Commentaries on the Laws of England*, 1765 ed., Vol. II, p. 67.

before whom it was tried in Philadelphia stated that it was "a case of the first impression in the *United States,*" and that "it must be determined on the principles of the laws of nations which form a part of the municipal law of *Pennsylvania.*" [1]

The gravity of the offense is indicated by the following sentence which the Chief Justice, on behalf of the court, pronounced as follows:

> That you pay a fine of one hundred French crowns to the commonwealth; that you be imprisoned until the 4th day of *July* 1786, which will make a little more than two years imprisonment in the whole; that you then give good security to keep the peace, and be of good behaviour to all public ministers, secretaries to embassies, and consuls, as well as to all the liege people of *Pennsylvania,* for the space of seven years, by entering into a recognizance, yourself in a thousand pounds, and two securities in five hundred pounds each: that you pay the costs of this prosecution, and remain committed until this sentence be complied with.[2]

It was natural for Pennsylvania to indict and to sentence De Longchamps, inasmuch as the law of nations was a part of the common law, and the law, criminal as well as civil, was in force in Pennsylvania. There might have been some difficulty in regarding the law of nations as a part of the law of the United States; but that difficulty seems to have been obviated by section eight of the first article of the Constitution, authorizing in express terms the Congress "To define and punish Piracies and Felonies committed on the high Seas, and Offenses against the Law of Nations." As nations have trouble enough in administering their domestic laws, without seeking to enforce within their limits foreign laws as such, the law of nations, therefore, became by this provision of the Constitution, by implication if not by express statement, the law of the land, This has been universally held from the first to the last decision of the Supreme Court, especially in the case of *The Paquete Habana,* (175 U. S. 677, 700), decided in 1900, in which Mr. Justice Gray, speaking for the court, said: "International law is a part of our law, and must be ascertained and administered by the courts of justice of appropriate jurisdiction, as often as questions of right depending upon it are duly presented for their determination." As the law of the land it is the law of each State of the Union, as well as of the Union, and as such, it is administered in all courts, in all cases involving its principles.

The judicial power, therefore, extends to cases in law and equity, admiralty and maritime jurisdiction, and the law of nations.

[1] 1 Dallas, 114.
[2] *Ibid.,* 118.

XXII

IMMUNITY OF STATES AND NATIONS FROM SUIT

It is an established principle of jurisprudence in all civilized nations that the sovereign cannot be sued in its own courts, or in any other, without its consent and permission; but it may, if it thinks proper, waive this privilege, and permit itself to be made a defendant in a suit by individuals, or by another State. And as this permission is altogether voluntary on the part of the sovereignty, it follows that it may prescribe the terms and conditions on which it consents to be sued, and the manner in which the suit shall be conducted, and may withdraw its consent whenever it may suppose that justice to the public requires it. (*Chief Justice Taney in Beers v. State of Arkansas, 20 Howard, 527, 529, decided in 1857.*)

It is a familiar doctrine of the common law, that the sovereign cannot be sued in his own courts without his consent. The doctrine rests upon reasons of public policy; the inconvenience and danger which would follow from any different rule. It is obvious that the public service would be hindered, and the public safety endangered, if the supreme authority could be subjected to suit at the instance of every citizen, and consequently controlled in the use and disposition of the means required for the proper administration of the government. The exemption from direct suit is, therefore, without exception. This doctrine of the common law is equally applicable to the supreme authority of the nation, the United States. They cannot be subjected to legal proceedings at law or in equity without their consent; and whoever institutes such proceedings must bring his case within the authority of some act of Congress. Such is the language of this court in *United States v. Clarke, 8 Peters, 444.*
The same exemption from judicial process extends to the property of the United States, and for the same reasons. As justly observed by the learned judge who tried this case, there is no distinction between suits against the government directly, and suits against its property.
But although direct suits cannot be maintained against the United States, or against their property, yet, when the United States institute a suit, they waive their exemption so far as to allow a presentation by the defendant of set-offs, legal and equitable, to the extent of the demand made or property claimed, and when they proceed *in rem*, they open to consideration all claims and equities in regard to the property libelled. They then stand in such proceedings, with reference to the rights of defendants or claimants, precisely as private suitors, except that they are exempt from costs and from affirmative relief against them, beyond the demand or property in controversy. (*Mr. Justice Field in The Siren, 7 Wallace, 152, 153-154, decided in 1868.*)

While the United States as a government may not be sued without its consent, yet with its consent it may be sued, and the judicial power of the United States extends to such a controversy. Indeed, the whole jurisdiction of the Court of Claims rests upon this proposition. (*Mr. Justice Brewer in State of Minnesota v. Hitchcock, 185 United States Reports, 373, 386, decided in 1902.*)

Sec. 145. The Court of Claims shall have jurisdiction to hear and determine the following matters:
First. All claims (except for pensions) founded upon the Constitution of the United States or any law of Congress, upon any regulation of an Executive Department, upon any contract, express or implied, with the Government of the United States, or for damages, liquidated or unliquidated, in cases not sounding in tort, in respect of which claims the party would be entitled to redress against the United States either in a court of law, equity, or admiralty if the United States were suable: *Provided, however,* That nothing in this section shall be construed as giving to the said court jurisdiction to hear and determine claims growing out of the late civil war, and commonly known as "war claims," or to hear and determine other claims which, prior to March third, eighteen hundred and eighty-seven, had been rejected or reported on adversely by any court, department, or commission authorized to hear and determine the same.

Second. All set-offs, counterclaims, claims for damages, whether liquidated or unliquidated, or other demands whatsoever on the part of the Government of the United States against any claimant against the Government in said court: *Provided,* That no suit against the Government of the United States, brought by any officer of the United States to recover fees for services alleged to have been performed for the United States, shall be allowed under this chapter until an account for said fees shall have been rendered and finally acted upon as required by law, unless the proper accounting officer of the Treasury fails to act finally thereon within six months after the account is received in said office.

Third. The claim of any paymaster, quartermaster, commissary of subsistence, or other disbursing officer of the United States, or of his administrators or executors, for relief from responsibility on account of loss by capture or otherwise, while in the line of his duty, of Government funds, vouchers, records, or papers in his charge, and for which such officer was and is held responsible. (*The Judicial Code of the United States, 1911, 36 Statutes at Large, 1136.*)

CHAPTER XXII

IMMUNITY OF STATES AND NATIONS FROM SUIT

In the exercise of judicial power and judicial discretion a judgment, it may be supposed, has been rendered in a case between actual litigants involving a principle of law or equity. As there existed between the parties a difference of opinion — a contest — it is the duty of the court, in the exercise of judicial power and judicial discretion, to decide that controversy, settling finally and without appeal the rights of the litigants in the matter of the dispute, whether it be by a court of first instance, from which no appeal is taken or allowed, or whether it be the court of last resort upon appeal. The result in either case is an adjudication or culmination of jurisdiction. In the exercise of the judicial power a judgment of the court is not only a final determination but one which, when determined, can be or is to be enforced by appropriate process of that court. For, according to the conception of judicial power in the United States, a judgment of a court, to be final, is one which can be executed under process from the court. This statement, however, is to be understood in the sense that the decision is final as to the rights of the parties in a judicial matter and is to be executed against individual litigants; and in this respect American practice may be said to accord with the practice of other nations.

Suits
Against
States

There is, however, a matter in which the practice of the United States differs from that of other countries, in that a State may, under certain circumstances, be sued as of right in the Supreme Court of the United States in controversies involving law or equity, and the rights of the litigating parties fixed by a judgment of the court. As this is an extension of judicial power beyond precedent at the time of the adoption of the Constitution of the United States, we are prepared to expect that, in the exercise of this new right, there may be limitations or qualifications of it unknown in suits between individuals. For in this instance we are dealing with peoples in their political capacity. It would not necessarily follow that the process obtaining in the one would obtain in the other case or that the procedure applicable to the individual would be applicable to the aggregation which we call a state and which, although it be a person, is an artificial person. A careful examination of the records of the Constitutional Convention of 1787 and of the proceedings of the conventions of the different States ratifying the Constitution, fails to disclose any intent on the part of the framers of the Constitution, or

452

of the States ratifying it, that a judgment against a State was to be executed by the force of the United States. Yet it was doubtless the feeling of the framers and of those advising the ratification of the Constitution that, in extending the judicial power to controversies against States, they were not doing a useless thing, and that the exercise of judicial power in controversies against States would be obeyed, whatever the sanction.

Mr. Chief Justice Taney, to cite only one illustrious example, recognized the distinction between a judgment against an individual and a judgment against a State in its political capacity. It is to be presumed that he had this distinction in mind when he drafted the opinion for the court in the case of *Gordon* v. *United States*, because four years before, in 1860, he had solemnly declared, on behalf of the court, in delivering its unanimous opinion in the case of *Kentucky* v. *Dennison* (24 Howard, 66, 109–10), that, " If the Governor of Ohio refuses to discharge " a duty imposed upon him by the Constitution and regulated in its exercise by an act of Congress, " there is no power delegated to the General Government, through the Judicial Department, or any other department, to use any coercive means to compel him." Coercion of States

In view of the importance of this matter, the exact language of Chief Justice Taney in the case of *Gordon* v. *United States* (117 U. S., 697, 701–2) is quoted:

> It was to prevent an appeal to the sword and a dissolution of the compact that this Court, by the organic law, was made equal in origin and equal in title to the legislative and executive branches of the government: its powers defined, and limited, and made strictly judicial, and placed therefore beyond the reach of the powers delegated to the Legislative and Executive Departments. And it is upon the principle of the perfect independence of this Court, that in cases where the Constitution gives it original jurisdiction, the action of Congress has not been deemed necessary to regulate its exercise, or to prescribe the process to be used to bring the parties before the court, or to carry its judgment into execution. The jurisdiction and judicial power being vested in the court, it proceeded to prescribe its process and regulate its proceedings according to its own judgment, and Congress has never attempted to control or interfere with the action of the court in this respect.

In so far as States are concerned, the Constitution provides that the judicial power of the United States shall extend (1) to controversies to which the United States shall be a party; (2) to controversies between two or more States (3) between a State and citizens of another State; (4) between citizens of different States (5) between citizens of the same State claiming lands under grants of different States; (6) and between a State, or the citizens thereof, and foreign States, citizens or subjects. It further provides that " in all cases . . . . in which a State shall be a party, the Supreme Court shall have original jurisdiction." Judicial Power over States

The consent to be sued is a general consent on behalf of the States which does not have to be renewed on any particular occasion; and, given in the Constitution, it can not be withdrawn by any of the United States. The consent to be sued in a court other than the Supreme Court is a special consent which may be given by statute in general or for a particular purpose; and in giving it the State may express the conditions upon which it is given and may revoke it according to its pleasure at any time after the beginning of the suit and before final judgment.

In this latter case, however, we are not dealing with the consent given by the Constitution but with the consent of a State, in its original capacity, unaffected by the provisions of the Constitution. In order to have a clear understanding of this subject, it may be well to consider in this place whether a State in international law, which is generally called a nation, may be sued without its consent, and whether the States which, by their delegates, drafted, and, by their conventions, ratified the Constitution were to be considered as nations in the sense of international law, or as possessing, in the matter of suits, the same rights and privileges. Because, if the States under the Confederation stood on an equality with the nations at large; and if they renounced an immunity by the Constitution which they possessed as States before its ratification; it follows that the right of suit is in derogation of their sovereignty, and that it is therefore to be strictly construed, as in every grant against a sovereign, and is to be exercised according to and within the limits of the grant.

There is no need to quote authority for the statement that any and every nation under international law is exempt from suit without its express consent, for consent is not and can not in such cases be implied. The reason why a nation should be exempt from suit has been variously and differently stated, but the fact of immunity is not open to argument. Mr. Justice Gray, whose learning often appalled while it convinced, said in the case of *Briggs* v. *Light-Boats* (11 Allen, Mass., 157), decided in 1865, on the question of the immunity of the State from suit, that " the broader reason is that it would be inconsistent with the very idea of supreme executive power and would endanger the performance of the public duties of the sovereign, to subject him to repeated suits as a matter of right at the will of any citizen, and to submit to the judicial tribunals the trial and disposition of his public property, his instruments and means of carrying on his government, in war and in peace, and the moneys in his treasury." And in a more recent case, Mr. Justice Gray's successor on the Supreme Court, Mr. Justice Holmes, said, in delivering its opinion in the case of *Kwananakoa* v. *Polyblank* (205 U. S., 349, 353), decided in 1907:

Some doubts have been expressed as to the source of the immunity of a sovereign power from suit without its own permission, but the answer has been public property since before the days of Hobbes. (Leviathan, c. 26, 2.) A sovereign is exempt from suit, not because of any formal conception or obsolete theory, but on the logical and practical ground that there can be no legal right as against the authority that makes the law on which the right depends. *" Car on peut bien recevoir loy d'autruy, mais il est impossible par nature de se donner loy."* Bodin, Republique, 1, c. 8. Ed. 1629, p. 132. Sir John Eliot, De Jure Maiestatis, c. 3. *Nemo suo statuto ligatur necessitative. Baldus., De Leg. et Const., Digma Vox.* (2d ed., 1496, fol. 51 B. Ed. 1539, fol. 61.)

It is thus clear that by the law of nations a sovereign State was exempt from suit; and it was also clear that the particular sovereign State, to wit, England, from which country the colonists had derived their laws and institutions, was immune from suit except with its own consent. It remains to be considered if the States whose independence was proclaimed by the immortal Declaration believed themselves free from suit. In this great document the united colonies are declared to be " free and independent States." After specifying certain powers which independent States may exercise, it is further asserted that they have the power " to do all other acts and things which independent States may of right do." The Articles of Confederation, approved by the Congress in 1777, but not ratified by the last of the thirteen States, and therefore not binding upon any of them, until March 1, 1781, declares in its second article the States to be sovereign, free and independent and possessed of every power, jurisdiction and right which it did not grant to the United States in Congress assembled. In Article 9, the States forming the Confederacy allowed themselves to be sued by one another for specified purposes and in a prescribed manner.

But it is evident, from the case of *Simon Nathan* v. *the Commonwealth of Virginia* (1 Dallas, 77, Note A), tried in the Court of Common Pleas of Philadelphia in the September term of 1781, that, apart from the Articles of Confederation and the right of suit according to the method there prescribed, a sovereign, free and independent State of the Confederacy was immune from suit. The facts of the case are thus stated by the reporter:

A foreign attachment was issued against the Commonwealth of Virginia, at the suit of Simon Nathan; and a quantity of clothing, imported from France, belonging to that state, was attached in Philadelphia. The delegates in Congress from Virginia, conceiving this a violation of the laws of nations, applied to the Supreme Executive Council of Pennsylvania, by whom the sheriff was ordered to give up the goods. The counsel for the *plaintiff,* finding that the sheriff suppressed the writ, and made no return of his proceedings, obtained, September 20, 1781, a rule that the sheriff should return the writ, unless cause was shown.

Upon the argument, the Attorney General, on the part of the sheriff and by direction of the Supreme Executive Council, " showed cause," to quote again the reporter, " and prayed that the rule might be discharged." The Attorney General, it will be observed, took his stand upon the law of nations. Thus:

Sovereignty
not Always
an Exemption

> He premised, that though the several states which form our federal republic, had, by the confederation, ceded many of the prerogatives of sovereignty to the United States, yet these voluntary engagements did not injure their independence on each other; but that each was a sovereign, " with every power, jurisdiction and right, not expressly given up." He then laid down two positions. 1. That every kind of process issued against a sovereign, is a violation of the laws of nations; and is, in itself, null and void. 2. That a sheriff cannot be compelled to serve or return a void writ.[1]

Leaving out the balance of the argument supporting these positions, it is to be observed that counsel for the plaintiff admitted the sovereignty of Virginia, but insisted that sovereignty was not a defense against an act of injustice. Thus, to quote the language of the reporter:

> The counsel for the *plaintiff* insisted, that though Virginia was a sovereign state, yet this ought not to exempt her property in every case from the laws and jurisdiction of another state. The sovereignty should never be made a plea in bar of justice; and that the true idea of prerogative, was the power of doing good, and, not, as it had sometimes been expressed, " the divine right of doing ill." [2]

Without considering the balance of the plaintiff's contention, which, as has been seen, recognized the sovereignty of Virginia, it is sufficient to quote the judgment of this case in the words of the reporter:

> The Court held the matter some days under advisement; and at their next meeting, the President delivered it as the judgment of the court:
> " That the rule made upon the sheriff, to return the writ issued against the commonwealth of Virginia, at the suit of Simon Nathan, should be discharged." [3]

The meaning of this is free from doubt. The Commonwealth of Virginia, sovereign under the Articles of Confederation, could not be sued except in the manner prescribed by the Articles of Confederation; that a writ of attachment, if issued, would be dissolved; and that an order of the court directing the sheriff to return the writ would be discharged as inconsistent with the rights of a sovereign State.

It can therefore be confidently stated, and without fear of successful contradiction, that the States represented by their delegates in the Philadelphia

[1] 1 Dallas, 78.
[2] *Ibid.*, 79.
[3] *Ibid.* 80.

Conference were sovereign, and possessed of all sovereign powers except in so far as they had been pleased to renounce the exercise thereof; that one of the powers of sovereignty inherent in a State was immunity from suit, except as the States had renounced the exemption in the Articles of Confederation; and that they were exempt from suit under the new and more perfect Union drafted by their delegates in conference and ratified by the States, except in so far as they renounced the immunity.

It is frequently said that, under the 9th of the Articles of Confederation, a State could be sued by a State only in the matter of boundary; but this is so glaringly inconsistent with the express language of the articles that it is hard to see how anyone at all familiar with its text could fall into such an error. And yet Mr. Justice McLean, delivering the opinion of the Supreme Court in the case of *Briscoe* v. *Bank of Kentucky* (11 Peters, 257, 321), said in January, 1837:

> But was a state liable to be sued? . . . . No sovereign state is liable to be sued without her consent. Under the articles of confederation, a state could be sued only in cases of boundary.

Suit without Consent Inconsistent with Sovereignty

The fact is that, upon the ratification of the Constitution and the institution of the government under it, the Articles of Confederation dropped out of sight, and they have not yet been treated by historians and publicists as they deserve. The material portion of the 9th Article reads:

> The United States in Congress assembled shall also be the last resort on appeal in all disputes and differences now subsisting or that may hereafter arise between two or more States concerning boundary, jurisdiction, or any cause whatever.

But the nature and extent of this power and its exercise need not detain us here. It is merely mentioned in passing to show that the States had consented generally to suit and had prescribed the method.

The immunity of a State of the American Union from suit was discussed in *Beers* v. *State of Arkansas* (20 Howard, 527), decided in 1857. In this interesting and leading case it appeared that the constitution of the State of Arkansas authorized the General Assembly to direct " in what courts and in what manner suits may be commenced against the State; " and, in pursuance of this provision of the constitution, an act was passed. Under the permission of this act, suit was brought against the State which, after the suit had begun, passed an act requiring the plaintiff to file in open court the bonds on which the suit was brought. This the plaintiff refused to do, and the court dismissed the suit. On writ of error carried to the Supreme Court of the United States, the judgment of the court of last resort of Arkansas was

Waiving of Sovereignty

affirmed, and, in the course of the unanimous opinion of the court announcing judgment, Mr. Chief Justice Taney said:

> It is an established principle of jurisprudence in all civilized nations that the sovereign cannot be sued in its own courts, or in any other, without its consent and permission; but it may, if it thinks proper, waive this privilege, and permit itself to be made a defendant in a suit by individuals, or by another State. And as this permission is altogether voluntary on the part of the sovereignty, it follows that it may prescribe the terms and conditions on which it consents to be sued, and the manner in which the suit shall be conducted, and may withdraw its consent whenever it may suppose that justice to the public requires it.[1]

Considering the question whether the law of the General Assembly permitting suit was, when acted upon by the plaintiff, in the nature of a contract, which could not be repealed without injury to the plaintiff's rights, the Chief Justice said, speaking for the court:

> Arkansas, by its Constitution, so far waived the privilege of sovereignty as to authorize suits to be instituted against it in its own courts, and delegated to its General Assembly the power directing in what courts, and in what manner, the suit might be commenced. And if the law of 1854 had been passed before the suit was instituted, we do not understand that any objection would have been made to it. The objection is, that it was passed after this suit was instituted, and contained regulations with which the plaintiff could not conveniently comply. But the prior law was not a contract. It was an ordinary act of legislation, prescribing the conditions upon which the State consented to waive the privilege of sovereignty. It contained no stipulation that these regulations should not be modified afterwards, if, upon experience, it was found that further provisions were necessary to protect the public interest; and no such contract can be implied from the law, nor can this court inquire whether the law operated hardly or unjustly upon the parties whose suits were then pending. That was a question for the consideration of the Legislature. They might have repealed the prior law altogether, and put an end to the jurisdiction of their courts in suits against the State, if they had thought proper to do so, or prescribe new conditions upon which the suits might still be allowed to proceed. In exercising this latter power, the State violated no contract with the parties; it merely regulated the proceedings in its own courts, and limited the jurisdiction it had before conferred in suits when the State consented to be a party defendant.[2]

In like manner, the State having a right to appear in court and sue naturally determines when it shall exercise that right. Otherwise, the possession of the right would be an empty privilege. This was briefly but adequately stated in the case of *Clark* v. *Barnard* (108 U. S., 436, 447–8), decided by

---

[1] 20 Howard, 529.
[2] *Ibid.*, 529–30.

the Supreme Court in 1883, in which Mr. Justice Matthews, speaking for a unanimous court, said:

> The immunity from suit belonging to a State, which is respected and protected by the Constitution within the limits of the judicial power of the United States, is a personal privilege which it may waive at pleasure; so that in a suit, otherwise well brought, in which a State had sufficient interest to entitle it to become a party defendant, its appearance in a court of the United States would be a voluntary submission to its jurisdiction; while, of course, those courts are always open to it as a suitor in controversies between it and citizens of other States. In the present case the State of Rhode Island appeared in the cause and presented and prosecuted a claim to the fund in controversy, and thereby made itself a party to the litigation to the full extent required for its complete determination. It became an actor as well as defendant. . . .

If, however, the State appears, it waives its immunity to the extent of its appearance, and judgment may be had against it to this extent. It may, for example, decide it to be in its interest to object to the jurisdiction of the court. If it appear for this purpose it is and can only be a party to that extent. For, being exempt from process, it determines for itself the extent to which it can safely renounce the immunity inherent in sovereignty, and that is withdrawn from the court which the State has not authorized it to exercise. In *The Siren* (7 Wallace, 152), decided in 1868, the Supreme Court had occasion to consider not merely the general question but a specific application of it. The vessel was captured in the harbor of Charleston in February, 1865, in the attempt to violate the blockade of that port. It was put in charge of a prize master and crew and ordered to Boston for adjudication. Passing through Long Island Sound, it ran into and sank the sloop *Harper*. The court found that the collision was the fault of the *Siren*. Arriving at Boston, the *Siren* was libeled, condemned as lawful prize, sold, and the proceeds were deposited with the Assistant Treasurer of the United States in compliance with an act of Congress, where they remained subject to the order of the court.

In this state of affairs, the owners of the *Harper* claimed a portion of the fund because of the collision, due to the fault of the *Siren,* and intervened by petition for this purpose. On the general phase of the question, Mr. Justice Field said:

> It is a familiar doctrine of the common law, that the sovereign cannot be sued in his own courts without his consent. The doctrine rests upon reasons of public policy; the inconvenience and danger which would follow from any different rule. It is obvious that the public service would be hindered, and the public safety endangered, if the supreme authority could be subjected to suit at the instance of every citizen, and consequently con-

trolled in the use and disposition of the means required for the proper administration of the government. The exemption from direct suit is, therefore, without exception. This doctrine of the common law is equally applicable to the supreme authority of the nation, the United States. They cannot be subjected to legal proceedings at law or in equity without their consent; and whoever institutes such proceedings must bring his case within the authority of some act of Congress. Such is the language of this court in *United States* v. *Clarke*. [8 Peters, 444.]

The same exemption from judicial process extends to the property of the United States, and for the same reasons. As justly observed by the learned judge who tried this case, there is no distinction between suits against the government directly, and suits against its property.[1]

But, while this is no doubt true, the learned Justice, speaking for the court, recognized that it was a harsh doctrine, that it should not be extended beyond the principle, and that exceptions should be allowed to it in the interest of justice, where such exceptions were consistent with principle or sanctioned by practice. He therefore continued:

But although direct suits cannot be maintained against the United States, or against their property, yet, when the United States institute a suit, they waive their exemption so far as to allow a presentation by the defendant of set-offs, legal and equitable, to the extent of the demand made or property claimed, and when they proceed *in rem,* they open to consideration all claims and equities in regard to the property libelled. They then stand in such proceedings, with reference to the rights of defendants or claimants, precisely as private suitors, except that they are exempt from costs and from affirmative relief against them, beyond the demand or property in controversy.[2]

Referring to the particular case, Mr. Justice Field stated that in admiralty law a lien is created in favor of the injured party against the vessel in fault, and that the inability of the private person to enforce the lien against the Government, without its consent, does not invalidate the claim; but only prevents its allowance in an ordinary judicial proceeding. For this he refers to the adjudged cases of English and American courts, holding that a court would enforce a mortgage upon land conveyed by the Government, which the Government had taken subject to the mortgage of the previous owner; and that claims would be enforced by judicial process against the proceeds of property belonging to the Government, but which had been sold, under decree of the court, and the proceeds placed within its jurisdiction. After stating that, in accordance with the principles of maritime law, claims upon a vessel extend equally to and are satisfied out of the proceeds of the sale, the learned Justice thus applies this doctrine to the facts of the *Siren:*

[1] 7 Wallace, 153-4.
[2] *Ibid.,* 154.

Assuming, therefore, that the Siren was in fault, and that by the tort she committed a claim was created against her, we do not perceive any just ground for refusing its satisfaction out of the proceeds of her sale. The government is the actor in the suit for her condemnation. It asks for her sale, and the proceeds coming into the registry of the court, come affected with all the claims which existed upon the vessel created subsequent to her capture. There is no authority, that we are aware of, which would exempt them under these circumstances, because of the exemption of the government from a direct proceeding *in rem* against the vessel whilst in its custody.[1]

In support of these views, he refers to *United States* v. *Wilder* (3 Sumner, 308), decided in 1838, in which Mr. Justice Story, sitting at circuit, held, to quote Mr. Justice Field's summary of the case, that " goods of the United States were subject to contribution, equally with goods of private shippers, to meet the expenses incurred in saving them; " and also to the case of *The Schooner Davis and Cargo* (6 Blatchford, 138), decided in 1868 in the circuit court for the southern district of New York, which was later, upon appeal, affirmed by the Supreme Court of the United States (10 Wallace, 15), in 1869. In the case upon appeal it was held that, to meet salvage services in saving vessel and cargo, cotton belonging to the United States was liable to contribution as would have been the property of private persons. After referring to *The Siren* (7 Wallace, 152) and *Briggs* v. *The Light Boats* (11 Allen, 157), " as perhaps the two most authoritative and well considered cases on that subject," Mr. Justice Miller thus concluded his opinion on behalf of a unanimous court:

> The United States, without any violation of law by the marshal, was reduced to the necessity of becoming claimant and actor in the court to assert her claim to the cotton. Under these circumstances we think it was the duty of the court to enforce the lien of the libellants for the salvage before it restored the cotton to the custody of the officers of the government.[2]

Cotton not only troubled the American but the English courts, in which the United States of America appeared as plaintiff in order to recover the property of the Confederacy found within the jurisdiction of England. The Confederate States had entered into a contract with the firm of Fraser, Trenholm & Co., of which Prioleau was the English member, by virtue of which it was to sell all the cotton of the Confederacy sent to Europe, to buy eight steamships to be engaged in the transportation of the cotton and to pay out of that very necessary commodity the expenses incident to the contract and the undertaking, advancing in first instance the necessary moneys. Twenty thousand pounds had already been expended for this purpose. A

[1] 7 Wallace, 159.
[2] 10 Wallace, 22.

particular consignment of 1365 bales of cotton had been received in Liverpool after the collapse of the Confederacy, and the United States filed its bill in the court of chancery, praying to have the cotton delivered to its agents and for an injunction and receiver.

Leaving out the very interesting points discussed in the argument and decision of this case, it is sufficient for present purposes to state that the court decreed that the United States was entitled to the cotton by the law of succession, and that it was therefore the property of the United States government, but that it must take it subject to the obligations entered into respecting it by the *de facto* Confederate government. The defendant, Prioleau, was therefore appointed receiver, with power to sell the cotton; but he was properly required to give security for its value beyond £20,000, that being the amount of the defendant's lien (*2 H. & M.*, 559).

If the matter had ended here, this case would not be cited, as we are dealing with States not as plaintiffs but as defendants, for it is universally admitted that a sovereign can sue. We say, off-hand, that one story is good until another is told. The same is true in courts. The case of the United States was clear until Prioleau told his story, which he did by filing a crossbill to obtain discovery from the United States, as a private suitor would be

A Plaintiff
Sovereign
Relinquishes
a Degree of
Sovereignty

required to give under the circumstances. Therefore, in the second phase of this case, entitled *Prioleau* v. *United States and Andrew Johnson* (2 Law Rep., Eq., 659), decided in 1866, Vice-Chancellor Page Wood, later Lord Chancellor Hatherley, held that the United States, suing in an English court, subjected itself to the jurisdiction of the Court; that it stood in the same position as a foreign sovereign, and that it could only obtain relief subject to the rules of practice of the court in which it sued, according to which every suitor, be he a private suitor, a foreign sovereign, or a corporate body, is entitled to discovery upon oath concerning the matters of the suit, and to file a cross-bill for the purpose of obtaining such discovery. Proceedings were therefore stayed in the case of *Prioleau* v. *The United States,* suing in its corporate capacity, until an answer should be put in to the cross-bill of the defendant.

In the course of his decree, Vice-Chancellor Wood intimated that a demurrer should have been filed to the bill of the United States in that cause, as no public officer was put forward as representing its interests or who could be called upon to give discovery upon the cross-bill. Taking advantage of this decision, in the case of *United States* v. *Wagner* (2 Law Rep., Chancery App. Cases, 582), decided in 1867, the defendant, Wagner, demurred to the bill, praying that an account be taken of the moneys, goods and ships which had come into the possession of the defendants and which were claimed by the United States as successor to the Confederacy, on the ground that it should have put forward the President of the United States or some other official of that Government upon whom process could be served by the defendants and who might answer to the cross-bill. The demurrer was allowed by Vice Chancellor Wood, but from this decree the plaintiffs appealed. In the course of very interesting individual opinions, it was held by Lord Chancellor Chelmsford and the great Lord Cairns, destined shortly to succeed him as Lord Chancellor, that a foreign State adopting the republican form of government can sue in the courts of Great Britain in its own name; that such a State is not bound to sue in the name of any officer of the Government or to join as co-plaintiff any official of the Government, or to join as co-plaintiff any other official upon whom process may be served and who may be called upon to give discovery upon a cross-bill; but that the court may stay proceedings in the original dispute until the means of discovery are secured in the cross suit.

In what may be called the third and final phase of this suit, for although the three were separated in form they were related in fact, *United States of America* v. *McRae* (8 Law Rep., Eq., 69), decided in 1869, Vice Chancellor James thus disposed of the entire matter, for the reasons briefly stated in the head-note to the case:

> Upon the suppression of a rebellion, the restored legitimate government is entitled, as of right, to all moneys, goods, and treasure which were public property of the government at the time of the outbreak; such right being in no way affected by the wrongful seizure of the property by the usurping government.
>
> But with respect to property which has been voluntarily contributed to, or acquired by, the insurrectionary government in the exercise of its usurped authority, and has been impressed in its hands with the character of public property, the legitimate government is not, on its restoration, entitled by title paramount, but as successor only (and to that extent recognising the authority) of the displaced usurping government; and in seeking to recover such property from an agent of the displaced government can only do so to the same extent and subject to the same rights and obligations as if that government had not been displaced, and was itself proceeding against the agent.
>
> Therefore, a bill by the *United States* government, after the suppression of the rebellion, against an agent of the late *Confederate* government, for an account of his dealings in respect of the *Confederate* loan, which he was employed to raise in this country, was dismissed with costs; in the absence of proof that any property to which the Plaintiffs were entitled in their own right, as distinguished from their right as successors of the *Confederate* government, ever reached the hands of the Defendant, and on the Plaintiffs declining to have the account taken on the same footing as if taken between the *Confederate* government and the Defendant as the agent of such government, and to pay what on the footing of such account might be found due from them.

The
Sovereign
Becomes
Subordinate
to Law

From these cases, purposely chosen from a foreign jurisdiction, it appears: that a foreign State may freely sue, but that, in doing so, it waives its sovereignty as such for the purposes and to the extent of the suit; that it can only claim rights against the defendant accorded to a private suitor; that it must recognize the rights of the defendant according to the laws of the country in which the suit is brought and that it may be made a defendant in a cross-bill or other action springing out of the transaction. It is interesting to note in this case, that the illustrious plaintiff, having failed to comply with the local law of which it sought the benefit, was taxed in costs as any other unsuccessful or unwilling litigant.

Further
Renunciation
of Immunity
from Suit
by a
Sovereign
Power

In view of the fact that a sovereign waives its immunity by appearing as plaintiff in a court of justice, and of the further fact that in asking justice, it is obliged to do it at the instance of a defendant, the question arises whether a State, stepping down from the pedestal of a sovereign by engaging in industry or trade, may not, because thereof, be held to renounce its immunity from suit and subject itself to suit as a corporation or private person would be subjected in like circumstances. This question has been much discussed, and must be decided if the State as such is, in the future as in the past, to enter into competition with its subjects or citizens in the ordinary business of life.

Thus, in *Bank of United States* v. *Planters' Bank of Georgia* (9 Wheaton, 904, 907–8) decided as long ago as 1824, Mr. Chief Justice Marshall said:

> It is, we think, a sound principle, that when a government becomes a partner in any trading company, it divests itself, so far as concerns the transactions of that company, of its sovereign character, and takes that of a private citizen. Instead of communicating to the company its privileges and its prerogatives, it descends to a level with those with whom it associates itself, and takes the character which belongs to its associates, and to the business which is to be transacted. Thus, many States of this Union, who have an interest in Banks, are not suable even in their own Courts; yet they never exempt the corporation from being sued. The State of Georgia, by giving to the Bank the capacity to sue and be sued, voluntarily strips itself of its sovereign character, so far as respects the transactions of the Bank, and waives all the privileges of that character. As a member of a corporation, a government never exercises its sovereignty. It acts merely as a corporator, and exercises no other power in the management of the affairs of the corporation, than are expressly given by the incorporating act.
>
> The government of the Union held shares in the old Bank of the United States; but the privileges of the government were not imparted by that circumstance to the Bank. The United States was not a party to suits brought by or against the Bank in the sense of the constitution. So with respect to the present Bank. Suits brought by or against it are not understood to be brought by or against the United States. The government, by becoming a corporator, lays down its sovereignty, so far as respects the transactions of the corporation, and exercises no power or privilege which is not derived from the charter.

We think, then, that the Planters' Bank of Georgia is not exempted from being sued in the federal Courts, by the circumstance that the State is a corporator.

But, in national as well as in international law, the United States is not subject to suit without its consent, either at the instance of a citizen or subject, of a foreign citizen or subject, or of a foreign State or nation; but, by the Constitution of the United States, State may sue State, and has often done so.[1] As originally drafted and as construed by the Supreme Court, a citizen of one of the States could sue another State of the Union; but its exercise in the case of *Chisholm* v. *Georgia* (2 Dallas, 415), decided in 1793, led to the passage of the 11th Amendment, to the effect that the judicial power of the United States should not extend to such a suit. The United States may sue a State of the American Union. The United States are, for purposes of suit, regarded as a State within the meaning of the Constitution, as solemnly adjudged in *United States* v. *Texas* (143 U. S., 621), decided in 1892; but it is equally well settled that the Government of the United States is not made by the Constitution suable, without express consent, by State or citizen. However, by various acts of Congress, the Federal Government has consented to be sued, in a limited category of cases, in the Court of Claims, created in 1855 for this purpose. These acts are in terms broad enough to include States as well as private persons. As amended in 1912, they thus define and state the jurisdiction of the present Court of Claims:

A State May Sue a State

> Sec. 145. The Court of Claims shall have jurisdiction to hear and determine the following matters:
> First. All claims (except for pensions) founded upon the Constitution of the United States or any laws of Congress, upon any regulation of an Executive Department, upon any contract, express or implied, with the Government of the United States, or for damages, liquidated or unliquidated, in cases not sounding in tort, in respect of which claims the party would be entitled to redress against the United States either in a court of law, equity, or admiralty if the United States were suable. . . .
> Second. All set-offs, counterclaims, claims for damages, whether liquidated or unliquidated, or other demands whatsoever on the part of the Government of the United States against any claimant against the Government in said court.[2]

[1] For collection of cases, see J. B. Scott, *Judicial Settlement of Controversies Between States*, 2 vols.
[2] 36 Statutes at Large, 1136–7.

XXIII

A MORE PERFECT SOCIETY OF NATIONS

It is a favourite maxim of mine that history, while it should be scientific in its method, should pursue a practical object. That is, it should not merely gratify the reader's curiosity about the past, but modify his view of the present and his forecast of the future. (*Sir John R. Seeley, The Expansion of England, American edition, 1883, p. 1.*)

To be right, to set for the world a standard of true liberty and true justice: that is the great mission of democracy! . . .
. . . It is for us whose lives are cast in such lines that we can see and feel the difference between that high function and the ordinary things of life, to teach our friends and neighbors the secret of the great judgment of our free democracy, that they may reverence it and preserve it always. (*Elihu Root, The Spirit Which Makes a Nation Live, Addresses on Government and Citizenship, 1916, pp. 500-502.*)

We wish for no victories but those of peace; for no territory except our own; for no sovereignty except sovereignty over ourselves. We deem the independence and equal rights of the smallest and weakest member of the family of nations entitled to as much respect as those of the greatest empire; and we deem the observance of that respect the chief guaranty of the weak against the oppression of the strong. We neither claim nor desire any rights or privileges or powers that we do not freely concede to every American republic. We wish to increase our prosperity, to expand our trade, to grow in wealth, in wisdom, and in spirit; but our conception of the true way to accomplish this is not to pull down others and profit by their ruin, but to help all friends to a common prosperity and a common growth, that we may all become greater and stronger together. (*Elihu Root, Address to the Third Conference of the American Republics at Rio de Janeiro, July 31, 1906, Latin America and the United States, 1917, p. 10.*)

There are no international controversies so serious that they cannot be settled peaceably if both parties really desire peaceable settlement, while there are few causes of dispute so trifling that they cannot be made the occasion of war if either party really desires war. The matters in dispute between nations are nothing; the spirit which deals with them is everything. (*Elihu Root, Address at the Laying of the Corner Stone of the Building for the Pan American Union, Washington, May 11, 1908, in Latin America and the United States, 1917, pp. 230-231.*)

It is the proper end of government to reduce this wretched waste to the smallest possible amount, by taking such measures as shall cause the energies now spent by mankind in injuring one another, or in protecting themselves against injury, to be turned to the legitimate employment of the human faculties, that of compelling the powers of nature to be more and more subservient to physical and moral good. (*John Stuart Mill, Principles of Political Economy, 1848, Vol. 2, p. 560.*)

CHAPTER XXIII

A MORE PERFECT SOCIETY OF NATIONS

THE Society of Nations is approximately composed of fifty States claim- The Great Problem
ing to be sovereign, free and independent. The more perfect Union of the
United States is composed of forty-eight States. The official delegates of
twelve of the then thirteen sovereign, free and independent American States
who met in Federal Convention in the city of Philadelphia in 1787, were
faced by the problems which confront every international conference in which
an attempt is made to bring and to keep the nations in closer relations. The
greatest of these problems is that of renouncing in the common interest the
exercise of certain sovereign rights, while retaining unimpaired the exercise
of all sovereign rights not so renounced. The line of demarkation between
what may be safely renounced in the interest of all and what it is essential
to retain in the interest of each is always difficult to draw. That the problem is in itself not insuperable is shown by the success of those delegates of
twelve of the thirteen American States, for, as Benjamin Franklin, a delegate from the State of Pennsylvania, said, "we had many interests to
reconcile." The delegates to that memorable assembly established in fact and
in form, a union for legislative purposes, a union for administrative purposes, and a union for judicial purposes, which, taken together and acting
in cooperation as they must, since each depends upon the other, form a more
perfect Union than that of the Society of Nations.

The delegates in Federal Convention did not merge the States in a union,
but formed a union of the States. They vested the legislative branch
with eighteen powers of legislation only, so that the Union is from this
standpoint one of enumerated powers merely. The executive branch of the
Union possesses no powers save those specified in the instrument of its creation, and any attempt on the part of the legislative or the executive branch to
exercise powers in excess of the grant contained in the Constitution is declared null and void and of no effect by the judicial branch of the Union. An
attempt on the part of the Union to exercise a power in excess of the grant
is, in an appropriate and specific case presented for its decision, declared to
be null, void and of no effect by the Supreme Court of the United States.
This is accomplished without the use of force against the Union on the part

of a State or combination of States. Only the individual is coerced. The statute may remain unrepealed, for it has ceased to possess legal validity.

A
Possible
Solution

The Society of Nations may not be willing, and indeed even with good will may not be able, to go so far now or at any time as have the States forming the American Union. But however many steps they may take or however few toward the closer Union, the experience of the framers of the Constitution who traversed the entire path should be as a lamp to their feet.

Yet we must not imagine that the Society of Nations is a mere phrase. It is a body politic if it care to consider itself as such, for which statement we have the authority of *Respublica* v. *Sweers* (1 Dallas, 41), decided by the Supreme Court of Pennsylvania in 1779, at a time when the Articles of Confederation were still unratified, the court saying that " from the moment of their association the United States necessarily became a body corporate; for, there was no superior from whom that character could otherwise be derived." On two occasions, in 1899 twenty-six nations and in 1907 forty-four nations solemnly recognized in the Pacific Settlement Convention of The Hague " the solidarity which unites the members of the society of civilized nations," thus bringing the Society of Nations within the rule of law defining the association of the American States. They can, if they will, frame the law for the Society through delegates of their own choice meeting in conference at stated intervals and submitting the draft of their labors for ratification to each of the States participating in the conference, thus making of themselves a legislature *ad referendum*. In like manner delegates of the Nations may in conference assembled establish a court of the Nations, for which they have a precedent in the Supreme Court of the American Union, which can declare and apply the law of Nations now existing or as made by their delegates in conference and ratified by each of the Nations. Delegates of twenty-six Nations in 1899, delegates of forty-four Nations in 1907 in the Pacific Settlement Convention declared it to be " expedient to record in an international agreement the principles of equity and right on which are based the security of States and the welfare of peoples." It can be added that an international court of justice " accessible to all in the midst of the independent Powers " would not only extend " the empire of law " and strengthen " the appreciation of international justice," but to quote still further from the Pacific Settlement Convention of 1899 and 1907, that it would also make for " the maintenance of the general peace."

Should the Powers desire, they may take a third and further step by vesting their diplomatic representatives residing in any city, such as The Hague, under the presidency of the resident minister of foreign affairs, with such powers of supervision and of initiative as to them shall seem meet and proper. The delegates of the Nations may, if they are willing, enter into a more perfect Union, and in conference assembled render the Society of Nations, as delegates in convention rendered the Articles of Confederation, " adequate to the exigencies of government and the preservation of the Union."

APPENDIX

A. PLANS OF UNION FOR THE COLONIES AND THE STATES OF NORTH AMERICA.[1]

I. THE NEW ENGLAND CONFEDERATION OF 1643 [2]

Articles of Confederation (ratified September 7, 1643).

ARTICLES
of
Confederation betwixt the Plantations under the Government of the
Massachusets, the Plantations under the Government of *Plimouth,*
the Plantations under the Government of *Connectecut,* and the
Government of *New Haven,* with the Plantations in
Combination therewith.

Whereas we all came into these parts of *America,* with one and the same end and ayme, namely, to advance the Kingdome of our Lord Jesus Christ, and to enjoy the liberties of the Gospel, in purity with peace; and whereas in our settling (by a wise providence of God) we are further dispersed upon the Sea-Coasts, and Rivers, then was at first intended, so that we cannot (according to our desire) with convenience communicate in one Government, and Jurisdiction; and whereas we live encompassed with people of severall Nations, and strange languages, which hereafter may prove injurious to us, and our posterity: And forasmuch as the Natives have formerly committed sundry insolencies and outrages upon severall Plantations of the English, and have of late combined themselves against us. And seeing by reason of the sad distractions in *England,* which they have heard of, and by which they know we are hindred both from that humble way of seeking advice, and reaping those comfortable fruits of protection which, at other times, we might well expect; we therefore doe conceive it our bounden duty, without delay, to enter into a present Consotiation amongst our selves, for mutuall help and strength in all our future concernments, that, as in Nation, and Religion, so, in other respects, we be, and continue, One, according to the tenour and true meaning of the ensuing Articles.

[1] For the texts of the various plans and scholarly comment upon them, see Frederick D. Stone, Plans for the Union of the British Colonies of North America, 1643–1776, in Carson's *100th Anniversary of the Constitution of the United States,* 1889, Vol. ii, pp. 439–503. For a summary of early plans and suggestions of Colonial Union see also Chapter IV in Richard Frothingham's *Rise of the Republic of the United States,* 1872, pp. 109–120.

[2] Reprinted from the *Records of the Colony or Jurisdiction of New Haven,* C. J. Hoadly, ed., 1858, pp. 562–6.

I. Wherefore it is fully Agreed and Concluded by and between the parties, or Jurisdictions above named, and they doe joyntly and severally by these presents agree and conclude, That they all be, and henceforth be called by the name of, *The United Colonies of New-England.*

II. The said United Colonies for themselves, and their posterities doe joyntly and severally hereby enter into a firm and perpetuall league of friendship and amity, for offence and defence, mutuall advice and succour, upon all just occasions, both for preserving and propagating the truth, and liberties of the Gospel, and for their own mutuall safety, and wellfare.

III. It is further agreed, That the Plantations which at present are, or hereafter shall be settled within the limits of the *Massachusets,* shall be forever under the Government of the *Massachusets.* And shall have peculiar Jurisdiction amongst themselves, as an intire body; and that *Plimouth, Connecticut,* and *New-Haven,* shall each of them, in all respects, have the like peculiar Jurisdiction, and Government within their limits. And in reference to the Plantations which already are setled, or shall hereafter be erected and shall settle within any of their limits respectively, provided that no other Jurisdiction shall hereafter be taken in, as a distinct head, or Member of this Confederation, nor shall any other either Plantation, or Jurisdiction in present being, and not already in combination, or under the Jurisdiction of any of these Confederates, be received by any of them, nor shall any two of these Confederates, joyne in one Jurisdiction, without consent of the rest, which consent to be Interpreted, as in the sixt ensuing Article is expressed.

IV. It is also by these Confederates agreed, That the charge of all just Wars, whether offensive, or defensive, upon what part or Member of this Confederation soever they fall, shall both in men, provisions, and all other disbursements, be born by all the parts of this Confederation, in different proportions, according to their different abilities, in manner following, namely, That the Commissioners for each Jurisdiction, from time to time, as there shall be occasion, bring a true account and number of all the Males in each Plantation, or any way belonging to, or under their severall Jurisdictions, of what quality, or condition soever they be, from sixteen years old, to threescore, being inhabitants there. And that according to the different numbers, which from time to time shall be found in each Jurisdiction, upon a true, and just account, the service of men, and all charges of the war, be born by the poll: Each Jurisdiction, or Plantation, being left to their own just course, and custome, of rating themselves, and people, according to their different estates, with due respect to their qualities and exemptions among themselves, though the Confederation take no notice of any such priviledge. And that, according to the different charge of each Jurisdiction, and Plantation, the whole advantage of the War (if it please God so to blesse their endeavours) whether it be in Lands, Goods, or persons, shall be proportionably divided among the said Confederates.

V. It is further agreed, That if any of these Jurisdictions, or any Plantation under, or in Combination with them, be invaded by any enemy whomsoever, upon notice, and request of any three Magistrates of that Jurisdiction so invaded.

The rest of the Confederates, without any further meeting or expostulation, shall forthwith send ayde to the Confederate in danger, but in different proportion, namely the *Massachusets* one hundred men sufficiently armed, and provided for such a service, and journey. And each of the rest five and forty men, so armed and provided, or any lesse number, if lesse be required, according to this proportion. But if such a Confederate may be supplyed by their next Confederate, not exceeding the number hereby agreed, they may crave help there, and seek no further for the present. The charge to be born, as in this Article is expressed. And at their return to be victualled, and supplied with powder and shot (if there be need) for their journey by that Jurisdiction which imployed, or sent for them. But none of the Jurisdictions to exceed these numbers, till by a meeting of the Commissioners for this Confederation, a greater ayde appear necessary. And this proportion to continue, till upon knowledge of the numbers in each Jurisdiction, which shall be brought to the next meeting, some other proportion be ordered. But in any such case of sending men for present ayde, whether before or after such order or alteration, it is agreed, That at the meeting of the Commissioners for this Confederation, the cause of such war or invasion, be duly considered, and if it appear, that the fault lay in the party so invaded, that then, that Jurisdiction, or Plantation, make just satisfaction, both to the invaders, whom they have injuried, and bear all the charges of the war themselves, without requiring any allowance from the rest of the Confederates toward the same.

And further, if any Jurisdiction see any danger of an invasion approaching, and there be time for a meeting, That in such case, three Magistrates of that Jurisdiction may summon a meeting, at such convenient place, as themselves shall think meet, to consider, and provide against the threatned danger. Provided, when they are met, they may remove to what place they please, onely while any of these four Confederates, have but three Magistrates in their Jurisdiction, a request or summons, from any two of them, shall be accounted of equall force, with the three mentioned in both the clauses of this Article, till there be an increase of Magistrates there.

VI. It is also agreed, That for the managing and concluding of all affaires proper to, and concerning the whole Confederation, two Commissioners shall be chosen by, and out of the foure Jurisdictions, namely two for the *Massachusets,* two for *Plimouth* two for *Connecticut,* and two for *New-haven,* being all in Church-fellowship with us, which shall bring full power from their severall generall Courts respectively, to hear, examine, weigh, and determine all affaires of war, or peace, leagues, aydes, charges, and numbers of men for war, division of spoyles, or whatsoever is gotten by conquest, receiving of more confederates, or Plantations into Combination with any of these Confederates, and all things of like nature, which are the proper concomitants, or consequences of such a Confederation, for amity, offence, and defence, not intermedling with the Government of any of the Jurisdictions, which by the third Article, is preserved intirely to themselves. But if these eight Commissioners when they meet, shall not all agree, yet it is concluded, That any six of the eight agreeing, shall have power to settle, and determine the businesse in question. But if six doe not agree, that then such Propositions, with their Reasons, so far as they have been debated, be sent, and referred to the foure Generall Courts, *viz.* The *Massachusets, Plymouth, Connectecut,* and *New-haven.* And if at all the said Generall Courts, the businesse so referred, be concluded, then to be prosecuted by the Confederates, and all their Members. It is further agreed, That these eight Commissioners shall meet once every year, besides extraordinary meetings, according to the fifth Article to consider, treat, and conclude of all affaires belonging to this Confederation, which meeting shall ever be the first *Thursday* in *September.* And that the next meeting after the date of these presents, which shall be accounted the second meeting, shall be at *Boston* in the *Massachusets,* the third at *Hartford,* the fourth at *New-haven,* the fifth at *Plimouth,* the sixth and seventh at *Boston;* and then *Hartford, New-haven,* and *Plymouth,* and so in course successively. If in the mean time, some middle place be not found out, and agreed on, which may be comodious for all the Jurisdictions.

VII. It is further agreed, That at each meeting of these eight Commissioners, whether ordinary or extraordinary; they all, or any six of them agreeing as before, may choose their President out of themselves, whose Office and work shall be, to take care, and direct for Order, and a comely carrying on of all proceedings in the present meeting. But he shall be invested with no such power or respect, as by which, he shall hinder the propounding or progresse of any businesse, or any way cast the scales, otherwise then in the precedent Article is agreed.

VIII. It is also agreed, That the Commissioners for this Confederation hereafter at their meetings, whether ordinary or extraordinary, as they may have Commission or opportunity, doe endeavour to frame and establish Agreements and Orders in generall cases of a civil nature, wherein all the Plantations are interested, for preserving peace amongst themselves, and preventing (as much as may be) all occasions of war, or differences with others, as about the free and speedy passage of Justice in each Jurisdiction, to all the Confederates equally, as to their own, receiving those that remove from one Plantation to another, without due Certificates, how all the Jurisdictions may carry it towards the *Indians,* that they neither grow insolent, nor be injuried without due satisfaction, least War break in upon the Confederates, through such miscarriages. It is also agreed, That if any Servant run away from his Master, into any other of these Confederated Jurisdictions, That in such case, upon the Certificate of one Magistrate in the Jurisdiction, out of which the said Servant fled, or upon other due proof, the said Servant shall be delivered either to his Master, or any other that pursues, and brings such Certificate, or proof. And that upon the escape of any Prisoner whatsoever, or fugitive, for any Criminall Cause, whether breaking Prison, or getting from the Officer or otherwise escaping, upon the Certificate of two Magistrates of the Jurisdiction out of which the escape is made, that he was a prisoner or such an offender, at the time of the escape. The Magistrates, or some of them, of that Jurisdiction where for the present the said prisoner or fugitive abideth, shall forthwith grant such a Warrant, as the case will bear, for the apprehending of any such person, and the delivery of him into the hand of the Officer, or other person who pursueth him. And if help be required for the safe returning of any such offender, it shall be granted unto him that craves the same, he paying the charges thereof.

IX. And for that the justest Wars may be of dangerous consequence, especially to the smaller Plantations in these *United Colonies,* it is agreed, That neither the *Massachusets, Plymouth, Connecticut,* nor *New-Haven,* nor any of the Members of any of them, shall at any time hereafter begin undertake or engage themselves, or this Confederation, or any part thereof in any War whatsoever (sudden exigents with the necessary consequences thereof excepted, which are also to be moderated, as much as the case will permit) without the consent and agreement of the forenamed eight Commissioners, or at least six of them, as in the sixt Article is provided. And that no charge be required of any of the Confederates in case of a defensive War, till the said Commissioners have met, and approved the Justice of the War, and have agreed upon the sum of money to be levied; which sum is then to be paid by the severall Confederates, in proportion, according to the fourth Article.

X. That in extraordinary occasions, when meetings are summoned by three Magistrates of any Jurisdiction, or two as in the fifth Article, if any of the Commissioners come not, due warning being given, or sent, it is agreed, That foure of the Commissioners shall have power to direct a War which cannot be delayed, and to send for due proportions of men, out of each Jurisdiction, as well as six might doe, if all met, but not lesse then six shall determine the justice of the War, or allow the demands, or Bills of charges, or cause any levies to be made for the same.

XI. It is further agreed, That if any of the Confederates shall hereafter break any of these present Articles, or be any other way injurious to any one of the other Jurisdictions such breach of Agreement, or injury shalbe duly considered, and ordered by the Commissioners for the other Jurisdictions, that both peace, and this present Confederation, may be intirely preserved without violation.

Lastly, this perpetuall Confederation, and the severall Articles and Agreements thereof, being read and seriously considered, both by the Generall Court for the *Massachusets,* and by the Commissioners for *Plymouth, Connecticut,* and *New-Haven,* were presently and fully allowed and confirmed by three of the fore-named Confederates, namely the *Massachusets, Connecticut,* and *New-Haven;* in testimony whereof, the Generall Court of the *Massachusets* by their Secretary, and the Commissioners for *Connecticut* and *New-Haven* subscribed them the 19 day of the third month, commonly called *May, Anno Domini,* 1643.

Only the Commissioners from *Plymouth,* having brought no Commission to conclude, desired respite to advise with their Generall Court, which was granted, and at the second meeting of the Commissioners for the Confederation, held at *Boston* in *September* following, the Commissioners for the Jurisdiction of *Plymouth,* delivered in an Order of their Generall Court, dated the 29 of *August,* 1643, by which it appeared that these Articles of Confederation were read, approved and confirmed by the said Court, and all their Townships, and their Commissioners authorized to ratifie them by their subscriptions, which they accordingly did, the 7 day of *September,* 1643.

II. WILLIAM PENN'S PLAN FOR A UNION OF THE COLONIES, FEBRUARY 8, 1698.[1]

[Plantation General Entries, XXXIV A. 102]

A Briefe and Plaine Scheam how the English Colonies in the North parts of America Viz: Boston Connecticut Road Island New York New Jerseys, Pensilvania, Maryland, Virginia and Carolina may be made more usefull to the Crowne, and one anothers peace and safty with an universall concurrence.

1st. That the severall Colonies before mentioned do meet once a year, and oftener if need be, during the war, and at least once in two years in times of peace, by their stated and appointed Deputies, to debate and resolve of such measures as are most adviseable for their better understanding, and the publick tranquility and safety

2. That in order to it two persons well qualified for sence sobriety and substance be appointed by each Province, as their Representatives or Deputies, which in the whole make the Congress to consist of twenty persons.

3. That the Kings Commissioner for that purpose specially appointed shall have the Chaire and preside in the said Congresse.

4. That they shall meet as near as conveniently may be to the most centrall Colony for ease of the Deputies.

5. Since that may in all probability, be New York both because it is near the Center of the Colonies and for that it is a Frontier and in the Kings nomination, the Gov[r] of that Colony may therefore also be the Kings High Commissioner during the Session after the manner of Scotland.

6. That their business shall be to hear and adjust all matters of Complaint or difference between Province and Province. As 1st where persons quit their own Province and goe to another, that they may avoid their just debts thô they be able to pay them, 2[d] where offenders fly Justice, or Justice cannot well be had upon such offenders in the Provinces that entertaine them, 3dly to prevent or cure injuries in point of commerce, 4th, to consider of ways and means to support the union and safety of these Provinces against the publick enemies In which Congresse the Quotas of men and charges will be much easier, and more equally sett, then it is possible for any establishment made here to do; for the Provinces, knowing their own condition and one anothers, can debate that matter with more freedome and satisfaction and better adjust and ballance their affairs in all respects for their common safty.

---

[1] Reprinted from *Documents Relative to the Colonial History of the State of New York,* J. R. Brodhead, 1851 ed., Vol. IV, pp. 296–7.

7ˡʸ That in times of war the Kings High Commissioner shall be generall or Chief Commander of the severall Quotas upon service against the Common enemy as he shall be advised, for the good and benefit of the whole.

III. BENJAMIN FRANKLIN'S PLAN FOR A UNION OF THE SEVERAL COLONIES, ADOPTED AT ALBANY, JULY 10, 1754.[1]

PLAN OF UNION

ADOPTED BY THE CONVENTION AT ALBANY; WITH THE REASONS AND MOTIVES FOR EACH ARTICLE OF THE PLAN.[2]

It is proposed that humble application be made for an act of Parliament of Great Britain, by virtue of which one general government may be formed in America, including all the said colonies, within and under which government each colony may retain its present constitution, except in the particulars wherein a change may be directed by the said act, as hereafter follows.

PRESIDENT-GENERAL AND GRAND COUNCIL

That the said general government be administered by a President-General, to be appointed and supported by the crown; and a Grand Council, to be chosen by the representatives of the people of the several colonies met in their respective Assemblies.

It was thought that it would be best the president-general should be supported as well as appointed by the crown, that so all disputes between him and the grand council concerning his salary might be prevented; as such disputes have been frequently of mischievous consequence in particular colonies, especially in time of public danger. The quit-rents of crown lands in America might in a short time be sufficient for this purpose. This choice of members for the grand council is placed in the house of representatives of each government, in order to give the people a share in this new general government, as the crown has its share by the appointment of the president-general.

[1] Reprinted, with the permission of The Macmillan Company of New York, from Albert Henry Smyth, *The Writings of Benjamin Franklin,* 1907, Vol. iii, pp. 207–227. See also *Documents Relative to the Colonial History of New York,* Vol. vi, pp. 889–891.

[2] Dr. Franklin accompanied the text of the Articles with comments here reproduced in Italics. The several *Articles,* as originally adopted are printed in Roman type.

It is to be observed, that the union was to extend to the colonies of New Hampshire, Massachusetts, Connecticut, Rhode Island, New York, New Jersey, Pennsylvania, Maryland, Virginia, North Carolina, and South Carolina, (being all the British Colonies at that time in North America, except Georgia and Nova Scotia,) "for their mutual defence and security, and for extending the British settlements in North America." Another plan was proposed in the Convention, which included only New Hampshire, Massachusetts, Connecticut, Rhode Island, New York, and New Jersey. This was printed in the volume of the COLLECTIONS of the Massachusetts Historical Society for 1800. It is a rough draft of the above Plan, with some unimportant variations. It would seem, by the *Hints* communicated to Mr. Alexander, that Franklin himself did not at first contemplate anything more that a union of the northern colonies. (Mr. Smyth's note.)

But it being proposed by the gentlemen of the council of New York, and some other counsellors among the commissioners, to alter the plan in this particular, and to give the governors and council of the several provinces a share in the choice of the grand council, or at least a power of approving and confirming, or of disallowing, the choice made by the house of representatives, it was said,

" That the government or constitution, proposed to be formed by the plan, consists of two branches; a president-general appointed by the crown, and a council chosen by the people, or by the people's representatives, which is the same thing.

" That by a subsequent article, the council chosen by the people can effect nothing without the consent of the president-general appointed by the crown; the crown possesses therefore full one half of the power of this constitution.

" That in the British constitution, the crown is supposed to possess but one third, the lords having their share.

" That this constitution seemed rather more favourable for the crown.

" That it is essential to English liberty, that the subject should not be taxed but by his own consent, or the consent of his elected representatives,

" That taxes to be laid and levied by this proposed constitution will be proposed and agreed to by the representatives of the people, if the plan in this particular be preserved;

" But if the proposed alteration should take place, it seemed as if matters may be so managed, as that the crown shall finally have the appointment, not only of the president-general, but of a majority of the grand council; for seven out of eleven governors and councils are appointed by the crown;

" And so the people in all the colonies would in effect be taxed by their governors.

" It was therefore apprehended, that such alterations of the plan would give great dissatisfaction, and that the colonies could not be easy under such a power in governors, and such an infringement of what they take to be English liberty.

" Besides, the giving a share in the choice of the grand council would not be equal with respect to all the colonies, as their constitutions differ. In some, both governor and council are appointed by the crown. In others, they are both appointed by the proprietors. In some, the people have a share in the choice of the council; in others, both government and council are wholly chosen by the people. But the house of representatives is everywhere chosen by the people; and, therefore, placing the right of choosing the grand council in the representativs is equal with respect to all.

" That the grand council is intended to represent all the several houses of representatives of the colonies, as a house of representatives doth the several towns or counties of a colony. Could all the people of a colony be consulted and unite in public measures, a house of representatives would be needless, and could all the Assemblies conveniently consult and unite in general measures, the grand council would be unnecessary.

" That a house of commons or the house of representatives, and the grand

council, are thus alike in their nature and intention. And, as it would seem improper that the King or House of Lords should have a power of disallowing or appointing members of the House of Commons; so likewise, that a governor and council appointed by the crown should have a power of disallowing or appointing members of the grand council, who, in this constitution, are to be the representatives of the people.

" If the governors and councils therefore were to have a share in the choice of any that are to conduct this general government, it should seem more proper that they choose the president-general. But, this being an office of great trust and importance to the nation, it was thought better to be filled by the immediate appointment of the crown.

" The power proposed to be given by the plan to the grand council is only a concentration of the powers of the several Assemblies in certain points for the general welfare; as the power of the president-general is, of the powers of the several governors in the same points.

" And as the choice therefore of the grand council, by the representatives of the people, neither gives the people any new powers, nor diminishes the power of the crown, it was thought and hoped the crown would not disapprove of it."

Upon the whole, the commissioners were of opinion, that the choice was most properly placed in the representatives of the people.

ELECTION OF MEMBERS

That within   months after the passing such act, the house of representatives, that happen to be sitting within that time, or that shall be especially for that purpose convened, may and shall choose members for the grand council, in the following proportion, that is to say,

Massachusett's Bay,	7
New Hampshire,	2
Connecticut,	5
Rhode Island,	2
New York,	4
New Jersey,	3
Pennsylvania,	6
Maryland,	4
Virginia,	7
North Carolina,	4
South Carolina,	4
	48

It was thought, that if the least colony was allowed two, and the others in proportion, the number would be very great, and the expense heavy; and that less than two would not be convenient, as, a single person being by any accident prevented appearing at the meeting, the colony he ought to appear for would not be

*represented.   That as the choice was not immediately popular, they would be gen-
erally men of good abilities for business, and men of reputation for integrity; and
that forty-eight such men might be a number sufficient.   But though it was thought
reasonable that each colony should have a share in the representative body in some
degree according to the proportion it contributed to the general treasury, yet the
proportion of wealth or power of the colonies is not to be judged by the proportion here fixed; because it was at first agreed, that the greatest colony should not
have more than seven members, nor the least less than two; and the setting these
proportions between these two extremes was not nicely attended to, as it would
find itself, after the first election, from the sums brought into the treasury, as by
a subsequent article.*

PLACE OF FIRST MEETING

—— who shall meet for the first time at the city of Philadelphia in Pennsylvania,
being called by the President-General as soon as conveniently may be after his
appointment.

*Philadelphia was named as being nearer the centre of the colonies, where the
commissioners would be well and cheaply accommodated.   The high roads,
through the whole extent, are for the most part very good, in which forty or fifty
miles a day may very well be, and frequently are, travelled.   Great part of the
way may likewise be gone by water.   In summer time, the passages are frequently
performed in a week from Charleston to Philadelphia and New York; and from
Rhode Island to New York through the Sound, in two or three days; and from
New York to Philadelphia, by water and land, in two days, by stage, boats and
wheel carriages that set out every other day.   The journey from Charleston to
Philadelphia may likewise be facilitated by boats running up Chesapeake Bay
three hundred miles.   But if the whole journey be performed on horseback, the
most distant members, viz. the two from New Hampshire and from South Carolina may probably render themselves at Philadelphia in fifteen or twenty days; the
majority may be there in much less time.*

NEW ELECTION

That there shall be a new election of the members of the Grand Council every
three years; and, on the death or resignation of any member, his place should be
supplied by a new choice at the next sitting of the Assembly of the colony he
represented.

*Some colonies have annual assemblies, some continue during a governor's
pleasure; three years was thought a reasonable medium, as affording a new member time to improve himself in the business, and to act after such improvement,
and yet giving opportunities, frequently enough, to change him, if he has mis-
behaved.*

PROPORTION OF MEMBERS AFTER THE FIRST THREE YEARS

That after the first three years, when the proportion of money arising out of each colony to the general treasury can be known, the number of members to be chosen for each colony shall from time to time, in all ensuing elections, be regulated by that proportion, yet so as that the number to be chosen by any one province be not more than seven, nor less than two.

By a subsequent article it is proposed, that the general council shall lay and levy such general duties, as to them may appear most equal and least burthensome, &c. Suppose, for instance, they lay a small duty or excise on some commodity imported into or made in the colonies, and pretty generally and equally used in all of them, as rum perhaps, or wine; the yearly produce of this duty or excise, if fairly collected, would be in some colonies greater, in others less, as the colonies are greater or smaller. When the collector's accounts are brought in, the proportions will appear; and from them it is proposed to regulate the proportion of representatives to be chosen at the next general election, within the limits however of seven and two. These numbers may therefore vary in the course of years, as the colonies may in the growth and increase of people. And thus the quota of tax from each colony would naturally vary with its circumstances thereby preventing all disputes and dissatisfaction about the just proportions due from each; which might otherwise produce pernicious consequences, and destroy the harmony and good agreement that ought to subsist between the several parts of the Union.

MEETINGS OF THE GRAND COUNCIL, AND CALL

That the Grand Council shall meet once in every year, and oftener if occasion require, at such time and place as they shall adjourn to at the last preceding meeting, or as they shall be called to meet at by the President-General on any emergency; he having first obtained in writing the consent of seven of the members to such call, and sent due and timely notice to the whole.

It was thought, in establishing and governing new colonies or settlements, regulating Indian trade, Indian treaties, &c., there would be every year sufficient business arise to require at least one meeting, and at such meeting many things might be suggested for the benefit of all the colonies. This annual meeting may either be at a time or place certain, to be fixed by the president-general and grand council at their first meeting; or left at liberty, to be at such time and place as they shall adjourn to, or be called to meet at by the president-general.

In time of war it seems convenient, that the meeting should be in that colony, which is nearest the seat of action.

The power of calling them on any emergency seemed necessary to be vested in the president-general; but, that such power might not be wantonly used to harass the members, and oblige them to make frequent long journeys to little purpose, the consent of seven at least to such call was supposed a convenient guard.

CONTINUANCE

That the Grand Council have power to choose their speaker; and shall neither be dissolved, prorogued, nor continued sitting longer than six weeks at one time, without their own consent or the special command of the crown.

The speaker should be presented for approbation; it being convenient, to pre-vent misunderstandings and disgusts, that the mouth of the councils should be a person agreeable, if possible, both to the council and president-general.

Governors have sometimes wantonly exercised the power of proroguing or continuing the sessions of assemblies, merely to harass the members and compel a compliance; and sometimes dissolve them on slight disgusts. This it was feared might be done by the president-general, if not provided against; and the incon-venience and hardship would be greater in the general government than in par-ticular colonies, in proportion to the distance the members must be from home during sittings, and the long journeys some of them must necessarily take.

MEMBERS' ALLOWANCE

That the members of the Grand Council shall be allowed for their service ten shillings sterling per diem, during their session and journey to and from the place of meeting; twenty miles to be reckoned a day's journey.

It was thought proper to allow some wages, lest the expense might deter some suitable persons from the service; and not to allow too great wages, lest unsuit-able persons should be tempted to cabal for the employment, for the sake of gain. Twenty miles were set down as a day's journey, to allow for accidental hindrances on the road, and the greater expenses of travelling than residing at the place of meeting.

ASSENT OF PRESIDENT-GENERAL AND HIS DUTY

That the assent of the President-General be requisite to all acts of the Grand Council, and that it be his office and duty to cause them to be carried into exe-cution.

The assent of the president-general to all acts of the grand council was made necessary, in order to give the crown its due share of influence in this govern-ment, and connect it with that of Great Britain. The president-general, besides one half of the legislative power, hath in his hands the whole executive power.

POWER OF PRESIDENT-GENERAL AND GRAND COUNCIL; TREATIES OF PEACE AND WAR

That the President-General, with the advice of the Grand Council, hold or direct all Indian treaties, in which the general interest of the colonies may be concerned; and make peace or declare war with Indian nations.

The power of making peace or war with Indian nations is at present supposed to be in every colony, and is expressly granted to some by charter, so that no new power is hereby intended to be granted to the colonies. But as, in consequence of this power, one colony might make peace with a nation that another was justly engaged in war with; or make war on slight occasions without the concurrence or approbation of neighbouring colonies, greatly endangered by it; or make par-ticular treaties of neutrality in case of a general war, to their own private advan-tage in trade, by supplying the common enemy; of all which there have been instances; it was thought better, to have all treaties of a general nature under a general direction, that so the good of the whole may be consulted and provided for.

INDIAN TRADE

That they make such laws as they judge necessary for regulating all Indian trade.

Many quarrels and wars have arisen between the colonies and Indian nations, through the bad conduct of traders who cheat the Indians after making them drunk, &c., to the great expense of the colonies, both in blood and treasure. Particular colonies are so interested in the trade, as not to be willing to admit such a regulation as might be best for the whole; and therefore it was thought best under a general direction.

INDIAN PURCHASES

That they make all purchases, from Indians for the crown, of lands not now within the bounds of particular colonies, or that shall not be within their bounds when some of them are reduced to more convenient dimensions.

Purchases from the Indians, made by private persons, have been attended with many inconveniences. They have frequently interfered, and occasioned uncertainty of titles, many disputes and expensive law suits, and hindered the settlement of the land so disputed. Then the Indians have been cheated by such private purchases, and discontent and wars have been the consequence. These would be prevented by public fair purchases.

Several of the colony charters in America extend their bounds to the South Sea, which may be perhaps three or four thousand miles in length to one or two hundred miles in breadth. It is supposed they must in time be reduced to dimensions more convenient for the common purposes of government.

Very little of the land in those grants is yet purchased of the Indians.

It is much cheaper to purchase of them, than to take and maintain the possession by force; for they are generally very reasonable in their demands for land; and the expense of guarding a large frontier against their incursions is vastly great; because all must be guarded, and always guarded, as we know not where or when to expect them.

NEW SETTLEMENTS

That they make new settlements on such purchases, by granting lands in the King's name, reserving a quit-rent to the crown for the use of the general treasury.

It is supposed better that there should be one purchaser than many; and that the crown should be that purchaser, or the Union in the name of the crown. By this means the bargains may be more easily made, the price not enhanced by numerous bidders, future disputes about private Indian purchases, and monopolies of vast tracts to particular persons (which are prejudicial to the settlement and peopling of the country), prevented; and, the land being again granted in small tracts to the settlers, the quit-rents reserved may in time become a fund for support of government, for defence of the country, ease of taxes, &c.

Strong forts on the Lakes, the Ohio, &c., may, at the same time they secure our present frontiers, serve to defend new colonies settled under their protection; and such colonies would also mutually defend and support such forts, and better secure the friendship of the far Indians.

A particular colony has scarce strength enough to extend itself by new settlements, at so great a distance from the old; but the joint force of the Union might suddenly establish a new colony or two in those parts, or extend an old colony to particular passes, greatly to the security of our present frontiers, increase of trade and people, breaking off the French communication between Canada and Louisiana, and speedy settlement of the intermediate lands.

The power of settling new colonies is therefore thought a valuable part of the plan, and what cannot so well be executed by two unions as by one.

Laws to Govern Them

That they make laws for regulating and governing such new settlements, till the crown shall think fit to form them into particular governments.

The making of laws suitable for the new colonies, it was thought, would be properly vested in the president-general and grand council; under whose protection they must at first necessarily be, and who would be well acquainted with their circumstances, as having settled them. When they are become sufficiently populous, they may by the crown be formed into complete and distinct governments.

The appointment of a sub-president by the crown, to take place in case of the death or absence of the president-general, would perhaps be an improvement of the plan; and if all the governors of particular provinces were to be formed into a standing council of state, for the advance and assistance of the president-general, it might be another considerable improvement.

Raise Soldiers and Equip Vessels, &c.

That they raise and pay soldiers and build forts for the defence of any of the colonies, and equip vessels of force to guard the coasts and protect the trade on the ocean, lakes, or great rivers; but they shall not impress men in any colony, without the consent of the legislature.

It was thought, that quotas of men, to be raised and paid by the several colonies, and joined for any public service, could not always be got together with the necessary expedition. For instance, suppose one thousand men should be wanted in New Hampshire on any emergency. To fetch them by fifties and hundreds out of every colony, as far as South Carolina, would be inconvenient, the transportation chargeable, and the occasion perhaps passed before they could be assembled; and therefore that it would be best to raise them (by offering bounty-money and pay) near the place where they would be wanted, to be discharged again when the service should be over.

Particular colonies are at present backward to build forts at their own ex-

pense, which they say will be equally useful to their neighbouring colonies; who refuse to join, on a presumption that such forts will be built and kept up, though they contribute nothing. This unjust conduct weakens the whole; but the forts being for the good of the whole, it was thought best they should be built and maintained by the whole, out of the common treasury.

In the time of war, small vessels of force are sometimes necessary in the colonies to scour the coasts of small privateers. These being provided by the Union will be an advantage in turn to the colonies which are situated on the sea, and whose frontiers on the landside, being covered by other colonies, reap but little immediate benefit from the advanced forts.

Power to Make Laws, Lay Duties, &c.

That for these purposes they have power to make laws, and lay and levy such general duties, imposts, or taxes, as to them shall appear most equal and just (considering the ability and other circumstances of the inhabitants in the several colonies), and such as may be collected with the least inconvenience to the people; rather discouraging luxury, than loading industry with unnecessary burthens.

The laws which the president-general and grand council are empowered to make are such only as shall be necessary for the government of the settlements; the raising, regulating, and paying soldiers for the general service; the regulating of Indian trade; and laying and collecting the general duties and taxes. They should also have a power to restrain the exportation of provisions to the enemy from any of the colonies, on particular occasions, in time of war. But it is not intended that they may interfere with the constitution and government of the particular colonies; who are to be left to their own laws, and to lay, levy, and apply their own taxes as before.

General Treasurer and Particular Treasurer

That they may appoint a General Treasurer and Particular Treasurer in each government, when necessary; and from time to time may order the sums in the treasuries of each government into the general treasury; or draw on them for special payments, as they find most convenient.

The treasurers here meant are only for the general funds, and not for the particular funds of each colony, which remain in the hands of their own treasurers at their own disposal.

Money, How to Issue

Yet no money to issue but by joint orders of the President-General and Grand Council; except where sums have been appropriated to particular purposes, and the President-General is previously empowered by an act to draw such sums.

To prevent misapplication of the money, or even application that might be dissatisfactory to the crown or the people, it was thought necessary, to join the president-general and grand council in all issues of money.

ACCOUNTS

That the general accounts shall be yearly settled and reported to the several Assemblies.

By communicating the accounts yearly to each Assembly, they will be satisfied of the prudent and honest conduct of their representatives in the grand council.

QUORUM

That a quorum of the Grand Council, empowered to act with the President-General, do consist of twenty-five members; among whom there shall be one or more from a majority of the colonies.

The quorum seems large, but it was thought it would not be satisfactory to the colonies in general, to have matters of importance to the whole transacted by a smaller number, or even by this number of twenty-five, unless there were among them one at least from a majority of the colonies; because otherwise, the whole quorum being made up of members from three or four colonies at one end of the union, something might be done that would not be equal with respect to the rest, and thence dissatisfaction and discords might rise to the prejudice of the whole.

LAWS TO BE TRANSMITTED

That the laws made by them for the purposes aforesaid shall not be repugnant, but, as near as may be, agreeable to the laws of England, and shall be transmitted to the King in Council for approbation, as soon as may be after their passing; and if not disapproved within three years after presentation, to remain in force.

This was thought necessary for the satisfaction of the crown, to preserve the connexion of the parts of the British empire with the whole, of the members with the head, and to induce greater care and circumspection in making of the laws, that they be good in themselves and for the general benefit.

DEATH OF THE PRESIDENT-GENERAL

That, in case of the death of the President-General, the Speaker of the Grand Council for the time being shall succeed, and be vested with the same powers and authorities, to continue till the King's pleasure be known.

It might be better, perhaps, as was said before, if the crown appointed a vice-president, to take place on the death or absence of the president-general; for so we should be more sure of a suitable person at the head of the colonies. On the death or absence of both, the speaker to take place (or rather the eldest King's governor) till his Majesty's pleasure be known.

OFFICERS, HOW APPOINTED

That all military commission officers, whether for land or sea service, to act under this general constitution, shall be nominated by the President-General; but the approbation of the Grand Council is to be obtained, before they receive their commissions.   And all civil officers are to be nominated by the Grand Council, and to receive the President-General's approbation before they officiate.

It was thought it might be very prejudicial to the service, to have officers appointed unknown to the people, or unacceptable, the generality of Americans serving willingly under officers they know; and not caring to engage in the service under strangers, or such as are often appointed by governors through favour or interest.   The service here meant, is not the stated, settled service in standing troops; but any sudden and short service, either for defence of our colonies, or invading the enemy's country; (such as the expedition to Cape Breton in the last war; in which many substantial farmers and tradesmen engaged as common soldiers, under officers of their own country, for whom they had an esteem and affection; who would not have engaged in a standing army, or under officers from England.)   It was therefore thought best to give the council the power of approving the officers, which the people will look upon as a great security of their being good men.   And without some such provision as this, it was thought the expense of engaging men in the service on any emergency would be much greater, and the number who could be induced to engage much less; and that therefore it would be most for the king's service and general benefit of the nation, that the prerogative should relax a little in this particular throughout all the colonies in America; as it had already done much more in the charters of some particular colonies, viz. Connecticut and Rhode Island.

The civil officers will be chiefly treasurers and collectors of taxes; and the suitable persons are most likely to be known by the council.

VACANCIES, HOW SUPPLIED

But, in case of vacancy by death or removal of any officer civil or military under this constitution, the Governor of the province in which such vacancy happens may appoint, till the pleasure of the President-General and Grand Council can be known.

The vacancies were thought best supplied by the governors in each province, till a new appointment can be regularly made; otherwise the service might suffer before the meeting of the president-general and grand council.

EACH COLONY MAY DEFEND ITSELF ON EMERGENCY, &C.

That the particular military as well as civil establishments in each colony remain in their present state, the general constitution notwithstanding; and that on sudden emergencies any colony may defend itself, and lay the accounts of expense thence arising before the President-General and General Council, who may allow and order payment of the same, as far as they judge such accounts just and reasonable.

Otherwise the union of the whole would weaken the parts, contrary to the design of the union.   The accounts are to be judged of by the president-general and grand council, and allowed if found reasonable.   This was thought necessary to encourage colonies to defend themselves, as the expense would be light when borne by the whole; and also to check imprudent and lavish expense in such defences.[1]

IV. BENJAMIN FRANKLIN'S SKETCH OF ARTICLES OF CONFEDERATION [2]

Read before Congress July 21, 1775.

ARTICLES OF CONFEDERATION AND PERPETUAL UNION, ENTRED IN BY THE DELEGATES OF THE SEVERAL COLONIES OF NEW HAMPSHIRE, ETC., IN GENERAL CONGRESS [3]

Met at Philadelphia May 10. 1775.

ART. I.

The Name of this Confederacy shall henceforth be THE UNITED COLONIES OF NORTH AMERICA.

[1] In Carey's *American Museum*, 1789, February (pp. 190–194), March (pp. 285–288), April (pp. 365–368), there is an elaborate article, "Albany Plan of Union," at the conclusion of which appears the following: —

"Remark February 9, 1789.

"On Reflection it now seems probable, that if the foregoing Plan or something like it had been adopted and carried into Execution, the subsequent Separation of the Colonies from the Mother Country might not so soon have happened, nor the Mischiefs suffered on both sides have occurred perhaps during another Century. For the Colonies, if so united, would have really been, as they then thought themselves, sufficient to their own Defence, and being trusted with it, as by the Plan, an Army from Britain, for that purpose would have been unnecessary; The Pretences for framing the Stamp Act would then not have existed, nor the other Projects for drawing a Revenue from America to Britain by Act of Parliament, which were the Causes of the Breach & attended with such terrible Expense of Blood and Treasure; so that the different Parts of the Empire might still have remained in Peace and Union. But the Fate of this Plan was singular. For then after many Days thorough Discussion of all its Parts in Congress it was unanimously agreed to, and Copies ordered to be sent to the Assembly of each Province for Concurrence, and one to the Ministry in England for the Approbation of the Crown. The Crown disapproved it, as having placed too much Weight in the Democratic Part of the Constitution; and every Assembly as having allowed too much to Prerogative. So it was totally rejected."

The above, as printed in *The Museum*, omits the word "Remark," but bears date at the bottom, Philadelphia, April 9, 1789. It was written by Dr. Franklin and accompanied the following letter: —

"Sir

"I thank you for the Opportunity you propose to give me of making Alterations in those old Pieces of mine which you intend to republish in your *Museum*. I have no Inclination to make any Changes in them; but should like to see the Proof Sheet, supposing your Copies may possibly be incorrect.— And if you have no Objection, you may follow the Albany Plan with the enclosed *Remark* but not as from me.

"I am, Sir

"Your humble Servant,

(Signed) "B. FRANKLIN."

Addressed on the back: —

"Mr. Mathew Carey

"Printer of the Museum."

The originals of the above papers, in the handwriting of Dr. Franklin, are in my possession.

HENRY CAREY BAIRD,

PHILADELPHIA.   — ED.

[2] Reprinted from Albert Henry Smyth, *The Writings of Benjamin Franklin* (New York, The Macmillan Co.), Vol. vi, pp. 420–426.

[3] A contemporary copy exists among the papers of the Continental Congress (vol. 47,

ART. II.

The said United Colonies hereby severally enter into a firm League of Friendship with each other, binding [on] themselves and their Posterity, for [their common] Defence against their Enemies, for the Security of their Liberties and Properties, the Safety of their Persons and Families, and their mutual and general Welfare.

ART. III.

That each Colony shall enjoy and retain as much as it may think fit of its own present Laws, Customs, Rights, Privileges, and peculiar jurisdictions within its own Limits; and may amend its own Constitution, as shall seem best to its own Assembly or Convention.

ART. IV.

That for the more convenient Management of general Interests, Delegates shall be annually elected in each Colony, to meet in General Congress at such Time and Place as shall be agreed on in the next preceding Congress. Only, where particular Circumstances do not make a Duration necessary, it is understood to be a Rule, that each succeeding Congress be held in a different Colony, till the whole Number be gone through; and so in perpetual Rotation; and that accordingly the next [Congress] after the present shall be held at Annapolis, in Maryland.

ART. V.

That the Power and Duty of the Congress shall extend to the Determining on War and Peace; the entring into Alliances, [sending and receiving ambassadors] (the reconciliation with Great Britain); the settling all Disputes and Differences between Colony and Colony, [about Limits or any other cause,] if such should arise; and the Planting of new Colonies; when proper. The Congress shall also make such general [ordinances] as, tho' necessary to the General Welfare, particular Assemblies cannot be competent to, viz. [those that may relate to our general] Commerce, or general Currency; the establishment of Posts; [and] the Regulation of [our common] Forces. The Congress shall also have the appointment of all General Officers, civil and military, appertaining to the general Confederacy, such as General Treasurer, Secretary, &c.

ART. VI.

All Charges of Wars, and all other general Expences [to be] incurr'd for the common Welfare, shall be defray'd out of a common Treasury, which is to be supply'd by each Colony in proportion to its Number of Male Polls between 16 and 60 Years of Age; the Taxes for paying that Proportion [are] to be laid and levied by [the] Laws of each Colony.

folios 1–7), L. C. It is endorsed by Franklin: "Sketch of Articles of Confederation," and, in a different hand, "Read before Congress July 21, 1775."— Smyth's note.

ART. VII.

The Number of Delegates to be elected and sent to the Congress by each Colony shall be regulated, from time to time, by the Number of [such] Polls return'd; so as that one Delegate be allowed for every 5000 Polls. And the Delegates are to bring with them to every Congress an authenticated return of the number of Polls in their respective Provinces, [which is] to be $\frac{\text{triennially}}{\text{annually}}$ taken for the Purposes above mentioned.

ART. VIII.

At every Meeting of the Congress, one half of the Members return'd, exclusive of Proxies, be necessary to make a Quorum; and each Delegate at the Congress shall have a Vote in all Cases, and, if necessarily absent, shall be allow'd to appoint [any other Delegate from the same Colony to be his] Proxy, who may vote for him.

ART. IX.

An executive Council shall be appointed by the Congress [out of their own Body,] consisting of 12 Persons; of whom, in the first appointment, [one third, viz.] (four,) shall be for one Year, (four) for two Years, and (four) for three Years; and as the said terms expire, the Vacancies shall be filled by appointments for three Years; whereby one Third of the Members will be changed annually. And each Person who has served the said Term [of three Years] as Counsellor, shall have a Respite of three Years, before he can be elected again. This Council, [of whom two thirds shall be a Quorum] in the Recess of Congress, is to execute what shall have been enjoin'd thereby; [to] manage the general [Continental] Business and Interests; to receive applications from foreign Countries; [to] prepare Matters for the Consideration of the Congress; to fill up, [pro tempore,] [continental] offices, that fall vacant; and to draw on the General Treasurer for such Monies as may be necessary for general Services, and appropriated by the Congress to such Services.

ART. X.

No Colony shall engage in an offensive War with any Nation of Indians without the Consent of the Congress, or great Council above mentioned, who are first to consider the Justice and Necessity of such War.

ART. XI.

A perpetual Alliance, offensive and defensive, is to be entred into as soon as may be with the Six Nations; their Limits to be ascertain'd and secur'd to them; their Land not to be encroach'd on, nor any private [or Colony] Purchases made of them hereafter to be held good; nor any [Contract for Lands] to be made, but between the Great Council [of the Indians] at Onondaga and the General Congress. The Boundaries and Lands of all the other Indians shall also be [ascertain'd and] secur'd to them [in the same manner,] and Persons appointed to reside among them in proper Districts; who shall take care to prevent Injustice in the Trade with them; [and be enabled at our general Expence,] by occasional small supplies, to relieve their personal Wants and Distresses. And all Purchases from them shall be by the Congress, for the General Advantage and Benefit of the United Colonies.

ART. XII.

As all new Institutions may have Imperfections, which only Time and Experience can discover, it is agreed, that the General Congress, from time [to time,] shall propose such amendments of the Constitution as may be found necessary; which, being approv'd by a Majority of the Colony Assemblies, shall be equally binding with the rest of the Articles of this Confederation.

ART. XIII.

Any and every Colony from Great Britain [upon the continent of North America,] not at present engag'd in our Association, may, upon application [and joining the said Association,] be receiv'd into the Confederation, viz. [Ireland,] the West India Islands, Quebec, St. John's, Nova Scotia, Bermudas, and the East and West Floridas; and shall [thereupon] be entitled to all the advantages of our Union, mutual Assistance, and Commerce.

These Articles shall be propos'd to the several Provincial Conventions or Assemblies, to be by them consider'd; and if approved, they are advis'd to impower their Delegates to agree to and ratify the same in the ensuing Congress. After which the Union thereby establish'd is to continue firm, till the Terms of Reconciliation proposed in the Petition of the last Congress to the King are agreed to; till the Acts since made, restraining the American Commerce [and Fisheries,] are repeal'd; till Reparation is made for the Injury done to Boston, by shutting up its Port, for the Burning of Charlestown, and for the Expence of this unjust War; and till all the British Troops are withdrawn from America. On the Arrival of these Events, the Colonies return to their former Connection and Friendship with Britain: But on Failure thereof, this Confederation is to be perpetual.

READ BEFORE CONGRESS JULY 21, 1775

Whereas.[1] It hath pleased God to bless these countries with a most plentiful

---

[1] The Resolutions which follow were printed by Mr. Bigelow ("The Complete Works of Benjamin Franklin," Vol. V, p. 554) from the original Ms. in D. S. W. They had been earlier printed in the Archives of New Jersey, Vol. X, p. 691. The use of brackets, etc., in the following text is thus explained by Mr. Worthington C. Ford. "As I find some differences between the articles as printed in the New Jersey Archives, I have taken the original on the enclosed sheets, giving the parts erased, and also distinguishing the carets or interlinear words thus []. The 'free-trade' resolutions were brought in on the same day as the articles, are written on the same paper, and all in B. F.'s Ms. I am quite sure they originally formed a part of the articles (although not numbered and placed in a different volume in the records of the Continental Congress). They were even endorsed 'Articles of Confederation,' though a pen was afterwards run through the endorsement."— Smyth's note.

harvest, whereby much corn and other provisions can be spared to foreign nations who may want the same, Resolved, That [after the expiration of Six Months] from (*and after*)[1] the [20th of July Instant,] (*being one full year after*)[1] [being] the Day appointed by a late Act of the Parliament of Great Britain, for restraining the Trade of the Confederate Colonies, all Custom-Houses [therein] (if the Act be not first rescinded) shall be shut up, and all officers of the same discharged from the Execution of their several Functions, and all the Ports of the said Colonies are hereby declared to be thenceforth open to the Ships of every State in Europe that will admit of our Commerce and protect it; who may [*torn off*] and expose to sale free of all Duties their respective Produce and Manufactures, and every kind of Merchandize, excepting Teas, and the Merchandize of Great Britain, Ireland, and the British West India Islands.

Resolved, That we will to the utmost of our Power, maintain and support this Freedom of Commerce for [two] years certain after its Commencement, any reconciliation between us and Britain notwithstanding; and as much longer beyond that term, as the late Acts of Parliament for restoring the Restraining the Commerce and fisheries, and altering the Laws and Charters of any of the Colonies, shall continue unrepealed.

ENDORSED — No. 2. (*Articles of Confederation*) A proposal for opening the ports of N. A. bro[t] in by committee — read July 21, 1775 — on motion postponed for future consideration.

V. THE DECLARATION OF INDEPENDENCE, JULY 4, 1776.[2]

The unanimous Declaration of the thirteen united States of America.

WHEN in the Course of human events, it becomes necessary for one people to dissolve the political bands which have connected them with another, and to assume among the Powers of the earth, the separate and equal station to which the Laws of Nature and of Nature's God entitle them, a decent respect to the opinions of mankind requires that they should declare the causes which impel them to the separation.

We hold these truths to be self-evident, that all men are created equal, that they are endowed by their Creator with certain unalienable Rights, that among these are Life, Liberty and the pursuit of Happiness. That to secure these rights, Governments are instituted among Men, deriving their just powers from the consent of the governed, That whenever any Form of Government becomes destructive of these ends, it is the Right of the People to alter or to abolish it, and to institute new Government, laying its foundation on such principles and organizing its powers in such form, as to them shall seem most likely to effect their Safety and Happiness. . . .

We, therefore, the Representatives of the united States of America, in General Congress, Assembled, appealing to the Supreme Judge of the world for the recti-

---

[1] The words in italics show the erasures in the original Ms.
[2] Revised Statutes of the United States, 1878, pp. 3–6.

tude of our intentions, do, in the Name, and by Authority of the good People of these Colonies, solemnly publish and declare, That these United Colonies are, and of Right ought to be Free and Independent States; that they are Absolved from all Allegiance to the British Crown, and that all political connection between them and the State of Great Britain, is and ought to be totally dissolved; and that as Free and Independent States, they have full Power to levy War, conclude Peace, contract Alliances, establish Commerce, and to do all other Acts and Things which Independent States may of right do. And for the support of this Declaration, with a firm reliance on the Protection of Divine Providence, we mutually pledge to each other our Lives, our Fortunes and our sacred Honor.

JOHN HANCOCK.

New Hampshire
JOSIAH BARTLETT
WM. WHIPPLE
MATTHEW THORNTON

Massachusetts Bay
SAML. ADAMS
JOHN ADAMS
ROBT. TREAT PAINE
ELBRIDGE GERRY

Rhode Island
STEP. HOPKINS
WILLIAM ELLERY

Connecticut
ROGER SHERMAN
SAM'EL HUNTINGTON
WM. WILLIAMS
OLIVER WOLCOTT

New York
WM. FLOYD
PHIL. LIVINGSTON
FRANS. LEWIS
LEWIS MORRIS

New Jersey
RICHD. STOCKTON
JNO. WITHERSPOON
FRAS. HOPKINSON
JOHN HART
ABRA. CLARK

Pennsylvania
ROBT. MORRIS
BENJAMIN RUSH
BENJA. FRANKLIN
JOHN MORTON

GEO. CLYMER
JAS. SMITH
GEO. TAYLOR
JAMES WILSON
GEO. ROSS

Delaware
CAESAR RODNEY
GEO. READ
THO. M'KEAN

Maryland
SAMUEL CHASE
WM. PACA
THOS. STONE
CHARLES CARROLL OF CARROLLTON

Virginia
GEORGE WYTHE
RICHARD HENRY LEE
TH. JEFFERSON
BENJA. HARRISON
THOS. NELSON, JR.
FRANCIS LIGHTFOOT LEE
CARTER BRAXTON

North Carolina
WM. HOOPER
JOSEPH HEWES
JOHN PENN

South Carolina
EDWARD RUTLEDGE
THOS. HEYWARD, Junr.
THOMAS LYNCH, Junr.
ARTHUR MIDDLETON

Georgia
BUTTON GWINNETT
LYMAN HALL
GEO. WALTON

VI. ARTICLES OF CONFEDERATION ADOPTED BY CONGRESS, NOVEMBER 15, 1777, RATIFIED BY THE LAST OF THE THIRTEEN STATES, MARCH 1, 1781.[1]

To all to whom these Presents shall come, we the undersigned Delegates of the States affixed to our Names send greeting.

Whereas the Delegates of the United States of America in Congress assembled did on the fifteenth day of November in the Year of our Lord One Thousand

---

[1] Revised Statutes of the United States, 1878, pp. 7–12.

Seven Hundred and Seventyseven, and in the Second Year of the Independence of America agree to certain articles of Confederation and perpetual Union between the States of Newhampshire, Massachusetts-bay, Rhodeisland and Providence Plantations, Connecticut, New York, New Jersey, Pennsylvania, Delaware, Maryland, Virginia, North-Carolina, South-Carolina and Georgia in the Words following, viz.

"Articles of Confederation and perpetual Union between the States of New-hampshire, Massachusetts-bay, Rhodeisland and Providence Plantations, Connecticut, New-York, New-Jersey, Pennsylvania, Delaware, Maryland, Virginia, North-Carolina, South-Carolina and Georgia.

ARTICLE I.   THE stile of this confederacy shall be " The United States of America."

ARTICLE II.   Each State retains its sovereignty, freedom and independence, and every power, jurisdiction and right, which is not by this confederation expressly delegated to the United States, in Congress assembled.

ARTICLE III.   The said States hereby severally enter into a firm league of friendship with each other, for their common defence, the security of their liberties, and their mutual and general welfare, binding themselves to assist each other, against all force offered to, or attacks made upon them, or any of them, on account of religion, sovereignty, trade, or any other pretence whatever.

ARTICLE IV.   The better to secure and perpetuate mutual friendship and intercourse among the people of the different States in this Union, the free inhabitants of each of these States, paupers, vagabonds and fugitives from justice excepted, shall be entitled to all privileges and immunities of free citizens in the several States; and the people of each State shall have free ingress and regress to and from any other State, and shall enjoy therein all the privileges of trade and commerce, subject to the same duties, impositions and restrictions as the inhabitants thereof respectively, provided that such restrictions shall not extend so far as to prevent the removal of property imported into any State, to any other State of which the owner is an inhabitant; provided also that no imposition, duties or restriction shall be laid by any State, on the property of the United States, or either of them.

If any person guilty of, or charged with treason, felony, or other high misdemeanor in any State, shall flee from justice, and be found in any of the United States, he shall upon demand of the Governor or Executive power, of the State from which he fled, be delivered up and removed to the State having jurisdiction of his offence.

Full faith and credit shall be given in each of these States to the records, acts and judicial proceedings of the courts and magistrates of every other State.

ARTICLE V.   For the more convenient management of the general interest of the United States, delegates shall be annually appointed in such manner as the legislature of each State shall direct, to meet in Congress on the first Monday in November, in every year, with a power reserved to each State, to recall its delegates, or any of them, at any time within the year, and to send others in their stead, for the remainder of the year.

No State shall be represented in Congress by less than two, nor by more than seven members; and no person shall be capable of being a delegate for more than three years in any term of six years; nor shall any person, being a delegate, be capable of holding any office under the United States, for which he, or another for his benefit receives any salary, fees or emolument of any kind.

Each State shall maintain its own delegates in a meeting of the States, and while they act as members of the committee of the States.

In determining questions in the United States, in Congress assembled, each State shall have one vote.

Freedom of speech and debate in Congress shall not be impeached or questioned in any court, or place out of Congress, and the members of Congress shall be protected in their persons from arrests and imprisonments, during the time of their going to and from, and attendance on Congress, except for treason, felony, or breach of the peace.

ARTICLE VI. No State without the consent of the United States in Congress assembled, shall send any embassy to, or receive any embassy from, or enter into any conference, agreement, alliance or treaty with any king prince or state; nor shall any person holding any office of profit or trust under the United States, or any of them, accept of any present, emolument, office or title of any kind whatever from any king, prince or foreign state; nor shall the United States in Congress assembled, or any of them, grant any title of nobility.

No two or more States shall enter into any treaty, confederation or alliance whatever between them, without the consent of the United States in Congress assembled, specifying accurately the purposes for which the same is to be entered into, and how long it shall continue.

No State shall lay any imposts or duties, which may interfere with any stipulations in treaties, entered into by the United States in Congress assembled, with any king, prince or state, in pursuance of any treaties already proposed by Congress, to the courts of France and Spain.

No vessels of war shall be kept up in time of peace by any State, except such number only, as shall be deemed necessary by the United States in Congress assembled, for the defence of such State, or its trade; nor shall any body of forces be kept up by any State, in time of peace, except such number only, as in the judgment of the United States, in Congress assembled, shall be deemed requisite to garrison the forts necessary for the defence of such State; but every State shall always keep up a well regulated and disciplined militia, sufficiently armed and accoutered, and shall provide and constantly have ready for use, in public stores, a due number of field pieces and tents, and a proper quantity of arms, ammunition and camp equipage.

No State shall engage in any war without the consent of the United States in Congress assembled, unless such State be actually invaded by enemies, or shall have received certain advice of a resolution being formed by some nation of

Indians to invade such State, and the danger is so imminent as not to admit of a delay, till the United States in Congress assembled can be consulted: nor shall any State grant commissions to any ships or vessels of war, nor letters of marque or reprisal, except it be after a declaration of war by the United States in Congress assembled, and then only against the kingdom or state and the subjects thereof, against which war has been so declared, and under such regulations as shall be established by the United States in Congress assembled, unless such State be infested by pirates, in which case vessels of war may be fitted out for that occasion, and kept so long as the danger shall continue, or until the United States in Congress assembled shall determine otherwise.

ARTICLE VII.   When land-forces are raised by any State for the common defence, all officers of or under the rank of colonel, shall be appointed by the Legislature of each State respectively by whom such forces shall be raised, or in such manner as such State shall direct, and all vacancies shall be filled up by the State which first made the appointment.

ARTICLE VIII.   All charges of war, and all other expenses that shall be incurred for the common defence or general welfare, and allowed by the United States in Congress assembled, shall be defrayed out of a common treasury, which shall be supplied by the several States, in proportion to the value of all land within each State, granted to or surveyed for any person, as such land and the buildings and improvements thereon shall be estimated according to such mode as the United States in Congress assembled, shall from time to time direct and appoint.

The taxes for paying that proportion shall be laid and levied by the authority and direction of the Legislatures of the several States within the time agreed upon by the United States in Congress assembled.

ARTICLE IX.   The United States in Congress assembled, shall have the sole and exclusive right and power of determining on peace and war, except in the cases mentioned in the sixth article — of sending and receiving ambassadors — entering into treaties and alliances, provided that no treaty of commerce shall be made whereby the legislative power of the respective States shall be restrained from imposing such imposts and duties on foreigners, as their own people are subjected to, or from prohibiting the exportation or importation of any species of goods or commodities whatsoever — of establishing rules for deciding in all cases, what captures on land or water shall be legal, and in what manner prizes taken by land or naval forces in the service of the United States shall be divided or appropriated — of granting letters of marque and reprisal in times of peace — appointing courts for the trial of piracies and felonies committed on the high seas and establishing courts for receiving and determining finally appeals in all cases of captures, provided that no member of Congress shall be appointed a judge of any of the said courts.

The United States in Congress assembled shall also be the last resort on appeal in all disputes and differences now subsisting or that hereafter may arise between two or more States concerning boundary, jurisdiction or any other cause whatever; which authority shall always be exercised in the manner following. Whenever the legislative or executive authority or lawful agent of any State in controversy with another shall present a petition to Congress, stating the matter in question and praying for a hearing, notice thereof shall be given by order of Congress to the legislative or executive authority of the other State in controversy, and a day assigned for the appearance of the parties by their lawful agents, who shall then be directed to appoint by joint consent, commissioners or judges to constitute a court for hearing and determining the matter in question: but if they can not agree, Congress shall name three persons out of each of the United States, and from the list of such persons each party shall alternately strike out one, the petitioners beginning, until the number shall be reduced to thirteen; and from that number not less than seven, nor more than nine names as Congress shall direct, shall in the presence of Congress be drawn out by lot, and the persons whose names shall be so drawn or any five of them, shall be commissioners or judges, to hear and finally determine the controversy, so always as a major part of the judges who shall hear the cause shall agree in the determination: and if either party shall neglect to attend at the day appointed, without showing reasons, which Congress shall judge sufficient, or being present shall refuse to strike, the Congress shall proceed to nominate three persons out of each State, and the Secretary of Congress shall strike in behalf of such party absent or refusing; and the judgment and sentence of the court to be appointed, in the manner before prescribed, shall be final and conclusive; and if any of the parties shall refuse to submit to the authority of such court, or to appear or defend their claim or cause, the court shall nevertheless proceed to pronounce sentence, or judgment, which shall in like manner be final and decisive, the judgment or sentence and other proceedings being in either case transmitted to Congress, and lodged among the acts of Congress for the security of the parties concerned: provided that every commissioner, before he sits in judgment, shall take an oath to be administered by one of the judges of the supreme or superior court of the State, where the cause shall be tried, " well and truly to hear and determine the matter in question, according to the best of his judgment, without favour, affection or hope of reward:" provided also that no State shall be deprived of territory for the benefit of the United States.

All controversies concerning the private right of soil claimed under different grants of two or more States, whose jurisdiction as they may respect such lands, and the States which passed such grants are adjusted, the said grants or either of them being at the same time claimed to have originated antecedent to such settlement of jurisdiction, shall on the petition of either party to the Congress of the United States, be finally determined as near as may be in the same manner as is before prescribed for deciding disputes respecting territorial jurisdiction between different States.

The United States in Congress assembled shall also have the sole and exclusive right and power of regulating the alloy and value of coin struck by their own authority, or by that of the respective States.— fixing the standard of weights and measures throughout the United States.— regulating the trade and managing all affairs with the Indians, not members of any of the States, provided that the legislative right of any State within its own limits be not infringed or violated — establishing and regulating post-offices from one State to another, throughout all the United States, and exacting such postage on the papers passing thro' the same as may be requisite to defray the expenses of the said office — appointing all officers of the land forces, in the service of the United States, excepting regimental officers — appointing all the officers of the naval forces, and commissioning all officers whatever in the service of the United States — making rules for the government and regulation of the said land and naval forces, and directing their operations.

The United States in Congress assembled shall have authority to appoint a committee, to sit in the recess of Congress, to be denominated " A Committee of the States," and to consist of one delegate from each State; and to appoint such other committees and civil officers as may be necessary for managing the general affairs of the United States under their direction — to appoint one of their number to preside, provided that no person be allowed to serve in the office of president more than one year in any term of three years; to ascertain the necessary sums of money to be raised for the service of the United States, and to appropriate and apply the same for defraying the public expenses — to borrow money, or emit bills on the credit of the United States, transmitting every half year to the respective States an account of the sums of money so borrowed or emitted,— to build and equip a navy — to agree upon the number of land forces, and to make requisitions from each State for its quota, in proportion to the number of white inhabitants in such State; which requisition shall be binding, and thereupon the Legislature of each State shall appoint the regimental officers, raise the men and cloath, arm and equip them in a soldier like manner, at the expense of the United States; and the officers and men so cloathed, armed and equipped shall march to the place appointed, and within the time agreed on by the United States in Congress assembled: but if the United States in Congress assembled shall, on consideration of circumstances judge proper that any State should not raise men, or should raise a smaller number than its quota, and that any other State should raise a greater number of men than the quota thereof, such extra number shall be raised, officered, cloathed, armed and equipped in the same manner as the quota of such State, unless the legislature of such State shall judge that such extra number cannot be safely spared out of the same, in which case they shall raise officer, cloath, arm and equip as many of such extra number as they judge can be safely spared. And the officers and men so cloathed, armed and equipped, shall march to the place appointed, and within the time agreed on by the United States in Congress assembled.

The United States in Congress assembled shall never engage in a war, nor grant letters of marque and reprisal in time of peace, nor enter into any treaties or alliances, nor coin money, nor regulate the value thereof, nor ascertain the sums and expenses necessary for the defence and welfare of the United States, or any of them, nor emit bills, nor borrow money on the credit of the United States, nor appropriate money, nor agree upon the number of vessels of war, to be built or purchased, or the number of land or sea forces to be raised, nor appoint a commander in chief of the army or navy, unless nine States assent to the same: nor shall a question on any other point, except for adjourning from day to day be determined, unless by the votes of a majority of the United States in Congress assembled.

The Congress of the United States shall have power to adjourn to any time within the year, and to any place within the United States, so that no period of adjournment be for a longer duration than the space of six months, and shall publish the journal of their proceedings monthly except such parts thereof relating to treaties, alliances or military operations, as in their judgment require secresy; and the yeas and nays of the delegates of each State on any question shall be entered on the journal, when it is desired by any delegate; and the delegates of a State, or any of them, at his or their request shall be furnished with a transcript of the said journal, except such parts as are above excepted, to lay before the Legislatures of the several States.

ARTICLE X.   The committee of the States, or any nine of them, shall be authorized to execute, in the recess of Congress, such of the powers of Congress as the United States in Congress assembled, by the consent of nine States, shall from time to time think expedient to vest them with; provided that no power be delegated to the said committee, for the exercise of which, by the articles of confederation, the voice of nine States in the Congress of the United States assembled is requisite.

ARTICLE XI.   Canada acceding to this confederation, and joining in the measures of the United States, shall be admitted into, and entitled to all the advantages of this Union: but no other colony shall be admitted into the same, unless such admission be agreed to by nine States.

ARTICLE XII.   All bills of credit emitted, monies borrowed and debts contracted by, or under the authority of Congress, before the assembling of the United States, in pursuance of the present confederation, shall be deemed and considered as a charge against the United States, for payment and satisfaction whereof the said United States, and the public faith are hereby solemnly pledged.

ARTICLE XIII.   Every State shall abide by the determinations of the United States in Congress assembled, on all questions which by this confederation are submitted to them.   And the articles of this confederation shall be inviolably observed by every State, and the Union shall be perpetual; nor shall any alteration at any time hereafter be made in any of them; unless such alteration be agreed to in a Congress of the United States, and be afterwards confirmed by the Legislatures of every State.

And whereas it hath pleased the Great Governor of the world to incline the hearts of the Legislatures we respectively represent in Congress, to approve of, and to authorize us to ratify the said articles of confederation and perpetual union.   Know ye that we the undersigned delegates, by virtue of the power and authority to us given for that purpose, do by these presents, in the name and in behalf of our respective constituents, fully and entirely ratify and confirm each and every of the said articles of confederation and perpetual union, and all and singular the matters and things therein contained: And we do further solemnly plight and engage the faith of our respective constituents, that they shall abide by the determinations of the United States in Congress assembled, on all questions, which by the said confederation are submitted to them. And that the articles thereof shall be inviolably observed by the States we re[s]pectively represent, and that the Union shall be perpetual.

In witness whereof we have hereunto set our hands in Congress. Done at Philadelphia in the State of Pennsylvania the ninth day of July in the year of our Lord one thousand seven hundred and seventy-eight, and in the third year of the independence of America.

On the part & behalf of the State of New Hampshire.

JOSIAH BARTLETT,
JOHN WENTWORTH, Junr.,
August 8th, 1778.

On the part and behalf of the State of Massachusetts Bay.

JOHN HANCOCK,
SAMUEL ADAMS,
ELDBRIDGE GERRY,
FRANCIS DANA,
JAMES LOVELL,
SAMUEL HOLTEN.

On the part and behalf of the State of Rhode Island and Providence Plantations.

WILLIAM ELLERY,
HENRY MARCHANT,
JOHN COLLINS.

On the part and behalf of the State of Connecticut.

ROGER SHERMAN,
SAMUEL HUNTINGTON,
OLIVER WOLCOTT,
TITUS HOSMER,
ANDREW ADAMS.

On the part and behalf of the State of New York.

JAS. DUANE,
FRA. LEWIS,
WM. DUER,
GOUV. MORRIS.

On the part and in behalf of the State of New Jersey, Novr. 26, 1778.

JNO. WITHERSPOON,
NATHL. SCUDDER.

On the part and behalf of the State of Pennsylvania.

ROBT. MORRIS,
DANIEL ROBERDEAU,
JONA. BAYARD SMITH,
WILLIAM CLINGAN,
JOSEPH REED, 22d July, 1778.

On the part & behalf of the State of Delaware.

THO. M'KEAN, Feby. 12, 1779.
JOHN DICKINSON, May 5th, 1779.
NICHOLAS VAN DYKE.

On the part and behalf of the State of Maryland.

JOHN HANSON, March 1, 1781.
DANIEL CARROLL, Mar. 1, 1781.

On the part and behalf of the State of Virginia.

RICHARD HENRY LEE,
JOHN BANISTER,
THOMAS ADAMS,
JNO. HARVIE,
FRANCIS LIGHTFOOT LEE.

On the part and behalf of the State of No. Carolina.

JOHN PENN, July 21st, 1778.
CORNS. HARNETT,
JNO. WILLIAMS.

On the part & behalf of the State of South Carolina.

HENRY LAURENS,
WILLIAM HENRY DRAYTON,
JNO. MATHEWS,
RICHD. HUTSON,
THOS. HEYWARD, Junr.

On the part & behalf of the State of Georgia.

JNO. WALTON, 24th July, 1778.
EDWD. TELFAIR,
EDWD. LANGWORTHY.

VII. THE CONSTITUTION OF THE UNITED STATES ADOPTED SEPTEMBER 17, 1787, IN EFFECT FROM AND AFTER MARCH 4, 1789.[1]

WE THE PEOPLE of the United States, in Order to form a more perfect Union, establish Justice, insure domestic Tranquility, provide for the common defence, promote the general Welfare, and secure the Blessings of Liberty to ourselves and

---

[1] The text of the Constitution, and the amendments thereto, are taken from the Revised Statutes of the United States, 1878, and Senate Document No. 12, 63d Congress, 1st Session.

The numbers prefixed to the clauses of the Constitution, and here placed in parentheses, do not appear in the original text.

our Posterity, do ordain and establish this CONSTITUTION for the United States of America.

ARTICLE I

SECTION 1. All legislative Powers herein granted shall be vested in a Congress of the United States, which shall consist of a Senate and House of Representatives.

SECTION 2. (1) The House of Representatives shall be composed of Members chosen every second Year by the People of the several States, and the Electors in each State shall have the Qualifications requisite for Electors of the most numerous Branch of the State Legislature.

(2) No Person shall be a Representative who shall not have attained the Age of twenty-five Years, and been seven Years a Citizen of the United States, and who shall not, when elected, be an Inhabitant of that State in which he shall be chosen.

(3) * [Representatives and direct Taxes shall be apportioned among the several States which may be included within this Union, according to their respective Numbers, which shall be determined by adding to the whole Number of free Persons, including those bound to Service for a Term of Years, and excluding Indians not taxed, three fifths of all other Persons.] The actual Enumeration shall be made within three Years after the first Meeting of the Congress of the United States, and within every subsequent Term of ten Years, in such Manner as they shall by Law direct. The Number of Representatives shall not exceed one for every thirty Thousand, but each State shall have at Least one Representative; and until such enumeration shall be made, the State of New Hampshire shall be entitled to chuse three, Massachusetts eight, Rhode-Island and Providence Plantations one, Connecticut five, New-York six, New Jersey four, Pennsylvania eight, Delaware one, Maryland six, Virginia ten, North Carolina five, South Carolina five, and Georgia three.

(4) When vacancies happen in the Representation from any State, the Executive Authority thereof shall issue Writs of Election to fill such Vacancies.

(5) The House of Representatives shall chuse their Speaker and other Officers; and shall have the sole Power of Impeachment.

SECTION 3. [(1) The Senate of the United States shall be composed of two Senators from each State, chosen by the Legislature thereof, for six Years; and each Senator shall have one Vote.] †

(2) Immediately after they shall be assembled in Consequence of the first Election, they shall be divided as equally as may be into three Classes. The Seats of the Senators of the first Class shall be vacated at the Expiration of the second Year, of the second Class at the Expiration of the fourth Year, and of the third Class at the Expiration of the sixth Year, so that one-third may be chosen every second Year; and if Vacancies happen by Resignation, or otherwise, during the

---

* The clause included in brackets is amended by the fourteenth amendment, second section.

† The first paragraph of section three of Article 1, of the Constitution of the United States, and so much of paragraph two of the same section as relates to filling vacancies are amended by the seventeenth amendment to the Constitution.

Recess of the Legislature of any State, the Executive thereof may make temporary Appointments [until the next Meeting of the Legislature, which shall then fill such Vacancies].

(3) No Person shall be a Senator who shall not have attained to the Age of thirty Years, and been nine Years a Citizen of the United States, and who shall not, when elected, be an Inhabitant of that State for which he shall be chosen.

(4) The Vice President of the United States shall be President of the Senate, but shall have no Vote, unless they be equally divided.

(5) The Senate shall chuse their other Officers, and also a President pro tempore, in the Absence of the Vice President, or when he shall exercise the Office of President of the United States.

(6) The Senate shall have the sole Power to try all Impeachments. When sitting for that Purpose, they shall be on Oath or Affirmation. When the President of the United States is tried, the Chief Justice shall preside: And no Person shall be convicted without the Concurrence of two thirds of the Members present.

(7) Judgment in Cases of Impeachment shall not extend further than to removal from Office, and disqualification to hold and enjoy any Office of honor, Trust or Profit under the United States: but the Party convicted shall nevertheless be liable and subject to Indictment, Trial, Judgment and Punishment, according to Law.

SECTION 4. (1) The Times, Places and Manner of holding Elections for Senators and Representatives, shall be prescribed in each State by the Legislature thereof; but the Congress may at any time by Law make or alter such Regulations, except as to the Places of chusing Senators.

(2) The Congress shall assemble at least once in every Year, and such Meeting shall be on the first Monday in December, unless they shall by Law appoint a different Day.

SECTION 5. (1) Each House shall be the Judge of the Elections, Returns and Qualifications of its own Members, and a Majority of each shall constitute a Quorum to do Business; but a smaller Number may adjourn from day to day, and may be authorized to compel the Attendance of absent Members, in such Manner, and under such Penalties as each House may provide.

(2) Each House may determine the Rules of its Proceedings, punish its Members for disorderly Behaviour, and, with the Concurrence of two thirds, expel a Member.

(3) Each House shall keep a Journal of its Proceedings, and from time to time publish the same, excepting such Parts as may in their Judgment require Secrecy; and the Yeas and Nays of the Members of either House on any question shall, at the Desire of one fifth of those Present, be entered on the Journal.

(4) Neither House, during the Session of Congress, shall, without the consent of the other, adjourn for more than three days, nor to any other Place than that in which the two Houses shall be sitting.

SECTION 6. (1) The Senators and Representatives shall receive a Compensation for their Services, to be ascertained by Law, and paid out of the Treasury of the United States. They shall in all Cases, except Treason, Felony and Breach of the Peace, be privileged from Arrest during their Attendance at the Session of their respective Houses, and in going to and returning from the same; and for any Speech or Debate in either House, they shall not be questioned in any other Place.

(2) No Senator or Representative shall, during the Time for which he was elected, be appointed to any civil Office under the Authority of the United States, which shall have been created, or the Emoluments whereof shall have been encreased during such time; and no Person holding any Office under the United States, shall be a Member of either House during his Continuance in Office.

SECTION 7. (1) All Bills for raising Revenue shall originate in the House of Representatives; but the Senate may propose or concur with Amendments as on other Bills.

(2) Every Bill which shall have passed the House of Representatives and the Senate, shall, before it become a Law, be presented to the President of the United States; If he approve he shall sign it, but if not he shall return it, with his Objections to that House in which it shall have originated, who shall enter the Objections at large on their Journal, and proceed to reconsider it. If after such Reconsideration two thirds of that House shall agree to pass the Bill, it shall be sent, together with the Objections, to the other House, by which it shall likewise be reconsidered, and if approved by two thirds of that House, it shall become a Law. But in all such Cases the Votes of both Houses shall be determined by Yeas and Nays, and the Names of the Persons voting for and against the Bill shall be entered on the Journal of each House respectively. If any Bill shall not be returned by the President within ten Days (Sundays excepted) after it shall have been presented to him, the Same shall be a Law, in like Manner as if he had signed it, unless the Congress by their Adjournment prevent its Return, in which Case it shall not be a Law.

(3) Every Order, Resolution, or Vote to which the Concurrence of the Senate and House of Representatives may be necessary (except on a question of Adjournment) shall be presented to the President of the United States; and before the Same shall take Effect, shall be approved by him, or being disapproved by him, shall be repassed by two thirds of the Senate and House of Representatives, according to the Rules and Limitations prescribed in the Case of a Bill.

SECTION 8. The Congress shall have Power (1) To lay and collect Taxes, Duties, Imposts and Excises, to pay the Debts and provide for the common Defence and general Welfare of the United States; but all Duties, Imposts and Excises shall be uniform throughout the United States;

(2) To borrow money on the credit of the United States;

(3) To regulate Commerce with foreign Nations, and among the several States, and with the Indian Tribes;

(4) To establish an uniform Rule of Naturalization, and uniform Laws on the subject of Bankruptcies throughout the United States;

(5) To coin Money, regulate the Value thereof, and of foreign Coin, and fix the Standard of Weights and Measures;

(6) To provide for the Punishment of counterfeiting the Securities and current Coin of the United States;

(7) To establish Post Offices and post Roads;

(8) To promote the Progress of Science and useful Arts, by securing for limited Times to Authors and Inventors the exclusive Right to their respective Writings and Discoveries;

(9) To constitute Tribunals inferior to the supreme Court;

(10) To define and punish Piracies and Felonies committed on the high Seas, and Offenses against the Law of Nations;

(11) To declare War, grant Letters of Marque and Reprisal, and make Rules concerning Captures on Land and Water;

(12) To raise and support Armies, but no Appropriation of Money to that Use shall be for a longer Term than two Years;

(13) To provide and maintain a Navy;

(14) To make Rules for the Government and Regulation of the land and naval Forces;

(15) To provide for calling forth the Militia to execute the Laws of the Union, suppress Insurrections and repel Invasions;

(16) To provide for organizing, arming, and disciplining the Militia, and for governing such Part of them as may be employed in the Service of the United States, reserving to the States respectively, the Appointment of the Officers, and the Authority of training the Militia according to the discipline prescribed by Congress;

(17) To exercise exclusive Legislation in all Cases whatsoever, over such District (not exceeding ten Miles square) as may, by Cession of particular States, and the Acceptance of Congress, become the seat of the Government of the United States, and to exercise like Authority over all Places purchased by the Consent of the Legislature of the State in which the Same shall be, for the Erection of Forts, Magazines, Arsenals, dock-Yards, and other needful Buildings; — And

(18) To make all Laws which shall be necessary and proper for carrying into Execution the foregoing Powers, and all other Powers vested by this Constitution in the Government of the United States, or in any Department or Officer thereof.

SECTION 9.   (1) The Migration or Importation of such Persons as any of the States now existing shall think proper to admit, shall not be prohibited by the Congress prior to the Year one thousand eight hundred and eight, but a tax or duty may be imposed on such Importation, not exceeding ten dollars for each Person.

(2) The Privilege of the Writ of Habeas Corpus shall not be suspended, unless when in Cases of Rebellion or Invasion the public Safety may require it.

(3) No Bill of Attainder or ex post facto Law shall be passed.

* [4] No Capitation, or other direct, Tax shall be laid, unless in Proportion to the Census or Enumeration herein before directed to be taken.

[5] No Tax or Duty shall be laid on Articles exported from any State.

[6] No Preference shall be given by any Regulation of Commerce or Revenue to the Ports of one State over those of another: nor shall Vessels bound to, or from, one State, be obliged to enter, clear, or pay Duties in another.

[7] No Money shall be drawn from the Treasury, but in Consequence of Appropriations made by Law; and a regular Statement and Account of the Receipts and Expenditures of all public Money shall be published from time to time.

[8] No Title of Nobility shall be granted by the United States; and no Person holding any Office of Profit or Trust under them, shall, without the Consent of the Congress, accept of any present, Emolument, Office, or Title, of any kind whatever, from any King, Prince, or foreign State.

SECTION 10. [1] No State shall enter into any Treaty, Alliance, or Confederation; grant Letters of Marque and Reprisal; coin Money; emit Bills of Credit; make any Thing but gold and silver Coin a Tender in Payment of Debts; pass any Bill of Attainder, ex post facto Law, or Law impairing the Obligation of Contracts, or grant any Title of Nobility.

[2] No State shall, without the Consent of the Congress, lay any Imposts or Duties on Imports or Exports, except what may be absolutely necessary for executing its inspection Laws: and the net Produce of all Duties and Imposts, laid by any State on Imports or Exports, shall be for the Use of the Treasury of the United States; and all such Laws shall be subject to the Revision and Control of the Congress.

[3] No State shall, without the Consent of Congress, lay any duty of Tonnage, keep Troops, or Ships of War in time of Peace, enter into any Agreement or Compact with another State, or with a foreign Power, or engage in War, unless actually invaded, or in such imminent Danger as will not admit of delay.

ARTICLE II

SECTION 1. [1] The executive Power shall be vested in a President of the United States of America. He shall hold his Office during the Term of four Years, and, together with the Vice President, chosen for the same Term, be elected, as follows:

[2] Each State shall appoint, in such Manner as the Legislature thereof may direct, a Number of Electors, equal to the whole Number of Senators and Representatives to which the State may be entitled in the Congress: but no Senator or Representative, or Person holding an Office of Trust or Profit under the United States, shall be appointed an Elector.

† [The Electors shall meet in their respective States, and vote by Ballot for two persons, of whom one at least shall not be an Inhabitant of the same State with themselves. And they shall make a List of all the Persons voted for, and of the Number of Votes for each; which List they shall sign and certify, and

* See XVI Amendment.
† This clause has been superseded by the twelfth amendment.

transmit sealed to the Seat of the Government of the United States, directed to the President of the Senate. The President of the Senate shall, in the Presence of the Senate and House of Representatives, open all the Certificates, and the Votes shall then be counted. The Person having the greatest Number of Votes shall be the President, if such Number be a Majority of the whole Number of Electors appointed; and if there be more than one who have such Majority, and have an equal Number of Votes, then the House of Representatives shall immediately chuse by Ballot one of them for President; and if no Person have a Majority, then from the five highest on the List the said House shall in like Manner chuse the President. But in chusing the President, the Votes shall be taken by States, the Representation from each State having one Vote; A quorum for this Purpose shall consist of a Member or Members from two thirds of the States, and a Majority of all the States shall be necessary to a Choice. In every Case, after the Choice of the President, the Person having the greatest Number of Votes of the Electors shall be the Vice President. But if there should remain two or more who have equal Votes, the Senate shall chuse from them by Ballot the Vice President.]

(3) The Congress may determine the Time of chusing the Electors, and the Day on which they shall give their Votes; which Day shall be the same throughout the United States.

(4) No Person except a natural born Citizen, or a Citizen of the United States, at the time of the Adoption of this Constitution, shall be eligible to the Office of President; neither shall any Person be eligible to that Office who shall not have attained to the Age of thirty five Years, and been fourteen Years a Resident within the United States.

(5) In Case of the Removal of the President from Office, or of his Death, Resignation, or Inability to discharge the Powers and Duties of the said Office, the Same shall devolve on the Vice President, and the Congress may by Law provide for the Case of Removal, Death, Resignation or Inability, both of the President and Vice President, declaring what Officer shall then act as President, and such Officer shall act accordingly, until the Disability be removed, or a President shall be elected.

(6) The President shall, at stated Times, receive for his Services, a Compensation, which shall neither be encreased nor diminished during the Period for which he shall have been elected, and he shall not receive within that Period any other Emolument from the United States, or any of them.

(7) Before he enter on the Execution of his Office, he shall take the following Oath or Affirmation:—"I do solemnly swear (or affirm) that I will faithfully execute the Office of President of the United States, and will to the best of my Ability, preserve, protect and defend the Constitution of the United States."

Section 2. (1) The President shall be Commander in Chief of the Army and Navy of the United States, and of the Militia of the several States, when called into the actual Service of the United States; he may require the Opinion, in writing, of the principal Officer in each of the executive Departments, upon any Subject relating to the Duties of their respective Offices, and he shall have Power to grant Reprieves and Pardons for Offences against the United States, except in Cases of Impeachment.

(2) He shall have Power, by and with the Advice and Consent of the Senate, to make Treaties, provided two thirds of the Senators present concur; and he shall nominate, and by and with the Advice and Consent of the Senate, shall appoint Ambassadors, other public Ministers and Consuls, Judges of the supreme Court, and all other Officers of the United States, whose Appointments are not herein otherwise provided for, and which shall be established by Law: but the Congress may by Law vest the Appointment of such inferior Officers, as they think proper, in the President alone, in the Courts of Law, or in the Heads of Departments.

(3) The President shall have Power to fill up all Vacancies that may happen during the Recess of the Senate, by granting Commissions which shall expire at the End of their next Session.

SECTION 3.   He shall from time to time give to the Congress Information of the State of the Union, and recommend to their Consideration such Measures as he shall judge necessary and expedient; he may, on extraordinary Occasions, convene both Houses, or either of them, and in Case of Disagreement between them, with Respect to the Time of Adjournment, he may adjourn them to such Time as he shall think proper; he shall receive Ambassadors and other public Ministers; he shall take Care that the Laws be faithfully executed, and shall Commission all the Officers of the United States.

SECTION 4.   The President, Vice President and all civil Officers of the United States, shall be removed from Office on Impeachment for, and Conviction of, Treason, Bribery, or other high Crimes and Misdemeanors.

ARTICLE III

SECTION 1.   The judicial Power of the United States, shall be vested in one supreme Court, and in such inferior Courts as the Congress may from time to time ordain and establish.   The Judges, both of the supreme and inferior Courts, shall hold their Offices during good Behaviour, and shall, at stated Times, receive for their Services, a Compensation, which shall not be diminished during their Continuance in Office.

SECTION 2.   (1) The judicial Power shall extend to all Cases, in Law and Equity, arising under this Constitution, the Laws of the United States, and Treaties made, or which shall be made, under their Authority; — to all Cases affecting Ambassadors, or other public Ministers and Consuls; — to all Cases of admiralty and maritime Jurisdiction; — to Controversies to which the United States shall be a Party; — to Controversies between two or more States; — between a State and Citizens of another State; — between Citizens of different States; — between Citizens of the same State claiming Lands under Grants of different States, and between a State, or the Citizens thereof, and foreign States, Citizens or Subjects.

(2) In all Cases affecting Ambassadors, other public Ministers and Consuls, and those in which a State shall be Party, the supreme Court shall have original Jurisdiction. In all the other Cases before mentioned, the supreme Court shall have appellate Jurisdiction, both as to Law and Fact, with such Exceptions, and under such Regulations as the Congress shall make.

(3) The Trial of all Crimes, except in Cases of Impeachment, shall be by Jury; and such Trial shall be held in the State where the said Crimes shall have been committed; but when not committed within any State, the Trial shall be at such Place or Places as the Congress may by Law have directed.

SECTION 3.   (1) Treason against the United States, shall consist only in levying War against them, or in adhering to their Enemies, giving them Aid and Comfort. No Person shall be convicted of Treason unless on the Testimony of two Witnesses to the same overt Act, or on Confession in open Court.

(2) The Congress shall have Power to declare the Punishment of Treason, but no Attainder of Treason shall work Corruption of Blood, or Forfeiture except during the Life of the Person attainted.

ARTICLE IV

SECTION 1.   Full Faith and Credit shall be given in each State to the public Acts, Records, and judicial Proceedings of every other State. And the Congress may by general Laws prescribe the Manner in which such Acts, Records and Proceedings shall be proved, and the Effect thereof.

SECTION 2.   (1) The Citizens of each State shall be entitled to all Privileges and Immunities of Citizens in the several States.

(2) A Person charged in any State with Treason, Felony, or other Crime, who shall flee from Justice, and be found in another State, shall on Demand of the executive Authority of the State from which he fled, be delivered up, to be removed to the State having jurisdiction of the Crime.

(3) No Person held to Service or Labour in one State, under the Laws thereof, escaping into another, shall, in Consequence of any Law or Regulation therein, be discharged from such Service or Labour, but shall be delivered up on Claim of the Party to whom such Service or Labour may be due.

SECTION 3.   (1) New States may be admitted by the Congress into this Union; but no new State shall be formed or erected within the Jurisdiction of any other State; nor any State be formed by the Junction of two or more States, or Parts of States, without the Consent of the Legislatures of the States concerned as well as of the Congress.

(2) The Congress shall have Power to dispose of and make all needful Rules and Regulations respecting the Territory or other Property belonging to the United States; and nothing in this Constitution shall be so construed as to Prejudice any Claims of the United States, or of any particular State.

SECTION 4.   The United States shall guarantee to every State in this Union a Republican Form of Government, and shall protect each of them against Invasion; and on Application of the Legislature, or of the Executive (when the Legislature cannot be convened) against domestic Violence.

ARTICLE V

The Congress, whenever two-thirds of both Houses shall deem it necessary, shall propose Amendments to this Constitution, or, on the Application of the Legislatures of two thirds of the several States, shall call a Convention for proposing Amendments, which, in either Case, shall be valid to all Intents and Purposes, as part of this Constitution, when ratified by the Legislatures of three fourths of the several States, or by Conventions in three fourths thereof, as the one or the other Mode of Ratification may be proposed by the Congress; Provided that no Amendment which may be made prior to the Year One thousand eight hundred and eight shall in any Manner affect the first and fourth Clauses in the Ninth Section of the first Article; and that no State, without its Consent, shall be deprived of its equal Suffrage in the Senate.

ARTICLE VI

[1] All Debts contracted and Engagements entered into, before the Adoption of this Constitution, shall be as valid against the United States under this Constitution, as under the Confederation.

[2] This Constitution, and the Laws of the United States which shall be made in Pursuance thereof; and all Treaties made, or which shall be made, under the Authority of the United States, shall be the supreme Law of the Land; and the Judges in every State shall be bound thereby, any Thing in the Constitution or Laws of any State to the Contrary notwithstanding.

[3] The Senators and Representatives before mentioned, and the Members of the several State Legislatures, and all executive and judicial Officers, both of the United States and of the several States, shall be bound by Oath or Affirmation, to support this Constitution; but no religious Test shall ever be required as a Qualification to any Office or public Trust under the United States.

ARTICLE VII

The Ratification of the Conventions of nine States, shall be sufficient for the Establishment of this Constitution between the States so ratifying the Same.

Done in Convention by the Unanimous Consent of the States present the Seventeenth Day of September in the Year of our Lord one thousand seven hundred and Eighty seven, and of the Independence of the United States of America the Twelfth. **IN WITNESS** whereof We have hereunto subscribed our Names.

G°.: WASHINGTON
Presidt and deputy from Virginia

New Hampshire.

JOHN LANGDON   NICHOLAS GILMAN

Massachusetts.

NATHANIEL GORHAM   RUFUS KING

Connecticut.

WM. SAML. JOHNSON   ROGER SHERMAN

New York.

ALEXANDER HAMILTON

New Jersey.

WIL: LIVINGSTON   WM. PATTERSON
DAVID BREARLEY   JONA: DAYTON

Pennsylvania.

B. FRANKLIN   THOMAS MIFFLIN
ROBT. MORRIS   GEO. CLYMER
THOS. FITZSIMONS   JARED INGERSOLL
JAMES WILSON   GOUV MORRIS

Delaware.

GEO: READ   GUNNING BEDFORD Jun
JOHN DICKINSON   RICHARD BASSETT
JACO: BROOM

Maryland.

JAMES McHENRY   DAN of ST THOS JENIFER
DANL. CARROLL

Virginia.

JOHN BLAIR—   JAMES MADISON Jr.

North Carolina.

WM. BLOUNT   RICHD DOBBS SPAIGHT
HU WILLIAMSON

South Carolina.

J. RUTLEDGE   CHARLES COTESWORTH PINCKNEY
CHARLES PINCKNEY   PIERCE BUTLER

Georgia.

WILLIAM FEW   ABR BALDWIN

Attest   WILLIAM JACKSON *Secretary*

B. AN ORDINANCE FOR THE GOVERNMENT OF THE TERRITORY OF THE UNITED STATES NORTHWEST OF THE RIVER OHIO[1]

SECTION 1. *Be it ordained by the United States in Congress assembled,* That the said territory, for the purpose of temporary government, be one district, subject, however, to be divided into two districts, as future circumstances may, in the opinion of Congress, make it expedient.

SEC. 2. *Be it ordained by the authority aforesaid,* That the estates both of resident and non-resident proprietors in the said territory, dying intestate, shall descend to, and be distributed among, their children and descendants of a deceased child in equal parts, the descendants of a deceased child or grandchild to take the share of their deceased parent in equal parts among them; and where there shall be no children or descendants, then in equal parts to the next of kin, in equal degree; and among collaterals, the children of a deceased brother or sister of the intestate shall have, in equal parts among them, their deceased parent's share; and there shall, in no case, be a distinction between kindred of the whole and half blood; saving in all cases to the widow of the intestate, her third part of the real estate for life, and one-third part of the personal estate; and this law relative to descents and dower, shall remain in full force until altered by the legislature of the district. And until the governor and judges shall adopt laws as hereinafter mentioned, estates in the said territory may be devised or bequeathed by wills in writing, signed and sealed by him or her in whom the estate may be (being of full age), and attested by three witnesses; and real estates may be conveyed by lease and release, or bargain and sale, signed, sealed, and delivered by the person, being of full age, in whom the estate may be, and attested by two witnesses, provided such wills be duly proved, and such conveyances be acknowledged, or the execution thereof duly proved, and be recorded within one year after proper magistrates, courts, and registers, shall be appointed for that purpose; and personal property may be transferred by delivery, saving, however, to the French and Canadian inhabitants, and other settlers of the Kaskaskies, Saint Vincents, and the neighboring villages, who have heretofore professed themselves citizens of Virginia, their laws and customs now in force among them, relative to the descent and conveyance of property.

SEC. 3. *Be it ordained by the authority aforesaid,* That there shall be appointed, from time to time, by Congress, a governor, whose commission shall continue in force for the term of three years, unless sooner revoked by Congress; he shall reside in the district, and have a freehold estate therein, in one thousand acres of land, while in the exercise of his office.

SEC. 4. There shall be appointed from time to time, by Congress, a secre-

---

[1] *Revised Statutes of the United States,* 2d ed., 1878, pp. 13–16.

tary, whose commission shall continue in force for four years, unless sooner revoked; he shall reside in the district, and have a freehold estate therein, in five hundred acres of land, while in the exercise of his office. It shall be his duty to keep and preserve the acts and laws passed by the legislature, and the public records of the district, and the proceedings of the governor in his executive department, and transmit authentic copies of such acts and proceedings every six months to the Secretary of Congress. There shall also be appointed a court, to consist of three judges, any two of whom to form a court, who shall have a common-law jurisdiction, and reside in the district, and have each therein a freehold estate, in five hundred acres of land, while in the exercise of their offices; and their commissions shall continue in force during good behavior.

SEC. 5. The governor and judges, or a majority of them, shall adopt and publish in the district such laws of the original States, criminal and civil, as may be necessary, and best suited to the circumstances of the district, and report them to Congress from time to time, which laws shall be in force in the district until the organization of the general assembly therein, unless disapproved of by Congress; but afterwards the legislature shall have authority to alter them as they shall think fit.

SEC. 6. The governor, for the time being, shall be commander-in-chief of the militia, appoint and commission all officers in the same below the rank of general officers; all general officers shall be appointed and commissioned by Congress.

SEC. 7. Previous to the organization of the general assembly the governor shall appoint such magistrates, and other civil officers, in each county or township, as he shall find necessary for the preservation of the peace and good order in the same. After the general assembly shall be organized the powers and duties of magistrates and other civil officers shall be regulated and defined by the said assembly; but all magistrates and other civil officers, not herein otherwise directed, shall, during the continuance of this temporary government, be appointed by the governor.

SEC. 8. For the prevention of crimes and injuries, the laws to be adopted or made shall have force in all parts of the district, and for the execution of process, criminal and civil, the governor shall make proper divisions thereof; and he shall proceed, from time to time, as circumstances may require, to lay out the parts of the district in which the Indian titles shall have been extinguished, into counties and townships, subject, however, to such alterations as may thereafter be made by the legislature.

SEC. 9. So soon as there shall be five thousand free male inhabitants, of full age, in the district, upon giving proof thereof to the governor, they shall receive authority, with time and place, to elect representatives from their counties or townships, to represent them in the general assembly: *Provided,* That for every five hundred free male inhabitants there shall be one representative, and so on, progressively, with the number of free male inhabitants, shall the right of representation increase, until the number of representatives shall amount to twenty-five;

after which the number and proportion of representatives shall be regulated by the legislature: *Provided,* That no person be eligible or qualified to act as a representative, unless he shall have been a citizen of one of the United States three years, and be a resident in the district, or unless he shall have resided in the district three years; and, in either case, shall likewise hold in his own right, in fee-simple, two hundred acres of land within the same: *Provided also,* That a freehold in fifty acres of land in the district, having been a citizen of one of the States, and being resident in the district, or the like freehold and two years' residence in the district, shall be necessary to qualify a man as an elector of a representative.

SEC. 10.   The representatives thus elected shall serve for the term of two years; and in case of the death of a representative, or removal from office, the governor shall issue a writ to the county or township, for which he was a member, to elect another in his stead, to serve for the residue of the term.

SEC. 11.   The general assembly, or legislature, shall consist of the governor, legislative council, and a house of representatives.   The legislative council shall consist of five members, to continue in office five years, unless sooner removed by Congress; any three of whom to be a quorum; and the members of the council shall be nominated and appointed in the following manner, to wit: As soon as representatives shall be elected the governor shall appoint a time and place for them to meet together, and when met they shall nominate ten persons, resident in the district, and each possessed of a freehold in five hundred acres of land, and return their names to Congress, five of whom Congress shall appoint and commission to serve as aforesaid; and whenever a vacancy shall happen in the council, by death or removal from office, the house of representatives shall nominate two persons qualified as aforesaid, for each vacancy, and return their names to Congress, one of whom Congress shall appoint and commission for the residue of the term; and every five years, four months at least before the expiration of the time of service of the members of the council, the said house shall nominate ten persons, qualified as aforesaid, and return their names to Congress, five of whom Congress shall appoint and commission to serve as members of the council five years, unless sooner removed.   And the governor, legislative council, and house of representatives shall have authority to make laws in all cases for the good government of the district, not repugnant to the principles and articles in this ordinance established and declared.   And all bills, having passed by a majority in the house, and by a majority in the council, shall be referred to the governor for his assent; but no bill, or legislative act whatever, shall be of any force without his assent.   The governor shall have power to convene, prorogue, and dissolve the general assembly when, in his opinion, it shall be expedient.

SEC. 12.   The governor, judges, legislative council, secretary, and such other officers as Congress shall appoint in the district, shall take an oath or affirmation of fidelity, and of office; the governor before the President of Congress, and all other officers before the governor.   As soon as a legislature shall be formed in the district, the council and house assembled, in one room, shall have authority, by joint ballot, to elect a delegate to Congress, who shall have a seat in Congress, with a right of debating, but not of voting, during this temporary government.

Sec. 13. And for extending the fundamental principles of civil and religious liberty, which form the basis whereon these republics, their laws and constitutions, are erected; to fix and establish those principles as the basis of all laws, constitutions, and governments, which forever hereafter shall be formed in the said territory; to provide, also, for the establishment of States, and permanent government therein, and for their admission to a share in the Federal councils on an equal footing with the original States, at as early periods as may be consistent with the general interest.

Sec. 14. It is hereby ordained and declared, by the authority aforesaid, that the following articles shall be considered as articles of compact, between the original States and the people and States in the said territory, and forever remain unalterable, unless by common consent, to wit:

ARTICLE I

No person, demeaning himself in a peaceable and orderly manner, shall ever be molested on account of his mode of worship, or religious sentiments, in the said territories.

ARTICLE II

The inhabitants of the said territory shall always be entitled to the benefits of the writs of *habeas corpus,* and of the trial by jury; of a proportionate representation of the people in the legislature, and of judicial proceedings according to the course of the common law. All persons shall be bailable, unless for capital offenses, where the proof shall be evident, or the presumption great. All fines shall be moderate; and no cruel or unusual punishment shall be inflicted. No man shall be deprived of his liberty or property, but by the judgment of his peers, or the law of the land, and should the public exigencies make it necessary, for the common preservation, to take any person's property, or to demand his particular services, full compensation shall be made for the same. And, in the just preservation of rights and property, it is understood and declared, that no law ought ever to be made or have force in the said territory, that shall, in any manner whatever, interfere with or affect private contracts, or engagements, *bona fide,* and without fraud previously formed.

ARTICLE III

Religion, morality, and knowledge being necessary to good government and the happiness of mankind, schools and the means of education shall forever be encouraged. The utmost good faith shall always be observed towards the Indians; their lands and property shall never be taken from them without their consent; and in their property, rights, and liberty they never shall be invaded or disturbed, unless in just and lawful wars authorized by Congress; but laws founded in justice and humanity, shall, from time to time, be made, for preventing wrongs being done to them, and for preserving peace and friendship with them.

ARTICLE IV

The said territory, and the States which may be formed therein, shall forever remain a part of this confederacy of the United States of America, subject to the Articles of Confederation, and to such alterations therein as shall be constitutionally made; and to all the acts and ordinances of the United States in Congress assembled, conformable thereto. The inhabitants and settlers in the said territory shall be subject to pay a part of the Federal debts, contracted, or to be contracted, and a proportional part of the expenses of government to be apportioned on them by Congress, according to the same common rule and measure by which apportionments thereof shall be made on the other States; and the taxes for paying their proportion shall be laid and levied by the authority and direction of the legislatures of the district, or districts, or new States, as in the original States, within the time agreed upon by the United States in Congress assembled. The legislatures of those districts, or new States, shall never interfere with the primary disposal of the soil by the United States in Congress assembled, nor with any regulations Congress may find necessary for securing the title in such soil to the *bona fide* purchasers. No tax shall be imposed on lands the property of the United States; and in no case shall non-resident proprietors be taxed higher than residents. The navigable waters leading into the Mississippi and Saint Lawrence, and the carrying places between the same, shall be common highways, and forever free, as well to the inhabitants of the said territory as to the citizens of the United States, and those of any other States that may be admitted into the confederacy, without any tax, impost, or duty therefor.

ARTICLE V

There shall be formed in the said territory not less than three nor more than five States; and the boundaries of the States, as soon as Virginia shall alter her act of cession and consent to the same, shall become fixed and established as follows, to wit: The western State, in the said territory, shall be bounded by the Mississippi, the Ohio, and the Wabash Rivers; a direct line drawn from the Wabash and Post Vincents, due north, to the territorial line between the United States and Canada; and by the said territorial line to the Lake of the Woods and Mississippi. The middle State shall be bounded by the said direct line, the Wabash from Post Vincents to the Ohio, by the Ohio, by a direct line drawn due north from the mouth of the Great Miami to the said territorial line, and by the said territorial line. The eastern State shall be bounded by the last-mentioned direct line, the Ohio, Pennsylvania, and the said territorial line: *Provided, however,* And it is further understood and declared, that the boundaries of these three States shall be subject so far to be altered, that, if Congress shall hereafter find it expedient, they shall have authority to form one or two States in that part of the said territory which lies north of an east and west line drawn through the southerly bend or extreme of Lake Michigan. And whenever any of the said States shall have sixty thousand free inhabitants therein, such State shall be admitted, by its delegates, into the Congress of the United States, on an equal footing with the original States, in all respects whatever; and shall be at liberty to form a permanent constitution and State government: *Provided,* The constitution and government, so to be formed, shall be republican, and in conformity to the principles contained in these articles, and so far as it can be consistent with the general interest of the confederacy, such admission shall be allowed at an earlier period, and when there may be a less number of free inhabitants in the State than sixty thousand.

ARTICLE VI

There shall be neither slavery nor involuntary servitude in the said territory, otherwise than in the punishment of crimes, whereof the party shall have been duly convicted: *Provided always,* That any person escaping into the same, from whom labor or service is lawfully claimed in any one of the original States, such fugitive may be lawfully reclaimed, and conveyed to the person claiming his or her labor or service as aforesaid.

Be it ordained by the authority aforesaid, That the resolutions of the 23d of April, 1784, relative to the subject of this ordinance, be, and the same are hereby, repealed, and declared null and void.

Done by the United States, in Congress assembled, the 13th day of July, in the year of our Lord 1787, and of their sovereignty and independence the twelfth.

C. DOCUMENTS FROM WHICH THE CONSTITUTION WAS EVOLVED.

I. TEXT OF MR. RANDOLPH'S RESOLUTIONS, PRESENTED TO THE CONVENTION MAY 29, 1787.[1]

1. Resolved that the articles of Confederation ought to be so corrected & enlarged as to accomplish the objects proposed by their institution; namely. "common defence, security of liberty and general welfare."

2. Res^d. therefore that the rights of suffrage in the National Legislature ought to be proportioned to the Quotas of contribution, or to the number of free inhabitants, as the one or the other rule may seem best in different cases.

3. Res^d. that the National Legislature ought to consist of two branches.

4. Res^d. that the members of the first branch of the National Legislature ought to be elected by the people of the several States every   for the term of   ; to be of the age of   years at least, to receive liberal stipends by which they may be compensated for the devotion of their time to public service; to be ineligible to any office established by a particular State, or under the authority of the United States, except those peculiarly belonging to the functions of the first branch, during the term of service, and for the space of   after its expiration; to be incapable of re-election for the space of   after the expiration of their term of service, and to be subject to recall.

5. Resol^d. that the members of the second branch of the National Legislature ought to be elected by those of the first, out of a proper number of persons nominated by the individual Legislatures, to be of the age of   years at least; to hold their offices for a term sufficient to ensure their independency, to receive liberal stipends, by which they may be compensated for the devotion of their time to the public service; and to be ineligible to any office established by a particular State, or under the authority of the United States, except those peculiarly belonging to the functions of the second branch, during the term of service, and for the space of   after the expiration thereof.

6. Resolved that each branch ought to possess the right of originating Acts; that the National Legislature ought to be empowered to enjoy the Legislative Rights vested in Congress by the Confederation & moreover to legislate in all cases to which the separate States are incompetent, or in which the harmony of the United States may be interrupted by the exercise of individual Legislation; to negative all laws passed by the several States, contravening in the opinion of the National Legislature the articles of Union; and to call forth the force of the Union agst. any member of the Union failing to fulfill its duty under the articles thereof.

[1] *Documentary History of the Constitution*, Vol. iii, pp. 17–20.

7. Res^d. that a National Executive be instituted; to be chosen by the National Legislature for the term of   years, to receive punctually at stated times, a fixed compensation for the services rendered, in which no increase or diminution shall be made so as to affect the Magistracy, existing at the time of increase or diminution, and to be ineligible a second time; and that besides a general authority to execute the National laws, it ought to enjoy the Executive rights vested in Congress by the Confederation.

8. Res^d. that the Executive and a convenient number of the National Judiciary, ought to compose a Council of revision with authority to examine every act of the National Legislature before it shall operate, & every act of a particular Legislature before a Negative thereon shall be final; and that the dissent of the said Council shall amount to a rejection, unless the Act of the National Legislature be again passed, or that of a particular Legislature be again negatived by   of the members of each branch.

9. Res^d. that a National Judiciary be established to consist of one or more supreme tribunals, and of inferior tribunals to be chosen by the National Legislature, to hold their offices during good behaviour; and to receive punctually at stated times fixed compensation for their services, in which no increase or diminution shall be made so as to affect the persons actually in office at the time of such increase or diminution. that the jurisdiction of the inferior tribunals shall be to hear & determine in the first instance, and of the supreme tribunal to hear and determine in the dernier resort all piracies, & felonies on the high seas, captures from an enemy; cases in which foreigners or citizens of other States applying to such jurisdictions may be interested, or which respect the collection of the National revenue; impeachments of any National officers, and questions which may involve the national peace and harmony.

10. Resolv^d. that provision ought to be made for the admission of States lawfully arising within the limits of the United States, whether from a voluntary junction of Government & Territory or otherwise, with the consent of a number of voices in the National legislature less than the whole.

11. Res^d. that a Republican Government & the territory of each State, except in the instance of a voluntary junction of Government & territory, ought to be guaranteed by the United States to each State

12. Res^d. that provision ought to be made for the continuance of Congress and their authorities and privileges, until a given day after the reform of the articles of Union shall be adopted, and for the completion of all their engagements.

13. Res^d. that provision ought to be made for the amendment of the Articles of Union whensoever it shall seem necessary, and that the assent of the National Legislature ought not to be required thereto.

14. Res^d. that the Legislative Executive & Judiciary powers within the several States ought to be bound by oath to support the articles of Union.

15. Res^d. that the amendments which shall be offered to the Confederation, by the Convention ought at a proper time, or times, after the approbation of

Congress to be submitted to an assembly or assemblies of Representatives, recommended by the several Legislatures to be expressly chosen by the people, to consider & decide thereon.

II. OUTLINE OF THE PINCKNEY PLAN PRESENTED TO THE CONVENTION MAY 29, 1787.[1]

1. A Confederation between the free and independent States of N. H. etc. is hereby solemnly made uniting them together under one general superintending Government for their common Benefit and for their Defense and Security against all Designs and Leagues that may be injurious to their Interests and against all Forc[e] [?] and Attacks offered to or made upon them or any of them

2 The Stile

3 Mutual Intercourse — Community of Privileges — Surrender of Criminals — Faith to Proceedings etc.

4 Two Branches of the Legislature — Senate — House of Delegates — together the U. S. in Congress assembled

H. D. to consist of one Member for every thousand Inhabitants ⅗ of Blacks included

Senate to be elected from four Districts — to serve by Rotation of four Years — to be elected by the H. D. either from among themselves or the People at large

5 The Senate and H. D. shall by joint Ballot annually [septennially] chuse the Presid^t. U. S. from among themselves or the People at large.— In the Presd^t. the executive authority of the U. S. shall be vested.— His Powers and Duties — He shall have a Right to advise with the Heads of the different Departments as his Council

6 Council of Revision, consisting of the Presid^t. S. for for. Affairs, S. of War, Heads of the Departments of Treasury and Admiralty or any two of them tog^r w^t the Presid^t.

7 The Members of S. and H. D. shall each have one Vote, and shall be paid out of the common Treasury.

8 The Time of the Election of the Members of the H. D. and of the Meeting of U. S. in C. assembled.

9 No State to make Treaties — lay interfering Duties — keep a naval or land Force Militia excepted to be disciplined etc according to the Regulations of the U. S.

[1] This outline of the so-called Pinckney plan laid before the Federal Convention on May 29, 1787, immediately after that of Mr. Randolph, was found by Professor Andrew C. McLaughlin among the Wilson papers deposited in the Pennsylvania Historical Society and identified by him as in James Wilson's handwriting. It is believed to be a summary made by Mr. Wilson either during the reading of the Pinckney plan upon its introduction, or from the original draft referred to the Committee of Detail, of which Mr. Wilson was a member. For fuller particulars concerning the draft, see J. Franklin Jameson, Studies in the Federal Constitution, *Annual Report of the American Historical Association*, 1902, Vol. i, pp. 130–1.
   Plan here is reprinted from *The American Historical Review*, July, 1904, Vol. IX, pp. 741–747.

10. Each State retains its Rights not expressly delegated — But no Bill of the Legislature of any State shall become a law till it shall have been laid before S. and H. D. in C. assembled and received their Approbation.

11. The exclusive Power of S. and H. D. in C. assembled

12. The S. and H. D. in C. ass. shall have exclusive Power of regulating trade and levying Imposts — Each State may lay Embargoes in Times of Scarcity

13 ———— of establishing Post-Offices

14. S. and H. D. in C. ass. shall be the last Resort on Appeal in Disputes between two or more States; which Authority shall be exercised in the following Manner etc

15. S. and H. D. in C. ass. shall institute offices and appoint officers for the Departments of for. Affairs, War, Treasury and Admiralty.

They shall have the exclusive Power of declaring what shall be Treason and Misp. of Treason agt. U. S.— and of instituting a federal judicial Court, to which an Appeal shall be allowed from the judicial Courts of the several States in all Causes wherein Questions shall arise on the Construction of Treaties made by U. S.— or on the Laws of Nations — or on the Regulations of U. S. concerning Trade and Revenue — or wherein U. S. shall be a Party — The Court shall consist of   Judges to be appointed during good Behaviour — S and H. D. in C. ass. shall have the exclusive Right of instituting in each State a Court of Admiralty, and appointing the Judges etc of the same for all maritime Causes which may arise therein respectively

16. S and H. D. in C. Ass shall have the exclusive Right of coining Money — regulating its Alloy and Value — fixing the Standard of Weights and Measures throughout U. S.

17. Points in which the Assent of more than a bare Majority shall be necessary.

18 Impeachments shall be by the H. D. before the Senate and the Judges of the federal judicial Court.

19. S. and H. D. in C. ass. shall regulate the Militia thro' the U. S.

20. Means of enforcing and compelling the Payment of the Quota of each State.

21. Manner and Conditions of admitting new States.

22. Power of dividing annexing and consolidating States, on the Consent and Petition of such States.

23. The assent of the Legislature of   States shall be sufficient to invest future additional Powers in U. S. in C. ass. and shall bind the whole Confederacy.

24. The Articles of Confederation shall be inviolably observed, and the Union shall be perpetual: unless altered as before directed

25. The said States of N. H. etc guarrantee mutually each other and their Rights against all other Powers and against all Rebellion etc.

III. REPORT OF THE COMMITTEE OF THE WHOLE ON MR. RANDOLPH'S PROPOSITIONS, JUNE 13, 1787.[1]

1. Res^d. that it is the opinion of this Committee that a National Governm^t. ought to be established, consisting of a supreme Legislative, Executive & Judiciary.

2. Resol^d. that the National Legislature ought to consist of two branches.

3. Res^d. that the members of the first branch of the National Legislature ought to be elected by the people of the several States for the term of three years, to receive fixed Stipends by which they may be compensated for the devotion of their time to public service, to be paid out of the National Treasury: to be ineligible to any office established by a particular State, or under the authority of the U. States, (except those peculiarly belonging to the functions of the first branch), during the term of service, and under the national Government for the Space of one year after its expiration.

4. Res^d. that the members of the second branch of the Nat^l. Legislature ought to be chosen by the individual Legislatures, to be of the age of 30 years at least, to hold their offices for a term sufficient to ensure their independency, namely, seven years, to receive fixed stipends by which they may be compensated for the devotion of their time to public service to be paid out of the National Treasury; to be ineligible to any office established by a particular State, or under the authority of the U. States, (except those peculiarly belonging to the functions of the second branch) during the term of service, and under the Nat^l. Gov^t. for the space of one year after its expiration.

5. Res^d. that each branch ought to possess the right of originating Acts

6. Res^d. that the Nat^l. Legislature ought to be empowered to enjoy the Legislative rights vested in Cong^s. by the Confederation, and moreover to legislate in all cases to which the separate States are incompetent; or in which the harmony of the U. S. may be interrupted by the exercise of individual legislation; to negative all laws passed by the several States contravening in the opinion of the National Legislature the articles of Union, or any treaties subsisting under the authority of the Union.

7. Res^d. that the rights of suffrage in the 1st. branch of the National Legislature, ought not to be according to the rule established in the articles of confederation but according to some equitable ratio of representation, namely, in proportion to the whole number of white & other free citizens & inhabitants, of every age sex and condition, including those bound to servitude for a term of years, & three fifths of all other persons, not comprehended in the foregoing description, except Indians not paying taxes in each State:

8. Resolved that the right of suffrage in the 2^d. branch of the National Legislature ought to be according to the rule established for the first.

9. Resolved that a National Executive be instituted to consist of a single person, to be chosen by the Nat^l. Legislature for the term of seven years, with

[1] *Documentary History of the Constitution*, Vol. iii, pp. 120–3.

power to carry into execution the national laws, to appoint to offices in cases not otherwise provided for — to be ineligible a second time, & to be removeable on impeachment and conviction of malpractices or neglect of duty — to receive a fixed stipend by which he may be compensated for the devotion of his time to public service to be paid out of the national Treasury.

10. Resol^d. that the nat^l. Executive shall have a right to negative any Legislative Act, which shall not be afterwards passed unless by two thirds of each branch of the National Legislature.

11. Resol^d. that a Nat^l. Judiciary be established, to consist of one supreme tribunal, the Judges of which to be appointed by the 2^d. branch of the Nat^l. Legislature, to hold their offices during good behaviour, & to receive punctually at stated times a fixed compensation for their services, in which no increase or diminution shall be made, so as to affect the persons actually in office at the time of such increase or diminution.

12. Resol^d. that the Nat^l. Legislature be empowered to appoint inferior Tribunals.

13. Res^d. that the jurisdiction of the Nat^l. Judiciary shall extend to all cases which respect the collection of the Nat^l. revenue, impeachments of any Nat^l. Officers, and questions which involve the national peace & harmony.

14. Res^d. that provision ought to be made for the admission of States lawfully arising within the limits of the U. States, whether from a voluntary junction of Government & territory or otherwise, with the consent of a number of voices in the Nat^l. Legislature less than the whole.

15. Res^d. that provision ought to be made for the continuance of Congress and their authorities and privileges untill a given day after the reform of the articles of Union shall be adopted and for the completion of all their engagements.

16. Res^d. that a Republican Constitution & its existing laws ought to be guaranteed to each State by the U. States.

17. Res^d. that provision ought to be made for the amendment of the Articles of Union whensoever it shall seem necessary.

18. Res^d. that the Legislative, Executive & Judiciary powers within the several States ought to be bound by oath to support the articles of Union.

19. Res^d. that the amendments which shall be offered to the confederation by the convention ought at a proper time or times after the approbation of Cong^s. to be submitted to an Assembly or Assemblies recommended by the several Legislatures to be expressly chosen by the people to consider and decide thereon.

IV. TEXT OF THE NEW JERSEY PLAN, MOVED BY MR. PATTERSON JUNE 15, 1787.[1]

1. Res^d. that the articles of Confederation ought to be so revised, corrected, & enlarged, as to render the federal Constitution adequate to the exigences of Government, & the preservation of the Union.

[1] *Documentary History,* Vol. iii, pp. 125–8.

2. Res^d. that in addition to the powers vested in the U. States in Congress, by the present existing articles of Confederation, they be authorized to pass acts for raising a revenue, by levying a duty or duties on all goods or merchandizes of foreign growth or manufacture, imported into any part of the U. States, by Stamps on paper, vellum or parchment, and by a postage on all letters or packages passing through the general post-Office, to be applied to such federal purposes as they shall deem proper & expedient; to make rules & regulations for the collection thereof; and the same from time to time, to alter & amend in such manner as they shall think proper: to pass Acts for the regulation of trade & commerce as well with foreign nations as with each other: provided that all punishments, fines, forfeitures & penalties to be incurred for contravening such acts rules and regulations shall be adjudged by the Common law Judiciaries of the State in which any offense contrary to the true intent & meaning of such Acts rules & regulations shall have been committed or perpetrated, with liberty of commencing in the first instance all suits & prosecutions for that purpose in the superior Common law Judiciary in such State, subject nevertheless, for the correction of all errors, both in law & fact in rendering judgment, to an appeal to the Judiciary of the U. States.

3. Res^d. that whenever requisitions shall be necessary, instead of the rule for making requisitions mentioned in the articles of Confederation, the United States in Cong^s. be authorized to make such requisitions in proportion to the whole number of white & other free citizens & inhabitants of every age sex and condition including those bound to servitude for a term of years & three fifths of all other persons not comprehended in the foregoing description, except Indians not paying taxes; that if such requisitions be not complied with, in the time specified therein, to direct the collection thereof in the non complying States & for that purpose to devise and pass acts directing & authorizing the same; provided that none of the powers hereby vested in the U. States in Cong^s. shall be exercised without the consent of at least   States, and in that proportion if the number of Confederated States should hereafter be increased or diminished.

4. Res^d. that the U. States in Cong^s. be authorized to elect a federal Executive to consist of   persons, to continue in office for the term of   years, to receive punctually at stated times a fixed compensation for their services, in which no increase nor diminution shall be made so as to affect the persons composing the Executive at the time of such increase or diminution, to be paid out of the federal treasury; to be incapable of holding any other office or appointment during their time of service and for   years thereafter; to be ineligible a second time, & removeable by Cong^s. on application by a majority of the Executives of the several States; that the Executives besides their general authority to execute the federal acts ought to appoint all federal officers not otherwise provided for, & to direct all military operations; provided that none of the persons composing the federal Executive shall on any occasion take command of any troops, so as personally to conduct any enterprise as General, or in any other capacity.

5. Res^d. that a federal Judiciary be established to consist of a supreme Trib-

unal the Judges of which to be appointed by the Executive, & to hold their offices during good behaviour, to receive punctually at stated times a fixed compensation for their services in which no increase nor diminution shall be made, so as to affect the persons actually in office at the time of such increase or diminution: that the Judiciary so established shall have authority to hear & determine in the first instance on all impeachments of federal officers, & by way of appeal in the dernier resort in all cases touching the rights of Ambassadors, in all cases of captures from an enemy, in all cases of piracies & felonies on the high seas, in all cases in which foreigners may be interested, in the construction of any treaty or treaties, or which may arise on any of the Acts for regulation of trade, or the collection of the federal Revenue: that none of the Judiciary shall during the time they remain in Office be capable of receive or holding any other office or appointment during their time of service, or for   thereafter.

6. Res^d. that all Acts of the U. States in Cong^s. made by virtue & in pursuance of the powers hereby & by the articles of confederation vested in them, and all Treaties made & ratified under the authority of the U. States shall be the supreme law of the respective States so far forth as those Acts or Treaties shall relate to the said States or their Citizens, and that the Judiciary of the several States shall be bound thereby in their decisions, any thing in the respective laws of the Individual States to the Contrary notwithstanding: and that if any State, or any body of men in any State shall oppose or prevent y^e. carrying into execution such acts or treaties, the federal Executive shall be authorized to call forth ye power of the Confederated States, or so much thereof as may be necessary to enforce and compel an obedience to such Acts, or an Observance of such Treaties.

7. Res^d. that provision be made for the admission of new States into the Union.

8. Res^d. that the rule for naturalization ought to be the same in every State.

9. Res^d. that a Citizen of one State committing an offence in another State of the Union, shall be deemed guilty of the same offence as if it had been committed by a Citizen of the State in which the offence was committed.

V. ALEXANDER HAMILTON'S SKETCH OF A GOVERNMENT FOR THE UNITED STATES, PRESENTED JUNE 18, 1787.[1]

I " The Supreme Legislative power of the United States of America to be vested in two different bodies of men; the one to be called the Assembly, the other the Senate who together shall form the Legislature of the United States with power to pass all laws whatsoever subject to the Negative hereafter mentioned.

II The Assembly to consist of persons elected by the people to serve for three years.

III. The Senate to consist of persons elected to serve during good behaviour;

---

[1] *Documentary History,* Vol. iii, pp. 149–151.

their election to be made by electors chosen for that purpose by the people: in order to this the States to be divided into election districts. On the death, removal or resignation of any Senator his place to be filled out of the district from which he came.

IV. The supreme Executive authority of the United States to be vested in a Governour to be elected to serve during good behaviour — the election to be made by Electors chosen by the people in the Election Districts aforesaid — The authorities & functions of the Executive to be as follows: to have a negative on all laws about to be passed, and the execution of all laws passed, to have the direction of war when authorized or begun; to have with the advice and approbation of the Senate the power of making all treaties; to have the sole appointment of the heads or chief officers of the departments of Finance, War and Foreign Affairs; to have the nomination of all other officers (Ambassadors to foreign Nations included) subject to the approbation or rejection of the Senate; to have the power of pardoning all offences except Treason; which he shall not pardon without the approbation of the Senate.

V. On the death resignation or removal of the Governour his authorities to be exercised by the President of the Senate till a Successor be appointed.

VI The Senate to have the sole power of declaring war, the power of advising and approving all Treaties, the power of approving or rejecting all appointments of officers except the heads or chiefs of the departments of Finance War and foreign affairs.

VII. The supreme Judicial authority to be vested in   Judges to hold their offices during good behaviour with adequate and permanent salaries. This Court to have original jurisdiction in all causes of capture, and an appellative jurisdiction in all causes in which the revenues of the general Government or the citizens of foreign nations are concerned.

VIII. The Legislature of the United States to have power to institute Courts in each State for the determination of all matters of general concern.

IX. The Governour Senators and all officers of the United States to be liable to impeachment for mal- and corrupt conduct; and upon conviction to be removed from office, & disqualified for holding any place of trust or profit — all impeachments to be tried by a Court to consist of the Chief or Judge of the Superior Court of Law of each State, provided such Judge shall hold his place during good behavior, and have a permanent salary.

X All laws of the particular States contrary to the Constitution or laws of the United States to be utterly void; and the better to prevent such laws being passed, the Governour or president of each State shall be appointed by the General Government and shall have a negative upon the laws about to be passed in the State of which he is the Governour or President.

XI No State to have any forces land or Naval; and the Militia of all the States to be under the sole and exclusive direction of the United States, the officers of which to be appointed and commissioned by them

VI. MR. RANDOLPH'S RESOLUTIONS AS REVISED AND ENLARGED BY THE CONVENTION AND REFERRED JULY 26, 1787, TO THE COMMITTEE OF DETAIL.[1]

Journals,
June 20.

    I. Resolved, That the government of the United States ought to consist of a supreme legislative, judiciary, and executive.

June 21.

    II. Resolved, That the legislature consist of two branches.

    III. Resolved, That the members of the first branch of the legislature ought to be elected by the people of the several states, for the term of two years; to be paid out

June 22.

of the publick treasury; to receive an adequate compensation for their services; to be of the age of twenty-

June 23.

five years at least; to be ineligible and incapable of holding any office under the authority of the United States (except those peculiarly belonging to the functions of the first branch) during the term of service of the first branch.

June 25.

    IV. Resolved, That the members of the second branch of the legislature of the United States ought to be chosen by the individual legislatures; to be of the age of thirty

June 26.

years at least; to hold their offices for six years, one third to go out biennially; to receive a compensation for the devotion of their time to the publick service; to be ineligible to and incapable of holding any office, under the authority of the United States (except those peculiarly belonging to the functions of the second branch) during the term for which they are elected, and for one year thereafter.

    V. Resolved, That each branch ought to possess the right of originating acts.

Postponed 27.

    VI. Resolved, That the national legislature ought to possess the legislative rights vested in Congress by the confed-

July 16.

eration; and moreover, to legislate in all cases for the general interests of the union, and also in those to which

July 17.

the states are separately incompetent, or in which the harmony of the United States may be interrupted by the exercise of individual legislation.

    VII. Resolved, That the legislative acts of the United States, made by virtue and in pursuance of the articles of union, and all treaties made and ratified under the authority of the United States, shall be the supreme law

[1] *Journal, Acts and Proceedings of the Federal Convention,* 1819, pp. 207–213.

July 17.

of the respective states, as far as those acts or treaties shall relate to the said states, or their citizens and inhabitants; and that the judiciaries of the several states shall be bound thereby in their decisions, any thing in the respective laws of the individual States to the contrary, notwithstanding.

July 16.

VIII. Resolved, That in the original formation of the legislature of the United States, the first branch thereof shall consist of sixty-five members; of which number

New Hampshire shall send....three,
Massachusetts ....eight,
Rhode Island ....one,
Connecticut ....five,
New York ....six,
New Jersey ....four,
Pennsylvania ....eight,
Delaware ....one,
Maryland ....six,
Virginia ....ten,
North Carolina ....five,
South Carolina ....five,
Georgia ....three.

But as the present situation of the states may probably alter in the number of their inhabitants, the legislature of the United States shall be authorized, from time to time, to apportion the number of representatives; and in case any of the states shall hereafter be divided, or enlarged by addition of territory, or any two or more states united, or any new states created within the limits of the United States, the legislature of the United States shall possess authority to regulate the number of representatives, in any of the foregoing cases, upon the principle of their number of inhabitants according to the provisions hereafter mentioned, namely — Provided always, that representation ought to be proportioned according to direct taxation. And in order to ascertain the alteration in the direct taxation, which may be required from time to time by the changes in the relative circumstances of the states —

IX. Resolved, That a census be taken within six years from the first meeting of the legislature of the United States, and once within the term of every ten years afterwards, of all the inhabitants of the United States, in the manner and according to the ratio recommended by Congress in their resolution of April 18, 1783; and that the legislature of the United States shall proportion the direct taxation accordingly.

X. Resolved, That all bills for raising or appropriating money, and for fixing the salaries of the officers of the government of the United States, shall originate in the first branch of the legislature of the United States, and shall not be altered or amended by the second branch; and that no money shall be drawn from the publick treasury, but in pursuance of appropriations to be originated by the first branch.

XI. Resolved, That in the second branch of the legislature of the United States, each state shall have an equal vote.

July 26.
XII. Resolved, That a national executive be instituted, to consist of a single person; to be chosen by the national legislature, for the term of seven years; to be ineligible a second time; with power to carry into execution the national laws; to appoint to offices in cases not otherwise provided for; to be removable on impeachment, and conviction of mal-practice or neglect of duty; to receive a fixed compensation for the devotion of his time to the publick service; to be paid out of the publick treasury.

July 21.
XIII. Resolved, That the national executive shall have a right to negative any legislative act, which shall not be afterwards passed, unless by two third parts of each branch of the national legislature.

July 18.
July 21.

July 18.
XIV. Resolved, That a national judiciary be established, to consist of one supreme tribunal, the judges of which shall be appointed by the second branch of the national legislature; to hold their offices during good behaviour; to receive punctually, at stated times, a fixed compensation for their services, in which no diminution shall be made, so as to affect the persons actually in office at the time of such diminution.

XV. Resolved, That the national legislature be empowered to appoint inferior tribunals.

XVI. Resolved, That the jurisdiction of the national judiciary shall extend to cases arising under laws passed by the general legislature; and to such other questions as involve the national peace and harmony.

XVII. Resolved, That provision ought to be made for the admission of states lawfully arising within the limits of the United States, whether from a voluntary junction of government and territory, or otherwise, with the consent of a number of voices in the national legislature less than the whole.

XVIII. Resolved, That a republican form of government shall be guarantied to each state; and that each state shall be protected against foreign and domestick violence.

July 23.   XIX. Resolved, That provision ought to be made for the amendment of the articles of union, whensoever it shall seem necessary.

XX. Resolved, That the legislative, executive, and judiciary powers, within the several states, and of the national government, ought to be bound, by oath, to support the articles of union.

XXI. Resolved, That the amendments which shall be offered to the confederation by the convention ought, at a proper time or times after the approbation of Congress, to be submitted to an assembly or assemblies of representatives, recommended by the several legislatures, to be expressly chosen by the people to consider and decide thereon.

XXII. Resolved, That the representation in the second branch of the legislature of the United States consist of two members from each state, who shall vote per capita.

July 26.   XXIII. Resolved, That it be an instruction to the committee, to whom were referred the proceedings of the convention for the establishment of a national government, to receive a clause or clauses, requiring certain qualifications of property and citizenship, in the United States, for the executive, the judiciary, and the members of both branches of the legislature of the United States.

VII.   REPORT OF THE COMMITTEE OF DETAIL, AUGUST 6, 1787.[1]

"We the people of the States of New Hampshire, Massachusetts, Rhode-Island and Providence Plantations, Connecticut, New-York, New-Jersey, Pennsylvania, Delaware, Maryland, Virginia North-Carolina, South-Carolina, and Georgia, do ordain, declare, and establish the following Constitution for the Government of Ourselves and our Posterity.

Article I

The stile of the Government shall be, " The United States of America "

II

The Government shall consist of supreme legislative, executive, and judicial powers.

[1] *Documentary History,* Vol. iii, pp. 444–458.

III

The legislative power shall be vested in a Congress, to consist of two separate and distinct bodies of men, a House of Representatives and a Senate; each of which shall in all cases have a negative on the other. The Legislature shall meet on the first Monday in December every year.

IV

SECT. 1. The members of the House of Representatives shall be chosen every second year, by the people of the several States comprehended within this Union. The qualifications of the electors shall be the same, from time to time, as those of the electors in the several States, of the most numerous branch of their own legislatures.

SECT. 2. Every member of the House of Representatives shall be of the age of twenty five years at least; shall have been a citizen of the United States for at least three years before his election; and shall be, at the time of his election, a resident of the State in which he shall be chosen.

SECT. 3. The House of Representatives shall, at its first formation, and until the number of citizens and inhabitants shall be taken in the manner herein after described, consist of sixty five Members, of whom three shall be chosen in New Hampshire, eight in Massachusetts, one in Rhode-Island and Providence Plantations, five in Connecticut, six in New-York, four in New-Jersey, eight in Pennsylvania, one in Delaware, six in Maryland, ten in Virginia, five in North-Carolina, five in South-Carolina, and three in Georgia.

SECT. 4. As the proportions of numbers in different States will alter from time to time; as some of the States may hereafter be divided; as others may be enlarged by addition of territory; as two or more States may be united; as new States will be erected within the limits of the United States, the Legislature shall, in each of these cases, regulate the number of representatives by the number of inhabitants, according to the provisions herein after made, at the rate of one for every forty thousand.

SECT. 5. All bills for raising or appropriating money, and for fixing the salaries of the officers of Government, shall originate in the House of Representatives, and shall not be altered or amended by the Senate. No money shall be drawn from the public Treasury, but in pursuance of appropriations that shall originate in the House of Representatives.

SECT. 6. The House of Representatives shall have the sole power of impeachment. It shall choose its Speaker and other officers.

SECT. 7. Vacancies in the House of Representatives shall be supplied by writs of election from the executive authority of the State, in the representation from which it shall happen.

V

SECT. 1. The Senate of the United States shall be chosen by the Legislatures of the several States. Each Legislature shall chuse two members. Vacancies may be supplied by the Executive until the next meeting of the Legislature. Each member shall have one vote.

SECT. 2.   The Senators shall be chosen for six years; but immediately after the first election they shall be divided, by lot, into three classes, as nearly as may be, numbered one, two and three.   The seats of the members of the first class shall be vacated at the expiration of the second year, of the second class at the expiration of the fourth year, of the third class at the expiration of the sixth year, so that a third part of the members may be chosen every second year.

SECT. 3.   Every member of the Senate shall be of the age of thirty years at least; shall have been a citizen in the United States for at least four years before his election; and shall be, at the time of his election, a resident of the State for which he shall be chosen.

SECT. 4.   The Senate shall chuse its own President and other officers.

VI

SECT. 1.   The times and places and manner of holding the elections of the members of each House shall be prescribed by the Legislature of each State; but their provisions concerning them may, at any time, be altered by the Legislature of the United States.

SECT. 2.   The Legislature of the United States shall have authority to establish such uniform qualifications of the members of each House, with regard to property, as to the said Legislature shall seem expedient.

SECT. 3.   In each House a majority of the members shall constitute a quorum to do business; but a smaller number may adjourn from day to day.

SECT. 4.   Each House shall be the judge of the elections, returns and qualifications of its own members.

SECT. 5.   Freedom of speech and debate in the Legislature shall not be impeached or questioned in any Court or place out of the Legislature; and the members of each House shall, in all cases, except treason felony and breach of the peace, be privileged from arrest during their attendance at Congress, and in going to and returning from it.

SECT. 6.   Each House may determine the rules of its proceedings; may punish its members for disorderly behaviour; and may expel a member.

SECT. 7.   The House of Representatives, and the Senate, when it shall be acting in a legislative capacity, shall keep a Journal of their proceedings, and shall, from time to time, publish them: and the yeas and nays of the members of each House, on any question, shall at the desire of one-fifth part of the members present, be entered on the journal.

SECT. 8.   Neither House, without the consent of the other, shall adjourn for more than three days, nor to any other place than that at which the two Houses are sitting.   But this regulation shall not extend to the Senate, when it shall exercise the powers mentioned in the   article.

SECT. 9.   The members of each House shall be ineligible to, and incapable of holding any office under the authority of the United States, during the time for which they shall respectively be elected: and the members of the Senate shall be ineligible to, and incapable of holding any such office for one year afterwards.

SECT. 10. The members of each House shall receive a compensation for their services, to be ascertained and paid by the State, in which they shall be chosen.

SECT. 11. The enacting stile of the laws of the United States shall be, " Be it enacted by the Senate and Representatives in Congress assembled."

SECT. 12. Each House shall possess the right of originating bills, except in the cases beforementioned.

SECT. 13. Every bill, which shall have passed the House of Representatives and the Senate, shall, before it become a law, be presented to the President of the United States for his revision: if, upon such revision, he approve of it, he shall signify his approbation by signing it: But if, upon such revision, it shall appear to him improper for being passed into a law, he shall return it, together with his objections against it, to that House in which it shall have originated, who shall enter the objections at large on their journal and proceed to reconsider the bill. But if after such reconsideration, two thirds of that House shall, notwith-standing the objections of the President, agree to pass it, it shall together with his objections, be sent to the other House, by which it shall likewise be reconsidered, and if approved by two thirds of the other House also, it shall become a law. But in all such cases, the votes of both Houses shall be determined by yeas and nays; and the names of the persons voting for or against the bill shall be entered on the journal of each House respectively. If any bill shall not be returned by the President within seven days after it shall have been presented to him, it shall be a law, unless the legislature by their adjournment, prevent its return; in which case it shall be a law.

VII

SECT. 1. The Legislature of the United States shall have the power to lay and collect taxes, duties, imposts and excises;

To regulate commerce with foreign nations, and among the several States;

To establish an uniform rule of naturalization throughout the United States;

To coin money;

To regulate the value of foreign coin;

To fix the standard of weights and measures,

To establish Post-offices;

To borrow money, and emit bills on the credit of the United States;

To appoint a Treasurer by ballot;

To constitute tribunals inferior to the Supreme Court;

To make rules concerning captures on land and water;

To declare the law and punishment of piracies and felonies committed on the high seas, and the punishment of counterfeiting the coin of the United States, and of offences against the law of nations;

To subdue a rebellion in any State, on the application of its legislature;

To make war;

To raise armies;

To build and equip fleets;

To call forth the aid of the militia, in order to execute the laws of the Union, enforce treaties, suppress insurrections, and repel invasions;

And to make all laws that shall be necessary and proper for carrying into execution the foregoing powers, and all other powers vested, by this Constitution, in the government of the United States, or in any department or officer thereof;

SECT. 2. Treason against the United States shall consist only in levying war against the United States, or any of them; and in adhering to the enemies of the United States, or any of them. The Legislature of the United States shall have power to declare the punishment of treason. No person shall be convicted of treason, unless on the testimony of two witnesses. No attainder of treason shall work corruption of bloods nor forfeiture, except during the life of the person attainted.

SECT. 3. The proportions of direct taxation shall be regulated by the whole number of white and other free citizens and inhabitants, of every age, sex and condition, including those bound to servitude for a term of years, and three fifths of all other persons not comprehended in the foregoing description, (except Indians not paying taxes) which number shall, within six years after the first meeting of the Legislature, and within the term of every ten years afterwards, be taken in such manner as the said Legislature shall direct.

SECT. 4. No tax or duty shall be laid by the Legislature on articles exported from any State; nor on the migration or importation of such persons as the several States shall think proper to admit; nor shall such migration or importation be prohibited.

SECT. 5. No capitation tax shall be laid, unless in proportion to the Census hereinbefore directed to be taken.

SECT. 6. No navigation act shall be passed without the assent of two thirds of the members present in each House.

SECT. 7. The United States shall not grant any title of Nobility.

VIII

The acts of the Legislature of the United States made in pursuance of this Constitution, and all treaties made under the authority of the United States shall be the supreme law of the several States, and of their citizens and inhabitants; and the judges in the several States shall be bound thereby in their decisions; any thing in the Constitution or laws of the several States to the contrary notwithstanding.

IX

SECT. 1. The Senate of the United States shall have power to make treaties, and to appoint Ambassadors, and Judges of the Supreme Court.

SECT. 2. In all disputes and controversies now subsisting, or that may hereafter subsist between two or more States, respecting jurisdiction or territory, the Senate shall possess the following powers. Whenever the Legislature, or the Executive authority, or lawful Agent of any State, in controversy with another, shall by memorial to the Senate, state the matter in question, and apply for a hearing; notice of such memorial and application shall be given by order of the Senate, to the Legislature or the Executive authority of the other State in Controversy. The Senate shall also assign a day for the appearance of the parties, by their agents, before the House. The Agents shall be directed to appoint, by joint consent, commissioners or judges to constitute a Court for hearing and determining the matter in question. But if the Agents cannot agree, the Senate shall name three persons out of each of the several States; and from the list of such persons each party shall alternately strike out one, until the number shall be reduced to thirteen; and from that number not less than seven nor more than nine names, as the Senate shall direct, shall in their presence, be drawn out by lot; and the persons whose names shall be so drawn, or any five of them shall be commissioners or Judges to hear and finally determine the controversy; provided a majority of the Judges, who shall hear the cause, agree in the determination. If either party shall neglect to attend at the day assigned, without shewing sufficient reasons for not attending, or being present shall refuse to strike, the Senate shall proceed to nominate three persons out of each State, and the Clerk of the Senate shall strike in behalf of the party absent or refusing. If any of the parties shall refuse to submit to the authority of such Court; or shall not appear to prosecute or defend their claim or cause, the Court shall nevertheless proceed to pronounce judgment. The judgment shall be final and conclusive. The proceedings shall be transmitted to the President of the Senate, and shall be lodged among the public records, for the security of the parties concerned. Every Commissioner shall, before he sit in judgment, take an oath, to be administered by one of the Judges of the Supreme or Superior Court of the State where the cause shall be tried, " well and truly to hear and determine the matter in question according to the best of his judgment, without favor, affection, or hope of reward."

Sect. 3. All controversies concerning lands claimed under different grants of two or more States, whose jurisdictions, as they respect such lands shall have been decided or adjusted subsequent to such grants, or any of them, shall, on application to the Senate, be finally determined, as near as may be, in the same manner as is before prescribed for deciding controversies between different States.

X

Sect. 1. The Executive Power of the United States shall be vested in a single person. His stile shall be, " The President of the United States of America;" and his title shall be, " His Excellency." He shall be elected by ballot by the Legislature. He shall hold his office during the term of seven years; but shall not be elected a second time.

Sect. 2. He shall, from time to time, give information to the Legislature, of the state of the Union: he may recommend to their consideration such measures as he shall judge necessary, and expedient: he may convene them on extraordinary occasions. In case of disagreement between the two Houses, with regard to the time of adjournment, he may adjourn them to such time as he thinks proper: he shall take care that the laws of the United States be duly and faithfully executed: he shall commission all the officers of the United States; and shall appoint officers in all cases not otherwise provided for by this Constitution. He shall receive Ambassadors, and may correspond with the supreme Executives of the several States. He shall have power to grant reprieves and pardons; but his pardon shall not be pleadable in bar of an impeachment. He shall be commander in chief of the Army and Navy of the United States, and of the Militia of the Several States. He shall, at stated times, receive for his services, a compensation, which shall neither be increased nor diminished during his continuance in office. Before he shall enter on the duties of his department, he shall take the following oath or affirmation, " I —— solemnly swear, (or affirm) that I will faithfully execute the office of President of the United States of America." He shall be removed from his office on impeachment by the House of Representatives, and conviction in the supreme Court, of treason, bribery, or corruption. In case of his removal as aforesaid, death, resignation, or disability to discharge the powers and duties of his office, the President of the Senate shall exercise those powers and duties, until another President of the United States be chosen, or until the disability of the President be removed.

XI

SECT. 1. The Judicial Power of the United States shall be vested in one Supreme Court, and in such inferior Courts as shall, when necessary, from time to time, be constituted by the Legislature of the United States.

SECT. 2. The Judges of the Supreme Court, and of the Inferior Courts, shall hold their offices during good behaviour. They shall, at stated times, receive for their services, a compensation, which shall not be diminished during their continuance in office.

SECT. 3. The Jurisdiction of the Supreme Court shall extend to all cases arising under laws passed by the Legislature of the United States; to all cases affecting Ambassadors, other Public Ministers and Consuls; to the trial of impeachments of Officers of the United States; to all cases of Admiralty and maritime jurisdiction; to controversies between two or more States, (except such as shall regard Territory or Jurisdiction) between a State and Citizens of another State, between Citizens of different States, and between a State or the Citizens thereof and foreign States, citizens or subjects. In cases of impeachment, cases affecting Ambassadors, other Public Ministers and Consuls, and those in which a State shall be party, this jurisdiction shall be original. In all the other cases before mentioned, it shall be appellate, with such exceptions and under such regulations as the Legislature shall make. The Legislature may assign any part of the jurisdiction above mentioned (except the trial of the President of the United States) in the manner, and under the limitations which it shall think proper, to such Inferior Courts, as it shall constitute from time to time.

SECT. 4. The trial of all criminal offences (except in cases of impeachments) shall be in the State where they shall be committed; and shall be by Jury.

SECT. 5. Judgment, in cases of Impeachment, shall not extend further than to removal from Office, and disqualification to hold and enjoy any office of honour, trust or profit, under the United States. But the party convicted shall, nevertheless be liable and subject to indictment, trial, judgment and punishment according to law.

XII

No State shall coin money; nor grant letters of marque and reprisal; nor enter into any treaty, alliance, or confederation; nor grant any title of Nobility.

XIII

No State, without the consent of the Legislature of the United States, shall emit bills of credit, or make any thing but specie a tender in payment of debts; nor lay imposts or duties on imports; not keep troops or ships of war in time of peace; nor enter into any agreement or compact with another State, or with any foreign power; nor engage in any war, unless it shall be actually invaded by enemies, or the danger of invasion be so imminent, as not to admit of delay, until the Legislature of the United States can be consulted.

XIV

The Citizens of each State shall be entitled to all privileges and immunities of citizens in the several States.

XV

Any person charged with treason, felony or high misdemeanor in any State, who shall flee from justice, and shall be found in any other State, shall, on demand of the Executive power of the State from which he fled, be delivered up and removed to the State having jurisdiction of the offence.

XVI

Full faith shall be given in each State to the acts of the Legislatures, and to the records and judicial proceedings of the Courts and Magistrates of every other State.

XVII

New States lawfully constituted or established within the limits of the United States may be admitted, by the Legislature, into this Government; but to such admission the consent of two thirds of the members present in each House shall be necessary. If a new State shall arise within the limits of any of the present States, the consent of the Legislatures of such States shall be also necessary to its admission. If the admission be consented to, the new States shall be admitted on the same terms with the original States. But the Legislature may make conditions with the new States, concerning the public debt which shall be then subsisting.

XVIII

The United States shall guaranty to each State a Republican form of Government; and shall protect each State against foreign invasions, and, on the application of its Legislature, against domestic violence.

XIX

On the application of the Legislatures of two thirds of the States in the Union, for an amendment of this Constitution, the Legislature of the United States shall call a Convention for that purpose.

XX

The members of the Legislatures, and the Executive and Judicial officers of the United States, and of the several States, shall be bound by oath to support this Constitution.

XXI

The ratification of the Conventions of   States shall be sufficient for organizing this Constitution.

XXII

This Constitution shall be laid before the United States in Congress assembled, for their approbation; and it is the opinion of this Convention, that it should be afterwards submitted to a Convention chosen, under the recommendation of its legislature, in order to receive the ratification of such Convention.

XXIII

To introduce this government, it is the opinion of this Convention, that each assenting Convention should notify its assent and ratification to the United States in Congress assembled; that Congress, after receiving the assent and ratification of the Conventions of   States, should appoint and publish a day, as early as may be, and appoint a place, for commencing proceedings under this Constitution; that after such publication, the Legislatures of the several States should elect members of the Senate, and direct the election of members of the House of Representatives; and that the members of the Legislature should meet at the time and place assigned by Congress, and should, as soon as may be, after their meeting, choose the President of the United States, and proceed to execute this Constitution."

VIII. PROCEEDINGS OF CONVENTION REFERRED TO THE COMMITTEE OF STYLE AND ARRANGEMENT, SEPTEMBER 10, 1787.[1]

We the People of the States of New-Hampshire, Massachusetts, Rhode-Island and Providence Plantations, Connecticut, New-York, New-Jersey, Pennsylvania, Delaware, Maryland, Virginia, North-Carolina, South-Carolina, and Georgia, do ordain, declare and establish the following Constitution for the Government of Ourselves and our Posterity.

Article I

The stile of this Government shall be, " The United States of America."

II

The Government shall consist of supreme legislative, executive and judicial powers.

III

The legislative power shall be vested in a Congress, to consist of two separate and distinct bodies of men, a House of Representatives, and a Senate. The Legislature shall meet at least once in every year, and such meeting shall be on the first Monday in December unless a different day shall be appointed by law.

IV

Sect. 1. The Members of the House of Representatives shall be chosen every second year, by the people of the several states comprehended within this Union. The qualifications of the electors shall be the same, from time to time, as those of the electors in the several States, of the most numerous branch of their own legislatures.

Sect. 2. Every Member of the House of Representatives shall be of the age of twenty-five years at least; shall have been a citizen of the United States for at least seven years before his election; and shall be, at the time of his election, an inhabitant of the State in which he shall be chosen.

Sect. 3. The House of Representatives shall, at its first formation and until the number of citizens and inhabitants shall be taken in the manner herein after described, consist of sixty-five members, of whom three shall be chosen in New-Hampshire, eight in Massachusetts, one in Rhode-Island and Providence Plantations, five in Connecticut, six in New-York, four in New-Jersey, eight in Pennsyl-

---

[1] Compiled by Professor Farrand and with his permission reprinted from Farrand, *The Records of the Federal Convention*, vol. ii, pp. 565–579.

vania, one in Delaware, six in Maryland, ten in Virginia, five in North-Carolina, five in South-Carolina, and three in Georgia.

Sect. 4.   As the proportions of numbers in the different states will alter from time to time; as some of the States may hereafter be divided; as others may be enlarged by addition of territory; as two or more States may be united; as new States will be erected within the limits of the United States, the Legislature shall, in each of these cases, regulate the number of representatives by the number of inhabitants, according to the rule hereinafter made for direct taxation not exceeding the rate of one for every forty thousand.   Provided that every State shall have at least one representative.

Sect. 6.[1]   The House of Representatives shall have the sole power of impeachment.   It shall choose its Speaker and other officers.

Sect. 7.   Vacancies in the House of Representatives shall be supplied by writs of election from the executive authority of the State, in the representation from which they shall happen.

V

Sect. 1.   The Senate of the United States shall be chosen by the Legislatures of the several States.   Each Legislature shall chuse two members.   Vacancies happening by refusals to accept, resignations or otherwise may be supplied by the Legislature of the State in the representation of which such vacancies shall happen, or by the executive thereof until the next meeting of the Legislature.   Each member shall have one vote.

Sect. 2.   The Senators shall be chosen for six years; but immediately after they shall be assembled in consequence of the first election they shall be divided, by lot, into three classes, as nearly as may be, numbered one, two and three.   The seats of the members of the first class shall be vacated at the expiration of the second year, of the second class at the expiration of the fourth year, of the third class at the expiration of the sixth year, so that a third part of the members may be chosen every second year.

Sect. 3.   Every member of the Senate shall be of the age of thirty years at least; shall have been a citizen of the United States for at least nine years before his election; and shall be, at the time of his election, an inhabitant of the State for which he shall be chosen.

Sect. 4.   The Senate shall chuse its own President and other officers.

VI

Sect. 1.   The times and places and the manner of holding the elections of the members of each House shall be prescribed by the Legislature of each State respectively; but regulations in each of the foregoing cases may, at any time, be made or altered by the Legislature of the United States.

Sect. 3.[2]   In each House a majority of the members shall constitute a quorum

---

[1] Sect. 5 was struck out.
[2] Sect. 2 was struck out.

to do business; but a smaller number may adjourn from day to day, and may be authorised to compel the attendance of absent members in such manner and under such penalties as each House may provide.

Sect. 4.   Each House shall be the judge of the elections, returns and qualifications of its own members.

Sect. 5.   Freedom of speech and debate in the Legislature shall not be impeached or questioned in any court or place out of the Legislature; and the members of each House shall, in all cases, except treason, felony and breach of the peace, be privileged from arrest during their attendance at Congress, and in going to and returning from it.

Sect. 6.   Each House may determine the rules of its proceedings; may punish its members for disorderly behaviour; and may, with the concurrence of two thirds, expel a member.

Sect. 7.   The House of Representatives, and the Senate, shall keep a journal of their proceedings, and shall, from time to time, publish them, except such parts thereof as in their judgment require secrecy; and the yeas and nays of the members of each House, on any question, shall, at the desire of one-fifth part of the members present, be entered on the journal.

Sect. 8.   During the session of the Legislature neither House, without the consent of the other, shall adjourn for more than three days, nor to any place than that at which the two Houses are sitting.

Sect. 9.   The Members of each House shall be ineligible to any civil office under the authority of the United States created, or the emoluments whereof shall have been encreased during the time for which they shall respectively be elected — and no person holding any office under the United States shall be a Member of either House during his continuance in Office.

Sect. 10.   The members of each House shall receive a compensation for their services, to be paid out of the Treasury of the United States, to be ascertained by law.

Sect. 11.   The enacting stile of the laws of the United States shall be.   " Be it enacted, by the Senate and Representatives in Congress assembled.

Sect. 12.   All Bills for raising revenue shall originate in the House of representatives: but the Senate may propose or concur with amendments as on other bills.   No money shall be drawn from the Treasury but in consequence of appropriations made by law.

Sect. 13.   Every bill, which shall have passed the House of Representatives and the Senate, shall, before it become a law, be presented to the President of the United States, for his revision; if, upon such revision, he approve of it, he shall signify his approbation by signing it: But if, upon such revision, it shall appear to him improper for being passed into a law, he shall return it, together with his objections against it, to that House in which it shall have originated, who shall enter the objections at large on their Journal, and proceed to reconsider the bill.   But if, after such reconsideration, three-fourths of that House shall, notwithstanding the objections of the President, agree to pass it, it shall, together with his objections be sent to the other House, by which it shall likewise be reconsidered, and, if approved by three-fourths of the other House also, it shall become a law.   But, in all such cases, the votes of both Houses shall be determined by Yeas and Nays; and the names of the persons voting for or against the bill shall be entered in the Journal of each House respectively.   If any bill shall not be returned by the President within ten days (Sundays excepted) after it shall have been presented to him, it shall be a law, unless the Legislature, by their adjournment, prevent its return; in which case it shall not be a law.

Sect. 14.   Every order, resolution or vote, to which the concurrence of the Senate and House of Representatives may be necessary (except on a question of adjournment, and in the cases hereinafter mentioned) shall be presented to the President for his revision; and before the same shall have force, shall be approved by him, or, being disapproved by him, shall be repassed by the Senate and House of representatives, according to the rules and limitations prescribed in the case of a bill.

VII

Sect. 1.   The Legislature shall have power to lay and collect taxes, duties, imposts and excises, to pay the debts and provide for the common defence and general welfare of the United States.

To regulate commerce with foreign nations, and among the several States; and with the Indian tribes.

To establish an uniform rule of naturalization throughout the United States;

To coin money;

To regulate the value of foreign coin;

To fix the standard of weights and measures;

To establish post-offices and post-roads;

To borrow money on the credit of the United States;

To appoint a Treasurer by joint ballot;

To constitute tribunals inferior to the supreme court;

To make rules concerning captures on land and water;

To define and punish piracies and felonies committed on the high seas, to punish the counterfeiting of the securities, and current coin of the United States, and offences against the law of nations;

To declare war; and grant letters of marque and reprisal.

To raise and support armies; but no appropriation of money to that use shall be for a longer term than two years.

To provide & maintain a navy;

To make rules for the government and regulation of the land and naval forces.

To provide for calling forth the militia to execute the laws of the Union, suppress insurrections, and repel invasions;

To make laws for organizing, arming, and disciplining the militia, and for governing such part of them as may be employed in the service of the United States, reserving to the States, respectively, the appointment of the Officers, and the authority of training the militia according to the discipline prescribed by the United States.

To establish uniform laws on the subject of bankruptcies.

To exercise exclusive legislation in all cases whatsoever over such district (not exceeding ten miles square) as may by cession of particular States and the acceptance of the Legislature become the seat of the Government of the United States, and to exercise like authority over all Places purchased, by the consent of the Legislature of the State, for the erection of Forts, Magazines, Arsenals, Dock Yards and other needful buildings.

To promote the progress of science and useful arts by securing for limited times to Authors and Inventors the exclusive right to their respective writings and discoveries.

And to make all laws that shall be necessary and proper for carrying into execution the foregoing powers, and all other powers vested, by this Constitution, in the government of the United States, or in any department or officer thereof.

All [1] debts contracted and engagements entered into, by or under the authority of Congress shall be as valid against the United States under this constitution as under the confederation.

Sect. 2. Treason against the United States shall consist only in levying war against them, or in adhering to their enemies, giving them aid and comfort. The Legislature shall have power to declare the punishment of treason. No person shall be convicted of treason, unless on the testimony of two witnesses to the same overt act, or on confession in open court. No attainder of treason shall work corruption of blood, nor forfeiture, except during the life of the person attainted. The Legislature shall pass no bill of attainder nor any ex post facto laws.

Sect. 3. The proportions of direct taxation shall be regulated by the whole number of free citizens and inhabitants, of every age, sex, and condition, including those bound to servitude for a term of years, and three fifths of all other persons not comprehended in the foregoing description (except Indians not paying taxes) which number shall, within three years after the first meeting of the Legislature, and within the term of every ten years afterwards, be taken in such manner as the said Legislature shall direct.

Sect. 4. No tax or duty shall be laid by the Legislature on articles exported from any State. The migration or importation of such persons as the several States now existing shall think proper to admit shall not be prohibited by the Legislature prior to the year 1808 — but a tax or duty may be imposed on such importation not exceeding ten dollars for each person. Nor shall any regulation of commerce or revenue give preference to the ports of one State over those of another, or oblige Vessels bound to or from any State to enter, clear, or pay duties in another.

[1] The correct location of this clause is uncertain. It was considered and adopted in connection with the "powers of Congress," and so is inserted here.

And all duties, imposts, and excises, laid by the Legislature, shall be uniform throughout the United States.

Sect. 5. No capitation tax shall be laid, unless in proportion to the census herein before directed to be taken.

Sect. 7.[1] The United States shall not grant any title of nobility. No person holding any office of profit or trust under the United States, shall without the consent of the Legislature accept of any present, emolument, office, or title of any kind whatever, from any king, prince or foreign State.

VIII

This Constitution and the Laws of the United States which shall be made in pursuance thereof, and all treaties made or which shall be made under the authority of the United States shall be the supreme law of the several States, and of their citizens and inhabitants; and the judges in the several States shall be bound thereby in their decisions; any thing in the constitutions or laws of the several States to the contrary notwithstanding.

IX

Sect. 1. The Senate of the United States shall have power to try all impeachments: but no person shall be convicted without the concurrence of two thirds of the Members present: and every Member shall be on oath.

X

Sect. 1. The Executive power of the United States shall be vested in a single person. His stile shall be, " The President of the United States of America; " and his title shall be, " His Excellency." He shall hold his office during the term of four years, and together with the Vice President, chosen for the same term, be elected in the following manner.

Each State shall appoint, in such manner as its legislature may direct, a number of Electors equal to the whole number of Senators and Members of the House of representatives to which the State may be entitled in the Legislature. But no Person shall be appointed an Elector who is a member of the Legislature of the United States, or who holds any office of profit or trust under the United States.

The Electors shall meet in their respective States and vote by ballot for two Persons of whom one at least shall not be an inhabitant of the same State with themselves.— and they shall make a list of all the Persons voted for, and of the number of votes for each, which list they shall sign and certify, and transmit sealed to the seat of the general Government, directed to the President of the Senate.

The President of the Senate shall in the presence of the Senate and House of representatives open all the certificates and the votes shall then be counted.

[1] Sect. 6 was struck out.

The Person having the greatest number of votes shall be the President (if such number be a majority of the whole number of the Electors appointed) and if there be more than one who have such a majority, and have an equal number of votes, then the House of representatives shall immediately choose by ballot one of them for President, the representation from each State having one vote — But if no Person have a majority, then from the five highest on the list, the House of representatives shall, in like manner, choose by ballot the President — In the choice of a President by the House of representatives a quorum shall consist of a Member or Members from two thirds of the States, and the concurrence of a majority of all the States shall be necessary to such choice.— and, in every case after the choice of the President, the Person having the greatest number of votes of the Electors shall be the vice-President: But, if there should remain two or more who have equal votes, the Senate shall choose from them the Vice President

The Legislature may determine the time of chusing the Electors and of their giving their votes — But the election shall be on the same day throughout the United States

The Legislature may declare by law what officer of the United States shall act as President in case of the death, resignation, or disability of the President and Vice President; and such Officer shall act accordingly, until such disability be removed, or a President shall be elected

Sect. 2. No Person except a natural born Citizen, or a Citizen of the U. S. at the time of the adoption of this Constitution shall be eligible to the office of President; nor shall any Person be elected to that office, who shall be under the age of 35 years, and who has not been in the whole, at least 14 years a resident within the U. S.

Sect. 3. The Vice President shall be ex officio, President of the Senate, except when they sit to try the impeachment of the President, in which case the Chief Justice shall preside, and excepting also when he shall exercise the powers and duties of President, in which case, and in case of his absence, the Senate shall chuse a President pro tempore — The Vice President when acting as President of the Senate shall not have a vote unless the House be equally divided

Sect. 4. The President by and with the advice and consent of the Senate, shall have power to make treaties: and he shall nominate and by and with the advice and consent of the Senate shall appoint Ambassadors, other public Ministers and Consuls, Judges of the supreme Court, and all other officers of the U. S. whose appointments are not otherwise herein provided for. But no Treaty shall be made without the consent of two thirds of the Members present.

The President shall have power to fill up all vacancies that may happen during the recess of the Senate by granting commissions which shall expire at the end of the next session of the Senate.

Sect. 2.[1] He shall, from time to time, give to the Legislature information of the State of the Union: and recommend to their consideration such measures as he shall judge necessary, and expedient: he may convene both or either of the

---

[1] Original numbering, the sections above numbered 2–4 were insertions.

Houses on extraordinary occasions, and in case of disagreement between the two Houses, with regard to the time of adjournment, he may adjourn them to such time as he shall think proper: he shall take care that the laws of the United States be duly and faithfully executed: he shall commission all the officers of the United States; and shall appoint to all offices established by this constitution except in cases herein otherwise provided for, and to all offices which may hereafter be created by law. He shall receive Ambassadors, other public Ministers and Consuls. He shall have power to grant reprieves and pardons except in cases of impeachment. He shall be Commander in Chief of the Army and Navy of the United States, and of the Militia of the several States when called into the actual service of the United States; and may require the opinion in writing of the principal officer in each of the executive departments upon any subject relating to the duties of their respective offices. He shall, at stated times, receive for his services, a compensation, which shall neither be encreased nor diminished during his continuance in office. Before he shall enter on the duties of his department, he shall take the following Oath or Affirmation, " I ——————— solemnly swear (or affirm) that I will faithfully execute the Office of President of the United States of America, and will to the best of my judgment and power, preserve, protect and defend the Constitution of the United States." He shall be removed from his office on impeachment by the House of representatives, and conviction by the Senate, for treason or bribery or other high crimes and misdemeanors against the United States; the Vice President and other civil Officers of the United States shall be removed from Office on impeachment and conviction as aforesaid; and in case of his removal as aforesaid, death, absence, resignation or inability to discharge the powers or duties of his office the Vice President shall exercise those powers and duties until another President be chosen, or until the inability of the President be removed.

XI

Sect. 1. The Judicial Power of the United States both in law and equity shall be vested in one Supreme Court, and in such Inferior Courts as shall, when necessary, from time to time, be constituted by the Legislature of the United States.

Sect. 2. The Judges of the Supreme Court, and of the Inferior courts, shall holds their offices during good behaviour. They shall, at stated times, receive for their services, a compensation, which shall not be diminished during their continuance in office.

Sect. 3. The Judicial Power shall extend to all cases both in law and equity arising under this Constitution and the laws of the United States, and treaties made or which shall be made under their authority; to all cases affecting Ambassadors, other Public Ministers and Consuls; to all cases of Admiralty and Maritime Jurisdiction; to Controversies to which the United States shall be a party, to controversies between two or more States (except such as shall regard

Territory and Jurisdiction) between a State and citizens of another State, between citizens of different States, between citizens of the same State claiming lands under grants of different States, and between a State or the citizens thereof and foreign States, citizens or subjects. In cases affecting Ambassadors, other Public Ministers and Consuls, and those in which a State shall be party, the Supreme Court shall have original jurisdiction. In all other cases beforementioned the Supreme Court shall have appellate jurisdiction both as to law and fact with such exceptions and under such regulations as the Legislature shall make.

Sect. 4. The trial of all crimes (except in cases of impeachments) shall be by jury and such trial shall be held in the State where the said crimes shall have been committed; but when not committed within any State then the trial shall be at such place or places as the Legislature may direct.

The privilege of the writ of Habeas Corpus shall not be suspended; unless where in cases of rebellion or invasion the public safety may require it.

Sect. 5. Judgment, in cases of Impeachment, shall not extend further than to removal from office, and disqualification to hold and enjoy any office of honour, trust or profit under the United States. But the Party convicted shall nevertheless, be liable and subject to indictment, trial, judgment and punishment, according to law.

XII

No State shall coin money; nor emit bills of credit, nor make anything but gold or silver coin a tender in payment of debts; nor pass any bill of attainder or ex post facto laws; nor grant letters of marque and reprisal, nor enter into any treaty, alliance, or confederation; nor grant any title of nobility.

XIII

No State, without the consent of the Legislature of the United States shall lay imposts or duties on imports or exports, nor with such consent but for the use of the treasury of the United States; nor keep troops or ships of war in time of peace; nor enter into any agreement or compact with another State, or with any foreign power; nor engage in any war, unless it shall be actually invaded by enemies, or the danger of invasion be so imminent, as not to admit of a delay, until the Legislature of the United States can be consulted.

XIV

The citizens of each State shall be entitled to all privileges and immunities of citizens of the several States.

XV

Any person charged with treason, felony, or other crime in any State, who shall flee from justice, and shall be found in any other State, shall, on demand of the Executive Power of the State from which he fled, be delivered up and removed to the State having jurisdiction of the offence.

If any Person bound to service or labor in any of the United States shall escape into another State, He or She shall not be discharged from such service or labor in consequence of any regulations subsisting in the State to which they escape; but shall be delivered up to the person justly claiming their service or labor.

XVI

Full faith and credit shall be given in each State to the public Acts, records, and judicial proceedings of every other State, and the Legislature may by general laws prescribe the manner in which such acts, records, and proceedings shall be proved and the effect thereof.

XVII

New States may be admitted by the Legislature into this Union: but no new State shall be hereafter formed or erected within the jurisdiction of any of the present States, without the consent of the Legislature of such State as well as of the general Legislature. Nor shall any State be formed by the junction of two or more States or parts thereof without the consent of the Legislatures of such States as well as of the Legislature of the United States.

The Legislature shall have power to dispose of and make all needful rules and regulations respecting the territory or other property belonging to the United States: and nothing in this Constitution contained shall be so construed as to prejudice any claims either of the United States or of any particular State.

XVIII

The United States shall guaranty to each State a Republican form of government; and shall protect each State against invasions, and, on the application of its Legislature or Executive, against domestic violence.

XIX

The Legislature of the United States, whenever two thirds of both Houses shall deem necessary, or on the application of two thirds of the Legislatures of the several States, shall propose amendments to this Constitution which shall be valid to all intents and purposes as parts thereof, when the same shall have been ratified by three fourths at least of the Legislatures of the several States, or by Conventions in three fourths thereof, as one or the other mode of ratification may be proposed by the Legislature of the United-States: Provided that no amendments which may be made prior to the year 1808 shall in any manner affect the 4th and 5th Sections of article the 7th

XX

The Members of the Legislatures, and the executive and judicial officers of the United States, and of the several States, shall be bound by oath or affirmation to support this Constitution.

But no religious test shall ever be required as a qualification to any office or public trust under the authority of the United States.

XXI

The ratification of the Conventions of nine States shall be sufficient for organising this Constitution between the said States.

XXII

This Constitution shall be laid before the United States in Congress assembled, and it is the opinion of this Convention that it should be afterwards submitted to a Convention chosen in each State, under the recommendation of its Legislature, in order to receive the ratification of such Convention.

· XXIII

To introduce this government, it is the opinion of this Convention, that each assenting Convention should notify its assent and ratification to the United States in Congress assembled; that Congress, after receiving the assent and ratification of the Conventions of nine States, should appoint and publish a day, as early as may be, and appoint a place for commencing proceedings under this Constitution; that after such publication, the Legislatures of the several States should elect Members of the Senate, and direct the election of Members of the House of Representatives; and that the Members of the Legislature should meet at the time and place assigned by Congress and should, as soon as may be, after their meeting, proceed to execute this Constitution.

IX. THE CONSTITUTION AS REPORTED BY THE COMMITTEE ON STYLE, SEPTEMBER 12, 1787, AND AS SIGNED, SEPTEMBER 17, 1787.

Report of the Committee on Style.[1]

We, the people of the United States, in order to form a more perfect union, to establish justice, insure domestic tranquillity, provide for the common defence, promote the general welfare, and secure the blessings of liberty to ourselves and our posterity, do ordain and establish this Constitution for the United States of America.

ARTICLE I

Sect. 1. ALL legislative powers herein granted shall be vested in a Congress of the United States, which shall consist of a Senate and House of Representatives.

Sect. 2. The House of Representatives shall be composed of members chosen every second year by the people of the several states, and the electors in each state shall have the qualifications requisite for electors of the most numerous branch of the state legislature.

(a) No person shall be a representative who shall not have attained to the age of twenty-five years, and been seven years a citizen of the United States, and who shall not, when elected, be an inhabitant of that state in which he shall be chosen.

(b) Representatives and direct taxes shall be apportioned among the several states which may be included within this Union, according to their respective numbers, which shall be deter-

The Constitution as signed.[2]

We the People of the United States, in Order to form a more perfect Union, establish Justice, insure domestic Tranquility, provide for the common defence, promote the general Welfare, and secure the Blessings of Liberty to ourselves and our Posterity, do ordain and establish this Constitution for the United States of America.

ARTICLE I

Section 1. All legislative Powers herein granted shall be vested in a Congress of the United States, which shall consist of a Senate and House of Representatives.

Section 2. The House of Representatives shall be composed of Members chosen every second Year by the People of the several States, and the Electors in each State shall have the Qualifications requisite for Electors of the most numerous Branch of the State Legislature.

No Person shall be a Representative who shall not have attained to the Age of twenty five Years, and been seven Years a Citizen of the United States, and who shall not, when elected, be an Inhabitant of that State in which he shall be chosen.

Representatives and direct Taxes shall be apportioned among the several States which may be included within this Union, according to their respective Numbers, which shall be deter-

[1] *Documentary History*, Vol. iii, pp. 720–733.
[2] *Documentary History*, Vol. ii, pp. 3–20.

Report of the Committee on Style.	*The Constitution as signed.*
mined by adding to the whole number of free persons, including those bound to servitude for a term of years, and excluding Indians not taxed, three fifths of all other persons. The actual enumeration shall be made within three years after the first meeting of the Congress of the United States, and within every subsequent term of ten years, in such manner as they shall by law direct. The number of representatives shall not exceed one for every forty thousand, but each state shall have at least one representative: and until such enumeration shall be made, the state of New-Hampshire shall be entitled to chuse three, Massachusetts eight, Rhode-Island and Providence Plantations one, Connecticut five, New-York six, New-Jersey four, Pennsylvania eight, Delaware one, Maryland six, Virginia ten, North-Carolina five, South-Carolina five, and Georgia three.	mined by adding to the whole Number of free Persons, including those bound to Service for a Term of Years, and excluding Indians not taxed, three fifths of all other Persons. The actual Enumeration shall be made within three Years after the first Meeting of the Congress of the United States, and within every subsequent Term of ten Years, in such Manner as they shall by Law direct. The Number of Representatives shall not exceed one for every thirty Thousand, but each State shall have at Least one Representative; and until such enumeration shall be made, the State of New Hampshire shall be entitled to chuse three, Massachusetts eight, Rhode-Island and Providence Plantations one, Connecticut five, New-York six, New Jersey four, Pennsylvania eight, Delaware one, Maryland six, Virginia ten, North Carolina five, South Carolina five, and Georgia three.
(c) When vacancies happen in the representation from any state, the Executive authority thereof shall issue writs of election to fill such vacancies.	When vacancies happen in the Representation from any State, the Executive Authority thereof shall issue Writs of Election to fill such Vacancies.
(d) The House of Representatives shall choose their Speaker and other officers; and they shall have the sole power of impeachment.	The House of Representatives shall chuse their Speaker and other Officers; and shall have the sole Power of Impeachment.
Sect. 3. The Senate of the United States shall be composed of two senators from each state, chosen by the legislature thereof, for six years: and each senator shall have one vote.	Section 3. The Senate of the United States shall be composed of two Senators from each State, chosen by the Legislature thereof, for six Years: and each Senator shall have one Vote.
(a) Immediately after they shall be assembled in consequence of the first election, they shall be divided as equally as may be into three classes. The seats of the senators of the first class shall be vacated at the expiration of the second year, of the second class at the expira-	Immediately after they shall be assembled in Consequence of the first Election, they shall be divided as equally as may be into three Classes. The Seats of the Senators of the first Class shall be vacated at the Expiration of the second Year, of the second class at

Report of the Committee on Style.	*The Constitution as signed.*
tion of the fourth year, and of the third class at the expiration of the sixth year, so that one-third may be chosen every second year: and if vacancies happen by resignation, or otherwise, during the recess of the Legislature of any state, the Executive thereof may make temporary appointments until the next meeting of the Legislature.	the Expiration of the fourth Year, and of the third Class at the Expiration of the sixth Year, so that one third may be chosen every second Year; and if Vacancies happen by Resignation, or otherwise, during the Recess of the Legislature of any State, the Executive thereof may make temporary Appointments until the next Meeting of the Legislature, which shall then fill such Vacancies.
(b) No person shall be a senator who shall not have attained to the age of thirty years, and been nine years a citizen of the United States, and who shall not, when elected, be an inhabitant of that state for which he shall be chosen.	No Person shall be a Senator who shall not have attained to the Age of thirty Years, and been nine Years a Citizen of the United States, and who shall not, when elected, be an Inhabitant of that State for which he shall be chosen.
(c) The Vice-President of the United States shall be, ex officio, President of the senate, but shall have no vote, unless they be equally divided.	The Vice President of the United States shall be President of the Senate, but shall have no Vote, unless they be equally divided.
(d) The Senate shall choose their other officers, and also a President pro tempore, in the absence of the Vice-President, or when he shall exercise the office of President of the United States.	The Senate shall chuse their other Officers, and also a President pro tempore, in the Absence of the Vice President, or when he shall exercise the Office of President of the United States.
(e) The Senate shall have the sole power to try all impeachments. When sitting for that purpose, they shall be on oath. When the President of the United States is tried, the Chief Justice shall preside: And no person shall be convicted without the concurrence of two-thirds of the members present.	The Senate shall have the sole Power to try all Impeachments. When sitting for that Purpose, they shall be on Oath or Affirmation. When the President of the United States is tried, the Chief Justice shall preside: And no Person shall be convicted without the Concurrence of two thirds of the Members present.
(f) Judgment in cases of impeachment shall not extend further than to removal from office, and disqualification to hold and enjoy any office of honor, trust or profit under the United States: but the party convicted shall nevertheless be	Judgment in Cases of Impeachment shall not extend further than to removal from Office, and disqualification to hold and enjoy any Office of honor, Trust or Profit under the United States: but the Party convicted shall nevertheless

Report of the Committee on Style.

liable and subject to indictment, trial, judgment and punishment, according to law.

Sect. 4. The times, places and manner of holding elections for senators and representatives, shall be prescribed in each state by the legislature thereof: but the Congress may at any time by law make or alter such regulations.

(a) The Congress shall assemble at least once in every year, and such meeting shall be on the first Monday in December, unless they shall by law appoint a different day.

Sect. 5. Each House shall be the judge of the elections, returns and qualifications of its own members, and a majority of each shall constitute a quorum to do business: but a smaller number may adjourn from day to day, and may be authorized to compel the attendance of absent members, in such manner, and under such penalties as each house may provide.

(a) Each house may determine the rules of its proceedings; punish its members for disorderly behaviour, and, with the concurrence of two-thirds, expel a member.

(b) Each house shall keep a journal of its proceedings, and from time to time publish the same, excepting such parts as may in their judgment require secrecy; and the yeas and nays of the members of either house on any question shall, at the desire of one-fifth of those present, be entered on the journal.

(c) Neither house, during the session of Congress, shall, without the consent of the other, adjourn for more than

The Constitution as signed.

be liable and subject to Indictment, Trial, Judgment and Punishment, according to Law.

Section 4. The Times, Places and Manner of holding Elections for Senators and Representatives, shall be prescribed in each State by the Legislature thereof; but the Congress may at any time by Law make or alter such Regulations, except as to the Places of chusing Senators.

The Congress shall assemble at least once in every Year, and such Meeting shall be on the first Monday in December, unless they shall by Law appoint a different Day.

Section 5. Each House shall be the Judge of the Elections, Returns and Qualifications of its own Members, and a Majority of each shall constitute a Quorum to do Business; but a smaller Number may adjourn from day to day, and may be authorized to compel the Attendance of absent Members, in such Manner, and under such Penalties as each House may provide.

Each House may determine the Rules of its Proceedings, punish its Members for disorderly Behaviour, and, with the Concurrence of two thirds, expel a Member.

Each House shall keep a Journal of its Proceedings, and from time to time publish the same, excepting such Parts as may in their Judgment require Secrecy; and the Yeas and Nays of the Members of either House on any question shall, at the Desire of one fifth of those Present, be entered on the Journal.

Neither House, during the Session of Congress, shall, without the Consent of the other, adjourn for more than

Report of the Committee on Style.	*The Constitution as signed.*
three days, nor to any other place than that in which the two houses shall be sitting.	three days, nor to any other Place than that in which the two Houses shall be sitting.
Sect. 6. The senators and representatives shall receive a compensation for their services, to be ascertained by law and paid out of the treasury of the United States. They shall in all cases, except treason, felony and breach of the peace, be privileged from arrest during their attendance at the session of their respective houses, and in going to and returning from the same; and for any speech or debate in either house, they shall not be questioned in any other place.	Section 6. The Senators and Representatives shall receive a Compensation for their Services, to be ascertained by Law, and paid out of the Treasury of the United States. They shall in all Cases, except Treason, Felony and Breach of the Peace, be privileged from Arrest during their Attendance at the Session of their respective Houses, and in going to and returning from the same; and for any Speech or Debate in either House, they shall not be questioned in any other Place.
(a) No senator or representative shall, during the time for which he was elected, be appointed to any civil office under the authority of the United States, which shall have been created, or the emoluments whereof shall have been encreased during such time; and no person holding any office under the United States, shall be a member of either house during his continuance in office.	No Senator or Representative shall, during the Time for which he was elected, be appointed to any civil Office under the Authority of the United States, which shall have been created, or the Emoluments whereof shall have been encreased during such time, and no Person holding any Office under the United States, shall be a Member of either House during his Continuance in Office.
Sect. 7. The enacting stile of the laws shall be, " Be it enacted by the senators and representatives in Congress assembled."	Section 7.
(a) All bills for raising revenue shall originate in the house of representatives: but the senate may propose or concur with amendments as on other bills.	All Bills for raising Revenue shall originate in the House of Representatives; but the Senate may propose or concur with Amendments as on other Bills.
(b) Every bill which shall have passed the house of representatives and the senate, shall, before it become a law, be presented to the president of the United States. If he approve he shall sign it, but if not he shall return it, with his objections to that house in which it	Every Bill which shall have passed the House of Representatives and the Senate, shall, before it become a Law, be presented to the President of the United States; If he approve he shall sign it, but if not he shall return it, with his Objections to that House in

Report of the Committee on Style.

shall have originated, who shall enter the objections at large on their journal, and proceed to reconsider it. If after such reconsideration two-thirds of that house shall agree to pass the bill, it shall be sent, together with the objections, to the other house, by which it shall likewise be reconsidered, and if approved by two-thirds of that house, it shall become a law. But in all such cases the votes of both houses shall be determined by yeas and nays, and the names of the persons voting for and against the bill shall be entered on the journal of each house respectively. If any bill shall not be returned by the President within ten days (Sundays excepted) after it shall have been presented to him, the same shall be a law, in like manner. as if he had signed it, unless the Congress by their adjournment prevent its return, in which case it shall not be a law.

(c) Every order, resolution, or vote to which the concurrence of the Senate and House of Representatives may be necessary (except on a question of adjournment) shall be presented to the President of the United States; and before the same shall take effect, shall be approved by him, or, being disapproved by him, shall be repassed by three-fourths of the Senate and House of Representatives, according to the rules and limitations prescribed in the case of a bill.

Sect. 8. The Congress may by joint ballot appoint a treasurer. They shall have power

(a) To lay and collect taxes, duties, imposts and excises; to pay the debts and provide for the common defence and general welfare of the United States.

The Constitution as signed.

which it shall have originated, who shall enter the Objections at large on their Journal, and proceed to reconsider it. If after such Reconsideration two thirds of that House shall agree to pass the Bill, it shall be sent, together with the Objections, to the other House, by which it shall likewise be reconsidered, and if approved by two thirds of that House, it shall become a law. But in all such Cases the Votes of both Houses shall be determined by yeas and Nays, and the Names of the Persons voting for and against the Bill shall be entered on the Journal of each House respectively. If any Bill shall not be returned by the President within ten Days (Sundays excepted) after it shall have been presented to him, the Same shall be a Law, in like Manner as if he had signed it, unless the Congress by their Adjournment prevent its Return, in which Case it shall not be a Law.

Every Order, Resolution, or Vote to which the Concurrence of the Senate and House of Representatives may be necessary (except on a question of Adjournment) shall be presented to the President of the United States; and before the Same shall take Effect, shall be approved by him, or being disapproved by him, shall be repassed by two thirds of the Senate and House of Representatives, according to the Rules and Limitations prescribed in the Case of a Bill.

Section 8. The Congress shall have Power

To lay and collect Taxes, Duties, Imposts and Excises, to pay the Debts and provide for the common Defence and general Welfare of the United

Report of the Committee on Style.

(b) To borrow money on the credit of the United States.

(c) To regulate commerce with foreign nations, among the several states, and with the Indian tribes.

(d) To establish an uniform rule of naturalization, and uniform laws on the subject of bankruptcies throughout the United States.

(e) To coin money, regulate the value thereof, and of foreign coin, and fix the standard of weights and measures.

(f) To provide for the punishment of counterfeiting the securities and current coin of the United States.

(g) To establish post offices and post roads.

(i) To promote the progress of science and useful arts, by securing for limited times to authors and inventors the exclusive right to their respective writings and discoveries.

(j) To constitute tribunals inferior to the supreme court.

(k) To define and punish piracies and felonies committed on the high seas, and punish offences against the law of nations.

(l) To declare war, grant letters of marque and reprisal, and make rules concerning captures on land and water.

(m) To raise and support armies: but no appropriations of money to that use shall be for a longer term than two years.

(n) To provide and maintain a navy.

(o) To make rules for the government and regulation of the land and naval forces.

The Constitution as signed.

States; but all Duties, Imposts and Excises shall be uniform throughout the United States;

To borrow Money on the credit of the United States;

To regulate Commerce with foreign Nations, and among the several States, and with the Indian Tribes;

To establish an uniform Rule of Naturalization, and uniform Laws on the subject of Bankruptcies throughout the United States;

To coin Money, regulate the Value thereof, and of foreign Coin, and fix the Standard of Weights and Measures;

To provide for the Punishment of counterfeiting the Securities and current Coin of the United States;

To establish Post Offices and post Roads;

To promote the Progress of Science and useful Arts, by securing for limited Times to Authors and Inventors the exclusive Right to their respective Writings and Discoveries;

To constitute Tribunals inferior to the supreme Court;

To define and punish Piracies and Felonies committed on the high Seas, and Offences against the Law of Nations;

To declare War, grant Letters of Marque and Reprisal, and make Rules concerning Captures on Land and Water;

To raise and support Armies, but no Appropriation of Money to that Use shall be for a longer Term than two Years;

To provide and maintain a Navy;

To make Rules for the Government and Regulation of the land and naval Forces;

Report of the Committee on Style.	*The Constitution as signed.*
(p) To provide for calling forth the militia to execute the laws of the union, suppress insurrections and repel invasions.	To provide for calling forth the Militia to execute the Laws of the Union, suppress Insurrections and repel Invasions;
(q) To provide for organizing, arming and disciplining the militia, and for governing such part of them as may be employed in the service of the United States, reserving to the States respectively, the appointment of the officers, and the authority of training the militia according to the discipline prescribed by Congress.	To provide for organizing, arming, and disciplining, the Militia, and for governing such Part of them as may be employed in the Service of the United States, reserving to the States respectively, the Appointment of the Officers, and the Authority of training the Militia according to the discipline prescribed by Congress;
(r) To exercise exclusive legislation in all cases whatsoever, over such district (not exceeding ten miles square) as may, by cession of particular States, and the acceptance of Congress, become the seat of the government of the United States, and to exercise like authority over all places purchased by the consent of the legislature of the state in which the same shall be, for the erection of forts, magazines, arsenals, dock-yards, and other needful buildings — And	To exercise exclusive Legislation in all Cases whatsoever, over such District (not exceeding ten Miles square) as may, by Cession of particular States, and the Acceptance of Congress, become the Seat of the Government of the United States, and to exercise like Authority over all Places purchased by the Consent of the Legislature of the State in which the Same shall be, for the Erection of Forts, Magazines, Arsenals, dock-Yards, and other needful Buildings; — And
(s) To make all laws which shall be necessary and proper for carrying into execution the foregoing powers, and all other powers vested by this constitution in the government of the United States, or in any department or officer thereof.	To make all Laws which shall be necessary and proper for carrying into Execution the foregoing Powers, and all other Powers vested by this Constitution in the Government of the United States, or in any Department or Officer thereof.
Sect. 9. The migration or importation of such persons as the several states now existing shall think proper to admit, shall not be prohibited by the Congress prior to the year one thousand eight hundred and eight, but a tax or duty may be imposed on such importation, not exceeding ten dollars for each person.	Section 9. The Migration or Importation of such Persons as any of the States now existing shall think proper to admit, shall not be prohibited by the Congress prior to the Year one thousand eight hundred and eight, but a Tax or duty may be imposed on such Importation, not exceeding ten dollars for each Person.
(a) The privilege of the writ of	The Privilege of the Writ of Habeas

Report of the Committee on Style.

habeas corpus shall not be suspended, unless when in cases of rebellion or invasion the public safety may require it.

(b) No bill of attainder shall be passed, nor any ex post facto law.

(c) No capitation tax shall be laid, unless in proportion to the census herein before directed to be taken.

(d) No tax or duty shall be laid on articles exported from any state.

(e) No money shall be drawn from the treasury, but in consequence of appropriations made by law.

(f) No title of nobility shall be granted by the United States. And no person holding any office of profit or trust under them, shall, without the consent of the Congress, accept of any present, emolument, office, or title, of any kind whatever, from any king, prince, or foreign state.

Sect. 10. No state shall coin money, nor emit bills of credit, nor make any thing but gold or silver coin a tender in payment of debts, nor pass any bill of attainder, nor ex post facto laws, nor laws altering or impairing the obligation of contracts; nor grant letters of marque and reprisal, nor enter into any treaty, alliance, or confederation, nor grant any title of nobility.

(a) No state shall, without the consent of Congress, lay imposts or duties on

The Constitution as signed.

Corpus shall not be suspended, unless when in Cases of Rebellion or Invasion the public Safety may require it.

No bill of Attainder or ex post facto Law shall be passed.

No Capitation, or other direct, Tax shall be laid, unless in Proportion to the Census or Enumeration herein before directed to be taken.

No Tax or Duty shall be laid on Articles exported from any State.

No Preference shall be given by any Regulation of Commerce or Revenue to the Ports of one State over those of another: nor shall Vessels bound to, or from, one State, be obliged to enter, clear, or pay Duties in another.

No Money shall be drawn from the Treasury, but in Consequence of Appropriations made by Law; and a regular Statement and Account of the Receipts and Expenditures of all public Money shall be published from time to time.

No Title of Nobility shall be granted by the United States: And no Person holding any Office of Profit or Trust under them, shall, without the Consent of the Congress, accept of any present, Emolument, Office, or Title, of any kind whatever, from any King, Prince, or foreign State.

Section 10. No State shall enter into any Treaty, Alliance, or Confederation; grant Letters of Marque and Reprisal; coin Money; emit Bills of Credit; make any Thing but gold and silver Coin a Tender in Payment of Debts; pass any Bill of Attainder, ex post facto Law, or Law impairing the Obligation of Contracts, or grant any Title of Nobility.

No State shall, without the Consent of the Congress, lay any Imposts or

Report of the Committee on Style.	*The Constitution as signed.*
imports or exports, nor with such consent, but to the use of the treasury of the United States: nor keep troops nor ships of war in time of peace, nor enter into any agreement or compact with another state, nor with any foreign power. Nor engage in any war, unless it shall be actually invaded by enemies, or the danger of invasion be so iminent, as not to admit of delay until the Congress can be consulted.	Duties on Imports or Exports, except what may be absolutely necessary for executing it's inspection Laws: and the net Produce of all Duties and Imposts, laid by any State on Imports or Exports, shall be for the Use of the Treasury of the United States; and all such Laws shall be subject to the Revision and Controul of the Congress. No State shall, without the Consent of Congress, lay any Duty of Tonnage, keep Troops, or Ships of War in time of Peace, enter into any Agreement or Compact with another State, or with a foreign Power, or engage in War, unless actually invaded, or in such imminent Danger as will not admit of delay.

II

Sect. 1. The executive power shall be vested in a president of the United States of America. He shall hold his office during the term of four years, and, altogether with the vice-president, chosen for the same term, be elected in the following manner:

(a) Each state shall appoint, in such manner as the legislature thereof may direct, a number of electors, equal to the whole number of senators and representatives to which the state may be entitled in Congress: but no senator or representative shall be appointed an elector, nor any person holding an office of trust or profit under the United States.

(b) The electors shall meet in their respective states, and vote by ballot for two persons, of whom one at least shall not be an inhabitant of the same state with themselves. And they shall make a list of all the persons voted for, and of the number of votes for each; which

ARTICLE II

Section 1. The executive Power shall be vested in a President of the United States of America. He shall hold his Office during the Term of four Years, and, together with the Vice President, chosen for the same Term, be elected, as follows

Each State shall appoint, in such Manner as the Legislature thereof may direct, a Number of Electors, equal to the whole Number of Senators and Representatives to which the State may be entitled in the Congress: but no Senator or Representative, or Person holding an Office of Trust or Profit under the United States, shall be appointed an Elector.

The Electors shall meet in their respective States, and vote by Ballot for two Persons, of whom one at least shall not be an Inhabitant of the same State with themselves. And they shall make a List of all the Persons voted for, and of the Number of Votes for each; which

Report of the Committee on Style.

list they shall sign and certify, and transmit sealed to the seat of the general government, directed to the president of the senate. The president of the senate shall in the presence of the senate and house of representatives open all the certificates, and the votes shall then be counted. The person having the greatest number of votes shall be the president, if such number be a majority of the whole number of electors appointed; and if there be more than one who have such majority, and have an equal number of votes, then the house of representatives shall immediately chuse by ballot one of them for president; and if no person have a majority, then from the five highest on the list the said house shall in like manner choose the president. But in choosing the president, the votes shall be taken by states and not per capita, the representation from each state having one vote. A quorum for this purpose shall consist of a member or members from two-thirds of the states, and a majority of all the states shall be necessary to a choice. In every case, after the choice of the president by the representatives, the person having the greatest number of votes of the electors shall be the vice-president. But if there should remain two or more who have equal votes, the senate shall choose from them by ballot the vice-president.

(c) The Congress may determine the time of chusing the electors, and the time in which they shall give their votes; but the election shall be on the same day throughout the United States.

(d) No person except a natural born citizen, or a citizen of the United States,

The Constitution as signed.

List they shall sign and certify, and transmit sealed to the Seat of the Government of the United States, directed to the President of the Senate. The President of the Senate shall, in the Presence of the Senate and House of Representatives, open all the Certificates, and the Votes shall then be counted. The Person having the greatest Number of Votes shall be the President, if such Number be a Majority of the whole Number of Electors appointed; and if there be more than one who have such Majority, and have an equal Number of Votes, then the House of Representatives shall immediately chuse by Ballot one of them for President; and if no Person have a Majority, then from the five highest on the List the said House shall in like Manner chuse the President. But in chusing the President, the Votes shall be taken by States, the Representation from each State having one Vote; A quorum for this Purpose shall consist of a Member or Members from two thirds of the States, and a Majority of all the States shall be necessary to a Choice. In every Case, after the Choice of the President, the Person having the greatest Number of Votes of the Electors shall be the Vice President. But if there should remain two or more who have equal Votes, the Senate shall chuse from them by Ballot the Vice President.

The Congress may determine the Time of chusing the Electors, and the Day on which they shall give their Votes; which Day shall be the same throughout the United States.

No Person except a natural born Citizen, or a Citizen of the United States,

Report of the Committee on Style.

at the time of the adoption of this constitution, shall be eligible to the office of president; neither shall any person be eligible to that office who shall not have attained to the age of thirty-five years, and been fourteen years a resident within the United States.

(e) In case of the removal of the president from office, or of his death, resignation, or inability to discharge the powers and duties of the said office, the same shall devolve on the vice-president, and the Congress may by law provide for the case of removal, death, resignation or inability, both of the president and vice-president, declaring what officer shall then act as president, and such officer shall act accordingly, until the disability be removed, or the period for chusing another president arrive.

(f) The president shall, at stated times, receive a fixed compensation for his services, which shall neither be encreased nor diminished during the period for which he shall have been elected.

(g) Before he enter on the execution of his office, he shall take the following oath or affirmation: " I ——, do solemnly swear (or affirm) that I will faithfully execute the office of president of the United States, and will to the best of my judgment and power, preserve, protect and defend the constitution of the United States."

Sect. 2. The president shall be commander in chief of the army and navy of the United States, and of the militia of the several States: he may require the opinion, in writing, of the

The Constitution as signed.

at the time of the Adoption of this Constitution, shall be eligible to the Office of President; neither shall any Person be eligible to that Office who shall not have attained to the Age of thirty five Years, and been fourteen Years a Resident within the United States.

In Case of the Removal of the President from Office, or of his Death, Resignation, or Inability to discharge the Powers and Duties of the said Office, the Same shall devolve on the Vice President, and the Congress may by Law provide for the Case of Removal, Death, Resignation or Inability, both of the President and Vice President, declaring what Officer shall then act as President, and such Officer shall act accordingly, until the Disability be removed, or a President shall be elected.

The President shall, at stated Times, receive for his Services, a Compensation, which shall neither be encreased nor diminished during the Period for which he shall have been elected, and he shall not receive within that Period any other Emolument from the United States, or any of them.

Before he enter on the Execution of his Office, he shall take the following Oath or Affirmation:—" I do solemnly swear (or affirm) that I will faithfully execute the Office of President of the United States, and will to the best of my Ability, preserve, protect and defend the Constitution of the United States."

Section 2. The President shall be Commander in Chief of the Army and Navy of the United States and of the Militia of the several States, when called into the actual Service of the

Report of the Committee on Style.

principal officer in each of the executive departments, upon any subject relating to the duties of their respective offices, when called into the actual service of the United States, and he shall have power to grant reprieves and pardons for offences against the United States, except in cases of impeachment.

(a) He shall have power, by and with the advice and consent of the senate, to make treaties, provided two-thirds of the senators present concur; and he shall nominate, and by and with the advice and consent of the senate, shall appoint ambassadors, other public ministers and consuls, judges of the supreme court, and all other officers of the United States, whose appointments are not herein otherwise provided for.

(b) The president shall have power to fill up all vacancies that may happen during the recess of the senate, by granting commissions which shall expire at the end of their next session.

Sect. 3. He shall from time to time give to the Congress information of the state of the union, and recommend to their consideration such measures as he shall judge necessary and expedient: he may, on extraordinary occasions, convene both houses, or either of them, and in case of disagreement between them, with respect to the time of adjournment, he may adjourn them to such time as he shall think proper: he shall receive ambassadors and other

The Constitution as signed.

United States; he may require the Opinion, in writing, of the principal Officer in each of the executive Departments, upon any Subject relating to the Duties of their respective Offices, and he shall have Power to grant Reprieves and Pardons for Offences against the United States, except in Cases of Impeachment.

He shall have Power, by and with the Advice and Consent of the Senate, to make Treaties, provided two thirds of the Senators present concur; and he shall nominate, and by and with the Advice and Consent of the Senate, shall appoint Ambassadors, other public Ministers and Consuls, Judges of the supreme Court, and all other Officers of the United States, whose Appointments are not herein otherwise provided for, and which shall be established by Law: but the Congress may by law vest the Appointment of such inferior Officers, as they think proper, in the President alone, in the Courts of Law, or in the Heads of Departments.

The President shall have Power to fill up all Vacancies that may happen during the Recess of the Senate, by granting Commissions which shall expire at the End of their next Session.

Section 3. He shall from time to time give to the Congress Information of the State of the Union, and recommend to their Consideration such Measures as he shall judge necessary and expedient; he may, on extraordinary Occasions, convene both Houses, or either of them, and in Case of Disagreement between them, with Respect to the Time of Adjournment, he may adjourn them to such Time as he shall think proper; he shall receive Ambassadors

Report of the Committee on Style.

public ministers: he shall take care that the laws be faithfully executed, and shall commission all the officers of the United States.

Sect. 4. The president, vice-president, and all civil officers of the United States, shall be removed from office on impeachment for, and conviction of treason, bribery, or other high crimes and misdemeanors.

III

Sect. 1. The judicial power of the United States, both in law and equity, shall be vested in one supreme court, and in such inferor courts as the Congress may from time to time ordain and establish. The judges, both of the supreme and inferior courts, shall hold their offices during good behaviour, and shall, at stated times, receive for their services, a compensation, which shall not be diminished during their continuance in office.

Sect. 2. The judicial power shall extend to all cases, both in law and equity, arising under this constitution, the laws of the United States, and treaties made, or which shall be made, under their authority. To all cases affecting ambassadors, other public ministers and consuls. To all cases of admiralty and maritime jurisdiction. To controversies to which the United States shall be a party. To controversies between two or more States; between a state and citizens of another state; between citizens of different States; between citizens of the same state claiming lands under grants of different States, and between a state, or the citizens thereof, and foreign States, citizens or subjects.

The Constitution as signed.

and other public Ministers; he shall take Care that the Laws be faithfully executed, and shall Commission all the Officers of the United States.

Section 4. The President, Vice President and all civil Officers of the United States, shall be removed from Office on Impeachment for, and Conviction of, Treason, Bribery, or other high Crimes and Misdemeanors.

ARTICLE III

Section 1. The judicial Power of the United States, shall be vested in one supreme Court, and in such inferior Courts as the Congress may from time to time ordain and establish. The Judges, both of the supreme and inferior Courts, shall hold their Offices during good Behaviour, and shall, at stated Times, receive for their Services, a Compensation, which shall not be diminished during their Continuance in Office.

Section 2. The judicial Power shall extend to all Cases, in Law and Equity, arising under this Constitution, the Laws of the United States, and Treaties made, or which shall be made, under their Authority;— to all Cases affecting Ambassadors, other public Ministers and Consuls;— to all Cases of admiralty and maritime Jurisdiction;— to Controversies to which the United States shall be a Party;— to Controversies between two or more States;— between a State and Citizens of another State;— between Citizens of different States,— between Citizens of the same State claiming Lands under Grants of different States, and between a State, or the Citizens thereof, and foreign States, Citizens or Subjects.

Report of the Committee on Style.

In cases affecting ambassadors, other public ministers and consuls, and those in which a state shall be a party, the supreme court shall have original jurisdiction. In all the other cases before mentioned, the supreme court shall have appellate jurisdiction, both as to law and fact, with such exceptions, and under such regulations as the Congress shall make.

The trial of all crimes, except in cases of impeachment, shall be by jury; and such trial shall be held in the state where the said crimes shall have been committed; but when not committed within any state, the trial shall be at such place or places as the Congress may by law have directed.

Sect. 3. Treason against the United States, shall consist only in levying war against them, or in adhering to their enemies, giving them aid and comfort. No person shall be convicted of treason unless on the testimony of two witnesses to the same overt act, or on confession in open court.

The Congress shall have power to declare the punishment of treason, but no attainder of treason shall work corruption of blood nor forfeiture, except during the life of the person attainted.

IV

Sect. 1. Full faith and credit shall be given in each state to the public acts, records, and judicial proceedings of every other state. And the Congress may by general laws prescribe the manner in which such acts, records and proceedings shall be proved, and the effect thereof.

Sect. 2. The citizens of each state

The Constitution as signed.

In all Cases affecting Ambassadors, other public Ministers and Consuls, and those in which a State shall be Party, the supreme Court shall have original Jurisdiction. In all the other Cases before mentioned, the Supreme Court shall have appellate Jurisdiction, both as to Law and Fact, with such Exceptions, and under such regulations as the Congress shall make.

The Trial of all Crimes, except in Cases of Impeachment, shall be by Jury; and such Trial shall be held in the State where the said Crimes shall have been committed; but when not committed within any State, the Trial shall be at such Place or Places as the Congress may by Law have directed.

Section 3. Treason against the United States, shall consist only in levying War against them, or in adhering to their Enemies, giving them Aid and Comfort. No Person shall be convicted of Treason unless on the Testimony of two Witnesses to the same overt Act, or on Confession in open Court.

The Congress shall have Power to declare the Punishment of Treason, but no Attainder of Treason shall work Corruption of Blood, or Forfeiture except during the Life of the Person attainted.

ARTICLE IV

Section 1. Full Faith and Credit shall be given in each State to the public Acts, Records, and judicial Proceedings of every other State. And the Congress may by general Laws prescribe the Manner in which such Acts, Records and Proceedings shall be proved, and the Effect thereof.

Section 2. The Citizens of each

Report of the Committee on Style.	*The Constitution as signed.*
shall be entitled to all privileges and immunities of citizens in the several states.	State shall be entitled to all Privileges and Immunities of Citizens in the several States,
A person charged in any state with treason, felony, or other crime, who shall flee from justice, and be found in another state, shall on demand of the executive authority of the state from which he fled be delivered up, and removed to the state having jurisdiction of the crime.	A Person charged in any State with Treason, Felony, or other Crime, who shall flee from Justice, and be found in another State, shall on Demand of the executive Authority of the State from which he fled, be delivered up, to be removed to the State having Jurisdiction of the Crime.
No person legally held to service or labour in one state, escaping into another, shall in consequence of regulations subsisting therein be discharged from such service or labor, but shall be delivered up on claim of the party to whom such service or labour may be due.	No Person held to Service or Labour in one State, under the Laws thereof, escaping into another, shall, in Consequence of any Law or Regulations therein, be discharged from such Service or Labour, but shall be delivered up on Claim of the Party to whom such Service or Labour may be due.
Sect. 3. New states may be admitted by the Congress into this union; but no new state shall be formed or erected within the jurisdiction of any other state; nor any state be formed by the junction of two or more states, or parts of states, without the consent of the legislatures of the states concerned as well as of the Congress.	Section 3. New States may be admitted by the Congress into this Union; but no new State shall be formed or erected within the Jurisdiction of any other State; nor any State be formed by the Junction of two or more States, or Parts of States, without the Consent of the Legislatures of the States concerned as well as of the Congress.
The Congress shall have power to dispose of and make all needful rules and regulations respecting the territory or other property belonging to the United States: and nothing in this Constitution shall be so construed as to prejudice any claims of the United States, or of any particular state.	The Congress shall have Power to dispose of and make all needful Rules and Regulations respecting the Territory or other Property belonging to the United States; and nothing in this Constitution shall be so construed as to prejudice any Claims of the United States, or of any particular State.
Sect. 4. The United States shall guarantee to every state in this union a Republican form of government, and shall protect each of them against invasion; and on application of the legislature or executive, against domestic violence.	Section 4. The United States shall guarantee to every State in this Union a Republican Form of Government, and shall protect each of them against Invasion; and on Application of the Legislature, or of the Executive (when the Legislature cannot be convened) against

Report of the Committee on Style.

V

The Congress, whenever two-thirds of both houses shall deem necessary, or on the application of two-thirds of the legislatures of the several states, shall propose amendments to this constitution, which shall be valid to all intents and purposes, as part thereof, when the same shall have been ratified by three-fourths at least of the legislatures of the several states, or by conventions in three-fourths thereof, as the one or the other mode of ratification may be proposed by the Congress: Provided, that no amendment which may be made prior to the year 1808 shall in any manner affect the —— and —— section of article

VI

All debts contracted and engagements entered into before the adoption of this Constitution shall be as valid against the United States under this Constitution as under the confederation.

This constitution, and the laws of the United States which shall be made in pursuance thereof; and all treaties made, or which shall be made, under the authority of the United States, shall be the supreme law of the land; and the judges in every state shall be bound thereby, any thing in the constitution or laws of any state to the contrary notwithstanding.

The Constitution as signed.

domestic Violence.

ARTICLE V

The Congress, whenever two thirds of both Houses shall deem it necessary, shall propose Amendments to this Constitution, or, on the Application of the Legislatures of two thirds of the several States, shall call a Convention for proposing Amendments, which, in either case, shall be valid to all Intents and Purposes, as Part of this Constitution, when ratified by the Legislatures of three fourths of the several States, or by Conventions in three fourths thereof, as the one or the other Mode of Ratification may be proposed by the Congress; Provided that no Amendment which may be made prior to the Year One thousand eight hundred and eight shall in any Manner affect the first and fourth Clauses in the Ninth Section of the first Article; and that no State, without its Consent, shall be deprived of it's equal Suffrage in the Senate.

ARTICLE VI

All Debts contracted and Engagements entered into, before the Adoption of this Constitution, shall be as valid against the United States under this Constitution, as under the Confederation.

This Constitution, and the Laws of the United States which shall be made in Pursuance thereof; and all Treaties made, or which shall be made, under the Authority of the United States, shall be the supreme Law of the Land; and the Judges in every State shall be bound thereby, any Thing in the Constitution or Laws of any State to the Contrary notwithstanding.

Report of the Committee on Style.

The senators and representatives beforementioned, and the members of the several state legislatures, and all executive and judicial officers, both of the United States and of the several States, shall be bound by oath or affirmation, to support this constitution; but no religious test shall ever be required as a qualification to any office or public trust under the United States.

VII

The ratification of the conventions of nine States, shall be sufficient for the establishment of this constitution between the States so ratifying the same.

The Constitution as signed.

The Senators and Representatives before mentioned, and the Members of the several State Legislatures, and all executive and judicial Officers, both of the United States and of the several States, shall be bound by Oath or Affirmation, to support this Constitution; but no religious Test shall ever be required as a Qualification to any Office or public Trust under the United States.

ARTICLE VII

The Ratification of the Conventions of nine States, shall be sufficient for the Establishment of this Constitution between the States so ratifying the Same.

X.   LETTER TRANSMITTING THE CONSTITUTION TO CONGRESS, SEPTEMBER 17, 1787.[1]

We have now the honor to submit to the consideration of the United States in Congress assembled, that Constitution which has appeared to us the most adviseable.

The friends of our country have long seen and desired, that the power of making war, peace, and treaties, that of levying money and regulating commerce, and the correspondent executive and judicial authorities should be fully and effectually vested in the general government of the Union: But the impropriety of delegating such extensive trust to one body of men is evident — Hence results the necessity of a different organization.

It is obviously impracticable in the federal government of these states, to secure all rights of independent sovereignty to each, and yet provide for the interest and safety of all: Individuals entering into society, must give up a share of liberty to preserve the rest. The magnitude of the sacrifice must depend as well on situation and circumstances, as on the object to be obtained. It is at all times difficult to draw with precision the line between those rights which must be surrendered, and those which may be reserved: and on the present occasion this difficulty was encreased by a difference among the several states as to their situation, extent, habits, and particular interests.

In all our deliberations on this subject we kept steadily in our view, that which appears to us the greatest interest of every true American, the consolidation of our Union, in which is involved our prosperity, felicity, safety, perhaps our national existence. This important consideration, seriously and deeply impressed on our minds, led each state in the Convention to be less rigid on points of inferior magnitude, than might have been otherwise expected; and thus the Constitution, which we now present, is the result of a spirit of amity, and of that mutual deference and concession which the peculiarity of our political situation rendered indispensible.

That it will meet the full and entire approbation of every state is not perhaps to be expected; but each will doubtless consider, that had her interest been alone consulted, the consequences might have been particularly disagreeable or injurious to others; that it is liable to as few exceptions as could reasonably have been expected, we hope and believe; that it may promote the lasting welfare of that country so dear to us all, and secure her freedom and happiness, is our most ardent wish.

[1] *Documentary History,* Vol. ii, pp. 1–2.

XI. RESOLUTION OF THE CONVENTION, SEPTEMBER 17, 1787, THAT CONGRESS TRANSMIT THE CONSTITUTION TO THE STATES FOR RATIFICATION.[1]

Resolved, That the preceeding Constitution be laid before the United States in Congress assembled, and that it is the Opinion of this Convention, that it should afterwards be submitted to a Convention of Delegates, chosen in each State by the People thereof, under the Recommendation of its Legislature, for their Assent and Ratification; [2] and that each Convention assenting to, and ratifying the Same, should give Notice thereof to the United States in Congress assembled.   Resolved, That it is the Opinion of this Convention, that as soon as the Conventions of nine States shall have ratified this Constitution, the United States in Congress assembled should fix a Day on which Electors should be appointed by the States which shall have ratified the same, and a Day on which the Electors should assemble to vote for the President, and the Time and Place for commencing Proceedings under this Constitution.   That after such Publication the Electors should be appointed, and the Senators and Representatives elected: That the Electors should meet on the Day fixed for the Election of the President, and should transmit their Votes certified, signed, sealed and directed, as the Constitution requires, to the Secretary of the United States in Congress assembled, that the Senators and Representatives should convene at the Time and Place assigned; that the Senators should appoint a President of the Senate, for the sole Purpose of receiving, opening and counting the Votes for President; and, that after he shall be chosen, the Congress, together with the President, should, without Delay, proceed to execute this Constitution.

By the Unanimous Order of the Convention

G° WASHINGTON Presid[t]

W. JACKSON Secretary.

---

[1] *Documentary History of the Constitution*, Vol. ii, pp. 20–21.

[2] In compliance with this resolution the Congress on September 28, 1787, transmitted the Constitution to the States, which called conventions and ratified it in the following order: Delaware, December 7, 1787; Pennsylvania, December 12, 1787; New Jersey, December 18, 1787; Georgia, January 2, 1788; Connecticut, January 9, 1788; Massachusetts, February 6, 1788; Maryland, April 28, 1788; South Carolina, May 23, 1788; New Hampshire, June 21, 1788; Virginia, June 26, 1788; and New York, July 26, 1788.   The President informed Congress, on January 28, 1790, that North Carolina had ratified the Constitution November 21, 1789; and he informed Congress on June 1, 1790, that Rhode Island had ratified the Constitution May 29, 1790.   Vermont, in convention, ratified the Constitution January 10, 1789, and was, by an act of Congress approved February 19, 1791, "received and admitted into this Union as a new and entire member of the United States."

D. AMENDMENTS TO THE CONSTITUTION.

I. THE FIRST TEN AMENDMENTS TO THE CONSTITUTION IN LIEU OF A BILL OF RIGHTS.

ARTICLES IN ADDITION TO, AND AMENDMENT OF, THE CONSTITUTION OF THE UNITED STATES OF AMERICA, PROPOSED BY CONGRESS, AND RATIFIED BY THE LEGISLATURES OF THE SEVERAL STATES PURSUANT TO THE FIFTH ARTICLE OF THE ORIGINAL CONSTITUTION.

ARTICLE I.[1]

Congress shall make no law respecting an establishment of religion, or prohibiting the free exercises thereof; or abridging the freedom of speech, or of the press; or the right of the people peaceably to assemble, and to petition the Government for a redress of grievances.

ARTICLE II.

A well regulated Militia, being necessary to the security of a free State, the right of the people to keep and bear Arms, shall not be infringed.

ARTICLE III.

No Soldier shall, in time of peace be quartered in any house, without the consent of the Owner, nor in time of war, but in a manner to be prescribed by law.

ARTICLE IV.

The right of the people to be secure in their persons, houses, papers, and effects, against unreasonable searches and seizures, shall not be violated, and no Warrants shall issue, but upon probable cause, supported by Oath or affirmation, and particularly describing the place to be searched, and the persons or things to be seized.

ARTICLE V.

No person shall be held to answer for a capital, or otherwise infamous crime, unless on a presentment or indictment of a Grand Jury, except in cases arising in the land or naval forces, or in the Militia, when in actual service in time of War or public danger; nor shall any person be subject for the same offence to be twice put in jeopardy of life or limb; nor shall be compelled in any Criminal Case to be a witness against himself, nor be deprived of life, liberty, or property, without due process of law; nor shall private property be taken for public use, without just compensation.

---

[1] The first ten amendments to the Constitution of the United States were proposed to the legislatures of the several States by the First Congress, on the 25th of September, 1789. They were ratified by the following States, and the notifications of ratification by the governors thereof were successively communicated by the President to Congress: New Jersey, November 20, 1789; Maryland, December 19, 1789; North Carolina, December 22, 1789; South Carolina, January 19, 1790; New Hampshire, January 25, 1790; Delaware, January 28, 1790; Pennsylvania, March 10, 1790; New York, March 27, 1790; Rhode Island, June 15, 1790; Vermont, November 3, 1791, and Virginia, December 15, 1791. There is no evidence on the journals of Congress that the legislatures of Connecticut, Georgia, and Massachusetts ratified them.

Article VI.

In all criminal prosecutions, the accused shall enjoy the right to a speedy and public trial, by an impartial jury of the State and district wherein the crime shall have been committed, which district shall have been previously ascertained by law, and to be informed of the nature and cause of the accusation; to be confronted with the witnesses against him; to have compulsory process for obtaining Witnesses in his favor, and to have the Assistance of Counsel for his defence.

Article VII.

In suits at common law, where the value in controversy shall exceed twenty dollars, the right of trial by jury shall be preserved, and no fact tried by a jury shall be otherwise re-examined in any Court of the United States, than according to the rules of the common law.

Article VIII.

Excessive bail shall not be required, nor excessive fines imposed, nor cruel and unusual punishments inflicted.

Article IX.

The enumeration in the Constitution, of certain rights, shall not be construed to deny or disparage others retained by the people.

Article X.

The powers not delegated to the United States by the Constitution, nor prohibited by it to the States, are reserved to the States respectively, or to the people.

II. SUBSEQUENT AMENDMENTS TO THE CONSTITUTION.

Article XI.[1]

The Judicial power of the United States shall not be construed to extend to any suit in law or equity, commenced or prosecuted against one of the United States by Citizens of another State, or by Citizens or Subjects of any Foreign State.

Article XII.[2]

The Electors shall meet in their respective states, and vote by ballot for President and Vice-President, one of whom, at least, shall not be an inhabitant of the same state with themselves; they shall name in their ballots the person voted for as President, and in distinct ballots the person voted for as Vice-President, and they shall make distinct lists of all persons voted for as President, and of all persons

[1] The eleventh amendment was declared in a message from the President to Congress, dated the 8th of January, 1798, to have been ratified by the legislatures of three-fourths of the States.

[2] The twelfth amendment, in lieu of the original third paragraph of the first section of the second article, was declared in a proclamation of the Secretary of State, dated the 25th of September, 1804, to have been ratified by the legislatures of three-fourths of the States.

voted for as Vice-President, and of the number of votes for each, which lists they shall sign and certify, and transmit sealed to the seat of the government of the United States, directed to the President of the Senate; — The President of the Senate shall, in the presence of the Senate and House of Representatives, open all the certificates and the votes shall then be counted; — The person having the greatest number of votes for President, shall be the President, if such number be a majority of the whole number of Electors appointed; and if no person have such majority, then from the persons having the highest numbers not exceeding three on the list of those voted for as President, the House of Representatives shall choose immediately, by ballot, the President. But in choosing the President, the votes shall be taken by states, the representation from each state having one vote; a quorum for this purpose shall consist of a member or members from two-thirds of the states, and a majority of all the states shall be necessary to a choice. And if the House of Representatives shall not choose a President whenever the right of choice shall devolve upon them, before the fourth day of March next following, then the Vice-President shall act as President, as in the case of the death or other constitutional disability of the President.— The person having the greatest number of votes as Vice-President, shall be the Vice-President, if such number be a majority of the whole number of Electors appointed, and if no person have a majority, then from the two highest numbers on the list, the Senate shall choose the Vice-President; a quorum for the purpose shall consist of two-thirds of the whole number of Senators, and a majority of the whole number shall be necessary to a choice. But no person constitutionally ineligible to the office of President shall be eligible to that of Vice-President of the United States.

ARTICLE XIII.[1]

SECTION 1. Neither siavery nor involuntary servitude, except as a punishment for crime whereof the party shall have been duly convicted, shall exist within the United States, or any place subject to their jurisdiction.

SECTION 2. Congress shall have power to enforce this article by appropriate legislation.

ARTICLE XIV.[2]

SECTION 1. All persons born or naturalized in the United States, and subject to the jurisdiction thereof, are citizens of the United States and of the State wherein they reside. No State shall make or enforce any law which shall abridge the privileges or immunities of citizens of the United States; nor shall any State deprive any person of life, liberty, or property, without due process of law; nor deny to any person within its jurisdiction the equal protection of the laws.

SECTION 2. Representatives shall be apportioned among the several States according to their respective numbers, counting the whole number of persons in

---

[1] The thirteenth amendment was declared, in a proclamation of the Secretary of State, dated the 18th of December, 1865, to have been ratified by the legislatures of twenty-seven of the thirty-six States.

[2] The fourteenth amendment was, in a proclamation of the Secretary of State, dated the 28th of July, 1868, declared to have been ratified by the legislatures of thirty of the thirty-six States.

each State, excluding Indians not taxed. But when the right to vote at any election for the choice of electors for President and Vice-President of the United States, Representatives in Congress, the Executive and Judicial officers of a State, or the members of the Legislature thereof, is denied to any of the male inhabitants of such State, being twenty-one years of age, and citizens of the United States, or in any way abridged, except for participation in rebellion, or other crime, the basis of representation therein shall be reduced in the proportion which the number of such male citizens shall bear to the whole number of male citizens twenty-one years of age in such State.

SECTION 3. No person shall be a Senator or Representative in Congress, or elector of President and Vice-President, or hold any office, civil or military, under the United States, or under any State, who, having previously taken an oath, as a member of Congress, or as an officer of the United States, or as a member of any State legislature, or as an executive or judicial officer of any State, to support the Constitution of the United States, shall have engaged in insurrection or rebellion against the same, or given aid or comfort to the enemies thereof. But Congress may by a vote of two-thirds of each House, remove such disability.

SECTION 4. The validity of the public debt of the United States, authorized by law, including debts incurred for payment of pensions and bounties for services in suppressing insurrection or rebellion, shall not be questioned. But neither the United States nor any State shall assume or pay any debt or obligation incurred in aid of insurrection or rebellion against the United States, or any claim for the loss or emancipation of any slave; but all such debts, obligations and claims shall be held illegal and void.

SECTION 5. The Congress shall have power to enforce, by appropriate legislation, the provisions of this article.

ARTICLE XV.[1]

SECTION 1. The right of citizens of the United States to vote shall not be denied or abridged by the United States or by any State on account of race, color, or previous condition of servitude.

SECTION 2. The Congress shall have power to enforce this article by appropriate legislation.

ARTICLE XVI.[2]

The Congress shall have power to lay and collect taxes on incomes, from whatever source derived, without apportionment among the several States, and without regard to any census or enumeration.

---

[1] The fifteenth amendment was declared, in a proclamation of the Secretary of State, dated March 30, 1870, to have been ratified by the legislatures of twenty-nine of the thirty-seven States.

[2] The sixteenth amendment was declared, in a proclamation by the Secretary of State, dated February 25, 1913, to have been ratified by the legislatures of thirty-eight of the forty-eight States.

Article XVII.[1]

[1] The Senate of the United States shall be composed of two Senators from each State, elected by the people thereof, for six years; and each Senator shall have one vote. The electors in each State shall have the qualifications requisite for electors of the most numerous branch of the State legislatures.

[2] When vacancies happen in the representation of any State in the Senate, the executive authority of such State shall issue writs of election to fill such vacancies; *Provided,* That the legislature of any State may empower the executive thereof to make temporary appointments until the people fill the vacancies by election as the legislature may direct.

[3] This amendment shall not be so construed as to affect the election or term of any Senator chosen before it becomes valid as part of the Constitution.

Article XVIII.[2]

Section 1. After one year from the ratification of this article the manufacture, sale, or transportation of intoxicating liquors within, the importation thereof into, or the exportation thereof from the United States and all territory subject to the jurisdiction thereof for beverage purposes is hereby prohibited.

Sec. 2. The Congress and the several States shall have concurrent power to enforce this article by appropriate legislation.

Sec. 3. This article shall be inoperative unless it shall have been ratified as an amendment to the Constitution by the legislatures of the several States, as provided in the Constitution, within seven years from the date of the submission hereof to the States by the Congress.

---

[1] The seventeenth amendment was declared, in a proclamation by the Secretary of State, dated May 31, 1913, to have been ratified by the legislatures of thirty-six of the forty-eight States.

[2] The eighteenth amendment was declared, in a proclamation by the Acting Secretary of State, dated January 29, 1919, to have been ratified by the legislatures of thirty-six of the forty-eight States.

INDEX

INDEX

579

over territories until their admission to union, 295; power of, to recognize State governments. 303 note, 380-2, 392; to propose amendments to Constitution, 300-1; defined extent of power of Supreme Court, 342; act of, respecting pensions, 350, 365; act of, authorizing judges to adjust claims under treaty with Spain, 354; act of, respecting jurisdiction of Supreme Court, 366-8; act of, respecting drawing of lotteries in District of Columbia, 409. *See also* Legislative Branch.

Congressional Committee on Appeals. *See* Committee on Appeals, Congressional.

Connecticut, settlers of, 4, 5; Fundamental Orders of, 4, 5; member of New England Confederation, 7; represented at Albany Congress, 11; governed under a charter, 22; charter of, 84 note, 103, 119, 121, 131, 348; representative assemblies of, 84 note, 96; charter provisions of, in force after Declaration of Independence, 84; legislative power of, 96, 97, 101, 119; boundary disputes, 101-9, 114, 118, 231-4, 237, 292 note; Act of 1699 respecting settlement of intestate estates, 119 *et seq.*, 348; constitution of, 131; colonial governor of, elected by people, 138; courts of, elected by colonial authorities, 138; delegates of, to Federal Convention, 147, 152; in favor of equal representation and suffrage of States in Senate, 179-80, 184; claim of, to Northwest Territory, 292 note; opposed to popular ratification of Constitution, 305, 308.

Conquest, rights of, *v.* rights of discovery, 91, 92; Blackstone's interpretation of, 92; laws of, 93 note, 95.

Constitution of the United States, prescribes equal representation of States, 11; a compromise, 41, 46, 172, 332; government under, acts directly on people of States, 43; powers vested in union by, 43, 161, 165-8; three-fold division of government a principle of, 45; amendments to, 46, 137, 299 *et seq.*, 323 *et seq.*, 572-6; ratification of, 46, 164, 301 *et seq.*, 312, 321-2; Articles of Confederation and State constitutions bases of, 53, 131; Articles of Confederation replaced by, 53, 58, 147, 161; adoption of, 58; a result of progressive history, 64; colonial charters foundation of, 64; laws inconsistent with, 65, 101, 200, 361; judicial power conferred by, 65, 102, 108, 119 note, 121, 125, 126, 190, 211-12, 374-5, 398 *et seq.*, 427, 429, 430, 438 *et seq.*, 453, 454; a charter of union, 84; legislative powers conferred by, 137, 172 *et seq.*, 280, 342, 376, 467; instructions respecting, to delegates to Federal

Convention, 150-3; Randolph plan basis of, 158; other plans for, 163-4; drafted by Committee of Detail, 164, 260, 532-40; *The Federalist*, classic exponent of, 164, 315; international law in, 167; established a government of laws and not of men, 168; seat of government under, 168; established a government of limited powers, 168; supremacy of, enforced, case of *The Active*, 222 note; " supreme law of the land," 276-9, 302 *et seq.*, 375; devised primarily for the thirteen confederated States, 290; officers of States and United States bound by oath to support, 304; derives its validity from ratification of the States, 309; government under, begun, 322; ratified by State conventions, 331; Madison's letter to Hayne respecting, 335-7; text of, 502-11, 552-69; transmitted to Congress, 570; transmitted to States for ratification, 571.

Constitutions, British constitution, 64; government more perfect under, than under charters, 139.

Constitutions, State, three-fold division of government in, 45, 133 *et seq.*; influence of colonial charters on, 130-2; bills of rights prefixed to, 137; governments under, 139-40; courts under, 139; the Constitution of the United States given precedence over, 276, 302 *et seq.*, 375; of Arkansas, 457-8; of Connecticut, 131; of Delaware, 126; of Maryland, 196, 307; of Massachusetts, 131 *et seq.*, 138, 156, 201, 274 *et seq.*; of New Jersey, 349; of New York, 136, 137, 201; of Pennsylvania, 136, 365; of Rhode Island, 131, 380; of South Carolina, 198; of Vermont, 290; of Virginia, 76-7, 133.

Constitutional Convention. *See* Federal Convention.

Continental Congress, First, 1774, a forerunner of, in Penn's plan of union, 10; foresaw necessity for some form of government, 129-30; Franklin's second plan presented to, 15; met at Philadelphia, 23; delegates to, 23, 24; Randolph president of, 24; Declaration and Resolves of, 24-6; views of members respecting Navigation Acts and Acts of Trade, 26; advocated association to cut off trade with Great Britain, 26.

Continental Congress, Second, independence declared by, 22, 29 *et seq.*; recommends adoption of some form of government, 28-9, 129 *et seq.*; met at Philadelphia, 26, 129; president of, 26; election of commander-in-chief by, 26-7; adopted Declaration of the Causes and Necessity of Taking up Arms, 27; efforts of, at concilia-

Articles of Confederation similar to, 18, 41-2.

Franklin, William Temple, proposed as secretary, Federal Convention, 149; not elected, 149-50.

French and Indian War, Washington in, 14; expenses of New York in, 115; States parties in, 213.

French Revolution, and influence of Rousseau, 31.

Frothingham, Richard, on Franklin's first plan of union, 6; on principle underlying New England Confederation, 9 note; on representative assemblies, 83-6 notes.

Fuller, Mr. Chief Justice, on case involving action of political departments of government, 379 note; opinion of, in case involving distinction between suits of a civil nature and suits coming under law of nations, 440 note.

Fundamental Orders of Connecticut, first written constitution, 4; preamble to, 5; provisions of, 5.

Garcia v. Lee, 379, 379 note.

General Assemblies, of East India Company, 70; of Virginia, 74, 75, 76; of Massachusetts, 80, 82-3; of Grenada, 94, 96, 247; of Jamaica, 95; of Connecticut, 96; of New York, 137.

George III, grievances suffered by colonies at hands of, 30; proclamation of, respecting General Assembly of Grenada, 94, 96, 247.

Georgia, excluded from Albany plan of union, 11; not represented at First Continental Congress, 23, 24; represented at Second Continental Congress, 26; wars and treaties of, with Indians, 49; appointed delegates to Federal Convention, 57, 146; representative assemblies in, 86 note; instructions to delegates, Federal Convention, 152; vote divided on question of equal suffrage of States in Senate, 176, 176 note, 184; opposed to equality of States in Senate, 185; in favor of popular ratification of Constitution, 305, 308; ratification of Constitution by, 310, 571 note.

Georgia v. Stanton, 386-9.

Germans, customs of, depicted by Tacitus, 76.

German States, customs union in, 55.

Gerry, Elbridge, on representation of States in two branches of legislature, 130; favored compromise, Senate suffrage controversy, 184-5; chairman compromise committee, Senate suffrage controversy, 185; urged establishment of prize jurisdiction in Massachusetts, 216; proposed a bill of rights to Constitution, 328; in favor of

separation of judicial and other powers, 314, 418, 419.

Gibbons v. Ogden, 59-60.

Gladstone, Wm. E., statement of, regarding British and American constitutions, 64.

Gloucester, The, 224 note.

Goldsborough, Robert, member of court, South Carolina-Georgia boundary dispute, 237.

Gordon v. United States, 356-60, 453.

Gorham, Nathaniel, on commercial motive to union of Eastern States, 188, 189-90; called attention of Federal Convention to method of appointment of public officials in Massachusetts, 199; in favor of appointment of Supreme Court judges by executive with consent of the Senate, 258; member, Committee of Detail, 260; considered special provision for settling suits between States unnecessary, 269; in favor of separation of judicial and other powers, 418, 419.

Government, under Constitution, a government of laws, 168; seat of, 168; a government of limited powers, 168; per interim, 321; new government begun, 322; relation of Court to, 369.

Governor, signature of, to statutes and bills required by State constitutions, 136; member of council for revision of bills to be passed by legislature, 136-7; powers entrusted to by States, 197.

Governor and Company of the Massachusetts Bay in New England, creation of by charter of 1628-9, 79, 80.

Governor and Company of Merchants of London Trading to the East Indies. See East India Company.

Gray, Mr. Justice, decision, case involving action of political departments of the government, 379 note; on interpretation of terms of Constitution in light of common law, 444; decision indicating gravity of offense against law of nations, 449; on reason for exemption of State from suit, 454.

Great Britain, conquest of Canada by, 14, 23; efforts of colonies at reconciliation with, 16, 18, 23, 27, 28, 29; regarded colonies from imperial standpoint, 22-3; proclamation of rebellion issued by, 28; renunciation by, of right to impose taxes on a colony, 28; Treaty of Peace with United States, 49, 60, 276, 277; Island of Granada ceded to, by treaty of 1763 with France, 94; conflict of interests of, with those of colonies, 99; western territory ceded to, by France, 292.

"Green Mountain Boys," defeated Hessians at battle of Bennington, 239.

Greene, Nathaniel, declined position as member of court, Pennsylvania v. Connecticut, 232.

Grenada, legislative authority vested in general assembly of, 94, 96; ceded to Great Britain by France, 94, 347.

Grenville's Act, 1770, for trial of disputed elections, 230.

Grier, Mr. Justice, on prize cases and power of president under international law, 382-3.

Griffin, Cyrus, Judge, Court of Appeals in Cases of Capture, 223; member of court, Pennsylvania v. Connecticut, 232, 233.

Guizot, F., on assemblies, 76.

Habana, The Paquete, 449.

Hague Conference, Pacific Settlement Convention of, 269, 468.

Hamilton, Alexander, on coercion of States, 55, 204, 205; delegate of New York to Annapolis Convention, 56; proposed Major Jackson for secretary of the Federal Convention, 149-50; suggestion for a constitution by, 164, 527-8; secured ratification of Constitution in New York, 164, 314-15; and *The Federalist,* 164, 204, 205, 314-15, 362; on independence of Vermont, 241; on defective judicial system under Confederation, 247-8; on immunity of sovereign from suit, 248-9; member, Committee on Style, 277 note; views of, respecting a conditional ratification of the Constitution, 309; views of, on interpretation of Constitution, 332; on power of judiciary to declare laws unconstitutional, 363-4; held judicial power to be concurrent, 414-15.

Hamilton, John, member Massachusetts-New Hampshire boundary commission, 119 note.

Hancock, John, succeeded Randolph as president of Second Continental Congress, 26, 216, 310; signed Declaration of Independence as president of Congress, 30, 310; views of, respecting amendments to Constitution, 310.

Hans v. Louisiana, 419.

Hanson, Alexander Contee, member of court, South Carolina-Georgia dispute, 237.

Hardwicke, Lord. *See* Yorke, Sir Philip.

Harlan, Mr. Justice, on right of United States to withhold moneys received by it under a treaty, 432-3.

Harris, William, pretensions of, subject of Holden & Green petition, 102-9.

Harrison, Benjamin, on influence of New Englanders in Congress, 41.

Hayburn's Case, 352, 353, 365.

Haymilton, Otho, member, Massachusetts-New Hampshire boundary, 119 note.

Heathfield v. Chilton, 448.

Henry, Patrick, opposed to Constitution, 312; declined appointment to Federal Convention, 312.

Henry IV, project of, respecting establishment of European diet, 9, 333.

Hessians, defeated at battle of Bennington, 239.

Hobart, Sir Henry, on by-laws of corporations, 67; drafted second Virginia charter, 71; drafted third Virginia charter, 72.

Holden and Green, petition of, 101-9.

Holland, Treaty of, with United States, October 8, 1782, 49, 60.

Holland, Samuel, member of New York-New Jersey boundary commission, 1767, 116.

Holmes, Mr. Justice, on source of immunity of sovereign power from suit, 454-5.

Holmes v. Walton, 349, 363.

Holt, Chief Justice, on jurisdiction of a corporation, 68; on rights of discovery and conquest, 92.

Holton, S., agent, Massachusetts-New York boundary dispute, 235.

Hooker (Richard), influence of doctrines of, on Declaration of Independence, 35.

Hooker, Thomas, on spirit of Pilgrims, 3.

Hosmer, Titus, Judge, Court of Appeals in Cases of Capture, 223.

House of Burgesses, Virginia, 23, 83, 84 note; colonial assemblies sometimes called, 132.

House of Representatives, represents people of States according to population, 172; great debate on, question of representation in, 173 *et seq.;* compromise respecting proportional representation in, 156-7; rule of suffrage for, 187; and presidential election, 196; debate in, on Madison amendments, 325. *See also* Legislative Department.

Houston, William Churchill, member of court, Pennsylvania v. Connecticut, 235, 236.

Hudson Bay Company, a joint-stock company, 68.

Hunter, governor of New York, 110; commissions issued by, respecting New York-New Jersey boundary dispute, 110, 113.

Hutchinson, Thomas, on Virginia House of Burgesses, 23; on original charter of Massachusetts, 65; on representative institutions in Massachusetts, 82-3; plan of, for treaty-making with Indians, 198 note.

northern colonies modeled upon charter and institutions of, 71; the Plymouth Company, 78-9; Council of, 79; charter annulled in 1684, 82; royal charter of 1691, 82; Jefferson on colonial laws of, 97; grant of, by Charles II to Duke of York, 122.

New England Company. *See* Plymouth Company.

New England Confederation, 1643, indicates existence of idea of colonial union, 6; aims of, 6, 7; summary of articles of, 6-9; subscribed to by commissioners of colonies, 9; prescribes equal representation of colonies, 11; advantages of union shown by, 11; complaint of Rhode Island against, 101-9; text of, 471-6. *See also* Commissioners of New England Confederation, *and* Confederates, New England.

New England Restraining Act, 1775, 27.

New Hampshire, represented at Albany Congress, 11; establishment by, of revolutionary government recommended, 29, 129; late attendance of, at Federal Convention, 58, 175, 176, 185; representative government set up in, 85 note; boundary disputes, 115, 118 note, 238-41, 421; instructions to delegates to Federal Convention, 150; in favor of equal suffrage of States, 175, 185; New Hampshire grants, 238 *et seq.;* recognized independent statehood of Vermont, 241; in favor of popular ratification of Constitution, 308; ratification of Constitution by, 312, 315, 571 note; amendments to Constitution proposed by, 330; ratification by, of first ten amendments, 572 note.

New Haven, member of New England Confederation, 7.

New Jersey, compact of, with Pennsylvania, an encroachment on Federal authority, 49; commercial situation of, 55; represented at Annapolis Convention, 56, 146; delegates of, to Federal Convention, 57, 146; representative assemblies in, 85 note; boundary disputes, 109-18, 238 *et seq.;* grant of, to Lord Berkley and Sir George Carteret, 116; in favor of equal representation of States in Congress, 174; in favor of equal suffrage of States in Senate, 184; in favor of independence of Rhode Island, 241; vote of, on popular ratification of Constitution, 305, 308; ratification of Constitution by, 309, 310, 571 note; constitution of, 349; statute of New Jersey of 1778 declared unconstitutional, 349; ratification by, of first ten amendments, 572 note.

New Jersey v. Virginia, 238, 239, 242-4.

New Jersey Assembly Acts relative to boundaries, Act of 1719, 110, 111; Act of 1748, 111, 114; Act of 1764, 101; Act of 1772, 117.

New Jersey Plan. *See* Patterson Plan.

New York, represented at Albany Congress, 11; address of Provincial Congress of, to Washington, 27 note; laws of, favoring own citizens, 49; represented at Annapolis Convention, 56, 146; charter of, 86 note; representative assemblies in, 86 note; conquered from Dutch and ceded to Great Britain by teaty, 91; boundary disputes, 109-18, 118 note, 234-6, 237, 238-41, 292 note, 387; constitution of, 136-7, 201; senate, court of appeals in, 139; appointed delegates to Federal Convention, 147; instructions to delegates, Federal Convention, 152; ratification of Constitution by, secured by Hamilton, 164, 164 note; vote of, respecting equal suffrage of States in Senate, 184, 185; and independent statehood of Vermont, 241, 290; claim of, to Northwest Territory, 244, 292, 292 note; opposed to popular ratification of Constitution, 305; ratification of Constitution by, 312, 314-15, 571 note; amendments to Constitution proposed by, 330; ratification by, of first ten amendments, 572 note.

New York Assembly Acts relative to boundaries, Act of 1717, 109, 110, 111, 113, 114; Act of 1719, 114; Act of 1754, 114, 115; Act of 1771, 117.

New York v. Connecticut, 386.

New York City, first seat of government under Constitution, 322.

Non-Importation, Non-Consumption and Non-Exportation Agreement, considered by Congress, 26.

Norris v. Staps, 67.

North, Lord, Conciliatory Resolution of February 27, 1775, 27; rejected, 28.

North and South, distrust between, 41; distinction between, 77; colonial development contrasted, 83.

North Carolina, delegates of, to First Continental Congress, 24; commercial situation of, under Confederation, 55; ratification of Constitution by, 46, 309, 571 note; appointed delegates to Federal Convention, 49, 146; instructions to delegates Federal Convention, 150; charter of, 85 note; representative assemblies in, 85 note; boundary disputes, 118 note, 119 note; vote of, respecting equal suffrage of States in Senate, 184, 185; in favor of popular ratification of Constitution, 305, 308; ratifica-

Sergeant, Jonathan Dickinson, agent, case of Pennsylvania *v.* Connecticut, 232.

Seven Years' War. *See* French and Indian War.

Shaw, Mr. Chief Justice, on interpretation of terms of common law, 445-6.

Shay's Rebellion, 1787, Madison on, 50.

Sherman, Roger, member, drafting committee of Declaration of Independence, 30; Connecticut delegate, Federal Convention, 152; remarks on question of equal representation, of States, 180-1, 184; views of, respecting power of Congress to negative State legislation, 201; in favor of limitation of judicial power of United States to one supreme tribunal, 252; in favor of appointment of supreme court judges by legislature, 255; opposed to creation of inferior tribunals by Congress, 259; considered special provision for settling suits between States unnecessary, 269; in favor of extending judicial power, 271; in favor of equality of Western States, 294; considered popular ratification of Constitution unnecessary, 305; in favor of separation of judicial and political powers, 419.

Shiras, Mr. Justice, on finality of decree of Supreme Court, 360-1.

Shirreft, William, member, Massachusetts-New Hampshire boundary commission, 119 note.

Siren, The, 459-60.

Sitgreaves, John, member of court, Massachusetts-New York boundary dispute, 235; District Judge, North Carolina Circuit Court, 351.

Skeene, William, member, Massachusetts-New Hampshire boundary commission, 119 note.

Slaves, as affecting basis of representation in legislature, 187; three-fifths rule respecting, 187; right to continue slave-trade, insisted on by Southern States, 187, 189; provision of Constitution relative to importation of, 188-90, 299-300.

Smith *v.* Alabama, 443, 444.

Smith, Isaac, member of court, Massachusetts-New York boundary dispute, 235.

Smith, Melancthon, opposed to Constitution, 314; finally voted for Constitution, 315.

Smith, Sir Thomas, named in royal charter as first governor of East India Company, 69.

Society of Nations, question of large and small states in, 41; union under Articles of Confederation an example for, 47; membership of United States in, recog-

nized by treaties, 60; difficulty of conferring upon an agent the exercise of large sovereign powers, 99; more perfect union under Constitution a model for, 147; standing rules and orders in Federal Convention a precedent for future conferences of the, 156; provisions for judicial settlement under Confederation capable of application to, 213; a permanent court of the, 282; political questions of, may become judicial, 424; sovereignty, the great problem of, 467; compared with the union of the United States, 467-8; a possible solution of the problems of, 468-9.

South and North, distrust between, 41; distinction between, 77; colonial development contrasted, 83.

South Carolina, representative government set up in, 85 note; boundary disputes, 118 note, 234, 236-7; steps taken by, to prevent anarchy during Revolution, 129; appointed delegates to Federal Convention, 147; instructions to delegates, Federal Convention, 152; opposed to equal suffrage of States in Senate, 184, 185; constitution of, 198 note; charter of, 236; in favor of popular ratification of Constitution, 305, 308; ratification of Constitution by, 311, 312, 571 note; amendments to Constitution proposed by, 330; ratification of first ten amendments, 572 note.

South Carolina *v.* Georgia, 236-7.

South Carolina *v.* United States, 335.

South Carolina, The, 224 note.

Southern States, and regulations of commerce, 188-9.

Sovereignty, passed to people of colonies as result of the Declaration of Independence, 33; certain powers of, renounced by States under Confederation, 42-3; Madison on, 52; of States, under Articles of Confederation, 58; of States, under Constitution, 161, 333-4; problem of, in establishment of a judiciary, 248-9; not amenable to suit without consent, 249, 335; of the people by Constitution, 308; division of sovereign powers, 334-5; States protected from attempts of Government to infringe upon, 359-60; not always immune from suit, 456; suit without consent inconsistent with, 457; waiving of, 457; degree of, relinquished by a plaintiff sovereign, 462-3, 464-5; cases when sovereign becomes subordinate to law, 464; the great problem of the Society of Nations, 467.

Spaight, Richard Dobbs, motion of, on procedure in Federal Convention, 155.

Spain, ceded Florida to United States by